The

"I Love My Bible"

Commentary

Copyright

Jean Heizer

Outskirts Press, Inc.
Denver, Colorado

The opinions expressed in this manuscript are solely the opinions of the author and do not represent the opinions or thoughts of the publisher. The author represents and warrants that s/he either owns or has the legal right to publish all material in this book.

The "I Love My Bible" Commentary

All Rights Reserved.
Copyright © 2007 Jean Heizer
V1.0

Cover Photo © 2007 J Jean Heizer Corporation. All rights reserved - used with permission.

This book may not be reproduced, transmitted, or stored in whole or in part by any means, including graphic, electronic, or mechanical without the express written consent of the publisher except in the case of brief quotations embodied in critical articles and reviews.

Outskirts Press, Inc.
http://www.outskirtspress.com

ISBN: 978-1-4327-1283-9

Outskirts Press and the "OP" logo are trademarks belonging to Outskirts Press, Inc.

PRINTED IN THE UNITED STATES OF AMERICA

Library of Congress Control Number: 2007931721

This book is, first of all, dedicated to my Lord who is ever present in my heart!
It is also dedicated to my husband, Woodrow, who is now present with the Lord, along with my Mother and Daddy, brother and sister. And I must include my two children, (and their spouses) Corky and Kaye (Bavouset) Wreay, and Ed and Becky (Baxter) Bavouset, and my six grandchildren, Jeff and Cara Bavouset, Kim, Delaina, Ashley and Amanda Wreay, and Elizabeth Kaye Wreay-Watts, my great grand daughter who keeps me company everyday(well, almost). *She keeps me young at heart!* Also I want to dedicate this to my three stepsons, Don(and Ruth Ann), Dennis(and Sandy), and Richard (and Sara) and their children-especially Christel Heizer Brenner and little Madison(who I get to see on a regular basis) and also all my great grand babies! I cannot forget to mention my former Sunday School attendees for their eager response to my lesson comments have encouraged me to continue this work. And–of course to my many great friends (many of who attended my Sunday School classes!) especially Jean Robbins Pinner who has faithfully encouraged and supported me in this great work! And, I dedicate this to you, my readers, and my prayer is that it will inspire you to read **God's precious Holy Word, the Bible**. Jesus said, "Heaven and earth will pass away, but my words will not....." Can you think of a better reason than that to read His 'love letter' to us?

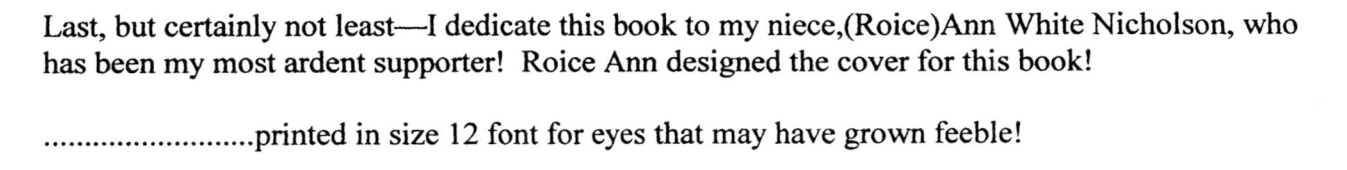

Last, but certainly not least—I dedicate this book to my niece,(Roice)Ann White Nicholson, who has been my most ardent supporter! Roice Ann designed the cover for this book!

..........................printed in size 12 font for eyes that may have grown feeble!

I want to emphasize that I did not write this book to be read primarily alone. I hope you will always read God's Precious Word first, then read my comment on whatever scripture passage you have just read. God's love whispers through every passage (even the harsh ones) and we should always have the ears of our hearts open, searching for that great love! We must remember God is the God of the things we often cannot see-His great love, the hope, the joy, the peace, and of course the love He plants in our hearts. Unless we search His Word we will fail to see all these great things he has for us......and we can discover them all through His Word-The Holy Bible. So----for your sakes-----read The Bible. God bless you as you do!!!

©Copyright 2003 by Jean Heizer

Printed in the United States of America August 2006

Copyright #   TXu-085-068

Table of Contents

I Want To Know..
Preface..
Introduction To Old Testament..

The Old Testament

Part One–The Books of Moses
(Comment on Genesis-Deuteronomy)

Genesis..P. 15
The Ten Commandments
Exodus..P. 39
Leviticus..P. 59
Numbers..P. 73
Deuteronomy..P. 89

Part Two–The Blossoming Kingdom
(Comment on Joshua-2nd Samuel)

Joshua..P. 105
Judges..P. 113
Ruth..P 119
!st Samuel..P 121
2nd Samuel..P 131

Part Three-Israel's Rise and Demise)
(Comment on 1st Kings-Esther)

1st Kings..P 141
2nd Kings..P 149
1st Chronicles..P 157
2nd Chronicles..P 167
Ezra..P 179
Nehemiah..P 183
Esther..P 187

Part Four–The Poetic Books
(Comment on Job-Song of Solomon)

Job..P. 193
Psalms..P. 205
Proverbs..P. 247
Ecclesiastes..P 257
Song of Solomon..P. 261

Part Five–The Major Prophets
(Comment on Isaiah-Daniel)

Isaiah..P. 267
Jeremiah..P. 289
Lamentations..P. 307
Ezekiel..P. 309
Daniel..P. 326

Part Six-The Minor Prophets
(Comment on Hosea-Malachi)

Hosea..P. 333
Joel..P. 337
Amos..P. 339
Obadiah..P. 343
Jonah..P. 345
Micah..P. 347
Nahum..P. 351
Habakkuk..P. 353
Zephaniah..P. 355
Haggai..P. 357
Jechariah..P. 359
Malachi..P. 363

Introduction to New Testament

The Blessed New Testament

Part Seven-The Morning Star Arises
(Comment on Matthew-Acts)

Matthew..P. 371
Mark..P. 385
Luke..P 393
John..P. 403
Acts..P. 413

Part Eight–The Loving Letters And Final Farewell
*(*Comment on Romans-Revelations)

Romans..P. 425
1st Corinthians..P. 431
2nd Corinthians..P. 437
Galations..P. 443
Ephesians..P. 447
Phillipians..P. 451
Colossians..P. 453
1st Thessalonians..P. 455
2nd Thessalonians..P. 456
1st Timothy..P. 459
2nd Timothy..P. 461
Titus and Philemon..P. 463
Hebrews..P. 465
James..P. 471
1st Peter..P. 473
2nd Peter..P. 474
!st John..P. 477
2nd and 3rd John..P. 478
Jude..P. 481
Revelation..P. 483
Closing Comment..P. 493

I Want To Know

*I want to read God loves me
over and over and over again!
I'll never be able to learn enough
about this glorious salvation
God has given every man.
I want to embrace
that anticipation in the air
and to cherish a love
that is beyond compare!
I need to know God's plan for me
and the reason He has set me free!
Oh how I want to pick up those
feelings between the lines
and be able to discern
why His Light shines!
I want to look beyond
those distant hills
and see what David saw
when he discovered so much grace
hidden in the law!
And I want to know why Paul said
"For me to live is Christ
and to die is gain!"
<u>Because of that</u>
I'll read this Precious Holy Book
until God Himself makes it plain!*

Preface

Dear, Dear People,

Have you ever wished for a different type commentary-one written to let God's love shine through? Have you ever wanted to stand on the mountaintop with Sarah, or with David beside the Still Waters? Or, maybe you would wish to stand with Paul who was beaten, stoned, threatened, and run out of so many places he lost count, yet would say, "I've been down but I'm not out!" Have you ever longed to look at others with the same love, kindness, and patience that Jesus did? That why I'm writing this commentary! I want to encourage you to seek that golden thread of love that weaves its way through the Bible's precious pages.

The Lord Jesus said, "My Words, they are Spirit and they are Life!" Surely they are! And we desperately need the surgical knife of Spiritual Truths to debride contaminates from our souls. In the many years I've been writing this book, I've kept that thought foremost in my mind realizing I must examine myself carefully through diligent study, in continual prayer, and, of course through love!

God wants to build integrity, strength, endurance, and, most of all love in His people. That, too, is my reason for writing this commentary. I am 78 years old and have spent my life studying God's Word. I have attended numerous Bible Conferences, read many commentaries and too many devotionals to count.

Remember what God once said to Ezekiel(Chpt. 3:v10)? "Apply these words to your own heart first!" My, that has been one BIG challenge! But I have never been unhappy when I have lived in obedience to HIS will(revealed through prayer and His Word). Passing that on has been the basis for my teaching, my writing, and(hopefully)the good example I set in the way I try to live from day to day. I want you to be happy also. God guarantees that—when we trust and obey His will for our lives.

We live in a time when skepticism surrounds God's Word. Its accuracy is questioned, its authenticity ridiculed and its meaning often obscured. Unless God's people replace suspicion of God's Word with faith, we will never understand His purpose for our lives. His purpose is to draw us closer to Him. He is Magnificently Holy and Omnipotently Loving and Kind. When we question His Word, we need to remember Jesus said, "Seek and you shall find." ***The choice is ours!***

I am not writing my book to the intellect but to the heart (with the heart man believeth unto righteousness). Millions are hungry for the promises that wind through the Bible and are the ones I want to reach and the irony is, though we faithfully fill the pews of our great churches, we fail to realize the most beautiful flowers of faith are those we pick ourselves! To those who consider the Bible to be harsh I say, "One must find a way around the thorns if he wants to pick a rose!"

I hope to encourage you to re-discover the Bible, to study it, to cherish it and to find happiness in following the ONE it describes so lovingly. He is–beyond all doubt *the source of incredible joy*!

No commentary can do justice to God's love or His Word, but it can and should praise Him! I hope as I present this Commentary, mine will do just that. Please read God's Word for no other book can give you as much strength, as much hope or more wonderfully abiding grace as will this perfect, precious Word of God. At no time in this world have we needed it more. Surely you will learn to love, honor, and obey this ONE who is described in its pages, this ONE whose love is magnified even *between* the lines. No other love can equal His. No other words can compare. Although man's defeat and failures are depicted in many ways, God's precious love remains gloriously victorious!

I will be presenting this "I Love My Bible" Commentary in eight parts.

They are:

The Old Testament

Part One: The Books of Moses
(Genesis–Deuteronomy)

Part Two: The Blossoming Kingdom
(Joshua–2nd Samuel)

Part Three   Israel's Rise And Demise
(1st Kings–Esther)

Part Four: The Poetic Books
(Job–Song of Solomon)

Part Five: The Major Prophets
(Isaiah–Daniel)

Part Six: The Minor Prophets
(Hosea–Malachi)

The New Testament

Part Seven: The Morning Star Arises
(Matthew–Acts)

Part Eight: The Loving Letters and Final Farewell
(Romans–Revelation)

And the Great Fantastic Hello!!!

Introduction To The Old Testament

*We know the New Testament displays
the prophecies foretold in the Old.
Dear Christian, please don't neglect
these Old Testament writings.
They are more precious than purest gold!
Many an Old Testament prophet
and countless saints who did God's will
were privileged to see
the "Promise of the Ages"
stand on Zion's Hill.
Through the centuries the truths
of both Testaments intertwine.
Both are consistently precious .
Both are equally divine!
We have had the advantage
of double treasure
from both the Old and the New
and with them we see the beautiful
panorama of the wider view!
Search these Ancient Scriptures
whatever you do
for they provide the dramatic truths
from which those Word Artists
of the New Testament so eloquently drew!*

PART ONE

THE BOOKS

OF

MOSES

The Book of Genesis

In The Beginning God Created

The Heavens and the Earth

The "I Love My Bible" Commentary

GENESIS 1

In the beginning God created the heavens
And the earth. It was a chaotic mass.
But by the time He finished It was
A-No.1 class!
With tenderness He placed each star
Because He knew man would gaze
In wonder from afar!
Then He stepped back to look
At His creation
And all heaven
Joined in a joyous celebration!
Someday, we'll be able
to search the universe
But we'll never be able to find
As beautiful a garden as the one
In Which God placed mankind.
For God would give Adam His best
Before He would take time to rest!

Genesis 2

Then God created Eve with material
Extracted near Adam's heart
So they would have a close relationship
From the start!
It was a tender admonition.
Love for her must be of Adam's
Own volition.
And we see the story of creation
Repeated in chapter two
Because God knew man would
Prefer the evolutionary view.
But..though countless armies
Should stand belligerent with their flags
 unfurled
We say with STRONG conviction
"This is our Father's World!"

GENESIS 3

Remember Eve was created
With material already perfected!
Her beauty must have been something to see.
Why was she left unprotected?
What was Adam doing when Satan insisted
Eve do that which Adam could have resisted?
Maybe Adam knew he wouldn't
And left it up to Eve because he knew
She couldn't.
Then he could blame his wife for all
His troubles the rest of his life!
But think of the hope God would spur
When He said the "Seed" of all the ages
Would come through her!
And for all women who feel down trod
Remember Eve was forgiven by God!
But still they were driven
From *the garden* because
Both had developed character flaws.
Since we would continue to feel that
   tragic loss
The "*God of the Garden* would become
The "God of The Cross!"
God gave Our Savior as a
Bridge across the gap
And because we needed directions
Back to Him God provided
The Bible as our map!

GENESIS 4

The hatred in Cain's heart erupted
When he killed his brother
And his denial to the Father was
They didn't answer for one another!
But he could not fool the Lord
Of all the earth.

Comments On Genesis

And he was excommunicated from God,
His parents, and the land of his birth.
Can't you hear the heartbreak in Cain's voice?
Walking with the Lord could no longer be his choice .
Oh to be separated from my God forever
I have no doubt
Though the fires of hell should die
The fire in my soul would never go out!
Like Cain, I would die a little every day
If God wasn't near
And every day I walk this earth would be
A day of fear!
I don't think Cain knew how hard
It would be to spend
The rest of his life away from the Lord
And I have no doubt
Somewhere he walks with a fire in his soul
That will *never* go out!

GENESIS 5

Adam—this man was made in the image
Of God yet he fell. That day he lost God's
God's image must have brought its own
Particular brand of hell.
After that Adam was never the same
And all his descendants would bear
His shame.
How could one born in the image of God
Stoop to being a sinner
When God had created him perfect
A man made to be a *winner!*
And how could Adam know his weakness
Would start
All those awful devastating ravages
Of the heart?

The perversion that began in Adam's Day
Continues to thrive and it grew like a cancer
Affecting all those named in chapter Five.

GENESIS 6

Giants were born in those day
But wouldn't walk in God's ways.
Sexual laws must have been perverted
And it broke God's heart when He saw
That His Loving laws were skirted.
The crime rate was rising rapidly
And God could see these men were
Full of depravity.
But Noah was a different sort
Truly a man after God's own heart!
Had it not been for Noah there would be
No trace
Of what we know as the Family tree of the
Human race.
Noah and his family survived extinction with
The protection our Lord and Savior gives.
Because Noah was found to be righteous
In the Lord's sight,
The story *of the Garden lives!!*

GENESIS 7

The Ark was big enough for all
Who wanted to board it.
There was no question as to
Who could afford it!
But they thought Noah was crazy
And those who pounded on the ark's side.
Taunted Noah until he must have wanted
To run away and hide.
None of these men could see an inch

The "I Love My Bible" Commentary

Beyond his nose
Or else they would have known one day
That door in the ark would close.
These arrogant men who refused to bathe in
Holiness would drown in pain
Learning way too late of the horrors of
Torrential merciless rain.
But look what was done for Noah!
God kept him away from harm..
Noah knew for sure God was God
Even of the Storm!

GENESIS 8

Forty days and nights!
What an awful mess to see!
So many people washed into eternity!
Time would drag on for this family
And its ark-confined farm
In hearing the animals roar
They must have felt great harm!
Would you want to be there
Packed like sardines in a can
Along side animals dangerous to man?
And those men also confined
Had to listen to those wives
Who all must have whined!
One day a little dove would find
A tiny leaf and they all would rejoice
For soon they'd be able once again
To roam trails of their own choice.
And once they disembarked
The ark would stay there parked
On an earth now scarred
While Noah and his family sacrificed
To the Lord.
God promised Noah that never again
Would He send such a deluge .
To punish the most wicked man.

We must remember that promise
Every time we see a rainbow!
To know our FATHER is ever present Should
give our hearts an eternal glow!

GENESIS 9

God commands the sons of Noah
To replenish the earth's population.
He had already given the sign that
Reminds us of His great salvation.
God's people know He will supply
Glorious hope for His people
Whenever that symbol appears in the sky!
Now may the closing words
Of this chapter teach us all
Not to be too critical of those who fall
Under the debilitating, dehumanizing
Effects of alcohol!

GENESIS 10

It is hard to believe so many came
From so few.
From Shem, Ham and Japeth nations grew.
The first king mentioned was Nimrod
Some said he was a man blessed of God.
But it doesn't seem Nimrod ever had
A personal relationship with God
Still–in his time the nations greatly expanded
Multiplying the earth as God commanded.
But faith was not multiplied and we see
Man resorted to devious truancy!
Thus it has always been.
We find it so easy to commit sin!

Comments On Genesis

GENESIS 11

Man has always patted himself on the back.
Thinking he could climb God's upward track
But his climb was to glorify himself.
He didn't want God on the "Top Shelf"
But somewhere below
And that isn't the way God had it planned!
So mankind thought he could take a stand
But watch as his walls come tumbling down.
Common clay cannot replace Holy Ground.
Only with God's permission can we climb
Can we climb heaven bound!
What we have here
Is a break down in Communication..
God wasn't invited to their dedication.
It was no feat for God to confuse these men
For confused is what they'd had always been.
Now brother would turn against brother
Because they couldn't understand each other.
Through the years God has been dishonored
By man's dishonesty, greed, and awful hate.
Will he ever learn to cherish our Creator
Before it becomes too late?

GENESIS 12

God has an "Abraham" for every generation,
One who rises to fame above the population,
One who is faithful despite what
Might be the cost.
This Abraham was sure God
Could supply much more than he lost!
We must not forget God has a "Sarah" too
Whom He uses to pass His blessings through!
Sarah was a remarkable lady brave and strong
Who stood by Abraham her whole life long!
But–there is a spot on Abraham's reputation
For he put Sarah in a dangerous situation.
If Abraham truly trusted in God's protection
He wouldn't have jeopardized
Sarah's perfection.
But God intervened for Sarah's sake
And no one could touch
This elegantly beautiful lady
Whom God loved so much!
I'm sure God must have said
"Shame on you, Abraham for letting Sarah go
To live in the presence of that decadent
Romeo!"

GENESIS 13

Abraham and Lot stood on a hill
Viewing the lush green valley below
Ah, look at that!" Lot must have thought
How thick the grass would grow!
But death was there
Around every corner beyond the town square.
What path should they take?
Would the local people be loving and kind?
What would he really find?
Lot sought his future in this pagan valley.
Abraham climbed the barren mountains
Beyond
Would separation breach that family bond?
Did Lot have any idea lust lurked in Sodom's
Shadowy dust filled streets
And horrible devastation
Would petrify her primeval sweets?
God knew Abraham could have chosen
That lush green valley below
But he gave it to his nephew
Who really wanted to go
And God told Abraham "You made
A wise choice in trusting me
So I'll give your Descendants
This vibrant land as far as you can see!"

The "I Love My Bible" Commentary

God knew that gross grass in the valley
Would soon burn
And Sodom would become a place
For which no man would ever yearn.

GENESIS 14

War is inevitable it seems
When men cause nightmares
Instead of noble dreams.
Though Sodom and its many alliance kings
Had not walked in the "light!"
They considered freedom to be
Their inalienable right
But they failed because they did not ask
God's help for their impossible task!
True freedom is freedom of the soul
And history shows us the men of Sodom
Were never spiritually whole!
It took righteous Abraham to set them free
A man whose faith in God was plain to see!
In spite of the noble names
This chapter stressed
Only this man Abraham was truly blessed.
He went to war for love–not greed.
Someone he dearly cherished
Found himself in dire need!
Only once is Melchizedek mentioned.
God sent him to bless a man well-intentioned!
War is merely a symbol that man has cursed
God's desire that we should
Put another's rights and welfare first.
The prisoners of pain cry for release
And to help them is our path to peace!

GENESIS 15

Abraham and Sarah's descendants future
Would be a very dismal one
God said it before He gave them a son.
Those who would call them
Father Abraham and Mother Sarah
Would live in bondage four hundred years.
They would experience back breaking labor
And shed heartbreaking tears.
Many times they doubted God would
Bring them out, make them brave and strong
And someday they would all sing
The victor's song!
This was because God would show
Mercy to these people whose faith
Would *never* grow!
He gave the Amorites four hundred years
To repent but they never did
And it was into a well deserved pit
They eventually slid!
This should be a lesson to us for we also
Try His patience, mercy and grace
Not realizing His great love
Is one we can *never* replace!
We can't be like an Amorite.
We must hold His love ever so tight!!!

GENESIS 16

God told Sarah *she* would have a son.
But it seems she didn't believe she was
God's appointed and favorite one.
And so she chose Hagar to bear
Abraham's first heir
And it was to herself she was so unfair.
Abraham had loved Sarah for so long
Expecting him to hold
Another woman's son was definitely wrong.
Why? Because God had said the "heir"
Would come *through both of them*
It was the *son of her love* that would bless

Comments On Genesis

Abraham!
But it was all those years she didn't conceive
That built her fears!
Look at the trouble she caused
And she blamed poor old Abraham.
Makes me want to say, "You're the one
Who gave him Hagar, Ma'am!"
God would not permit Sarah to claim
Ishmael as her own
The heir must be her flesh and her bone!
Hagar needed pity though she acted *smart*
Whatever judgement Sarah passed should
Have been on her own doubtful heart!
But maybe we shouldn't judge
Sarah too harshly for if we had walked
Those trails she trod
Would we have reached ninety eight years
Still full of faith in God?
And its quite possible we would also
Have sent Hagar away
To walk in confusion and fear
Day after day!

GENESIS 17

God blessed Abraham and we should
Have no doubt!
We can still see the incredible blessings of
Abraham have never run out!
Though the world hates the Jews,
God still blesses them.
I can say with confidence there will always be
A Jerusalem !
Because Abraham cherished God
God stayed by his side.
There is no doubt in my mind
Abraham was a man perfectly satisfied!
Abraham put God before every thing

Even his own son
And as for shadows of disobedience
There were absolutely none!
So the Jews remain even to this day
Because our God definitely wants it that way!
Those who doubt that will *never* see
The purpose in Gethsemane!

GENESIS 18

Sarah laughed at the promise God made.
Many times she had hoped for a son
And many times that hope would fade.
Suppose you had one foot in the grave
And the other on a banana peel!
How in the world could you believe
What you heard was real?
Sarah didn't believe but yet she cringed
In fear.
She laughed but she was hoping
God didn't hear.
She couldn't believe God would give her
A son so late in life.
It seemed a hundred years she'd been
Abraham's wife.
Despite all her charms
God had never given her a baby of her own
To hold in her arms!
She just didn't understand God's time table
And she didn't understand if God wanted to
Give her a son He was certainly able!
God had power to spare
And by the following year
That precious baby, Isaac, would be there
In her arms, in her heart, in her life
And needless to say
Abraham would have a very happy wife!

The "I Love My Bible" Commentary

GENESIS 19

The angels had until the setting of the sun
To find ten righteous men. They found *one!*
And we wonder why a righteous man would
Want to live around such deviate awful sin.
He had been around godly Abraham so long
How could he tolerate such awful wrong.
It wasn't meant to be.
Their was evil God didn't want Lot
Or his family to see
And soon God would take matters
Into His own hands
For the men who surrounded Lot
Made too many unholy demands.
They were blind to God's truth and light
And God gave them a future dark as midnight
But the training Lot's lovely daughters
Had in Sodom was certainly not the best.
Where else could they have learned about
The sin of incest?
Their descendants and the Jews
Were never friends
For deceit brings a rift that never ends.
I bet they didn't know
You always reap what you sow!

GENESIS 20

Sarah stands on the pages of time as possibly
The most beautiful woman who has ever
Walked this earth,
Blessed of God, admired by men,
Lovely at ninety nine at a time close
To Isaac's birth!
You'd think a man who had a wife
This gorgeous those many years
Would die to protect her
But he sought only to protect himself
And his reputation suffers its greatest slur.
And we wonder if she had to be
A pawn in man's oldest most cruel game
Possessed by a foolish king
Who would only bring her shame.
We know Abraham fought several kings
To save his nephew
But when it came to his precious wife
It seems there was nothing he would do.
           Priorities!
Women were at the bottom of the totem pole.
Even this one who loved Abraham
With all her heart and soul!
But again God would let no one touch
This elegantly beautiful lady
Whom He loved so much!
No wonder Abimelech sent them
Away with a reprimand
And tells them rather harshly to leave his land
So Abraham's lie was discovered, this mister
Who passed his wife off as only his sister!
It is deadly for us to look fear in the eye
Just the looking bids us
Bid our faith goodbye.
Such was Abraham's sin.
No matter how great they were
He was *never* to be afraid of men!

GENESIS 21

Look at Isaac, Sarah and remember
His is a Miracle birth promise God kept!
Look at Sarah, people and don't marvel
Why she wept!
Ninety nine years she waited
To give Abraham a baby boy
And though her eyes were full of tears,
Her heart was full of joy!

Comments On Genesis

But Sarah refuses to share her joy
With hagar, her maid
And she sent Hagar and her son away
Lonely and afraid.
But God promised Abraham
He would bless Ishmael, too
And Hagar knew God had given her a hope
He would constantly renew!
It is quite possible that the all season hatred
And the all season fear
Between the Arabs and Jews started
Because of the hatred between Hagar
And Sarah manifested here.
Isn't it a shame that their hatred
Was so strong
That it has created havoc to humble people
To humble people for this long!

GENESIS 22

Everything Isaac did was precious,
And everything he did was fun!
He was a miracle, a wonder, Abraham's
Favorite son!
Now God says sacrifice Isaac.
    Say what?
After all these years Abraham waited,
God puts Him on the spot!
Abraham and God were so closely related
We don't see even for a moment that
He even paused or hesitated.
No argument! No appeal?
He didn't even ask,"God, are you for real?"
We would have wouldn't we!
We'd cry like a baby. "Oh Lord," we'd say,
"You can't do that to me!"
"Don't forget the promise,"Abraham must
Have thought."Don't forget the vow."

God would deliver Isaac some way,
    some how!
You know, we're like a Computer.
We hear what God has to say and
Then our "hard drive crashes"
And quicker than you can say "Scat"
We forget those little "*dots and slashes!*"
Faith knocks at the door but we
Move faith over and let fear in instead.
But Abraham knew better
And he followed God's directions
To the letter.
Boy, that blows my mind!
And the first thing we would ask
Ourselves is how could God be so unkind.
Well, maybe its not unkind
To check out a person's heart.
To see if his love is real
And he if he possesses a loving
Loyalty that is vibrantly strong
And a comfort to feel!!
No doubt about Abraham!
He would willingly do
All the Heavenly Father would tell him to!
And if you look at the blessings
Of Abraham still evident today
You will not wonder why Gods love Is a love
That will never go away!
God certainly satisfied this loyal man,
Abraham
When he supplied that sacrificial ram
And he certainly brought Isaac total relief
And must have multiplied
Many times over, Isaac's faltering belief!
We would like further explanation
But none is there
Only when God supplies a sacrifice,
He does it with unassuming flair!

The "I Love My Bible" Commentary

GENESIS 23

Sarah stood on the mountain top
Knowing it was time to go.
She had walked beside her man
In desert sands and winter snow.
Twice she had risked the sanctity
Of her marriage to save Abraham's life.
She must have been sure
God was with her.
Truly Abraham had a marvelous wife!
Now Abraham would be left
Pondering his loss
Because Sarah had one more mountain
She had to cross.
It never entered Abraham's mind that his
Precious Sarah would leave him behind.
Death never comes easy never comes
Welcomed. It just comes to take those
We love to a better, more beautiful place.
And it seems those we love
Disappear without a trace
But God knows where they are
And someday we too can walk
The same trails our loved ones do!
So as a picture of their togetherness
Here and someday on the other side
And so he could be close to this beautiful lady
In whom he felt so much pride
Abraham bought a burial plot
So in the resurrection they could rise
Hand in hand from the very same spot!
He made sure they would be together in death
As well as they had been in life
And he bought that field to bury Sarah
His precious wife!

♡♡♡♡♡♡♡♡♡♡♡

GENESIS 24

It provided more than water this well
He stood beside
Because he had asked the Lord,
"Please send me Isaac's bride.
And almost before he asked
The answer was there!
She was gracious and beautiful.
God had answered his prayer!
Sometimes a love story begins
Before two lovers meet.
The FATHER knows which one will
Make our lives complete!
'Tis said Isaac's love for her was great
This one God chose to be Isaac's soul-mate!
Her family sent her away
With a blessing they hoped God would fulfill
Confident that Rebekah's marriage to Isaac
Was truly in God's will!

GENESIS 25

It seems to me after having had Sarah so long
Abraham's heart should have been filled
With a lovely song
But the memory of her melody brought
A heartache loneliness could not erase.
So Abraham looked for the music
Of another pretty face.
He had other sons by Keturah
but they only proved to be competitive
To Isaac, Sarah's son.
God had already warned Abraham the great
Inheritance could not go to just anyone
So Abraham gave his and Keturah's sons gifts
Gifts one day
And then sent them to the East far away.

Comments On Genesis

Ishmael already had land of his own
And now Canaan would be Isaac's
And his descendants alone.
Ishmael's descendants were like some of us.
All they did was fight & fuss
They couldn't get along with each other.
And they didn't cherish Isaac's descendants
Though He was Ishmael's brother.
And neither could Isaac's sons get along
For Jacob, being sneaky,
Certainly did Esau wrong!

GENESIS 26

Isaac was a "chip off the old Block,"
A pretty big chip!
And his rating with his wife
Probably took a big dip!
And he certainly made a big mistake
When he hid
Behind his wife's skirt
In just the way Abraham did!
Abimelech should have been wise
To this old scam.
After all, hadn't it been instigated
By Isaac's father crafty old Abraham?
Putting one's wife in harm's way wasn't wise.
Evidently Isaac didn't consider her
To be much of a prize.
And as the saying goes
Here we go again!
Another beautiful woman.
Another lousy plan.
And another greedy king
Wanting more than his share
Just because the "package"
Was incredibly fair!
Lust gave him the itch
And Isaac was obliged

To make the switch.
Well God watched over Rebekah too
And He allowed some "hanky panky"
Between Isaac and Rebekah right smack in
Abimelech's view.
Isaac's future wasn't Abimleck's
To command
But he did tell Isaac to get off his land.
And he was wise enough
To see the hand writing on the wall!
God had convinced him not to harm
Isaac and Rebekah *at all!*
God was protecting them
For they were his own
And no one could harm them
Not even this man who ruled
From an earthly throne.
God's throne was higher still
And no one could supercede God's
omniscient will!

GENESIS 27

This chapter does not relate a pretty picture
As it contains
Treachery when Jacob takes advantage
Of Esau's hunger pains.
And Esau was gone for meat for his blessing
When Jacob approached Isaac
With "venison" and dressing.
He had help from his Mother
Who advised him how to take
The blessing from his brother.
Did you notice the flaw?
Rebekah loved Jacob
And Isaac loved Esau.
Each one wanted to help
The one they loved the most
So Rebekah stealthy provided

The "I Love My Bible" Commentary

Jacob's roast.
Well, I suppose it wasn't too wise
Because she paid
When Esau's terrible anger made her afraid.
In effect she lost Jacob because he had to flee.
It was "pay back" time for their treachery!
What we sow–we reap
And in loneliness for her son
Rebekah would often weep!
It was a short lived victory
For Jacob could no longer sit
At his Mother's knee!
Wealth was but a token
That left Esau heart-broken.
The family would never be the same
After that day Jacob lived "Up to his name."
Not only did he steal Esau's birthright
But his blessing as well and because of his
Treachery he had to sneak
Away during the night.and he didn't know
When Laban offered him a retreat
He would inadvertently pay for his deceit!

GENESIS 28

It is not the journey that pivots Jacob's life.
It was the angels he saw
As he walked to meet his future wife.
And it took a pillow of stone to enable him
To see angels descending from The Throne
Never was a ladder used for such glory!
And I'm sure Jacob emphasized its use
Whenever he told this story!
Even though he was running away from pain
God's promises pictured dramatic
Earthly gain.
How could God ever want
To use a liar and a cheat?
It's called "Grace!"
That sweetens any defeat.

A marvel it must have been.
God had already forgiven
Jacob's deceitful hearted sin!
God said He would not depart until
He had given all He'd spoken of.
Great is God's grace
But even greater is His love!
Jacob offered God a tenth
In humble adoration
And we've reason to believe
It was a lifetime dedication!

GENESIS 29

Jacob makes use of another stone
This one covers a well.
where sheep and shepherds dwell.
It was by sheer force he removed the rock.
Surely he was showing off
When he watered Laban's flock!
But then, a pretty girl has that effect
And here Jacob must have
Felt his heart eternally wrecked.
This is the day that begins pay-back time.
Can you imagine Jacob working
Seven years without making a single dime?
It had been so easy to cheat Esau
But Laban made no money
Available on which he could draw.
He was certainly bit by the love bug.
Seven years of work before
He could even get a hug!
And then to make matters worse
His work was in vain
And he was being repaid
For holding Esau in disdain.
I feel sorry for Leah!
The only thing that brought her joy
Was she–not Rachel–presented
Jacob with his first baby boy!

Comments On Genesis

But though her sons grew to number four
Jacob didn't love her one bit more!
It must have torn her apart.
To know love is not love that is not
From the heart.

GENESIS 30

Rachel couldn't help but see
God had left her out.
His blessing of Leah fed Rachel's doubt.
But it was in sympathy God had increased
Leah's sons to four.
For Jacob would always love Rachel more.
In desperation because of her barreness,
Rachel blamed her spouse
And that didn't bring harmony to her house!
Well, it was easier to blame Jacob
Instead of the Lord.
She couldn't understand His will
Though she tried so hard.
Jealously widened the wedge
Between Jacob's wives
Sisters whose bitterness saddened their lives.
But Jacob had bigger problems
One-how to solve that poverty he was in.
And now again we see deceit between these
Two men when Jacob used manipulation
To rob Laban of his animal population.
Certainly Laban never did encourage Jacob
And Jacob never changed.
Though they worked together
They were emotionally estranged!

GENESIS 31

When you play a "one-up" game
You can end up losing your good name.

Now all Laban's sons grew
Aware of Jacob's tricks
And their countenance warned Jacob
Their hearts had turned hard as bricks.
It was time to run again
And he advised Leah and Rachel
Of his departure plan.
It really was time to go.
Chances are he was in deeper trouble
Than he could possibly know!
So away they went on the double
Before Laban grew aware of their absence
They'd be long gone and away from trouble.
But Laban wasn't through with Jacob yet
And if God hadn't stepped in he might have
Done something he'd always regret!
The problem was worked out and
Laban went home satisfied
Leaving Jacob to travel safely home
With his family by his side.

GENESIS 32

Jacob's road back home was paved with fear.
He trembled as he watched to see
When Esau would appear.
Stealing Esau's birthright and his blessing
Had been a vice around Jacob's heart
And now it tightened slowly and his
World was falling apart.
Guilt has a way of bringing the chickens
Home to roost
Just at the inopportune time
That one's ego needs a boost
We can understand why Jacob's
Mind was so full of doubt.
He now had a big family to worry about.
But why did he think God would lead him
Into despair?

The "I Love My Bible" Commentary

Every time he needed God, God was always
There!
Jacob faced the greatest struggle of his life
But it was not what he anticipated.
This ONE Jacob wrestled with had power
Jacob grossly underrated!
It also gave Jacob courage though it seemed
Rather ambivalent.
Jacob still didn't thoroughly understand
This rescue that was truly Heaven sent!
I think God shows us here in a way very plain
To give Him our problems and then worry
Is to worry in vain.
We can say this much for Jacob.
He wouldn't let go
And he knew the courage God gave him
Would continue to grow!

GENESIS 33

It is wonderful for brothers to be reconciled
And when Jacob and Esau greeted one another,
All the Angels must have smiled!
Esau came with pomp and power but his heart
Was meek
And Jacob truly humbled already had the
Forgiveness he thought he had to seek.
Happiness often brings tears to our eyes
And joy hangs on every word
Of a lost brother's replies!
They were kindly solicitous these two
Gladly accepting this reconciliation
Long over due.
Forgiveness turned Esau
From an enemy to a friend
And God brought their animosity to an end.
And when Jacob erected an altar at Bethel
It was to thank God for his emotional health
As well!

GENESIS 34

Maybe if Jacob had gone with Esau, Dinah
Would not have been abused
And it would not have been necessary to
Reprimand Levi and Simeon for the treachery
They had used.
That word "if" can turn lives around
Or end them prematurely
As these men of Shechem found.
Their deaths made other problems
Jacob didn't want to face
And it only diluted the joy Jacob had
Received by grace!
Remember God had called Jacob a "prince"
With power
And since that came from God, Jacob didn't
Have to run or cower!
But Jacob did run again though he ran
In anger this time.
Simeon and Levi insisted they were right
To punish Shechem for his crime.
They felt the world must learn
It makes no sense
To rape the daughter of a "Prince!"

GENESIS 35

"Go back to Bethel," God said.
"Remember who greeted you there!
Think about our relationship
That was badly in need of repair.
Think about the love, the forgiveness,
Think about the grace
You received the day you met me
Face to face!"
There were no idols then to throw away
Only fear.

Comment on Genesis

Think how awe-struck you felt when you said,
'God is here!' "
God knew Jacob was facing great sorrow.
God comes to us in our today
To say He is with us in our tomorrow!
In Jacob's tomorrow he would lose his loving
Companion, his favorite wife.
And treachery would cut through his heart
Like a deadly rusty knife.
We don't think of Jacob as having
Many redeeming qualities
But God held him dear!
And no matter his problems, no matter his
Weaknesses God would always be near!
Let us, too, go back to our Bethel
One more time
And walk in the light of God's own
Glorious sunshine!

GENESIS 36

One chapter is devoted to Esau
And then he and Jacob's paths would part
And then the Bible follows Jacob's trail for
God lived in Jacob's heart!
There is one big difference we need to draw.
Esau was concerned with only 'self' and
Jacob dearly loved The 'birthright!'
Because he accepted God's great promise
Jacob's soul took flight!
And Jacob's descendants are still around
Because Jacob chose to walk
On Holy Ground!
Its hard for me to say much about Esau.
He comes!   He goes!
And his descendants dilemma
Was later they would disappear
Because they became one of Israel's foes.

But then-they hated each other, too
There was nothing noble in their lives
God would want to renew.
The Lord was not Esau's birthright
For he failed to keep God's love in sight.
And there's not much this chapter can say
About one who could have followed God
Yet chose to turn away.

GENESIS 37

Joseph is proof that a big mouth can get
Even a good man in dutch!
Its true he had beautiful dreams,
But he bragged about them way too much!
No brother wants to bow to another
And certainly neither did his father or mother.
Joseph was a smart alec kid with a giant ego
And he needed a lesson in humility so his
Spirit would have a chance to grow.
Later, Joseph was able to see God's hand
In his brothers deceit
And no matter how much pain or how bitter
The problem God would make it sweet!
We must look for deep purpose
When someone is unkind.
Is God there to open eyes
That have become spiritually blind!
The greater a person's position
The more humble he must be
And don't we all ask the question when
Accused of being proud or arrogant,
         "Who?"   "Me!"
Joseph was born a favorite son but became an
Indigent slave
But think of the many people
This arrogant boy would someday save!
Mostly his people, that is true.
But he saved the whole nation of Egypt

The "I Love My Bible" Commentary

GENESIS 38

Judah, through whom Shiloh would come
Followed a path utterly dumb.
He left his family and married a Canaanite
Which according to custom wasn't right.
Did he forget the prophesy
That "Shiloh" would come through him?
Are God's people supposed to marry
On the basis of a momentary whim?
My mother used to say such a person
Couldn't see an inch beyond his nose
And isn't it true our decisions
Determine which way the wind blows?
It seems he hadn't gotten the picture
Of God's grace
And wanted to be involved
With someone from a heathen race.
But, then, there's a sweeter picture
Hidden in this story
Jesus, himself, would extend His invitation
Even to heathen to share His glory!
Judah reached out through human desire
But our Savior's purpose was *much* higher!
And someday relationships will revolve back
To that day of Creation
Back to the ONE who was and *is*
Our perfect heavenly relation!

GENESIS 39

Joseph's journey ends in Egypt
Where he is sold to be a slave
But he kept his honor despite he faced
A future very grave.

It was a strange country with customs
Stranger still
And a promiscuous woman
Who meant to bend Joseph's will.
But he stood steadfast in grace
Her invitation would bring a dishonor
He didn't want to face
She was a woman he couldn't trust.
Unlike his sister, this woman was full of lust.
Still he suffered when she lied
About the pleasure she was denied.
Joseph must have been
The first *innocent* man Accused of rape.
Her lie held a viciousness
He was unable to escape.
So this innocent man was thrown in jail
For a crime he didn't commit.
And though he was falsely imprisoned
It seems his faith did not waiver one bit!
How beautifully God uses His people
Whose faith is strong.
No matter man's or woman's intention,
God can always right a wrong!
Only God can change a prisoner to a prince!
We can never be defeated
When God comes to our defense!
It seems we all must face some measure
Of trouble and strife
But we can say "God is my protector
And will for all the rest of my life!"

GENESIS 40

Soon two men joined Joseph in his cell block.
But one was involved in an assassination plot.
Yet, they had both displeased
Egypt's peevish Pharaoh.
One served him rancid wine but he

Comments On Genesis

Should have checked the baker's sourdough!
Joseph was assigned to care for their needs
While they languished there
Because of their questionable deeds.
It didn't take long to discover the guilty party.
The baker was impaled but
The other was restored hale and hardy!
Joseph begged not to be forgotten
When the cupbearer was freed
But he immediately forgot Joseph
And Joseph's good deed!
So Joseph would have two more years
To fret and fume
Wondering when he, too, would be freed
From his musty room!

GENESIS 41

Dreams can imprison our minds
Or dreams can free our hearts
And dreams can promise a future
That ignites a million sparks!
But Pharaoh's dream was so ambivalent
He didn't know what to think.
Dreams aren't always what they seem
And he was smart enough to know
His was no silly irrelevant dream
But skinny cows eating fat ones!
And fat corn swallowing the lean!
Who in the world would know
What that could possibly mean?
But as dramatic were the dreams
They still faded from his mind
And his wise men could find
No solution of any kind.
It took a humble youth
Who was a righteous man
To enlighten Pharaoh to God's future plan.

We must have the spirit of God to know
God's spirit of loving care
To know just when we need Him most
Our God will surely be there.
Years earlier ten brothers thought
They had Joseph's future figured out
But then they had not considered the One
Who has powerful unchangeable clout!
Pharaoh would discover Joseph's greatness
Before his brothers would
And what they couldn't accomplish
Joseph would assure them--*God could!*
They wanted to accomplish Joseph's demise
But God readied them for a colossal surprise!
Pharaoh was certainly surprised when Joseph
Told him what the future would bring.
Seven years would be productive
But seven more years
Would bring no crops in the Spring
No harvest in the fall
No hope for any people there at all.
But God told Joseph what must be done
And God was ready to honor
Jacob's favorite son.
The measure of a man is not in his wisdom
But in the God of all the ages - Joseph's God
Who knew every path Joseph trod.
His steps were always in the steps of the Lord
And he measured up to this life that could
Have been incredibly hard.
How easy it is for God to move in our favor
And how thankful we should be
For our mighty precious Savior!

Genesis 42
(Past-Present)

Sadness flies on shifting desert winds
Following ten men unaware of their fate

The "I Love My Bible" Commentary

And it was because of a hidden deed
To a brother of whom they felt only hate.
When Jacob sent his sons to Egypt for food
He never imagined what would take place
Or a ruler who could be so terribly rude
Was only disguising God's incredible grace!
Hunger will force these men to roam
To a distant land far from home.
It was their father's insistence they go
To a future they couldn't know.
Well, suffice it to say the chickens came home
To roost.
And these men who bowed before Joseph
Must have given his ego a monumental boost!
The memory of his dreams returned
And to see them restored all those years
Joseph had yearned.
Yet, watch what he does when the
Demon of revenge raises its ugly head
As he sees his brothers discomfort
And listens to what his brothers said.
He held Simeon prisoner so he could
Be certain they would come back.
And with the news they brought Jacob
He felt a future only eternally black!
He couldn't face losing Benjamin also
"No," he said. "Benjamin can't go!"

GENESIS 43

It must have felt as if they were tearing
Out his heart
As he watched Benjamin and the others
Depart.
Benjamin must have thought life unfair
As he looked back and saw his father
Standing there.
Benjamin left his heart behind
And shuddered to think of one so unkind.
How could this stranger ask so much?
Did he have a heart no one could touch?
Did you ever notice when you travel
Somewhere the first time, it seems forever
Getting there?
I bet Benjamin noticed every shrub, every dry
Water hole and starving animals everywhere.
But of course he wasn't in a rush
To meet a man he surely didn't trust.
The welcome he received must have been
Quite a surprise.
Five portions more than his brothers
Indicated a reason he couldn't surmise.
Who was this man and what was his game?
Benjamin–what favor could be connected
To his own name?
When seeking an answer becomes too hard
Then is the time to seek the Lord.
We don't read that Benjamin did
But surely he hid in the shadow of the One
In which his father hid.
God had given Joseph his power
And neither Benjamin or his brothers
Needed to cower.
Over and over in these precious pages
We learn to trust our Rock of Ages!

GENESIS 44

Joseph had one more trick up his sleeve
But it was just a test.
He would never put Benjamin in jeopardy
Not even in jest!
It must have been quite a scare
For Benjamin who had never left home
    before!
He had been wined, dined and entertained
And given all the goodies Joseph held in
    store.
And here comes this steward bearing down

Comment on Genesis

On them wanting Benjamin to be restrained.
What a hoax some people play
And we never suspect
In Joseph's case it was based
On his continuing feeling of reject.
Surely he was aware of how he felt
And he wanted to be sure his brother's
Hearts would melt.
Well, they did–melted in fear
Retribution was much too near!
But, then, maybe I should mention
Joseph only wanted their undivided attention!

GENESIS 45

Trouble has a way of coming through
The back door but God sends it out the front.
Love takes trouble and reshapes it
Into only a harmless stunt.
Can't you hear that l-o-n-g sigh of relief
When news of Joseph's forgiveness
Strengthened their belief?.
Benjamin hadn't been guilty but the others had
And finally they could take the best of news
To their grieving Dad!
Guilt and fear fed their doubt
But when love comes along fear fizzles out!
They had left for Canaan in a hurry
Still holding on to a guilt they needed to bury.
That is one reason Joseph brought them back.
It was time to put the troubled hearts
Of his brothers on the right track.
And though Judah's plea was eloquent
It wasn't needed
And all these brothers were so shocked
At Joseph's revelation
The truth didn't register and had to be
Repeated.

This couldn't be Joseph!
Their guilt had convinced them he was dead.
But he was so convincing they finally
Believed what he said!
Joseph alive! Joseph is alive!
Even Egypt rejoiced now that Joseph
And his brothers were reunited
And were no longer haunted by a guilt
That had long been unrequited.
They returned to Jacob with overflowing
Good news and numerous gifts
And we can see how high Jacob's spirit lifts!

GENESIS 46

It must have been a bright sunny day.
Egypt may be a far distance
But they were on their way!
Those carts must have rattled the dishes
As they rumbled down the ruts
And leaving their familiar territory
Must have taken a healthy helping of guts!
But the hungrier you get the gutsier you grow
And in their minds they must have smelled
Fresh risen dough!
But leaving the territory was no big threat
Although it haunted them to see trees dying
That should have been dripping wet,
To feel dust in their faces, to see how sadness
Dried other places.
For sadness was in the drought
And sadness slowly followed them south.
They came to the Egypt so many people loved
But to them it was unloved, unknown
And though it felt strange
It was sweet not being there alone.
What started out as a sad story
Suddenly glows
For love, assurance, peace, and faith grows!

The "I Love My Bible" Commentary

After all they had Joseph as next of kin.
If not for him where would they have been?
And if they easily settled in
It was because God, Himself, had reserved
Joseph for these men!

GENESIS 47

With Joseph–it was Jacob's golden year
Jacob in Egypt with Joseph standing near.
Seeing Joseph had been beyond his dreams,
Dreams that had been locked in grief and pain
And though Jacob might have thought it
A miracle, it was a result of years without rain.
We forget God moves in mysterious ways
His wonders to perform.
Though His people had to move from home
They would face no harm.
You see they had a brother who was wise
Whom God, not them, had sent ahead
And though Jacob had spent years in sorrow
Now he knew for sure Joseph wasn't dead!
His heart was so full he blessed Pharaoh
And told him all he wanted to know.
Now Jacob was humble though once
He had not been
But remember that struggle he had with God?
It made him the best of men.
I'm sure Pharaoh was really impressed
And probably wondered why he was blessed.
Surely it was in more ways than one.
I have a sneaky suspicion he thought
Jacob had passed wisdom to every son.
Maybe he thought them all smart as Joseph
And he would have the best.
These gifted sons the old man brought
Would make Egypt prouder than any country
Better than all the rest!
Sure they were good workers, proud men too

But it was Joseph who affected Pharaoh's
Point of view.
Because God had sent Joseph to save a nation
All people *who came to him* were provided
An ample ration.
Can you get the picture in this story?
Our greater "Brother" provides for us
From His home in glory.
We *come to Him* for hope and grace
For the lost position He can replace.
The Egyptian lost their wealth, their homes,
Their cattle, their freedom just to stay alive.
But the ones who had a *righteous brother*
To intercede continued to multiply and thrive!
Joseph never prospered from Egypt's loss.
It was Pharaoh who was truly Egypt's boss.
Remember that younger Jacob who lied,
Stole, connived and manipulated?
Now we see a humble old man who learned
Honesty is much less complicated.
He passed that on to Joseph somehow!
And for the holiness he taught Joseph
He and his family are safe in "Egypt" now!

GENESIS 48

He was feeble so they propped him up in bed
But he was strong enough to ignore what
Joseph said.
And again we see him manipulate
Just a little bit
And when he crossed hands
He exhibited a little family wit!
Many years have passed but he still remembers
And his hands hold steady despite the tremors.
At least he knew what Isaac didn't know
Wisdom of the heart told him which way
Those boys future must go!
He had been a conniver, manipulator, & cheat

Comment on Genesis

But God loved him anyway.
Jacob had grown in grace and integrity
Because he had wrestled with God
  (*Actually he was holding on*)
     one eventful day!
That was one battle he lost *and yet he won!*
For having been doubly blessed of God
He was able to do the same
For Joseph's youngest son!

GENESIS 49

Jacob turns to his other sons for their blessings
And the mood changed and it is easy to see
How much his emotions ranged.
From those of whom he was justly proud
To the two of whom he was ashamed
He ran the gamut of emotions to show
His displeasure
But in his pride for Judah and Joseph
He was generous with God's treasure.
He couldn't give Reuben his rightful place
The sin he committed with Bilhah
Was a terrible disgrace!
And the pity is that Simeon and Levi lost
So much because they were such violent men.
This father loved them but *love* can't reward
These two who left behind a family reputation
Badly scarred.
But I love what he said about Judah·
The scepter would remain until Shiloh appears
And he must have known
Our Lord would not come for many years!
Still the kingdom waits until Christ will fulfill
Every jot and every tittle of the Father's will!
Jacob moves on to bless the others
But theirs seemed almost insignificant
Compared to their brothers.
That precious man, now godly, was feeble
And old
But he was ready to walk those streets of gold!
The time had come for him to die
And his greatest blessing was that he was able
To tell all his sons goodby!

GENESIS 50

It takes awhile to mourn one who has been
Around so long.
You want to rehash so many things
All that was right and all that was wrong!
Sadly the brothers remember their mistake
And their guilt convinced them Joseph
Might still be full of hate.
Guilt is like a puppy dog that chases shadows
Of fear
And causes its victims to convince themselves
"We'll find no safety here!"
In a way they hurt Joseph even more.
He thought he had convinced them
His love for them had erased that score.
He wasn't keeping records but was holding
On to a love that truly never would let go!
Because love would hold this family together
And in time would help it grow.
Now Genesis is ended and we must move on
And those people of Israel march forward
To another time zone!
Note: What can I say about Genesis? It moves from creation to man's chaos, from structure to strangeness, from delight to despair and through it all God gently guides men back to godliness and hope, love and labor, to blue skies and peaceful valleys, rainbows and gentle rains, togetherness and harmony, joy and goodness and it is simply because He loves us--<u>and will forever!!!</u>
There is nothing as great as God's love!!!

The Ten Commandments

1. Thou shalt have no other gods before Me.

   We must love our God with *all* our hearts
   souls and might
   For God is *Love* and God is *life* and God
   is *Light!*

2. Thou shalt not make unto thee any graven image.

   Nothing man makes will make my spirit *whole!*
   My allegiance is to the Father.
   Only God can save my soul!

3. Thou shalt not take the name of the Lord thy God in vain.

   To use God's name in vain is a shame
   For *Holy is that Precious Name!*

4. Remember the Sabbath Day to keep it holy.

   How wonderful that we have a day to pause
   And ponder the way our lives
   Are held together by God's loving laws!

5. Honor thy Father and thy Mother That thy days may be long on the earth.

   This rule is worth repeating
   For to dishonor our parents is self defeating!

6. Thou shalt not kill!

   To take another's life is to say we don't care
   If we choose to gaze on death's unholy stare!

7. Thou shalt not commit adultery.

   Only the end of time can tell
   Of the horrors adultery has caused
   For its blatant wholesale disobedience
   Has *far* surpassed the breaking of
   Any of God's other laws!

8. Thou shalt not steal.

   Stealing shows a faulty decision
   Resulting from doubting God's provision.

9. Thou shalt not bear false witness.

   False witness leaves us bare
   To the awful winds of unprovidential care!

10. Thou shalt not covet.

    To desire a neighbor's spouse or wealth
    Is to expose ones self to envy's deadly stealth!

I AM the Lord thy God

Thou shalt have no other gods before me
(kjv-Ex:20:1-2)

The Book Of Exodus

*And GOD said unto Moses,
I AM THAT I AM:
and he said, thus shalt thou say
unto the children of Israel,
I AM
hath sent me unto you.*

*And God said moreover unto Moses,
thus shalt thou say unto the children of Israel,
the Lord God of your fathers,
the God of Abraham,
the God of Isaac,
and the God of Jacob,
hath sent me unto you:
this is my name forever
and this is my memorial unto all generations.*

*......I have surely visited you,
and seen that which is done to you in Egypt:*

*And I have said,
I will bring you up out of the affliction of Egypt....
......unto a land flowing with milk and honey.*

(Exodus 3:14,15, 16b and 17kjv)

The "I Love My Bible" Commentary

EXODUS 1

Sometimes to add luxury is to subtract comfort
And sometimes to multiply is to divide.
God knew He would need to separate
The Egyptians and Israelis
Because of the Egyptians fierce pride.
Pharaoh wanted Egypt great
But God would bring it to its knees
And before His people called God was ready
To answer their frantic pleas!
But He never gets in a hurry
When He interacts with mankind.
Maybe that is why we are so impatient
And so spiritually blind.
God raised up two midwives in that hour
And protected them by His power.
They knew more than Pharaoh did
When they told him those Israeli mothers
Had their babies and then hid.
These midwives may have trembled in fear
But faith held their heads up high.
They would not look for the mothers
Nor stop to hear a baby's cry!
And because they would not help
Pharaoh set his traps
God gave them babies of their own
To hold joyfully on their laps!.

EXODUS 2

Pharaoh wanted all the little boys thrown away
But God sent along a princess to rescue Moses
On an uplifting, life changing, glorious day!
Moses's Egyptian experience began
In a basket on the river Nile
When a lonely Egyptian princess lifted him
Far above the 'rank and file!'
Moses, born to slavery yet destined for more
Met his destiny along that river shore.
There would be a time much later
When our Savior would come in humility
Like a slave yet gloriously and completely free!
Somehow He was there with Moses and He
And this one born in slavery joined hands.
Moses would be a conqueror though his path
Led through harsh desert sands.
Raised as an Egyptian prince but a Hebrew at heart
His true heritage came through
When he took the wrong man's part.
Had he killed the Israeli it would not have mattered
But his aura of glory faded as his victim's blood scattered!
Still Moses was a giant of a man
Though destined to walk in a lonely place
And for forty years he would long for
a familiar face!

EXODUS 3

Don't you think in those second forty years
Moses sadly focused on himself only.
He would remember his glory in Egypt
And inevitably felt sad and lonely?
Maybe that is why God burned
Yet did not burn that bush one day .
Moses would never succeed on his own
Because God had another, better way!
"The "Great I Am" the One who knew
Their future and their past
Wrapped His hands around their hearts
And gave them an incredible future
    Guaranteed to last!
    Do your plans fail?
    Is your labor in vain?
    Does your light pale
    And you collapse in pain?
Take your burdens to the Lord where they

Comments on Exodus

belong.
He is the One who took a defeated man
And then made him brave and strong!
God gives victory and no one needed it more.
Moses went striding into Egypt
Greater than he had ever been before!
God was his banner, his inspiration, his shield.
Moses had no power until he witnessed
The power God revealed.
And if we want to walk out of our 'desert'
    on our toes
There is a way for us that only God knows!
We're like Moses who needed a push.
And the Holy Spirit is our 'burning bush!'

EXODUS 4

Can you imagine it? This man called Moses
Stood there and argued with the Lord.
He couldn't speak! He wouldn't go!
He just *knew* it would be way too hard.
I suspect he lost all that confidence
He once enjoyed as Egypt's prince.
And since he had once killed an Egyptian
He thought it *just* recompense.
He had left Egypt in fear.
And now God was saying, "Go back!"
Go back to what? Go back to disgrace?
Go back to a dangerous and unholy place!
But God wouldn't take no for a reply.
Whether or not Moses realized it God had
Prepared him to bid the desert goodby.
Ahead was a great challenge.
Ahead were people in great need.
Would Moses go? Oh, yes indeed!
I thank God He has refused to accept
A "no" from me.
I thank Him there were blessings
Waiting ahead I could not see.
I thank Him for giving me tasks
He won't let me shirk.
And I thank Him for involving me
In His blessed work!

Though Moses argued, he went.
How could he not go for he was
Truly blessed in being sent?
And God gave him support.
He had sent Aaron on his way
And what Moses needed
God had already sent him that day.
Why do we hesitate? Don't we know
God has already opened the way
Whenever He says, "Go!"

EXODUS 5

Now two giants meet who were worlds apart.
One was a man after God's own heart
And the other was Egypt's great Pharaoh
And he wasn't about to let God's people go!
Instead he made it harder on the Israelis
And then refused to listen to their pleas.
Before the rainbow comes the rain
And their was plenty about which to complain.
God's people need to realize a setback
Can be a move forward when God is in control
He knows the outcome when He sets a goal!
Don't you know the night is always darkest
Just before the dawn breaks through.
There would be many dark days before
Pharaoh would learn how much God can do!
Now those Israelis had to hunt their own straw
And they worked until their hands were raw
Because the men who once gathered sticks
Added that chore to those who made the bricks.
And talk about the straw that broke
The camel's back
This one truly did, for the Israelis were the
'Camels' and heavy was their task!
"Its your fault," they told Moses.
"Its your fault," Moses told the Lord.
Isn't it just like us humans to pass the buck
When times are hard?

The "I Love My Bible" Commentary

EXODUS 6

God has to reiterate His intent once again
For Moses needed reassurance and maybe
Moses really didn't understand God's plan.
How many times would God have to say
He would surely rescue them one day.
It must be in His own time and His own way!
"I AM God," He says! "I AM God!"
But our memory banks fail to hold
A truth so marvelous and so bold!
He is my God. Can I contain
Such knowledge presented so simply plain?
He would tell them over and over again
Hoping it would 'soak' in to every tribe
Every clan and every man.
Even Moses had a problem seeing that
For God had to order him to go back.
Moses didn't want to face
Pharaoh, Egypt's king in the first place.
God still has reluctant servants who can't see
The incredible joy serving Him can be!
I suppose this chapter names all those tribal
Heads so we can understand
Why Moses would have such a problem
Convincing them thy could leave this land!
Egypt had been their home so long
And they seemed to accept their servitude.
Why should Moses 'rock the boat' and make
Pharaoh not only cruel but viciously rude?
And why should Moses confront such a man?
Because God told him to and he must
He had to prove to the people their God
Was a God they could fully trust!
Now God says, "This is what I want you to do.
Give Pharaoh the message I have given you!"

EXODUS 7

When Jehovah said, "You *will* be my
Ambassador," Moses could not refuse.
He had been raised as a prince, and had lived
As a shepherd, two qualities God could use.
So, two mighty men stood face to face.
One lived for himself. One lived for others.
Moses said to Pharaoh, "I demand in the name
Of Jehovah that you release my brothers."
These two men who faced each other certainly
Did not agree.
Pharaoh said to Moses, "You'll never get what
You want from me!
Who is this so called God of yours anyway
Who thinks I will release these slaves today?"
Pharaoh was unimpressed because he could
Only see this man called Moses.
Pharaoh– so much like us–who often listen
To a man of God and fail to see the truth
He discloses.
Though Pharaoh wouldn't listen, Aaron still
Threw down that *"rod!"*
"Pharaoh *must learn*," Jehovah says,
    "That I AM God!"
God said He would multiply His signs and
Wonders in the land.
This so called great and mighty Pharaoh
Would have to listen to God's
Imperial command!

EXODUS 8

It wasn't a giant frog that God sent but a
Bunch of little ones
God would show His power in words while
All Pharaoh's were as useless puns.
Besides, Pharaoh never kept his word.
Every 'yes' turned to a 'no.'
And He absolutely refused to let God's
People go!
All those frogs may as well have been a giant
Because this Pharaoh refused to be compliant.
First water-now dust-God adds a little spice.
Frogs were not convincing.
How about some lice?

Comments on Exodus

Pharaoh would not even listen to his magicians
Who said, "This is the Hand of God!"
They were smart enough to realize only God
Could put His power into Aaron's rod!
His hard head was like a blind-folded horse.
He was unable to see any need of remorse!
So God sent flies like homing pigeons
Sent on a mission
But only to each Egyptian living room, bed
Room and kitchen!
God has His own special bug controlling 'raid'
And no Israeli suffered from this plague.
Yet Pharaoh considered Israel the diamond
In his crown
And no matter how many times Moses
'set him up'
He'd respond by 'setting his foot down!'
He never learned it was Moses's God
He couldn't handle
And his rebellion was Egypt's biggest scandal!

EXODUS 9

Did Pharaoh have a choice? Did Egypt have
To be destroyed?
Who was the villain here? Who was this God
With whom Pharaoh toyed?
He certainly didn't know
Or he would have let God's people go!
Did you ever happen to sit on your front porch
And happen to see where the rain cut off?
There–God cut it off from Goshen
Though He knew Pharaoh would scoff!
But Egyptian cattle died, and men too
And everywhere they looked death laid in view.
How can a man be so hard hearted and his
Vision so dim
That he cannot see the judgement given him?
God will go to all lengths to save His own
And *that* has always been known!
My God sends boils to some as He did then
And keeps others free of pain.

Pharaoh definitely had a choice–horror
To suffer or peace to gain.
Even boils did not truly change his mind.
After all the plagues
After all that death, Pharaoh continued to rage.
We begin to wonder what God must do
In order to bring His people through.
And in seeing do we still need to ask
Why in the world was Egypt trashed?
God's judgements were not only tailored
To chastise
But so the hope of the impoverished
Might have reason to rise!
I ask again. Did Pharaoh have a choice
Whether or not to let God's people go?
Sure he did-and he made his choice.
And God answered in a strong
And mighty voice!

EXODUS 10

All those plants! Lettuce for locusts!
Cereal to be devoured!
Nothing left to eat, and briefly-very briefly
Pharaoh cowered!
Surely Pharaoh had
Spiritual Attention Deficit Disorder!
God wanted His people free.
Pharaoh wouldn't let them cross the border!
But the harder Pharaoh's heart,
The tougher the Lord became.
God still had more "tricks up His sleeve."
Even Pharaoh would have to honor His Name!
When God sets His people free
He frees their children, their animals, their
Possessions-borrowed though they may be!
God *never* does *anything* halfway!
That's the kind of God we still worship today!
I think God also sent darkness
For He needed to show
Pharaoh didn't even have one dying ember
Left to glow.

The "I Love My Bible" Commentary

But, Moses was wrong when he left his side.
Pharaoh was yet to take his wildest
Most destructive ride!
Moses must set his heart on the right track
For God's people needed to be free
And Moses had to go back!

EXODUS 11

They say, "The quiet comes before the storm,"
But this time the storm came first.
Israel wanted freedom and only freedom
Could quench their thirst.
God would give them what they wanted
And Pharaoh couldn't hold them back.
The freedom train was *coming down the track!*
Moses thought his task would be easy
Because God was by his side
But it was nine plagues later and freedom
Continued to hide like a reluctant bride.
Only death could rescue those indigent slaves.
Freedom waited-freedom for which every soul
Wanting wholeness craves!
Death to bondage! Death to fear!
Death to all that holds us here!
That must have been on Moses's mind
Only death could force Pharaoh
To be reluctantly kind!
To think—God did all that—and to boot
They all walked out with Egypt's loot!
Small pay for long hours.
Egypt's jewelry for people stripped of
Earthly powers
And we should remember ever after
What our God did in the next chapter!

EXODUS 12

Joy to some, and pain. Beware of midnight!
It was dark. It was fearful. Yet there was light..
For with the rising sun freedom beckoned!
The night passed with more havoc than Pharaoh
And all his worldly wise men
Could have reckoned.
But "day" was here and Israel, slaves though
They were, had no more to fear!
Their shoes were on, walking sticks ready
And they left Egypt happy, sure, and steady!
They were spared by the blood of lambs
Seen by the death angel on their door jambs!
He was death to Egypt, life to the Hebrews.
No wonder there were many people
Who would walk away with the Jews!
They were ready–from the greatest to the least
–strengthened by that freedom feast!
Notice, God first provided the feast
And the Passover sacrifice.
Hope comes when God provides the "spice!"
So close to death! So far away!
Blood made the difference on that holy day.
God saves and cleans,
Whatever the reason, whatever the means!
In Israel's most desperate need
God performed His greatest deed!
So joy for the Israelis came one morning
After God had given Pharaoh ample warning.
Pharaoh HAD to let God's people go.
Now who would dig those ditches
For this evil, decadent old Pharaoh?
But those whom God spares
Can walk away shouting, "Who Cares!"

EXODUS 13

God said, "I want to be an integral part
Of your Life, but this is the way it must be.
You <u>must</u> be sanctified by Me!"
To sanctify our "firstborn" means
Our firstborn love, our firstborn hopes, means
To dedicate to Him all our *firstborn* resources!
Our love, our loved ones, our fortunes, a true
Wholesome relationship
Are those things God never forces.

Comments on Exodus

It must be our willing choice
But it's the only way to walk with Him
To hear His glorious voice!
God dipped His love when those Israeli's
Dipped the blood and placed it on those doors.
Now they must dip their hearts in His love
And follow a higher holy trail
That would lead them to His home above!
We can see the trail just so far
But it ends somewhere beside
That wondrous "Morning Star"!
He waits to see if we'll come *His* way!
It is a brighter, fresher trail
He gives us to follow no matter what the day.
He tells us to come out of "Egypt" as He did
The Jews.
We know incredible joy when we do
But ultimate sorrow if we refuse.
Oh the glory on the trail ahead
When we choose to walk
With that living "Passover Bread!"

EXODUS 14

Afraid of the water?
There it is and no way back!
There is an army back there,
Egyptians beginning to worry about
Those slaves they now lacked!
So they came, charioteers menacing and tall
But God's angel clouded their view
And told those Israelis not to worry at all!
This is where faith comes in and fear
Slithers out.
When God takes action on His promises
There is no room left for doubt!
But who would ever, in their wildest dreams,
Dream up such a feat,
Water dividing like curtains, the sea's bed
Drying complete?
Who but God could do such a thing
And who could vision the hope it would bring?
No matter, though the miracles they had seen

They spotted the Egyptians and knew
The horror that could mean!
So God must teach them not to look
At circumstances or the obvious threat.
Our God is greater than any army
And He didn't want them to fret.
So the waters parted like a badly sewn seam
And that light on the other side
Drew them like a hypnotic beam!
Afraid of the "water?" Or whatever the fear
God still says to His people,
"Do not be afraid. I AM here.
(He calls Himself the GREAT I AM)
And-always-no matter the force of the water
It can't surmount His impregnable dam!

EXODUS 15

Victory writes a sweeter song for those on
The winning side
And while they sang they knew they could not
Have taken losing in stride!
I notice those Israelis immediately discovered
Who the True Victor was
And we who read about it can also see
The great things our Heavenly Father does!
What made the song truly sweet was its quality
Not its length.
"The Lord," they sang, "The Lord is my song,
My salvation, and my strength".
Had they sang no more, it would have been
Enough!
This Jehovah who would reign forever,
This Jehovah, was definitely tenderly tough!
It must have been marvelous to see His power,
To see the waters rise like a tunneling tower!
Just to know what God did at the Red Sea
Would quiet the battle cries of Moab, Edom,
Canaan, or any other enemy.
Though those Israelis danced, sang, and
Rejoiced about God's victory
Their joy turned to bitterness almost instantly.

The "I Love My Bible" Commentary

Why didn't they realize God who had made
Their rescue complete
Could turn even bitter waters utterly sweet?
Strange how quickly they forgot God's grace
And wanted to go back to the same old muddy
Pits, to die in the same old place!
After all those miracles they had seen
They still couldn't picture how very much
True freedom could mean!
But, still our Lord was willing to please
For He led them to a place of rest
By twelve springs and seventy Palm trees!
Yes, we can sing a sweeter song
We trust the ONE who is gently loving,
Graciously tender and magnificently strong!

EXODUS 16

Griping must be in our genes. Listen!
"Why did it happen to me?" You hear it still.
"Why did God do that," not wanting His will!
Then, again, He handed dominion over to us.
Look at world conditions today. Who is
Responsible? At whom should we fuss?
As attitudes go–it was the same in those days
And so they griped and failed
To give our Lord any praise.
So easily forgotten–they had been shackled.
So easily forgotten–the overwhelming
Problems The Father successfully tackled!
And–so easily forgotten they were walking free
Washed of the dust and awful slavery
As they passed through that Red Sea.
Their stomachs grumbled and so did they.
It was the pattern they followed every day.
But God did provide them a food
Which looked like coriander seed
And sometimes Quail–whatever their need.
But if you were to weigh the praise against
Their many complaints
Then I guess you could say these people were
Far from being saints!

Praise puts us on the upward trail!
To complain is but to fail.
It seems *that* is what we do best
And then wonder why we never succeed
To experience the spiritual comfort
We so desperately need!

EXODUS 17

We have to hold God's banner high to win
The war with our "selves."
But we won't realize the help we have
If we leaves our Bibles on our shelves.
Our "banner" is God's word given to
Strengthen our souls.
To hold it high, to obey our Lord brings us
Assurance we'll reach our goals
–goals of grace surrounding us all about
–goals of love we can't do without
–goals of peace so needed today
–and goals of faith which grows when we pray!
As Moses held God's rod up high
We, too, must give it a try.
Hold His word high for all to see
Best done by living righteously!
Those Israeli's needed water from the rock.
Don't we all!
Face it folks! Without that needed sustenance
We are all likely to faint and fall!
Why did God tell Moses to strike the rock?
Had He not, in tenderness, fed His flock?
Well maybe–and this is just a hunch,
It was just a way for Moses to take out
His frustration on that grumbling bunch!
Now I ask you which was harder when
Amalek attacked.
Was it harder for Joshua to stand and fight
Or for Moses to sit and pray?
Did you notice it was Moses
who had to have help lifting his arms that day?
And as if it is relative for those who complain
God sent evil relatives like a thundering train.

Comments on Exodus

Their distant cousins meant to destroy Israel
Once and for all!
But through Moses's perseverance and prayer
Those Amalekites were destined to fall.
Amalek is only a picture of how consistently
Evil rages
And how badly we need the help of our
Heavenly "Rock" of ages!

EXODUS 18

God's people can rejoice in that wisdom
God gives His own
Always there, always ready, always great,
Given by God alone!
But there are others given to benefit humanity
Such as Jethro wise and willing as could be!
Jethro was open to the wisdom of our Lord.
And he had seen Moses working way too hard.
His concern for Moses shows what love he had
And he knew too much of a good thing
Could turn out extremely bad!
How long could Moses stand the strain?
How long could he tenderly listen to these
People complain?
Ever hear of burn out?
When you are surrounded by negativity
You, yourself will begin to doubt!
How many time must we solve another's
Conflict
Without thinking, "My God, all this griping
Is making me sick?(!)
I think Jethro must have known the score
Having been a priest of Midian he'd faced
The same experiences many times before!
Love makes him pass on good advice to Moses
And today our leaders follow the practical
Advice he discloses.
I suspect Jethro didn't come based on a
Hasty decision.
God sent this man who could resolve

A seemingly impossible condition.
For our Father watches over us every day
And from the President to the pauper
He shows His love in every way!
But don't forget the greatest way God shows
His concern
Is to give His *survival laws* for us to learn.
Moses would tell his people, "You have a
Choice! Choose death OR choose life!"
Obedience brought joy but to disobey
Would only bring strife!
But Moses needed help and the pattern was set
And now he had the extra time to give
Quality service with no regret!
As we read through this precious book
Let us remember the rules God has given
For OUR sakes!
If everyone obeyed them, there would be
No broken homes, no need to fear
And no heartaches!
I call that positive power
That brings the "Jethro" help we need
For even our darkest hour!

EXODUS 19

Now its time to climb the mountain
To obtain that cleansing from God's
Holy fountain!
Only Moses could go to receive those laws.
Others were possessed with too many flaws!
It seems their hearts were hollow
Because of those laws they failed to follow!
God knew those Israeli's would need guidance
And restraint
And without it not one, not even Moses
Could be a worthy saint.
Essentially He was saying to Moses
"All must be clean to come to me."
To bathe and wash their clothes showed
The outward cleansing to picture the

The "I Love My Bible" Commentary

Inward cleansing they needed so desperately!
God had saved them from fear and distress.
Now they needed to be clean, and to be pure!
        Sin was their disease!
        Sanctification was the cure!
God knew they needed direction. Did they?
It seems so as we hear them say
"All the Lord says we will do!"
And evidently-of the rebellion that lay in their
Hearts-they didn't have a clue!
But God knew how insidious and dangerous
Rebellion can be
And He must have said,"Those rebels cannot
Come close to me!
He knew those that declared such loyalty
Would, almost immediately, commit idolatry.
The mountain pictured pureness they needed
That day
Because, instead of being snow white,
Their hearts were a dingy gray!

EXODUS 20

Here we see God's majesty is greater than the
Mountains, purer than the skies!
To put Him first invites a splendor far beyond
Where any eagle flies!
Put Him first and you will understand the peace
And joy that comes by obeying this command.
Oh, people, if you really thirst
You can find joy putting Him first!
Every command God gives is for our benefit.
It is glorious joy we need and God is willing
To give it!
And we'll never be sorry for honoring
Our Mothers and Dads
The ones who gave us all the love they had!
And to simply love each other
Like we'd love a sister or a brother
Is to experience a life content.
Don't you think that's what our Father meant?
A life lived pure and just
 Frees us from crippling lust.

True happiness is an open mind
--open to God
Always loving and kind
And don't envy the Jones's next door.
Joy doesn't come from having more.
What really sets life apart
Is to walk with love in your heart!

EXODUS 21

What is it about bondage that frightens us so?
Is it because we can't do what we want to do
        go where we want to go?
Does it make us less human than we are?
Can't a slave attach his hopes to a shining star?
It seems that way in this chapter!
Did someone miss the point we're really after?
Did Moses misunderstand the Lord
And destine some for lives incredibly hard?
Then, again, Paul says we are the bond servants
Of Christ though *we are free*!
Ambivalent as it seems what is the meaning
 For you and me?
My FATHER set me free yet we are bonded
        together!
    Free to love Him
    Free to do His will
    Free to worship Him forever!!!
    No seven year itch here
    I don't want to be free
    Even in seven million years!
For I am bonded to the One who saved me
    From all my sins
    All my doubts
    All my fears!
(And I will praise His Name forever!)

EXODUS 22

Responsibility! Oh how we hate that word!
This chapter is full of it!
It tells us we are responsible.

Comments on Exodus

For the errors we commit.
A thief robs someone and when caught says
"Who? Me?
And if he is shot at the wrong time(daytime)
The shooter can't cop an innocent plea!
But if the thief is caught he must make
Full restitution,
A great idea we should add
To our own constitution!
There are so many "do nots" and "can nots"
It is hard to assimilate them all.
They are simply telling us
There are countless ways we can fall!
        Details! Details! Details!
Responsibilities in which so many of us fails.
God is concerned with the little things
And knows the heartaches failure brings.
Now-a-days right and wrong are not
Laid out so plain
For holiness is a word we are taught to disdain.
Higher education has often led to lower morals
And some assume responsibility is outdated
AND *sowing* and *reaping* are not related!
But, through it all, with the problems
Mankind rehashes
Responsibility keeps rising from the ashes!

EXODUS 23

God offers us a way to grab on to sweet life
And go along for the ride
And we will find it much easier to do
With our Heavenly Father by our side.
God knows little mistakes can hurt
And troubles can come in an unwanted spurt!
So He gives mini-instructions and mini-advice.
He knows just when our lives need
A little added spice!
And, remember, when we are blessed by God
We mustn't think its good luck giving us a nod.
God's blessings come, maybe from osmosis,
While we are holding His heart in ours!
And if we don't perhaps we'll find how life
Without our Heavenly Father quickly sours!
It is He who promises to take sickness away
As we *walk with Him* from day to day!
Sometimes we may think His laws are unreal
      but everything He does
        everything He says
          is for our benefit
No matter what we think or how we feel!
Sometimes such truth is hard to understand
Because we are on a different wave-length
But-always-He wants to give us
His love, His protection and His strength!
And our pilgrimages are not just three yearly.
Everyday is a pilgrimage of love
Sent from our Precious Father who lives
In Heavenly splendor up above!
        Love!   Mercy!
          Blessing! Grace!
They make it much sweeter-this life we face!

EXODUS 24

Picture an altar with twelve pillars round about
To circle the Father in love is to leave
No Room For Doubt!
It is certainly a symbol of worship
And the joy worship brings.
Twelve tribes looped like inseparable rings!
We are speaking of a time when everything
Was strange and new.
God had to tell them point-by-point
What He wanted them to do.
It seemed easy for them to say
How willingly they would obey.
But it was easier said than done
And they would soon reject holiness
For what they thought was a little fun.
Lets not judge! Would our faith last forty days
Without the presence of the Lord?
Can we criticize people whose souls

The "I Love My Bible" Commentary

Were so easily scarred?
The influence of holy men goes a long way
And we need them just as badly in this
Gospel-doubting day.
So it is necessary that we truly understand
Why God calls men (or women) apart
For sin, impatience, and doubt are still
Failures of the heart.

EXODUS 25

God said, "Bring me the best!"
Somehow, giving our **best** to God
Sanctifies the rest.
He only asked *for a little of what He already
 gave*
And He did it through the Egyptians
When each of them was but a slave!
Notice, God had a pattern for whatever
They made or built
From an awesome tabernacle to a tiny quilt!
God's pattern had already been perfected
And it was to be faithfully followed
When the tabernacle was built and erected.
 PATTERNS!
God lovingly gives one to you and me.
Our pattern is the Bible
And our materials are His supply!
Don't forget, everything comes from Him
No matter what we make or buy!
And when we follow His directions
He fills our lives with His perfections!
In day to day living we can honor our Lord
And should we forget He watches over us
Nature is our "cue card!"
The stars twinkle His love.
Until time ends, we'll see that moon up above!
God gives us rippling rivers and quiet streams
And He even walks through our dreams!
We can bounce through life or merely plod.
It all depends on how closely
We follow the patterns of our God

EXODUS 26

Jesus is my "pillar of strength," my curtain
Of holiness!
We are connected by His *clasps of love*
He gives all of Himself to heal my brokenness!
There is beauty in His presence
Strength in His grace.
He provides everything I need
For all the problems I might face!
His great truth is very simple.
All I need is in *His* temple!
There are colors of joy there
Which no gold, silver, or jewels can compare!
In His love–even when we are on the outside–
 we're still "in!"
Jesus is the "courtyard," the sacrifice
 for our sin.
However, those Israelis had to come
To the courtyard
And it was there they received forgiveness
From the Lord!
Today our *courtyards* are our hearts
Which are surrounded by love and grace
And the mercy our loving God imparts!
He has already provided for our needs
And gives us strength for kind, noble deeds!
Through us, God calls everyone who strays
And He continues to show His great love
In glorious gentle ways!

EXODUS 27

If they wanted to walk with God
They must walk the narrow road
And holy must be the materials
For God's earthly abode.
They were often punished when they balked.
They must not trash this perfect road
On which God and they walked.
More directions are coming, more plans to give
For only special materials could be used

Comments on Exodus

In this place our Lord would live.
It would be a hallowed place
Filled with His love, mercy, and grace!
He had given them Egypt's best
And in the proportional giving back
They would be truly blessed!
God did the planning. They did the work!
They all came willing to share their gifts.
Not one soul showed a desire to shirk.
Matter of fact, God had to say, "No more!"
The walls were bursting with materials
They had brought to store!
Oh that His people today would do the same
And in showing our love for God
Bring glory to His Name!
We can all say, "God used the best materials
        In making me,
        His love for my heart
        His peace for my mind
        His joy for the rest of me.
        And He gave me wisdom
        To walk 'His walk'
        And do it lovingly!
He has clothed me in His garments of salvation
        And robed me in humility!
On this eternally vibrant sea of life I sail
I have no excuse to quit or fail.
Salvation is God's gossamer lace
Delicately strong, sewn together by His grace!
We must never be afraid.
Our garments of salvation are Heavenly made!

EXODUS 28

Now we are told in chapter twenty eight
Where God will abide must be made
Strong and straight!
It must have been the most glorious tent
Ever erected.
Even the garments the priests wore
Would be closely inspected.
Imagine building a life of which God approves,
No ugly glitches, nor unseemly grooves!

Just a life of beauty clean and pure
Following His directions brings happiness
    for sure!
Beautiful materials expertly designed
The Father will present us to Himself
Gloriously refined!
Gold and silver, purple and blue
Pictures of souls, tried and true!
Our foundation is Christ Himself
Our walls the love He gives
His grace the canopy.
He is the complete covering for you and me!
It is a permanent ordinance,
This thing called grace
That will take us to our Heavenly Father's
Most Holy Place!
Oh think of the torment
Facing those who have refused
To wear His wedding garment!

EXODUS 29

Let's not become weary with the many details
For a beautiful house must have perfect plans!
Our Great Architect sees the smallest splinter
And knows a builder's many demands.
From tiny boards to windows that give light
From frames that need nails to hold them tight
From all the many items a 'house' needs
To the land and to its 'deeds'
All are joined together with heavenly expertise
And in that perfection God gives us peace.
It is His-this body we call our "house"
A place of joy if he abides.
No one can even imagine
This place of beauty to which He guides!
"I am with you always," We can hear Him say!
And *that* is the glorious "house"
We live in today!
Take heart Dear Christian,
The Pattern is still around!
And His love will keep us
On heavenly solid ground!

The "I Love My Bible" Commentary

EXODUS 30

My heart is a small altar
And I'm incensed when goodness fails.
Yet, when we think we're so pure
We have to admit, in His presence
How quickly our pureness pales.
It took a lot of burning, a lot of ashes to purify
Even one sinner for which
Many an animal had to die.
Still, the Bible fully notes
Purity never comes from the deaths
Of bulls, lambs, or goats!
There's a better way. Jesus died once for all
      the Perfect Sacrifice
The pure Lamb of God guilty of no sin or vice!
The priest had to follow orders
But our Savior's life was in *perfect order!*
The priest's heart might be flawed
But God's love has no border!
No ransom paid could save a soul
Only Jesus could give Himself
To make our spirits whole.
Complete love needs no details.
Anything less completely fails.
We must make our hearts altars
Where God can dwell
And then He can whisper softly
"I am here and all is well!"

EXODUS 31

When God saw the need
He Sent Bezaleel and Aholiab to resolve it.
He wanted beauty for the altar
But knew ashes needed only a pit.
He gave directions from the sublime
To the least
From the care of the altar to the use of the beast
And for the instruction of the people
God gave them a priest.
They were to remember God filled different
People with talents for the task
And what they needed He had already given
So no one had to ask.
Some to work, Some to teach.
Levites to serve. Priests to preach.
And In empathy He gave them a day to rest
For bodies weaken that are stressed.
He seems to be saying, " I rested one day
      out of seven."
It was a picture of eternal rest someday,
Somehow, somewhere in Heaven.
But rest is not a picture of inactivity.
Rest is the vehicle that encourages constancy!
And the law was a covenant reminder
      -written on stone
There to teach Israelis to worship God alone!

EXODUS 32

In this chapter we see the difference
Between Aaron and Moses.
Aaron wanted to please the people
And brings trouble before this chapter closes.
Hearts hardened like dried plaster
Can only bring themselves disaster.
Aaron proved his humanness inside and out
And left this whole nation dangling in doubt.
But he hadn't yet been consecrated.
He had not been prepared.
He was guilty too, but there is a reason
He was spared.
All those years in Egypt he had become weak.
He had struggled for acceptance
And it was this he continued to seek.
But the people's acceptance should not have
Been his goal
For it resulted in an unsteady heart
And a damaged soul.
Had it not been for Moses
Who fell on his face before God
To save Israel from the Lord's destroying rod.
Even Aaron would have ceased to exist
-a whole nation gone like morning mist!

Comments on Exodus

But we must look beyond the sin
To see the power of prayer.
When this nation needed deliverance
God found Moses kneeling there.
Moses humbled himself because his people
Were disgraced
And they needed prayer to save them
From the punishment they faced.
But always remember *sin is unsightly*
And God can not-will not-take it lightly!

EXODUS 33

I used to think God knew everything
But I wondered how He could possibly know
How getting to see Him even once
Could give my heart an instant glow!
How can He-being God-really feel
The tremendous surge in my heart
Seeing *for myself* He is more than real!
So many people question God's existence.
Maybe they did back then.
And still today, so many people flaunt their sin.
God couldn't tolerate such blatant disbelief.
And who of us can understand
Why they brought themselves so much grief?
They couldn't see this Great Jehovah God
But they could see His power
And knew God considered Moses his friend
Thus chose him as the *man of the hour!*
But this man felt his was no choice at all
And unless God walked with him
He would surely fall.
And because my need is so great I can see
Why God needed a place called Calvary.
    Why!
To send His Son to rescue me!
And that is why my soul can sing.
I know my God knows everything!

♡ ♡ ♡ ♡ ♡ ♡ ♡ ♡

EXODUS 34

Moses's greatness wasn't based on fate.
It was GOD Himself who made Moses great!
    Our God is the "GREAT I AM"
    God of Love   God of Power
    God of Grace   God of Hope
        King of the Ages
    The unseen One who never dies!
This God took an ordinary man and made him
            extraordinary!
    Took this man raised to be great
        vanquished to be humble
    and put him back together again!
Moses had walked the halls of palaces
And had trudged lonely desert trails
And back in the desert now was readied
To serve this Glorious One who never fails!
And God once again had to reiterate
He-and only He-was truly great.
He walked before Moses in His splendor
        and grace
And Moses came away from that encounter
        with a glow on his face.
        Lift up your head!
        Put on a smile!
    When God goes with you
    You can go the second mile!
The second mile is service, a daily commitment,
        a daily task
And like Moses, when we need Him
All we have to do is ask!
The people's sin had been so great
God had angrily said, "NO!
They are so wicked I won't go!"
But Moses was a man of prayer
And God wouldn't turn away
And just leave him there!
HE went, but there were rules they must follow
And the lesson here?
Without God, life is empty and hollow

The "I Love My Bible" Commentary

Without Him, our heartbeat wanes lifeless
    and flat!
And you can bet Moses knew that!

EXODUS 35

All the supplies that would be needed
They had borrowed and brought from Egypt.
So when God called for tabernacle supplies
They were more than amply equipped!
In the previous chapter they knew
They had seen this man who had seen God
And that must have jolted the uninspired.
God had erased their sin
And cold hearts had been fantastically fired!
They needed a man true to the "Great IAM"
If they were to survive
And oh how badly they needed guidance
To keep their faith alive!
This nation had danced into danger
And carelessly provoked God's anger.
It had exposed a sin well hidden
And worshiped an idol expressly forbidden!
So this nation needed a great man
To lead them to the promised land.
In the meantime work must be done
    materials supplied.
The place must be glorious where God
    would abide.
God-in just being there made that dismal desert
    fair
-just being there, turned this nation around
And put their feet on solid ground.
Their greatest need was a man who would lead
And this man could say "I have seen God and
He walks with us today!"
It is great to see people with great skill
Who knew they could do their best
And knew their best was in doing
  The Heavenly Father's will!

♡ ♡ ♡ ♡ ♡ ♡ ♡

EXODUS 36

The supplies would have done no good
Unless men's hearts were stirred..
These men with many talents must use them
According to God's Word.
No matter how elaborate the plans
No matter how glorious the gold
The tabernacle would not have one ounce
    of glory
Unless they built it just like they were told.
Talent is no good unless one is willing
Unless work is well done life is not fulfilling.
But Bazaleel and Aholiab were dedicated
Spirit filled, wise hearted men
Thankful for how very generous
Their fellow Israelis had been.
And inspiration and dedication made their work
    so much better
Especially because they followed God's
    blueprints to the letter!
The tabernacle-pictured as one unit-would unite
Their hearts and souls
And as they listened to the God of all the ages
They would surely meet their goals!
We sit back and look at the pictures
Painted on linen spun with pure gold
And see the glory of the greatest story ever told!
For every stitch and every jewel of God's design
Would picture the day I can call Him mine!
My God, my Father, my Savior
Wrapped up in a picture of love
A picture painted first
In that glorious home above!
Call Him yours ? That's for sure!
Nothing else can ever make us feel so secure!
And security is the 'apple pie' that satisfies
Our spiritual appetite.
It is God putting all the 'ingredients' together
And making sure the 'pie' comes out right!
It is knowing God gives His best
To give our souls eternal rest.

Comments on Exodus

EXODUS 37

The Law was given by a heart of gold
And pure gold must surround it
    must protect it
    must support it.
Nothing else God gave them was as important
    not the air we breathe
    not the water we drink
    not the food we eat
    not even this earth on which we walk!
The Law, the Word, will never pass away!
    All else will!
There is something better up ahead
    something eternal!
This earth is but a haystack
And men have reduced the law to just a needle
    hidden there.
But-though not seen-gold still surrounds it
    -molded, moving, melted gold!
It was golden love that gave the law
So man could know true love.
Paul knew that! "Love," he said, "causes
No ill to its neighbor!"
To Paul, love and law were inseparable.
And the law is still our pattern because
God's ark of love surrounds it.
The 'hay' will blow away some day
And the 'needle' will be found
-still mighty, still gold, still relevant
Because it was given
By God's precious heart of gold!

EXODUS 38

The tabernacle would not be finished
Until the priests were fully clothed
According to God's Holy plan.
We, too, are not finished until we are clothed.
What is our clothing?
The garments of salvation
The robe of righteousness
-both made by God's design.
How definitely we need to see
How great His design for us can be!
Should we not wear His 'wedding garment'
    He will say
"You cannot enter here. You must go away!"
There is a response! What must it be?
What must be our RSVP?
It is simply, "Lord I do accept the garment
You've so graciously given me!"
That is our purpose. That is our identity.
That garment is our label, our ticket to eternity!
Clothed by the Lord, the best designer of all!
I hope this doesn't sound irreverent but
Someday we're going to have a ball!
And we'll certainly be well dressed.
Through that dressing, we'll be forever blessed!
Then, this 'tabernacle' will be glorified.
I will be there because it was for me He died!

EXODUS 39

How glorious the priests were clothed
With garments to picture holiness
And hopefully-hearts to fit that holy mold!
We'll see God's instructions were intended
To picture hearts needing to be mended!
We see beauty in the Lord
Ugliness in His chosen few.
Yet He knew what they needed
And He told them what to do!
His brand of life is the *best!*
Hearts and hands must follow the rules.
Hearts and hands must pass the test.
In Genesis we see the birth and growing pains.
In Exodus we see the solutions
To clean man's guilty stains!
Its just like our Heavenly Father
Whose love is ever real
To give us His love and His brand of hope
AND that joy we so desperately need to feel!
And that is why I tell this story.
The law is the Old Testament vehicle
    of His glory!

The "I Love My Bible" Commentary

EXODUS 40

It has all come together, the work finished now.
The ark, the tabernacle, the clothes
The symbol placed on Aaron's brow
The table, the lamps to chase away the dark
The veil to enclose the Holy of Holies
The precious commandments placed in the ark
Were arranged the way God decreed
And that glorious help gave them hope indeed!
We must get that true picture
Of what our God has supplied.
Our 'ark,' our 'tabernacle' is a precious place
Where His people can triumphantly abide
Rested and forever by the Father's side!
He gave His salvation design
And in that place there was a purpose
For every line!
His glory filled the tabernacle portraying
His pleasure.
And close to that tabernacle
We live a life we can treasure
For His gems of life glow within
And the love of all the ages shows us
How to overcome our sin.
It is the tabernacle of eternal love
Sent from the Father up above!

NOTE: He has given us the pictures of His holiness.   He has shown us His purity. We have seen His power through out the Bible, but have we obeyed Him? Look at the history of man's disobedience through these many centuries. Consider the blatant disobedience of *even Christians* today who consider the Bible outdated, who mock God's commandments against adultery, who seem to have problems with honesty and integrity, who support an industry that glamorizes every sin this precious book has condemned-over and over! And because we break the greatest of all the commandments to truly, honestly love one another, we hurt each other terribly. Have we forgotten God does not change, His laws have not changed, and His word is still as relevant today as it was more than two thousand years ago? Shouldn't we wonder how many times our Lord has come close to losing patience with us when we step outside the bounds of His love, show contempt for His commandments, ignore the Holy Spirit, and treat our Savior with disdain? Yet, *despite our sins His mercies fail not. They are new every morning!*

Every time we sin our Lord graciously forgives us(whenever we ask with repentant hearts). Every time we stray He sends someone to show us the way. Every time we have shown hatred, He has shown us love! And for every time we doubt, He shows us amazing compassion! But we still keep doubting Him—and so we hurt deeply. But our Lord has a love bandage for our hurts. Its fibers of healing are bonded by grace!

Evidently He doesn't doubt us nearly as much as we doubt Him!

Surely He must know something we don't know!

*Then a cloud covered the tent
of the congregation
and the glory of the Lord
filled the tabernacle*

*and Moses was not able to enter
into the tent of the congregation
because the cloud abode thereon*

*and the glory of the Lord
filled the tabernacle.*
(Exodus 40:34-35kjv)

THE BOOK OF LEVITICUS

These are

The Commandments

which the Lord

commanded Moses

for the children of Israel

in Mount Sinai.
(Leviticus 27:34 kjv)

The "I Love My Bible" Commentary

LEVITICUS 1

Day after day, year after year
the same old thing.   *The Law!*
Love wrapped in black paper
Love without a single flaw
Love substantiated by Grace
beautiful, beautiful love
to conquer the problems we face.
It is deeper, wider, higher than we can ever
comprehend
this Law sent from God to give us life
without end.
This Law, this soul protection is given by
God's love!
If we are to keep life's hands clean
the Law is our glove!
Yet, as we walk into Leviticus it seems
we walk into a life mundane
but structure, purity, purpose is given
in order to keep us sane!
Is the Law personal? Yes indeed!
To touch the sacrifice is to admit our need
and to admit when our life is scarred
how very badly we need our Lord.
Today we touch Him by prayer.
Prayer is His tabernacle
and He meets us lovingly there!
Take Leviticus apart.
Put it under love's microscope.
And we'll see God's ultimate purpose
is to give us a life of glorious hope!

LEVITICUS 2

To say one picture is worth a thousand words
Is no good if people won't look.
Who cares enough about old fashioned virtues
Customs introduced in this book?
To some its like wearing a girdle
Which gives too much restraint.
God gave(gives)guidelines to follow but
They(we) said either, "we won't or we can't!"
Maybe God was saying, "Before your sins
Can spoil
Get rid of them with a dose of Spiritual
Castor Oil!"(& who likes castor oil?)
To come to God's altar, to be personally
Involved
Was a substitutionary way
To have their problems solved.
Let's face it! The biggest problems yet remain
Because we fail to come to Christ
And ask Him to remove every single stain.
If you know Him and that must be willingly
You will long for Him to walk with you
And you will never know the end
Of all the miracles He can do!
"Come unto me," He says, "and I will give
You rest!"
Close to His "altar" is where we live
Totally blessed!

LEVITICUS 3

Thanksgiving! A sacrifice? No Way!
It should be joy coming from the heart
An exuberant response to God's love
That fills our hearts every day!
So! What are we to be thankful for?
Every blade of grass, every twinkling star
Every time the sun rises and sets
All the blessings in between
For which man kind forgets!
We must remember that kind words spoken
Mend many a heart that has been broken!
God gives us fresh morning air!
We can smell the fragrant flowers
See beauty every where!
Even the hard times, the dark days
Can make us strong
And of course we should be thankful
When God cleanses us from every wrong!
Think about the new born babies
That bring innocence to earth

Comments on Leviticus

And the happy brides and bridegrooms
Who fill it with their mirth!
Listen to every little girl and boy
Grace the day with laughter
Fill it with their joy!
> *Thanksgiving
> A sacrifice?
> How can it be?*

Think of the peace, the joy, the blessings,
The incredible love
God has given you and me!
We must not forget when we pray
To think Him for the blessings
He sends us every day!.

LEVITICUS 4

Now we're down to personal responsibility.
Even the priest was not exempt!
> General sin!
> Private sin!

Any transgression of the Divine Law
Any sin digs deep into the soul
And, generally speaking, only that
Private Power of God
Can reach down to make us whole!
All those details in Chapter 4 merely meant
When a soul is injured by self or others
It needs more than a 'splint!'
That which is frightening in this day
Is we cannot claim ignorance in any way.
We have so much knowledge and grace.
What can we do about the consequences
We face?
We must admit our sins are presumptuous
Because we've been taught so much
Yet it seems insanity of the soul
Has put us and God out of touch.
Like the priests of old we are not exempt.
And it is truly dangerous today
To hold God's Grace in contempt.
God's laws have not expired.
To whom much is given much is required!
But beyond this Law stands a thing called

LOVE
And if we tremble in expectation
It should be because
He has sent so much of it
From His Home up above!

LEVITICUS 5

In the case of holy things we are still so dumb.
We have not studied to show ourselves
Approved unto God
Thus our souls are pitifully numb!
At the cross Jesus prayed, "Father forgive them
For they know not what they do!"
He was speaking of a wisdom deeper
Than human knowledge
A wisdom contained by a very few!
So it is the deep wisdom of the soul
For which we must be aware.
Sin against our precious Lord can
Only bring despair!
This chapter is careful to show
Arrangement for forgiveness was extended
To the very poor.
Its not the wealth or money we give
In which our God is keeping score!
So He provided help for those in poor
Spiritual *and material* health
For one soul is worth much more
Than all the world's accumulated wealth!
God's expectations of us still remains the same
And He provides a way for all of us
To stand on a higher, nobler plain!
His Law and Love stand hand in hand
And lead us to His Promised Land.
In this chapter is His Holy advice.
And even though we don't understand it
His forgiveness comes through sacrifice.
But its already been done.
One day, He gave His Marvelous Son!!!

✝ ✝ ✝ ✝ ✝ ✝ ✝ ✝ ✝

The "I Love My Bible" Commentary

LEVITICUS 6

Just as we need the nourishment of daily food
We need daily guidance as well.
"Hear instruction and be wise,"Solomon said
And those who didn't listen, fell
    with a thud!!!
Life, that should have been holy and vibrant,
Without the power of obedience
    became(becomes) a *dud!*
One cannot lie or steal even by default.
If honesty is not 100 percent
It can be costly to repent.
God says restore 20 percent more plus
An offering of what the priest would demand.
It is only proof we will have to pay
When a cheating heart takes command.
"What goes around, comes around" *they* say
And whether we like it or not
That restitution rule still applies today.
And, then again, an ounce of prevention
Is worth a pound of cure!
Staying 100 percent honest helps to keep
Or at least makes us feel secure!
Well, I for one, have missed the mark
And if you did too, we have an *ark.*
It is an ark called *life anew!*
God's mercies are *new* every morning
And they give life fresh as the morning dew!
Burnt offerings and guilt offerings
Are mentioned too.
Holiness must be lived back then
According to God's point of view!
Some day it really would be, when Jesus came
To take away our guilt, our fear, and shame.
Yes—someday Jesus would pay it all
And His eternal love reaches down
To lift us when we fall!

LEVITICUS 7

Who would think of peace as a sacrifice?
It brings such quality to life!
We all talk about peace and quiet
But do we want it badly enough
To put an end to useless strife?
What this chapter tells me is peace
Begins with me.
Oh, if only I could spread a virus called peace
How blessed this whole world would be!
One must deny his own will
With an elegant loving style
But it seems so hard to do for many think
That would be going the "second mile!"
Look at the involvement pictured here,
God, priest, and personhood
Coming together at the altar
With the person bringing what he could!
God does not demand what He doesn't supply
To do our best brings a gift God will not deny.
Is peace available to all? Of course!
Is it not better than wars deadly force?
To truly want peace is to seek it with all
Our heart
And to have it takes every one doing
His own part!
But think of the years we've studied the Bible
Think of the time we've spent.
Instead of having peace we are plagued
With the virus of discontent!
We must examine our hearts to see
Is it because of you or is it because of me?
Since the world began it's been the same.
Peace comes only when we glorify His Name

LEVITICUS 8

I'm clothed in the garments of salvation
And I didn't sew a single stitch!
It is a pleasure singing praises to Him
Salvation harmony in perfect pitch!
And to keep me from growing cold
God covers me with His robe of righteousness
Always keeping me warm
Even when life may taunt me with
Its meanest strongest storm!

The Book of Leviticus

Amazing what God does for His people.
Amazing is His grace!
And I became aware of it years ago
In a sawdust floored tabernacle
Which I remember as a happy, holy place!
My life really began there in that place
That was anointed with His presence, power.
Grace, mercy, and salvation
All sent in love's gentle shower!
God still sends us directions, patterns
We are to follow.
Without Him, without His love
We experience a life empty and hollow.
When it all began God had to be specific.
I bet they couldn't see how soon their lives
Would grow strong, would be terrific!
Every goal God set for them
He helped them meet.
He gave them light at night
And protected them from noon day heat.
Same now!
In our darkness, He comes to guide the way
Even in our sorrow
His presence makes a perfect day!
But we need His anointing oil.
We need to feel that blessed presence
When the Holy Spirit hovers!
We need to realize it is He who clothes us
And blessed are we, the ones He covers!
Life, *true life,* begins at His tabernacle door.
It is always open and He waits!
Behind Him, beyond that door
We catch a glimpse of those gone before
Through His wide open welcoming gates!
We are clothed, anointed, blessed!
Even in darkest times
God gives our souls eternal rest!

LEVITICUS 9

I used to wonder why we needed to bring
A guilt offering when the priests had already
Accepted the offering for sin.
But I slowly learned it is holding to our guilt
That puts us in a situation which is 'no-win!'
We hold feverishly to it-our heart rending guilt
But we find no comfort in this
Dark patch-work quilt.
So God made it one of the offerings
We must bring to Him
For as long as we hold on to guilt
We face a future only grim.
Its like we turn to a 'pillar of salt'
Looking back keeps us *full of our fault.*
It is the guilt we hold on to that torments us
The most.
It becomes an unreal creature
An unfriendly ghost!
Paul said, "All our guilt is gone.
      GONE!
So we see when God demanded a sin offering,
He demanded a guilt offering as well
      Think about it!
Tormenting guilt makes us face a daily hell.
Guilt! A piece of this puzzle of life
We definitely don't need
If we'll only put it on God's altar
We'll find peace, joy and comfort indeed!
In Christ, God's glory shines through.
It is His daily gift to me and you!

LEVITICUS 10

Right at the first just so we won't forget
God teaches His people a lesson
Even we haven't learned as yet.
For so many suffer with the *Big Head* disease
And often believe they can do as they please.
Like Nadab and Abihu!
After all, weren't they big men they thought?
When God wanted someone special
It was them He had sought!
But look at the trouble for them
That kind of thinking brought.
"Oh God doesn't mean what He says, you say"
But when we foolishly question His rules

The "I Love My Bible" Commentary

We will find ourselves in trouble some day.
God dislikes making an example of anyone
But even Nadab and Abihu had to face
What they had done
All the rules of worship had been laid out
        Plain to see!
        Too Holy to doubt!
What is it about human nature that says
"It won't happen to me?!
And then the charred remains of failure
Is all that is left to see.
Too whom much is given, much is required.
We must treat those souls holy
Whom God has spiritually fired!
Nadab and Abihu had no recompense
When they carelessly burned unholy incense.
And those who sit high in the holy echelon
(or who *think* they do)
Must make sure their holiness
Is holiness according to God's point of view!
It is very easy for a Christian to fall
When He steps into the trap of thinking
He knows it all
Let us remember if we want to wear a crown
The ego that goes up
Must come tumbling down!
Look at Nadab and Abihu and hear God say.
"Man, if you want to come to Heaven,
You're going to come *My Way!*"

LEVITICUS 11

Here we go again with the details
We don't have to worry about
But God had to lay the foundation
For His House of Holiness
Must be strong and stout!
He is teaching people who had lived among
Idols-dead gods with no power
He had to built the little faith in Him
That had often turned sour.
They mistakenly thought He was like
The dead gods of their masters

And still didn't realize why God send Egypt
Those dreadful disasters!
He was wiping out every visage of every
Helpless god
Man made, they were falling apart
As easily as a dried-out clod.
"I Am God, " He declared
And evil must be squashed; nothing spared!
If a bowl was defiled, it must be smashed
Anything that couldn't be cleaned
Would have to be trashed!
"I Am Holy," God says and He is in
The business of making us holy, too.
But it is according to what **HE** says
And *that* is what He expects us to do!
But times have changed!
The Eternal Sacrifice has been given.
Jesus Christ our Savior took our place!!!
The details have merged and submerged
In God's sea of love and grace!
But God is still holy, still hasn't changed
Still sets the rules
And to go our own way, to do our own thing
Has often made us into blubbering fools.
David says, "The fool has said in his heart-
    'there is no God'"
But when we make fools of ourselves
We can say like David,
"I have found comfort in God's staff
And strength in His unbending rod!"

LEVITICUS 12

Blood is contaminating no matter the sex
But is there an injustice this idea reflects?
Maybe so but why?
In old times little girls would not be
considered
Equals no matter how hard they would try.
Even if women were smarter they had no
    brute force
And sad to say man mis-used just *that*
To spiral this world on its downward course.

The Book of Leviticus

But-back to the cleansing
Maybe it took twice as long for a mother
To prepare
Her daughter to live in a culture so obviously,
Pitifully, wrongfully unfair!
When God created Eve it was to *help* her man
But man demoted women to second class
Though that was *never* God's plan.
He made Eve perfect.
It was man He made from dust.
But the man was physically stronger
And the weaker sex became victims
Of his lust.
They were to compliment one another-
    man and wife
And share the joy of togetherness
Bringing oneness to life!
Surely we will never understand
The culture of that time.
It is as if having a little girl was some
Devilish crime.
Have we sometimes misunderstood
God's great directions
And imposed on others our imagined
Imperfections?
God never intended inequality among us so
This chapter will always be hard to understand
Because He had made man and woman
To walk lovingly together hand-in-hand!

LEVITICUS 13

A plague! What is it but grief?
It must have been a constant itch
From which there was no relief.
Think of the eye sore; think of the pain.
Think of the trauma for those
Held in shuddering disdain!
Patches of carelessness plague us today.
Scabs of neglect have come to stay.
You can see leprosy in the skin
But how about leprosy of the soul
That peels away the blessed hope

We carry hopefully within?
How about the pain of being alone,
Pain that seeps into the marrow
And cuts through the bone?
How about the deep pain for which there
Seems no cure?
Ah! But we have a priest that promises
To make us completely pure!.
Our High Priest is a Priest of love
Not merely one who is hired
He knows those with leprosy of the soul
Are needing desperately to be inspired.
His main objective is healing you and me.
For in Heaven there will be
No form of leprosy.

LEVITICUS 14

I can imagine one bird saying, "Its not
My turn," when one had to die!
One was a sacrifice, the other free to fly!
Perhaps we need to see the obvious here.
Jesus had to die so we could 'fly'
    with out fear!
But in that day and time details were a part
Of cleansing the sins of a troubled heart.
And seven days had to come into play
Before all that residue could be washed away.
Seven days must pass before one would be
    Considered clean.
We often wonder about the depth of cleansing
And what did it mean!
There is so much involved here.
Was leprosy the victims fault?
How could he have prevented it without
Placing himself in a separate sterile vault?
The contamination must have been so great
It took a triple whammy
But all those details seem to border on being
Just a slightly bit 'hammy,'
Like over staging a screen script
When we see how often the sacrifice had to be
    dipped!

The "I Love My Bible" Commentary

It is so easy to be contaminated
By our environment especially today,
And the Environmental Protection Agency
Has failed to hold it at bay.
If outer contamination is so hard to sterilize
Think how hard it is to cleanse our souls.
But not for our 'High Priest' who helps us
Set high and lofty goals!
A question now! How many times
Has He had to cleanse us?
Since we need it daily,
Many more times than seven!
But His great desire is to get us all
Safely to Heaven!
Though even our spiritual contamination
May be grim
There is great healing when we turn
This infection over to Him!

LEVITICUS 15

Picture this!
Living close to God is a sterile situation
A high rise, clean living, top floor location!
Even those things we sweep into a corner
Must be brought into the center.
Even in our unstructured moments
God still wants to be our Mentor!
But what we often fail to see is
He was (and is) their (our) center
The 'dot' in the circle
The 'hub' of the wheel!
When God involves Himself in our lives
Our most intimate moments become
Part of the deal!
He *cares* so much. He *knows* so much!
There is no part of our lives
Which He does not want to touch!
After all He created us lovingly
So He is interested in anything
That concerns you and me!
If we were as interested in soul cleanliness
As is our Lord

Ridding this world of Aids, Gonorrhea, and
Syphilis wouldn't be so hard.
But to cleanse the outward parts in which
We take so much pride
Takes 'scrubbing' the desires that often
Haunt us deep, deep inside!
Anything wrong can be changed to the right
When we place it under the inspection
Of God's incredible light!

LEVITICUS 16

The most high and holy moment
In all the Holy Days Israel observed
Was the *Day of Atonement*!
Everything must be hallowed
No stone left unturned!
Every sin, every idle thought
The evil lying deep in every soul
Must be thoroughly 'burned!'
Like a surgeon's knife that scrapes away
    debris
The surgeons of holiness must make the alter
    dirt free!
God is thorough. We can do no less.
My heart must be cleansed and open
Waiting to be blessed.
We are building *life!*
Every 'nut' and 'bolt' must be examined
And the faulty ones rejected.
Remember to install the 'Fruits of the Spirit'
For without them how can we consider
This 'tabernacle' totally perfected?
God says He casts our sins into the depths
    Of the sea
But on that day they were 'laid' on a goat
That was led into the wilderness
To wander aimlessly.
And therein lies a picture of what happens
When we hold on to our sins.
Our wandering in the wilderness
Of fear and doubt never ends!
Look at the deeper meaning here.

The Book of Leviticus

God provides a way for us to walk
Without doubt and without fear!
What does this chapter—
This Day of Atonement really mean?
Well, it shows us, with God's help
We can shine 'squeaky clean!'

Leviticus 17

In the days of the Law when meat was
A sacrifice
A life had to be taken
But they had to realize, in drinking the blood,
They would be terribly mistaken.
It was not holy, but holy is our God who said,
"Don't drink the blood of that which is dead."
The blood had sustained life.
It was liquid treasure
Not to be treated lightly.
Not for another's pleasure.
God knew they needed food but the blood
Must be drained.
And those who had become cannibalistic
Had to be re-trained..
Perhaps men had become like animals
Regressing to a lower life form
Living only for gluttony from those
They could harm.
Or had they become like devils
Resigned to existence on basement levels?
But whatever they perceived as personal fate
God didn't make them to be cannibals.
God made them to be great!
As we fast forward through the ages
And have repeatedly searched God's Word
We find nothing was ever said
To deny transfusing someone who
without
This life sustaining fluid might soon be dead.
Blood! Life's gentle intrusion!
It was God who gave doctor's the knowledge
Of transfusion!
It is amazing the wisdom man still gains

About blood and the life it sustains!
But remember God felt it necessary to shout
When you eat or drink, "Leave the blood out!"

LEVITICUS 18

And the Lord spoke........
That is the way our days should begin!
Our Lord speaks to us and we should be
listening in!
His greatest desire is we be an *engine*
not a caboose!
We are not to follow the evils the old train
of life has set loose!
Many times He reiterated, "I *AM* the Lord!"
In life He is the Dealer who holds the ace card!
Why is it so difficult to be good to each other?
There is no more enmity between enemies
Than is often shown to a 'sister' or a 'brother.'
Strange times now and even way back then
When God had (has) to say,
"Be nice, folks, be nice to your next of kin!"
No form of incest would be allowed
And it seems God was really perplexed
When any of His people
Performed any act of perverted sex!
And when He says, "Don't defile yourselves,"
He puts down His ace card!
Over and over He reminded them
And still reminds us through His Word,
"I AM THE LORD!".

LEVITICUS 19

In this chapter God leaves no corners unturned
For His laws concerning relationships
With Him and each other *must be learned!*
No excuse to be dishonest; no excuse to
cheat or defraud
One who did those things He hated
Could face the danger of being outlawed!
Look deep into God's heart and you will see

The "I Love My Bible" Commentary

If lived for Him, how great your life can be!
When our Lord walks close to us
He expects more
Because He knows we have more honesty,
More joy, more love to share
Than we've ever had before!
They never saw Him as He really is.
Completely loving, completely powerful
        completely whole!
And He is willing to share all that He is
To give true life to every living soul!
Now let us think of the ONE who lived
Completely, fantastically victorious.
Many hated Jesus but He was truly glorious!
He was rich in love, impatient with hate.
He lived like God wanted—for others
And He had *not one unkind trait!*
"So they killed Him," you say.
No they didn't! They slowed Him down
For a fraction of a second!
Our Lord had power for which they had
    never reckoned!
He never broke a commandment mentioned
   in this chapter.
He showed us evil should never be our captor.
But it all depends on these guidelines
   God laid out.
Unless we follow Him our lives will always be
Haunted by fear and doubt.
He who gives us life can take us to the "peak"
      Do we want life?
      Do we want joy?
      Do we want peace?
    Remember what our Savior said.
     "You find what you seek!"
    Why do we find it so hard
    To seek the one who says,
     "I AM Your LORD"
He wants to be our soul mate,
And He wants to make our lives
    truly great!
And He can because
   HE IS GOD!

LEVITICUS 20

There is a difference between good and evil.
No gray lines exist.
But we have blended black and white
And cannot see the truths we've missed.
We cannot claim ignorance though
Few read the Bible today.
It seems as even more Bibles are printed
Even more people turn away!
Maybe the reason lies in this chapter
That describes our misuse of sex.
There would be no children without homes
Without hope, without love
If only we obeyed this Holy Text!
World wide we see the horror
Of children left to roam in sorrow.
Because humanity refuses to obey these rules
This world is stuffed full of fools!
It is like closing the gate after the horses
      get out
To claim ignorance of what all these horrors
    are about.
   They are about lack of love.
   They are about endless lust.
  They are about people thinking
    I'll have my way or bust!
   They are about not thinking
    God has a better way.
It is about loving Him and each other
That will bring us a peaceful, holy, happy day!
    To not observe His rules
   Is to fall far below perfection
    But God has a remedy.
Listen closely to your heart and you will hear
The sweetest words ever spoken as He says
    "I want you to come to me!"
  Why? Because He wants us to be free,
    Free of guilt, free of shame,
   Free to treat each other lovingly!
    That is what His rules are for.
   For keeping them is like latching
    To His brightest perfect star!

The Book of Leviticus

LEVITICUS 21

How holy is God?
The High Priest
The one who came into the Holy of Holies
Could have no blemish at all.
Between God's holiness and man's defects
Was an awesome wall!
Here we see the picture that only
A perfect man, perfect body, clean heart
Could stand before a perfect God.
Anyone unqualified
Would feel God's appalling judgement rod!
Only one could come into the Holy of Holies
 Only one!
He must be a man among men
Devoid of, or thoroughly cleansed from all sin.
This place, this room beyond the veil
Was an reverent testament
God dwelt inside and it was no ordinary tent!
All the grandeur of the ages
All the descriptions in these precious pages
Barely scratch the surface
Of truths that still lie hidden in space
But then Paul said, "We will know
 as we are known
When we can look on His face!"

LEVITICUS 22

It is hard for us who live in the Christian era
To think of these words as inspired.
But here lies the perfect indications of
"To whom much is given, much is required."
Perfection seems to be the operative word
Even in creatures, beef to bird!
God would accept no less
From these people He wanted to bless.
He has the right to set the standards here.
In holiness and awe and reverence
We must hold Him dear.
Man has grown far beyond the minute details
Yet in consistently loving each other
He constantly fails!
Once we have the pattern memorized
Once we've felt His love
Once we've received forgiveness
And once we've known His grace
We can understand the responsibility
Of such a high and holy place.
Perfect? No! Perfected!
God does that consistently
Only when we come to Him in true humility!

LEVITICUS 23

Special days should remind us
Of the greatness of our Lord
A time to pause and ponder
In the blessings He gives us daily
Makes life itself its own reward.
People need a time to sit and reflect
Of all the joy available
To give thanks with deep respect!
Life loses its glitter
When we take it for granted.
Thankfulness keeps the glow alive
And our souls are heavenly transplanted.
The special times, the special sabbaths
Would keep them aware.
Through all the drudgeries of life
God enlightened them with loving care!
He is worthy of remembrance
He is worthy of great reverence!
To cut Him off from our thoughts, our lives
Is to suffer a self-defeating severance.
It seemed difficult for them to put God first
And because they didn't
They often felt their days were cursed!
Sometimes God left them all alone
And doesn't that thought chill us to the bone?
When God pictured a person being cut off
From Him, He pictured it as a curse.
In all our pictures of horror and dread
We could never imagine anything worse!
Remember what I said about Cain?

The "I Love My Bible" Commentary

Oh to be separated from my God forever
I have no doubt
Though the fires of hell would die
The fire in my soul would never go out!
Life that should be glorious turns so grim
When we deny ourselves the joy and peace
That only comes from Him!
Surely we can see His great eternal love
      Erases all our sorrow!
      That is why we honor Him
          Yesterday!
          Today!
          Tomorrow!

LEVITICUS 24

What a day when God speaks!
He lifts our souls beyond the mountain peaks!
Of course most of us can't see that
Because our thoughts are elsewhere
  -because our faith is flat!
When God detailed the things they must do
He knew their cataracted faith
Had limited their point of view!
To know Him in your heart
Is to see Him in your mind!
Behind every command He gave
Was to show us He is loving and kind.
Ah! There is glory in this life I want to find
And when my Father wants to direct me
I surely don't mind!
I want to see His grace and glory!
I want to share this grand old story!
I know He had to teach these people in detail.
They knew so little.
Their lives were so tedious.
Their faith had become brittle.
His commands were given so they could know
Their life could smooth into an even flow!
      Everything He taught
      Everything He said
Indicated their were good times
On the trail up ahead!
And if we want life to have an added spice
We would do well to follow His advice!
We know we are not under the law
      as were they
But we have so much grace
We have more reason to follow Him today!

LEVITICUS 25

One does not have to wait fifty years
To obtain freedom of the soul.
It is available instantaneous
If we should desire to be made whole!
But in those days one would have to wait
Fifty years long
Before he could sing even one stanza
Of freedom's glorious song!
When our Savior came to set us free
He began remodeling this culture
That would someday change tremendously!
But in these days many were bonded
And poverty was often resolved
In the ways they responded.
An Israeli would sell himself only for a while.
Keeping him enslaved would be but to defile.
God cared about the land and how they used it
And He would not bless them if they abused it.
In all aspects of our lives God wants
To be involved.
We must be open to His wisdom
If we want our problems solved!
And He is the great environment protection
Agent who knows
The temper of the times, the needs of the land,
The way each river flows!
God does have a workable environmental plan.
After all, He is the one who made the earth
      for man!

The Book of Leviticus

LEVITICUS 26

The most precious promise in this chapter
Is when God says, "I will walk before you."
He would clear the way for them
And they would continue to see
All the miracles He could do!
But there was a condition He had a right
    to demand.
It would be only if they obeyed His command.
It was as if they would reap what they sowed.
He laid out the guidelines for failure
    or great success!
And somehow they failed to get the message
They were people He truly wanted to bless!
When they obeyed Him all went well
But their negative response time and again
Turned their lives into a living hell.
There is a hell on earth. Look at today!
Man hooks the hellish worms of deceit
Still fishing for his own way!
Would you say,
Because we hold God's Word
To be in error
We are hounded by murder, rape,
And every other kind of terror?
In cars, in clothes, *in life*,
We need to follow the pattern, the design.
It just makes it easier walking
"Up the perfection line!"
If we want to be blessed, truly blessed
Then we would do well to remember
Our God knows, really knows what is best!

NOTE:

As I searched through Leviticus
I found my God is a *keeper*!
He keeps me close; He keeps me warm;
He keeps me safe from all harm!
And believe me, it takes much study,
Much looking deeper and deeper!
Many truths are hidden here.
Many truths to hold dear!
We must leave no stone unturned
To find this deep love mankind has spurned.
Why do we turn away from life so real,
This life that offers us the deep security
God wants us to feel?
Reality! Ah, there it lies
Worthy to be sought but we have blindfolded
    our eyes!
Seeing we see not. Hearing is deafened too.
Still our Lord guides us through this maze
    of life
And shows us what to do.
He wants us to see life is greater
When you love me and I love you!
And to love God puts icing on the "cake!"
    Love!   There it is!
The greatest choice we can ever make!
This love can be so easy to give
And is meant to pass through our hearts
Like a heavenly sieve!
And God won't mind one bit
When you decide since you've got it
You may as well *flaunt it!*

THE

BOOK OF

NUMBERS

These are the commandments

and the judgements

which the LORD commanded

by the hand of Moses

unto the children of Israel

in the plains of Moab

by Jordan near Jericho.

(Numbers 36:13kjv)

The "I Love My Bible" Commentary

NUMBERS 1

Don't you know you are number one to God?
Your name is written in the palm of His hand
And on this ladder of life
It doesn't matter where you stand!
In his vision of the ladder
Jacob was looking up
And when David contemplated
On the One who made the stars
He said, "Lord, fill my cup!"
It wasn't as if they had to be
At the top of the ladder.
These men who loved the Lord
Knew their position didn't matter!
So many people anxiously striving
To be number one
Find themselves full of derision
Not knowing the effort almost always
Dulls and obscures our *vision*.
But, be the best you can be
No matter how small the task.
Putting your heart into your work
Is not too much to ask!
Yes, we are numbered and God even knows
The number of our hairs!
But when He wants us to climb
The ladder of life
He provides the stairs!
He had His reasons for counting these men
And He wanted them to see
No matter their number-large or small
It is He who would provide the victory.
It seems this life on earth
Can be a constant war
But God is helping us
No matter what number we are!
And it seems no matter how hard we work
Or what great things we may have done
We know our precious Lord and only Him
Can ever truly be number one!

NUMBERS 2

Take a peek at this folks
And maybe you will see the meaning of life!
It is God loving, directing us
Giving us power over our problems
To conquer pain and strife–
At the *center* where He wants to be.
When He is in control of our lives
Our hearts are completely happy, truly free!
Oh how I love my blessed Savior
And oh how my Savior loves me!
Life is so much sweeter
When He occupies the throne of my heart
Thoroughly in control, helping me lovingly!
He does not want to be on the outside
    looking in.
Is that where you want Him
Never to know the joy that might have been?
Every word He speaks, every deed,
Every thought He extends
Is to show the blessings of knowing
God and I are closely related,
Are true and loving friends!
"Come unto me!" He said.
Put Him at the center of your lives
Where amazing joy exists.
But think how many in this world
Unknowingly or stupidly resists,
Never to experience the wonders of this love
They have foolishly missed.
Be sure to understand the picture here.
With God at the center of your life
You will have nothing to fear.
But the even greater picture is someday
We will gather around His glorious throne
And there we will see the greatest love
This world has ever known!
How very precious it will be to enter
Into the presence of
The One who is our Center!

Comments On Numbers

NUMBERS 3

They were a Baker's dozen we might say
But the Levites were not counted
With other tribes in that ancient day.
They were a tribe apart
Surrounding the tabernacle
Living closely to God's heart!
So don't worry when you are not counted
    with the crowd.
Not being counted with others
Can make us humble instead of proud!
And they were not to be an army!
Maybe they were destined to sing
About all the mighty miracles
This loving God could bring.
Isn't it true everyone who serves Him knows
The longer we serve Him
The greater and sweeter He grows?
Every man in this tribe of Levi had a place
And no matter how great or small
Each was filled with His grace.
Some had a lofty calling
Some the hard labor detail
But lofty or mundane,
In their many responsibilities
None were permitted to fail.
No job was too low, no task too hard
For life is lifted to a higher plane
Whenever we serve our Lord!

NUMBERS 4

Life has a pre-existant order
And each task has its own border.
Even the Levites who could approach
    near to God
Could only come so far, do so much.
There were articles some couldn't carry
And some they definitely couldn't touch!
We often wish for another's job, his money

His power, his fame
But if we are happy where God puts us
We are famous just the same!
He knows how highly He regards His own.
I am His 'diamond,' not someone else's
    stepping stone!
God was very specific in naming
Each person's area of responsibility.
It will make us less anxious if we only realize
We are exactly where God wants us to be!
Do you think they fretted
When one could carry the altar
The other merely a board?
Certainly to be out of place
Brought a punishment none could afford.
When the Kohathites carried
The most holy things
Those articles had to be covered
For it was over these
God's Holy Spirit had hovered!
These descendants of Levi, Gershon,
Kohath, and Merari,
Each had special items only they could carry.
What do I carry through life?
What do you?
We can know if we carry ourselves humbly
Following God's directions
We can make it safely through!
Our Lord always paves the way
To give us a significantly lovely day!

NUMBERS 5

I've always wanted to skip this chapter
Whenever I read the Bible
Think of how this woman would be hurt
If she wasn't liable!'
A jealous husband can cause too much strife
When he is unjustly suspicious of his wife.
And he certainly didn't think much of her
If embarrassing her was his goal.

The "I Love My Bible" Commentary

Think of how much trauma he could inflict
On a(could be)innocent soul.
But first the priest assumes her innocence
And 'if' there is guilt
The ominous warnings of punishment
Are quickly built
Line upon line
Here a little, there a little.
It was a time when proof of sin
Could be very hard and brittle.
But why shouldn't the man rot too?
It takes two to *tango*
If *tango* is what you want to do.
Boy! Is there ever inequality here!
What about the man who was at fault?
Was his way out just to disappear?
Regardless–a jealous husband
Could put his wife through wrenching pain.
Well, my point of view is
That *turkey* could live forever out in the rain!

NUMBERS 6

Oh how precious and holy is a vow!
We don't have to go through those steps
A Nazarite did.
In fact we don't know how.
But isn't a vow to the Lord
Just as important to His people now?
And perhaps more so, because grace
Is so much greater than the law.
Because, you see, His love has covered us
And buries every damaging flaw!
With His love and grace we have even more!
He takes our vows to His heart
And then gives us wings to soar!
No soul can be truly happy.
No life is ever grand
Unless we vow in our hearts
To walk this earth holding God's hand!
It is like taking a trip to the mountain top
And gazing on an incredible view.
And beauty turns to comfort in my heart
For I *know* what God is willing to do!

NUMBERS 7

Don't you wonder about this?
Even those 'slaves' had a *pecking order!*
When did they become princes?
Ah-it must have been
When they crossed Egypt's border!
Freedom has a way of separating
The Captain from the crew.
Even then, the 'go-getters' must have been
Numbered among the very few.
There has always been an order to observe
Some to be leaders, some just to serve.
We know responsibility weighs heavily
    on the mind
And those willing to carry the burdens
Have always been hard to find.
Those leaders were willing to give first
    -to give more.
Somehow-even though slaves
-those with talent are never poor!
But now they were slaves no more
And one who is free is always rich
Free to find his way
Free to journey without a single hitch!
So all of them needed to say
"Thanks to God, I'm free today!"
They needed to look at freedom's reality
And shed their defeating slave mentality!
Those 'princes' of freedom did give first
Of their silver and their gold
-gave wagons and meat and loyalty untold!
The others would see these princely gifts
And would bring theirs later
Bearing in mind those princes, too
Were giving to that glorious One
Who is much, much greater!

Comments On Numbers

NUMBERS 8

Even the high priest-Aaron
Must observe protocol,
Little details-like which way
The light must fall!
It must always be forward to light the way.
It must be kept burning night and day.
For God's people must always have a light,
Must always know
There are heavenly goals to keep in sight!
Our God who is utterly divine
Wanted that light to always shine!
First comes the light that will always curve
Around the hearts of those who serve.
And, second, the servers are dedicated.
These Levites must show the people
They are truly consecrated!
Men of honor are set aside,
Men of valor purified!
Their work was never hard
These men who served Aaron
Who served the Lord!
Their service was seen as an atonement
    for sin.
It was rampant among the people
And this 'plague' kept them at a distance
-always on the outside looking in.
Those who consider sin lightly today
Need to know
God never looks at it that way!
Sin holds us at long-arm length
And we don't feel the warmth of His love
Or the power of His strength.
So when you look at these rules in detail
Consider they are just road maps
To guide us along God's heavenly trail!

NUMBERS 9

There was an urgency in the first Passover
An urgency that said, "Lets get out of here!"
It was an urgency to God also.
He had promised to rescue His people
And it had been time for them to go.
Now they knew God was a God
Who was powerful and omnipotent
One they could revere!
    The Passover
It was the best day of the rest of their lives,
To walk out, to walk up with their God.
Ahead there were wild and beautiful trails
They were now destined to trod!
They were to always remember
What God did one night
How He made a difference between
That which is evil and that which is right!
Egypt had to learn it was wrong
To hold God's people in bondage for so long.
And the people must hold that Passover feast
To celebrate the day they were released!
They were to always to remember it was God
Who *paved the road and cleared the way!*
    Rescued!
   Free to walk with God each day!
And they knew for sure God was there
    Because of the fire
    Because of the cloud
   It was a time to be humble
   And a time to be proud!
    God said
"You must go where I go, stay where I stay!"
Wouldn't we feel an incredible comfort
If we walked with Him that way today!
    And wouldn't we
    Less restless be?

NUMBERS 10

    Move out!
    Move on!
    Move up!

The "I Love My Bible" Commentary

God is telling them when to move
When to rest, when to sup!
God told them when to move on
And showed them they would not be alone!
He was involved in the most minute detail
Because He wanted order along the trail.
'Order' is God's theme song.
Order molds a nation and makes it strong!
They had not been viewed as a nation before
-just a bunch of slaves extremely poor.
But look what God does when He takes hold.
Shivering servants become extremely bold.
They could move with joy
With each step they took.
They would see hope and promise
In every direction they would look.
And it was because God was their King!
And freedom was a lovely song
Each man, woman, and child could sing!
It is the sweetest story ever told.
Life is heaven on earth when God takes hold!

NUMBERS 11

What happens in one's heart
When he complains?
We know his heart holds no light
And we hear him griping when it rains.
A thankless heart is like a tight pair of shoes.
Though one walks a happy trail'
He(and his feet)still has the blues.
Had these people been given turkey to eat
They would have cried for beans.
Had they been given chocolate cake
They would have wanted turnip greens.
In the state of doubt we cannot travel far.
We walk in the circle of God's love
But cannot see how blessed we are!
It displeased God because these people
Could not see their riches considering
The poverty of doubt clouding their eyes.

The could not feed the glory of love
Because fogs of discontent
Obscured God's heavenly blue skies!
The horizon held no promise
Sunshine no warmth, soft breezes no hope.
They had not trusted God's Word
-indeed ignored Him when He spoke.
Some day surely they would learn
A nation that thinks only of its belly
Will find the strength it needs
Turning swiftly to jelly.

NUMBERS 12

Both Aaron and Miriam criticized Moses.
Then why was only Miriam punished?
Why was only Miriam struck with leprosy?
Had only she spoken so defiantly?
      Stop!
      Remember!
Aaron had been cleaned, clothed, consecrated
And stood before the Lord wholly dedicated.
He could not be defiled even in the least
For he was chosen to be Israel's High Priest.
Even though Aaron was as guilty as she
God would not afflict Aaron with leprosy.
Not that He loved Aaron more than Miriam
But his 'position' must be highly esteemed.
The consensus, the hidden truth was
Aaron had truly been redeemed!
God had set Aaron up.
He would not put Aaron down.
But you can bet Aaron, too,
Felt the fury of God's frown.
We never know how highly or closely
God holds His servants in His heart
But we do know insulting a man of God
Cannot be considered very smart.
Aaron! What can we say about this man?
Except that we don't see him
Questioning Moses's authority ever again!

Comments On Numbers

NUMBERS 13

Remember my quoting, "To whom much
Is given much is required?"
Great men of Israel searched Canaan
And came back gloriously inspired.
But they started a big dispute.
Those men of Canaan were to Israel
Like the grapes they compared to grapefruit.
"We can't defeat those giants," They said.
Except for two, they were all afraid.
They felt sure they would all be crushed
No matter how hard they prayed.
But Caleb and Joshua disagreed.
"Its our land to take," they must have said.
"Isn't that why we were freed?"
But the other ten remained defiant
"How," they wondered, "could a grasshopper
Defeat a giant?"
Yet a giant is smaller than an ant
When compared to God's power!
Joshua and Caleb knew this was their dream
Their long awaited hour.
But ten men can talk louder than two
So those fearful people accepted
The cowardly's point of view.
It wasn't that they needed to be brave
They only needed to remember
Our God is the One who is mighty to save!

NUMBERS 14

Can you imagine possessing a land
Of milk and honey?
As great as it was-it wouldn't cost
An ounce of sweat or any amount of money.
The Israelis couldn't either.
They certainly didn't want to sweat!
And they thought it an useless battle
They would soon regret.
They banged their heads against a wall of fear
And the majority of them said,
"Lets get out of here!"
Well, it noticeably displeased the Lord
That their faith was so easily jarred.
They had crossed the Red Sea,
Now they could cross the Jordan River
But after all His miracles
All they could do was stand and quiver.
God does not recognize even the first letter
In the word *defeat!*
All they had to do was to trust Him
To conquer every challenge they would meet.
To reject God's help was to have it denied
And for forty years these people cried.

NUMBERS 15

Think how small a pimple is but it mars
　the skin
And likewise God sees the imperfection
Caused by even the slightest sin.
It was a pity these people didn't know
"You will always reap what you sow."
If they were to picture God's holiness
His rules had to be made specific.
Otherwise how would they know
God is utterly holy, absolutely terrific!
God has a pattern for success
A way to make sure we are blessed.
A designer original can only be made
The way the designer planned
Or its worth will be minimal
And it will be re-routed to the bargain stand.
But people are no bargain
Who bargain away God's gift.
Whether it is great purpose, great life,
Or great companionship
Each gives our hearts a lift!
God recreates us to be beyond the usual,
Beyond the mundane
And calls us to possess souls

The "I Love My Bible" Commentary

Without a single stain!
Called to drink *living water,*
Called to walk high and holy trails
And when one rejects that holy calling
One utterly fails.
It seems this chapter sets the goals too high
 but yet
There is a joy, a marvel waiting for us
None of us dares forget!

NUMBERS 16

Did you ever attend a boot camp?
That is where these people were!
God's marine boot camp no less!
One can't get by with a hair out of place
And you can bet much more is expected
In God's completely holy, heavenly
Marine boot camp of grace!
Here we don't see His grace exampled
Because it was His Holy Commandments
On which they had trampled.
You think marines are tough?
Sure! But not nearly as much as this One
Who was offering His people
A heavenly sized bushel of 'The right stuff!'
We know the awful things
Haughty, belligerent people can do
But it is hard to imagine the punishment
These insolent people went through.
These men shook their fists in God's face
And they were banished with out a trace!
It is written here so we can see
How awful God sees disobedience to be.
How many of us will have learned
When we see Him face to face
There is no such thing as cheap grace?
We are in 'boot camp' still
But we can say with a sigh of relief
The One who gave His life for us
Is now our Blessed Commander-in-chief!

NUMBERS 17

Only God can make a piece of dead wood
 bloom.
Only God can plant a garden in your heart
Only if you give him room.
And only God can use extreme measures
To exalt the One He treasures.
Don't think God wasn't appalled
When these people said Aaron wasn't called!
Remember the many times these people
Questioned Moses?
It seems they couldn't see an inch
Beyond their purulent noses.
Great princes brought their rods
And laid them down
And then felt they were doomed
When only Aaron's bloomed!
God was weary of their complaints.
It must have seemed impossible
Turning these complainers into saints!
I wonder if they ever understood
Why God gave life only
To Aaron's piece of wood?

NUMBERS 18

Only the best must be given to talented men.
 Only the best!
Second class effort must not be given
 to first class men
And it was the best these people brought in!
Scarlet and blue linen, very fine
Gold and silver polished to make it shine!
And don't ever forget we, too, are polished
 by love divine!
Would these men have done their best
With inferior supplies
And would the finished products
Have sparkled in their eyes?
What would Our Father have thought

Comments On Numbers

If it had been only shoddy materials
These people would have brought?
And what does He think today
When we bring our *second-hand sweat*
-when bargain table love is all He can get?
No wonder our Christianity
Leaves little to be desired
When instead, our luke-warm love
Was meant to be *heavenly fired!*
Sad to say, our souls will never be at rest
Until we learn to give our Heavenly Father
Our all, our very best!

NUMBERS 19

Death is so final.
It pictures ultimate defeat.
It contaminates all it touches
And its devastation is complete.
It is the opposite end of the spectrum
-a thorn in the side of life,
-a closing chapter in good and evils
    constant strife.
Death cannot approach unto God.
Satan wishes it could.
If he could find a way
You can bet he would.
Even in small ways, even on rainy days
Death cannot draw near.
God will not tolerate it
And we have nothing to fear.
It is obnoxious to Him.
It is darkness of the soul.
They must be cleansed to come to Him
-every whit made whole.
But He showed them the way
And wonder of wonders
He still guides us today.
But He guides us much more tenderly
For He gave the sacrifice Himself
    to set us free!

NUMBERS 20

Even in anger we should show restraint.
And even in fear we have no reason to faint.
These people complained in fear and thirst.
How many times had they moaned
And groaned and cursed?
It seems Moses took it personal every time
Because he knew complaining against God
Was their greatest crime.
He probably wanted to strike them
Instead of the rock
For his patience had sprung like a tightly
    wound clock!
God had wanted him to speak gently, kindly
With love in his voice
But bitterness had overwhelmed him
And he made the wrong choice.
Would we have done any differently than he?
How do we react when angry as can be?
Well if we are wise
We'll take a deep breath and count to ten
Because God shows us
This kind of anger makes it easy to sin.
Just one little sin
Kept Moses out of the promised land
For God took it personal
When Moses disobeyed that one command.
And Aaron never got to see the land at all.
His rebellion at '*the rock*' caused him to fall.
Actually the Bible doesn't mention his sin.
But he must have encouraged Moses
    to strike the rock
And God wasn't about to let him in.

NUMBERS 21

It was time to take care of the business
    at hand
And *that* was to go in and *possess the land!*

The "I Love My Bible" Commentary

They had skirted it for forty years.
Dead were those who had voiced their fears!
It had been like kids circling a candy store
-licking their lips, unable to do more!
That land they had trampled for so long
Must have been like concrete
Pounded daily by those with longing hearts
And tired aching feet!
Now those days were almost over.
Ahead was a land full *of four-leaf clover*!
The giants didn't look like giants anymore
In their eyes.
Years of dejection had whittled
Those monsters down to size!
Yes, they were eager to take care
Of the business at hand
And they bounced in like eager gymnasts
Tumbling to possess the land!

NUMBERS 22

Once upon a time there lived a donkey
Smarter than its master.
Three times it saved that smart-aleck idiot
From certain disaster!
I think perhaps we are all stupid
When we press God for His approval.
In Balaam's case, he was too eager to please
The prince who sought Israel's removal.
"Curse them!" Balak said.
"If you don't, I'm good as dead!"
But *Someone greater, Someone grander*
Had talked to Balaam first!
And he told Balak, "I can not curse
Whom God has not cursed."
And we can see as Balak rages
He had *never met* the King of All the Ages!
No matter who he called.
No matter who he sent
He would never be able to control
The direction Israel went!

It was Israel's triumphant hour
And Balak could never overcome
God's great power!
Israel sped through like a fast freight train
And Balak's hopes went down the drain.
It is sad to say that Balaam would
Soon be destroyed
Because he failed to see
By whom he was really employed!

NUMBERS 23

Oh what a wish Balaam made!
He must have had a great heritage himself
But he was willing to make a trade.
"Oh that I may be like Jacob in the end!"
God had blessed them and God
Would not bend!
No greater blessings have been given anyone
Except God's great promise of salvation.
It goes far beyond the bounds
Of the *Everlasting Hills*
For those who live in righteous dedication.
But no one on this earth has received
Greater material blessings
Than Balaam gave Israel that day
Straight from the heart of God
And they couldn't be changed in any way!
And they would not live alone
Though they would live apart
-away from others, surrounded and cherished
By God's great, magnificent heart!
And the next blessing was sweeter still.
World, Remember your cursing Israel
Will never be in God's will.

NUMBERS 24

Well, Balaam finally learned
No matter how many altars
No matter how many sacrifices he burned

Comments On Numbers

He could never change God's mind.
But it was a truth to which Balak
Was utterly blind.
Balak saw only himself in the mirror of time
And could never imagine the power
And glory of this One who was so sublime!
He wasn't up against Israel.
He was up against a wall
And like old Humpty Dumpty
Balak was destined for a fall!
No where in history, no time, no way
Has any people received the great blessings
Israel received that day.
Though they failed God time and time again
And though they have tried to destroy
Many of this earth's most righteous men
Yet God still loves His chosen race.
For, you see, you will never find a *period*
After this word called grace!

NUMBERS 25

Think God doesn't hate sin?
Then think of the 24,000 killed!
They mocked our Father's commandments
And a *lot* of their blood was spilled.
Two things God hates,
Idolatry, the sin against Him
And adultery, the sin we sin
Against each other.
He considers worshiping idols to be awful
And adultery is to hold contempt for another.
Nations considered it acceptable in that era
But not our Lord
Who had to teach His people a lesson
Who had sinned with no holds barred!
Seems strange doesn't it?
Today people consider adultery no more
Than two ships bumping in the night.
The god of this world(Satan)
Has blinded the minds of people
Who should be walking in God's light.
Twenty four thousand lives snuffed out
Like a candle
Because their lust had grown
Much too big for them to handle.
Notice God punished His own people first
For He had told them to do evil
Was to be cursed!
They did to themselves
What Balaam couldn't do
When they did what God told them not to!
But the Midianites, too, felt His wrath
For they had put temptation
Right in Israel's path.

NUMBERS 26

Now it comes to pass that God speaks again.
He did not give up on His people
Nor of that glorious plan.
Do you think they earned the promised land?
No! But His mercy would take them there.
Now He tells Moses to number them again
For their's was an inheritance to declare.
How their hearts must have been troubled
Because this later census could have
Been doubled!
Remember, over six hundred thousand men
Had eventually perished when they refused
To go in and conquer the land.
They had no faith to conquer the enemy
Nor but two of them would take a stand!
So many did not stand in that final count.
Had they stood tall in God's eyes
There would have been over a million
In that final amount.
Oh, think of the cost!
It seems when one has no faith, all is lost!
But the land was still theirs to be taken
And God's people knew
They had NOT been forsaken!

The "I Love My Bible" Commentary

NUMBERS 27

Heretofore it had been for the men
Life had been going 'great guns!'
That is why I think sometimes
God would not allow them to have sons.
      Sons!
         Daughters!
What difference did it make?
This Land was for all of them to take!
But God had something new
For Moses's final act.
Daughters, too, must be remembered
With diplomacy and tact!
Moses's mission is now complete.
He did lead them TO the Promised Land!
But for one moment of disobedience
It became the place he couldn't stand.
God did let him see it from a mountain top.
So close. He must have seemed to him
Just a skip, jump, and a hop!
But close is not close enough
And a miss by an inch is as bad as by a mile!
In a moment of anger and despair
He had become excessively riled.
The people would go in but not him
But He would watch them
    from the other side!
For this man who had served the Lord
The gates of heaven would open wide!

NUMBERS 28

All the sacrifices should have meaning
-a meaning burned deep in their hearts.
It wasn't in the animals they burned.
Or any of their various parts.
Why? Why would God go to such detail?
Had they walked with Him hand in hand
There was no way they could have failed.
In repetition, over and over,
God made it plain,
The sacrifices were necessary
To cleanse their sins' awful stain.
He couldn't have made it plainer
Had He hit them over the head
With a baseball bat!
But did they ever learn any of that?
The sacrifices were to keep the way to Him
Free and clear.
The pure in heart never have reason to fear!
Should we sit back and judge these people
When all that most of the world sees
    of the church
Is just a view of its steeple?
Many-many through the ages
Never where they should have been
Always on the outside of the church
Occasionally passing by and only
    looking in!

NUMBERS 29

The 'main event' was not the sacrifices
    they brought
They were only a symbol of the One
They should have sought.
In the back of their minds
In the depth of their hearts
The knowledge of His closeness
Should have spurred them onward
To that strange land's unknown parts.
People need reminding
And it does seem strange they would
And I wonder, with God's arms around them,
If they ever knew how really tall they stood?
And should we need reminding of His love?
Have we not read often enough
Of why He left His home above?
How much repetition do we need?
How many times do we have to read
That to live in the circle of His love

Comments On Numbers

Is more a reminder than a warning?
Truly our Heavenly Father's mercies
    fail not.
They are new every morning!
And *if that is repetitious give me more!*
For such knowledge makes each day
Sweeter than the day before!

NUMBERS 30

How earnestly do we take vows today
And how seriously can others take what
    we say?
I remember a time when one's word
    was enough
A promise to keep-no matter how tough!
A vow was the measure of a man
A way to state, "I will do what I can!"
It was in those days, too,
More so a promise through and through!
A vow to God was even more so.
In a way two hearts are bound together
And if broken certainly God would know.
Once our Father made a vow
It was as if it was written in stone
And He never, never broke it
Once He'd made it to His own!
Remember the vow He made to Abraham?
And He keeps it still!
And that is why it is so important to Him
That we do what we say we will.
It seems the woman wasn't as responsible
Because the man was the 'head' of the house
And if he wouldn't allow her to make a vow
God wouldn't blame his spouse.
Who knows today who will take the blame
When one breaks a vow
Carelessly taken in His name?
Think about this thing called fate.
Today we gals can't hide behind our mate!

NUMBERS 31

Again God reminds Moses of the need
    for retribution.
Midian had mislead His people
And now comes complete restitution!
Midian could not curse whom God had not
    cursed
Yet they tempted the Israelis with adultery
Like a stage play wildly rehearsed.
So the Midianites were destroyed
Because of this sin so easily deployed.
They may have considered it a joke
The way God's people fell
But it was they who were consigned
To punishment's deepest, darkest well.
We don't like to read this because it seems
    so strong
And we have greyed the lines between
That which is right and that which is wrong.
But God has not changed.
He still considers evil to be horribly deranged.
How different today when we surmise
How glamorous are the 'bad' guys
So—we all still need to know
Eventually we are going to reap what we sow?
(Unless we have truly repented
  and been forgiven)

NUMBERS 32

Reuben and Gad and some of Manasseh
Must have remembered what God had said,
That the land clear to the Euphrates River
Would be taken from the inhabitants
And given to them instead.
All they had to do was to stake a claim
And in taking possession, they would glorify
    His Name!
But Israel never took hold
Of all the land promised to them

The "I Love My Bible" Commentary

On the condition they must be bold!
Yet, they must also go across the Jordan too.
West, laid the great city of Jerusalem(Jebus)
The picture of life anew!
It was theirs for the taking!
It is a picture of Heaven, a place promised
To His people through all generations.
And it is a promise He keeps on making!
But still Reuban must help his brothers out.
Their promises must be kept-their faith stout!
Possession was a family affair.
Not one could own an inch of land
Until all were settled there!
Jesus made sure salvation was not for Jews
    alone
Because of Him, His people in all nations
Will rejoice around the throne.
For there is a "Land" to be possessed
And countless numbers yet remaining
    to be blessed!

NUMBERS 33

God knows about our journeys
-knows every inch we take
-knows the land He has for us
But we must 'drive' the stake!
In the old days man had to stake his claim.
Land was at the heart of the life he pictured
And the borders were its frame!
Whether the picture was large or small.,
Whatever the size, he must claim it all!
God had said, "Wherever you walk
Will be yours to keep
But they had to consider taking it
With a commitment pure and deep.
But first, it seems they could only circle
    and camp
In a wilderness that could only serve
As Canaan's entrance ramp.

Doubt had robbed them of instant success
But they remained a people God was willing
    to bless!
It is almost over now .
The trauma of forty years will be left behind.
There was great life to be lived
And great treasures to find!
And we must not tire of our journey here.
His land is ours.
When our wilderness wondering is over
We will walk among God's heavenly flowers!

NUMBERS 34

There was a specific area for a specific tribe.
Every man had a place always with a way
    to expand
For in the bigger picture, the wider scope
God's plan for them was utterly grand.
Even though the area now was really small
There was more available
And they should have claimed it all!
This was to be a land never polluted
Once it was purified
-a land set apart for God's people
-a land of humble beginnings
-a godly inheritance in which to take pride!
It was not what they were, but who they were
-sons of Abraham!
No people on earth could say with such vigor,
"How very lucky I am!"
Except we who have been born anew.
For we can say it is truly a miracle
What our Heavenly Father can do!
What can we say? Ah!!
"There is a place in Heaven
Where my name is on a stake.
It was purchased by my Savior
Who died for my sake!"
(And did I hear you say, "Amen!")

Comments On Numbers

NUMBERS 35

In this land there was to be a special place
For those who ministered God's grace
-a special inheritance of the inheritance gained
And since God does not limit His blessings
A uniquely special blessing still remained!
In giving a share to God's servants made
These people able to see
To share their blessings with others
Showed how important their blessings
Turned out to be!
A blessing is not a blessing until
It becomes a blessing shared.
Now they were learning just how much
Their Heavenly Father cared!
So their gifted cites were in turn
Given to the Levites for cities of refuge
For, being human, these people could make
Mistakes that were incredibly huge!
And if one harmed another but not with
Vicious intent,
Those responsible for judging him
Must ascertain what he really meant.
For justice must prevail
And justice should demand guilt deserves
A punishment with no bail
Our 'liberals' need to understand
Murder still pollutes the 'land!'

NUMBERS 26

The daughters of Zelophehad must take care.
It was a holy inheritance they would share.
They were not to marry outside their tribe
And now it seems it was only a bribe.
Yet their identity must remain intact.
And their genealogy must be a proven fact.
One tribe must not take the land of another
God would not want an Israeli taking
Land from his ' brother.'
It happened every now and then
But to do it was considered a sin.
God wanted tight-knit families dedicated
To each other
And it was faithfully taught by every mother!
Holy, loving, righteous families were
Truly important back then.
It was loving closeness and knowledge of God
That would keep these people away from sin.
God wanted them to be a nation apart
And He knew how easy it is to contaminate
    the heart!
Godliness leads to humility and to be humble
Is to dodge the sin of pride
That has caused countless souls to stumble!
Meekness was to be the pavement on the roads
    they trod
For precious is *any inheritance* that comes
  from the hand of God!

Note: There can be an end to judgement as
long as hope rises with the sun and never sets
and unfortunately these people would see
many sunsets before their hope would rise.
Sin does that to us. It takes away our faith and
our hopes. It makes each day seem like a
month and each year endless, but as long as
we have our God(and that will be for always)
hope will rise, but somewhere during that span
of time of punishment, repentance must knock
on God's heart--because it is always open and
forgiving. Unrepentance is like a black hole
that has no bottom and it keeps us tumbling
away from God. I think He stands on the edge
of that black hole longing for His people to
return. "Repent and be saved!" How often
we've heard that through the years. And it is
still as true as it was thousands of years ago.
        How do I know?
My Bible says God does NOT change!
And that is why hope rises with the sun!

THE

BOOK OF

DEUTERONOMY

(Just a reminder)

And these words which I command thee this day

shall be in thine heart

and thou shalt teach them diligently

unto thy children

and shalt talk of them when thou sittest in thine house

and when thou walkest by the way

and when thou liest down and when thou risest up,

and thou shalt bind them for a sign upon thine hand

and they shall be a frontlets between thine eyes.

And thou shalt write them on the posts of thy house

and on thy gates.
(Deuteronomy 6:6-9kjv)

The "I Love My Bible" Commentary

DEUTERONOMY 1

Deuteronomy means twice-told
And Moses repeats the Commandments
Because they are far more precious than gold!
Important enough to be repeated
Told again to these people
Whose wanderings have been completed.
To be successful they must obey
Every single command.
These Commandments were the 'ink'
Of God's map to the Promised Land.
Blessings-*or*-curses would be their choice
Based on whether or not they listened to
And obeyed God's voice.
His voice was the 'Word'
And His Word was the means
That would enable His people
To walk calm pastoral scenes!
What was the question? To be or not to be!
To remember God had said
"You will be successful if you follow me!"
Actually that is still the 'recipe.'
And if you will study this nations history
You will agree.
When they followed God they were blessed
And when they lived in sin
They failed at the simplest quest.
Life is fashioned after the Great Designer
And His design holds no flaws.
We install them when we refuse
To follow His life-saving laws!
Often Israel forgot their holy station
And many times sin dismantled this nation.
Now they are once again at Canaan's border
Where their courage had spit and sputtered.
And Moses reminded them
Of the negative words they had uttered.
He was afraid they might do as their parents
Had done once before
When they had stood hesitant at Canaan's shore
He reminded them of what happened
 that awful day
When doubt caused their parents to turn away.
That moment of doubt led to forty years
 of decay
And their children had no joyful place to play.
And one thing you can bet
Not even one of them ever enjoyed
Those forty years of hideous sweat.

DEUTERONOMY 2

Moses said, "Then we turned back."
Failure is always a sad story.
But it was their parents who had turned down
The chance to live in God's glory.
Instead they trampled that desert floor
Until every foot was sore
And--until their time on earth was ended
For their disobedience could not be mended!
It had taken forty l-o-n-g years of training
Before Moses was able to endure
Their constant complaining.
Now their children are ready to move on.
Forty years! I bet they counted every stone!
This time they would obey God's order
And eagerly cross Canaan's border.
I presume those kings they defeated
On Jordan's eastern shore.
Just whet their appetites to conquer more!
Canaan-now in sight-and they could enter in
Because now they truly believed
God would help them win!

DEUTERONOMY 3

Even the Giants could not defeat them
With God on their side!
This time you will not see even one of them
Running away to cower and hide.

Comments On Deuteronomy

The lands they conquered on Jordans east
Were given to the half-tribe of Manasseh
And the tribes of Reuben and Gad.
There they would build shelters for the sheep
    they already had.
Still, there was a condition applied.
They must help their brothers
To conquer land on the other side.
Now here they were in the valley
    of Beth-peor
Viewing the land they had been looking for!
With the help of the settled tribes
They would conquer this land that Moses
    describes!

DEUTERONOMY 4

Obedience to the law would bring
A reputation for wisdom and intelligence.
It was God's will that they reverence Him
And He would give them *uncommon*
    common sense!
Moses reminds them no other nation
Had heard the voice of God and survived.
If God had not kept His promise to Abraham
Surely they would have been tragically
    deprived.
But!! God's people------don't lose any sleep!
God *never* made a promise He didn't keep!
The HIGH point in this chapter
Was their thought for the day.
Jehovah was(is)God both in Heaven and earth
    and there was
NO OTHER GOD LIKE HIM
IN ANY WAY!
And, dear people, *that* is still true today.

DEUTERONOMY 5

I stand in awe of this chapter
How precious are its laws!
Given to us by the Father
To help us eliminate all our flaws.
Our Lord was very pleased
When the people said they would obey.
"Oh that my people would always have
Such a heart for me," God replied that day.
These Israelis could not attain perfection
Unless they closely followed God's direction.
It still applies to you and me.
True success comes only as we follow Him
    faithfully!

DEUTERONOMY 6

Moses said, "God told me to tell you this.
Following Him will gently lead all of you
Into a life of hallowed bliss!"
"What is the purpose," your descendants
Will ask, "of these laws you tell us about?"
"They are to honor the Lord," you must say
"Who reached down into Egypt
And brought us out?"
"And when you are full," Moses said,
"You must not let it got to your head!"
He was afraid they would fail to realize
How important it was to be right
    in the Lord's eyes!
He wanted them to think constantly
Of the laws he reviewed that day
And he added, "don't ever forget what I say."
But they did many times
And Israel became a nation
Full of hideous crimes.
Much like America today
Whose judges have kicked prayer
    out of school
And where many parents fail to teach
Their children *the golden rule!*
America–where television and the movies
Glorify violence and adultery
And where many children do not get to see

The "I Love My Bible" Commentary

Their parents living in Christian harmony.
It is all there in the precious Book
Glorious advice if we will only look.
And *if* we look we will turn from our past
To accept God's sweeter, gentle love,
-the only kind that will really last!

DEUTERONOMY 7

(Note: I consider this chapter so great I have **bolded** my comment on it. Read this chapter in your Bible slowly and carefully and you will-I hope-understand why I did!)

*No thought
no feeling
no expression
of this body of sod
no word
no sound
no melody
can ever express
or explain
the magnificent holiness
of Jehovah our God!
His love reaches out
to a <u>thousand</u> generations
of those who do His will!
He promised
to take away the diseases
of Egypt.
His people must not be ill!
They were destined
to live under
God's loving care!
Divine intervention
surrounded, protected them
and it would always be there!
But there was a requirement!
This God of the what
where, when, why, and how, said
"You must obey me!"
Obedience was the link
that would keep them safe
continuously!
And remember
<u>wisdom</u> does <u>not</u> touch
anything God has cursed.
For to do so
was to look for the worst!
It is plain to see
this body of sod
was created for the joy
of honoring
our Blessed Holy God!*

DEUTERONOMY 8

This is a chapter of remembrance
Of what the Lord had done.
These people's strength, their power,
Their provision had come *only* from this One!
God fed them with manna and gave them
    water to drink.
It was to make them humble and cause them
    to pause and think.
They were to think about God's love
And how His provision was so very real
And what our Father does for us
Is never based on how we feel!
God said real life comes from following Him.
If they were relying on wealth and fame
Their chances would be very slim.
In the final analysis, if we do not cherish
This One who so willingly helps us
Our hopes, our dreams, our plans,
    will eventually perish.
Without Him what can we do?
I need Him always and so do you.
We seek His help where ever we are.
Because He is our Bright and Morning Star!

Comments on Deuteronomy

DEUTERONOMY 9

"Why are you here?" Not so strange that
    Moses asked.
Haven't you ever asked, "Why am I here?"
Why are you? Why were they?
Why should they follow Him day after day?
I bet it was a question they often asked
And their peevishness made leading them
An almost impossible task.
I believe Moses must have said to them,
"You don't know how stubborn you are
And only God Himself could have brought
You miserable people this far!"
He told them God had not helped them
Because they were good.
Many times they had failed
To do what they should.
Had not Moses interceded in prayer
None of them would be standing there!
We know God considers prayer very pleasing
And answers come when we pray
    without ceasing!
Moses prayed fervently and Moses prevailed.
He trusted God and God never failed!
But He must have listened harder
To Moses's prayers than he did
The Israelis complaints
And today we know He listens closely
To the prayers of His saints.
When we pray God meets us there
For He wants us to see there really is
    power in prayer!

DEUTERONOMY 10

*Moses reminds them
of those precious tablets
on which God had written
by Himself alone!
And Moses said
"He is your God
and He is your praise!
Remember that
the rest of your days!
Always strive
to walk in His ways
for He is your God
and He is your praise!"
Isn't that magnificent?
God IS our praise,
wonderful
forgiving
loving always!
God is like this
more than a soft breeze's
gentle kiss
more consistent
than the seasons,
guiding us
like seaside beacons!
God is every thing
I've always wanted to be
and He makes me better
at being me!
That is why He deserves
our worship and praise.
He gives us His love
now and always!
And that is what Moses
wanted these people to see.
God is a God
who should be praised
constantly!*

DEUTERONOMY 11

We often wonder why Moses repeated
The same thing so many times.
Did these people have too much ear wax?
Were they too blind

The "I Love My Bible" Commentary

To follow those well laid tracks?
Had he put it in black and white
Would they have done any better?
And when they did learn to read
They didn't follow God's laws 'to the letter!'
God had slain their enemies,
Calmed their seas.
Their shoes were not worn out
And they had no patches on their knees!
It seems the more people are blessed
The worse their memory grows.
So–God's love is great
–a truth everybody knows.
So why must they be reminded?
Does lust and pride cause many to be blinded?
You can't live with someone forty years
And not know them inside and out
And, sad to say, after all this time
Moses knew they were full of doubt.
Doubt does not lead to worship
Or reverence or thanksgiving.
And even pride which Moses warned about
Would bring them bargain-table living.
And if we will carry these commandments
In our heart as Moses said.
We will not have to live even one day
In fear and dread!

DEUTERONOMY 12

Through the centuries, time after time,
Year after year God has said,
Do NOT worship idols
For idols are lifeless; *idols are dead..*
You can't get blood from a turnip
And you can't get life from an idol!
He said that many times
In this blessed book, the Bible!
Why do we find it hard
To believe words so real?

Can any idol soothe our pain
Or calm the fears we feel?
Heathen claim the idols have magic
But love is missing and that is tragic.
Something formed from a tree
Can never satisfy me.
And its no better made from stone
"Worship God," Moses said.
"Worship God alone."
There were no idols on creation day
Only God could bring life
From a clump of clay.
And idols can't talk, can't smell, can't speak.
God is the only God we should seek!
Moses had told them over and over
How to worship Him!
Worship was the pavement
On that super highway to Jerusalem!
.

DEUTERONOMY 13

In this chapter we get a clear picture
Of how merciless is the law.
We see how vicious justice can seem
-how very raw!
No one has the right to mislead another.
He must never confuse his brother.
These holy rules are plain and clear
To keep them is to have no reason to fear.
But to people who say it makes no difference
What you believe we must say
"If that is so then it makes no difference to you
Where you go!"
Well it does to me and I want you to know
I believe God when He says, "There is
No other God but me!"
And I constantly need His help to make me
All I want to be!
Of all the love in the world, His is the best!
Just worship Him and forget about the rest!

Comments On Deuteronomy

DEUTERONOMY 14

God's exclusive possession!
That is what we are-chosen to be His own!
Someday Jesus would say, "You have not
Chosen me, but *I have chosen you!"*
How many times had Moses told them
They were a chosen race?
Up until that time no other nation had received
Such a marvelous portion of God's grace!
Then-in contrast-we see the law
Something we see as a monstrous geek
And if we break God's laws we receive
A punishment we didn't mean to seek!
It is because we don't believe God's Word
Like those people who seemed not to believe
Any thing they heard.
Having ears they hear not Isaiah would write
And seeing wasn't easy when they kept
Their eyes closed tight.
It goes back to the beginning of the
Mistaken belief, "It can't happen to me."
Oh yeah! Guess what? We often find out
We are as mistaken as we can be.
Any penalty is the law clothed in justice
And it will surely be performed
For the sake of those who are harmed.
We don't always see justice carried out
And that is why many are so full of doubt.
But a famous preacher once said,
"Payday someday!"
And whether we believe it or not
That 'sowing' rule will be applied anyway.
I'm talking about the unrepentant
Who is never sorry for his sins
Who spends a lifetime wrecking havoc
And never makes amends.
These ones will never find satisfaction
    or comfort
Under the judgement rod
Of an angry avenging God!

DEUTERONOMY 15

It was always God's will that His people be
    debt free.
And when some of them needed help
He wanted them to see
Those most fortunate must help the others.
What better way could a nation show love
For its brothers.
They were not to worry about having less.
Their sharing was the tool God used to bless!
Every seven years they were to cancel each
    debt.
It was to keep from discouraging the poor,
That time was set!
You know, it seems strange, a man would
Choose not to be free
But sometimes in those days they would
Decide not to be.
But maybe what changed his attitude
Was that his family would stay in servitude.
We are so used to being free it seems strange
And we need to really thank the Lord
Those kinds of times have changed!

DEUTERONOMY 16

There was power in the blood-of that there is
    no doubt
Especially after God destroyed Egypt's idols
But led His children out!
God's *ways* seem strange to earth bound
    creatures
Who do not understand *their* many features
    The way His love goes on and on
    The many miracles He has shown
    The way He lives in peoples hearts
    The wonderful knowledge
        He imparts!
He came to those Israelis a long time ago

The "I Love My Bible" Commentary

And rescued them so they would know
He is a God who can do ALL things
-whatever the situation brings.
And the festivals they were to observe
   each year
As they lived in the land *without* fear
Were to remind each and everyone
Of the *great things* the Lord had done!
God also cautioned them justice must prevail
And-once again-demands they destroy
All idols without fail!

DEUTERONOMY 17

God will not accept the mediocre.
He demands our best!
Why should we hog our greatest blessing
And give him a portion of the worst
   of the rest?
God's covenant must not be violated.
There must be pure worship from those
God, Himself, had consecrated.
No man could reject the judge's verdict.
Death to the rebels was God's edict!
And if the people wanted a king to rule
From an earthly throne
He must be faithful to the Lord
If he wanted his sons to carry on.
This chapter has several subjects
But only ONE theme.
It is our Lord who reigns supreme!

DEUTERONOMY 18

God did not overlook the Levites.
He said they must not be denied their rights.
God also warned the Israelis
Not to sacrifice their children
For He would not accept such evil behavior.
And those who sought evil spirits etc.
Would not live under His favor.

He also promised to provide another prophet
At the time of Moses's demise.
And they were warned not to believe a false
   prophet's lies.
How could they test a prophet's integrity?
There would be just one clue.
Only God's messages to *His* prophets
Were guaranteed to come true.
From the Levites whom God fed
To the common man whom Moses led
There was the same message for all.
Follow the Lord constantly-Winter, Summer
   Spring and Fall!

DEUTERONOMY 19

Murder was a very serious offense not to be
   overlooked.
A man must pay for the fragile life he took.
But before the man could be punished
They would make sure!
In the meantime, until they knew his motive,
He could be secure.
But they could have no pity
If the death was discovered to be deliberate
He was found guilty.
God said to kill him-a definite command!
Only his death would purge the land.
My, how times have changed.
Now criminals are often turned loose
On the street
To intimidate others they might meet.
It seems responsibility is only a fun fest
And what once was considered a crime
Is looked on as a harmless jest.
And why do so many get by with murder
While the victims cringe?
Our courts do not protect the innocent
And so the ruthless binge.
Lawyers and judges must share the blame
When hardened criminals feel no shame.

Comments on Deuteronomy

DEUTERONOMY 20

Life was a constant warfare.
They had to remain on guard.
But the Lord would always be with them
Particularly when times were hard.
Remember God had already given
These Israelis the Promised Land
But they still had to do their part.
They were to go in and *claim* their inheritance
And it was now time to start!
To the man who was about to marry
God said, "Marry before you join the army
Whether to fight, or to roam.
And if there are cowards present
They will frighten the others.
Send those weaklings home!"
He said they could take captives
In the distant cities but not the Promised Land
For it must be purged completely
According to God's command.
It was the place where He would dwell
And His presence has always been like
A thirst-quenching, deep abiding well!
And if they truly wanted God's presence
They must strive to be godly men
For our Heavenly Father will not stay
In a land steeped with sin.
That truth still applies in this time, this day
For God who abhors sin will simply walk
    away.
Oh people we should go to any length
To assure ourselves the presence of
    His strength.
His Word says the nation that commits
Multiple sins shall be turned into hell
And so we should examine ourselves
In these times when so little is going well.
Our nation is full of distrust and crime.
We need a great revival and we can all agree
If we ever needed it, *now is the time!*

DEUTERONOMY 21

The Promised Land is a fragile picture
Of God's home- His Holy Heavenly place.
Because it is, no sin would be allowed.
There should be no trace!
To live in God's presence, man must be
Spiritually clean
And no manner of sin could be seen.
A man must respect a captive wife
-not treat her like a fool.
And if she bore his oldest son
Fairness to him must be the rule.
Remember this chapter *states the cold facts!*
Man will be judged by the way he acts.
If a man was worthy of death
In those days he was hung on a tree
But they must lower his body at sundown
And cut it free.
To leave him hanging would defile the land.
That wasn't allowed in this holy place
Where the King of All The Ages would stand!

DEUTERONOMY 22

God was concerned how they handled their
    relationships.
He said they should help their neighbors
And even their animals if they were needy.
And robbing a bird's nest would only show
A man to be cruel and greedy.
Don't think God is overwhelmed by details.
To overlook the small things is when a man
    often fails.
And don't let anyone tell you
God is not concerned with the *small stuff!*
In any way He can show he loves you,
Even the small ways is big enough!
The need may be small but His love is great!
Big or small the needs, He is faithful
And that gives us many reasons to celebrate!

The "I Love My Bible" Commentary

DEUTERONOMY 23

In all instances, in every case
To be impure would put one *out of place!*
For God was too holy to be defiled
And that is the reason even seemingly
Unimportant laws were compiled.
Details! Details! Details! Oh, Boy!
But keeping them insured a life of joy!
We can still see how very precious
Is His Holy Name!
And Christ assures us we can all stand
Before Him free of any blame!
Now for more compassionate commands!
If a slave should escape, they were to leave
    him alone
And show the same mercy for him
Our Lord had once shown
For they had been slaves in Egypt
When God intervened and set them free
So He told them, "If a slave escapes
From you, then let him be!

DEUTERONOMY 24

He who knows the future of all mankind
Also knows his past
And though God had told man to put
Him *First*, man had placed Him last!
Last-put God where man failed to see
    God's love
    God's mercy
    God's strength
    God's abiding presence
    And God's plan for His life!
And all through the ages instead of the peace
God wants us to have, we've opted for strife!
"You must think of others," God was saying.
    "Think of others!"
We are not to forget, because of Him,
    all mankind are brothers!

DEUTERONOMY 25

It seems as if Moses knew he was running
    out of time
And he had so much to reiterate.
To compact what he says in this chapter
Was-in obeying the Lord-they would
Become noble and great!
He was giving them rules one line at a time
Because they were too necessary to overlook.
And because future Israelis would need them
He wrote them in a(scroll)book!
There is only one way to eliminate the details
And that is to live
According to the rule of love!
Love was exampled by the One who died
    on the cross!
To fail to love others is to suffer great loss!
I have always told my classes that Christianity
Is a glorious relationship!
To know the Father's love and to share it
Is to not let one holy moment slip.
Every minute is a jewel of great splendor
A time of incredible peace.
And life-true eternal life-becomes a great gift
Rather than a elusive lease!

DEUTERONOMY 26

What we see here is a "holy" land grant!
There would be no limit to the food supply.
But God expects a return on His investment.
A tenth wasn't too much to ask!
They could have given more and still
Have been incredibly blessed.
For full stomachs make work an easy task!
But it wasn't long before they would forget
Who gave them the food and the land,
--gave them scenery that was utterly grand.!
Not long before worship was by rote
And every sacred song sung with a sour note.

Comments On Deuteronomy

But they should have been sweetly singing
That the Lord had given them a land flowing
With milk and honey
A place so fantastic its worth could not be
Compared with any amount of money!
I wonder how many of them gave the Lord
Tithes and offerings from their wealth
And how many truly thanked Him
For their splendid health!
They were in a land where blessings,
Peace, and joy never ends.
It was the Promised Land and was to be
Celebrated with their families and friends.
Some where along the way they lost
That holiness they were to defend at any cost.
Some where along the way
They simply forgot who gave them
All this "*milk and honey*" land.
And somehow they managed to break
Every precious holy command.
It seems they didn't care
And those are the saddest words
In the universe-"I don't care!"
They didn't care about God, about honesty,
About love, about prayer.
And they hit bottom with a thud
But God always leaves a seed of love
Just waiting to bud!
Man has fallen many times
And as many times, God has responded
And when He does, His love and ours
Is graciously re-bonded!
How can we not love our God?
He 'hugs' us considerably more
Than He ever uses His rod!
Like a river His love keeps rolling on and on.
Because of my Father, I will never be alone!
I don't know about you but I will sing
Of His grace
Until He allows me the joy
Of gazing on His blessed face!

DEUTERONOMY 27

Here we see two mountains, both the same
One merely stone to pronounce their shame
And the other known as a wasteland
But because of the blessings
It must have been considered grand!
Blessings and curses could not share
 the same mountain
For curses are like a dry well
And blessings nourish like a spring-fed
 fountain!
Sin is like tumbling down mountain slopes
But blessings grab and renew our hopes.
It was a fifty-fifty situation; they were
Divided six and six.
What we should see is blessings and curses
Never mix!
You're either on one mountain or the other
Depending on what you do.
There were a lot more curses than blessings
 listed
But it must be that way
Because day after day
Man strays like a blind horse
And fails to see the reasons for remorse.
This is not an encouraging chapter for it has
No gentle facts.
It reminds us over and over mankind will pay
For the way he acts.
The choices are there and gentle men
Will choose the 'blessing' mountain
And walk away from sin!

DEUTERONOMY 28

This seems to be one of the harshest chapters
In the Bible but lets look at it this way
Positive-or-negative, the universal laws
God set in motion do not sway!
When we choose to ignore these laws

The "I Love My Bible" Commentary

Morals run amuck
And instead of admitting our responsibility
We just *'pass the buck.'*
But the chain of events cannot be ignored.
Still, in those days(and even now),
God demonstrates how rapport with Him
Can be restored!
We must read this chapter again and again
Until we understand
We, ourselves, set the results in motion
When we refuse to obey our Lord's command!

DEUTERONOMY 29

How many times would God have to affirm
That these people were His own?
After all they had been through you'd think
By now their love for him would have grown.
He knew they still didn't realize how little
He had grown in His people's eyes!
He was a giant but they were spiritually blinded
And over and over again they had to be
    reminded.
Continuity lined that holy contract
But they treated it as fables instead of fact!
The warnings listed in previous chapters
Remained in effect
And any who sinned were unworthy of respect.
God knew they would sin and knew the result,
Knew frustration would reign along with
    anger and tumult.
He warned He would boot them out of the land
If they refused to obey His command.
We still refuse to believe what He really said.
"IF you *live in sin* you are as good as dead."
They would be dead to emotion, dead to hope
-too many holding to the end of their rope.
Many of them would go without sleep
Still refusing to admit what ever we sow
Is what we are going to reap!

DEUTERONOMY 30

Whenever Moses told the Israelis about
God's judgement, he always told them
About God's great mercy too.
For without mercy there is no hope-no chance
To *'cleanse your plate'* and start life anew!
Later the prophet Jeremiah would say,
"God's mercies fail not. They are new
    every morning!"
So hope rides on the *coat tails* of every
    warning!
God never locks a door but He closes it
Sometimes so we can see
That not to be able to look on His face
Brings only misery!
Of course we can't see Him but we can always
See His love
And we have the promise we will meet Him
Face to face when we reach that home above!
God's word has told us, God's glory departs
Whenever we carry sin in our hearts.
We know people listened to Moses
But still they didn't hear
For their griping and complaining
Made every word unclear.
Essentially all that Moses said
Was to obey the Lord and when they did
They saw glory on the trails ahead!
But how much do we retain from these words?
Does unbelief carry them away like
Migratory birds?
Now we know grace is the foundation for
    every law
But how many laws can we break
Before God says.
"Well, that's the *last straw!"*
We don't know when that time will be
And since I know I don't
I want to live in such a way
That God will always welcome me!

Comments On Deuteronomy

DEUTERONOMY 31

Moses told the people he would not be
With them but the Lord would remain.
They were not to fear but remember
The great kings they had already slain!
They would have to remember to be brave
    and strong
For hadn't the Lord been with them all along?
How many times did He rescue them?
How many times did they doubt?
How many times did He have to remind them
The many times He had brought them out!
God was tender yet they called Him stern.
So now He gives them a new song to learn!
It was a song of reminder.
Did any know a god who was kinder?
Did any know a god who expected so much
Or One who could help them with just
His gentle touch?
Yes, this was a song every Israeli could sing!
No other nation knew so great a King!
No other nation had been so blessed!
No other god existed who could lead them
With so much power and so much zest!
This God gave them a song
To sing at the *top of their lungs*
Their whole life long!

DEUTERONOMY 32

The beat goes on and as they marched
Many were stung
By *the bees of discontent* so the song goes
And discord would bring their happiness
To an untimely close.
I don't suppose they believed all this prophecy
Moses gave in his song.
So much had gone right
Why should they believe so much
Would go wrong?
They would fall away *like flies*
    blown by the wind
Battered by the hail of judgement
When God's wrath would descend.
They were warned before they sinned
That their evil must come to an end!
Yet the Word tells us they did as they pleased
And because they did their blessings ceased!
How many of us learn from the past?
We say,"It won't happen to me!"
Then we wonder why our hearts, our lives,
Our futures seem as empty as can be.
The Word tells us why.
Souls that sin are destined to cry.
There will be no singing in our souls
Unless we learn to strive for higher goals.
And unless we put our Father first
These souls of ours will continue to thirst.
That was the essence of this song!
Stay close to God where you belong!

DEUTERONOMY 33

Israel often complained that times were hard
But Moses asked them
What other nations had been saved by the Lord.
He had just given them his final blessing
And had told them of the great riches
In the land they would soon be possessing!
He prayed that Israel's strength would match
The length of her days
Knowing they would be protected as they
Walked in God's ways!
The greatest thought in this chapter states
How much God loves His people and
Mighty as is the Lord, love is at the top
Of His many blessed traits!
Because of their great blessings
Israel was to endeavor
To love our Heavenly Father forever and
    forever!

The "I Love My Bible" Commentary

DEUTERONOMY 34

This man Moses's life of service
Began on a mountain top
And he was on a mountain top as it ended!
He was with our Blessed Lord when he
Viewed that land and he never descended!
To be with God, what a mountain top experience!
What a beautiful way for life to end!
In the presence of the One who was
His *dearest friend*!
It was a beautiful panorama
God unfolded before Moses
But God had a better plan in mind
For this man
As his life of service closes!
Could we say his life of service was hard
When to be absent from the body
Is to be present with the Lord!

I have listed the books of Moses separately to emphasize our beginning, our responsibility and of course the basis for our blessed future! The way is to walk with God, so—we start with Salad of the Soul!

Genesis is for Grace!
Exodus is for Eternity!
Leviticus is for L-O-V-E!
Numbers is for Newness(of life)
and
Deuteronomy is for Devotion!
Quite a salad!

And even in Genesis we look to our Savior who is indeed, the dressing for the Salad of our Souls! So there it is, from the garden of our beginnings, the inward vitamins and minerals that existed in the heart of God before He planted all we would need on this earth, before He created man. He provided food and then He provided clothing and then He provided a covering for our sins. Later He would say, "Without the shedding of blood there is no remission for sin." Think He didn't know *that* when He killed those animals to clothe and cover Adam and Eve?

I am amazed at how little awe and reverence we show Him. You would think in this day of great knowledge man would have learned to see Him as He is–as He is described in Isaiah. Among other things He is called our Counselor, Our God, the Prince of Peace, The Everlasting Father. But hearing we hear not and seeing we see not. We are like graduate students of humanity not ready for our final test, wanting a degree in holiness but failing to qualify! One day our Savior would come and qualify in our behalf. Only He has a PHD in perfection! Only He can stand in that 'gap' I mentioned at the beginning of Genesis. Without Him we can do *nothing*. With Him *nothing* can defeat us. We might lose a few 'skirmishes' but the battle is already won!

Even before we get to Revelation, you will know for certain who the winner is!

*And there arose
not a prophet since
in Israel
like unto Moses
whom the LORD knew
face to face,
in all the signs and the wonders
which the LORD sent him to do
in the land of Egypt to Pharaoh
and to all his servants
and to all his land.
And in all that mighty hand
and in all the great terror
which Moses showed
in the sight of all Israel.*
(Deuteronomy 34:10-12kjv)

PART 2

The Blossoming

Joshua through 2nd Samuel

KINGDOM

*Now after the death of Moses the servant of the Lord
it came to pass, that the Lord spake unto Joshua
the son of Nun, Moses' minister, saying
Moses my servant is dead:
now therefore arise, go over this Jordan,
thou and all this people
unto the land which I do give to them
even to the children of Israel.
.....only be thou strong and very courageous,
that thou mayest observe to do according to all the law,
which Moses my servant commanded thee:
turn not from it to the right hand or to the left,
that thou mayest prosper whithersoever thou goest.
This book of the law shall not depart out of thy mouth;
but thou shall meditate therein day and night,
that thou mayest observe to do
according to all that is written therein:
for then thou shalt make thy way prosperous,
and then thou shalt have good success.
Have not I commanded thee?
Be strong and of a good courage,
be not afraid, neither be dismayed:
for the Lord thy God is with thee
whithersoever thou goest.*
(Joshua 1:1-2;7-9kjv)

The "I Love My Bible" Commentary
(Book of Joshua)

JOSHUA 1

God was no stranger to Joshua.
Joshua had spent time with Him
In the tabernacle!
Therefore he knew there was no task
Too big for him to tackle!
Our Lord is faithful to each generation.
When Israel needed a man for any hour
God would raise one for this nation.
But He had to remind Joshua to be brave.
Again God would show He is mighty to save!
Joshua knew it was one thing to bring Israel
Out---another to take her in!
There would be many obstacles to conquer
Many battles to win!
God had appeared to Moses as a burning bush
But Joshua needed to be bolder
So God would soon appear to him
As a mighty soldier!

JOSHUA 2

Strange that it would be a prostitute
Who rescued those Israeli spies.
She blatantly told the Jericho police
A bunch of lies.
But she was honest with the Israelis
When she said,
"If you do not spare my family,
We're as good as dead!"
"You are to stay in the house," they replied.
She was to do what they said
And all her family would be safe inside!
If a scarlet rope was hung in view
She would be safe and her family too.
She could trust them for they believed
In the supreme God
And she had heard of their valor in defeating
The kings of Sihon and Og.

The spies returned to Joshua
With a positive report!
Israel could move ahead.
The ball was in their court!

JOSHUA 3

Opportunity knocks but once.
It was time to go.
When the priests stepped into the water
The Jordan River ceased to flow.
God chooses not to do His work alone.
Joshua had to step out and keep God's people
    moving on!
The Israelis were seen leaving Acacia early
    in the morning
And when they camped at the Jordan river
All Jericho took warning.
For three days and more Jericho would watch
    and quiver
Dreading the day those Israelis would cross
    the river.
How many of them saw that river divide
As the Israelis crossed the river to their side?
Once again Israel could be found
Crossing what should have been soggy ground.
But God had interceded once before
And now He does it just once more!
The catalyst for that miracle was the ark
God would not leave His people in the *'dark!'*

JOSHUA 4

People should never forget God's great feats
Especially those of such magnitude
As this miracle which He repeats!
Now He tells them each should take a stone
To build a monument before they entered
The battle zone.
That monument would remind them

Comments on Joshua

Of God's power
To rescue them-even in their darkest hour!
The stones would be there year after year
Teaching future generations to rise above fear.
And as they walked in His light
Israel would succeed.
God would be with them whatever their need!

JOSHUA 5

God told Joshua to circumcise all the men.
They had to fulfil His covenant.
Not to do it would be sin.
Israel would soon enter the Promised Land
And their lives would never be the same!
The circumcision covenant had not been kept.
They must do it to remove their shame.
And they would observe the Passover before
They crossed to Jordan's other shore!
It was the last day manna was supplied.
Remember how much they hated it
And how often they moaned and cried!
I suppose Joshua was weary clear to the bone
And so he goes away just to be alone.
But he sees a stranger who gets his attention.
There stood the One too marvelous to mention!
Joshua saw Him with his own eyes!
Thus he would know
God was with him too.
Now watch his courage grow!

JOSHUA 6

God sees our enemy defeated
Long before we do!
Especially when He leads the battle
His army marches through!
The Israelis are a case in point.
They followed God's battle plan
And they won the battle without losing a man!
Now they kept their promise
To Rahab and her family
Joshua directs them to go and set them free!
It was time for her to know
God had changed her *status quo!*
All the precious metals they confiscated
Were consigned to priestly care.
And we read God was with Joshua
Who became famous everywhere!
This God, who set fire to the burning bush
Can set a fire in our souls
And He who knocked down
The walls of Jericho
Can direct our feet toward nobler goals!
As we walk with Him in spirit and truth
The world is at our feet.
God will not let us quit
Until our victory is complete!

JOSHUA 7

Israel sinned!
Someone kept what wasn't his to keep.
He affected the whole nation when he stole
And buried his treasure deep.
It was a secret he thought, but God knew!
And Israel lost her next battle.
"We can beat Ai,"they said. "They are so few."
What a shock it was to Joshua who fell on
    his face
Crying to the Lord, "Why did you lead us to
    this place?"
God told him He wouldn't help Israel
Because there was sin in their camp
And he demanded that they punish
That sneaky scamp!
So that theft was discovered
And Achan's guilt was uncovered!
His punishment was swift and strong.
It can be dangerous to be wrong!
Though God loves all men
He will NOT live in the presence of sin.

The "I Love My Bible" Commentary

JOSHUA   8

Sometimes-though a problem is small-
We're unable to do a thing at all.
Israel couldn't defeat little Ai
No matter how hard she would try.
Facing responsibility was a bitter pill
But Israel must learn true victory won't come
When they fail to do God's will.
But that was resolved and God said
"Go take the city!"
Destroy them all. You must show no pity!"
This seems harsh but it was God's land.
A picture of Heaven on which
They would stand!
Once more the people reviewed
The blessings and the curses
Moses had written down
Knowing God's Word would strengthen them
As they marched into each town!

JOSHUA   9

Six kingdoms arm themselves to fight
For their lives.
It was their belief-only the brave survives!
But the Gibeonites pulled a fast one
We would say.
They told Israel they had come a long way.
The leaders erred not knowing
The Gibeonites meant to deceive
Which means don't trust your eyes.
You could be in error what you believe.
When you're not sure what others seek
Think-no, pray- before you speak!
The Israeli leaders had to keep their vow.
What else would their holy God allow?
Most of the Israelis were angry
Because they disagreed with the peace treaty.
Those lying Gibeonites were not truly needy.
But the Israeli leaders would retort
"We didn't know their journey was so short."
Because of Gibeon's deceit
Joshua pronounced a curse.
They would be Israel's servants.
They didn't mind because they knew
Their fate could have been much worse!

JOSHUA   10

Hush my soul!
Let time stand still!
Stand as still as the earth did that day
When God intervened in an unusual way!
Bask in the glory of this Mighty One
Who could twist His little finger around
           the sun!
And God caused the moon to hang
Over the valley of Aijalon
As the heathen died from Goshen to Gibeon!
So God over ruled His universal laws
To hold the earth suspended
Fighting for His people until the battle ended!
There was not one Israeli casualty–not one
All because of what the Lord had done!
      So when I stand in His presence
           I say, "Hush my soul
           I stand in the presence
               Of the One
            Who made me whole!"
            And when we climb
             That last holy hill
              It will be as if
              Time stood still!

JOSHUA   11

The Kings of the federation march to the
           Springs of Merom
And none of these kings lived to return
To the cities they had traveled from.

Comments on Joshua

Too bad they didn't know their enemy
Was the Lord of Hosts.
He told Joshua those sinners would die.
That would teach those men not to boast!
There would never be enough kings
To defeat the Lord's army
Because this God of all the universe
Was Israel's Commander-in-chief!
Those kings walked into God's ambush
And died still sinners full of unbelief.
Joshua defeated other cities
With the help of his and Israel's God!
The only cities still left undefeated
Were Gaza, Gath, and Ashdod.

JOSHUA   12

From The Arnon Gorge to Mount Hermon
The cities succumbed.
Even the cities of the eastern desert
Fell helpless, confused, be-numbed!
Count them-31 in all
Though they didn't believe it
Were destined to fall!
The Israelis conquered the land
From the hill country to the desert.
And everywhere the boils of defeat festered!
Those kings didn't have a chance.
The Israeli victories brought them
Only defeat choreographed to a somber dance.

JOSHUA   13

There were many lands left to conquer
And Joshua was growing old.
He had done what God said and was
Strong, courageous, and bold!
Now events have changed and time has
    passed.
Having conquered most of the land
They could celebrate at last!

The tribal boundaries were mentioned again
Time to be reviewed because they were
    settling in!
The tribe of Levi seems to be ignored
But God was their inheritance and
He would take care of them in different ways.
Their lives would not be lived helter-skelter!
God would see to it they always had food,
    clothing, and shelter.

JOSHUA   14

Caleb was named specifically in this chapter.
How faithful he had been!
He and Joshua had been faithful spies
Who stood against the other men.
He reminds Joshua of their stand
And Joshua gave him the portion he wanted
In the promised land!
Though others cringed in fear,
Caleb wouldn't cater.
Now his reward proves
Courage pays off-sooner or later!

JOSHUA   15

Look at the boundaries for Judah!
That tribe received the *lion's share!*
I suspect the other tribes were jealous
Because Judah had blessings to spare!
It must have been great belonging
To this tribe.
Think of the tremendous pride this people
Carried inside!
Proud enough to be humble they had
Received so much!
Surely they must have felt the *Midas touch*!
Caleb who is now mentioned again
Wanted Kiriath Sepher as if he didn't
    have enough
And he offered his daughter to the man

The "I Love My Bible" Commentary

Who could prove himself exceptionally tough
And guess who did that? Othniel!
That offer Caleb made must have been
An easy sell!
Not much is told of Acsah but she brings
Love and happiness to her marriage
And a couple of flowing springs.
She wanted Othniel to ask for a field
But she wanted something too.
She asked for water because trees and flowers
Would enhance their view.
Ever see a woman who didn't want flowers
In her garden and surrounding her land.
Flowers take an ordinary home and turns it
Into something grand!
But for all the power Judah had, her victory
Was incomplete.
The Jebusites held on to Jerusalem
And claimed every street.
But they did live side by side.
And that was no comfort to Judah's pride!

JOSHUA   16

The tribe of Ephraim receives land
In this chapter
But they couldn't defeat the people
They went after!
The people in Gezer were never driven out.
What happend to Ephraim who should have
Won without a doubt?
Silent were the praises they once had sung.
And they were fearful of these people
They had to live among!
Maybe they were afraid to reach out and take
The victory God had promised
Victory they should have won for
His Name's sake!
God didn't take them by the hand
And set them down in the Promised Land.
"We're partners," He must have said.

"Now it is yours if you will just move ahead!"

JOSHUA   17

The tribe of Manasseh would eventually
Reside in the area listed
Though the Canaanites continually resisted.
Again, Zelophehad's daughters complained
So their uncles were restrained.
These men were not trying to be cruel.
They thought the inheritance always going
To the men had always been the rule.
But God never intended for His daughters
To be slighted.
The daughters of Zelophehad were examples
Of wrongs righted!
Had not God intervened to give them land
They would not have received an inch.
God loves His daughters–that's a cinch!
It was mentioned in this chapter for
Future women to see
They, too, could be eligible for their father's
    property!
Now we see Joseph's descendants
Were no better than the other tribes.
They could not drive out the Canaanites
By force, threats, or bribes!

JOSHUA   18

Seven tribes have not possessed their lands.
"Move on , move out, move up,"
    Joshua commands!
But first he sends spies to scout the territory
Remember the beauty those previous
    Spies described?
They must have repeated the same story!
The remainder of this chapter describes
What the tribe of Benjamin got
For Joshua divides this holy land
By sacred lot!

Comments On Joshua

JOSHUA 19

The rest of the tribes are mentioned
In chapter nineteen.
These blessed people were receiving
The most glorious land they had ever seen!
It was the land where God would live.
His presence was more important
Than any other present He could give!
God chose each area and whatever
    He decided
Was the way the land was divided!

JOSHUA 20

Cities of refuge were listed because
Not every death is intentional.
Sometimes it is an accident
And harm to another was not one's intent.
But think how a person might feel.
Fearing the consequences of a death
Can be very real!
The first thing a grieving person might want
    to do
Is to say, "You killed him and I will kill you!"
Our Heavenly Father knows our earthly frame
And how readily we like to lay the blame.
But if there is no intent to kill
Killing that man is against God's will.
But let's remember God says
The *intentional* murderer must be found.
There is nowhere for him to run.
He must pay inch for inch-pound for pound!

JOSHUA 21

After Israel was settled
After they had conquered all the land
They remembered the Levites
And obeyed God's command.
But of course they had to be reminded!
When people get what they want
When they are *riding high*, they can be
    blinded!
But they willingly gave the cities and the lands
Requested by the Levites.
Now all God's people had been given
And received their rights!
These people who had walked so many miles
Now radiated God's glory through their
    smiles!
Now their peace, their joy, their hopes
Should never fade
Because our Blessed Lord had kept
Every single promise He made!

JOSHUA 22

Our lives can be an altar of witness to others
If we stand tall like that monument
Reuben, Gad, and Manaasseh built
For their brothers!
Even the river could not be too wide
That brothers could not live side by side!
They had been faithful to their brothers
In every battle
But the first ones to see that monument
Had to run and tattle!
"Look what our brothers did," they cried.
"God will kill us for sure!"
And they trembled inside!
"No its not an altar for sacrifice." They replied.
"That is not what we meant!
It is so you will know God is our God, too.
That is why we built this monument!"
And rejoicing because the Lord was so kind
They returned to their homes with peace
    of mind!
It is only the land the river parts
And the Lord would see
They would be blessed with undivided hearts!

The "I Love My Bible" Commentary

JOSHUA 23

When Joshua was very old he called
The people together and said
"I've done all I can for you
And you know very well that God's promises
To you have all come true!"
He reminds them to follow
 Moses's instructions and not deviate.
Then the Lord would remain with them
And they would have reason to celebrate!
The heathen made many idols.
There was not one of them worthy to cherish.
Should Israel do so, they would surely perish!
To turn away from God is to steadily decline.
But think of the joy to be able to say
"I am His and He is mine!!!"

JOSHUA 24

His last words in this book were
Israel should worship God alone.
He reminded them God had given them
 now and later
Every thing they would ever own!
And he added, "Whatever you do
We WILL serve the Lord, my family and I !"
Then to their reply he said
"You must serve Him or you will die!"
And again he has to say
"Destroy all your idols this very day!"
It seems someone was always telling them
"Destroy your idols," but did they ever?
Long years in the distant future
God would sever
All ties with these people who failed
 to understand
Life would be empty without Him
As empty as He would strip their land!

When Joshua said, "As for me and my house, we will serve the Lord, it wasn't because he was a hard task master, but it was because he loved the Master of All the Ages! And he must have felt he had taught his children right—had been a good example—and had earnestly taught them to love the Lord.

Joshua was a great man and he was great because he was filled with God's grace!

Even Moses could not have made a better confession than Joshua made! Here was a man true to the Lord and no better thing can be said whether that man was Moses or Elijah or David!

He was not as dramatic as Moses but he was just as devoted!

He was not as powerful as Elijah but he was just as prayerful!

And he was not as poetic as David but he praised God just as beautifully!!

Joshua was truly one of God's great men!

As for me

and my house

we WILL serve

the Lord

(Joshua 24:15b-kjv)

The "I Love My Bible" Commentary
(Judges)

JUDGES 1

Joshua had said, "You're here at last!
Now possessing the land will be your task."
Caleb believed him and took control.
Taking 'his' mountain had been his goal!
But look at the half-hearted victory
Of the other tribes,
The unwillingness to conquer the land
This Chapter describes.
Caleb is the only bright spot here.
What stopped the others-laziness or fear?
God had given them this land to possess.
When He told them to take it
How could they have done any less?
Fear should have been forsaken
And the promises of God gladly taken!
How many of us have been deprived
Of victories we refused to accept
And like them fail to see
The many promises God has kept.
Our vision is limited because we look
In faith through a tiny *peep hole*
And is it any wonder we fail to reach one goal?
We must broaden our vision, let faith grow
And then only God knows how far we can go!

JUDGES 2

It was a sad day for Israel
When the Angel said in essence
"God is no longer with you,
You have lost His presence!"
From then on He would reveal Himself
To only a very few.
Only those who would *really listen*
Would He tell what to do!
He withdrew the loving counsel He supplied
When Joshua and his generation died.
Because Israel worshiped idols
They were a people scorned and shamed.
It was against these disobedient people
God's anger flamed.
God's holiness demanded
Discipline for their refusal to do what
He commanded.
From then on Israel failed to move
In giant strides
For God left the heathen to be thorns
In their sides.

JUDGES 3

Most of Judges could be called
 the See-saw book!
We see this nation up, then down
Every where we look.
We see this *see-saw* beginning in this chapter
And for years she couldn't make up her mind
Who or what she was after!
Except for Othniel, Ehud, and Shamgar
The people of Israel follow God from afar.
Israel often listened to a *different drum*
And we will see that in the chapters to come.

JUDGES 4

Deborah and Jael stand out in this chapter
--like two beacon lights!
One destroyed a general while the rest
 of Israel fights.
Deborah led Israel to victory
While King Jabin's general goes down
As defeated by a woman in ancient history!
She spoke softly to Sisera, this woman
 named Jael
He ran to her for protection and that
 is why He fell!
Spiritual and physical were his hurts
Because he hid behind a woman's skirts!

Comments on Judges

JUDGES 5

How can you beat a song that has everything,
That tells how God helped two women
And gave them reason to sing?
Battles are supposed to be won by the strong
 and the brave!
But this time it was different.
Sly Jael didn't behave!
So the third woman, a mother, waits
For treasures she will not receive.
Her son will never come home to his mother
And she is left alone to grieve.
According to the song, the stars of heaven
Fought for Israel
The time Sisera fell!
When Israel turned to God
He subdued all their fears
And there was peace in Israel for forty years!

JUDGES 6

Oh Israel, what was wrong with you?
Once again you refused to follow orders.
Once again you suffered at the hands
Of those heathen marauders.
You're lucky God appeared to Gideon
As he was treading the grapes
Reassuring Gideon when he asked.
"Lord what are you going to do for our sakes?"
It seems Gideon was the kind
Who had great trouble making up his mind.
First he wanted the fleece wet on dry ground
And then he wanted the fleece dry
The second time around.
But God patiently honored his request
In order to put Gideon's mind at rest!

JUDGES 7

Look at those armies down in the valley
Waiting to slaughter Israel!
And there were thirty two thousand men
With Gideon yearning for the kill!
But God said, "No, You will boast of *your*
 strength; send some of them home.
There are too many of you to fight!"
And so that Gideon wouldn't fear
God sent him spying in the night!
It wasn't a battle Gideon would seek
For with only three hundred men,
They seemed awfully weak!
His confidence certainly needed restoring
And when he heard of the soldier's dream
It sent his hopes soaring!
He got his troops together knowing
Now they would win.
It was an easy battle for Gideon and his men!
"We fight for God and Gideon
They proclaimed!"
With God's help and only three hundred men
The over confident Midianites were shamed!

JUDGES 8

The battle was over and some didn't agree
It was because of God's help
Gideon had set Israel free!
But Gideon made a big mistake when he made
An ephod and God didn't like it one bit
When all of Israel bowed and worshiped it.
I'd like to crawl into Gideon's soul
And see why he would do such a thing
For when he defeated the Midianites
I bet you could have heard the angels sing!
This man who had been brave and bold
Foolishly caused many to worship
That ephod he made of tarnished gold.
How many times has man climbed
To the pinnacle of faith only to fall from grace
And then lost the glory of standing
In God's high and holy place?

The "I Love My Bible" Commentary

JUDGES 9

Nothing good could be said of Abimelech
And many in the town of Shechem refused
To show him any respect.
Gaal led the revolt hoping to take Abimelech
    by surprise.
But Zebul taunted him with snide remarks like
"You can't believe your eyes!"
Gaal thought he saw men marching toward the
    city.
He was unaware that Abimelech was planning
To attack and would show them no pity.
But vicious Abimelech slaughtered his enemies
As far as Thebez and that was his big mistake!
Since a *woman* killed him with a stone
It was the last one he would make!
The words of Jotham came true.
He told Abimelech, "I placed a curse on you!"
Abimelech had shown extreme cruelty
When he killed his seventy brothers foolishly.
Jotham was right when he said,
"As sure as there is a God in heaven,
Abimelech will pay for his crime!"
So maybe he had seventy levels of Hell
To go through
Before he would pay for all those horrors
He managed to do!
And I bet he suffered many more times
For committing all those vicious crimes.

JUDGES 10

Think of the heartbreak it caused the Lord
When He had to say
"I won't help you anymore, for you love
Your idols so much; go to them and pray."
What a shock that must have been!
It got the attention of those evil men.
They confessed they sinned and pleaded
With such anguish Our Lord conceded!
Once again His heart was touched by
His people's misery
And once again He would give them victory!

JUDGES 11

Gideon's son by a prostitute was not accepted
By his brothers
Who chased him from the presence
Of their mothers.
They drove him into being a mal-content
Living off the land
Yet when they needed a leader,
They asked him to take command.
When he agreed, Jephthah told King Sihon,
"Why all this fuss
You keep what your gods give you
And we will keep what our God gives us."
He lived to regret the vow that he'd sacrifice
The first one out of his house in trade.
And he couldn't renege on this vow he made.
God had told his people never to make
A foolish vow and this one topped the list.
It seems it was amended but his daughter
Mourned for the joys she had missed!
And the girls of Israel lamented each year
As they gathered for her from far and near.
Today we often fail to keep our word
As if we believe surely no one heard.
But it meant something back then
And making a foolish vow was considered sin!

JUDGES 12

It is sad that men must fight among themselves
After such a glorious victory.
Jephthah and his men had to kill
Forty two thousand of those Ephraimites
To prove Jephthah's nobility.
He and his men had been called
The scums of the earth and lowly outcasts

Comments On Judges

And their tempers boiled hotter
Than a furnace blast!
Think of the carnage of one so mad.
Think of at least 42,000 relatives
Whose hearts were broken and sad!
Those men still victorious
From a hot headed war
Couldn't stop killing and went t-o-o-o far!
No more was said
Of this man who died
And was buried in Gilead.
There were other judges mentioned
Such as Ibzan and Elon
And one that the Bible says had forty sons
Whose name was Abdon.
Those men must have been having a contest
And I bet he thought he proved
He was the very best!

JUDGES 13

Because Israel had turned to idols again
She had been in subjection to the Philistines
And had felt hopeless for forty years.
But then Manoah's wife received
A heartening message
When the angel of God appears!
He tells her she will have a son
Who will be a Nazarite
And he would rescue Israel
From her uncomfortable plight.
She and Manoah did not realize
He was the angel of the Lord
Until he ascended in the fire.
It was not meant for show.
He did it to inspire!
This couple had been childless all their life
And until he saw the angel
Manoah did not believe his wife.
Samson's birth had been announced
In an unusual way.

It was only natural he would find life
More exciting every passing day!
Samson loved to visit the parade grounds
Of the army of Dan.
Strength and power enchanted him
Even before he grew
To be a huge and powerful man!

JUDGES 14

When Samson made up his mind
It was impossible to change.
His parents disapproved of his fiancee.
In fact they thought he was acting strange.
Surely a beautiful girl of Israel would suffice!
No! He wanted one from a nation with not
A quality that could be considered nice!
Hadn't God told them not to mix
With a nation always up to dirty tricks?
They proved *that* by the way they solved
His riddle
"Shame on you!" He said. "I'll teach you
Not to fiddle
With my heifer"(who was his intended bride).
He knew they couldn't solve it without help
No matter how hard they tried.
Well he paid his debt
But had to kill thirty men
To pay off his foolish bet.
Her faithless act put those thirty men in danger
And then Samson rejected her
Because of his anger!

JUDGES 15

It seems Samson never rose above
A personal vendetta as he took revenge
First on his (?)Father-in-law and his wife
And then when they were killed
He went on a murderous binge.
Who else could brag of killing a thousand men

The "I Love My Bible" Commentary

With the jawbone of a donkey?
No one else has ever done that again!
And we can see the Lord had been with him.
He also gave Samson water when he prayed.
And He continually showed this wayward son
Mercy when he strayed!

JUDGES 16

Because Samson had a weakness in his heart
He revealed to Delilah
The symbol of his strength was in his hair
And she betrayed him to the Philistines
Whose razors left him none to spare.
Sometimes people of God choose to lead
An ambivalent lifestyle.
Samson was one of these!
And it does seem very questionable
Who this man wanted to please.
I wonder if his parents failed to explain
Samson's noble purpose in life
For it seems he continually got himself
    in trouble
And caused constant strife.
Yet Samson was not afraid to reach out
And get involved
Though they were of his own making
These problems he solved.
Samson judged Israel twenty years
Yet the Philistines controlled the land.
He never conquered them
Though thousands died at his hand.
He had 'played around' despite the gift he had
But I suppose we must admit
This fellow Samson wasn't always bad!

JUDGES 17

Micah stole a thousand dollars from his Mother
But he confessed.
It was a humble admission which she blessed.

The idol she gave Micah would enhance
His other idols she surmised
But how could she justify doing
What the Lord despised?
Soon a Levite became involved
And Micah thought his need for a priest
Had finally been resolved!
Had these people forgotten God hated idols
Of any kind?
We wonder what could have possessed
This Israeli's mind!
But there is no critique of how Micah acts.
This chapter simply states the facts.

JUDGES 18

The tribe of Dan meet Micah's priest
And it soon becomes known,
"Dan has joined himself to idols.
Leave him alone!"
But for now Micah started it all
When the men stayed at his home.
Soon they would steal his priest and his idols
To take wherever they would roam.
Yet they wanted to settle down in their own
    territory.
How they destroyed Laish and its inhabitants
Is not a pretty story.
They appointed another priest who is said
To be the grandson of Moses
And they were still worshiping idols
As this chapter closes.

Judges 19

The Bible can be brutally frank and it includes
The horror of human attitudes.
I guess I wanted to skip what I read here
For when I came to this to print
I had written not a word.
And I still shudder to think how awful

Comment on Judges

This woman was treated
And how easily lust is stirred.
These were men of Benjamin, people of God
Who had succumbed to the devil
And his divining rod.
He has always perverted this thing called sex
And these men must have welcomed
His evil hex.
Sin is a mountain made of paper maiche
And will easily burn to the ground some day.

JUDGES 20

Israel takes vengeance on its brother tribe
To an unknown man they would subscribe!
What state of mind was the tribe
Of Benjamin in
To allow these sex perverts to get by
With such a sin?
They fought as if it was a holy cause
They must defend
And it almost brought Benjamin's tribe
To an untimely end!
People were slaughtered like cattle
In that vicious unnecessary battle.
Numerous were the blessings in which
God's people had been the receivers.
Why would the tribe of Benjamin
Act like such evil unbelievers?
Today, courts release the guilty
Putting them back on the street
So we've learned no lesson from Benjamin
And probably won't until
God's style of judgement is complete!

JUDGES 21

Well if this doesn't beat all!
They almost destroyed Benjamin
And then they cried.
Perhaps their consciences hurt
So they couldn't be satisfied.
How they solved the problem was almost
As asinine
As how they drew the battle line!
And then they destroyed Jabesh-Gilead
Because they wouldn't take part
In the travesty that ripped this nation's heart.
Custom mandated they not supply a bride
To those six hundred young men
Even though Israel was guilty
Of almost committing genocide.
And it all started with a vicious rape
That led to this nation's sad, sad shape!
Why did Israel end up in such a plight?
Its there in this chapter's last sentence.
*"Every one did that
which **he** thought was right!"*

Note: If we've ever learned any thing about
    ambivalence, it is that it gets us no
    where. Israel never truly made up
    her mind whom to worship so she
    did not grow in grace during this
    time. She was like stagnant water
    with no movement. She was up one
    day and down the next and she did
    not move forward. Maybe that is why
    the book is called Judges.
    There is no movement when
    one(or many) must be judged. As
    no movement brings stagnant water,
    it also brings stagnant hearts! Israel
    had many great leaders during Judges
    but sadly, their influence died with
    them. None of them seemed to have
    a lasting effect on the people.
    Surely God must have wondered
    "Why am I so easy to forget?"
    Maybe, just maybe, He may be
    asking Himself that question today.

The "I Love My Bible" Commentary
(The Book of Ruth)

RUTH 1

Elimelech took his wife and two sons to Moab.
He and their two sons died there.
Naomi changes her name to Mara
Because she thought the Lord had been unfair.
To lose all the men of her household
Left her heart broken, bitter, and old.
It was a terrible blow Naomi was dealt.
Yet the ashes of grief held a beauty
Much too gracious for her not to have felt!
She would hear Ruth say, "I won't leave you."
And she didn't want Naomi to fuss.
"May the Lord do awful things to me," she said,
"If I allow anything but death to separate us!"
Naomi must have shown her daughter-in-law
Great love that Ruth would say,
"I want to go where you go,
Stay where you stay
So please don't turn me away!"
The Naomi-Ruth story remains to testify
Their love for each other was the best,
An example of why we can lay
Those in-law horror stories to rest!
Permit me to brag yet showing nothing fancy
Or much aplomb
Just to humbly say, I too, know the wonder
Of a daughter-in-law who quietly shows and
Says, "I love you Mom!"

RUTH 2

Have we ever thanked God for in-laws?
Don't we know it is often
They who support our cause?
Observe how Boaz treated Ruth.
He told her how he had heard of her love
For Naomi and knew of its truth!
Then he told the reapers to leave
Some of the grain they would beat
So Ruth and Naomi would have plenty to eat,
Not only for that day but for the whole season.
There is a basic law that tells the reason!
For those who do well its good to know,
As sure as there is a God in Heaven
We will reap just what we sow!
Ruth sowed kindness and love
And received the same!
We will always think of the word *love*
Whenever we hear her name!

RUTH 3

When it came to Israeli customs I'm afraid
Ruth was stupid!
Bur Naomi knew what she was doing
When she played *cupid*!
She knew where Boaz would be
Out on the threshing floor winnowing barley.
She thought since he was next of kin
He could be a replacement for her men.
As the closest kin he could make it known
Mahlon's name could live on!
But there was a closer relative
Boaz gave the chance
To offer Ruth another opportunity for romance.
Boaz's feelings for Ruth were more than pity
When he confronted that other relative
In the city!

RUTH 4

So Boaz marries Ruth and the Lord
Gave her a little boy
And Ruth, who had been better to Naomi
Than seven sons restored her faith and joy!
And they named him Obed
This child who became Grandfather to David!
So what comes around goes around.
Love puts our faith on solid ground!

The Book of Ruth

Note: "Ruth" is such a little book, but there is nothing little about the love described in its pages, nothing mundane, nothing spiteful! It is one of the best magnifying mirrors of how marvelous love can be. It disputes all the horror stories about mothers-in law . It says we fail to look below the surface of a special love available to all! Trust me Ruth wouldn't have loved Naomi so much had Naomi fit the description of ridiculed mothers-in-law today.

You see Naomi giving Ruth advice. So! Is that so bad? Do(or did) young wives know it all? Do(or did)we go into a marriage with the attitude we're not going to accept (or listen to)our in-laws? Ask yourself that! Be honest. I bet you will agree with me that the most maligned person in all history is a mother-in-law. But there are the lucky ones(who still have to bear the cruel jokes)who love and are loved by their daughters-in-law.

So-the book of Ruth is special. It is strictly about love between two women who are two (of the many)female creatures on this earth who are least expected to love one another. Ruth proves otherwise! That is what makes it so great! (Besides-it doesn't take long to read this book that is so l-o-n-g on love)!

The "I Love My Bible" Commentary
(The Book of 1ˢᵗ Samuel)

1ˢᵗ SAMUEL 1

Little Samuel had a mother who believed
She'd have a son even before she conceived.
On her knees she asked for a son
And there she stayed
Until she knew God answered
The prayer she prayed.
How many years had she prayed this hard?
And still she promised to give him to the Lord!
She always went to see Samuel once a year
To take him clothes.
He grew into a man of integrity who chose
To always follow the Lord.
Hannah loved the Lord so much
It wasn't hard to keep the promise she made
And the FATHER gave her five more children
Simply because she prayed!
Truly, this Mother had felt the FATHER'S touch!
She knew what she gave away would return seven-fold
And God did give her other children to hold.
You see, faith looks beyond 'today'
And FAITH compels God to answer
The <u>fervent</u> prayers we pray!
Not casual, not hurried, but heart felt
These prayers cause God's heart to melt!
Be not discouraged, God knows our need
And hears every prayer we plead!
Dedicated to the Lord,
Samuel lived a life of grace and truth.
What a marvelous life to behold!
And he faithfully guided the people
Even when he grew feeble and old!

1ˢᵗ SAMUEL 2

Hannah's verse of praise would be hard to beat.
She considered having so many children
quite a feat!
This woman who had been barren many years
Who had sought the Lord through many tears
Considered herself amply blessed
After she had put our Lord to the test!
But she promised God she'd give
Samuel back to Him
And now that she has many children
She feels her cup is filled to the brim!
She proclaims, "she that is barren is barren
    no more!"
Now she has more to praise the Father for
Than she ever had before!
Its strange to note the contrast here.
Eli's sons' contempt for the Lord
    held no fear.
They would not listen to their father Eli.
They were so wicked God said they would die.
Hannah had started this chapter with praise.
Now God says these wicked men
Would not live out their appointed days.
Quite a difference between an insignificant
    woman
And 'should be' holy priests!
God honored the woman
They would have honored the least.
The most important thing in this chapter
For us to see
Is God says, "I will only honor those
Who honor Me!"

1ˢᵗ SAMUEL 3

It must have been frightening for little Samuel
To say what God had told him.
No prophet, no priest, no preacher
Wants to give news so grim!
Even people with irreverent views
Want to hear the best of news!
But Samuel had none to give

Comment On 1st Samuel

And we see another example
Of how we must account for the way we live.
Eli had already been reprimanded
For not correcting his sons as God commanded.
He must have dreaded what God would say
Yet could hardly wait until the break of day.
If no news is good news then give me
No news at all
For I would not cherish the news
That I am destined to fall!
There is nothing tasty or nourishing
About life's *just desserts*
And that is a fact we must face
No matter how much it hurts!

1st SAMUEL 4

We still stumble down life's *'permissive'* trail
And yet ask our selves "Where did we fail?"
Its so easy to be easy in matters of the heart.
Our children often *get under our skin*
And when we should be faithful to discipline
We find ourselves giving in!
God, Himself, had to discipline Phinehas
and Hophni
And it broke the heart of old Eli.
When man takes his eyes
Off the One who made the stars
He inflicts himself with many spiritual scars.
Even Phinehas's wife cried
"We've lost the glory of God
Name my son Ichabod!"

1st SAMUEL 5

Everywhere the ark went
The Philistines suffered a plague
Ashdod, Ekron, Gath, where ever it stayed.
Or where ever it was moved trouble followed
close behind
And every where it went people whined!

God would not allow the presence of His Ark
To honor the heathen idol, Dagon
So they entreated the mayor to send it back
These inhabitants of Ekron..
Since the Philistines were afraid they would
all die
They were more than eager
To bid the Ark of God goodbye!

1st SAMUEL 6

The heathen people felt the power of God
He had destroyed many of them
From Gath to Ashdod.
They knew they needed to send a gift
Hoping those cloudy plagues of persecution
Would quickly lift!
And look at these people's ingenuity!
Just in case these plagues were *just a lark*
They hitched two mother cows together
To return the Ark!
They still wanted to prove
God had not caused their trouble
But the cows showed He did
For they headed to Israel *on the double!*
They wasted no time taking the ark back home.
In spite of their calves, they would still roam
Proving God could still use their cunning
To fulfill what He planned
That day the Philistines returned the ark
To the Holy Land!

1st SAMUEL 7

People who turn from the Lord know sorrow.
Their 'day' can not pass quickly enough
And they can't wait for 'tomorrow!'
These people's yesterdays brought only shame
And unless they returned to God
Their days to come would be the same.
The people of Israel knew only despair

The "I Love My Bible" Commentary

Until they went to Mispeh
And Samuel met them there.
They felt the Lord had abandoned them
But it was the other way around.
It was only when they returned to the Lord
They found themselves on solid ground!
Samuel would often plead for these people
But I bet he never had a hunch
They'd end up being such a rowdy, unholy bunch!
Yet he loved them anyway
And intervened for them each day.

1st SAMUEL 8

Remember Eli's sons?
It seems Samuel's were a carbon copy
For they, too, were greedy
And accepted bribes in stead of helping
The poor and needy.
Because of them Israel begs for a king
When they had the One Great King already
One who had guided them through the years
With a hand stout and steady.
Samuel told them a king would confiscate their fields
And those who kept their lands
Would be taxed on yearly yields.
But they wanted to be like other nations
With a king to establish political relations.
And it was the beginning of their downfall.
God told Samuel "They have never
Really followed me at all!"
This God, *their noble righteous King*
Was the very best
Yet He told Samuel to fulfill their request.

1st SAMUEL 9

Kish was not a name easy to recall.
His only claim to fame was a son named Saul
Who stood head and shoulders
Above the rest of his clan.
The first time Samuel saw him he must have
Thought Saul was a whale of a man!
Someone had forgotten to tether
The wandering donkeys that eventually
Brought Samuel and Saul together.
God used those donkeys to bring them face to face
So Saul could be His instrument
To save the future of his race.
Even though the Israelis wailed
Not wanting the Lord's leadership
God's mercy still prevailed.
Notice God gave them a tall man
They(figuratively) had to look UP to
But Saul was a midget in his heart
Never realizing he and God
Walked a million miles apart!

1st SAMUEL 10

That great prophet Samuel blesses Saul
Before he sends him away
And tells Saul of the many things
That will happen to him that day.
He told Saul he would be filled
With the Holy Spirit
And would have a new attitude
And he should base his decisions on that fact.
With God's guidance, Saul should change
The way he would act.
At first Saul seemed to be humble
Because of what He did.
The day Samuel was to reveal him to Israel
He ran away and hid!
He found out hiding could be tough
When God told Samuel Saul was hiding
"among the stuff!"
When they found this noble looking fellow
The people would sing

Comment on 1st Samuel

"We have found him!
"God save the king!"
Samuel replied Saul was the king of <u>their</u>
    choice
Then he sent them home to rejoice.
He did not want to see them turn
From the King of Eternity!

1ST SAMUEL   11

The citizens of Jabesh-giliad asked for peace
With Nahash
But the Ammonite treated the people
Of Israel like common trash.
Because he thought the rest of Israel
Would not answer these people's cry
Nahash threatened to gouge out
Every man's right eye.
Nahash was not aware God had given
Iarael a king at their request
And he thought there was little
Israel could do even at her best.
But there was love in Israel's camp
And what happened to Jabesh really mattered.
Hahash was beaten so badly
All his army was widely scattered!
Now Samuel and all the people re-confirm
Saul as king after the Ammonites retreated
And all Israel rejoiced because
The enemy had been defeated!
They had taught Nahash and his beaten batch
"Don't count your chickens before they hatch!"

1st SAMUEL   12

Samuel has to ask. . "Have I ever been bad?
I'm a gray haired old man and
I've served you since I was a lad.
Who have I ever defrauded?"
"No one," the people said.
And Samuel's integrity was reluctantly lauded.

Samuel tells the people it was evil for them
To ask for a king so he called down thunder
And it also rained
Because, he told them, it was against
The Lord they had complained.
They trembled as they asked Samuel to pray.
"It was wrong of us to ask for a king
And we admit our sin today!"
Again Samuel reminded them not to respond
With their usual belligerence and sarcasm
But to follow the Lord with *true* enthusiasm!
Once more he prays for this nation
And tells them to remember the Lord
Has chosen them to be His very own relation!

1ST SAMUEL. 13

What can I say about Saul and the lessons
He should have learned?
Being a king was a gift from God
Not a right he had earned.
Though he appeared to be courageous
Strong and tall
The image he projected was not true at all.
He deceived himself when he offered
Sacrifices to the Lord
And Samuel tells him he has lost his reward.
Remember when the people shouted
"God save the king?"
From that time Saul began to encroach
On Samuel's territory
And he used his influence to act as if
He was above reproach, and then strived
To attain his own *personal* glory
God saw it and said Saul's dynasty was ended
(almost before it had begun).
And it was because of Saul's disobedience
And other irrational things he had done.
His son would never ascend to the throne
Because of Saul's aberrant behavior
That God had to disown!

The "I Love My Bible" Commentary

1st SAMUEL 14

Jonathon was the son of king Saul
Yet he had no future
Because Saul's disobedience of God
Caused a rip no one could suture.
But even though his father was noticeably
Ill-tempered
Jonathon's courage would always be
Remembered!
Jonathon and his body guard sneaked off
Into the night
And were challenged by the Philistines
To come up and fight!
Because of Jonathon's bravery
The Philistines were subdued
And the morale of Israel's army
Was instantly renewed!
Yet Saul's edict had made matters worse.
He had weakened his army
With a foolish curse.
For Saul had said no one could eat
Until all his enemies died
And Saul would have destroyed his own son
Had not his troops replied
"No, we were saved today
By your son Jonathon!"

1st SAMUEL 15

Saul is supposed to kill all the Amalekites
But he spares Agag, the king.
Once again his disobedience has a familiar ring.
Man's behavior has always been the same
Abhorring God's presence and blaspheming
His glorious and Holy Name!
"Well," Saul said. "It wasn't me
Who committed that sin!"
And would you believe He blamed his men?
The only good thing about Saul's appeal
Was he gave his people national zeal!
The message Samuel carried to Saul seemed
Unusually harsh and stern
Yet he constantly mourned
Showing his love and concern!
It grieved Samuel to give Saul such bad news
Yet he knew he would soon anoint a king
God, Himself, would choose!

1st SAMUEL 16

The Lord told Samuel not to mourn
For Saul anymore.
He considered Saul wicked to the core.
He told Samuel to go find a man named Jesse
Who had a son God had selected.
The Lord would not continue to bless
The king he had rejected.
Samuel trembled as he replied,
"I'll be in a jam
For Saul will wonder why
I've gone to Bethlehem!"
But God told him how
To justify his presence there.
Samuel was impressed with Jesse's sons.
Some where tall and fair
But was disappointed when God said, "NO!"
God was looking for a man with a pure heart
And He knew men looked for *show!*
Finally Samuel sent for Jesse's youngest son
And the Lord said, "Anoint him. He's the one!"
What a shock it must have been to Samuel.
David was so young.
How could he challenge Saul
Who was now so high-strung?
But when Saul's temper became troublesome,
Nasty, and sharp
The sweet psalmist of Israel
Soothed Saul's temper with his harp!
As his fingers caressed the strings
He let the gentle rhythm roll
For David knew music quietly calms the soul!

Comment On 1st Samuel

1st SAMUEL 17

When Goliath challenged Israel
They thought, "We've been had
For that nasty looking man
Has got to be awfully bad!"
And they trembled as they watched him gloat.
"Send me any man," he bragged, "and
I'll get his *goat!*"
He shook his fist succeeding in looking mean.
And he had threatened Israel for forty days
When David came on the scene.
David asked, "Who is this heathen that defies
The armies of the Living God?
He claims to be so brave. Look how he's shod!"
Shocked by David's behavior, his brothers said
"Don't you talk like that!
You are nothing but a smart-alec brat!"
"And how can you fight him?" Saul asked.
"You are just a boy!"
But David and his slingshot became Israel's
Pride and joy.
That giant advanced with all his armor
But David used only a little stone.
"We will kill this Philistine!" He said,.
"Me and God alone!"
It happend just the way David said.
And the Philistines retreated
When David cut off Goliath's head!

1st SAMUEL 18

Saul made several attempts on David's life
But he never succeeded
For God had decided David was the king
Israel really needed.
Twice Saul sent David to fight the Philistines
Hoping he would be killed
Thinking they would eliminate his successor
And his wishes would be fulfilled.
Even though Saul had once offered David
Both of his daughters
He wanted to kill David so badly, He had
His men break into David's living quarters.
But Jonathon loved David as a brother
And they made a pact to be true to each other.
Jonathon didn't share his father's vicious hate
Instead, he and David shared a gentle trait.
It is obvious Saul's attempts against David
Were time ill spent
For the Heavenly Father protected David
Where ever he went!

1ST SAMUEL 19

Saul is still on his killing binge
Trying to use his aides to get revenge
On a youngster who meant Saul no harm
And Jonathon replied in emotional alarm
"Why? What has he done to you?
Hasn't he always done
What you have told him to?"
Saul relented momentarily
But a few days later
He tried to kill David with a spear.
Even Michal understood David's fright
And she helped him disappear into the night.
Afterwards Saul begins acting strange.
Prophesying certainly seems unrealistic
Coming from a man so deranged.

1st SAMUEL 20

David doubted Jonathon because of fear
But Jonathon recoiled.
Every attempt Saul made on David's life
Jonathon had spoiled!
They developed a plan to find out for sure
To find out if Saul's anger was deadly
Or if David was merely insecure.
Jonathon knew his father meant to kill David
When Saul threw his spear at him

The "I Love My Bible" Commentary

And he left his Father's presence feeling
Humiliated, angry and grim!
He met David and then they parted
Certain they'd never see each other again.
For Jonathon did not want to lead assassins
To David who would fulfill Saul's evil plan.
These two friends would give their lives
For each other.
Truly, a friend *can be* closer than a brother!

1st SAMUEL 21

David goes to the priest Ahimelech
And unknowingly put a 'noose' around
His neck,
For Doeg the Edomite was there
And it was a time for David to beware!
David even asked for Goliath's sword to use
A request Ahimelech could not refuse.
He thought David was on duty for Saul.
Unfortunately, that was not the case at all!
David was fleeing for his life, looking for a
Place to rest.
He finally found refuge in Gath
But soon became an unwelcome guest.
The servants of Achish remembered
David's reputation
And knew he was a man of zealous dedication.
So David feigned insane behavior
When he heard those men asking
Was not David Israel's savior!
His feigned insanity secured his release
And then he sneaked into Israel seeking peace.

1st SAMUEL 22

David escaped to a cave called Adullam
And was joined by many of the discontented
All hoping to return home if and when
Saul repented.
But Saul, who still wanted David's head
Rewarded the Edomite who said
That he had seen David asking Ahimelech
For Goliath's spear.
An adament Saul responded, "Bring
That rascal here!"
Saul showed the priest no mercy
Though his men refused to harm the clergy.
But Doeg willingly did Saul's dirty work
His hatred for David evidenced in his smirk.
Doeg killed other priests and only
Abiathar got away
And he was able to tell David what happened
That awful day.
David considered Doeg cheap and shoddy.
He told Abiathar to stay with him
For any harm to Abiathar would have to be
Over David's own dead body!

1st SAMUEL 23

The men of Keilah could not be trusted
Though David had fought in their behalf.
Even the men of Gath conferred with Saul
And his staff.
But David knew they would because he had
Heard from God!
The intentions of these men were revealed
Through Abiathar and the ephod!
David and Jonathon face each other again
Cognizant of the fact
Saul would never find David no matter
How the odds were stacked!
Even so, David had almost been caught
Until Saul withdrew because of news
His men had brought.
Once again Saul failed, it seemed
Because God, Himself, had intervened!
When Saul left to fight the Philistines
It gave David a break.
Therefore, the place where David hid
Was called the "Rock of Escape!"

Comment on 1st Samuel

1st SAMUEL 24

Sometimes it was almost comical the way
David was stalked.
Yet when his men wanted to kill king Saul
David balked.
He meant no harm when he cut off the hem
Of Saul's robe.
If anything, David had the patience of Job!
There must have been an eager silence
When Saul entered that cave
But David had strong control of his men
And made them behave.
David's demeanor was above reproach
Even with Saul so near.
He could have killed his enemy
And taken the throne that year
But David refused to endanger his soul.
Vengeance was not his goal.
He refused to get even with Saul
Even though Saul was alone.
David could wait because he knew for sure
God had already promised him the throne!

1st SAMUEL 25

Samuel dies and David goes into the
Wilderness of Paran.
While there, David sent his men to Nabal
To ask for anything he might have on hand.
But Nabal, who answered roughly, was known
To be crude.
David was so angry, he said, "We'll teach
That man a lesson. He'll rue the day
He was so rude."
Hearing of Nabal's response to David
Filled Abigail with remorse and shame.
She hurried to intervene, telling David
She was to blame.
She reminded David he would not want
A guilty conscience when he gained the throne.
David accepted her gifts and thanked the Lord
For the wisdom of this woman he had never
Known.
It seems Nabal was punished for he soon died
Of a stroke
Perhaps because of the intensity of the words
Abigail spoke!
David was told Nabal had lost his life
And he wasted no time in making Abigail
His wife.

1st Samuel 26

Saul had three thousand soldiers
He considered to be noble and elite!
Surely they would be the ones to cinch
A victory glorious and complete!
Saul had not been honest with David before.
There was no score to settle yet he was
Determined to *settle the score.*
No one had ever proved that David meant
Saul harm,
Any accusation he made against David
Proved to be a false alarm.
Now he learns from the Ziphites
That David is hiding on Hachilah Hill.
He follows David and moves in for the 'kill.'
Once more David proves he is no thug.
He refused to kill Saul
Instead takes his shield and jug!
Then David taunts Abner for being remiss
Raising Saul's spear and asking
"How do you think I got hold of this?"
David wants Saul to remember the hour
That God placed Saul in David's power.
David's wish was that God would spare
His life as he had spared Saul that day.
Yet, because of Saul's ambivalence
David knew he had to get away.
Life was way too sweet
To be Saul's latest 'treat!'

The "I Love My Bible" Commentary

1st SAMUEL   27

Saul's many attempts on David's life
Convinced David of Saul's rejection
So he took his six hundred men
And their families to king Achish
And asked for his protection.
Saul was told David's path
Led straight to king Achish at Gath!
David needed to worry no longer
About Saul's abuse.
Saul had given up searching for David
Thinking it was no use!
King Achish gave David the town of Ziklag
And whenever David saw the king he'd brag
About attacking Judah, the Kenites
And Jerahmeel
And Achish was certain how bitter all these
People would feel.
"David will have to stay and serve me forever!"
He thought.
But he didn't know David killed all the Amale-
-kites in other cities he raided
Thus was never caught.

1st SAMUEL   28

When Saul heard the Philistines
Were arming themselves panic set in!
And when God gave him no answer
His panic changed to frustration.
He finally went disguised to the witch of Endor
But she offered no cooperation.
"Saul will kill me," she said.
But he insisted. "I've got to talk
To a man who is dead!"
And when she saw Samuel, she was petrified.
"I'm in trouble now," she exclaimed.
You deceived me when you lied!"
Saul assured her she should feel no alarm.
He needed information
And would cause her no harm.
But the news Samuel gave Saul was bad, *bad!*
Not only was Samuel paralyzed with fright
From the news he had
It was so awful he lost his appetite.
But he and his men did eat before
They returned to the battle grounds to fight.
Still the news of his impending death
Was so dramatic
Every step he took must have been
Devastatingly traumatic!

1st SAMUEL   29

King Achish was certain he could use David
Against the Israeli army
But when his generals discovered
David's presence
Their protest was stormy.
When David objected to their attitude
King Achish replied politely
"Please don't upset my generals,
Just go quietly!"
So David honored the king's appeal.
He left for home while the Philistines
Headed for Jezreel.

1st SAMUEL   30

David's return took three days and nights
And he discovered Ziklag had been raided
By the Amalekites.
David's men threatened to kill him.
Losing their families brought them grief.
But God's reassurance gave them all relief!
It was a long almost fruitless search
Before they got their families back
Because those Amalekites were hard to track.
They recovered all the captured loot
And took some more to boot!
When they returned home they shared it

Comment on 1ˢᵗ Samuel

With some of the cities where they had been.
Proving love for Judah still lived in the hearts
Of David and his men!

1ˢᵗ SAMUEL 31

Now the tide turns and history changes.
Saul and his army are defeated!
When the Israelis learned Saul and his sons
Were dead, they hastily retreated.
As if it wasn't enough for the Philistines
To know Saul and his sons were dead
They returned to cut off Saul's armor
And his head.
But warriors from Jabesh traveled all night
To Bashan
To recover Saul's and his son's bodies
And buried them in their homeland!

Note: Over and over men hated, struggled, and committed heinous crimes against each other. This book just continues the story of man's inability to live together in harmony and and peace. But there is a deeper battle raging—one to cleanse evil from the Holy Land. That is why God told Israel to completely rid the Holy Land of the heathen. It was to be a *picture of Heaven* but like a jig saw puzzle with missing pieces this 'picture' was never completed..And the day would come that even Israel would be expelled. They had become liars, adulterers, idolaters, homosexuals, sorcerers and murderers. Such could not live in the Promised Land. Such WILL NOT live in Heaven!(Revelations 22:13-15) They did go back but fell into sin again and again, rejected God's Living Word and were scattered once more. But I will not criticize the Israelis. Many of us do not seem to get the picture either! Well, what are the missing pieces in the puzzle of life—pieces needed to make the picture complete.

THEY ARE:

1. Loving God with ALL our hearts!   2. Nothing before Him(no image-NO one)
3. Cherish that Name–Don't use it in vain(foolishly or to curse anyone) ever!
4. Honor The Lord's day!!   5. HONORING our Fathers and Mothers.
6. Mercy never kills(Thou shall not)!! 7. I (you) SHALL NOT commit adultery!
8. We must not steal.. *9. <u>Can't tell a vicious lie!!!</u>* 10. Don't envy the Jones's!!

What we do with these commandments affect our future, our hope, our happiness, and of course the happiness (or lack of it) of others in which we interact. The commandments protect us form others-if obeyed by them! It also protects others from us-if obeyed by us. If so—we'd have a wonderful circle of love and 99 and 99/100% assurance we'd have heaven on earth!

WOULDN'T THAT BE GREAT!!!!!!

The "I Love My Bible" Commentary
(The Book of 2nd Samuel)

2nd SAMUEL 1

David first hears of Saul's death
From an Amalekite
One who thought David would reward him
But he was far from right!
In the first place, he lied
When he told David how Saul died
So David tells his men to kill him
For his self-confessed deed
And for bringing news so grim.
David considered Saul and Jonathon
Mighty heroes
Who died undeservedly at the hands
Of their foes.
He wept for Jonathon who was his best friend
Because this mighty prince had come
To an untimely end.

2nd SAMUEL 2

David was much different than Saul.
He sought the Lord's advice
Before he would move on
And the Lord gave David instructions
To move to Hebron.
Then Abner suggests to Joab
That they watch their men
In some sword play
That neither side would win.
We wonder why such foolish skirmishes
Would be included
And why Abner was so vicious to Asahel
When he intruded
On Abner's right to be alone?
Such childish behavior for two men
Fully grown!
What a useless battle, dying for no cause
Showing two generals possessed gigantic
Character flaws.

Finally David's close relatives accept him
Without hesitancy
When he was crowned King of the Judean
Confederacy.

2nd SAMUEL 3

A long war existed between David and
Saul's dynasty and David grew stronger.
Had it not been for Abner's anger
Against Ishbosheth it could have lasted longer!
Abner swore allegiance to David
But all did not go well.
Joab killed Abner because he had killed Asahel
And once again foolishness prevails
As Joab leaves more bloody trails.
David was greatly displeased
At the infamous opportunity Joab had seized
For David had not willed
For this great General(Abner)to be killed.

2nd SAMUEL 4

It was unwelcome news for Ishbosheth
When he heard of Abner's death.
He trembled because the news was so bad.
But his biggest worry was Baanah and Rechab.
His army was now under their command
And they would take an unholy stand
When they killed Ishbosheth
And took David his head.
They didn't expect to hear what David said.
David was angry at their disloyalty
And he killed these men for showing
Their king such hostility.
Even though Saul had been so vicious
Toward David
He never considered Saul his enemy.
No matter what Saul did David felt secure
Because God protected him.

Comment on 2nd Samuel

Because He knew David's heart was pure.
David's priorities seemed to be strange
But his great love for, and loyalty to God
Would *never* change!

2nd SAMUEL 5

David–that great shepherd of Israel
Is crowned at last.
All the heartaches he endured because of Saul
Were now in the past!
But there were great challenges ahead
For God's beloved king
And disappointments too
Most of them brought on by himself
Because of what he would do.
But in the meantime God gave David victory
Making sure David had the power
To defeat every enemy.
This precious king knew his success
Came from the Lord and he exclaimed
"God gives me victory and all my enemies
Are shamed!"

2nd SAMUEL 6

That beautiful ark was a sight to behold
Because what it held was more precious
    than gold!
It seemed to be archaic and prim
But it opened the door to walk with *Him.*
It was God's way of saying, "I AM here!"
Knowing that, His people should not fear.
David was aware of that and he responded
In a jubilant prance
And a joyful, dynamic, but reverent dance!
For where God is, joy is in abundant supply!
And others would respond likewise
When the ark passed by.
Isn't it a pity Michal could not see
The power in that ark that had set Israel free?

David *did* and responded gloriously!
Sunrise to sunset, David knew
God would be with him the whole day
    through!

2nd SAMUEL 7

God turns down the plan David mentions
Though Nathan thinks David has good
    intentions!
God said, "I know what David meant.
But have I ever complained about
    living in a tent?"
David understood! God's temple must not
Picture or represent war.
His people had suffered so much
And had come so far!
War was so ugly and brutal.
Even though they were conquerors
War was still futile.
God's temple must be known as a refuge
    of peace
Where His people would receive confidence,
Quietness, and a harmonious release!
But the most important news in this chapter is
Though David had faced much enmity
His love for, and obedience to God
Had assured him an eternal dynasty!
God's beautiful promise has lived on
Through these many years
Though the Jews have faced many heartaches,
And have shed many tears!
But through the Messiah we can peer into
A future fantastically indescribable!
Truly, we have a God who is utterly reliable!
This God will never let us down!
Only He is worthy to wear that eternal crown!
Life is sweeter when He walks with me.
Because of that, I walk with Him willingly!
And David happily did the same!
His desire was to glorify the Father's Name!

The "I Love My Bible" Commentary

2nd SAMUEL 8

If David seemed heartless, it was
To God's enemies who had turned their backs
On God because they consistently refused
To face the facts.
God has a standard for people to obey.
He did and will punish the man who walks
In his own way.
But David never considered it hard
To walk worthy of our Lord!
Yet, some of David's deeds seem cruel
And unnecessary
And they should have made his enemies wary.
Still, they were enemies of the Lord too
And the spoils of war David received,
He dedicated to that Holy One
Who he followed and in whom believed!

2nd SAMUEL 9

Fear often produces cripples.
Mephibosheth(son of Jonathon) was one.
Because his nurse had dropped him
He barely walked and couldn't run.
David did not like to hear him talk
Of being a 'dead dog' who couldn't walk.
The love David had for Jonathon
Was carried on to his crippled son.
David's and Jonathon's friendship
Could not be destroyed by death
And David made it known to Mephibosheth!
True love is not an object one can disable.
And he would always eat at David's table
Though hatred must someday be destroyed
And nothing of it left, not even a trace
There will *never* be a time
When love is *out of place!*
Love is the sweetest 'fruit' on the vine.
Sweeter than grape nectar
And better than wine!

2nd SAMUEL 10

The Ammonite king dies and his son Hanun
Embarrassed David's men.
He refused to believe what good friends
His father and David had been.
He cut off each man's robe
And half of each man's beard
And then sent them home feeling weird!
An angry David attacked the Ammonites
For abusing the dignity of his men's
Human rights.
Even the Syrians could not help Hanun
Divert David's punishment for what this king
Had done.
When David defeats Hanun, his hostility ends.
Hanun's slavery was the result of his refusal
To be friends.

2ND SAMUEL 11

In the shadows of the evening
In the darkness of the night
David's faith faltered and he sinned
In God's sight!
It seems he didn't stop to think
His sin would take him to the brink
Of disaster
And he didn't consider how much
He would dishonor his Lord and Master.
And to make matters worse
His words to Joab were harsh and terse.
He told Joab to put Uriah at the front
Of the battle.
Bathsheba's pregancy might be revealed
And guilty David feared Uriah would tattle!
Uriah could have saved his own life
Had he not loved his fellow soldiers so much
And had he stayed and slept with his wife.
Now David couldn't hide the fact
That he had committed an adulterous act!

Comment on 2nd Samuel

But God said, "No!
This sin will haunt you wherever you go."
You see, David hadn't been minding his business.
His business was *minding the King!*
Had he done so he would not have suffered
All the heartaches this sin would bring.

2nd SAMUEL 12

David, the Sweet Psalmist of Israel fell
With a thud
And he dragged the *Father's Holy Name*
Down through the mud.
It saddened our *'Father'* that it would seem
David loved Him so little
That he would blaspheme
That Name that is above every name
And reduce it to merely common shame.
This man who had been a beacon light
For others to follow
Fell in such a way they must have thought
David's faith was definitely hollow.
David passed judgement on another
Showing no pity
But God said he was to suffer also
In view of everyone in the city.
God did forgive him but Bathsheba's baby died
Though David had refused to eat,
Mourned, prayed and cried.
Adultery has caused more of God's people
To fall than any other sin
And it must have caused
God's gentle shepherd to wonder
How much better and sweeter
His life could have been!

2nd SAMUEL 13

Abuse can happen in the best of families
As in the case of Tamar.
When Amnon raped his half-sister
He left a deep festering scar.
He could have asked her to be his wife.
Instead, the way he treated her
Ended up costing him his life.
Absalom never forget what Amnon did
And until he evened the score
His hatred for his half-brother Amnon
Only grew more and more.
Because of lust Tamar had to face
That awful treatment that brought her disgrace
All because of that one time David failed
To be faithful in his devotion
And his sin set some of his family
Into a spiral deadly downward motion!
Four sons(Bathesheba's baby, Amnon
Absalom and Adonijah) and Tamar paid
As a result of the one time David strayed.
We cannot view sin lightly.
The scars it leaves can be so unsightly!
But God helped His favorite wayward son
When he confessed and forsake
This awful thing he had done.
We never hear of David repeating this sin
And he is known as one of God's
Most faithful and noble men!

2nd SAMUEL 14

Absalom ran for his life and David seemed
To not want him back .
After all, Absalom's murder of Amnon
Threw this family notoriously *out of whack!*
Joab was displeased because he looked
At Absalom from a different perspective
And he tried fervently to encourage David
To be come more reflective!
But just to think about it caused David
To be deeply saddened
And he blamed himself for all that happened!

The "I Love My Bible" Commentary

Yet when David recalled Absalom
His forgiveness was incomplete
And Absalom's return was only bitter-sweet.
His home was not a happy place
As long as he could not see his father's face!
But with Joab's encouragement
David forgives Absalom at last.
Finally David assigns this heartache
To the past!
Even though David must have considered
Absalom a *feisty pup*
He and Absalom finally made up!
But Absalom had another trick *up his sleeve*
And again would cause his father to grieve!

2nd SAMUEL 15

We can see Absalom's revolt
Gave David quite a jolt!
For he left Jerusalem with his head covered
And walked barefoot as depression hovered.
He never thought this one so dear
Would be the one he'd have to fear.
David leaves, his heart breaking,
Fearing the chances his loyal friends
Were taking.
It was a bitter pill he swallowed
As he worried about those who followed.
He hoped Hushai could confuse Ahithophel
And he prayed it would be in God's will.
Though David's future seemed dark
He refused to allow Zadok to take the Ark.
David told him to take it back to Jerusalem
And if the Lord saw fit
Maybe someday he'd return to gaze on it.
David was an old man now
And he had trusted Absalom, his son.
No one can measure the harm
Absalom's treachery had done!
Maybe Absalom had never erased the scar
That began to grow

When Amnon victimized Tamar.

2nd SAMUEL 16

One would think this king who loved the Lord
Would not face such jeopardy.
Could the Lord have stopped
This awful carnage and David's heartbreak?
 Probably!
But the law of the universe had been
Put in motion
David had declared "four-to-one" punishment.
Thus he concocted his own *deadly potion*.
As he struggled up that hill
He must have thought
"Look at all the troubles I've bought!"
Yet he would not allow Abishai
To stop the stoning from Shime-I
Even though it seemed times were hard
David still depended
On the mercy of the Lord!

2nd SAMUEL 17

"We can get David," Athithophel surmised.
"We can throw him in a panic
If we can catch him by surprise!"
But Absalom wanted to ask Hushai who said,
"No! Your father is like a mighty bear.
He will slaughter your troops
And that wouldn't be fair.
If you truly want victory, then mobilize
So he can't defeat you
No matter how hard he tries!"
Meanwhile Ahithophel felt disgraced
Hung himself and died
While Hushai advised David to run and hide.
There were others who cared for David
And supplied his needs and stood by his side!
Dear David, magnificent and royal
Still had friends who were loyal!

Comment on 2nd Samuel

2nd SAMUEL 18

David did not want revenge.
Memories of this battle with his son
Would cause him to cringe.
In self-depredation, in horror, and remorse.
It seemed as if he considered Joab's victory
Merely a farce!
And though his faithful warriors put down
Absalom's revolt
His death struck David like a lethal
Lightening bolt!
King David felt he had not won
As he wept repeatedly
"O my son Absalom, my son,
My son Absalom, would God I had died
For thee, O Absalom, my son, my son!"

2nd SAMUEL 19

David's mighty army crept into town ashamed
Their jubilant battle cry hushed and tamed.
They knew their king would never be the same
Since he had heard his son was dead.
But Joab angrily reprimanded the king
When he said
"You act as if we have done something wrong
And seem to hate all who have faithfully
Served you for so long.
You cherish those who brought you pain
And strife.
Unless you apologize to your men
You will be worse off than you've ever been
In your entire life!"
David did forgive his enemies but
He also rewarded those faithful ones
He had luckily befriended.
Yet there would be more bitterness
Before his journey ended.
For war never ends in true joy.
Some mother will miss her little boy!

2nd SAMUEL 20

The split still existed. It seems as if David
Is starting all over again
Or else he must re-evaluate his people
And develop another plan.
The people would not welcome him
To Jerusalem
Until he dealt with the man who had
Perverted them.
David had already promised Amasa
The position that belonged to Joab
But his plans were thwarted when Amasa
Was viciously stabbed.
Once again, Joab was the *heavy*
And murder was the tax he would levy!
His mission was to capture Sheba
But he also a assassinated the king's nephew
Power had gone to his head as his conquests
 grew.
At last the rebellion was squashed
And Sheba was killed.
Now David reclaimed the throne
And the unrest in the land was stilled.

2nd SAMUEL 21

God sent a famine on the land
Because Israel made a pledge that didn't stand.
God told David Saul was guilty of treachery
And it must be corrected.
With murder hanging over her head
Israel would not be respected.
Many years in the past Israel had promised
Not to harm the Gibeonites
But Saul, in his nationalistic zeal
Had denied them their God given rights.
Saul considered these people insignificant
And thought his deed was hidden
But his descendants suffered
Because killing the Gibeonites was forbidden..

The "I Love My Bible" Commentary

Though only a few were involved
Justice must be done
Before the famine would be resolved.
Now David remembered the Gibeonites
Had been friends
And asked what he could do to make amends
And he did as they replied.
That is why so many of Saul's descendants
    died.

2nd SAMUEL 22

The greatest testimony a man can give
    of the One who says
"I AM! I LIVE!
Is
"His way is perfect
and
HIS WORD IS TRUE!

David said much, much more
And he elegantly described this One
He so faithfully followed after
And I suggest you slowly read this chapter.
There is such beauty in it
It was a song in which every note truly fit!
We've also learned there is *nothing*
Our Lord cannot do!
David knew his future was not left to fate.
It was the Lord's gentleness that made
David great!
When David thought of his own power
He had to take stock.
It was given to him by Jehovah his 'rock!'
David could not have sung a single note
Would never have had reason to gloat
Unless the Lord had caused him to walk
A steady tread.
And was the only reason David could have
For lifting his head

Was because the Blessed Rock of Ages
Was his guide.
No, David would have had no strength
Without our Savior by his side!
No one else can sing a greater song
Than David did about our Lord
Who stood by David his whole life long!

2nd SAMUEL 23

These are the last words of David.
He would have no more stories to tell.
But he speaks of his *Rock*
This sweet Psalmist of Israel!
He looked deep into the future
And saw a cloudless sunrise
Painted by the One who is *The Morning Star*
And David longed to see
This One who would come from so far!
David was a prophet and its not surprisin'
When he spoke of his descendants
He looked far beyond that day's horizon
And spoke of the future God had revealed
    When he said, God's covenant is
        Eternal!
        Final!
        Sealed!
This chapter also names those great men
In his army
Who helped him out when times were stormy.
And through all his battles David grew bolder
But it was the Lord
Who made him a mighty soldier!
God gave him other men who were
Great soldiers too.
No matter who he fought
They were by his side.
The enemy knew there was no place to hide
When they faced David and his men
For they were truly blessed
By the One who gave sweet David rest!

Comment on 2nd Samuel

2nd SAMUEL 24

David wanted a census so he sent Joab
Through out Israel-its width and its length.
But Joab said, "You have no right
To rejoice in the people's strength."
He knew God provided David's every desire.
This was a duty Joab preferred to retire!
David was *never* to rely on the people.
They were not his *source*!
When he took his eyes off the Savior
This godly king got off his course.
It is a shame the people had to suffer
Because of David's greed.
This was unnecessary knowledge
David didn't need.
But the census wouldn't have brought disaster
Had David fulfilled the instructions
Of his Lord and Master.
His troubles would not have mounted
If a ransom had been paid for each soul
    counted.
But God felt pity for the people
And that destructive decision was dropped
Then David offered a sacrifice
And the plague was stopped.

Have you noticed our God is completely impartial? Whether one is a pauper or a king, God will punish him when he sins. Doesn't sound like that which goes on in our courts today does it? The one who has the most money gets the best lawyers and often get by with even murder, extortion, crooked business practices and other vices because through the years justice has been *colored green*. But God has no color codes. Well, maybe He does but in His eyes *black is black, and white is white*. And there are no shades of gray. And certainly no green! He is completely just and fair. Though some may not recognize or know it, someday-at least for a thousand years, righteous rule will take precedence and no slick lawyers will be able to pervert justice or rescue the guilty. As the Bible says, "Be sure your sins will find you out"(Numbers 32:23-Moses speaking to the tribes of Reuben and Gad). David had to learn that, so did other kings-some the hard way! Paul once said it is an awesome thing to fall into the hands of the Living God. Be assured it is wonderful *to put yourself* into His hands. "Come unto me," He says, "....and I will give you rest....." Matthew 11:28. I get the picture here of a father holding his baby in his arms and the baby knows it is safe because it can hear its father's heart beating, "....love you, love you, love you" and so it rests its head on its fathers chest and feels secure. One of the prettiest pictures in the Bible(I believe)is the story of John leaning on Jesus' chest. In that precious instant he must have thought that God's heart was beating just for him.. And because God says, "I have loved you with an everlasting love," we can believe that too.
Over and over the Bibles tells of men's wickedness and God's forgiveness, but it was based on true repentance-always has and always will. I wonder why mankind has failed to learn that?

Part 3

ISRAEL'S

1ST KINGS THROUGH ESTHER

RISE AND DEMISE

Then King David
answered and said......
.....even as I sware unto thee
by the Lord God of Israel
saying,
assuredly Solomon thy son
shall reign after me,
and he shall sit on my throne
in my stead;
even so will
I certainly do this day.
....
And Zadok the priest took
an horn of oil
out of the tabernacle,
and anointed Solomon.
And they blew the trumpet
and all the people said
God save king Solomon.

(1st Kings 1: 28a, 30; and 39kjv)

The "I Love My Bible" Commentary
(1ST Kings)

1st KINGS 1

David is an old man now whose days
Are numbered.
He was given a beautiful young concubine
But still he slumbered.
And as he sleeps another conspiracy
Begins to unfold.
Absalom's younger brother wants the throne
And now he becomes bold.
Action must be taken Nathan tells Bathsheba
And she must move fast!
Whatever decision David makes
It will be his last.
David had promised Solomon the throne
And now fulfills his word.
Adonijah reacts in fear from the unwelcome
News he heard.
Reluctant forgiveness was King Solomon's
First official decree.
"If Adonijah behaves himself," Solomon said,
"He will have no trouble from me."

1st KINGS 2

Though surrounded by many, David felt alone.
Life was no longer a challenge.
It was time to move on!
This precious king who had done so much
Knew eternity beckoned from distant hills
And so he felt out of touch!
It was time to go and his heart felt warm
But first he must tell Solomon
He has a special duty to perform.
David has not forgotten the treachery shown
When his luck was at its worst.
He wanted revenge for Amasa and Abner's
Murders and remembers when he was cursed.
But he knew Solomon was wise and could
Handle these men with finesse.
Somehow Solomon would punish those
Who had betrayed David when he was
Under stress!
And then Adonijah, who wanted the throne,
Devised a sneaky plot.
He wanted Solomon to give him Abishag
But Solomon says, "I will not!"
He seemed to think Abishag could guarantee
Adonijah the throne.
Solomon was not about to give up this crown
He considered his alone!
So Adonijah, along with Joab and Shime-i,
Was killed.
He was only doing what his father willed!
Solomon destroyed those David(and he)
Considered to be impure
And now Solomon's grip on the throne
Becomes strong and secure!

1st KINGS 3

Marrying a princess from Egypt was
Solomon's first mistake.
She was one of the many wives he took
And it was his first *bad break!*
For sooner or later his heart would turn
Against *the Lord of all the universe*!
His wandering heart would yearn
For more heathen wives
And as he took them, his adulterous, idolatrous
Heart grew much, much worse!
But for now we see his first blunder
And we know it is no wonder
That later on he fell.
For a man who started at the top to fall so far
Is a story we hate to tell.
Yet he sometimes dwelt wisely
As with a prostitute
Who brought him his *first suit!*
And though the other prostitute was displeased

Comment on 1ˢᵗ Kings

He made no other provisions.
This was the beginning of Solomon's
Many wise decisions.
Still his wisdom was not as great as it seems
Because Solomon did not continue
To honor the Lord
Who had appeared to Solomon in his dreams.

1ˢᵗ KINGS 4

A nation needs great leaders
And some are listed here
But wisdom was given strictly to Solomon
And this chapter makes that clear.
It acknowledges his 3000 proverbs
And his 1000 plus songs.
All the people trusted in his wisdom
And judgements to right all wrongs.
Israel was a contented nation at this time.
They were not at war and feared no crime!
Solomon's reign was extensive
And his reputation was truly great.
God showed his love for Israel
When he made David and Bathsheba's son
Israel's noble *Head of State!*

1ˢᵗ KINGS 5

King Hiram would reach out and extend
His hand to a brand new friend.
He cherished Solomon
Because he was David's son!
And though using his men to cut timber
Might seem simple
It was a noble venture to furnish wood
For God's Holy Temple!
Hiram felt Israel was lucky to have a king
So wise
But little did he know!
That temple would be Israel's greatest prize!
God had promised to dwell there-in
Only then would it be special to all men.
Gold would not set that temple apart
But WHO it represented
And He would strengthen every heart!
Though Hiram furnished only wood
It is important to remember his intentions
Were honorable and good.
We know the gold had been supplied
By that precious king who died.
And though David desired to build
This great edifice it wasn't to be
God said, "It must be a man of peace
Who builds this temple to honor me."

1ˢᵗ KINGS 6

The people worked hard to build that temple
And it is described in detail.
Solomon made sure David's plans
Were followed without fail.
The most important fact we need to remember
Was the *quietness* there.
God says, "Let all the earth keep silent
Before me!"
So they had to take pains to build it
With loving care.
Quietness in the temple is still the only choice.
As my heart is rested and quiet
I find it easier to listen
To that *still, small, comforting voice!*
Silence in the temple
Silence in the heart
Listening, always listening
Longing for a tiny spark
For when I hear or feel
His presence
I won't be living in the dark!
Even a soul that is wounded
And badly scarred
Will fine glorious healing
In the house of the Lord!

The "I Love My Bible" Commentary

1ST KINGS 7

It took only seven years to build that temple
Of opulent splendor
A noble structure to convey the majesty
Of Israel's defender.
Israel's pride would be replenished
When they could see their glorious temple
Completely finished!
But every prayerful Israeli knew as he knelt
This temple was Jehovah's
And His presence must and would be felt!
Though Solomon's palace took twice as long
To build
It couldn't picture the promises
Of glorious hope fulfilled!
This temple had been David's dream
For so long
And was the end result of his faith
Which was very strong.
Solomon knew what his father was thinking of;
He may have built the temple
But David supplied the love!

1st KINGS 8

How can a fact so glorious
Be expressed so beautifully simple?
Truly, the most vibrant, holy period in a nation
Or individual is when God fills the 'temple!'
God fills the temple and makes it(or us)
Complete-- and gives joy to the soul.
And Solomon encourages all the people
To make godly living their foremost goal!
Every facet of life was mentioned in his prayer
And every hope explored.
Solomon prayed that should they sin
This *repentant* nation's glory be restored.
He knew it was difficult for the people
To comprehend
That sin against God would cause
The temple's untimely end.
But he also knew God's mercy was great
And if only the people would pray and wait
-wait for God's guidance and care
Then that temple would always be there!

1st KINGS 9

God warns Solomon to live pure and honestly.
He wanted Solomon to be like his father
Who had obey Him willingly!
God must have looked into Solomon's heart
And not found enough integrity there.
Had Solomon been perfectly honest
Would he have treated King Hiram so unfair?
These two men known to be friends
Which one is --depends
From which angle you view
The position of these two.
Hiram gave Solomon three million in gold
But Solomon gave him ghost towns
With dry desert sands.
Hiram considered it treachery
When he received what he called *waste lands*.
Surely Hiram then decided
His friendship with Solomon
Was only one-sided!
Yet Hiram remained Solomon's friend
And it must have been good news
To Solomon who needed gold
To know Hiram would send
Experienced sailors to accompany
Solomon's crews.

1st KINGS 10

The queen of Sheba came to test
Solomon's authenticity
And her awesome impression of him
Has gone down in history.
She arrived in sumptuous splendor

Comment on 1st Kings

Not so much to impress as to be impressed
And she exclaimed in astonishment
How beautifully his servants were dressed!
And though there were many gifts they shared
She found there was no one with whom
Solomon's wisdom could be compared.
The hand of God was on this man
Who passed every test
And she sensed all who listened to him
Were truly blessed.
There were many solutions she had sought
And with his wisdom to nurture her mind
She left with much more than she brought!

1ST KINGS 11

What a shame that Solomon thought
His shadow had grown so large
It overshadowed the Lord!
Now all he had was an empty future
With fear and trembling as his reward.
Solomon thought neither he nor his sons
Would ever lose the kingdom
But it was not his or theirs to keep.
It had always been the Lord's
Who would grieve as he watched idolatry creep
Into the heart of David's son.
And now the Lord had to tell him,
"Your descendants will lose ten of the tribes
Because of what you have done!"
The truth is, not even Solomon was exempt
When his worship of idols
Showed his contempt
Of God for there is no other worthy to hallow!
The man who forgets God
Will walk in his own shadow.
It is a sad state of affairs
When the affairs of state are out of order
And getting back in God's grace
Was something this idolater couldn't barter.
All his life Solomon had gotten by
On his father's goals
And so he leaves very little good influence
On other people's souls.
Now Israel had no place to go
But to go down hill
And it began with Solomon's refusal
To completely obey God's will.

1st KINGS 12

Rehoboam expected to carry on
As elegantly as his father had
But the people who longed for kindness
Would not accept news this bad
When he talked to them so rough.
"You think my father was harsh," he said.
"I'll be twice as tough!"
The told him to rule his own family
And then they seceded
From this king whose harshness was worse
Then these people thought they needed.
Then God gave Jeroboam a chance to rule
But this man's worship of idols
Marked him as a fool.
He placed one gold calf at Bethel
And another one at Dan.
It was not long before God was sorry
He had chosen this man.
Jeroboam did not cherish the Lord
Who had been so kind.
How could a man who had been blessed
So richly be so blind?
But look at the blessings God has poured
On people today!
Are we worshiping Him by putting Him first
Or are we going from pleasure to pleasure
-and going from bad to worse?
Are we taking responsibility for our decisions
Or blaming them on society
And in the process losing all sense
Of love and decency?

The "I Love My Bible" Commentary

1st KINGS 13

God knew where Jeroboam could be found
-at the altar of sin
Where his rejection of God showed what state
His rebellious heart was in.
God had wanted him to be as faithful as David
But that wasn't the case.
Instead of worshiping at God's altar
He was *'light years'* out of place!
Jeroboam provided himself gods
That were no gods at all
And it wasn't long before
This idolatrous king would fall.
But the saddest section in this chapter
Is a prophet's demise
Because he erroneously listened to
Another prophet's deceitful lies.
When God gives us a message have no doubt
Of the importance to detail in carrying it out!

1st KINGS 14

Not one good thing could be said
About Jeroboam–not one!
He was unholy and he certainly wasn't wise.
So when God told Ahijah to reprimand him
It should have been no surprise.
God had appeared to Jeroboam
Before his head grew bigger than his heart
And promised to bless him if he'd do his part
And it wasn't an impossible task.
It was so simple I'm ashamed to ask
"Why did he not obey?"
And don't you wonder why he made calf-idols
Which caused all Israel to stray?
Could there be no man found
Who could turn Israel around?
And Rehoboam of Judah was no better.
He also refused to follow the law of God
Strictly by the letter!

1st KINGS 15

After Israel seceded from Judah's rule
They could find no king better than a fool.
Israel had cut themselves off from Jerusalem
Though God had said to revere Him there
But since they didn't their worship
Became hazardous to them.
Nadab and Baasha both wore infamous titles
Because, like Jeroboam, they worshiped idols.
It was much different in Judah!
Asa's was a holy reign.
And he refused to treat God's law
With indifference and disdain.
There was constant war between Asa
And Israel's king Baasha because
It is inevitable when some are good
And others refuse to honor the purity
In God's holy laws.

1ST KINGS 16

We read that Baasha was so wicked
He wouldn't do–even in a crunch
And Elah, Zimri, Omri, and Ahab
Were all an unholy bunch!
God must have despised them all
For their sins led to Israel's fall.
Ahab was the worst of the lot
Because he was such a despot.
He married Jezabel whose influence
Pushed him over the edge
And because of her he forgot Israel's pledge.
They had told the Lord they'd be good
And always do what they should.
Yet when Ahab married Jezabel
He drew a *wild card*
And he ended up forsaking the Lord.
"Birds of a feather flock together," they say.
And these two *wild birds*
Didn't know how to pray!

Comment on 1st Kings

1st KINGS 17

Now Ahab fears Elijah and doesn't like
What he heard.
"There will be no rain," Elijah said,
"Until I say the word!"
Don't you know Ahab must have laughed
And said, "You will find out
You're just a puny prophet
Who can never produce a drought!"
But the rain didn't fall though every cloud
Must have brought eager anticipation
Even to a little widow who thought
Surely she would die of starvation.
But there was no hunger in her home.
She was spared
Because of her last piece of bread she shared!
Yet, she lost her son and she cried
"Prophet, My only son has died!"
She considered Elijah *man of the hour*
–a prophet who possessed amazing power!
Well, he did overcome her son's death
–one of life's most deadly storms
And he restored her son to her aching arms!

1st KINGS 18

The great prophet Elijah walks up to Ahab
And says, "So you think your troubles are passe
In spite of the sins you commit each day.
And why would you continue to balk
When it is your fault
Israel suffers? Bring those false prophets to me
I will show them who is God
And send them to hell where they ought to be."
God shows which sacrifice He approves
Sending fire that licks up the water
Even out of the grooves!
Then, after those false prophets were slain
Elijah outran Ahab's chariot
In order to get out of the rain!
Let us remember the words in this chapter
We just read
And let GOD BE GOD like Elijah said!

1st KINGS 19

The wind blew, and the earth shook
And an awesome fire raged
But God was not in any of these events
He staged!
He was in none of the above
Because He wanted to use a gentle whisper
To picture His Great Love!
Elijah had performed an almost impossible task
Yet he ran in fear and God had to ask
"Elijah, what are you doing here?"
And the claim Elijah made was grandiose.
"I'm the *only* one who worships you,"
He replied. " No one else is as close!"
"That is what you think!" God said.
"I have seven thousand men
Who have never bowed a knee or head
To anyone but me."
And I think He must have added
"And that is the way it will always be!"
Millions are free and hardy
Because God will never be
Just the God of a single party.
There are many on whom God's light has shone.
No, Elijah didn't worship Him alone!
Then God told him to anoint Elisha
To take his place
For Elijah would soon be able to look into
That precious, marvelous, holy face!
Elijah, like Enoch, was transported to heaven
To always be with the Lord.
I hope the people who read this realize
We, too, will some day gain our reward.
And what a day that will be
When we cross that river *Jordan*
And God welcomes you and me!

The "I Love My Bible" Commentary

1st KINGS 20

Benhadad of Syria was used of the Lord
To enlighten Ahab.
It started with Benhaded wanting anything
His troops could grab.
But God sent a prophet to Ahab to say
"You will know I am the Lord at last
The day Bendhadad discovers
I've got him way out-classed!"
Benhaded thought God was just a God
Of the hills
And he could beat God in the countryside.
But that braggart wimp of a king
Had to run away and hide!
Then Ahab, still unrepentant and ungrateful
Let Benhadad go
After all God did and it displeased Him so.
God said, "You will die in Benhadad's place
And I will destroy your family without a trace!
Harsh, maybe, but it was just recompense
For this obstinate king
Who showed not an ounce of common sense!

1st KINGS 21

There is probably no other story
In the Old Testament that will tell
Of two people any more vicious
Than Israel's King Ahab and Queen Jezebel.
Though he was already rich Ahab wanted
The vineyard of Naboth of Jezreel
And Naboth insisted on keeping his inheritance
Knowing it was land Ahab could not steal!
Ahab returned home sullen and angry
Refusing to eat
But Jezebel informed Ahab Naboth's vineyard
Was already his
For she had ways to manage Naboth's defeat.
Jezebel seemed to have no conscience at all
When she caused this good man's fall.
Murder was her expertise
And she used it to gain anything
She wanted to seize!
Had Ahab ever looked back in reflection
Would he have allowed this awful deception?
Jezebel gave him what he wanted
But he would gain no long-run satisfaction
For God would blame him for Jezebel's
Treacherous unholy action.
And He sent Elijah with bitter words
Of judgement
Which caused this evil king to tremble
And repent.
Those who claim our Old Testament God
Was vicious and brutal
Must look at His great mercy here
And admit that their unproven claims
Are worthless and futile!

1ST kings 22

Poor Ahab–was not his soul
More precious than his reign
–too precious to listen to Jezebel complain!
There would be no tranquility
For this man so full of iniquity.
He never did learn God's purpose for his life.
It seems all he and Jezebel caused
Was endless pain and strife..
Even King Jehoshaphat showed a hint
Of defiance
When he and Ahab formed an alliance.
Ahab wanted help to battle the Syrians
And he enticed Jehoshaphet to join him
On the campaign trail
Even though Micaiah warned Ahab
He was destined to fail.
Ahab went into battle wearing a disguise
But a Syrian soldier caught him by surprise.
Ahab was as vulnerable as a lonely sparrow
That day he died from a random arrow.

Comment on 1st Kings

And Jehoshaphat, too, could have died that day
But when he identified himself
The Syrian soldiers turned away.
All the evil in Ahab's life was stilled

That day Macaiah's prophecy was fulfilled.
Ahab's son, Ahaziah, took his father's place
But neither did he have an ounce
Of saving grace!

Now we've gone from aged King David's reign through the years to foolish young Ahaziah of Israel and these ensuing years brought far more gory than glory. It was not so in Judah who had seceded from Israel when Rehoboam, Solomon's son began to reign.

Life was not only down hill for Israel, it was a muddy slide almost to the bottom. Leaders have a strong influence on their citizens' morals and when their leaders sled into moral decay the people tumbled close behind.

Unfortunately we have people in high places today-supreme court judges etc.-who have little regard for God's Word, who deny school children prayer in school or any school activities and who have had a negative effect on the morals of our country. All because they have listened to perverts who confuse the subject of purity. *What we have done for 'arts' sake is only to put warts on our national conscience.*

As for separation of church and state—I'm a part of this state(or country) and you can't separate me into two parts. You can't separate me from the part that is 'state' and from the part that is 'church.' My mind and my spirit learn together! But look what I have to listen to now(I don't because I turn the raunchy TV programs off and I don't go to movies anymore because I don't want that trash in my mind. All *that* would do is turn me into a garbage dump).*You can't watch a movie or TV show without feeling as if you need to wash out your ears because of people who need to wash out their mouths.* And think of the sex acts blatantly shown, sex that used to be considered sacred and private. Truly, what we see or hear affects our hearts!

When I was young we thought only ignorant people cursed and lived recklessly. Now we have some PHD's whose morals haven't been promoted past kindergarten. and who can cuss as good as some who had little or no schooling and the ignorance here is spiritual ignorance and is much more deadly than lack of formal schooling. Well—I've been there done that(some of it anyway) and I've wept because of my mistakes. Why does no one weep for their sins today especially for those shown on TV or in the movies? Maybe—in the shadows of the heart people weep and don't know why!

Instead we like to blame our cussedness on society, on our parents, on our siblings, on anyone but our selves and we have failed to see God holds us(ourselves)responsible. I can't blame you for my mistakes and you sure can't blame me. Eternity will point its finger at me(at you)and say ok, lets look at what you did and, boy most of us are not going to want to look, but when we tumble into eternity there will be no other place to look but at ourselves. You can't run away from the brick wall of reality. What kind of movie will we see when we see ourselves? Thank God, because of my repentant heart, God has erased every unpleasant moment and every sin large or small because He has saved me by His grace and *that* is what you may call eternal ecstasy!

The "I Love My Bible" Commentary
(2nd Kings)

2nd KINGS 1

King Ahaziah would not ask our God
For advice
Though going to an idol god was riskier
Than throwing loaded dice.
Ahaziah longed to find someone
Who could ease the way he felt
But he did not trust the prophet
Who wore a wide leather belt.
And how could Ahaziah know Jehovah?
His mother was Queen Jezebel.
He only knew of idols who he thought
Could easily make him well.
This chapter tells of a strange confrontation.
One hundred die when Elijah calls down fire!
He would go see the king but his loyalty
Was not for hire.
He also had a message
Ahaziah would not want to hear.
God had decreed this king who was so evil
Would not live out the year.

2nd KINGS 2

Elijah's exit from this earth was climatic
Very appropriate for a man
Who had been so dramatic!
No one else had departed in quite the same way.
Elijah's illustrious transportation
Was God's chariots of fire that day.
And a double portion of Elijah's spirit
Was transplanted
When Elisha's wish was freely granted.
          Two miracles!
God allowed Elisha to see that heavenly vision
And he was able to part the Jordan river
Because God had made a favorable decision.
He was right there to help Elisha
When Elisha asked

"Where is the Lord God of Elijah?"
So God helped him perform his first task!
Yet Elisha ungraciously pouted
At five hundred young prophets who doubted
Who thought Elijah had died in the hills
And who thought it not fair
Just to leave such a noble prophet there.
They couldn't believe it when Elisha said
"Elijah is with God. He is not dead!"
After that, Elisha seems to start his ministry
On a sour note.
Read this chapter to see the negative event
I hesitate to quote.

2nd KINGS 3

There has always been evil such as Ahab's
And there has always been good.
But evil doesn't limit God who always sends
Someone to tell His people
How to live as they should.
Elisha was as dramatic as Elijah in his own way
And we still have dynamic men of God
On this earth today!
These men lovingly present the *"Water of Life"*
But then we also have 'men of moab'
Who cause sin and strife.
Yet the One who is majestic and glorious
Sees that His people are still victorious!
We praise our God with love and adulation
Because He has promised to be the God
Of every generation.
And He has kept every promise that He made.
The light of His love will never fade!

2nd KINGS 4

Now Elisha changes and grows in stature
Think of the great woman of Shunem
And what he did for her.

Comment on 2nd Kings

He had also provided enough oil
For a widow and her sons
Who knew they couldn't tolerate
Receiving so many unpayable duns!
Later he told some men what to do
When they claimed they had eaten
Poisoned stew.
And there's a picture of Jesus revealed
When Elisha fed
One hundred prophets from 20 pieces of bread.
So Elisha was busy indeed
Trying to keep up with every need!

2nd KINGS 5

A little servant girl was wise beyond her years.
Naaman feared he would die of leprosy
But she told him God could conquer
All his fears.
Naaman went to Israel to seek God's prophet
Who had healing power
But when Elisha said go bathe
In the Jordan River his faith turned sour.
But Naaman balked. He said "I'll not bathe
In that filthy river even one time.
At least the rivers in my country
Are not filled with slime.
What does Elijah mean?
Even soaking seven times
Won't make me clean!"
But his men convinced him to go
And the seventh time he came up
God would show
Obedience to his prophet was *the way to go!*
Naaman returned to Elisha humbled and healed
Though he had doubted the regimen
Elisha revealed.
He learned to worship the Lord
Because of a little servant girl who cared!
And as a result Naaman's life was spared.

2nd KINGS 6

There are invisible chariots on our hillsides
And we would not cower
If only we could see *that silent power!*
It is amazing what God lets His people see
And that inner vision needs faith as the key!
Faith overcomes the fear that blinds
To open our hearts and enlighten our minds.
Elisha's servant trembled in fear
And Elisha prayed
"Lord show him the help you've sent us here!"
The servant's eyes were opened.
The enemies' were closed.
Elisha led them to Samaria and there disposed
Of the threat they had been
And then he advised the king
To have mercy on these men.
Later Jehoram wanted to kill Elisha
And we wonder why he was so bullishly gritty.
Maybe it was because He was so displeased
(as if it were Elisha's fault)
When Benhadad besieged the city.

2nd KINGS 7

No one would expect good news
From four lepers waiting to die
But they thought it was useless
To sit and wonder why
They were so diseased and their future so drab.
Then, by accident, they found more food
And goodies than they were able to grab!
They had gone to the Syrian camp to surrender
But no one was there!
After their original gluttonous, greedy behavior
They decided they weren't being fair.
Their friends in Israel were going without food.
They feared terrible calamity for being so rude.
They hurried to tell of the Syrian's waste
Spilling the good news in frenzied haste!

The "I Love My Bible" Commentary

The food was as cheap as Elisha predicted
Though the king's officer ridiculed this scene
That Elisha had depicted!
The man who had doubted Elisha's forecast
Of such a glorious twist of fate
Was left behind when he was trampled,
Also like Elisha said, at the city gate.

2nd KINGS 8

Israel's King Jehoram is not all bad
In spite of the evil relatives he had.
He restored land to the widow of Shunem
When the story of her plight was told to him.
Then Hazael of Syria proved himself
An unworthy friend
For he caused King Benhadad's untimely end.
When he told Benhadad he would recover
      he lied!
He should have recalled Elisha's prediction
And how Elisha cried.
But he became king and that is all he cared
Because he showed no mercy to the man
He could have spared.
Time marches on as events change.
Men who should be godly now act so strange.
Jehoram of Israel and Jehoram of Judah
Form an alliance God did not command
So Jehoram of Israel is injured
Fighting soldiers under Hazael's command.

2nd KINGS 9

God told Elisha to anoint Jehu
And all he had to do
Was say the word
And Jehu pushed his horses toward Jezreel
As if they were running from a wild herd!
He would tell the watchmen
All they knew was stress
When they met him seeking only friendliness.

Nor did Joram of Judah and Ahaziah of Israel
Know what they'd go through
When they challenged this madman, Jehu!
At last the house of Ahab
Was punished for their crimes.
They had abused others many, many times.
And Jezebel met her waterloo
As Jehu's awful anger grew.
He told the palace eunuchs to throw her down
And at last her life was ended
In that evil, notorious town!

2nd KINGS 10

Ahab had seventy sons Jehu would slaughter
But it was Jehoiada the priest who later killed
Ahab's daughter.
Ahab's next task was to kill the prophets
Of Baal.
Indeed, it seems Jehu left a bloody trail.
But he lacked the most important quality.
His 'holiness' was not real.
He worshiped the golden calves
With what he thought was holy zeal.
God was displeased with what He saw
For Jehu did not walk in the ways
Of God's law.
This chapter simply closes with–when Jehu
Was dead
His son Jehoahaz reigned in his stead.
Jehu had been given the chance to become
Noble and great
But his unwillingness to obey
Left his son with an empty slate.

2nd KINGS 11

Athaliah—that dirty old bitty
Killed all the king's sons who lived in the city.
But with his aunt's help Joash hid.
He survived because of what she did!

Comments on 2nd Kings

She knew while he was in the temple
He had no need for alarm
And for six years he was kept safe from harm!
In the seventh year Joash was crowned
While Athaliah screamed, "Treason!"
The woman who had no right to rule
Was incapable of reason.
Judah's ruler must always be
A descendant of that *gentle shepherd boy*
And–like David–his heart should be
Always full of faith and joy!
Once again the people could rejoice
When the one they crowned was God's
Own choice!

2nd KINGS 12

Joash's concern for the temple was lovingly executed.
He reprimanded the priest because money
For rebuilding was not correctly computed.
He told them to keep the record simple.
It had once been his home, that precious temple.
From then on money for repairs
Was used for building materials, not precious wares.
Yet the temple was not completed
For when Hazael attacked Joash thought
He would be defeated.
He gave the gold from the temple treasuries
To buy off Hazael
Yet, in spite of that, his reign did not go well.
He would not die from Hazael's sporadic raids.
But was killed instead by his own trusted aids.

2nd KINGS 13

Jehoahaz of Israel reigned briefly and then
His son, Joash, who was unlike Joash of Judah.
Filled his life with unfruitful trash.
Much could be said of Joash but he did
Nothing worthy.
It could have been said of him
That he was evil and notoriously unearthly.
He sinned as did Jeroboam, Ahab, and others
In the past.
Knowing Elisha was not enough to guarantee
His victories would last.
Dear Elisha, this prophet whose life
Was bittersweet
Still had power in death
To bring a dead man to his feet!

2nd KINGS 14

As time passes the difference between
Israel and Judah seems to grow.
If there was any spiritual growth in Israel
It was impotently slim and awfully slow.
But Judah held on to Yahweh.
When she did she grew spiritually day by day!
The sons' of the two Joash's were
Quite a contrast.
Both were partly responsible whether or not
Their nations would last.
Though following the Lord is an individual choice
This chapter is one among many that shows us
People can listen to the wrong voice.

2nd KINGS 15

The contrast continues!
Uzziah was righteous and Zachariah was not
And his reign, too, was ended when he became
The victim of a vicious plot.
Several Israeli kings would come and go
During Uzziah's reign.
Three of those four kings were also slain.
But Uzziah reigned fifty two years

The "I Love My Bible" Commentary

One of the longest in Judah's history.
But once his pride got him in trouble.
That, itself should be no mystery!
It was pride–as destructive as when
A deadly cobra stings
–that was the downfall of many kings!
Then Uzziah's son and grandson
Each reigned sixteen years
And they were fairly good kings, it appears
But there is very little said about them.
This chapter closes as Jotham is buried
In the city of Jerusalem.

2nd KINGS 16

It seems Judah's King Ahaz possessed.
Absolutely no spiritual pizzaz!
He even copied the Assyrian king's altar
–a heathen king who was merely a cad.
When it came to holiness Ahaz would falter.
He was one of the few kings of Judah
Known to be bad.
He even offered his own son as a sacrifice.
God considered *that* an unforgivable vice.
But still he was not denied
His place in the royal cemetery when he died.

2nd KINGS 17

At last Israel's wickedness leads to her fall.
She became so wicked her kings,
Her people, even most of her prophets
Did not follow the Lord at all.
The people had built altars to other gods
Throughout the land.
Though the Lord had warned them many times
Still their wickedness got out of hand.
They continually provoked the Lord's anger
Until He would no longer rescue them
From danger.
God's people who were not to walk
In the darkness of night
Were emphatically swept from sight
Of the land they loved with all their might.
God had said, "You must never forget
The covenant I made with you!"
And they would no longer feel His Spirit
From that day He withdrew.
Now–those who withdraw from God
In our life span
Will only feel the emptiness of man.

2nd KINGS 18

Hezekiah was a good king who lived
In the days Israel was dispersed
But this king of Judah avoided all the evils
God had cursed.
He broke down the heathen altars
And the bronze serpent Moses had made.
He knew it had caused Israel's faith to fade.
God was with this king and would rescue him
From Sennacherib's power
All because Hezekiah had faith in God
When Judah faced this troubled hour!
God also knew Hezekiah's faith would sag
As he listened to those heathen men
Of Assyria boast and brag.
But Hezekiah did have enough faith
To tell his people to ignore
These braggart men who God would reduce
To the status of a bore!

2nd KINGS 19

Hezekiah received encouraging news
From the Lord who said,
"Don't worry about the king of Assyria.
He will soon be dead!"
Then Sennacherib boasted, "Don't believe
The God you trust in.
He cannot deliver you. Once again I'll win!"

Comment on 2nd Kings

But prayer does amazing things
Sennacherib knew nothing about!
As far as our Heavenly Father was concerned
This evil king had absolutely no clout!
God would stop this man who had defied Him
To defend His Name this man blasphemed.
There would be no victory for Assyria.
Ah, he would not have the victory of which
He dreamed!
God said, "Oh no you don't!
You will not gain the triumph
You so badly want."
God sent an angel who slew 185,000 troops.
I bet Sennacherib looked at all those bodies
And sadly exclaimed, "OOPS!"
He never managed to capture God's city.
In fact this vicious king died without pity.

2nd KINGS 20

Isaiah brought King Hezekiah bad news.
"Set your house in order anyway you choose."
God had told Isaiah Hezekiah was sick
And would not recover.
And I bet, like a cloud, Hezekiah could feel
That bad news hover!
But Hezekiah broke down, prayed and cried
And God wasted no time when He replied
By giving Hezekiah fifteen more years.
And then God gave Him a sign.
He pushed the shadow backwards ten points
And did it using the tool of His sunshine!
But when the king of Babylon sent greetings
Hezekiah acted curious.
He proudly showed his silver and gold
And it made God furious.
Even though Isaiah told Hezekiah
Of Babylon's intentions
He didn't seem to care.
This destruction of Judah would not come
In his lifetime. He would not be there.

No wonder Manasseh's faith was hollow.
His father had shown no concern
For the generations to follow.
Is our pollution of this once beautiful earth
Showing we do not care
If our descendants should live in pain
And hopeless despair?

2nd KINGS 21

Manasseh was twelve years old
When he began to reign.
So once more God sees an evil king
Of which He must complain.
Manasseh was even more wicked than the
Amorites who had lived there long ago.
And his murder of innocent people
Was a deadly unnecessary blow!
Even so, he ruled fifty five years.
Many times he was the cause of Judah's
Humiliation and tears.
God said His people had angered Him
From the time He had rescued them
From Egypt's abuse.
Now they left Him no choice but
To treat them like garbage and refuse!
But still God granted them a little respite
When Manasseh's grand son Josiah showed
God will shred the record of all our sins
Of which we honestly repent and quit!

2nd KINGS 22

For a little while Judah could rest.
Now she had a king who would do his best!
He loved the Lord as David did
And longed to do as the Lord would bid.
One day Hilkiah found a scroll
With God's laws written on it.
The King tore his clothes and exclaimed

The "I Love My Bible" Commentary

We haven't followed this one bit!"
But God understood his concern
And He promised Josiah bad times
Would not return
—at least not in his day
For God had heard Josiah pray!
And God in His Amazing Grace
Said, "Josiah will not linger here to see
The evil I will bring on this place!"

2nd KINGS 23

Judah's freedom was almost gone.
Josiah was her last great king!
Now there would be no freedom,
No reason to rejoice, no bells to ring.
There would be silence in the city
No children playing around.
The "FATHER" had departed.
There was no hallowed ground.
Judah had failed to hear her sister Israel's cries.
Instead she had listened to false prophet's lies.
Now there was no more remedy,
No balm in Gilead.
She could not be cured.
Her *'cancer'* was so bad.
Then Jehoahaz's reign was brief
And even under Jehoiakim
Judah would experience no relief.
She was about to expire from her terminal
    disease!
No one would come to her rescue
For she had no allies she could please.
Now Jehoiachin takes his father's place
But Babylon does not extend to him
Even an inch of grace.
He was taken prisoner along with the others.
Such was the fate of he and his brothers!
Judah had marched down hill way too long
And It catapulted her so strongly toward her fate
She was numb to the reality of doing wrong!

2nd KINGS 24

The enemy came and backed Judah to the wall
Took her prisoner and left no hope at all.
He was a vicious man, this Babylonian king.
The reigning nobles surrendered
And even God's temple was dismembered.
But Israel's sin had already dismembered it
Nothing left—not even a hint of God's spirit!
Only the very poor were left to carry on
When the Lord allowed Judah's destruction
By the hand of Babylon!
For years God had watched and pleaded
As the morals of Judah faded and receded.
They would not listen to His plea.
Now they faced a forced-march humility.
Their's was not the kind of humility faith
    demanded.
Judah would eat *humble pie* because
It was against God
All her leaders and people had banded!
Our God has ordinances for us to follow
Precious, holy, life rewarding guidelines
And we will surely find out
It is as dangerous to disobey as it is to doubt!

2nd KINGS 25

Judah ate the last bite of her home grown food
On July the 24th of that infamous year.
Nebuchadnezzar taught them the meaning
Of devastating, crippling fear.
But sadly, it didn't have to be.
Judah had sinned until there was no remedy!
In Babylon there would be no rejoicing or mirth
For Babylon had destroyed
All of Judah's treasures of any value or worth!
But King Jehoiachin was able to savor
Basking in king Evil-Merodach's favor.
God's forgiveness and grace would enable
Jenoiachin to eat at the king's table!

Comment on 2nd Kings

Note: Well, we have finished the "Kings" and I guess they thought the Lord was finished with them for good but He wasn't. He was just trying to teach them a lesson. It is such a pity that this nation(that has now been divided into two)that began with such promise now lay wounded with her enemies feet shoving her deep into dreary desert sands. But God's promises had been based on her loyalty to, and trust in Him. What is it that shows the Lord that we don't trust Him? What is it that says we don't love Him? What is the 'rule of thumb' here? Really want to know? Years and years later, our Lord would say to His disciples, "If you love me you **will** keep my commandments!" Simple, isn't it?

Did you know that since the beginning of time love has been the 'rule of thumb?' This hate business started with Cain and has haunted humanity ever since. Love doesn't kill. Love shows no ill to its neighbor(or brother). I think perhaps, when God kicked Adam and Eve out of the Garden, they forgot to take love with them-or maybe not enough to pass on to Cain. Whatever the problem, one can trace it back to a lack of love. The first commandment God gave to the Israelis was first to love Him. Later Jesus would say, "Thou shall love thy neighbor as thyself. They had the choice to obey Him and live and be prosperous and successful as a nation-or to disobey Him and lose their inheritance in the Promised Land. Jesus also said, "....not everyone that sayeth unto me, Lord, Lord, will enter the kingdom of heaven *but he that doeth the will of the Father!"* The Jews suffered because of their disobedience. We will too! The ten commandments are still in effect and we have a glorious reason to obey them since we are *saved by grace!*

We have accepted Jesus as our Savior, but have we accepted Him as our Lord? **One doesn't come without the other!** Do we truly follow Him? He says, *"I am the way, the truth and the life..."* We need to ask ourselves the same question Peter once asked our Lord. "...to whom shall we go Lord? Thou hast the words of life!"

It seems we Christians don't learn from history or our nation would not have easily turned so blatantly away from God to become a nation of alcoholics and drug addiction, of violence in our streets, our schools, and our homes. Have our leaders(and especially our Supreme Court judges)forgotten that Psalms says...... "The nation that forgets God shall be turned into hell?" How else can we describe America today? So many have accepted sex and violence in the movies and on TV. Well folks, it is **not** acceptable to God! (Remember Jeremiah said, *"Mine eye affects mine heart!"*)

When Christians watch such trash, they are, in effect, telling their children such lifestyles are acceptable and the violence and disregard for life seen today in such volume is a direct result of such careless programming, and irresponsible viewing. Proverbs says to raise a child in the way he should go and he will not depart thereof(of course 'raising them in the ways they should go is more than just taking them to church. It is the way we live in their presence). Do we make a practice of daily devotions, daily prayer, daily Bible reading? *Of course that takes time, but it is time well spent. Are not our children worth it?*

Obviously the people in the time of the 'Kings' didn't have the distractions we do. So, I suppose that means we must try twice as hard. *But we have twice the help. Jesus has sent us the Holy Spirit to help us in our Christian life. Remember, from the word 'go' life is meant to be so much sweeter and will be when we obey and honor Him. No desert sands for us!!!*

The "I Love My Bible" Commentary
(1st Chronicles)

1st CHRONICLES 1

This chapter goes back to the roots
Of the *"living tree!"*
And, beginning with Adam,
Traces all of Israel's pure ancestry.
Now the branches had grown thicker
And the tree taller
And there were almost too many to count!
They had walked many trails,
Thirsted in the desert and stood on God's
Holy mount!
It was time to look back and forward too.
They could see how many came from so few.
The descendants of Ishmael and Esau
Were named.
Many of them wanted Israel to be shamed.
Even Abraham's and Keturah's sons
Hated their distant kin
And all through history
That is the way it has always been!
Instead of being cherished and prized
God's people continue to be despised.
But, though countless horrors
Have been deployed
God's *"living tree"* cannot, *will not*
    be destroyed!

1st CHRONICLES 2

Who would think so many descendants
Would come from a little boy
Who stole his brother's birthright?
And not even Jacob would have dreamed
Some day he'd wrestle with an angel of God
In the darkness of the night!
So many names mentioned
So many hopes and dreams come and gone
Flesh and blood appearing on the stage of life
And then moving on.
But these were special people to the Lord
And these were special times
In which they starred!
What they did sometimes makes us wonder
About their sanity
But to the FATHER they were
The *cream of the crop* of humanity*!*
Remember–Judah was a prince among
    his brothers
And ONE would come from him
Who would give His Life for others!

1st CHRONICLES 3

King David's descendants named in this
    chapter
Would make a lengthy file
And it continues until their return
After the exile!
Had his sons and daughters been as faithful
    as he
None of the hardships they faced
Would have ever had to be!
Being a relative of the king does not count
Unless one's behavior is relevant.
They worshiped idols though God had said
    "You can't!
So this chapter simply names those
Who lived after David and makes no comment
    good or bad
But close scrutiny shows they seldom shared
David's joy in serving the Lord
From the time he was a lad!
Unlike David, who walked close to the Lord
They chose to walk a life time apart
And some of them never knew the joy
    of forgiveness
That comes to a repentant heart!
They failed to worship the ONE on the throne
And noncompliance kept them from moving on!

Comment on 1ˢᵗ Chronicles

1ˢᵗ CHRONICLES 4

There are many names in chapter four
Which traces Judah's descendants once more.
The name of Jabez stands out.
It could be said that his faith was stout!
Though his name meant 'distress'
He refused to be appalled.
He knew God would answer him
Whenever he called!
He often prayed that our *'Master'*
Would keep him from harm and disaster.
He was truly blessed
When God answered his request!
The sons of Simeon were also listed.
They destroyed the few remaining Amalekites
Though they strongly resisted.
And, the sons of Simeon also destroyed
The sons of Ham
And possessed all the land
That had belonged to them!

1ˢᵗ CHRONICLES 5

The indiscretion of Reuben is mentioned again.
Because of his sin, the official genealogy
Does not honor this man.
Instead, Joseph receives Reuben's birthright
But Judah is honored too.
It is from Judah's tribe
That untold blessings have come through!
Yet, the descendants of Reuben were proud.
Though they cried to God for help
None of them were cowed!
The half tribe of Manasseh was mentioned too
But this chapter has very little to say
About these idol worshipers who chose
To walk in their own misguided way.
They were taken captive
Along with the tribes of Reuben and Gad.
Disobedience turns what should have been
A happy ending
Into one that was very sad.

1ˢᵗ CHRONICLES 6

The most blessed tribe in times of old
Were the Levites who had treasure
For more precious than silver and gold.
The Lord God Himself was their treasure!
And that is a glorious wealth beyond measure.
The Levites listed here
Also had other riches they could not see
For God gave them a wealth of knowledge
To guide and set His people free.
Still the Levites were chosen
Because of the holiness of one man.
Because of their kinsman, Moses
They were chosen to reveal God's plan.
And What Is That?
Simply–that man may *know* God's purity
And walk with Him in truth and sincerity!
God, in love, provided cities of refuge
Where an innocent man could run!
There were to be no hasty decisions
To destroy anyone.

1ˢᵗ CHRONICLES 7

One way to recollect one's journey on earth
Is to recall the record of one's birth.
Though these were not significant tribes
Stouthearted warriors were among the people
This chapter describes.
Issachar, Benjamin, Manasseh, Ephraim,
And Asher–all
Had valued men and also some who would fall.
Ephraim must have felt much contention
From an unworthy act I hate to mention.
His sons Elead and Ezar
Were the first cattle rustlers. ever to be named
And because of them Ephraim was ashamed.

The "I Love My Bible" Commentary

It was futile to choose that dishonest path
For they were killed by the men of Gath.
And they paid dearly for that infamous crime.
Ephraim paid too for he mourned a long time.
Even in the best of families there is grief.
We must try our best to be holy and pure
For our time on earth is so very brief!

1st CHRONICLES 8

Benjamin was so close to Judah.
They were often considered one.
Israel's first king had come from Benjamin!
He was the tallest man in the nation
But was disobedient to God
Who had put him into such a noble station!
Benjamin was destined to be small.
As Saul said, it was the most insignificant
Tribe of all.
But she stayed close to Judah
Because the tribe of Judah would guard
Many of the leaders who loved the Lord!
It we observe closely we will find the reason
    is simple.
These two tribes were allotted land
Closest to that holy temple!
Though Benjamin was small
It rates a chapter of its own.
And-because of Benjamin-Judah
Never had to stand alone!

1st CHRONICLES 9

The annals of the kings of Israel
Carefully recorded every family tree.
God—who had their victories listed
Also included their failures for us to see.
He wanted them to know they all must depend
On facing the consequences when they sinned.
For seventy years their land lay silent
While they yearned

But it was a land of joy when they returned!
The duties of those who served in the temple
Are listed again
Also some of the responsibilities given
To each qualified (Levite)man.
And the tribe of Benjamin is mentioned
Once more
And it seems they had shrunk in size
And were even smaller than before!
The sin they had committed many years ago
Stunted them so they couldn't grow!

1st CHRONICLES 10

This chapter begins with Saul's defeat
and his last urgent plea.
He said, "Please don't let those heathen
get to me!"
His demise was far from grand
for he died at his own hand.
It was a pitiful day for Israel
when they heard the news.
Saul had died and it was because
The Lord and he so often had different views!
Disobedience was the vehicle that removed
Saul from the throne.
Generation after generation there are those
who just have to be shown!
Shown what?
Shown that God is God
and man is man!
Our God willingly shares His grace
but man can never take His place!
Saul was a tall man who was really very small
for a man who does not grow in spirit
really never grows at all!
Had Saul remained as meek as he seemed
at an earlier time
he and his sons would not have died
while still in their prime!

Comment on 1st Chronicles

1st CHRONICLES 11

David and Israel–an instant love affair!
They loved the way he fought
And saw he had plenty of energy to spare!
They already knew his faith was strong
And this man would never steer them wrong!
The noble men who fought for him
Were the very best!
They would put his enemies boasting to rest.
Joab was made Commander-in-chief
Because he was the first man to kill a Jebusite.
They had refused to let David enter Jebus
Mostly out of spite.
It seemed no one could stop David.
His power came from God above.
David's strength and motivation
Was the result of God's great love!

1st CHRONICLES 12

Famous warriors came to David
In enormous groups
Including Gad, Judah, Manasseh
And even Benjamin sent him troops!
They were swift as deer on the mountains
Strong as lions on the prowl
And experts with shield and spear.
These men were all faithful to David
And they all made that clear!
There was a special group known as the
 'thirty!'
Who came to stay.
The weakest was worth a hundred normal men
And the greatest could equal a thousand
On any given day.
They gave David their heart and their loyalty.
David must have been thinking of them
When he wrote of the 'true nobility!'
There was joy throughout the land
And they all would rejoice and sing
When they gathered in Hebron
To crown that noble shepherd king!

1st CHRONICLES 13

There is good reason for David to rejoice
Beginning with God's approval of his reign!
David and his officers gathered the people
To celebrate the return of the Ark.
It had been away from Jerusalem too long
And it seemed as is they were walking
In the dark!
God's ark would light up their hearts
When they could know it was near.
They had mourned for it many months.
And they watched anxiously for it to appear.
But once more they would have to wait.
Uzza touched it and that was a big mistake.
Oh that ark!
Made to ignite a perpetual spark!
Made to encourage the hearts of men!
But an ordinary man could not touch
Or even attempt to look in.
Who it represented
Was too holy to see
Too glorious to behold
More priceless than gold!
Love is what it held.
Love too holy to be felt!
The Law held man at bay
But Jesus changed that
On redemption day!
One day God would take away the 'wall'
When the 'law'
Was steadied by grace!
God was clouded in secrecy then
But soon we can all
Look on His face!
But the 'law' did not let them touch or see
What holy treasures it was that dwelt therein.
And if anyone did so, it was a deadly sin!

The "I Love My Bible" Commentary

1st CHRONICLES 14

God did not make David king
Because David was either strong or clever.
Nor did He use the criteria of any endeavor.
God made this soldier-shepherd king
Because his heart was pure!
God wanted His people to have joy
And to always feel secure!
David's effectiveness as a warrior or a king
Would never be reduced to a debit.
In every victory he would give God the credit!
The greatest weapon David had
  was his knee bone!
Down on his knees he learned
He would never have to fight alone!
Though they would boast and prance
The Philistines never had a chance.
God had given David power to spare
And David's fame quickly spread
Across the land everywhere!

1st CHRONICLES 15

David reminded the people that only Levites
Could carry the Ark.
Those who touched it without
God's permission.
Learned the results could be very stark!
Now that David was ready to bring the Ark
To Jerusalem
The Levites must be prepared
For moving it depended on them.
The people took part in a joyous celebration
All along the route
And while dancing to the clashing of cymbals
David entered Jerusalem with a shout!
It was an expression of his great love and trust
But his wife, Michal, looked on with disgust.
To say the least their relationship was bad.
She didn't have near the faith David had.

1st CHRONICLES 16

The Ark was now at home in the tabernacle
David built
And that precious, holy event
Was celebrated to the hilt!
At this time the using of choirs was begun
And there is no way we can surpass
That glorious song that was sung.
If only we would absorb
The marvelous advice in its lines
We would see how bright the love
Of our Heavenly Father shines!
Read this chapter over and over again
For great joy and promises are given
To raise the hopes of every man.
That celebration ended
When the people vowed to praise
Our Great God Jehovah
For the rest of their days!

1st CHRONICLES 17

The most prodigious time in Israel's history
Was during David's reign.
It was a time of spiritual maturity,
Of national zeal and of individual gain!
All God's people were prosperous
Because all God's people were led
By a king who truly loved God
And enjoyed *doing* what He said!
They were so close-this earthly king
And This Great God-that David would
Go in and sit before Him!
Many times David would be so overjoyed
He'd say, "God has filled my cup to the brim!"
He wanted to build God a glorious temple
But true glory does not come from war.
But God wanted someone else to build it.
He reminded David that he was a man of war!
God's temple must be built by a man of peace!

Comments on 1st Chronicles

It is through God's brand of peace
Man's soul gains release.
God promised David an eternal dynasty
Which would be fulfilled in Christ our King!
Someday He will sit on David's throne
And we will hear the angels sing!
The glory of that wonderful day
Is, we'll be singing too
Celebrating that era when God does
All the things
He told David He would do!

1st CHRONICLES 18

The Lord gives David victory
Everywhere he turns.
Many were the nations he 'pickled!'
He captured a thousand chariots and all
But one hundred of their horses
Were seriously crippled.
His victories came so easily
His enemies were grossly embarrassed!
But his strength came from His God
Whom David so lovingly cherished!
His enemies fought as men who
Must have been drowned in a deep sleep!
If David wanted their land,
It was land they knew they couldn't keep.
This shepherd king continued to leap
Like a deer across the mountain tops
Always jubilant, always victorious
Because God had pulled out all the stops!
No one could halt David's advance.
Even his enemies would have to admire
This king who took such a noble stance!
And sooner or later they would see
It was God who gave David the victory!

1st CHRONICLES 19

David sent his ambassador with a message
Of sympathy when King Hanun's father died
But Hanun's counselors' paranoia resulted
In his wounding the Israelis' pride.
King Hanun was unnecessarily rude
Because he thought they were spies
Wanting to intrude.
King Hanun had listened to perverted advice
At a time David was trying to be nice.
When a man acts like a fool he needs support
But Hanun couldn't find enough mercenaries
To effectively 'man the fort'!
Joab and Abishai were too strong no matter
How many men Hanun would gather.
His so-called men of defense
Could barely muster the fury of a feather!

1st CHRONICLES 20

In early Spring when battles heated up
And resistance melted down.
Joab successfully captured David
Another glorious, golden crown.
But David had a crown worth much more.
It was the crown of loyalty to our Lord
That David proudly wore!
It could not be measured in pounds.
Love for God is always weightier
Than it sounds!
As David grew older
He knew he could not shoulder
All the responsibilities that crown represented
And-as he thought of that
Many times he repented
Of the wars he won and the crowns he took
Because he felt he may never chance a look
At that temple he so strongly wanted to build.
For no crown could recall
All those people he had killed!
Much good can be said of David
For he was a shining star.
Still, he truly was a man of war!

The "I Love My Bible" Commentary

1st CHRONICLES 21

Even after a successful battle the devil attacks
Especially when people are celebrating victory
He sneaks up to their backs.
Why did David think he had to know
His kingdom's strength?
It was only God's strength he needed to show!
And did he forget a ransom must be paid?
God had decreed *that* in order to protect
All those souls He had made.
As the death angel neared Jerusalem
David could see clearly
His mistake had cost his people dearly!
But God repented of this destruction
His fervor caused
And God stopped the carnage
When the angel paused.
His mercy overcame His judgment
As it had many times before.
And David exclaimed,
"I'll build God's temple here,
On Ornan's threshing floor!"

1st CHRONICLES 22

David hears again he cannot build the temple
For he had been a man of war
Who had shed much blood.
And that news drowned David in despair
Again sweeping in like a mighty flood!
That temple would picture the Prince of Peace
The one purer than an innocent lamb's fleece!
Even though God had told his people
To conquer the heathen and cleanse the land
Peace must be the symbol of His temple
And that was His emphatic command!
  Peace for the body!
  Peace for the soul!
  Peace for these temples we live in
  must be our ultimate goal!
David's goal was to build the temple
But only the fortune he amassed
Could be used as Solomon built the temple
With a love that only David's love outclassed!
David had told Solomon to follow the Lord
With a pure and obedient mind.
Pure obedient worship!
God will accept no other kind!
There is no standard as pure and holy
As is our Lord's!
And, as we study His Word, we learn
Following Him brings its own special rewards!

1st CHRONICLES 23

In David's latter years he steps down
And hands his son, Solomon, his crown.
Now another census is taken
But this time David will not feel
Threatened or forsaken.
This census was taken to prepare the Levites
To oversee the work force.
Still, David must have felt some fear
Of course!
This time the census was to free the priests
To perform their holy unctions
And they could rely on the Levites
To perform all other functions.
Nothing must be left undone
David wanted to leave 'his house in order'
For Solomon his son!
If David could have bequeathed his faith
To Solomon the way he did his throne
Then truly, Solomon would have been
In his day, the greatest man ever known!

1st CHRONICLES 24

The priests were divided into 24 groups
In order to spread their expertise around.
God's people would need to know

Comment on 1st Chronicles

When they were standing on holy ground!
Though all the Levites were special
There was more leadership ability
In Eliezer's clan.
Since they were all famous, there was
No preference given to any particular man.
And–just so they would experience
No time loss
All their duties were assigned by coin-toss!
It was a time of holy zeal
And of great faithfulness to our Lord.
Oh think of the good fortune of those
Who could walk in holy corridors
Where other men were barred!

1ˢᵗ CHRONICLES 25

Back in the times
when times were simple
David started forming
choirs for the temple
And we can remember
when our times were quieter
we'd hear the church bells
ringing!
We knew they signified
a time of worship
a time of singing!
Now other noises occupy
our minds
and confusion of who to follow
has loosened
the tie that binds!
Singing!
It has always lifted
God's message in our hearts
and is often
the ignition that starts
the fire that builds
to a holy flame!
In our day when we fail
to lift our voices in praise
who is to blame?
Listen for the songs!
Put faith back
in our hearts
where it belongs!
Now, we fail to look
for joy, blessings, or peace
and storm clouds
cross our faces
and every brow
has it own unhappy crease.
We look at news
that makes us cringe in fear
and we forget the message
that our Lord is always near!
If we want to keep
our courage strong
let us be like David
and lift our voices
in joyful song!

1ˢᵀ CHRONICLES 26

There were priests who gave the message
And Levites who lifted their voices in song
And there were those who carried weapons
To keep the temple area strong.
All were needed in their own way.
All served the Lord faithfully every day.
It was an honor to help God's people
In such a way it seemed
God, Himself, was watching
Over those He had redeemed!
All areas of Israel were included
Under the Levite's rule.
God was using earthly men
As a heavenly tool!
Each person in Israel(and us too)
Was (and are)invited to be a soul mate
To the 'Great I Am' who is truly great!

The "I Love My Bible" Commentary

1st CHRONICLES 27

David also divided his troops
Into twelve regiments with 24,000 men each.
If anyone needed help
They would never be out of reach!
Each regiment served one month of the year
To assure God's people
They could live peacefully without fear.
There were also top political leaders
Something like a governor of state.
They served over each region
And all were known to be exceptionally great.
Somehow Gad and Asher were missed.
No one from their tribes were on the list.
Still David was adamant in his endless quest
To make sure his nation was the very best!

1st CHRONICLES 28

David's faith was a prime sample.
To live on the heights of faith he lived
We must(except for once)follow his example.
When he was depressed he called on God.
And when he felt triumphant, he exclaimed
"God is my staff and my rod!"
Whatever state of mind David was in
Victory was certain no matter
How bad the circumstances had been.
And because he loved the Lord
His life had been one of endless praise.
He knew when God was with him
The future held better days!
And he knew the plans for God's temple
Were heaven sent
And the people must honor the One
Whom that temple would represent!
He also felt trouble swirled
When God was dishonored by his people
And thus was mocked by the world.
He calls all the leaders together again
And tells them and Solomon their lives
Must be lived according to God's plan.
In effect he tell Solomon his life
Will come up short
Unless he follows the Lord with all his heart.
He knew times would be the worst
Unless God's people put Him first.
Yet Solomon would not do what David bid
And he did not walk the road his father did.
Like Solomon we will not follow that ideal
Unless our love for-and our faith in God
Is vibrant and real.
No more can be said about David
Except God loved him very much
And in everything David did
God gave him the 'Midas touch!'

1st CHRONICLES 29

David died at an old age
And his son Solomon reigned in his place.
He was known to be wise but he never
Achieved the level of his father's grace.
His father knew from whom his power came
And all his life David called on God's name!
David proved his love for God
Was beyond measure
When he left that precious temple
All his treasure!
He prayed that Solomon would be faithful
But isn't it strange
Instead of following David's example
Solomon's unfaithful heart would change.
David's final public appearance was
A pronouncement and a prayer
And his last words to his people
Was very good advice for us to share.
It was, "Give praise to the Lord your God"
For he knew God was full of love and power!
It was the best guidance he could give!
As he neared his final hour!

Comment On 1st Chronicles

There would be no more lands to conquer
Or hills to roam.

Soon his God would call him home!

Note: What can I say about David
that hasn't been said already?
He had a faith that was strong
and his loyalty was constant
and steady!
Even before David died
(long before)
he had set his affection
on things above
because he knew honor
is obedience
with a big dose of love!
He kept his eyes on the stars
because
he imagined the stars singing
the glories of the blessings
God's angels were bringing!
This earthly shepherd knew
the Heavenly Shepherd well!
Every time he sang
the Lord's praises
you can almost see
his heart swell!
The God of all the ages
loved this shepherd boy
and when David was old
and gray
God still gave him joy!

The "I Love My Bible" Commentary
(2nd Chronicles)

2nd CHRONICLES 1

Peace and godliness and an aura of grace
Fills the beginning of Solomon's reign!
Who could ever have imagined how much
Wisdom and knowledge he would gain?
There had been numerous wars and unrest
He wanted to dispel
So he asked the Lord to help him
Rule his people well!
Gold was in abundance and silver was
As numerous as rocks on the road.
Also expensive cedar to be used like
Cheaper wood was shipped in load after load.
Solomon could now easily afford
All those Egyptian horses he brought aboard.
Then those horses were resold
Bringing in more silver and gold!

2nd CHRONICLES 2

The tabernacle–now it was time to replace.
Solomon wanted an elegant building
That would gloriously portray God's grace!
153,000 men were involved in building
That magnificent edifice!
To be brilliantly beautiful it needed one man
Fully qualified to decorate it in detail.
It would need the expertise of Huramabi
And King Hiram knew he would not fail!
Huramabi was qualified to do exquisite work
With gold, silver, iron, or brass.
Man of many talents, he was known to be
Number one in his class.
King Hiram must have felt great love for Israel
For he stood behind his word
And he wished Solomon well!
That temple was built by good friends,
Cunning labor, and one who easily
Tied up all the loose ends!

Likewise, this temple I live in is being built
By the cunning labor of the One
Who builds nothing unsightly
His building is in the depths of my soul
And is done ever so quietly!
'Quietness in the temple-that makes it *sound!*
That is why workers in Solomon's temple
Were given no hammers with which to pound.
Lucky slave laborers!
They were the first to see
How glorious that temple was going to be!

2nd CHRONICLES 3

Anything of value requires work
Faithful to the least detail
And when we forget that, no wonder
Our feeble efforts fail!
The best of materials was used in this temple
Solomon and all those laborers built
And had their work been shoddy
God would have sensed their guilt!
Priceless materials required fervent labor
Or they would not have earned God's favor.
The material God gives us will surely
Shape and mold
Our souls into living treasures
Far more precious than silver or gold!
Listen to God's Word.
It is very important to hear it
For His Word is the material
That molds body, soul, and spirit!
We'll have quite a building when God finishes
One with absolutely NO blemishes!

2nd CHRONICLES 4

Materials for sacrifice were necessary
In the temple
But the light was its most intricate part!

Comment on 2nd Chronicles

It is God's light that brightens the soul
And illuminates the heart!
His sacrifice was to draw us near to Him.
We must not walk in spiritual darkness
Where the *soul light* is dim.
If we will follow His light
We will experience no trauma.
It is as if every negative circumstance
Is just meant to be an occasional comma!
Even if that light is just a candle
It is bright enough for the path we trod
Enough to guide us to the tender arms of God!

2nd CHRONICLES 5

I cannot describe that temple on my own.
but still it was undoubtedly inadequate
to picture our God
the greatest being ever known!
How can stone, silver, gold
or precious jewels express
the indescribable glory I'd like to stress?
Our Father is far more magnificent
than we can ever understand
even though that structure built to picture
His presence
was the most beautiful in the land!
People must have gazed at it in awe.
Certainly it was the most elegant building
they ever saw!
Can its splendor come to mind from the words
we read?
Does it truly picture our God
who is man's greatest need?
*Our most pressing need is that the
wisest temple builder of all eternity
build a memorial in our hearts
that we may know with certainty
the One who gave that graceful temple beauty
bestowed His grace
that darkest day on earth
when He died in our place!
His love
builds
restores
beautifies
And gives a fragrant essence
to these mortal temples
of we who live
in God's presence!
May God's glory be welcome
in these temples
of flesh and bone
and may our lives
be a living testimony
that we worship Him
and only Him alone!*

2nd CHRONICLES 6

It has always seemed strange to me
How we can walk so close to God
Yet feel so far away.
Solomon must have felt like that
For woven through his prayer
He begged God to walk with him each day.
Yet Solomon's spiritual wisdom regresses
When he chooses strange women
With shortened spirits and long tresses!
This man of God with heathen wives
Was adversely affected by their wicked lives.
His faith, his nerves, his temper
Must have frayed
And somewhere along the way
He forgot this beautiful prayer he prayed!
At the time he knelt before the people
He made it perfectly clear
He wanted to please the Lord
And he spoke the words
His people needed to hear.
Though these bodies are made of clay
God eagerly answers when we pray!

The "I Love My Bible" Commentary

2nd CHRONICLES 7

God's glory filled the temple so brilliantly
The priests could not enter
And fire from heaven flashed down
Burning the sacrifices and the wood
Down to the smallest splinter!
They all lifted their voices in praise
Because this was one of Israel's greatest days!
God had heard King Solomon pray
And here's the answer God gave him that day.
   "If my people which are called by My Name
           shall
      humble themselves
         and pray
     and seek my face
          and
  turn from their wicked ways
          then
    will I hear from heaven
  and will forgive their sin
  and will heal their land!
     There's the pattern!
      There's the hope!
     There's the recipe!
       God's way out!
      It's written down
       for you and me!
Even the justice that comes from God above
Is coated with His magnificent mercy and love!
But still God gives the warning.
Should Solomon's faith and obedience slacken
Many terrible calamities would surely happen!
What you sow is what you reap-timely then
And timely now.
Wouldn't you call that an *"un-sacred cow?"*
We cannot worship other gods instead
Maybe our Lord is trying to tell us
An *inanimate* is just another way of saying
You are worshiping something that is
        Dead, dead, dead!

Let's review the incredible beauty of what
    Our heavenly Father said!

"My People!"
"My People!"
Can you ever imagine
how much that means?
Claimed by the Great King
who loves
forgives
who cleans!
"My People!"
I am His
Made cream of the crop
Made to be a prince
or princess
truly royal.
"My people!"
Should we be less
than perfectly loyal?
Claimed by the
King of the Ages!
Proof?
It's here
all through these
sacred pages!
"My people"
AMEN!!!

We don't like this and we don't like that"
We like the game *but we don't want to bat!*
They were not faithful. What about us?
We can play ball in this game of life
Or we can just sit and fuss!
Remember what Samuel said to Saul?
"Behold rebellion is as witchcraft
And stubbornness is as iniquity and idolatry."
This game of holiness must be played
Joyfully and to the hilt.
No sitting on the bench in this marvelous
Game of life our Lord has built!

Comment on 2nd Chronicles

2nd CHRONICLES 8

Twenty years have passed
And the Lord's temple and Solomon's palace
Were both finished at last.
Then Solomon fortified various cities
And sent soldiers who were adept
At manning the supply centers
And guarding the places
Where Solomon's horses were kept.
He even built a palace for Pharaoh's daughter
Who was his wife.
Solomon felt David's palace was too holy
For one who'd led her kind of life.
The Ark of the Lord had been there.
It was holy ground she could not share.
He carefully followed David's organizational
    chart
And for awhile he, too, worshiped God
With a willing heart!
He also traveled to Edom's seaports to meet
King Hiram who had given him
A seaworthy fleet!
These ships brought gold from Ophir
And possibly jewels, frankincense and myrrh.
As time passed Solomon would amass
Riches untold
Including that 13 million in Gold!

2nd CHRONICLES 9

You would think the Queen of Sheba
Would glory
In listening to Solomon telling the story
Of the faith King David had
But instead she seemed interested only in
His opulence and how his servants were clad.
She had traveled for miles to look in his eyes
This man who was known to be truly wise.
But crooked paths are sometimes followed
By wisdom of the mind.

Placing one's faith in mere wisdom
Can cause one to become spiritually blind.
Solomon's life is one of many examples
When a man relies on his own wisdom
His life can and does fall into shambles!
The time would come when he would forsake
This Holy God David had considered so great!
Now Solomon passes on
And his son Rehoboam inherits the throne.
It may not be popular for me to say
But Solomon easily forgot to whom
He should pray.
His father David thought God's Words
Were sweeter than honey.
They were his favorite desserts!
Not so–his son Solomon
Who spent his life chasing skirts.
David's life ended in honor.
Solomon's did not!
Solomon looked to idols in his old age.
And because he worshiped idols
His record included an ugly blot.
We do not know for sure his end thereof
So we sadly question who was his true love?

2nd CHRONICLES 10

The seeds of discontent began to grow
In Solomon's time.
And almost with the flip of his advisor's coins
Rehoboam made the choice to warn the people
His little finger would be thicker
Than his father's loins!
Now the unrest and division that had
Stalked their hearts surfaced with rebellion
"Down with David's dynasty." They said.
They would not follow this evil hellion!
Thus Israel would not allow
David's descendants to rule
For in worshiping idols
Solomon and now his son had played the fool.

The "I Love My Bible" Commentary

2nd CHRONICLES 11

War never strengthens a divided nation
So Judah and Israel were not to fight.
War was not God's way
For these two nations to reunite.
Israel! Sin had devastated this nation.
War would only make it worse.
Could war cure their idolatrous curse?
Israel cut herself off from worshiping God
Strayed far from Him when she made that cut.
And she found her self wandering
Down a hopeless, endless rut!
Israel! Judah! Why was it so hard
For them to discover that unity comes
From faithfully following the Lord?
Those in Israel who loved the Lord
Moved to Judah to be
Close to the temple and close to God
Who they knew would keep them free.
As long a Rehoboam followed the Lord
He did nothing wrong
But, sad to say, his fervor didn't last very long.

2nd CHRONICLES 12

At the height of his power
Rehoboam forgot from whom his power came
And when the rest of Judah forsake the Lord
He was the one who was to blame.
Same old song–umpteenth verse!
Evil nations made their problems worse.
Sometimes when our spirits are out of order
We find our enemies parked on our 'border!'
Now we see Egypt and her allies
Surrounding Judah and were thick as flies.
Fortunately for Judah, God heard her cries!
They considered it was the Lord
Who raised this unholy alliance, this evil fuss
And they exclaimed,
"God was right in doing this to us!"
Rehoboam and his people repented
And though he did suffer a power reduction
The Lord did not send complete destruction.
But the king never gave the Lord his pledge.
When it came to total commitment
Rehoboam would hedge.
So the wars between Israel and Judah
Did not cease
And he, ambivalent, would know no peace!

2nd CHRONICLES 13

It would not have helped Jeroboam
Even if he should untruthfully plaster
News all over town that Jeroboam
And his people would worship our Master!
Not so! Jeroboam worshiped his self-made
Golden calves with zeal
Giving no thought to how God would feel.
What a difference between he and Abijah.
These two kings walked in different directions.
Abijah walked in the paths of the Lord
But Jereboam followed the shadow
Of those golden calves' reflections.
Israel should have known what we know.
Following the Lord is the *" way to go!!!"*

2nd CHRONICLES 14

Asa takes over when his father, Abijah, dies
And continues to worship our precious Lord
The One who Israel defies.
When idolatry is held in high esteem
    faith falters
And that is why Asa destroyed all those
Heathen idol-altars.
Asa loved the Lord and it appears
God gave him peace his first ten years.
But later Asa cried to the Lord in a panic-sweat
When Ethiopians became a disabling threat.
The Lord answered Asa's urgent call

Comment on 2nd Chronicles

And caused those arrogant Ethiopians to fall!
And when those million troops thundered
Guess who it was who Judah plundered?
God gave them victory!
The Ethiopians lust for Judah
Made God their enemy!

2nd CHRONICLES 15

This chapter shows us what leads to anarchy
And increasing crimes.
When people rebel against God
The result brings us vicious evil times.
Azariah warned Asa about that
And Asa speedily complied.
He didn't want to displease this precious God
On whom he had always relied.
Asa led his people into worshiping God only
With God by his side, he'd never be lonely.
He even removed his mother as queen
Because she made an idol.
That was one sin for which
He did not want to be held liable!
Her's was an infamous sin
And Asa refused to be
The idolater she had been.

2nd CHRONICLES 16

Asa's heart was perfect before God
Throughout his lifetime except at the end.
He died somewhat belligerent
And refusing to bend.
Nevertheless much good could be found
About this king who walked on holy ground!
Sad words sneak into this chapter.
Imagine God having to look for people
Whose hearts are still true blue!
It should be something One so grand
Would never have to do!
No fault can ever be found in our Lord!
Why do people turn away?
Oh my people, when I follow Him
He really *makes my day!*
We need his forgiveness so badly
And we must never forget to pray
Never forget where to find peace and His care.
Asa did and he ended his days
In pain and hopeless despair.

2nd CHRONICLES 17

Many, many times Judah had been terrorized!
To prevent a recurrence the king mobilized.
And the zeal of the surrounding nations
Quickly fell flat!
None of them had the courage to declare war
On King Jehoshaphat.
The Lord blessed him because he walked
In his father's earlier footsteps
And sought those principles which consisted
Of holy concepts.
He began to educate the people once again.
Teaching them the laws of God!
There could be no nobler plan!
By this time span God's Word had been
So misused
Countless people had become confused.
Jehoshaphat also kept over a million troops
In the holy city of Jerusalem.
He was totally prepared
Should any strange army
Attempt to conquer them.
But no armies would dare appear.
God had filled their hearts with fear!

2nd CHRONICLES 18

Jehoshaphat had done well through the years
But he made a marriage alliance for his son
With Ahab's daughter
Despite all the righteous people

The "I Love My Bible" Commentary

He and Jezabel had been known to slaughter.
Jehoshaphat and Ahab even went to war
Against Syria together
Hoping the evils of war would be easier to weather!
But though Ahab wanted good news
God send him a deceiver
For why should our Holy God encourage
This evil unbeliever?
Then Ahab imprisoned God's faithful prophet
Because he didn't believe what Micaiah said.
He had told Ahab, by the next day
The troops of Israel would be scattered
And Ahab would be dead.
Micaiah's prophecy came true at sundown
When the angel of death reached out
And removed Ahab's crown.

2nd CHRONICLES 19

This chapter should be the criteria
For every one who sits on the judges bench.
For a judge who takes bribes
Will sooner or later find God's reciprocal
Judgement an absolute cinch!
An honest judge will find it well not to rule
In favor of a rich and powerful
Dishonest fool.
No judge will ever be reprimanded
If he will judge in the fear of God
As Jehoshaphat commanded.
He knew how futile it was to help the wicked
For God was displeased when he helped Ahab.
And now that king was lying somewhere
On a cold lonely marble slab.
So Jehoshaphat warns the judges
To be fearless in their stand
For right judgement brings hope to any land.
Truth and integrity keeps God's people free!
    Truth and integrity!
    May they always be!

2nd CHRONICLES 20

When Jehoshaphat was threatened by
Ammon, Moab, and the Meunites
He prayed desperately for the Lord to protect
Him and his people's rights!
It was such a vast well trained army
He knew Judah didn't have a chance.
But he knew Judah's strength was not
In a soldier's sword or lance!
It was to the Lord he cried
And his prayer was not denied!
Notice this folks! Notice what praise can do!
When Judah began to sing and praise the Lord
He just took his big eraser
And erased those guys from view!
Yet this king who had so many needs
Seemed to forgot all of God's gracious deeds.
Though he had been full of praise
He, like his father, strayed from the Lord
In his latter days.
He "stumped his toe" somebody said.
No! He stumped his heart
When he limped away
From our God near his departure day!

2nd CHRONICLES 21

The man we know as Judah's Jehoram
Had no faith and no decorum!
How could a man who would kill his brothers
Be considered worthy to rule others?
He could have had the faith of Jehoshaphat
But his heart was as hard as a concrete slab
All because he had listened to king Ahab.
Jehoram ruled in Judah for eight years
And then died unmourned
But not before he had suffered horribly
As the Lord had sworn.
Maybe this was one of God's most costly fines
Because he had built so many idol shrines.

Comment on 2nd Chronicles

2nd CHRONICLES 22

Ahaziah was born 'between a rock
And a hard place'
Because neither one of his parents possessed
Any redeeming grace.
He formed an alliance with Jehoram of Israel
And from then on his luck slid down hill!
He was with Jehoram who was killed by Jehu
So Jehu stalked and killed him too.
I said Athaliah had no redeeming grace.
She proves it now for she kills
All her grandsons who could take his place.
She thought! Ah, one got away!
He would take her crown away some day!
Joash was hid in the temple
So Athaliah kills all but one.
Were any good deeds attributed to Athaliah?
    Absolutely none!

2nd CHRONICLES 23

In the seventh year of Athaliah's reign
She met her waterloo!
It was the precious little boy kept safe
From the time he withdrew.
He withdrew into holy ground
And, safe in the temple, he couldn't be found!
Now it was time for him to appear.
And it was Athaliah's most fateful year.
Jehoiada the priest had trained Joash
For this special season.
He would replace this evil queen
Who had committed treason.
At last Jehoiada had 'turned the tables'
When he had her killed at the palace stables.
They rejoiced because the queen was dead
And a righteous little boy reigned instead!
Her mother and father taught her well.
She was as vicious as Jezebel.
And no one cried the day she fell.

2nd CHRONICLES 24

During Joash's reign Judah worked on
The Temple's restoration
And as long as they worshiped the Lord
They had many reasons for celebration.
He was a godly king during Jehoiada's lifetime
But after Jehoiada's death
His murder of Zechariah was his worst crime!
He had ordered Zechariah killed as his reward
For Zecharaih had tried to turn Joash
Back to the Lord.
He, too, would be killed as recompense
For this murder that made no sense.

2nd CHRONICLES 25

Notice the mixed qualities Joash's son
Amaziah had?
In resentment, he killed those who killed
His dad!
But he tried to do that which was correct
And because of his desire to do right
He earned respect.
Pride, our greatest enemy, changed him.
You might say it came charging in again!
And he began to worship idols
Which changed the heart of this just man.
God sent a prophet to ask him
"Why have you worshiped gods
Who could not save their people from you?"
And he must have warned Amaziah
"You'd better watch what you do!"
It seemed Amaziah had lost his quality
And so his people had to kill this man
Who had fallen into idolatry.
Why does the pendulum swing so easily
From good back to evil deeds
And why does man make himself suffer
The treacherous results when he turns away
From the Righteous God he so badly needs?

The "I Love My Bible" Commentary

2nd CHRONICLES 26

Uzziah built towers around Jerusalem.
They formed a royal ring!
He wanted to protect his people
Those 52 years he reigned as king.
He had great herds of cattle
And was a man who loved the soil.
His army was full of men who were loyal.
Brilliant men invented engines of war
To shoot arrows from the towers.
The message of those arrows was
"You cannot take what is ours!"
But when Uzziah became powerful
He grew too proud for his own good.
He would never have had leprosy
Had he understood
He could never grow enough in God's eyes
To enter that sanctuary that held God's prize!
It was a holy place beyond compare
Because God's Holy Ark was there!

2nd CHRONICLES 27

It is unusual for people to become corrupt
When their king is holy
But for some reason Jotham was ineffectual
Though he followed the Lord solely.
He was careful to honor God though his
Power grew.
So little is said of this king
Who walked with God each day anew!
It seems he could only dream
Of the greatness that comes
From holding God in high esteem!
How sad considering the good things
He had done
That this man should die at age forty one.
Still this man planted holy, righteous seeds
Ah! His soul grew flowers instead of weeds!
And God noticed his good deeds.

2nd CHRONICLES 28

Ahaz traveled the down side of life
Not like his father who never caused Judah
Any unnecessary strife.
He sacrificed to idols and worshiped them
Those sixteen years he ruled in Jerusalem.
His warfare with Israel was the worst.
Israel devastated Judah yet they repented
Of capturing the 200,000 they had cursed.
God had sent Oded the prophet who told them
"Let those people go!"
Israel had gone too far and it was something
They needed to know.
Now Ahaz collapsed spiritually
And worshiped idols completely.
He was so brazen in his idolatry
It was not even done discreetly.
He was not buried in the royal tombs
When he died.
They were for kings who had tried
To please the Lord
And he had not qualified!

2nd CHRONICLES 29

Jotham's son Hezekiah knew why Judah
Had been defeated.
She had continued to sin even though
God's warnings had been repeated.
He wanted to open the temple doors
And bring people back to God.
Surely they had learned the futility
Of worshiping gods like Ashdod.
Opening the doors of the temple
Was a loving noble gesture.
Once again the high priest could
Offer sacrifices and don his holy vesture!
And the people could bow in worship
Rejoice and laugh
As they sang the joyful songs of Asaph!

Comment on 2nd Chronicles

2nd CHRONICLES 30

That precious Passover
Is going to be celebrated once again!
Think of the years of remembrance
It would span!
Could they really understand the glorious feat
God had accomplished
And that He would continue to do
All He promised?
And why did those people in Israel
Refuse to appear
After all God had done for them
Year after year?
Those who did come knew forgiveness
Strengthens and mends
And would guide them away
From the trajectory of evil winds!
Before, sin had weakened their dedication
And sin had led them in the wrong direction!
Now they could go back to that Holy Place
And once again enjoy God's grace!

2nd CHRONICLES 31

When we return to the Lord we often feel
It is a time of great joy that increases our zeal!
We want to do more for our Lord
For we discover peace of mind
Is more a gift than a reward!
These people must have felt the same.
When love for God takes charge
We'll tear down those shadows of shame.
Idols were just shadows to darken their paths
Imitation cleansing no better than spit baths!
How often our faith falters
When we worship at strange altars.
"We don't have idols," you say!
Well, what do we put before God today?
Fame or fortune or pleasure,
Are these the things we treasure?

God is on the Up Side of our lives
When we put Him first.
We are like the woman at the well.
Only Jesus can ease our thirst!
Hezekiah knew that and he worked very hard
To restore respect for the temple
And love for the Lord.
He knew godly living brings joy to the land
And he knew standing tall was the only way
   to stand!
Even though Hezekiah stumbled at the end
He never forgot his one true Great Friend!

2nd CHRONICLES 32

Though his father, Ahaz, had played the fool
Hezekiah's was a righteous rule!
He loved the Lord and sought his approval
And he demanded the heathen alters removal.
He needed a huge faith to erase the hysteria
Caused by the threats of the king of Syria.
Despite Sennacherib's boasting
And his many threatening puns
He was eventually destroyed by his own sons.
When God's people are threatened
He has always been around
To show the heathen armies
They cannot stand on holy ground.
God honored Hezekiah for he chose to obey
This remarkably wonderful Being who is
"The truth, the Life, and the Way!
God even restored Hezekiah's health
And He also gave him joy
And tremendous wealth!

2nd CHRONICLES 33

Manasseh began to reign when he was
A twelve year old brat.
His goals seemed to be based
On a philosophy of tit-for-tat!

The "I Love My Bible" Commentary

He finally learned when the tables were turned
That his defeat was partially because
He had his own children burned.
It was to evil gods who were no gods at all.
And his reliance on fortune tellers and witches
Also caused him to fall
Manasseh encouraged Judah to be more evil
Than any of the nations they had destroyed
And God used Babylon to issue
The same punishment Manasseh had deployed.
But Manasseh repented of the evil he had done
And God revoked the victory Babylon won.
Manasseh was set free to rule again
For God graciously showed mercy to this man!
Truly, this is *food for thought!*
We'd do well to remember all the forgiveness
True repentance has brought!
Manasseh discovered where true peace
Could be found
And God allowed him to be laid to rest
In his own burial ground.
But his son, Amon was *a royal pain.*
He was assassinated after only a two year reign
And his son Josiah would be the one
"Pulling the strings!"
Noble Josiah was known to be the last
Of Judah's righteous kings!

2nd CHRONICLES 34

Josiah was 8 years old when he took the throne.
His zeal for God and his righteousness
Was well known.
When God's Word was discovered
He reacted in fear
And he cried, "We have not obeyed
Any of these laws written here!"
He sent men to see Huldah the prophetess
Who told them, "Yes, this nation is in a mess!"
Because of Josiah's concern
Judah's judgement was delayed.

Once again she has a righteous king
Even though she had strayed.
Those storm clouds Josiah feared would not rumble
Because he had sought the Lord
And remained humble!
How many righteous men have been found
And how many of them
Have turned this world around?
The Billy Sundays, the John Wesleys,
The Billy Grahams. have set our feet
On faith's solid ground.
Loyalty to the Faith once delivered
To the saints
Is still the canvas on which the Holy Spirit paints.
We cannot describe this beauty
For this beauty lives in our souls.
It is this beauty painted by God
That encourages us to reach our goals!

2nd CHRONICLES 35

Josiah called for a Passover that involved
Many priests
Not one soul would be over looked
From the greatest to the least.
It is said no other Passover was held
In such a way
As that glorious Passover celebrated In
Josiah's day.
Judah stood on high and holy ground
Of the infinite faith God gives
For the man who worships Him
As long as he lives.
But Josiah left Jerusalem to battle at Megiddo
And he was killed by Egypt's King Necho.
And when this good man died
Even Jeremiah the prophet cried!
Now his name belongs
Only to those who compose sad songs!

Comment on 2nd Chronicles

2nd CHRONICLES 36

From here on, Judah would have no king
In whom she could boast.
And she went down hill faster
Than a roller coast can coast!
Over and over again she continued to back slide
Until there was no remedy to be found
And no place to hide.
Now the word of the Lord spoken
Through Jeremiah came true
And it would be seventy years before
They would effectively hear the words
"The Lord be with you!"
That was when Cyrus chose to indicate
Those who yearned to see Jerusalem
Would no longer have to wait.
Some would leave Babylon's restriction
The way it was told in Jeremiah's prediction!
And the closer they got to Jerusalem
The higher their hopes would rise
When Cyrus sent men back
With all those funds and supplies!

Now the stories of the kings have been told and repeated. The bankruptcies in the morals of both nations were often based on the influence of their kings and the failures far outnumbered the victorious lives of the many kings mentioned. If we search deeply, failure was often tied to the mothers of those kings. Many were heathen women who worshiped idols. God had told Israel not to mix with heathen unbelievers who worshiped idols. Evidently they didn't listen to him any better than most Christians today, only the heathen influence we've experienced is claimed to be in the name of "art" otherwise spelled *heathen!* What we see in the movies and on television today *has very little to do with godly morals!* We need to remember what Jeremiah said so many years ago still applies to us today. He said, "Mine eye affects mine heart!" My gosh, he didn't see nearly as much infidelity, adultery, violence and homosexuality, nor lies, nor theft as we see today. Nor did he see it as often. It blares at us from the big screen and the Boob tube 24 hours a day. Not all of it is bad, but the ratio is somewhat equivalent to that of the kings of Israel and Judah. The bad far outnumbers the good.

As far as human nature is concerned it is far easier to tumble downhill than it is to climb the heights of goodness. Same then as now. Do we ever learn from history? Evidently not. God does so much more for us in His New Covenant(testament) than He did in the Old but we have done no better than those who did not have the assurance of Salvation we have. When our books are opened in Heaven, how many people are going to shake their heads and say, "My oh my?" And they certainly won't be bragging! *What we see affects how we sow, and what we sow is what we reap. Maybe we'd better watch our "seed" purchases!* God says we are weak and we are, but we can be very, very thankful, He NEVER gives up on us! We may lose a bundle of skirmishes but He will see to it that we eventually win this great battle of life because, after all, *our God is in the winning business!*

The "I Love My Bible" Commentary
(The Book of Ezra)

EZRA 1

It was a long walk from Babylon
To Jerusalem's hills
So those who returned needed sturdy bodies
And strong wills!
More frightening than those strange trails
They would roam
Must have been not knowing
What they'd find in those hills back home!
But God had said He loved Jerusalem
And going back would mean
They were really, finally going home to Him!
"Good News!
We're going to Jerusalem!
Good news!"
They walked and clapped
and then some.
"Good news!
Sad songs.
No more time for
sad songs.
Glad songs
now to us belongs!
Good news!
Going to Jerusalem!
Good news!
Rivers not too wide
to cross now.
Sunshine
shining on us
somehow!
Good news!
Going to Jerusalem!
Good news!"
We pray we get to join them
some day, some way!
Going to Jerusalem!
Good news!
Going to Jerusalem!

EZRA 2

These are not just names listed here.
These are flesh and blood who just existed
In their enemies atmosphere.
They were afraid some proved their genelogy
Merely by stealth
And they thought others were able to return
Because they had great wealth.
Whatever–there were 42,000 who returned
Rejoicing in the freedom their loyalty to God
Had earned!
They came to build that precious temple again
Because King Cyrus had graciously lifted
    the ban
That kept the Jewish exiles from sacrificing
To our gracious Lord.
Cyrus allowed them to raise those temple walls
And to stand again in their own courtyard.!

EZRA 3

First the altar was built on its old site.
Now the sacrifices could be offered continually
Day and night!
Many Jews wept when that temple began to be
    rebuilt
But it seems some of these celebrants were
    split
Others shouted for joy that day
And their joy could be felt even far away!
The walls were not all up but the promise
    was there
And when they laid the foundations
They would declare Gods' love and devotion
So vibrantly, distant people heard the
    commotion!
Who says God's people should not shout
    or sing?
Didn't they have a loving, glorious King?

Comment on Ezra

EZRA 4

God's people have always had enemies
–always will!
And they will be consistent in trying to keep
God's people still.
The Jew's enemies began with their protests
To Cyrus
But the Jews replied, "King Cyrus sent us
And you can't fire us!"
But like a scorpion used its tail to sting
They used their words to poison the Jewish
Influence with each succeeding king.
They finally succeeded when Artaxerxes
    reigned
For he listened when these Jews enemies
    complained.
It must have brought sadness
When this bad news was dropped.
King Artaxerxes did say the Jewish work
Had to be stopped.

EZRA 5

When God's people picked up the pieces
And tried to mold them back together
They relied on their faith to get them through
Even the stormiest of political weather.
And during the ages we've found
We also need God's strength to hold our
    ground!
Many would contaminate our souls
And continually try to challenge our goals.
The malicious letters those dissidents sent
Were received with caution wherever they
    went.
Though the kings that received them knew
Jerusalem was a hot bed of insurrection
They had to admire those noble Jews
    dedication!
There will always be resistance
From those who are defiled.
    No matter!
God's work will slow to a turtle's pace
Only for a little while!
The Israelis learn that the God who gave us
The earth to occupy
Is the great "I AM" who is also able to supply.
God sent those baffled Jews word to resume
And He knew their enemies would fume!
It is *nothing* to God to overcome
Our enemies interference
And the Jews knew God's faithfulness
Deserved their adherence
To His word and to His servant Zerubbabel.
He encouraged them to do God's work
And to do it well!
God has been in the business of building
Temples since the world began
Not in bricks or stone but in the heart of man!

EZRA 6

King Darius ordered the governor and others
To leave the Jews alone.
He told them to supply the Jews from funds
They had considered to be their own.
It seemed these Jews could do nothing
Without their enemies intervention.
We can see their efforts were never based
On good intention!
Darius told Tatnai to let the work of the House
of God alone.
He was displeased with Tatnai and his allies
And he firmly made that known.
That precious temple was completed
And the Passover held.
Hearts full of joy, yet who could ever describe
How they truly felt?
Showers of blessings poured down!
God was back with His people again.
And Jerusalem rocked with a happy sound!

The "I Love My Bible" Commentary

EZRA 7

Ezra would reach many people through
The Words of the Scripture he would teach.
Even a king was impressed
By all God's noble deeds which Ezra
Proclaimed and professed!
His devotion may have seemed simple
Yet, because of it, he was allowed
To rebuild the temple.
Love for God is mightier than a nuclear
    reactor!
God used that love to reach out
And use Cyrus as an important factor!
Cyrus, this man the Jews called "heathen"
Truly loved the Lord and would say
"Whatever it takes to rebuild your temple,
We will pay!"
The Jews could not discount this king
Because God could arrange
To use the most unlikely
The one they considered strange!
Our God moves in mysterious ways
His wonders to perform
And is interested, *very interested*
In keeping His people safe from harm!

EZRA 8

During the reign of Artarxerxes more Jews
Accompanied Ezra to their homeland.
They refused protection from the king
Saying, "We are under the protection
Of God's own hand!"
They knew all they had to do was fast and pray
And God would protect them along the way!
They assembled at the Ahava River to see
If anyone had been missed
And Ezra noticed no Levites were on the list.
Ezra summoned them and they came
To keep the holy items in trust.
They wanted to get it safely to Jerusalem
For the king had said they must.
Valuable items were returned to the temple
    at this time.
And they passed through bandit infested
    territory
Without losing a single '*dime!*'
Sure–these men were honest and very astute
But they arrived in Jerusalem safely because
God's protection is absolute!

EZRA 9

We try to balance the tight rope of life
Along the great divide of our souls.
If and when we make it will be determined
By whether or not we've chosen worthy goals.
We should learn from these Israelis
What is truly best
Only when they followed God
Could they rejoice in perfect rest!
Ezra knew the consequences his people faced.
No wonder he was so unnerved.
His prayer would not change the guilty
But only the punishment they deserved.
Intense rain must have been the picture
Of what lay ahead.
Still these men were willing to do
What God, through Ezra, said!

EZRA 10

It seems Ezra continually dealt
With adolescent elders unsure of how they felt
And with their emotions loosely elastic
They were continually seeking the fantastic.
And once again these people perverted
Their basic desires
By seeking the heathen's lifestyles
Of strange alters and unholy fires.
God did not want their hearts to stray

Comment on Ezra

Yet it does seem inhuman that their sins
Caused innocent children to be sent away.
God's discipline is hard for us to understand
But we must remember this was a picture
Of Heaven, the true Holy Land.
Mixing God's people with heathen unbelievers
Is like mixing onions with ice cream.
That culinary combination makes
An awful unsavory team.
Same with the idolaters and the Jews.
People must be careful who they choose.
We need people with godly traits
Loving people to be our soul mates.
We'd have homes with an utopic essence
If we'd rejoice in God's holy presence.
Ah, just think the divorce rate would drop
And very few marriages would be a flop.
You can't beat God's way!
We should try His formula today,
Tomorrow, always!
Maybe then, we'd have
No children who become disobedient strays.
There would be no homes broken
No unkind words ever spoken
And no un-quenching thirst
If only Love came first!

I suppose that wish I just made is a BIG order but our God is in the BIG ORDER business. But this happens to be an order we must fill ourselves. We wish for Utopia but the pattern for Utopia lives in our hearts. We just <u>Don't</u> use the pattern. People don't buy exquisite material and then cut it at random. To maintain the beauty the pattern must be followed. The way for blessing is laid out, over and over, and over again----from Genesis to Revelation. God never left us without guidance. He has always sent someone to guide His people-Ezra in this case. How many has He sent? Read through the Bible and you will see. Actually that is a great assignment. You will be amazed at what you will learn about God's love, God's patience, God's grace, and God's daily involvement in our lives. He did give us dominion over this world but he has never left us without help. It is there for the asking! We've contaminated our planet, disregarded His laws, shamed each other, and live as if their will be no one to walk through the debris we leave behind. Oh, yes, it would be a big order to straighten this world out, *but we do have the pattern.* The question is—will we ever wise up enough to follow it. I hope so. The ball is in our lap! So---------------------!

The "I Love My Bible" Commentary
(The Book of Nehemiah)

NEHEMIAH 1

Before he consulted the king or said a word
Nehemiah cried to the Lord because he heard
The walls of Jerusalem were still torn down
And the gates were burned to his home town.
He asked for forgiveness first of all
And admitted how terrible were the sins
That had caused Israel and Judah to fall.
He also confessed his own sins
And before he closes
Nehemiah reminds the Lord
What He had said to Moses.
God had said He's send them home whenever
They chose to obey
And He said He'd set the wheels in motion
That very day!
I can say without error, the longer God lives
The greater He grows
And the more mercy He graciously gives!

NEHEMIAH 2

Nehemiah had made a strong impression
On King Artaxerxes who was concerned
About Nehemiah's apparent depression.
And he agreed to let Nehemiah depart
To check on that city so close to his heart.
Surely it was because of the years
Nehemiah had strived to do his best
That the king granted his request!
He wasn't in Jerusalem long
Before he checked to see what he needed
To make the walls of Jerusalem strong.
He began to build along with his brothers
Even though he was questioned
By Sanballat and others.
Nehemiah told the ungodly Sanballat
He could not share
In the work that was strictly God's affair.
Nehemiah would only choose
The help he needed from among the Jews!

NEHEMIAH 3

Many people were involved
In rebuilding the wall
And it is not necessary
That we name them all!
What matters is they cooperated
In their work
But the leaders of Tokia were known
Only to shirk.
Still, it wasn't long before
The work was done!
And we can see Nehemiah was proud
Of each and everyone!
It was a tremendous task
Yet most were eager to do what he asked.
Maybe what he did was the least
But they did have help from the high priest.
All in all it can be said
When God's people work together
They forge ahead!

NEHEMIAH 4

Though the enemy caused needless trouble
They still rebuilt that wall from discarded rubble.
Love made it first class merchandise!
And to them it would be twice as nice
As it was before! And the mockers
Would have to admit
They were jealous of it!
Instead they laughed and said those stones
Were as useless and brittle as dry bones.
It would take a major miracle
To eradicate the woes
That God's people have had to suffer daily

Comment on Nehemiah

At the hands of their foes.
But Sanballat and Tobiah could not stop
Nehemiah, who turned their viciousness
Into a total flop!

NEHEMIAH 5

Being a poor relative was no guarantee
That a man or his children would go free.
Because they had relatives greedy for gain
It wouldn't be long before the destitute
Would complain.
To the rich men, they were sheep to be shorn.
These rich men were the kind of people
Nehemiah held in scorn.
He made the greedy men restore
Property and children to those who were poor.
The rich had forgotten how it felt
To be enslaved
And were denying the poor the freedom
They craved.
Nehemiah charged no taxes and abused no one.
Surely God rewarded him for all the good
He had done!

NEHEMIAH 6

Sanballat, Tobiah, and Geshem devised a plot
Hoping to put Nehemiah on the spot!
They claimed Nehemiah's desire to be king
Was the reason
He was willing to involve others in his treason.
Notice they used a so-called message of God
To convince
Nehemiah all his labor made no sense.
And even Noadiah, the evil prophetess
Strived to keep Nehemiah under stress.
He and his people finished that wall anyway
Despite the frustrations they faced each day.
Actions based on faith make it clear
God's people WILL persevere!

NEHEMIAH 7

Jerusalem had to be governed by a man
Who would revere
Our Great God and who would not fear
To remember that noble cause
Encased, encouraged by God's great laws!
Then God told Nehemiah to register them
These men who had returned to Jerusalem!
These men who came with hope anew
Are also mentioned in Ezra chapter two.
They brought abundant supplies
Also silver and gold
Items for the temple, new and old!
All the people gave willingly of their wares.
We can discover-as well as they
Blessings come to the one who shares!

NEHEMIAH 8

It's meeting time when God's people
Gather again
To hear the Word of the Lord
And His purpose for each man.
They listened to those laws and wept
Mourning because of the many
They had not kept.
But Ezra told them it was no way to feel
For it was the time to celebrate
With a hardy meal!
The joy of the Lord was their strength
—ours, too!
It is a marvel and a wonder
What love for Him can do!
Why are we afraid to celebrate today
Rejoicing in that Holy Name
As we sing and pray?
Have we opted to make timidity our choice
Or, are we like those Israelis
Who knew the consequences of sin
And were too sad to rejoice?

The "I Love My Bible" Commentary

NEHEMIAH 9

Often the reading of the law
Causes people to weep.
Because the people strayed from holy paths
Their wounds were deep.
But the leaders tell them to stand
And praise the Lord and his glorious name.
Though He was greater
Than they could imagine
He loved them just the same.
Ezra confesses their sins
And reviews what God had done.
His faithfulness and His mercy
Could be equaled by no one.
Somehow their fervor to obey was fanned
When they had to admit their sins
Had caused them to be slaves
In their own land.

NEHEMIAH 10

God's presence is always needed
In order for the people to be inspired.
And if that *"bread of the presence"*
Was to be there, a donation was required.
Without it, people were prone to be lax
So Nehemiah instituted a temple tax.
People who love the Lord are willing to give!
And we know a benevolent heart inspires
A beautiful and a bountiful way to live!
   One other thing!
The Sabbath was *made for man*-made for man
To rest, to *wonder*, and to show reverence!
Otherwise we are incomplete as we would be
Should we have an arm or leg severanced!
And for them, keeping the laws of harvest
Was a necessary part
Of the marks of a loving and obedient heart!
It was a time of new oil and fresh wine
And a time when hearts were full of sunshine!

NEHEMIAH 11

There were many officials selected
To live in that city that was strongly protected.
Even volunteers came to stay
And to help finish that wall
That would hold their enemies at bay!
We can know God hears us when we call.
If we come *to our Jerusalem*
He keeps us safe within the *"wall!"*
Though their enemies resented
Those walls restraints
They were badly needed by the last of
The Old Testaments saints!

NEHEMIAH 12

The luckiest people ever known
Are those God has chosen for His own!
But the most fortunate of all
Were those who received the pastoral call!
These priests and Levites
Were given special rights!
Ezra and Nehemiah were among the few
Who were honor bound
To stand in God's presence on holy ground!
The day they finished the wall
And performed its dedication
Was not only a day of sharing
But of joyful recreation!
In those days the people gave willingly
To the Levites.
It was a time when religious fervor
Reached glorious new heights!
This was a time of gladness, of singing
Of continuous thanksgiving.
It was a time these people
Were oh so thankful they were living
Living to see the temple restored
Almost to its former beauty.
Indeed it was their most pleasant duty!

Comment on Nehemiah

NEHEMIAH   13

Foreigners who had cursed Israel
Were not allowed
To worship along with God's jubilant crowd.
Eliashib knew it was wrong to reserve
A room in the temple his friend didn't deserve.
Ehiashib was 'riding the fence'
And that created a fuss from either side
And he found himself with no place to hide.
And think of those saddle sores
From riding the fence with all those bores!
It seems holy living had been 'out of style'
And his 'holiness' was as fake as his smile.

He had a weakness he wouldn't confess
For a heathen in the temple made it
An unholy mess.
And we can see without a doubt
Nehemiah had to throw Tobias out!
He also demanded that the Jews
Preserve the Sabbath faithfully
And they were to cherish its sanctity.
Nehemiah consistently supplied
The people's needs
And he asked the Lord to remember
His good deeds!
I'm sure God did what he asked
For Nehemiah had been faithful to his task!

Two great men!

You might call them pillars of the community. That would fit! Truly they were. I doubt Jerusalem could have done much better had Moses and Aaron been there. Ezra and Nehemiah were men for that age for problems of that time. They were men who were faithful to God and faithful to their country as well. True it was not a country then, but the heart of the country was there.

Jerusalem!
Always in the heart of God!
It was known as the center of the earth to the Jews!
—if not actually, then emotionally—
Emotions have run heated there for centuries.
It has been a 'melt down' long enough!
Someday the King of the Ages will cool it down!
Someday the Jews will truly possess all the land that belongs to them!
Someday!
That is written!
That is decreed by God Himself!

The "I Love My Bible" Commentary
(The Book of Esther)

ESTHER 1

You'd think this king who ruled from India
To Ethiopia could decide
Who would rule his own home
Instead of asking Chauvinists whose
Opinions were 'cut and dried!'
Since they were his friends they would decide
In his behalf.
And naturally they would favor him
Because they were on his staff.
Vashti didn't have a chance
With this vulturous pact.
She had disobeyed them too
In her decision to react.
Why should she have to go with a bunch
Of drunks who were bull-headed
And why should she have to justify
Not doing what she dreaded?
Queen Vashti paid an awfully high price
When the king followed that bad advice!

ESTHER 2

Oh my! This king should have had
An endless case of the hives
Because this lustful stud
Ruined so many once hopeful lives.
Look at the many virgins
Who should have had homes of their own
Whose futures were perverted
Because of this sadistic sex maniac
Who just happened to sit on ths throne.
He threw out God's rule
That *one is a product of two*
And twisted countless lives
Before his live was through.
But good came out of bad this time
For Esther came along while her beauty
Was definitely in *high prime!*

God used her to set His people free
And once again proves *that* is His specialty!
She had already become the king's wife
When Mordecai was credited with saving
The king's life.
But that is not why she was there.
It was to be sure her people were treated
Just and fair!

ESTHER 3

Haman exulted in the reverence given him
As Prime Minister.
But he was furious when Mordecai
Refused to bow
Because Mordecai knew this man was sinister!
He devised a way to rid Persia of Mordecai
And all his relatives.
The edict he sent caused confusion and panic
Beyond the help of soothing sedatives.
What Haman had dictated
Was that the Jews would be killed
On the day he indicated.
He even offered twenty million dollars
To satisfy his urge
To ultimately destroy Mordecai in this
Unholy purge.
Think of the lives his destructive binge
Would touch
All because he despised one man so much!

ESTHER 4

Because Haman's edict was almost beyond
  belief
Mordecai donned mourning garments
And wailed loudly in total grief.
All the Jews through out the provinces wept.
Many lay in sackcloth and ashes
As their fear and misery swept!

Comment on Esther

Esther sent clothes to Mordecai who stood
Outside the palace gate
But his grief was so intense he refused
To cooperate.
He sent word for Esther to plead for the Jews
To appear before the king
But this was dangerous even for Esther
Unless it was a time the king would choose.
Esther sent word for Mordecai
To fast and pray.
And she swore to go in before Ahasuerus
Even if she died that very day!
She knew life was as fickle as the flicker
Of a candle
And facing the king without his invitation
Was almost more than she could handle!

ESTHER 5

What joy Esther must have felt
When she saw that shiny object
That the king held!
It was his golden scepter he extended
And much to her relief, her fears were ended!
He offered to give her anything she desired.
Surely his offer must have been truly inspired.
She offered a lively dinner for the king
And his friend.
What does Haman do?
He goes home and brags to his friends
About his good fortune and his esteem.
His head had grown much larger.
Of all those the king had honored
He thought he was the "cream!"
But this man whose plans were so deranged
Suddenly found his plans changed.
And, instead of Mordecai, he was hanged
Like a rag doll with no hope.
Now who was it who suffered
Because of his evil, cruel joke.
Yes, he would die instead of Mordecai!

ESTHER 6

King Ahasuerus had trouble sleeping
And decided to read awhile.
And there he found the report where Mordecai
Had saved his life-buried in the file.
Well, Haman would regret that report
And when he had to honor Mordecai
He took it like a spoiled-sport!
It took all the effort he could squeeze
To honor this man the king wished to please.
Haman had to wash the 'egg' off his face
And he went home in utter disgrace.
He went home bitter and pouting
After he and Mordecai took
What Haman considered an infamous outing!

ESTHER 7

How quickly this gourmet dinner turned sour
And we see this man quickly cower.
Imagine Haman's horror when he learned
Queen Esther was a Jew.
He stood there stripped of all hope
Knowing there was nothing he could do.
He fell at Esther's feet fearing foul play.
His fury had coiled like a snake and turned
On him that day.
He cringed when the king shouted
"What does he mean"
When he saw Haman prone beside the Queen.
We see how quickly retribution
Caught up with this man
Who had devised such an evil plan!

ESTHER 8

This great king loved Esther so much
No one in his kingdom was allowed to touch
Any of her people without reprimand.
And it would come from those joyful Jews

The "I Love My Bible" Commentary

Scattered throughout the land.
These Jews lives would not be lost.
They were permitted to protect themselves
At all cost.
So those Assyrians were filled with alarm
And they pretended to be Jews
In able to escape all harm.
Though this may be unkindly put
They found the shoe on the other foot!

ESTHER 9

Necessity caused the Assyrians to choose
Many friends among the Jews
And many rulers went out of their way
To help those they had wanted to slay.
Now, Mordecai was the man they wanted
To please.
This man of faith must have seemed
Just like Hercules!
He could not be destroyed
Because of the plan he and Esther deployed.
Because their plan was so successfully
Executed
The "Feast of Purim" was instituted!

It still reminds God's people they can depend
On the faithful protection
Of their dearest friend.
Why do you think the Jews are still around
In this day and age?
God is still protecting them
From their enemies' evil rage!

ESTHER 10

Ahasuerus had a mighty influence
On the Jews fate.
No wonder the Bible states
That this man was truly great.
It seems this man of tremendous power
Came on the scene at just the right hour!
Ahasuerus was deeply impressed
When Mordecai saved his life
And he loved the Jews simply because
He loved Esther, his wife!
Mordecai received great honor too.
This man is still spoken of as a righteous Jew!
He was a friend at court for his countrymen
Proving he was faithful to his own kin.
And Esther must not be overlooked.
Think of the great chance she took!

Esther was not a beauty whose beauty was skin deep.
A beautiful heart was behind all the promises she promised to keep!
Selfish beauty will have no place in the heavenly courts.
It is considered as unworthy as the hypocrisy it supports.
Why did the king love Esther so much?
It was her inner beauty with which he wanted to get in touch!
But Esther is remembered more for her faith than her beauty
because she, though fearful, remained true to her duty!
Was she great because she didn't want her people to fall?
No! She was great because she loved God most of all!
She chose to fast and pray
and she is lovingly remembered even to this day!
Beauty! Esther defines it!

And the king loved Esther and made her queen

Instead of Vashti (Esther 2:17 kjv)

Part Four

The Poetic Books

Job-Song of Solomon

The 23rd Psalm

The Lord is my Shepherd;
I shall not want.
He maketh me to lie down in green pastures;
He leadeth me beside the still waters.
He restoreth my soul;
He leadeth me in the paths of righteousness
for His Name's sake.
Yea though I walk through the valley
of the shadow of death,
I will fear no evil for thou art with me.
Thy rod and thy staff they comfort me.
Thou preparest a table before me in the presence of mine enemies;
Thou anointest my head with oil;
my cup runneth over.
Surely goodness and mercy shall follow me
all the days of my life
and I shall dwell in the house of the Lord
forever.

The "I Love My Bible" Commentary
(The Book of Job)

JOB 1

Was Satan a cry baby or wasn't he?
He cried to the Lord, "Job is righteous
Because you've always protected him
From me!"
Well Satan must have made a convincing case
Because this time God gave in
Mainly because He considered Job
The best of men!
And Satan had *a whale of a time*.
In fact what he did was definitely a crime!
But God set a limit on what Satan could do.
And He must have told Satan
"I'm not giving Job to you."
Still, Satan did his best
To see that Job had no rest.
Satan took everything Job had
Yet Job did not complain
And all of Satan's destruction did not cause
Job's faith to wane!

JOB 2

The old devil goes back to heaven
With a smirk on his face.
"Job is safe," he said, "because you've built
A hedge around his place."
"Okay" God said. "Cause him pain and strife
But you CANNOT take his life."
So why do we fear and tremble?
God protects us too
Even though we may have pain and heartache
Before our life is through.
But though the Lord's and Job's relationship
Was strongly bonded
When Job suffered personally
We see how he responded.
Even his friends joined him there
And they all wailed and cried in despair!

JOB 3

Job asked the impossible of God when he said
"Let the day of my birth be cursed
As if I were dead!"
God will never forget He has given life
To anyone,   and He would show Job
His brand of life can never be undone.
But Job's self pity sparks his regression
And he wearied his friends
In his unrealistic expression.
And he muttered-undoubtedly with a frown
"I was not fat and lazy
Yet the *trouble I feared* has struck me down!"
There you have it–the trouble Job feared
Sharpened the point on the devil's spear!

JOB 4

Eliphaz the Temanite said
"Job, what you say is far from right.
Shame on you Job for you said
We should be filled with trust
And to believe and obey God
Is definitely a must!
Now when trouble strikes you, you faint
And it's a sorry, helpless picture you paint."
He asks the question
"Is man more just than God, more pure?"
But we know if he was he'd not have
So many problems to endure!

JOB 5

What Eliphaz says is correct except for
The assumption
That Job 'took the wrong turn'
Somewhere at a lonely junction.
It was the opinion of this *purist*
That Job had become a sinful tourist!

Comment on Job

It must have been discouraging
When Job found out
His three noble 'friends' held him
In such questionable doubt.
And these men who were so genteel
Obviously didn't care how they made Job feel!
It seems Job got no respect
For their judgement of him
Was slanted and certainly incorrect!

JOB 6

Pain had eroded Job's patience
And he wanted to die.
"My sadness," he said, "is heavier than
The sand of a thousand sea shores
And that is why I cry!
There are no contented cows
And donkeys bray because the grass is gone.
God has deserted me
And I have no reason to carry on."
His friends, who should have comforted him,
Called him a crook
And they had proved as unreliable
As a meandering brook.
No wonder Job cried in desperation.
He had lived a life of dedication
But even his 'friends' assumed his guilt
And unjustly overlooked
The righteous reputation he had built.
Job said he would admit it if he had sinned
And though they pressed for his confession
He refused to bend!

JOB 7

This chapter contains
Some very foolish questions that Job asked.
Frustration made him forget
What God had done in the past.
"Oh God," he cried. "Am I some monster
That you should stalk?"
And he rambled on in his senseless talk.
He even went so far as to say
He hated his life.
Can you recall what he said to his wife?
He dreaded to see the sunset
And dared not look when the sun arose.
The longer one endures pain and suffering
The stronger his desperation grows!
His wife, his friends, and his pain
Worked on Job's mind
And almost drove him insane!

JOB 8

Bildad also showed hostility when he spoke.
He reminded Job that those who forget God
Have no hope.
There is much truth in what he said.
It is the main reason depression has spread.
For it still applies today
And only finds true healing when we pray.
Bildad's anger spread dangerous sparks
With his sharp tongue and irresponsible
    remarks.
But maybe man *can* determine
Whether or not his fate is good or rotten!
    God's Word says
The man who forgets God will be forgotten!

JOB 9

"Sure!" Job said.
"You're telling me nothing new!"
He knew arguing with God
Was something he couldn't do.
This God had stretched the heavens
And walked beside the sea.
Even if Job was sinless, he'd have
Not a single plea.
"Oh God! I have no mediator," Job cried

The "I Love My Bible" Commentary

"What will I do when I stand before my Judge
To be sentenced and tried?"
And man echoes that question
Down through each age
As he falters and stumbles across
Life's lonely stage.

JOB 10

It seems Job-in sorrow-strains
To seek the reason why confusion reigns.
He is almost belligerent in his self pity
And he repeatedly blames God for his misery!
It is a miracle Job was spared
After accusing God that He had never cared.
In fact he accused God of saving him
So he could destroy him if he sinned
Daring to form a breach
He, himself, could never mend!
Foolish accusations are rampant today
And untrusting hearts hold God at bay.
Blaming God for trouble is purely asinine
And as proof
Today's anarchy is a definite sign.
Man definitely plays the fool
When he refuses to put himself
Under God's righteous and loving rule!
We think we have *the right stuff*
But our righteousness is never good enough!

JOB 11

Zophar thinks Job was abhorrent
And wishes someone would stop
Job's wordy torrent!
He implies that Job 'stinks'
And he wishes God would tell Job
What HE thinks!
These so-called well wishers
Did not wish Job well
And as time went by
Their disgust for Job seemed to swell.
But verses thirteen through nineteen
Contain good news
Even though Zophar seems to condemn
And confuse.
He implies that those who are holy
Can make a welcome trade
And God will see to it His people
Can lie down unafraid.
Zophar says our troubles will be in the past
When we trust God at last.
Well, why not trust Him first?
Then our souls would never thirst!
But I think the longer Job's friends stayed
The further his faith strayed.
Read Job to see what I mean.
It looks to me like their faith was very lean.

JOB 12

What are good friends for?
Is this group a good example?"
Job seemed to be an injured man
On whom they could trample!
And all of them had questions
They failed to reconcile
Nor could they come up with any answers
Job could consider vaguely worthwhile.
Their foolish accusations made Job wonder
Had they come to help *or plow him under!*
His integrity was foolishly questioned
By his three friends
Who must have considered their judgement
A way to merely tie up a few loose ends.
He responds bitterly by saying,
"You must think wisdom will die with you!
When you discover God knows
What you are saying, what will you do?"
Job knew God was full of power and might
And man stumbled in his own feeble light

Comment on Job

He must have wished his friends
Would leave him alone
Or perhaps that the one *without* sin
Would dare cast the first stone
For like three buzzards sitting on a fence
Waiting for rigor mortis
Job's three '*friendly*' vultures
Were cruel, judgmental, and heartless!
They assumed he was evil
Because only the evil suffered!
Wasn't that so?
Had Job been innocent, they thought
This punishment from God
Would have been buffered!
They were the kind of friends
We don't need
And they came to Job with all speed!
    For what?
To tear him apart
When he was torn apart already
Left with a broken heart?
Like Job said
These three friends groped in the dark
And their so-called wisdom
Left them without a single spark!

JOB 13

Job considered his friends
To be physicians of no value!
"I'm not stupid," he said.
"I know as much as each of you."
And he knew the paths of knowledge
They had missed
And he warned them God's great truths
Were not given for them to twist.
He felt it was his turn to speak
And spoke of values they should seek.
But he foolishly asked why his Lord
Had turned away
And he could not understand
The terrible suffering he had to face each day.
Job must have been thin and pale
For he complained he felt so frail.
He was sure he'd given God his best
And now pleads for a little rest!
He hurt so bad he even pled
"Lord, plant me somewhere among the dead!"
But though his spirit was heavy and dark
He was able to make a memorable remark.
He told his friends they didn't have a case
Since their defense of God
Was as fragile as an useless clay vase.

JOB 14

Job asks God how can He demand purity
Of one born impure.
Job had looked at his *physical heritage*
And obviously felt insecure.
He knew he could never withstand
The Lord's scrutiny.
Yet he, and his friends questions
Almost bordered on spiritual mutiny!
Why should we question God when we are
    depressed?
Is it because our faith suffers when we are
    stressed?
Certainly foolish questions do nothing
To help our belief
And when we dwell on pain and misery
We can expect no relief.
Job makes it plain
He does not understand his pain.
But we who live in this day
Often question our pain in the same way!
The devil is the evil culprit
When it comes to doubt and fear.
He seems to push us away from God
Just at the time we need Him near!
So what can the answer be?
What is it that we need to see?
It is our God only does good to you and me!

The "I Love My Bible" Commentary

JOB 15

Eliphaz asks, "Have you no fear of God
No reverence?"
He must have known bitterness
Creates in us, a very painful severance.
Job, because of his pain, thought
God had left him and didn't care.
And, because he considered himself righteous
He felt God was being grossly unfair.
But Eliphaz told Job he was corrupt.
He had feigned kindness to Job
But continues to be abrupt.
To some extent, he was right
In what he was saying.
Instead of complaining, Job's best hope
Was down on his knees praying!
And the best advice Eliphaz gives
Is money bewitches
And no man-not even Job
-should trust in his riches!

JOB 16

Job thought his friends had an endless supply
Of foolish words
And he practically implied what they said
Was strictly *for the birds!*
He said if they were him, he'd try
To comfort them
But all their criticisms had been
A sermonizing scam.
Their counsel was to have been like
Gentle winds, pure and fresh.
Then Job would not have accused them
Of angrily tearing at his flesh.
But Job was smart enough to know
He had an Advocate on high
Who would be his defender
When it came his time to die
As he traveled that road of no return.

Meanwhile those *comforters with gaping jaws*
Had so very much to learn
For they had not encouraged him
As he thought they must
And because of them all his hopes
Lay buried in the dust!

JOB 17

Job was sick and near to death.
No wonder he found it hard to be brave!
And his friends who came to help him
Did nothing but rant and rave.
Job began to believe no one believed in him.
Now those who thought him guilty
Took happier days and turned them grim!
"My good days are in the past," he said
"And all I do is grieve."
And he wished those friends of his
Would hurry up and leave.
"Where is my hope?" Job asked.
Heshuddered to think all his good times
Were now in the past.
It seemed to Job, *He who is mighty to save*
Had abandoned him to a lonely grave.

JOB 18

I think if I had friends like Job, I'd tell them
"Go on back."
"If you don't believe in me, hit the road, Jack!"
It seems their accusations became more bold
And Job thought *that trash* was getting old.
No wonder Job grows more discouraged
As he listens to the remarks Bildad makes.
Why would he say there is a booby-trap
In every path Job takes?
Instead of their words building their friendship
    stronger
They made Job wish they would absolutely
Stay no longer!

Comment on Job

It seems their good intentions
Had turned into a curse.
Could any enemy of Job's have acted worse?
Don't think a sharp tongue
Can't destroy a life.
It can be deadlier
Than any fully sharpened knife!

JOB 19

If Job had said nothing more than he said
In verse twenty five
He would still have witnessed
That our Heavenly Father is very much alive!
"I *know* my Redeemer lives," he said,
"And will stand on this earth
And even though this body decays
I'll be regenerated as one in new birth!"
He added he wouldn't be in danger
For he was a friend of God
Who would never see him as a stranger!
He'd always found God was a place to hide.
The "Rock of Ages" would stand by his side!
If I don't comment on what comes
Before or after
Its because I find no greater confession
In any other verses of this chapter!

JOB 20

Zophar would give his advice freely.
He thought he knew all the answers!
But did he really?
If Job expected a gentle answer
His hopes would drop
For he found Zophar's innuendoes
Would not pause nor stop.
Why did these men automatically think
Job was so wicked his sins would bring him
To this disastrous brink?
Had they been looking for sin in Job so long

The hate in their hearts had actually grown
That strong?
How could Job justify himself against
Such rationale?
Instead of encouragement that gives a glow
Their faces held a vengeful scowl!

JOB 21

"Listen to me speak," says Job
"And afterwards mock on!
I am complaining about God
So no wonder I moan!"
Job knew the wicked lived to a ripe old age
Even though they mocked God in jestful rage.
"Who is almighty God?" They would fuss.
"And what does He think He can do to us?"
Job saw their irreverence and would say
God would not bother them
Even though they mocked Him day after day.
Yet Job would answer his own doubts
When he said
"The wicked will have nothing to enjoy
When he lies among the dead."
He also thought his friends whole premise
Was decisively wrong
Even though thy claimed
Their case against Job was strong!

JOB 22

The false accusations continue to fly
And Job's friends still refuse to listen
To his anxious reply.
When man is too opinionated to think
He causes the faith of others to shrink.
It is as if Eliphaz thinks he is speaking
In God's place and has a right to say
Job was so horribly wicked
He had lost his right to pray.
But Eliphaz was smart enough to exclaim

The "I Love My Bible" Commentary

If Job would only trust in God
He would know no shame!
God will save the humble with the light
Of His glory
And that is the basis for every Bible story!

JOB 23

Job knew God would ease his pain
Yet though he sought the Lord
It seemed to be in vain.
If Job's bank account had matched his ego
In these times of old
It would be safe to say
His worth was as matchless as solid gold!
Though Job boasted of his innocence
It was to 'thin air'
For those who listen had already passed
Judgements biased and unfair.
Job knew for sure he had not strayed
From his Dearest Friend
But he was surrounded by a terrible darkness
He could not comprehend.
Still he knew God would listen with sympathy
For Job's heart was NOT full of iniquity!
His friends might think he was deranged
But God's opinion of him had not changed!
And though their rage for him had boiled
God's love for him remained unspoiled!

JOB 24

God's court was closed and Job waited
In vain.
At least that was his belief and it brought
Him pain.
He felt the wicked were not acquainted
With the 'Light!'
Therefore they would continue to commit
Adultery, robbery and murder through out
The night!
But no matter the crimes those wicked men
Had rehearsed
Everything they did and everything they had
Would be cursed.
God would *never* help those men
Who were so steeped in deadly sin.
Job knew it seemed God preserved
Those who rejoiced in iniquity.
But why accuse God of a deed
So far beneath His dignity?
Our God is righteous and fair.
He has said He will NOT place the wicked
Under His loving care!

JOB 25

Bildad asked Job if anyone could brag
That he was clean.
When he said God was powerful and dreadful
He seemed to imply that God was mean
But that wasn't the case at all.
He knew the man who stood in opposition
To the Lord was headed for a fall!
The moon and stars were as nothing
When compared to the Lord
And man was as lowly as a worm buried
In his own back yard.
What else could man be in God's sight?
God is *never* wrong and man is *seldom* right!
God rules over an angelic host
And it is only in our God
That man can ever boast!

JOB 26

If his friends words were a deadly virus
Sent to punish wrong
I'm surprised that Job lived this long!
He disgustedly ridiculed their comments.
After all those empty words
He was right to think they had no sense!

Comment on Job

He resented their charge that he had lived
In iniquity
And he replied facetiously
"How you have enlightened my stupidity!"
He lists mighty things the Lord has done
    yet says they are
"Merely a whisper of His power!"
This God who no one can defeat
Will always be *Heaven's man of the hour!*
Yet few seem to understand
This world is still under His command!

JOB 27

Job begins his longest defense when he replies
"My lips shall speak no evil, my tongue
Shall tell no lies!"
He adds his conscience is clear
But those who are wicked will live in fear.
The wicked still has not learned
How much he lacks.
His 'house' is still as fragile as a spider web
And still as full of cracks!
Job promises the wicked will live to see
Others boo him into eternity.
The money he accumulated
Will do him no good
For he deliberately failed
To do what he should.
Not good news for the news is sad.
To have so much and then to lose
Every thing he had!

JOB 28

Job continues to say man has gained wisdom
But his wisdom is incomplete.
Man must learn to seek God's wisdom
To be able to stand on his own two feet.
Sad to say, most men do not know
If they lack wisdom

There is really only one place to go!
This wisdom Job is speaking of
Is knowledge based on God's power
And wisdom derived from God's love!
The one who wants to go to the head
Of the class
In the many tests of life, will fail or pass
Depending what he is willing to learn.
Will *our* wisdom stand God's test
Or will it burn?
And God has been trying to tell us
From time primeval
It takes His wisdom to forsake evil!

JOB 29

According to this chapter Job felt
He was full of good deeds
Never failing to supply widows and orphans
Their basic needs.
He had never expected this much strife
After having lived such a good life.
It seems Job trusted in *his* goodness
And would gripe instead of pray
And so there were many words of doubt
Job felt compelled to say.
When he experienced the dubious reward
Of one who never strays
He earnestly longed *for the good old days!*
He knew the Lord had been by his side
For he was successful at everything he tried!
He felt he was so good he'd earned the reward
Of the peaceful life given him by the Lord.

JOB 30

Job had been faithful but men of no reputation
Ridiculed this man.
These men blocked his path no matter
Which direction he ran.
He couldn't understand why men of low degree

The "I Love My Bible" Commentary

Would be allowed to place his life
In such jeopardy.
He reaffirms his righteousness
Yet his life is full of terror
Instead of peaceful bliss.
In place of respect Job had been scorned.
His goodness now seemed futile.
No wonder he mourned!
Job's friends talked too much and said too little
For their mouths were untamed
And their hearts were brittle.
These men who were known to be civil
Spent needless hours spouting useless drivel!

JOB 31

Job ends his defense with a chapter of ifs
And he tries to tell his friends his goodness
Has not been tales of untruthful myths.
He asks, "Do you want me to tear at my
Gut feelings and lay my wounded soul bare?
Do you think I should share my pain with you
When I know you don't even care?"
Maybe he didn't ask the above but if he had
Would they have changed their attitudes.
Possibly not because they were impressed
With their own goodness to the point
Of being prudes.
Narrow minded people seldom extend
A helping hand.
It is as if their actions
Are not under their command.
Perhaps they could not realize
They had been unkind
For that kind of knowledge
Takes a loving heart and an open mind!
Job was getting nowhere though he had talked
Until he was getting hoarse
For words bounce off a concrete block-head
As a matter of course.
Job's aching body had driven him
Almost to oblivion.
Now he would be driven further because
Of a new man's (Elihu) opinion.
Though Job's reputation had been great
He is being treated as a man of low estate!
It seems each man has shown how little
He knows
But except for Elihu, their questions of Job
Are coming to a close.
The lessons we should learn form them
Is though we question a man's intentions
And hold his integrity in doubt
It displeases the Lord for us to harangue
A fellow human when he's down and out!

Job 32

They were so angry they wouldn't
Answer Job anymore.
These self-righteous dignitaries
Failed to realize they didn't know the score!
And-had Job known they would be so rude
He would have said,
"Stay home. I prefer to suffer in solitude!"
Now we hear from a young 'upstart'
And we wonder where he learned his trade.
Surely it wasn't from the remarks
Job and his friends had made!
He did NOT approve of what these men said.
And he seems to shudder as he says
"Let me be frank lest God strike me dead!"
He added man need not be old to be wise.
This young man felt that anytime God gave
Wisdom it was His greatest prize!

JOB 33

Again we see God does not wait until
We are old to make us wise
Regardless of how we are seen
In other people's eyes.

Comment on Job

Elihu offered Job wisdom he hoped
Job would not reject.
In a way he was timid
And longed for Job's respect.
He must have walked close to *'The Father'*
For Elihu knew what God did
And it was important to him to explain
That God's deeds were never hid!
Sometimes the Lord will speak to us
In visions and dreams
Perhaps to illustrate that trouble
Is not what it seems.
Yet Elihu was afraid Job would think
He had no sense
And because of his age
He felt Job would be hard to convince.

JOB 34

Must God tailor His justice to give justice due?
Elihu seems to ask, "Should God alter
His judgements just to satisfy you?"
There are three choices he says we can make
    the food we eat
    the sounds we hear
    and the paths we choose to take!
    Job must have thought,
"Such wisdom this young one has
More than Bildad, Zophar, or even Eliphaz!"
There's no greater truth than found here.
Therefore we can freely live without fear!
We still need men who are faithful and true
So God sends us men like Elihu!

JOB 35

Elihu claims Job has a chronic complaint.
Job says he is without sin
Yet he is considered to be no saint!
Elihu asks Job if Job did sin
Would God be dethroned
Or would it cause God to lose all he owned?
Would God need Job's goodness
To give Him a lift
Or if Job was good, would it be a gift?
Through it all Elihu tries to bring out
Man should never live in fear and doubt.
Though God could be higher than distant skies
He will still hear His people's cries!

Job 36

Elihu states he does not have to defend
What God has done.
"God is almighty," he said, "yet does not
Despise anyone!"
He speaks of God's judgement but knows
Of God's loving trait
And of how it pleases Him
For His people to go 'straight!'
But man calls this earth God's school
Of hard knocks
Not realizing he has God's protection
Or the many troubles our Lord blocks!
Elihu was wrong in thinking he knew
All God had done.
Still he was right when he said
"God doesn't have to answer to anyone!"
Though man sees this earth as a school
Of hard knocks, His 'graduation' day
Will be one he cheers
And he won't have to worry
When the judgement day appears!

Job 37

Though Elihu is wise, he is almost inept
In describing all the promises God has kept.
God had promised mercy from the beginning.
The man who questions God
Find its his own web he is spinning.
Man's doubt creates his own travesty.

The "I Love My Bible" Commentary

"Thunder," Elihu says, "echoes the voice
Of God's majesty!"
What God wants has not changed in this day
-in this hour.
God wants man to comprehend
The greatness of His power!
Elihu had looked deep into the heart of God
And liked what he saw
And it had been the love and beauty of God
This verbal artist attempted to draw!
He could not understand why Job
And his friends would fuss.
In the final analysis he knew, God is so
Merciful and just, He will not destroy us!

JOB 38

Hold on, Job!
You had thought the interview was over
And it set your soul humming.
Now the Supreme Commander
Stands in the ball court
And there are more questions forthcoming
God asks Job why he uses his ignorance
To deny God's providence
And Job stood there helpless without
A word of defense.
God hit a 'home run' that put Him
Way out front
While Job stood embarrassed at home plate
Ashamed because he couldn't even 'bunt!'
He must have thought, "well shut my mouth!
I have been swinging at *foul balls*
When I should have been heading south!"
If he ran 'with the ball' at all
He must have been running slow
For his friends thought his heavenly
Batting average was way too low.
But God took matters in His own hands
When he decided to remedy *that*
And He, Himself, put Job 'up to bat!'

JOB 39

God is speaking of some of the wonders
Of His creation, some we don't understand
-how an ostrich runs so fast, and a horse's
Willingness to move at his rider's command.
God asks Job if he commands the eagle
To make her nest
In the mountains high above the rest.
And God emphasizes
How high the eagle rises.
(And though we have satellites in the skies
God still determines how high we can rise.)
The eagle, the ostrich, and others traits
Are attributed to Him.
How about God's other creations
On which man's questions stem?
When man thinks he knows the answer
-the answer changes.
Will we ever be able to understand
How far and how vast God's wisdom ranges?

JOB 40

Job, who had wanted to meet God face to face
Felt tremors he couldn't describe!
Now he had what he wanted, and the curtains
Of heaven had been drawn aside.
Job had talked about God's love and grace
But Job knew this time, God had come
To put him *in his place!*
During his pain he had gotten out of touch
And when he met God face to face
He had to say as much.
He could not answer even
One of the questions God had asked.
This man of wisdom found it to be
Way too big a task!
There was much about God Job didn't know
And God made it a point to tell him so.
God reminded Job of His great power

Comment on Job

And He reminded Job He did all things well!
And God dramatically brought Job out
Of his self-pity shell!

JOB 41

It may seem God asked
Strange questionsof Job.
And it may seem to be an unnecessary probe.
But in all those questions God had posed
It was a hint of His powers
He wanted disclosed.
This interview was not exactly what Job
Wanted it to be
For the Lords asked him,
"Who can stand before me?"
Job had to hang his head in shame
For he had failed to glorify God's holy name.
Job stood on ground dangerously unsteady.
Who could improve on God?
He was(and is)perfect already!
Job learned God's questions can be very astute
And awfully hard
And how we answer them in voice or action
Can appear on our final report card.
And no matter how many diplomas we hold
We will still be judged by how we respond
To the sweetest story ever told!

JOB 42

Job's words had sunk
To such a derogatory dimension
God had used a whirlwind to get his attention.
Yet God made allowances for Job
For Job had been in pain
A pain so severe, it almost drove him insane.
God tells Job's friends they have been wrong.
Even though Job had complained
God still considered his faith to be strong.
These judgmental people must make amends
And then when Job prays for them
His suffering ends!
God restores his health
And then doubles his wealth!
Job's friends only brought him strife.
Now God comes to reaffirm
His love takes the IF out of life!

If Job seems to be boring and depressing it is merely because man's wisdom is not deep enough to dig to the bottom of God's greatness nor can he search the highest heavens to find the end of it! Therefore man continues to question God. The more we learn the less we realize how little we know. Paul once said we will know 'completely. (Read 1st Corinthians chapter13). For me, to know God is not to know wisdom but to know love in its fullness. For love extends far beyond wisdom. Wisdom tells us how, but love says, "Go for it!" Wisdom is questions and answers entwined like a coiled rope and must be untangled to separate the one from the other. Where there is wisdom there will always be questions and, of course, wisdom will eventually find the answers. But where there is love we feel no need for questions. Perfect love casts out fear and, believe me, fear is based on questions. Why did I do that? What's going to happen next? What does tomorrow hold? Why am I here? So many questions for which we don't seem to have the answers. John said(in1st John 3:2)....when we see Him we shall be like Him for we shall see Him as He is! What an incredible statement this loving apostle makes!   Like Christ!
No more questions! Ever!

The "I Love My Bible" Commentary
The Book of Psalms
(Many written by the "sweet psalmist of Israel")

PSALMS 1

A tree by the river reaches
as far below ground as above
and the rustling of its leaves
whisper softly of God's love!
A man who follows godly advice
will be as 'tall' as that tree
and if he avoids the paths of sinners
his spirit will be free!
It is almost indescribable
how much he benefits
if He refuses to sit
where the scornful sits.
David starts the Psalms
with a 'Grand Slam'
and almost succeeds in creating
a celestial traffic jam!
He seems to create so much hope
for the reason
he is afraid holiness
will go out of season!
He chose this beautiful imagery
as a way to begin
because he wanted the book
of Psalms
to inspire all men!

PSALMS 2

Some men will shake their fists at God
Until they have no fists to shake.
And many will turn away from God
As long as they have the choice to make.
They will never tremble
Until life becomes a dead end street
And they will never admit God's great power
Until they face their last defeat.
Man will hold to this point of view
Because he prefers to think all God's Words
Will be proved untrue.
David knew those kind of man well
And-in effect-he said, they will
Motor-mouth their way to hell!
They will be destroyed by the
Ambivalent weapon of their own anarchy
Because they refuse to obey
Our Heavenly Monarchy!
But those who trust in God will live to see
The breathless panorama of eternity!

PSALMS 3

Where should we go when in trouble or afraid?
Do we think about the promises of protection
That our Lord has made?
David did! The Lord was his shield!
No matter how many arrows flew
He could be safe even in an open field!
Many sought to harm him, men full of hate
Because they wanted his position
As the regal head of state!
David always sought the Lord when he cried
And was never disappointed when the Lord
 replied!
In this Psalms we see our Great Artist paints
A beautiful picture of salvation for His saints!

PSALMS 4

Verse one begins with a terrific declaration!
Perfection is the epitome of salvation!
And we must pray, "Oh Lord help us realize
It is your salvation that makes us righteous
In your eyes!"
It is the Lord who sets the redeemed apart.
When I have faith I have a special peace
In my heart!

Comment on Psalms

We'll walk in the light of his love
Where he loves for us to be
Nothing on this earth can be so heavenly
Or fill us so full of mirth
As to walk with the Lord of all the earth!
David's hope is wrapped up in this fact.
When God's people cry *He will act!*

PSALMS 5

David knew to whom he should pray.
Therefore he expected God's help every day.
God's love is a shield no nuclear bomb
    can penetrate.
He gives peace that cannot be disturbed
No matter how many missiles
The enemy might activate!
And inner turmoil cannot rob me of peace.
God's safety valve of love gives me release!
I'm not attempting to ridicule the doubters.
I'm trying to encourage the saints!
God's own people must not listen
To doubters complaints.
No matter what we've done
Or what we've been
God will help us as we open our hearts
And He will let the fresh air of His spirit in!

PSALMS 6

"Oh come on, Lord and make me well.
In your kindness save me.
My sickness is a painful kind of hell
And it is hard to react bravely."
How many times has the Lord heard that
And cooled a fevered brow
Even as we wonder how much sickness
God will allow?
And if David thought he was disturbed
He should have lived today.
Talk about gloom and apprehension!
His must have been child's play.
But he knew that stress would age him
For he says his enemies had turned
His hair gray and caused his eyes to dim.
He warns those evil men to leave him alone.
God would strip them down *to the bone!*
A look at any Psalms will tell us so.
God protects us wherever we go!

PSALMS 7

If we ever needed God, we need Him now!
Still it seems those who reject Him
Appear to prosper anyhow.
It looks as if the more wicked man becomes
The more he makes
Though he blasphemes this God he forsakes.
He does not believe God is angry
With the wicked every day
So he takes the chance of being crumbled
As easily as clay.
Because he can't see God
He thinks God can't see him
And he walks the crest of despair
Dangerously close to the rim.
David warns the wicked
How just God's judgments are
And how deadly it is to turn from God
To wander dangerously afar!

PSALMS 8

The glory and majesty of our God fills the air.
How perfectly the earth is balanced
Because His power is everywhere!
And we should be like those little children
    who represent
How simplistically easy it is to be spiritually
    content!
God gives wisdom in response to our praises
And it shows on His happy children's faces!

The "I Love My Bible" Commentary

May the Lord give us faith like David had
And preserve us from those who are bad!
It was because he trusted God
That David's hopes were raised.
Oh how much he loved this God he praised!
The beauty hidden in this story
Is David knew we are made for God's glory.
Though He made us a lower than the angels
What little we lack
We'll receive when we see Him
And he gives us our real lives back!

PSALMS 9

Oh it sets my heart pounding
like the waves upon the shore
to know I love
"The Father"
yet to know He loves me
much
much more!
And I know, like David
that hope eternal flares
like an open flame
when God's people
live in such a way
as to glorify His Name!
David could never praise God enough
and he didn't have to fear
his enemies.
His God could be tough!
The enemy would stumble
into his own pitfall
and those who challenge God
just butt their heads
against the wall!
So, if we ever tremble
let us tremble for the wicked
who draw near
for our God will show them
What it is to fear.
But talk about our hearts pounding!
Just wait until we hear
God's mighty trumpet sounding!

PSALMS 10

I think sometimes we take God for granted
And think He should be *on call*
And I occasionally wonder if God thinks
His people have too much *gall!*
We think He should answer before we ask
And we never stop to wonder
About the hostility we mask.
Who are our enemies anyway?
Could they be of our own making?
Could they be the needy people
We, ourselves, have been forsaking?
Sure–there are people who plunder the poor
Our own government for example
Who creates loopholes for those with ample!
When David described the wicked
He included the haughty and the proud
Let us examine ourselves and like David
Stay away from that crowd!
But not to act could also be an admission
    of guilt
That we have not walked that road of love
Our precious Lord has built!
David knew God helps the humble
But He uses our hearts, our hands
And we need to remind ourselves
Love is one of His greatest commands!
If we truly love others we won't waste time
Praying for selfish things.
Helping others will help us discover
The perfect peace His presence brings!

PSALMS 11

David asks, "Why should I play *hide and seek*?
Did not God say He would protect the meek?"

Comment on Psalms

We also live in a time when law and order
Have seemed to collapse
But running from trouble
Only binds us tighter in trouble traps!
But wait!
God is still in His Holy Temple
And He still rules!
He still watches the proceedings on earth
And he will judge the evil, and greedy fools.
But He puts BOTH the righteous
And the wicked to the test.
Just being God's people is not enough for Him.
We must do our best!
Then others will know we are heaven sent
And will also learn to love this Holy God
We so willingly represent!

PSALMS 12

We still ask the question David asked
Almost in desperation.
Then he added, "everyone deceives
And flatters and lies" and that will lead
Us to a hopeless situation!
But our Lord speaks no careless word.
All He speaks is purest truth
Like silver seven times stirred!
Where can dependable men be found?
David knew it was near the Lord
Where they stood on holy ground!
But many lie to their hearts content.
Those men walk downwind
Of an unholy scent.
Vileness, on tv, in movies, and personally
Is praised by many throughout this land.
Yet we know such approval is contrary
To our Holy God's command.
Many say we have new guidelines to follow
As they walk down lanes in a vapid hollow.
These new 'guidelines'-do we feel empty, lost?
Away from God-ah, that's way too high a cost!

PSALMS 13

Strange!
When times are bad we think The Lord
Has turned away.
But to say He has-is an insolent way to pray.
We do feel alone when our faith turns sour
And fail to realize it is but a dainty flower!
Faith must look into the sunshine
Though sometimes watered by tears
And it must be nuzzled and nurtured
In order to grow through the years!
Then we won't ask for the 'Light'
For the 'Light' will live within
And then we won't be disadvantaged
By fear of evil men.
Even though David sunk to depths of despair
His special kind of faith was still very rare!
He was blessed and protected by the Lord.
So am I!
Like David, I can say He answers when I cry!

PSALMS 14

The man who tells himself there is no God
Lives in the eye of a hurricane.
It is a deadly circle in which
He has no place to run.
And he who feels there is no God
Has no urge to pray.
He has no inner strength
And he weakens day by day.
The Lord checks us out to see if we believe.
It is a truth beyond the 'earthbound' ability
Of unbelievers to conceive.
David said such people are not good.
Not even one!
"Terror will grip them," he says, "for our Lord
Sees what they have done!"
And we know that God knows every thing
That goes on under the stars *and* the sun!

The "I Love My Bible" Commentary

But there is hope for God's people.
Don't give up!
We need to remember how full the Lord
Filled David's cup!
What joy there will be in that final hour
When God saves His people
By His glorious power!

PSALMS 15

The righteous man is described.
He is like a rare, costly, beautiful jewel
And he has nothing to fear!
He is one who leads a blameless life
And is one who is truly sincere!
A man who strives to live in the 'spotlight'
Should heed God's definition of doing right.
We know it is easier to *stand tall*
When one's conscience is clear!
That man shall stand firm forever
For he knows our God is near.
If we would allow this chapter
To sink deep into our souls
Then there would be no Christians
Who would fail to meet their goals!

PSALMS 16

This chapter is fantastic!
It shows us all who the true nobility are!
And its not especially the rich, or athletic
Or even the world's most famous star.
The true nobility are those who are godly
In the Lord's eyes.
It is those who consider our Lord
To be their greatest friend and dearest prize!
Exuberance could barely describe
David's state of mind.
It is as if he thinks our Heavenly Father
Is more brilliant than all the stars
That have ever shined.!

And a constant focus on the Lord
Keeps us from falling.
For He has promised He will
Listen closely to hear us calling!
Life without God is like a song
That is tuneless and strident
But He gives His people a melody
That is softly and beautifully vibrant!
And God reserves a special sunrise
For those who love to be
In the presence of His great glory
Loved and safe constantly!

PSALMS 17

There is a hot line to heaven
for those who are pure and good!
David used it often!
But the pleas he made were not necessary
to make God's heart soften!
How eloquently David would hallow
this precious God
who hid David in His shadow!
The most beautiful pictures
of a relationship
between the human and Divine
have been painted with flair
in this priceless book of 'sunshine!'
David triumphed
through his knowledge
of God's grace
and his ultimate satisfaction
would be to see God
face to face!

PSALMS 18

David was surrounded by floods of ungodliness
And he was so weak.
He had treated his enemies with gentleness
And most of them knew he was meek!

Comment on Psalms

His enemies had been so heartless
David recoiled in shock
But even in his desperation
He remembered to "hide behind his Rock!"
"God is perfect," he said, "and true."
He was David's Savior.
There was *nothing* He couldn't do!
God is a shield to hide behind.
He is gentle when others are unkind.
This is the God David knew.
This is the God I present to you!

PSALMS 19

We cannot close our eyes
To God's testimony twinkling in the skies!
We cannot help but marvel
At how graceful and effortless an eagle flies!
We cannot gaze at the sun
Without feeling the heat it gives
And we do not doubt the proclamation
That our precious Savior lives!
His laws support the earth
And His laws make us wise!
His laws give joy and light and more
Than our minds can surmise!
If only we would remember
They are more desirable than silver or gold
We would not have so many sins
To grieve us when we grow old.
And if only we would remember
To obey Him as time goes by,
Our thoughts, words, and deeds
Would give us no reason to cry!
Our hearts would rise
Higher than the eagle flies
And the joy we would feel
Would reflect in the twinkle in our eyes!
We'd not close our hearts
To God's declaration
That He WILL provide us eternal salvation!

God save the king–and the beggar and the
Lonely child on the street.
God help us give His blessing
To all His children we chance to meet.
May He grant our hearts's desire
And may He be the desire of every heart!
He has this desire–that we worship Him
Whether at church or if we are apart.
    God save the king?
        He IS the King!
-has been through ages past
And He will greet us lovingly
When we see Him at last!
We will see Him as He is-this Great King
Then our God will no longer be a mystery.
He is the Alpha and Omega
The greatest King in all history!

PSALMS 21

A glimpse of eternity is open to all who read
Verses one through seven.
Rewards and eternal happiness await us
Who set our hopes on heaven!
But heaven's greatest joy
Is the joy of God's presence.
This joy that is beyond belief
Is full of a holy fragrant essence!
The joy He gives is just ONE reward
That comes from daily walking with our Lord!

PSALMS 22

David was surrounded by those who wanted
To shed his blood.
His faith was on a roller -coaster ride
And hit bottom with a thud!
But, despite his dire circumstances
He looked forward to the cross
Where he knew our Lord and Savior
Would suffer only temporary loss.

The "I Love My Bible" Commentary

This God would rescue him when he cried
And he felt like a child–safe and satisfied!
He proclaimed His God would not walk away.
He knew the Lord walked with him each day.
So many generations have come and gone
Yet the hope of the humble still lives on!
This God David described is always the same.
And those who seek the Lord
Will live eternally to praise His name!

PSALMS 23

This gentle shepherd knew a Shepherd
more gracious than he.
This gentle shepherd knew our God
was much greater
than he could ever be!
This gentle shepherd held lambs
in his arms
but God holds His lambs
in His heart!
On earth, He gives peace in the valley.
For me, He gives peace
in His arms,
peace that will never depart!
My gentle Shepherd
holds me close and protects me
from all life's storms!
Great is my Shepherd!
Great is His love!
It is as if I'm already
living in heaven above.
The Lord leads me through the valley.
Goodness and mercy walk behind.
My Shepherd, my gentle Shepherd
will never be unkind!
And David, who had carried
an injured lamb close to his heart
knew all about
God's loving care!

And when David felt like
a helpless lamb
he knew his Great Shepherd
would always be there!
God would be more protective
than he had been
would shelter him from wicked men!
The Lord would dress his wounds
anoint him with oil
and would strengthen him
for daily toil!
And as he sought the lamb
that strayed
he sensed his love was just a shadow
of a bond <u>no</u> one could sever.
From a boy this gentle shepherd knew
he would dwell in the
House of the Lord
forever and forever!

PSALMS 24

Open up oh ancient gates!
The King of Glory is coming home!
God had gone nowhere, but just maybe it was
An invitation to those who had chosen to roam!
But we wonder if God had searched the earth
And if He did, did He ever find
Just how many people actually possessed
A loving heart and a willing mind?
David loved the Lord because he knew
Life without God was hopeless, and askew!
David also knew God was mighty to save
And he often prayed that God would give him
Spiritual integrity strong enough
To make *his flesh* behave!
He said, "Open up oh ancient gates and let
The King of Glory in!"
David knew how badly we need our Lord
To keep us free from sin!

Comment on Psalms

PSALMS 25

David said , "Oh Lord, my sins are so many!"
And he felt if God counted his virtues
He would find hardly any!
He needed God's help in order to obey
And he knew God would redirect him
When he went astray.
"Oh see my sorrow," he said. "Feel my pain!"
He felt his many sins had left a terrible stain.
When he needed help he knew where to look
-down on his knees in his own private nook!
Then his joy would come from confessing
He lived within the circle of God's blessing!
David showed such love and confidence
In the Lord
No wonder he felt godliness was his own
Favorite bodyguard!

PSALMS 26

David hated hypocrites and he would not enter
The favorite haunts of the deceitful sinner.
Man had not learned his lesson in David's day.
Even then it seemed religion
Was just another game to play.
Same thing now!
What has man learned any how?
Holiness can be accomplished only one way
—God living through me!
David knew man needed God
Long before the age of Christianity!
We should be as dazzled at God's splendor
And remember-as did David-that God is
Our most faithful defender!
And wouldn't it be wonderful
If we all did as we should
And walked that path like David did
The path of doing good!
And we are 'David's in our day
So let us be good examples at work or at play!

PSALMS 27

David had nothing to fear; God was his light!
Like him, we who experience God's salvation
Will not stumble in evil demonic night.
We can be like David who longed to meditate
Out of the reach of his enemies in God's
(where God is)holy estate!
Oh, I would surely be as distressed as he
If my God would hide himself from me!
David never felt secure unless he knew
His precious, holy, mighty Lord was near!
It is obvious we feel the same way!
Who but the Lord can cure
The deep depression we see every day?
"Wait for the Lord," David said
And he encouraged us to be thinking of
  the ONE who can hide us
    in the shelter of His love!

PSALMS 28

If devastation should traumatize us
We all would cry
"Oh Rock of Safety, if not for you
We would surely die!"
To whom can we go
When the wicked taunt us so?
We know God sees our many needs
And will put an end to evil deeds.
David almost bursts into joyful song
When he declares God will protect us
From all wrong!
We will be safe someday from the evil
And the terrorism that alarms
God will carry us–forever in His arms!

PSALMS 29

David reminds us the Lord displayed
His power over the earth at the flood.

The "I Love My Bible" Commentary

Those who doubted him were found
To have decayed under many layers of mud!
Our God continues to show His majesty
To those who mock Him in their travesty.
The magnificent glory of my Lord
Is beyond my ability to describe.
And he honors the man-the good man
Who refuses to take a bribe!
I think it is impossible even to dream
Of the purity of our Lord and Savior
Who is utterly supreme!
Even the angels who stood in God's presence
Were commanded by David
To give God reverence!
Those angels must have done as David bid
But I bet even they could not praise God
As eloquently as David did!

PSALMS 30

The one who prances in pride often falls
On his face.
He has failed to learn that all he possesses
Is a result of God's incredible grace!
When he thought he was deserted by God
It frightened David out of his wits
And when he did, it tore his pride to bits!
David knew he couldn't speak from the grave
To tell others God is mighty to save!
He proclaimed God gave him garments
Festive and gay
To rejoice and celebrate in day after day.
Somehow he seemed to understand
He'd always been under the Lord's command.
Maybe some would say David was not clever
But he was smart enough to praise the Lord
    forever and forever!
    And that is smart
    Smart!
His wisdom was the kind
    that comes straight from the heart!

PSALMS 31

Only in God's presence would David's spirit
Have a chance to be sterile
And he certainly needed the 'Rock of Ages'
To guard him from peril!
God alone could pull David from the trap
His enemies had set.
God rescued him many times and they
Must have thought David was God's pet!
He needed God and would go to any length
To please the One who had given him strength.
David knew when he strayed
His sins weakened him and he became afraid.
But his trembling would cease at last
When God hid them in the abyss of the past!

Psalms 32

Happiness is to be forgiven!
Joy is to have one's record cleared!
And overwhelming victory comes
From Our God who we've always revered!
When God forgives, guilt is gone.
He gives us sunny days and commands clouds
To keep moving on!
He surrounds us with songs that are victorious
And gives us a life that is truly glorious!
Abiding love envelopes us as we do His will.
There is a hush in our hearts and a longing
   to be still!
Just to hear *(like Elijah did)* God's gentle voice
Will gives us all great reason to rejoice.
If we guard our lips and keep our hearts in line
    Then we can say, like David
    "I know that God is mine!"

PSALMS 33

Our God is worthy of our love and trust.
We have never known Him to be unjust!

Comment on Psalms

No wonder David would lie and watch
The stars above.
Each twinkle would remind him of God's
Tender love!
Our God yearns for His people to be kind
And he watches to see what He can find.
I hope He finds us living happily
Trusting in His name
And may we never disappoint Him
Or bring our Heavenly Father shame.
We must depend on Him to save us all.
His rope of love holds and will not let us fall!
From the beginning of time
Our Lord has shown
He will never turn away and make us
Walk this earth alone!

PSALMS   34

Oh, to praise the Lord like David
To speak of His glory and grace
To tell those who are discouraged
That they will look on His face
Will be our greatest goal
Because we know He loves every single soul!
We, who love the Lord, make the right selection
And ours will be no downcast look of rejection!
We can trust God's kindness
And if we put Him to the test
We will see His mercy as He gives us His best!
Do you want a long, good life?
Guard your lips and hold your tongue.
And be careful of the people you walk among.
The Lord will not forgive those people
Whose hearts are hardened
But the humble will be fully pardoned !
Truly our Lord is made of heaven's right stuff!
We will never be able to praise Him enough!
I consider it great that this One so *great*
Has looked down from heaven
And has chosen me to be His soul mate!

PSALMS   35

David wanted to say, "I'm not afraid of you
No matter what you plan to do
For the Lord is standing in front of me
And He will stop you in your killing spree!"
Yet David would also ask the Lord
Why He didn't act
Because he was sinking and near death
And *that* was a well known fact!
But the Lord knew David had too much pride
And I bet He wanted David to see how it felt
To have no place to hide!
But this dear gentle earthly shepherd knew
The Lord protects the weak
And the Great Commander of Heaven
Will walk closely to those who are meek!

PSALMS   36

One who is no longer good allows sin
Deep into his heart
So deeply rooted, it pulls him and God
Further and further apart!
What a shame he cannot see that his evil deeds
Deprive him of the very one he needs.
As David said," God is the fountain of life.
He is our delight!
That path He leads us on is smooth and bright!"
God pours His love from His unlimited well.
His is a story of victory too fantastic to tell!
His love is so strong and steadfast
We know it will last and last and last!
Our God is more solid than the mountains
He creates
Think of the wonders He does for our sakes!
David spoke of the complete assurance
God's salvation brings
And says we can take refuge under God's wings
And what more than that can I say
Than to advise you to walk with Him each day?

The "I Love My Bible" Commentary

PSALMS 37

What good is a Rolls Royce if it is wrecked
Twisted and bent?
Likewise, a soul that turns from God
Is headed for a colossal accident!
That is why David said, "Don't envy
The wicked no matter how rich!"
They will end up in a hole as dark as pitch!
If you truly want to be "the upper crust"
Give the Lord your whole hearted trust!
And don't worry if you need a little rest.
God gives it to those whom He has blessed.
What a joy to know God delights
In every step I take
And He will protect me for His Name's sake!
The evil man will always think it odd
That the righteous are protected when we put
Our trust in God!
We must commit our way to the Lord.
His salvation and eternal refuge assures us
Our protector is on constant guard!

PSALMS 38

Sometimes God's news is "show and tell"
Because there are many myths He must dispel.
One of the myths is "you're sick because
Of God's anger."
That is why David thought he was in danger.
And myth number two is God would desert
A sinful child.
Isn't that the complaint David filed?
Didn't he say, "Don't go away Lord; don't
　　　leave?"
Such an awful thought would cause
Anyone to grieve!
David's heart was broken because of his sin
And this *source of sorrow*
Threw his life into a tail-spin!
His repentant, broken hearted words
"Oh my Savior," should have told him
This very important thing.
God was his Savior and would never forsake
This gentle, shepherd king!

PSALMS 39

"Well, shut my mouth," David possibly said.
Maybe if he quit griping, he could get ahead.
Complaining sets up a negative connotation
That robs us of the joy of our salvation.
David couldn't help but groan.
He lost hope when he felt God left him alone.
Sin is like quick sand or a sink hole
That will mesmerize a troubled soul!
The deeper you sink, the less of
The glorious godly light you are able to see!
David knew he needed *that light*
To guide and set his spirit free!
Whenever David sensed God's absence
He was horrified!
He always cried for forgiveness
And the Lord always complied!

PSALMS 40

God is still the same as in David's day.
It is wonderful to know He hears and answers
When I pray!
God has put a new song in my heart also
And a spring in my step.
I wait patiently(but not always)for my Lord
Who has filled my trembling soul full of pep!
There is one thing for certain
My Lord is here when He knows I'm hurtin'
And my biggest hope
Is through my days and nights of uncertainty
My Lord will teach me how to cope!
It's a special joy to know He fills my needs
And I'm especially blessed when I follow
Where He leads.

Comment on Psalms

Truly, God set my feet upon a rock
And I feel no despair
Because I'm under the protection
Of His loving care!
Just think
Centuries later someone else may read
Of how God lovingly answers those who plead
And that someone will know
The awesome, holy, loving presence of God
Wherever they go.
Someone like me! Someone like you!

PSALMS 41

God's word has said it before.
But once again David says
"God blesses those who help the poor."
God saves us from our enemy's power
And in times of pain, keeps watch by the hour.
Many times David felt alone when he was ill
But he always believed that healing him
Was the Father's will!
He had known the desertion of friends
He held dear
And when he was down and out
Their intentions were made clear.
Still, he was blessed because of his loyalty
To the God whose majesty
Far surpasses any level of earthly royalty!

PSALMS 42

God's special gift made David want to shout.
It was a sunny day of incredible love
Steadily, blissfully pouring out!
How simple it would be to sing that song
Of praise for the Father all day long!
The deer could never long for water
As much as David longed for God
And David watched eagerly and longingly
For God's approving nod!
David loved the land where the Jordan river flowed.
He depended on God's faithfulness
And you can bet it showed!
He expected God to protect him from
His own doubts and any angry foe.
Surely his 'rock' would be by his side
Wherever he would go!

PSALMS 43

God is much higher
Than any of the High Supreme Court Judges
And His judgements stand no matter
How strong the fervor of other's grudges.
Therefore we will go to God's altar
To proclaim the wonder of our beloved Lord.
Just to feel the mercy our Father gives
Is its own exceedingly fantastic reward!
God leads His people to His holy mountain
To drink from His bottomless fountain.
David drank there to soothe his trouble heart.
He didn't know what to do but he knew
The best place to start.
His God would heal the soul cast down
And it would soar as he stood on holy ground!
God would quiet his disquieted soul
To soothe David's heart and make him whole.
No wonder his love for God was great.
"Trust in God!" David said.
You Betcha! I will always love
This One who died in my stead!

PSALMS 44

These charges the psalmist makes are untrue.
"Lord," he said. "You have deserted us
Despite our loyalty to you!"
It depressed him to say he had heard
Of God's miracles yet it was so long ago
How could this benevolent God love them so

The "I Love My Bible" Commentary

And not love people in David's day?
He obviously pleaded, "Please Lord
love us again!
Had God now turned away because of their sin
To leave them victims to the worst of men?
He complained, when their enemies cursed
They seemed to spit out the word "Jew."
Even now, those who love the Jews
Are counted among the very few!
They were and have been like sheep
Awaiting slaughter, needing God's grace
The psalmist pulls no punches
In proving their need for God
To be a very strong case.
Now why would the psalmist think
God needed a shove?
Hadn't God always showed His people
Evidence of His constant love?
He stands ready and anxious to perform
His good deeds
For God was, is, and will always be
The supplier who attends to our deepest needs.
God's power is greater than a mighty ocean
And we must remember our prayers
Are the activators that set His hand in motion!

PSALMS 45

David looks beyond the horizon to a reign
That will never end
And then looks deep into his own heart to find
The words to describe his Dearest Friend!
No one has ever depicted more beautifully
Than David did
This God who is so gloriously majestic
Many would do what He bid!
Justice has always been God's royal scepter
And is a mighty virtue to behold.
His truth, His honor, His justice, shines
With more brilliance than the purest gold.
Oh, to have the words like David

To glorify my King!
To stand with the holy angels and listen to
The millions sing
Would give me more joy than I could ever
Possibly contain!
Such eloquence would lift my life far beyond
The unsightly and the mundane.
Then I could look beyond the horizon too
And rejoice in what my God can do!

PSALMS 46

God is our refuge and strength, a soothing
Hope we must remember
When the world crumbles as the eons of time
Reaches its final December!
There is a river of joy flowing through
God's eternal city.
The psalmist says there will be no time
For anger or depression and no need for pity!
Joy will reign supreme
Because the God of the universe has come
To fulfill every dream!
The psalmist speaks in present tense.
Surely you can speak it and I can too.
Didn't our Savior say,
"I'll always be with you?"
And the psalmist seems to add clearly
"The Commander of the Armies of Heaven
Has come!   He is here to rescue us.
What in the world are you running from?"

PSALMS 47

The psalmist seems to think depression
Is a crime.
There is joy, *joy,* and now its "clapping time!"
There was wonderful news to be spread.
"Our God is awesome, beyond words!" he said.
Many nations will soon find out
God will ascend His throne with a strong shout!

Comment on Psalms

And when He does it will be time to sing
Eternal praises to our King!
God will be truly honored everywhere.
Some day the world will have to admit
God is the fairest of the fair!

PSALMS 48

The psalmist says, "God defends Jerusalem!
He is the city's glory."
Indeed, God's love for her is a beautiful story!
God has established Jerusalem forever.
Though it has fallen on many occasions
Its destruction is an impossible endeavor!
They were to walk around to count her towers
For blessings would fall on Jerusalem
Like gentle showers!
No city has known a greater love or protection.
Ah, it was a city full of God's perfection!
Her gates were strengthened by angels
As were her walls
And still her enemies are watching, waiting
Until she falls!
There is a dismal fate for every contender.
No one can defeat Israel's Defender!

PSALMS 49

One soul!   One world!
Can they be compared?   I think not!
He who believes his worth is based on wealth
Is undoubtedly "on the spot!"
(Jesus said, "What shall it profit a man if he
  gains the whole world and loses his soul?"
  ---so, friend, what should be your goal?)
Pomp and circumstance is a poor price to pay
And lonely is the soul who does not walk
With God each day.
There is nothing-*nothing*-on this earth
That can redeem a precious soul.
Man is priceless and knowing that
Should give us assurance from God

That only He can make us whole!
What do you think that will take?
The hidden message is
It took God's Son to die for my sake!
ONE only is what I need
And that One is known as David's seed!
David's descendant and David's ancestor
Are one and the same
And it was David's greatest desire
To praise His Holy Name!
David called Him, Lord. So do we!
Our souls are so precious to Him
He and He alone, can ransom you and me!
There are other hidden jewels in this chapter
I did not uncover or discuss
But, oh my people, the most important is
–how very much our Lord values us!
Read this chapter to see what you need
And I hope you learn from what you read!

PSALMS 50

God has to speak when the people refuse
To listen to the prophets' voices.
And because they wouldn't listen
They made a blind turn and the wrong choices.
That is when mankind begins to recite
Instead of receive.
That is when he seeks tradition
Instead of choosing to obey and believe.
Tradition makes God's word of none effect!
Tradition does not see the *glory light*
And really shows God no respect.
In fact it seems His reason for coming
Was to correct those misguided men
Who were spiritual slumming!
It has not been easy for God
To make it easy for all mankind.
Though God has given us His *light*
Man is still spiritually blind!
And the breezes carry the Father's sighs

The "I Love My Bible" Commentary

As He wonders, *"Why, oh why, won't you*
open your eyes?"
It has always displeased Our Lord to see
His people's tendency to roam
Because *home* is where the heart is
And with Him is truly *home sweet home!*

PSALMS 51

You never know how low you can get
until you sin against the Lord.
There is no other depression discovered yet
that can hit a soul so hard.
It is as if you've been covered
with tons of dirt.
Its as if you've been smothered
and never knew how much you could hurt.
You're standing now on shaky ground
and you hurt so bad you think
the Lord is surely no where around!
But God doesn't despise the repentant heart
and He will bless
those who humbly forsake
those sins they truly confess.
David wept before the Lord because
he knew he had wounded his own soul
but he also knew our Lord
would forgive and make him whole!

PSALMS 52

Doeg had no redeeming quality.
He was a man who practiced treachery.
This man who David called a beast
Had viciously killed eighty five priests.
Doeg was a smart aleck know it all
A delinquent spirit who was heading for a fall.
David said this man with a lying tongue
Was sharp as a tack
But obviously it was only at stabbing
Others in the back!

PSALMS 53

The man who says-in his heart-there is no God
Stalks an island called Ichabod!
This man wants to carry a god on his shoulder
Rather than welcome the Lord into his heart
And in his rambling will find himself
A victim of the devil's own deceitful dart.
David says only a fool would say
There is no God and foolishly risk
The consequences of saying God doesn't exist.
He implies the guy is corroded with sin
And doesn't realize the state he is in!
David states there is no one good
And those haters of God would be destroyed
Right where they stood!
They were so bad God would scatter their bones
-bones not even good enough
To be used for stepping stones!
God still looks down on the deeds of men
And not even a king will escape judgement
If he lives in unrepentant sin.
And he is left to stalk the island of Ichabod
As he wanders further and further
From our all mighty God!

PSALMS 54

The treacherous men of Ziph were worth
Much less than wood, hay, and stubble.
They conveniently forgot the many times
David had saved them from trouble.
They had told Saul David was at Hachilah hill
And with their help Saul could capture him
If that was his will!
David had protected all the people
Dwelling around Ziph in the country side.
Now because of the renegade men of Ziph
He had to run and hide!
These people he had tried to save
Tried to consign him to an early grave.

Comment on Psalms

Once more he knows where to go
* -to the One who made*
*   the Jordan river flow*
* -to the One who holds*
*   the world in His hands*
* -to the One whose love*
*   backs all His commands!*
And when we get in trouble
*   as we often do*
*   like David*
we can run to our Savior too!
For centuries it has been common knowledge
That the Lord will *never* face defeat
And He sends His people to the fox holes
Of His impregnable easy street.

PSALMS 55

Internal wickedness had entranced Jerusalem
In spiritual recession.
The desertion of the one friend David thought
Had been loyal, sent him into deep depression
And planted stark terror in his heart.
To make matters worse, David's own morals
Had come up pitifully short.
Wickedness was as volatile as a rocket's blast
And he felt goodness was destined not to last.
But David knew God would not fail him
—had not failed him in the past!
That is why David would pray
At least three times a day every day!
And he prayed that God would cut down
The wicked in their prime.
It seems his intercession for them was over
And the wicked had run out of time!
His ambivalence was like a jump rope
And he jumped to praying for the righteous
Who God would not allow to fall!
And no matter how low he felt
God would still be there after all!
Though murderers and liars would not live
Out even half their allotted days
The Lord would prolong the lives of those
Who walked in His ways!

PSALMS 56

When we fear, we should do like David did
—seek those everlasting arms where David hid!
David knew God had collected his tears
And stored them in a large fruit jar
To testify against his enemies whose hatred
Of the Lord and of David
Compelled them to declare war.
God protects us though we may be unaware
Of the similarities we and David share!
When there seems to be no peace and quiet
And my heavy heart yearns
He surely answers when I cry
And the tide of my inward battle turns!
Even now, when the earth is full of evil men
Men who are wicked and depraved
Who are bent on terrorism,
We can sing, "Thank God we are saved!"

PSALMS 57

David cries, "Pity me Lord!" and we wonder
Why did David seek God and cry so much.
Evidently he knew every day was a day
For God and him to keep in touch!
If David needed to hide in the shadow
Of God's almighty wings, can we do less?
We, too, live in a day of incredible stress!
If God is to be exalted
We must give our hearts to Him
And, like David, we will know where to turn
When trouble brews and hopes grow dim.
And we must never, never forget
When our hopes are raised
To do like David who knew beyond a doubt
Our God is worthy to be praised!

The "I Love My Bible" Commentary

PSALMS 58

Justice!
Oh my goodness!
How much equal justice do we really see?
Do the rich still pay their bribes
When God meant justice for all to be free?
David calls them cobras and deadly snakes
When judges take bribes from the wicked
To rule in their favor and for their sakes!
So! Bribery is nothing new!
We see this gentle shepherd faced it too!
David said injustice is a horrible sin
And someday the godly would observe
The stained fields of these wicked men.
Think! He is talking about men who judge!
Oh, judges, give an honest decision
No man or woman can begrudge!
And then the Lord will take delight in you
For He is the Supreme Judge
Who justly judges what you do!

PSALMS 59

Evil men slink like dogs prowling the city.
They insult and curse almighty God
And show their victims no pity.
Could these men be worthy to spare?
David thought not!
These men were so vicious and cruel
A penalty must follow their every evil plot!
David knew the protection of God's shield
Yet these men were so bad they would never
Know the joy of those that God concealed!
They searched for 'food' that didn't satisfy.
They never drank *water from the rock*
And so they were continually *dry!*
Despite his fear, David could sing praises
In his day of distress
For his enemies could *never* destroy
This one God was so willing to bless!

PSALMS 60

Why do God's people sink into depression
That is so deep
They believe God has rejected those
He has faithfully promised to keep!
Why is it so easy to look for the storm
And tremble as if we are facing harm?
We should draw on that endless strength
That commands us to be calm
And snuggle contentedly in our Savior's palm.
If we really believe God stands by our side
Testing and trouble won't leave us so terrified.
Instead, look at what David said
When he trembled and cried in fear.
"Give us a beacon, Lord and we will rejoice
Whenever you appear!"
Fear is common to man.
Faith is as scarce as gold!
But searching for it give us treasure to behold!
*Faith has moved mountains, calmed the seas
Helped us grow like deeply planted trees!*
Faith lifts us up and will continue to spring
As we dedicate our hopes, and our lives
In service to our heavenly King!

PSALMS 61

It is a cry that every man wants God to hear.
A cry winging its way through the atmosphere
And it seems to be a one way communication
Because we think the lines are clogged.
We often fail to see the answer through doubt
—darkened windows that are heavily fogged!
And we continue to cry,
"Lord why don't you hear our prayers?"
It seems He's gone so far away
And there's no one here who cares!
But God still guides all people He loves
By truth and loving kindness
So we have no excuse to wander around

Comment on Psalms

Through mazes of fear and spiritual blindness!
Never think God won't hear you cry
"Oh lead me to the Rock
that is higher than I!"

PSALMS 62

I picture David saying, "Silence my heart!
You are standing before the Lord.
Don't get impatient now and lose your reward."
One who doubts the Lord is an air-head
Who believes the lies God's enemies spread.
There is a *'rock'* no one can climb
Except God's own child!
It is inaccessible to those who are undisciplined
And spiritually wild.
The foothills are protected by the Rock of Ages
But are readily available when our storm rages.
He is there for the bold or the meek
And He will strengthen all who are weak.
Oh, Rock of Ages, why should I be tense?
David knew you would never
Keep your needy children in suspense!
That is holy knowledge meant for me
For keeping your people safe, oh Lord
Is your speciality!
Like David, I will stand in silence
And wait for the Lord to rescue me!

PSALMS 63

It may be nothing one can get his hands on.
It may be just a feeling that we are not alone.
Or, it must have been faith that made David say
"God's love and kindness grows better
    day by day!"
But he continually wanted more.
You would think David was keeping score!
He wanted to see God's strength and glory
And would make them the pivotal source
Of God's great salvation story!
It was David's desire to lift his voice in praise
And we notice once again
It was a promise he kept the rest of his days!

PSALMS 64

Now David seems to be complaining again.
He tires of the conspiracy of wicked men.
He felt their tongues were not made
To be bitter and sharp
Because the naive are so easy to warp.
It displeased this gentle shepherd to see men
Wait in ambush to harm another.
Man should not commit evil against a brother.
He was sure God would shoot them down.
God's arrows would protect David's crown.
He knew someday people would stand in awe.
Soon they would love and cherish God's law!
In this day, God is worshiped by so few
And only they will understand how much
How very much our Lord can do!

PSALMS 65

Shouldn't we in this age of *hurry* pause
Occasionally for a little while
And realize to honor our Lord
Is the only way to live in style!
Our God forgives all our mistakes and our sin
And He shows mercy to unrepentant men.
Joy awaits those who come to His courts
Like the prodigal son who had traveled
Far away to distant ports.
I think David is trying to say
God's heart keeps reaching out, no matter
How far you choose to run away!
The time we spend in God's presence
Is not time we waste.
Like the prodigal, when we realize
We are much too far away from home
We should return in haste!

The "I Love My Bible" Commentary

PSALMS   66

Melodic stories enrich the souls of men!
These songs praise the Lord and do it well!
Men, who tapped their feet as they wrote
Tap into our hearts by the stories they tell.
Songs like *Just As I am* turn many from sin!
But among the writers of the ages
I'd have to say, David was the best of men!
Didn't his songs soothe a troubled Saul?
Didn't he borrow the melody of the stars
To sing of the One he loved most of all?
Every song he ever wrote, or sang, or played
Has hummed its way into the hearts
Of ever redeemed sinner who ever strayed!
There were many more of course
Men and women who loved our Savior
And molded their notes in order to favor
The King of all the Ages, the Morning Star
The Prince of Peace, the Counselor
   The best by far!
Yet every song that's ever been written
   falls far short
Of describing how God's love and grace
Can heal a broken heart!
But writers— give us other songs to sing!
We must lift our voices in praise to our King!
And when we bless our God, we remember
David said He would never turn away
And-daily-God listens to answer as we pray!
Oh yes, David knew the glory of answered
   prayer
And he glorifies the Lord with fervent flair!

PSALMS   67

Such a short chapter!
Such an eloquent plea!
How many people have said through the ages
"Oh Lord, will you please look down on me!"
David wasn't the first and he wasn't the last

But his faith and consistency in asking
Will never be outclassed!
Oh Lord, look down on us as you did
That gentle shepherd boy
And we, like David, will thank you daily
For your incredible gift of joy!

PSALMS 68

David says the wicked must be destroyed.
Look who God chose to lead the way!
The little tribe of Benjamin would be used
To hold the giants of wickedness at bay.
God's people must not cower every time
The enemy sneezes!
Power belongs to God and He gives it
To whom he pleases!
David knew God gives strength and courage
To the timid and to the weak
Whose hearts are open to hear Him speak.
Now here is the world's greatest situation!
The God who bears our burdens
Also gives us His salvation!
The One who lassos the stars of heaven
And whose mighty voice thunders in the sky
   will prove beyond a doubt
   that His righteousness will triumph
   in the bye and bye!

PSALMS   69

Many of us have lifted our eyes to heaven
And said, "Save me oh my God!
Don't let me be a stumbling block
To those who travel the paths I've trod!"
And there will come a time when our hearts
   will break
When we are mocked for God's sake.
So we should emulate David who kept faith
And knew his zeal must remain
Even though he often felt rejection and pain.

Comment on Psalms

This psalm digs into the well of man's cruelty
To picture their defeat and insecurity.
Not one of them could justify their behavior
On that day men like them would crucify
    our Savior.
David inserted a beacon of truth
To show how our Savior's pain would
    intertwine
To join sinful man who is explicitly immoral
And the One who is *definitely divine!*
Because of His great sacrificial love
Someday we will be blessed to see
    the glory of this One
    who died for us on Calvary!

PSALMS 70

Again, David longs for God's first aid kit.
His enemies were hurting him
And he did not like it—*not one bit!*
Poor David must have seen more trouble
Than many twice his age
And many times he seemed to weaken
Under his enemies' rage.
But David was no coward even as a boy.
He knew God would rescue him
And that knowledge gave him joy!
We can also be filled with joy as we exclaim
"How glorious is our Lord and Savior
And we will always praise His Name!"
We plead as did that precious king who said
"Oh Lord, don't delay.
Come and pick us up today!"

PSALMS 71

There is one thing David knew for certain.
Fear of any kind created an iron curtain.
But he would never allow it to separate
Him from his God whom he considered great!
When fear struck David, he would hide
Always by his Savior's side.
From the time he was a carefree little child
Until he trembled with old age
He placed the Lord at his side.
His Savior would always be at center-stage!
David would not boast about himself
Even in his greatest hour
For he knew God had given him his power!

PSALMS 72

The psalmist used the word "gentle"
    numerous times
For he had been the victim of many crimes
And he revered such a blessed trait.
He considered it necessary for anyone
Who would claim the title, "*head of state!*"
But here this psalmist looks forward
To the most prestigious, powerful reign of all
To the rule of the Messiah, a blessed ruler
Where no good man would ever fall.
People around the world will praise His Name
For He will save his people from all shame!
    Kings who strive to be great
    will only struggle in vain
    for on one can ever equal
    the Messiah's holy reign!

PSALMS 73

If we would join hands, we who have been to
The edge of that cliff David wrote about
We would probably make a circle far, far out!
And wouldn't we eliminate a lot of cruelty
If we think about the slippery path they are on.
We'd realize they will be facing an eternity
Of terror away from God—all alone!
Who else is as great as the God of the universe
And He hears the joyful praises we rehearse!
As our circle of believers continues to grow
May He see our eager faces glow!

The "I Love My Bible" Commentary

PSALMS 74

One day he's up!
One day he's down!
One day he rejoices
But the next wears a frown!
Asaph could not stand for his God to be
Ignored or disobeyed or blasphemed.
And he grieved for those blessed people
On whom God's light had graciously beamed!
Why were they being treated so cruel now?
Had God turned away from them somehow?
Israel's enemies wanted to destroy God
And would leave no trace
Of the sanctuary that witnessed to His grace!
God's enemies' curses grew louder and louder
And Asaph compared them to chaff chowder!
He prayed for God at least
To come and protect his people
From those belligerent beasts!

PSALMS 75

Asaph is on the "thank you" wagon again
And rejoices to see God punish an evil man.
He imagines God saying the earth is secure
And promising He would protect the pure!
Once again God warns the one who strays
To lower his stubborn, insolent gaze!
It should be no surprise when the world
    comes to an end
That God will destroy His enemies
    and give the earth
To those on whom He can depend!
And it should be no surprise
When God rolls back the curtains of space
To show us how many
He has saved by His Amazing Grace!
Ah! There's nothing like being on His list!
—nothing as blessed as being there, so *never*
Let it be said that you have been missed!

PSALMS 76

No one has been able to answer the question
"Who can stand before an angry God?"
And who has ever been able to avoid
His awesome correcting rod?
Since God is so great its hard to conceive
How often our Lord intervenes for those
    who believe!
The psalmist says God should be feared
For though He forgives the meek
Those who continue in evil will not be cleared.
And there will be no court of appeals
In that final judgement day
When God brings His redeemed back home
And chases the evil ones away!
They will regret the paths they have trod
When they learn the answer to
"Who can stand before an angry God?"

PSALMS 77

There can be no joy for God's people
Without His intervention.
Asaph discovered the trials and tribulations
Heartaches, and headaches in his day
Were too many to mention!
There comes a time when we, too, are
Too distressed to pray
And, as Asaph said, that is an awesome, dark
And troublesome day!
Yet, that is the time to remember the good days
When God helped and blessed His people
Whose lips formed endless praise!
The message to us is–God is the God
Of our darkest hour
And He hasn't forgotten how to use His might
His miracles, and His spectacular power!
God provides a pathway for us to use
And if we are undecided, He'll be there
At the crossroads to show us which to choose!

Comment on Psalms

PSALMS 78

There are laws to obey and holy paths
We must follow.
Those who refuse to walk in them will wonder
Why their faith is hollow!
They forget about God's miracles
And we notice they cannot see
If they keep on living in rebellion and sin
God will never set them free!
It is not just words God wants to hear
But obedience that marks hearts firm and true!
Then each generation can set its hopes
On our glorious God anew!
His love overcomes the *generation gap*
And He provides the *water of life*
From an open, endless tap!
Yet over and over we see
God's people grieve for better days
That would have been given
If they had walked in His ways!
And from the time of Moses
It has been made known time and time again
God will not allow His people into heaven
Who walk in deliberate unrepentant, sin!

PSALMS 79

(I imagine David saying this-*just like me!*)
Oh God, heathen ways had conquered my heart
And I trembled in fear when I discovered
How far we'd grown apart.
I sunk so low I refused to pray
And I felt as if my life was slowly fading away!
I lived in fear and shuddered in shame
When I refused to pray or mention your name.
Sheep like me have cried before
And their starving souls begged for more
   -more of God
   -more of love
   -more of grace
And less of the terrible sins they would have
To beg God to erase!
These Israelis felt they should beware
Because their relationship with God
Was badly in need of immediate repair!
There has always been emptiness
Whenever God's people choose to stray
From the One who gives us life, and light
And a heaping measure of love each day
Who always answers when we pray
"Lord, lift us up and never let us stray!"

PSALMS 80

Their cries continue, "Oh Lord, we suffer
Because of the unholy ways we have behaved!
Turn us again to yourself, oh God.
Only then will we be saved!"
Every generation needs to make this plea.
Every generation must be made to see
Salvation is God and us joining hands
When we willingly obey His commands!
The psalmist earnestly asked God to turn
His people around.
It was as if they were walking on uneven
Unholy ground!
When Israel is too numb to beg for herself
He begs in place of her
And perhaps wonders how much
And how often will be the troubles
She will try to stir.
We must ask God to revive us
As did the Israelis long ago.
How else can the world look on us and see
Our faces all aglow?
We are merely a reflection of this great One
We are always thinking of
For our God has consistently been
God of joy and God of love!
Only He can give us ALL the love we crave
And our beloved Lord is always eager to save!

The "I Love My Bible" Commentary

PSALMS 81

*Vitamins and minerals
and calories galore
are good, maybe
but we need more!
We are told to eat the right stuff
but food just for our stomachs
is not enough.
Nutritionists are partly right
and partly wrong
but "The Word" states
It is the Lord who makes
us strong!
God says to open our mouths
wide
And He will see to it
that we are fully satisfied!
But he abhors the greedy
and the idol-monger.
God knows wrong ideals
and wrong goals
can never satisfy our hunger!
Stubbornness
and living according
to our desires
lead us down pathways
lit by wayward fires.
We'll find what we need
when we take stock.
What we really need is
"honey from the rock!"*

PSALMS 82

Stand up, oh Lord, like Asaph said.
Please don't let your people be mislead!
Judges must listen to an honest defense
And quit taking counsel that makes no sense.
Green backs in the hand
Bend the ear out of place!
How many times has money been used
To swing the verdict in a case?
Lord, though not seen, you sit on every docket
In the presence of every Judge!
Give each one an honest heart
That seeks justice and is unwilling to budge!
Truth and justice must prevail
Or the foundations of society will surely fail!
Please Lord, stand up for innocent people
And keep judges from the unjust sin
Of leaving the poor at the mercy
Of vicious, evil men!

PSALMS 83

The Israelis must have wondered if the Lord
Could still deliver.
He wasn't answering their prayers
Though He must have seen them quiver!
They were surrounded by enemies
With no help in sight.
Surely their enemies were evil vultures
Who would slay them merely out of spite!
He was asked to blow away their enemies
Like chaff or dust
For they were crafty murderers who were
Blind and unjust.
Remember these people were under the law
And thought the law to be harsh and strict.
And love, mercy and grace seems to be
Nothing it can ever depict.
But doesn't love protect its own?
Isn't it full of mercy for them and full grown?
Didn't God say He'd keep evil away?
He did! But they walked in evil every day.
I think He must have thought they were dumb
To walk in the evil they were to overcome
So He let them see how evil, evil can be
And let them be punished by their enemy!
They AND their enemies needed to learn
What you sow is what you(reap)earn!

Comment on Psalms

PSALMS 84

What the psalmist said is nothing new.
"Oh Lord of the armies of heaven
Blessed are those who trust in you!"
This psalm is full of praise
And lists the good things given
To those who walk in God's ways!
God still gives us hope and harmony.
He is still our protector!
We, who come to Him, must dread no enemy
Fear no earthly scepter.
He also gives us grace and glory
Just as He did the Israelis in this story!
A single day spent in God's house
Is worth a thousand spent else where!
Refreshing strength, blessing, and joy
Are some of the things we all can share!
Now, we should praise Him too!
Lord, blessed are all those who trust in You!

PSALMS 85

Amazing grace and amazing blessings
Go hand in hand.
It is through His love and forgiveness
That God blesses our land!
Tucked in the middle of this chapter
Almost hidden, is the fact
Repentance on our part causes God to act!
His salvation is near when we reverence
And follow Him each day
For God gives peace to His people
When we listen and obey!
He pours down a blessing that never stops
And the evidence is seen each year
In our huge profits and bountiful crops!
Oh that we would live lives of dedication
So that the Lord would never doubt
That we love Him, love Him, love Him
And that we cherish His salvation!

PSALMS 86

When David felt fear, he needed a sign
Of God's favor.
In his weakest hour he knew how badly
He needed the Savior!
Hatred takes our assurance away
But love is freely restored whenever we pray.
Every fiber of our being
Must unite in reverence to His Name!
God's kindness rescues us from depression
And keeps us free from blame!
No one can defeat us when we see
God's love is a love that will always be!
Those whose tongues were as sharp as saws
Would find God protects those who cherish
His holy laws!
David said to those beasts who were
So smug and conceited
"I have a God much bigger than you
And HE can NEVER be defeated!"

PSALMS 87

High on His holy mountain stands the city
God loves most!
Someday the ones born in that city will have
A glorious reason to boast!
It will be when God, Himself, takes pity
And renews the glory of this holy city.
And I can almost hear the Israelis sing
"Our God has returned to Jerusalem
Glory to our King!"
It WILL happen someday
No matter what the Arabs(or others)say!
And no matter if everyone deserts this nation
God will stand firm in His dedication.
And no matter what you've heard
God says He will restore Israel
And some glorious, wonderful day
Our God will keep His word!

The "I Love My Bible" Commentary

PSALMS 88

This psalm asks, "Can I praise God
From the grave?
Will I be able to tell others my God is mighty
To save?
In the land of shadows no one lifts his voice
To proclaim the amazing joy and wonder
Of making God his choice!"
Now we know-*if he does*-no one on earth
Will be able to hear
For his voice will be lost somewhere
Out in the distant atmosphere!
I think this man made one big mistake
When he accused God
Of filling his friends with hate.
He said terror surrounded him all day long!
Why is to so easy to lay the blame on God
When every thing we do seems to go wrong?
But we agree there is darkness everywhere
And it seems there is no one left to care.
That is the time we think there is no way out
And we begin to wonder
What in the world is this earthly life about?

PSALMS 89

Most of this chapter is so fantastic
It is hard to describe.
Judah finally realized the love God gave them
When the king was chosen from their tribe.
David would exclaim,
"Oh God
Strong is your love
Strong is your hand
Strong is your arm
Your throne is founded on righteousness.
Your mercy and truth will keep us from harm!"
Absolutely no one has ever praised God
As eloquently as David did!
Absolutely no one in his day was as fervent
In doing what Our Heavenly Father bid!
Because of that, God said, "I will love David
Forever, and will always be kind
For David loves me with all his heart
And keeps obedience for me on his mind!"
David was never too embarrassed to say
"God is my God and I will follow Him
Every minute, every hour, and every day!"
Oh to have such a love for my Lord
That walking with Him would be
My greatest joy and most coveted reward!
But David was discouraged and distressed
And it seems he forgot the many, many times
He had been gloriously blessed!
Yet, we must overlook his blatant cries
And try to understand
That David's questions were not a reprimand.
David knew that life at best is hard
And there would never be a time
He would not need our Lord!

PSALMS 90

What is home
or should I say
Who is home?
Well, God is home!
And no matter how far we roam
with God in our hearts
we'll never
be away from home!
When on the mountain top or the valley below
There is comfort in the news that our God
Will be with us wherever we choose to go.
Yet, like the Israelis, we continue to sin
And overlook this great responsibility to love
That God has given to all men.
We needn't worry about numbering our days
If we'd love the Lord and walked in His ways!
Then our hearts would cease to roam
And we'd know Our God is Home sweet Home!

Comment on Psalms

PSALMS 91

What a beautiful shadow that overshadows me
And what blessed hope this psalm shows me!
What I can't understand is why anyone
Would harden their hearts against the Lord
But then I have to admit I've done it too
Wanting my own way!
But that is when my heart grows hard
And I have to humbly repent and pray.
And then I do not have to be afraid!
Has not God said, He would come to my aid?
No one else's promises are as secure
As my sacred King whose every word is pure!
I can almost feel those mighty angels
Tender touch
And I wonder how my Heavenly Father
Could love me so much!
How can I thank Him for setting me free?
    I know!
    Like David
I will answer when He calls on me!

PSALMS 92

It is good to say, "Thank you," to God!
    It is good!
Actually, don't you think we should?
Can we even begin to recall what God has done?
Thankfulness is music to His ears!
We can sing no sweeter song? No, there is none!
The fool who doubts God cannot comprehend
How great it is to have such a glorious friend!
David says the Lord will live, LIVE, forever!
And-we have an eternal bond no one can sever!
Even in old age, God will keep us young
As we climb faith's ladder rung by rung!
This psalm guarantees our lives will not be grim
Because there is nothing but goodness in Him!
Imagine the glory when we see Him face to face
And really understand the wonder of His Grace!

PSALMS 93

A psalm does not need to be long in order
To praise our Lord!
This short psalm depicts beautiful memories
To lift up souls that may be scarred.
To remember God's greatness is best of all
And to remember He picks us up when we fall
Is worth more than any pot of gold!
Remember that as you grow old!
    Thankfulness!
How else can we take part in this triumphant
Proclamation of our great King?
How else can we lift our voices to sing
Of His glorious unending power?
And our love for God is to Him
Like a sweet, fragrant, ever blooming flower!
    David is saying
    Our God is always
    God of the present hour
    God of our hearts
    God of our lives
And no matter how hard another man strives
He can never surpass David's artful way
Of praising our Heavenly Father day after day!

PSALMS 94

Lord, through turmoil, let your glory shine out!
Please give me hope and cheer
When my mind is full of doubt.
This world is crowded with thieves, and liars
But help me seek your presence for what I need
Is anything-and everything-that truly inspires!
The Lord is my hope, my refuge, my joy!
Like the psalmist, I have a faith
God will allow no one to destroy!
Praise the Lord from everlasting ages past.
My Savior will never, never be out-classed!
And for those doubtful ones who scoff
Our precious Lord will cast them off!

The "I Love My Bible" Commentary

PSALMS 95

Since we have reason to rejoice and sing
Let God exult as we let joyful anthems ring!
Someday we'll stand with David and shout
The King of the Ages has brought us out!
We must not let our hearts harden
For we have been given a glorious pardon!
May we not lose the chance to stand
On the blessed shores of the Promised Land.
We must not grieve our Lord
-not for one minute
Without Him, life has no joy in it!
And if we expect God to bless this nation
We must return to being a godly generation!

PSALMS 96

David seems to wonder how we can forget
The redeeming work we must do yet.
Can we not see there are many depraved
Who wander in darkness and need to be saved?
We must praise the Lord and in a dramatic way
Continue to show others His love each day!
For He is great beyond description.
Obviously, David had the right prescription!
God's great love is utterly marvelous
But the message He gives us is simple.
Honor and majesty surround Him.
Strength and beauty are in His temple!
We should worship Him with holy lives
As our love for Him becomes the impetus
    that drives
Us into His everlasting arms
Safe from life's most destructive storms!
But until we reach those ageless plains
We are to remember we are saved
To tell the world why our Savior reigns!
This is our purpose, our dedication
Our devoted, consecrated, glorious occupation
Definitely this earth's greatest recreation!

PSALMS 97

Should we doubt Jehovah is our mighty King
When to question His holiness is such
A horrible thing?
His light shines for the godly
His love for those whose hearts are pure.
There is no place away from Him
Where we can feel safe and secure!
Every nation should cherish His glory.
Every child should know His story!
May we all learn to make Him our choice
And then as believers in Him, we can rejoice!
No one can ever take the place
Of this Holy One who saves us by His grace!
David was fervent and strong in his belief.
Only our great God can bring this earth relief!

PSALMS 98

We still sing about the Lord's mighty deeds
As we tell others how He provides our needs!
We gladly shout about victory after victory
As our great King marches through history.
The world cannot deny how we joyously reply
When even the seas roar with His praise
As He seeks the lamb that strays!
How can we fail to praise His Name?
Glory to God! He is always the same!

PSALMS 99

Here I am at Psalms 99 and that number is not
Enough to cover the times to praise our King!
Many are the times we should rejoice and sing.
For there are 99 ways and more we do wrong
And carelessly sin against Him all day long.
Though that number may be just the beginning
Still, Our Father forgives us for sinning!
Sin is a wild horse God can straddle
And justice is His unerring, powerful paddle!

Comment on Psalms

God seeks the wanderer to set him straight
Because His love is wonderfully great!
We will see Him in the Heavenly Jerusalem
And–WE WILL rejoice and worship Him!

PSALMS 100

*Oh people, try to realize
what this means
The One who created
and sustains pastoral scenes
is the Great Jehovah God!
And if we ever get
to enter into His presence
it will be because of
the faithful, obedient
holy paths we've trod!
He owes us nothing!
We owe Him our all!
Yet He reaches out
and assures us
He will answer when we call!
If we are looking for
a lasting sensation
we'll find it
in each succeeding generation!
Down and out!
Up and at 'em!
Rich and poor!
We can all praise Him
forever more!*

PSALMS 101

David longed to walk a path saints of the ages
    have sought
But he discovered it can only be found
By those who are willing to be taught.
The blameless path has a sign erected to guide
Those willing to walk by our Saviors side.
The One who pioneered that blessed path
Knew the counseling David needed.
It was the same as we who don't wish to be
    defeated!
God wants us to make the godly of the land
    our heroes.
We need the guidance God's Word bestows!
And-we need the common sense to lift up our
    heads
And walk in the light His Word sheds!
It is a daily task to rid ourselves of confusion
And to be vigilant enough to rid ourselves
Of negative soul-bruising contusion!
Like that gentle shepherd we must desire
The warmth of God-given spiritual fire!

PSALMS 102

David thought he was left all alone
To face those feelings he had feared.
He was discouraged because he thought
God had disappeared.
Though he moaned, complained, and cried
He had a faith that could not be denied.
David must have sit on the pinnacle
Of faith's mountain
And drank deeply from salvation's fountain.
Even when he was depressed, next to what
We feel, it was an emotional high.
Because he knew God would not let
The good times pass him by!
David knew he could find good news
In God's Holy Word
We're not as lucky in a way because
We shudder at the bad news we've heard!
No matter what channel we turn to
All we see and hear is continuing bad news.
We would welcome that lonely owl
Or follow that solitary sparrow
If only it would lead us toward the good path
The glorious news God leads us toward
-the good tidings of the straight and narrow!

The "I Love My Bible" Commentary

The King of all the ages walks there
And He has unlimited love to share!
David recorded this psalm for future
Generations to see
God wants us to live with Him no matter
Where He might be!
We can read over and over again
That God's years will never end
Therefore He will always be by our side
-always be our dearest friend.
May times I've called him friend
Because of what Jesus said.
"If you love me you are my friends"
-friends of the One who called himself
the living bread!

PSALMS 103

*All the things the Father is
all the things the Father does
and the reasons why
He can never be comprehended
are evident in this chapter!
We barely scrape
the surface of understanding
when we say
"His love is forever after!"
And we can never
travel far enough
to find our sins again!
Shame on those who doubt
God's great love for man!
"Bless the Lord," David said.
You bless Him too!
Ah!
And if you don't
shame on you!
Remember the Lord knows
we are made of dust.
He knows our frame!
And that's the reason*
*He forgive us!
Praise His Name!*

PSALMS 104

David says the earth is full of God's goodness
Mercy and riches
But man sneaks around at night looking for
The evil that bewitches.
God abundantly feeds us yet we turn away
And forget the many reasons we should pray!
David listed the blessings God had prepared
And he was convinced God made them
To be shared!
But what about those intangible blessings
We need the most?
Love, patience, and kindness
Are far more important
Than any riches in which we might boast.
When the hope of being loved by those
I love grows dim
I can still take hope because God's Word says
I am greatly loved by Him!

PSALMS 105

God has given us good memories so we can
    look back
When troubles and disappointments
Seem to grow and stack!
He can say, "Look at the blessings and pardon
I give
When we think we have no reason to live.
We are not to look down for we cannot see
The light
When our souls are as dark and heavy
As the darkest, endless night.
David reminded the people God fed them
With food others had planted
Because down through the years their minds
Had become perverted and slanted.

Comment on Psalms

It seems it took a special kind of bravery
To keep reminding these forgetful people
Of their rescue from slavery.
Man uses the crayons of his mind
And its strange conclusions he draws
As to the reasons we need to obey
God's holy, life enhancing laws!
The simple truth is, obedience draws us
Close to Him.
Only He can break the chains
That drag the hopeless to the brim.
The only true promises of hope
We've ever heard
Can definitely be found in *reading*
And *listening to God's Holy Word!*

PSALMS 106

If you are just and good to others, if you are fair
Then God has His special *"piece of cake"*
For you to share!
David knew that, but he said both he and
His people had sinned.
They had caused much heartache and pain
God had to step in and mend!
And though they had acted foolish and
Rebelled, to their shame
Our Heavenly Father saved them to defend
The honor of His Name!
Same thing for us! He saves us, too!
And I am amazed at the many times we fail
And the horrible things we sometimes do.

PSALMS 107

What is the most important thing
God's people can say?
It is, "I am redeemed
And I rejoice in that today!
Our Lord is loving and merciful and kind
And He even loved me when I was defiant
And spiritually blind!
We have left physical bondage behind
But there is still slavery of the mind!
There is death and darkness though we claim
To be so smart.
Somehow we overlook the pain and sorrow
That still lives in the heart.
Yet God satisfies the thirsty soul.
Only He can make our broken spirits whole!

PSALMS 108

I wish I could say, like David "My heart is ready
—ready to praise the Lord because my faith
Is strong and steady!"
But I can say, like David did
"Oh Lord, hear the cry of your beloved child!"
I, too, have had a disappointment that almost
Drives me wild.
I must remember God has given
His sacred promise even to me.
He can-and will-vanquish this deep depression
And wonderfully set me free!
I remind you David asked, "Lord, why have
You thrown us away?"
Well, that's the way I feel today.
"Oh Lord, I need you to help me climb out
Of this mood I'm in
Doubt and discouragement is an awful sin.
I ask as David did, come and lift me up.
Take away these awful feelings
And once again *fill my cup!"*
Over and over through the centuries
God has heard this cry
From many who have stood and watched
Their hopes and dreams die.
And as I've read this many times I've imagined
How God has answered all their prayers.
Its just so He can show how much He cares!

The "I love My Bible" Commentary

PSALMS 109

I was down hearted from false accusations
And implied curses
Until I read these first five verses!
And maybe now I can turn my fear to faith
And evil to good.
If I showed evil in return then I would
Not be doing as I should.
I can not show one how bad it feels
To be falsely accused.
Actually that is what this chapter reveals.
And even David thought he was abused.
He thought crime was a heathen invention
And they never had a good intention.
Here we see David's heart was defeated
It was a battle of faith in which he retreated.
He couldn't win looking at his circumstances.
And he made no noble, bold advances!
This chapter is so negative I shudder.
God forbid that I wish evil on anyone.
And I won't when I remember
All the mighty things my God has done!

PSALMS 110

There is healing
in God's love!
There is shelter
in His power!
So how could I have become
more depressed by the hour?
I used to wonder how
David could feel so low
yet come out
"smelling like a rose!"
I knew his faith was real
but I wondered
what is it he knows?
Well, this chapter says it all.
God would send His Messiah
on whom all men could call!
He will refresh the hearts
of men
when He rules from Jerusalem!
Now, observe very carefully
what I have to say.
Jesus WILL rule Jerusalem
in the future
but
He lives in our hearts
right now–today!
It is not a forceful rule
but a gentle reign!
He comes to heal
the broken spirit
and soothe us from our pain.
That will have to do
until He alone
comes to His holy city
to claim the throne!

PSALMS 111

"How can man be wise?" David asked.
Can universities and mighty men of science
Fulfill that task?
I think not!
Man, himself, performed the severance
From the wisdom of godly reverence.
Yet, God never forgets His promise to us.
Indeed, His love and provision is miraculous!
David said wisdom comes from obeying Him
Still, man turns away at the slightest whim.
Mankind forgets his most worthy endeavor
Is to praise this ONE who lives forever!
Man can take heart as long as he tries
To honor our God who is truly wise!
Spiritual wisdom is spiritually discerned and
That kind of expertise belongs to only one.
God said He would not give His glory
To another, but only to His Beloved Son!

Comment on Psalms

PSALMS 112

David implied there would be no spiritual depression
If we'd praise the Lord with delightful expression!
But, remember, life can move easily
Like a gently floating leaf
If, when you thank the Lord
You don't grit your teeth!!!
Ah! The day would hold no warning!
For we are told
God's mercies are new every morning!
Think about it!
Trust, obedience, and blessing
Are inseparable much like a golden triangle.
Try trust and obedience. God adds the blessing
Which no demon in hell or earth can mangle!
And happy is the man who delights
In doing God's will
For he knows just being healthy, wealthy
And wise, does not fill the heavenly bill!
Seek the golden triangle of trust, obedience
And God's blessing and you need not fear
For then you will learn how your
Remarkable future will be undoubtedly clear!
God's constant care of you
Will be evident for all to see
And that is all we need to feel completely free!

PSALMS 113

It is fantastic-the truths God reveals
And man would not despair
Of the loneliness he feels
If he would look and listen with his heart
And his ears, and keep his eyes open wide!
Deep in God's Word,
Sometimes between the lines, there is healing
For the hurts we carry buried inside!
As I've read through Psalms I've noticed
How David always bounced back.
He may have slipped and slid many times
But his faith stayed right on track!
Even though David's soul would fall
Into a horrible slump
And it seemed he was resigned to leave it
In a deserted garbage dump
He knew God would come and cleanse him again
For God loved this naive, and ambivalent
Yet noble, trustworthy man!
I challenge you to count the times David said
"Praise the Lord!"
And then you will see why David always
Walked along God's heavenly boulevard!

PSALMS 114

David once again reminded his people
where they had been.
They needed to remember the shape
they had once been in!
Today, we need to encourage each other also.
And as we do it should be no surprise
when we see the luster of our "Rock"
reflected in each others eyes!
Even in the darkest times
there is a golden glimmer
not found by anyone
who is a Bible skimmer!
Remember the adage about the old hay stack?
Well–if you want to find the needle
you have to keep going back!
And you will know when it is found
that needle holds the thread of truth
that keeps us heaven bound!
It may seem useless to review, review, review
but like King David knew
that is what it takes
to keep the love in our hearts
just as good as new!

The "I Love My Bible" Commentary

PSALMS   115

Israel's great shepherd king loved the Lord!
We should love Him just the same.
And if we do, we will pray like David did
"Lord, glorify your Name!"
Unless I see the *KING* in my life
I do not see the light.
Unless I love the *Lord*
True hope is completely out of sight!
And, unless the *Holy Spirit* reigns in my heart
Unshackled, full and free
I will fail to comprehend God's love for me!
Who is the man who says, "God is dead?"
Does he know how empty he is?
Certainly he cannot do what David said.
For one can only trust in one he believes
To be a LIVING God!
To trust like David is to walk the path he trod!
When there is praise, there is glorious life!
Without it, man walks in fear and strife.
Should God's people face defeat?   *!!Never!!*
Victory is already ours.
Praise the Lord forever and forever!

PSALMS   116

Communication keeps the flame of love alive!
Keeping it open makes a relationship thrive!
Just in case you wonder- *what is God's calling*
–here it is! *To deliver our souls from death!*
> *To dry the tears from our eyes!*
> *To keep our feet from falling!*
So our God made a way to accomplish this.
He simply says, "I will answer when you pray."
David said the Lord protects the child-like
And will walk with them along His own
Heavenly turnpike!
He wants us to know faith reaches its climax
Only when our souls trust God enough to relax.
David was not hesitant or tentative
When he said, "I am saved and <u>*meant to live!*</u>"
If only we will make adoration of the Lord
Our most precious, ultimate goal
We'll claim David's example and join him
In the "camp of the praise" super bowl!

PSALMS   117

This *shortest* chapter in the Bible
Has praise in *every* verse
Because God loves us for better or for worse!
And one thing we must not overlook
"Praise" is one of the sweetest words in this
   book!"
By now we know people who do not love
The "Great I AM"
Look for lies and hypocrisy
And the juicy slander of the latest scam!
The *scam* is in the people. Our God is pure!
Never forget, God's Word will always endure!
His strength will brighten our days
When we lift our thankful voices in praise!
> *This Chapter!*
> *Two verses only!*
> *Praise the Lord*
> *and you will*
> *never be lonely!*

PSALMS   118

"Oh Thank the Lord" the psalmist said.
Why grumble and complain?
We moan whenever its sunny and hot
And then, in showers, we gripe about the rain!
Maybe fewer of our souls would be scarred
If we had the presence of mind to praise
   the Lord!
Faith and thankfulness gives us the strength
Of a mighty elm
That stands rooted in God's holy realm!
David was deeply rooted in his love and belief

Comment on Psalms

And he would thank the Heavenly Father
Even before God sent him needed relief!

PSALMS 119

The longest chapter in the Bible starts with
A basic rule.
Blessed is the man who obeys the Lord.
The one who doesn't is a fool!
David truly wanted to succeed
And he knew exactly what he would need.
He would never have to fear.
When he kept God's laws, God would be near!
All through this chapter
We see David's love for God's laws
And it discouraged him because
He had to admit he possessed so many flaws!
And though he admitted to wandering away
He still remembered to keep
God's commandment's hidden in his heart
To help get him through each day!

PSALMS 120

Don't think troubles can trouble you.
Think only of what our Lord can do.
David knew the feeling of other men's hate
And he said, "...dark would be their fate!"
He often felt his pleas went unheeded
And his friends did not give him
The support he so badly needed.
When their denial of his rights seemed
Harsh and stern
This wise old king knew where to turn.
There was One on whom he could depend.
The "Rock of Ages" was his friend!
By now we should know what our God can do
And should realize, He is our friend too!
So, the troubles that try to trouble you
Definitely are limited by God's powerful grace
And He sends them all to outer space!

PSALMS 121

David asked, "Should I look to mountain gods
When my God is powerful and real?
And he knew no manufactured god
Could give any measure of love he could feel.
For God's love carried his soul heavenward
Easier than the wind carried a fragile feather!
David pictured God's love like a tranquil sea
While man's love is like stormy weather.
Nothing on this earth can surpass nor be
As great as the love God has for you and me!
Because of that we cannot sin against the Lord
As if there are "no holds barred!"
No one was ever more aware of God's love
Then David was
And he knew no one else can ever do
The great things our Lord does!
It was with realism he would paint
God's great love for every saint!
So don't be amazed at how wonderful
   you can feel
To know you can say like David
   "I know my God is real!"

PSALMS 122

David said, "I was glad when they said.
'Let us go into the House of the Lord'"
And he would exclaim he was saved
As he exulted in the love that God displayed!
Oh, to have his fervor to light a holy fire
That illuminates the soul with a fervent desire!
It seems Jerusalem was synonymous
With the temple
And it pictured God's love–plain and simple!
Oh Jerusalem, Jerusalem, no other city
   any where
Has known such love as you!
No other city has been privileged to see
Or feel the mighty things God can do!

The "I Love My Bible" Commentary

And what other city has ever known
Such honor, yet faced such defeat
That it would break the hearts
Of the prophets who loved every dusty street.
David must have circled her walls and cried
Over the times his Lord had been defied!
And he often *"blessed"* Jerusalem.
But, dear Jerusalem, we bless you, too
Just like David said we should do!
Blessed are they who bless Israel!
    Blessed are they!
Blessed are those who pray for her each day!
The more I read Psalms, the more I'm sure of
There wasn't a stone in Jerusalem's city limits
That David didn't love!

PSALMS 123

Oh how anxious I should be
    To keep my eyes lifted
        looking for the One
    who is abundantly gifted!
The greatest clue to the fact that our God lives
Lies in the wonderful gift of love that He gives!
    David said, "Oh God,
    I will lift my eyes to You!"
    To whom else could he go?
    What else could he do?
Had he not, David would not have possessed
    the great faith he had
Would have been desperate and constantly sad.
He had days of sorrow and pain. Such is life!
Just walking this earth seems to guarantee
    we will often face strife!
    Do we give up?
    No! We look up!
    Up beyond those distant hills
        —beyond what we can see
        to the God of all the ages
        whose love can make us
        what we long to be!

PSALMS 124

Christians can take comfort
    when trouble strikes.
We won't need to run and hide
    because the Commander
    of the armies of heaven
    walks by our side!
Even if we lose the skirmish
He takes us to be with Him
    and there, we'll walk
    with the angels
    and mighty cherubim!
Death is just a heavy fog
    we cannot see through
but beyond that obstruction
    is a very different view!
David declared he could not
    be destroyed
by other people's anger
and that should give us
    food for thought
when we are facing danger!
We need not walk in fear
in this land of our birth.
Our help comes from the Lord
who made heaven and earth!

PSALMS 125

The old devil can threaten, cavort and prance
But, we who trust God, will not be moved
By any of his plans or even circumstance!
Create a picture in your mind
Of Judah's mighty "lion"
And then try to be as steady as Mount Zion!
"I am surrounded," you can say in glee
And then joyously add, "It is the Lord who is
    surrounding me!"
God does good to those whose hearts are right
So, grab His hand and hold on tight!

Comment on Psalms

PSALMS 126

Do you think heaven is a dream
Or an evil scam God's people would employ?
If you do, you'll never laugh with the saints
And you'll never shout for joy!
Your soul will not be refreshed
As if by streams in the thirsty desert!
And you will remain dry and empty
No matter how much will you exert.
And, Christian, we'll never truly rejoice
Unless we extend to others the chance
To make a godly choice.
Tears in this chapter merely depict sincerity
Because they picture those who took
Their witness seriously!
And we'll truly have a right to sing
When we bring others to our righteous King!

PSALMS 127

Unless the Lord builds your 'house'
It will collapse in useless rubble.
It would be no stronger
Than sticks, hay, and stubble!
And do you think you should stand on guard?
Well that, too, is useless
Unless you are protected by the Lord!
We're also told not to worry about our fate
And we should not allow worry and fear
To keep us up late.
So now lets 'change gears' and think
Of God's sweetest gift-that of a little child!
In no other relationship
Except that of husband and wife
Can life be so happily profiled!
And of all God's creation every child
　　　is an aristocrat
someone to love and cherish!
　　　Please
　　please remember that!

PSALMS 128

Blessings!   Why are they so elusive?
Should I consider the first verse
　too conclusive?
How masterful David says it for us to read.
Blessings on all who reverence the Lord
And when He speaks, takes heed!
Why should I travel the world over
Looking for joy that God plants
In my own backyard?
It is reverence, trust, and obedience
　packaged in love
That brings my blessings from the Lord!
No 'if' 'and' 'buts'   or   'wherefore'
Just a simple, "Yes I will, Lord"
Brings blessings by the score!

PSALMS 129

The most persistent heritage that Israel
Has passed through the years from father to son
Has been the awful persecution seen even today
And we wonder if it will ever be over and done!
Since the grim reaper still carries his bag of fear
It seems doubtful that Israel will ever see
The 'light' burning bright and clear!
It WILL happen someday
When God comes to clean the debris
From His favored highway!
Those who hate Israel and Israel's faith in God
Are already as good as dead.
Someday love will rule where hate has been
For God will break the chains of evil men!
Though Israel is surrounded by those
Who mock and criticize
She remains, now and forever
God's greatest prize!
God has made her a promise He will not forget
And He will keep it someday
As sure as there is a sunrise and a sunset!

The "I Love My Bible" Commentary

PSALMS   130

Russian Roulette compares close to depression
And it seems cries go unheard as the soul
Continues in its regression.
But, somehow God's forgiveness takes hold
And it is more beautiful than we've ever
  been told!
David knew the blessed hope that the ages
  spawn
And he watched for the Lord
Like a sentinel watches for the dawn!
We *can* overcome the soul's Russian Roulette.
Does God still forgive and forget? You bet!
God did ransom Israel from sin
And He is *willing* to do the same for all men.
And it is obvious for me to see
He has also included me!

PSALMS   131

Oh Boy!
Shouldn't we all learn this chapter by heart?
If we did, we wouldn't rip our neighbors'
Reputations apart!
We certainly would not pretend to know it all
For haughtiness and pride usually precedes
Our own downfall.
We would be as quiet before the Lord
As a thoughtful child.
Maybe it was David's pattern for remaining
Undefiled!
Certainly, we will not grow bitter and hard
If we wait in willing dependence on our Lord!

PSALMS   132

Dear David did not have to pretend
That our blessed Lord was his friend.
His greatest desire was to please the Lord
So, he studied diligently and worked hard!

Though the temple would be beautiful
Its elegance rare
It would not be enough to depict the presence
Of He who is beyond compare!
Also, that blessed ark
That conveys God's presence
Would only be a spark
Compared to God's glory
For God's omnipotence cannot not be
Adequately pictured in any form, in any story!
And since only God can dress His priests
In robes that are truly white
All saints must wear His garments of salvation
In order to shed His light!
God would give David a *Mighty Son*!
That is what He decreed.
Only God could ease our heartaches
And fulfill our every need!
And one day That Ultimate King
Would stand in Jerusalem and declare
"I AM the Messiah," yet they thought they saw
Only a man standing there!
He was David's Lord yet came as David's son.
He was King of the ages yet came as a servant
To make salvation available to every one!
From Adam to 'Alpha,' from sinner to saint
Salvation is a picture only God can paint!

PSALMS   133

Harmony never caused a friendship to spoil
And is as refreshing as God's anointing oil!
David said it is a pleasure to see
Brothers living together in harmony!
I think its safe to say as love passes
From sister to sister and brother to brother
We'll find it much easier to help one another!
Love is a treasure sent from above
And life is sweeter that is filled with love!
And it seems God Himself will pour
His endless treasure of life on us forever more!

Comment on Psalms

PSALMS 134

You who serve the Lord day or night
Are truly His watchmen, walking in the light!
No wonder David said, "Lift up your hands."
Now, as we do that, may our hands perform
All of our Heavenly Father's commands!
May they be holy though aged or scarred
For the hands of every saint should be used
To praise the Lord!
May we lift them high for all to see
Our faithfulness to Him
So that we will not be ashamed when
He returns to rule in Jerusalem!

PSALMS 135

I know the omnipotence of the Lord is a fact.
His greatness shows in each and every act!
We still praise His name.
There is no other who can claim such fame!
It seems David gets carried away
When he recalls how much God helps
His people each and every day.
It pleases God for us to be thankful
For what we possess.
Time has proved no one can bless
As graciously as our Lord can bless.
If David walked this earth today
He would think we were vain
Not to thank the Father for all the blessings
Our lives contain!
He would not find it hard
To say, "Hallelujah, praise the Lord!"

PSALMS 136

One would certainly have to be stricken
With total un-reversible blindness
Were he not to see this chapter exclaims
God's magnificently loving kindness!
Over and over again David repeats
His heartfelt thanks for God's mighty feats!
He takes Israel back to the beginning of creation
And covers what he thinks is every situation.
And then he must have considered it was
Enough for Israel to know God created the universe
For then he names the nations God had cursed.
If you think his thankfulness was just a passing phase
Then count the many times David says to
Give God praise!

PSALMS 137

If I forget you, oh Jerusalem, shame on me!
David would say those who forget you
Will be disgraced throughout all history.
No other city on earth has felt such great love
Nor has been mourned with such fervor
Like that of a mourning dove!
Yet, Jerusalem knows to whom she belongs.
When God returns, there will be no sad songs!
She will need no one's pity
When the Lord returns to rule that city!
All the world will have to admit
Great is the King who will rule from it!
God will answer those who say He is overdue
With—*"Oh Jerusalem, I cannot forget you!"*

PSALMS 138

David isn't the only one who wants to
Thank you, Lord –and I do with all my heart
As I face *the temple of your love*
That tore that veil of secrecy completely apart!
God's love and his intentions are not fogged.
It is easy to see the blessings He logged!
Even in these days blessings are a 'log jam'
Coming from the Great I Am!

The "I Love My Bible" Commentary

Precious Holy King, how I love you!
There is not a single problem you have not
Brought me through!
May we continue to sing about God's
Glorious ways
And NEVER forget to lift our voices
In thankful praise!

PSALMS 139

The Lord makes a thorough
examination of my heart!
Not even the heights
of ecstasy
nor the depths of despair
can tear us apart.
For where I go
my Father goes
and what I face
my Father knows!
Even when I do not feel
His presence near
and even when
I hide in fear
I can be sure of one
marvelous thing.
I am under the watchful care
of my wonderful King!
I don't know how
but I know my Lord
is with me now!
It is in His shadow
I am hid.
We, who are God's people
can make the same claim
God's gentle shepherd did!

PSALMS 140

It is hard to be objective
when we are subjected
to bad news.
David prayed to be delivered
from men who held
violent negative views.
But, no matter what the situation
he did not have to yield
for he knew the Lord
was his Savior
his God
and his shield!
He prayed that liars
would not prosper.
Let us do the same.
We must listen to the godly
if we expect to praise
our Father's Holy Name!

PSALMS 141

Prayer can be a sweet smelling sacrifice
Better than incense offered at any price.
David seemed to have the same concern we do
For learning to control our tongues
Seems to be accomplished by very few!
He complains that greedy people have built
Their businesses based on lust
And taught millions to love 'things'
That will eventually turn to dust.
Don't say David wasn't smart.
He knew how 'things' could affect the heart.
He prayed to be disciplined by godly men.
Their reverent influence would keep him
From all known sin.
"Prayer," he said, "is what the wicked needs!"
To turn them from their evil deeds.
David looked to the Lord for refuge
Because his faith was incredibly huge!
Faith is the King's highway
Traveled eagerly by His saints each day
And we know, waiting at the other end
Is our glorious Father-friend!

Comment on Psalms

PSALMS 142

No one gives me a passing thought!
Do you ever feel that way?
And do you wonder if the Lord
will ever hear you
when you pray?
Do you-like David-feel
desperately overwhelmed
and alone?
Well then, look to the "Rock"
David was depending on!
And the times
we are conquered by fear
are the times we must
remember our Lord
is near!
David was imprisoned by fear
and other people's hate
but the Lord just came along
and opened that prison gate!
It was the Lord who helped him
through troubled days
and that is why
David would often
lift his voice in praise!

PSALMS 143

David said, "Lord, saving me
Will give glory to your name!
And he wanted the Lord to punish those
Who carelessly lived in shame.
Instead of climbing faith's mountain slope
He ran from his enemies, losing all hope.
But then he began to remember
All his blessings and all that God had done
And now he begs for God to intervene
And grant him at least another one!
He wanted the miracle of kindness
And, in effect, said, "Hurry!"

If not, he felt the world would have
One more victim to bury!
Now, we also must remember we should
Walk in those pathways God considers good!
And then, God will answer when we cry
And once more, will lift our spirits high!

PSALMS 144

David's closing remarks are, "Happy are those
Whose God is the Lord!"
But we must put Him first to encourage others
And to win a heavenly reward!
God was always first in David's heart
And he knew those who rejected God
Could actually never be considered smart!
He wondered why the Lord would bother
With the human race
And, in his self-pity
Forgot the purpose of God's amazing grace!
He goes on to describe a truly happy land
Stating happiness was based on people's
Willingness to obey our Lord's command.
"Happy are those whose God is the Lord"
Is worth repeating again!
For as long as humans walk this earth
God will show his love for man!

PSALMS 145

Now it becomes obvious-and lovingly so
That David cannot contain his zeal!
Time is getting short and he reminds Israel
God is real!
God IS real!
GOD IS REAL!
And it should not be surprisin'
that his praise reaches
far beyond the horizon!
Truly this shepherd king's feet were shod
With the marvelously invincible love of God!

The "I love My Bible" Commentary

PSALMS 146

Instead of slowing down
David's praise increased.
He would soon be leaving this body
His precious soul had leased!
We've always been told
These bodies we rent will soon grow old!
At best, life on this earth is a temporary
   occupation
Therefore, we should act with dignity
   in any situation.
     Going home!
     Going home!
What a joyful, wonderful thought!
We will make that heavenly transfer
If we live as we ought!
We will walk God's heavenly trails that list
No segregation nor restraining bars.
That is why God's people must keep
Their eyes on the One who made the stars!

PSALMS 147

Want to know how important gospel singing is?
Inspirational singing surrounds and uplifts
Those who are His!
I can hear(well, almost)God singing along
For Our Father loves to hear a gospel song!
Joy comes from beautiful gospel music.
And godly joy is not felt by those
Who refuse to choose it!
The soul who will not listen to it grows cold
-like a river of ice.
When we listen to gospel music
It seems to fill us with good advice!
It is one way to praise the Lord
And makes our troubles seems less hard!
Whoever said "let the anthems ring"
Knew singing is a lovely thing!
OK, folks! Turn loose! Now lets all sing!

PSALMS 148

David wants the heavens and all those angels
To join in
Just in case there is not enough praise
From earth's godly men!
The Lord must be praised for He is great.
Praising Him puts our minds in a godly state!
The heavens must have resounded
With unlimited joyful laughter
From all the praises listed in this chapter.
And if we don't praise God, that problem
Will be resolved, for so great is God's grace
That Jesus said the rocks would praise Him
If we don't-and would do it in our place!
     God alone is worthy!
     God alone is great!
Listen to the growing thunder of our praise
As we realize we walk by faith, not by fate!
Hallelujah, praise the Lord!
We can say we are in *a blessed holy state!*
We can say God controls us through love
And ALL those who follow Him will NEVER
Be possessed by hate.
Unless this Psalm(or any other)lifts up the Lord
It can not be considered a Psalm.
And knowledge of His presence
Is, now and always, more soothing
Than any earthly balm!

PSALMS 149

Singing and praising go together
They lighten our hearts better
Than the expectation that comes
From Springs balmy weather!
When Israel exulted in her Great King
With the accompaniment of drums and lyre
Even far off nations could feel the vibrations
Of her good cheer!
Praise the Lord, just like David said

Comment on Psalms

And we will walk in those same paths that led
By green pastures and still waters
That dear old David tread!
There is healing for hearts that are scarred
When our deeds and our voices praise the Lord!
Adoration lifts our hearts beyond the ordinary
And assures the world we love this God
Whose name we carry!

PSALMS 150

The Psalms close with
resounding praise!
"Hallelujah," David says
"Praise Him all your days!"
Every where you go
everything you do
remember to love
our blessed Lord
because our Lord loves you!
Every time he thought
of God's love
and life and light
David would let himself
get 'higher than a kite!'
He swore to follow the Lord
no matter what the price
and suggests we do the same
and that is good advice!
Now, if you are in deep
depression
if you are sad and blue
you will be pleasantly
surprised
what our God can do for you!

Note: I said once that no other Old Testament book has brought so much hope to so many lives. And that is because I believe this book has been read more than any other. People look for the still waters that David wrote about, seek the green pastures and the righteous trails where God walks. Only with God can we find the still waters, the green pastures, and the ones called "goodness and mercy" to follow us all our lives. Assurance is ours for the asking and it is found when we walk with the One who walks beside the still waters, in fact, the One who quiets the still waters. There is a peace, a quietness in the soul as we walk with Him. The Psalms, especially the 23rd Psalm is a dramatic picture of how soothing and peaceful life can be. Jesus said, "peace I leave with you, my peace I give unto you: not as the world giveth, give I unto you. Let not your heart be troubled, neither let it be afraid." (John 14:27kjv) He is the one David wrote of in the 23rd Psalm. He IS our still waters-our green pastures and our blessed hope. He is goodness and mercy who follows us. We can not adequately describe Him but we can walk with Him by faith-walk with Him in the green pastures and by the still waters. We can feel peace we can't explain, show joy that is real, experience love that surrounds and upholds us. All this is a gift from God and all this is described in the Psalms.. The more we understand God's love the more love means to us and certainly the more we will be willing to love others.
So—let it be. Let there be love!
Glorious, unending, eternal love!

The "I Love My Bible" Commentary
(The Book of Proverbs)

Note: In beginning Proverbs, I want to relate to you the change in <u>slant</u> from the "spirit" to the "Intellect." It's a change from the thoughts of the heart(David)to the musings of the mind(Solomon)and I can't resist giving you one more comment on Psalms and it may seem to you that I protest leaving Psalms. Maybe I do. Its so easy to identify with that "gentle shepherd" whose heart was full of God! I do believe, in the beginning of his reign, Solomon remembered David's joy as he worshiped the Lord. At first Solomon did too, but he never reached the spiritual level that David did....So now I'd like to remember David(and those other psalmists who had the spirit of David)one more time as I begin to comment on Proverbs. I want us to remember David's love for the Lord and there is <u>nothing</u> that can make life sweeter than loving Him! NOTHING!

I can imagine David wondering
"what in the world has happened?"
as he watches from one of
his 'distant' hills
wondering why God's people
have deserted the deep joy
of the spirit
and opted for cheap
empty thrills.
Don't you suppose he puzzled
why mankind has turned
from the "Light"
to walk spiritually blind?
David was certain
that a bitter, doubting atheist
would never know
the great love he had missed!
And he would call men fools
who doubt there is a God
and ignore God's awesome rules!
Those who do
think the thrill today
is to have a long lover's list
or to contort oneself in synch
to a musical(?) compact disc!
David sought the love
that would never change
and as he watches from above
he must think
we're acting awfully strange!
Today, so many have high IQ's
but that doesn't make us
spiritually smart.
It seems we are still
aboriginal
in matters of the heart!
And Solomon who was so wise
must have allowed lust
to cloud his eyes
and he forgot his duty
when he chose to
worship beauty.
Wisdom does not save a soul!
David knew
only God can make us whole!
Solomon–wiser than any one
forgot what it meant
to be David's son!
He was meant to carry
on the faith
once delivered to God's saints
but he worshiped beauty
and idols
apparently with no restraints!
We must remember
spiritual things are
spiritually discerned
and that was evidently something
Solomon never learned!

Comment on Proverbs

PROVERBS 1

Regardless of how Solomon's life ended
His beginning was "gung ho!"
"Following the Lord," he advised
  "is the only way to go!"
And he knew the Lord's kind of life
Was this earth's greatest prize.
God's nuggets of truth are absolutely necessary
If man wants to be wise
He advised young people to obey their fathers
And their mothers.
They'd not have so great a love
From cheats, toughs, or many others.
He also warns complacency can kill.
Its devious unconcern keeps people from doing
What they know to be God's will.
Doing God's will is the best choice
I ever made!
It helps me to live in peace and safety unafraid!

PROVERBS 2

King Solomon addressed
   the same astronomical problem
      we have today.
   Adultery is treated so lightly
   most people don't consider it sin
      but merely child's play.
   But, oh the troubles
      it has caused
   and degraded souls into
      possessing multiple flaws.
   Only wisdom from the Lord
      can save
   mankind from its hellishly
      ugly grave.
   God says the souls
   that commit adultery will die.
      Active voice!
      Present tense!
So, turning from adultery
   in repentance
   makes a lot of sense!
We may fly to the moon
and beyond in a space capsule
   but we get to heaven only
by obeying God's golden rule!

PROVERBS 3

The Lord mocks at mockers and
He will have the last laugh
On that final judgement day when
He blows away the "chaff!"
Solomon was right when he said God's love
For us is merciful and kind.
But He rejects the dissenters who choose
To be spiritually blind.
That has been said many times but needs
To be repeated.
Also—notice wisdom warns it is foolish
For man to be conceited.
Wisdom gives a long life, peace, riches
Honor and pleasure
And wise King Solomon considered that
Life's greatest treasure!
But—the most important advice in this
Or any other chapter is this.
   "Put God First!"
And if you do yours will be a life of bliss!

PROVERBS 4

Morning splendor overcomes the dawn
For we who walk in God's favor!
And we have no words to describe
The wonder, power, and love of our Savior!
He is wonderful! *Wonderful! Wonderful!*
Even Solomon could not over emphasize
God's benefits, the greatness of which
He could only surmise!

The "I Love My Bible" Commentary

Man seeks knowledge when it is wisdom
   he needs.
But when we worship God, His wisdom
Leads to a life of good deeds!
There is *no substitute* for the life
Our Savior gives!
Happy is the one who remembers *that*
As long as he(or she)lives

PROVERBS 5

The man who thinks doing his own thing
Is light, hearty, and jolly
Stands the chance of tripping into the trap
Of unthinkable folly.
God has not changed---will not! Cannot!
And, unless we are genuinely careful
We can get ourselves in an awful spot!
Solomon says God is closely watching you
And he weighs everything you(we)do!
In this chapter, the question
 "Why did I have to have my own way?"
Could be asked by you and I, if we're not
Careful what we do and say!
It is so easy to get in trouble, so hard to get out
Yet we all make the same mistakes because
We are so full of doubt.
We will have to be prepared to face
The consequences of what we choose
For it is the privilege of His presence
We should never want to lose!
Think of the bottomless trap we can spring
When we fail to realize eternity
Is a realistically awesome thing!
Again, Solomon seems to harp on adultery
And maybe it is for the reason
It can never take the place of God's love
Which will *never* go out of season!
God's love! Accept it! Hold it tight!
It is His sweepstakes ticket, made for us
So we can joyfully walk *in His light!*

PROVERBS 6

Solomon despises laziness and he adds
The Lord despises a liar.
And sowing discord among brothers
Starts a *raging fire*!
Also Solomon states there are seven things
The Lord hates.
Eagerness to do mischief, pride
And murder are some of those he relates!
Now, he's on adultery again when he implies
A man will blister his feet
Following a prostitute down a red-hot street!
He says it is the street to hell.
Man must be pure if he wants to do well.
Well, that is not a popular opinion today
For man has decided to go his own way.
He does not realize he's without the safety
Of God's ark
And he flounders directionless in the *dark!*
He(or she)who thinks adultery is ok
Will find God still despises it today!

PROVERBS 7

Solomon was *street smart*
In matters of the heart
And he knew which way to run
When challenged to *have a little fun!*
It has never been fun to be deceived
But some have learned that only in time
To know they've been betrayed and bereaved.
Solomon seemed to know about prostitutes
And this weakness of men that still causes
So many disputes!
I guess, in this case, the road to hell is paved
By lusty hearts willing to be depraved.
Obviously this is a sin we should not touch
Because it is one our Lord hates so much!
Jesus implied it is as bad and as unjust
Even to look on a woman and feel lust!

Comment On Proverbs

PROVERBS 8

Wisdom is not evasive!
Wisdom is not detained
except by foolish minds
unwilling to be trained!
It's value is far above rubies
far above wealth.
It can be said
the soul that rejects it
is in a state of ill health!
God used His wisdom
and then decided to share
a good measure of it
when He placed it in our care!
Solomon says whoever
finds wisdom finds life
but to reject it
leads us into strife.
For God's wisdom is
and God's wisdom was
and God's wisdom will
always be
His special way of setting
our despondent spirits free!

PROVERBS 9

To know the love of the Lord is more valuable
Than all the silver and gold in the world.
Those who are truly wise will admit it is
More precious than the most priceless pearl!
But, don't overlook the fact
Reverence and fear of God
Are basic to wisdom and affects how we act!
Notice what Solomon says about knowing God
Because it results in other kinds of wisdom
And smooths the lonesome paths we plod!
Wise men know *stolen melons* are not the best.
They know following our Lord
Will surely keep our souls at rest!

Read this chapter closely to see what I mean.
In the case of adultery, it is better to stay clear
And better to stay clean!
Solomon seems to have known it well!
A prostitute's guests are citizens of hell!
He must be trying to say man never learns
That _most_ of the problems he faces
Are merely those he earns!

PROVERBS 10

The next nineteen chapters of Proverbs
Is a study in contrasts.
Solomon congratulates the good
But says the bad are out-classed.
There are no gray lines–only black and white.
It is as if Solomon wanted to say
Riding the fence is never right!
In this chapter we can see
Verse thirty seems to summarize it well.
The good shall _never_ lose God's blessing
But the wicked shall lose everything.
What else can we expect
When we refuse to honor our great King?

PROVERBS 11

The rich can't use their riches on God's great
Judgement day.
God has already provided us another way!
If we have not counted on righteousness
Nothing will count!
Souls cannot be saved by any other amount!
There are those who become richer
When they give their money away.
Solomon knew the benevolent would live
To see a bright and shining day!
Of all the proverbs in this chapter
I love these the very best!
Loving people more than money
Is the surest way to be blessed!

The "I Love My Bible" Commentary

PROVERBS 12

There is so very little we can learn
Because we are unwilling to be taught.
It seems disobedience and spiritual ignorance
Is a highly contagious virus we have caught!
Solomon talks much about wisdom
Which is the basis
For all the virtues from which mankind races.
But to run from godliness brings us fear
And then we fail to feel God is ever near.
But, we have a King who is sublime!
And His knowledge truly stands
The test of time!

PROVERBS 13

The escalator of time takes the good man up
-the evil man down.
It all depends on whether or not
One takes advice with an unrelenting frown!
It seems Solomon had plenty of comparisons
   listed
And how wisdom escaped those who resisted
The great wisdom God has shared.
If mankind hears and obeys God's Word
He will be spared.
God's great wisdom refreshes like
A clear mountain spring!
And-look-Solomon even mentions
The good results discipline can bring!
It proves to your children that you love
   them dearly!
Just do it in a way they can see *that* clearly!
And I think we all would be smart
To take that last verse in this chapter to heart!

PROVERBS 14

Solomon builds to a very powerful argument.
Godliness exalts a nation and anyone can see

Godliness is certainly time well spent!
For to do right honors God and it leads
To the strength and perseverance
Every person needs!
Reverence is a fountain of life where
Cool waters
Form a 'moat' of protection around one's
Personal quarters!
Those who seem to 'worship' recreation
Fail to see, it is righteousness that truly
Exalts a nation.
But it begins with *number one!*
Collectively, our nation is only as good
As what we as individuals have done!

PROVERBS 15

If we profit from constructive criticism we
Will be added to the wise man's hall of fame!
But Solomon says to reject it is to live in such
A way that even fools will forget your name!
　　　　Stop!　Think!
Have we done what people choose not to
Honor or remember?
Will our passing leave---only a dying ember?
My Mother relied heavily on Proverbs.
It was her favorite Old Testament Book!
She felt we should live holy
No matter what it took!
I believe she had the wisdom of Solomon
And I hope I've lived as good as she
When my life on earth is done!
She knew a soft answer to a spiteful remark
Is like a breath of fresh Spring air
Because people need to know
We have a gentle love to share!
We do well to remember our Lord watches us.
He is looking for peace and harmony
And He certainly doesn't want to hear us fuss!
Evil, vicious people seem to be honored now
But some day the Lord will *clean their plow!*

Comment on Proverbs

PROVERBS 16

Through the centuries that time spans
Solomon says we should
Learn to honor God in all our plans!
We must always count on God's direction
Otherwise we fall so very short of perfection.
And we discover it is futile to look for
What we think is the wide and pleasant road
For it's the straight and narrow way
Where God lightens our load!
Pleasant words, he knew, were like honey
Sweet to the soul, better than money!
Solomon felt wisdom was the *fountain of life*
For wise words calmly spoken could ease
All manner of strife!
Sometimes his thoughts seem to be disjointed
But it was life itself to which he pointed!
He considered the undecided to be *flighty*
But he who ruled his own spirit was stronger
Than anyone considered rugged or mighty!
It is important to remember whatever our goal
To keep in our minds and in our hearts
That our Heavenly Father is in control!

PROVERBS 17

It is a sad thing when a friendship ends
So remember nagging parts the best of friends.
Perhaps we won't create the trouble it starts
When we rely on the Lord to purify our hearts!
Solomon may not have been
As joyous as his father, David was
But he consistently warned that man
Must answer for what he does.
He knew death held a fatal finality
When man would have to face ultimate reality.
Though he wrote many proverbs
Solomon admired the man of very few words.
And he held that point of view
When he warned what a broken spirit can do!

PROVERBS 18

This chapter contains a proverb none of us
Want to face
But Solomon knew the necessity of warning
That sin brings disgrace.
He hints as to what others have done
When he says the Lord is a strong fortress
To which we can run!
He talks of deadly rumors and of good advice
And added that rumors are deadly morsels
That come with an exorbitant price!
He warns men have died for saying the
Wrong thing
For words are *deadlier* than a scorpion sting.
Perhaps we should follow his advice
And be a friend
On whom it is a pleasure to depend!

PROVERBS 19

There is nothing man
dislikes to hear more
than it is better to be
honest and poor.
The "in" thing today
is quite a switch!
Man says it is better
to be rich!
When he is caught cheating
and goes down in shame
he spouts his innocence
and says others are to blame!
But Solomon tells us
who the Lord will bless
for He gives the ones
who love His wisdom
great success.
He warns against
what some teaching depicts
and wants us to study

The "I Love My Bible" Commentary

*the truths such teaching
contradicts.
Sometimes God's word
is shunted
so deliberately it leaves
God's people stunted!
Solomon is thinking of
mockers and rebels
when he says
"man proposes"
but he knows God
will do the disposing
when that man's life
on this earth closes!*

PROVERBS 20

Solomon starts this chapter implying
The false courage wine can give
And he should have warned it can haunt you
For as long as you live.
He adds, an intoxicated man loves to fight
And is unable to discern who is in the right.
And Solomon wonders who can say
"I have lived a sinless life today."
*We know Jesus knew men
And he would say none are without sin!*
I do believe at one time Solomon longed
To be good and pure
And he felt purity was the basis for making
His land and his people safe and secure!
Though he makes many ambivalent remarks
In this "book"
It is one we should not overlook!

PROVERBS 21

In sermon after sermon in most of Proverbs
Solomon teaches our actions determine
Our circumstances
And the quality of the rewards(or punishment)
God dispenses and enhances!
Solomon says the wicked will eventually lose
So we should be careful of the path we choose.
If life, righteousness, and honor, are the riches
We want to find
Solomon advises us to be good, loving,
Forgiving, and kind.
Such a life shows we have love to spare
And we know it pleases the Lord
When we are just and fair!
We make life wonderful when we reverence
Our loving Savior
And our love for Him has a way of showing
In our daily behavior!
The happiest words we can say
At the close of each day are
"my Lord still walks with me along the way!"

PROVERBS 22

*These are powerful words
Solomon wrote.
He did not have to bluff!
Had he written
only these four words
they would have been enough!
"Trust in the Lord!"
"Trust in the Lord!"
The necessity for that
has always been so.
We must trust in Him
and tell it wherever we go!
Yes, we must pass it on
this privileged life
we've known!
My people, we must not
let our light grow dim
for it is the light
we received from Him!
So, let it shine!
Let it shine!*

Comment on Proverbs

PROVERBS 23

If we could memorize and follow
All the advice Solomon gave
We'd have many wonderful memories
We'd all want to save!
But its so much easier said than done
And I bet, though Solomon's advice
And rules were many
He also wished he'd followed every one!
And there must be many a prostitute
Who wishes she'd been more astute
--many a man soused with wine
  who wishes he'd had more substance
  to his spine
–many a cheat who wishes he'd cheated no one
–and many a child of God who regrets
  many things he has done.
So many regrets! So much pain!
So many souls foolishly stained!
But God's love is bigger than our mistakes
And His mercy covers our relational breaks!
And I wonder how many times He has said
"I WILL forgive them!"
And we will see our God someday
When He returns to Jerusalem!

PROVERBS 24

Man's reasoning power is a marvelous asset
But after all these centuries he stumbles yet
And it seems to me he has atrophied
In that which he needs the most!
He can fly to the moon but has made
No great spiritual strides in which he can boast.
Knowledge becomes wisdom when it flows
In unison with universal love
And love becomes beautiful when we allow it
To descend unhampered from above!
Solomon tried to convince his people
Wisdom comes from an uncontaminated mind
And its vision reaches beyond this lifetime!
It reaches to a life of fulfilled golden dreams
And to God's promise that life can be
Much greater than it seems!
This chapter warns us we can not get by
With laziness or excessive slumber
And it seems to say that the Lord
already has our number!

PROVERBS 25

Do you have an enemy?
Feed him!
With such kindness
can he stay so grim?
And when he is thirsty
give him a drink.
It may cause him
to stop and think!
I'm not going to say
Solomon was a manipulator
but he knew the disposition
of others
and he was an excellent
illustrator!
He knew if we illustrated
kindness
we'd receive kindness
in return
and if we draw on
just one good deed
we'd supply
mankind's greatest need.
So—when was the last time
you gave a hungry soul
a meal
and was amazed
at how good you could feel?
To feed is to partner
with our Lord
who promises us a great reward!

The "I Love My Bible" Commentary

PROVERBS 26

Could there be a more harmful fetish
Than to pass on gossip with great relish?
And wouldn't it be safe to say
A careless tongue has destroyed
More lives than all the weapons ever deployed?
But can you believe what Solomon says
About flattery?
It may be about as useless
As an old run-down battery!
But I didn't realize it would hurt anyone
And thought it another way of having fun!
But Solomon says it is deadly fuel
That feeds hatred and is utterly cruel.
Run from flattery as fast as you can!
Don't let it fool you ever again.

PROVERBS 27

Like a bird wanders from its nest
Some men wander away from home.
There is an emptiness in their hearts
That causes them to roam.
But they fail to realize jealousy is worse
Than the strongest anger.
So if they ignore that, they could be in danger!
Throughout this chapter Solomon is warning
Us to act right and be sensible.
To be otherwise is to be indefensible.
He warns that ambition and death alike
Are never satisfied
And says, because of greed
Many a soul has cried!
And–a man's face is the mirror of his soul
And it often reveals his ultimate goal!
It seems all through this book
Solomon is in a hurry to say so much.
If its love we want we must keep in touch
-with our loved ones, our neighbors, our friends
 and therefore we'll find a joy that never ends!

PROVERBS 28

Solomon says to obey the law
is to fight evil.
Let the wicked flee!
Goodness is like a mighty lion
that protects you and me.
We should be concerned
about moral rot
in our nation
for it tears at the seams!
Anarchy
and disobedience
will destroy
all our life long dreams!
We cannot fight evil
unless we obey God's law.
Lust, cheating
and crime in our streets
reveals that we
possess a deadly flaw!
Solomon adds
that those who practice
God's wisdom are safe
and secure.
A nation will NOT fall
if its citizens are pure!

PROVERBS 29

Throughout all the excellent advice we've had
We learn—it is always useless to be bad.
In the end justice will succeed.
Someday, we'll have the peace we all need!
But–it comes from obedience to God's
Higher law. People cannot run wild!
Discipline must be taught and practiced
Beginning with a little child!
Learn most of all to be loving and kind.
Then God will willingly give us
Harmony, happiness, and peace of mind!

Comment on Proverbs

PROVERBS 30

An universal plea is made here
And it seems we all have the same fear.
There are two things for which Agur pleads.
One is for the Lord to satisfy his needs.
Two favors he asks—"before I die."
The second is–to help him never to tell a lie!
Agur speaks of dissatisfaction, of fear
And of perversion
And implies a fool surely needs conversion!
If we've learned anything from these lofty
Meditative words, some gentle, some hard
It is, if we have obeyed and trusted the Lord
We won't fear His awful rejection
When He comes to make His final inspection!

PROVERBS 31

This chapter takes a different turn
And describes a virtuous lady
Instead of listing the faults of so many
Solomon has described as "cheap and shady!"
It teaches us a woman of pure spiritual strength
Need not fear old age.
We need more 'stars' like her
If earth indeed is a stage!
Charm can be deceptive and beauty doesn't last
But a woman who has *truly been a lady*
Will never have to fear her past!
She, who cherishes and reverences God
Will receive great praise.
Lucky, lucky are the children
This woman is blessed to raise!
Lemuel's mother tells him such a women
Will take care of her children's needs.
We know her life will not be empty
And she will be known for her good deeds!
We should re-read Proverbs
And look for the goodness there
And then we'll see more clearly
How it teaches all mankind
To be loving, good and fair!

Note :Another comparison of these two books. David had loved the Lord and praised Him on every page. It was a special wisdom that grew even in his old age. Solomon's books are based on wisdom of the earthly kind and in them we see nourishment of the heart does not come from the mind. Solomon was great in his own way but when it comes to the glorious life of the spirit, he has so little to say. Remember when the prophet reprimanded him, Solomon acted in resentment. Therefore we cannot see if he ever possessed any heavenly contentment. It seems he was full of doubt. David's writings said, "Look Up" but Solomon's could only say, "Look out!" You see, David's book was one of praise, but Solomon's was merely prose! Whereas David said, "I know," Solomon could only say, "I suppose!" Though Solomon did not live like David on that "holy mount," still he possessed a wisdom we cannot discount, because, you see, what this book has said is that loyalty to The Lord is a must–no ifs, no ands, no buts, even though people may say we are a bunch of nuts! The world says, "do your own thing and go for the gusto!" I guess that makes no difference if it makes no difference to you where you go! But choices must be made by every living soul even though it is difficult in this age to choose the proper goal. But, know for sure, times have NOT changed. Life is still empty when we and God are estranged. Solomon was wise because he correctly surmised living close to the Heavenly Father was the only place to be prized! When man is concerned with merely social graces, He looks for love in all the wrong places. How is this for a start? Look for the love God has already placed in your heart!

The "I Love My Bible" Commentary
(The Book of Ecclesiastes)

ECCLESIASTES 1

This is a book that proves the futility
Of man's reasoning power.
Take a look at how the writer's depression
Seems to climb by the hour!
He has limited vision and can only see
How terrible his present situation can be.
He is like a horse with blinders
And can not see to follow
The spiritual path-finders!
We are blessed with the spirit of believing
And we know our eyes can be deceiving!
Solomon says there is nothing new
Under the sun
And he fails to look beyond the stars
To see what God has done.
This would not be such a book of warning
Had he realized God's mercies fail not.
They are new every morning!

ECCLESIASTES 2

"I said to myself" sets the tone and explains
Solomon's point of view.
He was looking at himself instead of God
And *that* limited what he knew.
Everything he did was for his own pleasure
Yet he did not enjoy his world
Or any earthly treasure.
And in desperation he would think
All man has to enjoy is his job, his food
And his drink!
But he finally realized God gave him that, too.
For joy, wisdom and everything good
Comes from pleasing God in what we do!
Solomon looked at life warily
And ended up fretting unnecessarily!
Our trust in the Lord overcomes the unknown
As we cherish the love our Lord has shown!

ECCLESIASTES 3

Solomon says there is a time for everything
And life will eventually have its "Spring!"
Maybe the troubles throughout the years
Have come because man doubts the things
He hears.
He *casts stones* at the wrong times
And is indiscriminate in committing crimes.
He laughs when he should cry
And allows his love for others
To gradually fade and die.
He tears apart and refuses to repair
So there are many who think
There is no one to care.
Give us a choice and we choose the wrong.
Give us a melody and we'll make it a sad song!
It is depressing to me
To 'hear' Solomon say
Whatever will be—will be!
It seems all he sees is strife
And he doesn't look forward to a future life.
It doesn't surprise me in the least
That he thinks man is no better than a beast!

ECCLESIASTES 4

One would think Solomon lived in 1989.
He looked at circumstances and thought
"Sad is this life of mine!"
He felt oppression and sadness prevailed
Throughout the earth
And man would be better off celebrating
His death rather than his birth!
Once again this ambivalent king stressed
Life was pointless and he was depressed!
He implied life is sad, un-fulfilling
And much like chasing the wind
And I find this a very discouraging way
For this chapter to end!

Comment on Ecclesiastes

ECCLESIASTES 5

Man should be silent in God's temple.
Should he speak–make his words few
And simple.
And Solomon seems to be describing
Our brand of democracy
When he speaks of matters being lost
In red tape and bureaucracy
And look what he says about being rich!
It seems wealth comes with a hitch.
Worship of God, freedom, and wealth
Are serious responsibilities
Which have puzzled men for ages.
The problems caused from
Men's interpretation of them still fools
This earth's greatest sages!
Finally–he says man has hope for tomorrow
And if he accepts his lot in life
He will not look back in sorrow!

ECCLESIASTES 6

We've got to make that *extra* push.
It seems a bird in the hand is worth
Two in the bush!
Likewise, fate and destiny go hand in hand.
They are so much better when we obey
God's command.
Trusting Him is time well spent
And we'll have less reason to repent.
It bothered Solomon not to know
What the future held.
Confusion could best describe the way he felt.
And he implied it was a hollow mockery
And a serious fault
For a man to die and leave his money
Laying in a vault!
And it is obvious his life of *few* days
Would have been much happier
Had he spent them giving God his praise!

ECCLESIASTES 7

Better to have a spine that is *limber*
Than to be a hard head with a high temper!
And Solomon also thought patience
Was better than pride
For it helped men to take
Disappointment in stride!
I don't suppose we'd have to be very smart
To realize one could not finish
What one does not start!
Solomon was simply saying to wait
Until you finish before you brag.
Man must have a very good reason
To wave his own flag!
Or–let's say it *this way*.
A hen must lay an egg before she cackles
And a man must take care to finish
Every task he tackles!
Now I wonder why Solomon called life silly
Unless it was because evil
Caused one to die prematurely
And we can say *that* certainly is a pity!
Now he closes with another sad remark.
Though man was made to walk with God
He chooses a path utterly stark.
And his soul would surely burn
Because he made a downward turn!

ECCLESIASTES 8

"Reason" can bring madness when man
Does not reason well.
The perversion of *reason* has almost made
This earth a living hell!
Humanists say its all right to sin
And do not realize the web of deceit
They are living in!
Because God does not send punishment
Instantly, they feel its all right to do wrong
And destine themselves to walk

The "I Love My Bible" Commentary

In treacherous *shadows* their whole life long!
Solomon knew wisdom *lights up a man's face*
And the greatest wisdom was to walk
The pathways of God's infinite grace!
Yet he spent so much time watching mankind
That it seems he ends his life walking
Spiritually blind!
Still, he did admit that God knows it all
And it is a man's own fault if he should fall!

ECCLESIASTES 9

Do you think David would ever have said
"Pray to stay alive–there is no hope
For the dead?"
How could Solomon say
 "One fate comes to all?
All must face death's ashen pall!"
Had he not been so concerned
With life's fleeting pleasures
His eyes could have been opened
To those endless heavenly treasures!
Man's opinion is faulty and incomplete
When he does not have a faith
That is as solid as concrete!
But Solomon did know that peace
Is an instrument that is better by far
Than all the destructive weapons of war!

ECCLESIASTES 10

A small mistake is like a cumbersome brick
That weighs heavy on the heart.
Wisdom and honor are ridiculed as many
Turn to idiocy instead of trying to be smart!
Solomon must be implying that a wise man
Is just a mistake away from being a fool
Who is easily persuaded to break
Just one beloved golden rule!
His heart will be broken and once clear eyes
Will grow misty

And it seems every venture he undertakes
Steadily grows more risky!
Every thing he says is carried by the wind
Or else a nosy little bird
Will tell the enemy everything it heard!
He'd better pray the one who might hear it
Has a gentle, quiet, forgiving spirit!

ECCLESIASTES 11

This chapter hits me right between the eyes!
Even when I keep going, how time flies!
But *my sitting* set a record
That beat the setting of the sun
And few were the times I got anything done!
How right Solomon turned out to be.
He who lived centuries ago, sure knew
A lot about me!
I like his advice to the young when he says
"Do what you want to do
But remember you'll have to answer to God
Because He is *watching* you!"
He told the young to be very careful
To avoid making bad mistakes.
He knew youth must be alert
To take advantage of life's good breaks!

ECCLESIASTES 12

This is my favorite chapter in this book,
The reality seems hard but it is really gentle
When we take a closer look!
What a joy it is to remember our creator
In the days of our youth.
The "key" to the enjoyment of living
Is this chapter's hidden truth!
It seems we will not fear so much
And we'll surely enjoy everything we touch!
But it's a shame he didn't know
God still gives joy to the old folks also!
I like Solomon's final conclusion

Comment on Ecclesiastes

As to the whole duty of man.
It is to do everything for the Lord
That we possibly can!

That is where happiness lies
And *that* is what it takes
To put the *light of glory* back in our eyes!

Note: Ecclesiastes is written from the viewpoint of <u>human</u> wisdom which never attains to the heights *which spiritual wisdom reaches.* God says, ' My ways are higher than your ways" and very few supposedly wise men of the ages will accept that! Jesus once said that a little child would lead us and maybe that is because man's interpretation of wisdom has not *colored his mind!* We've learned how to grow rich(some of us) and we've certainly learned how to kill, but how many of us have ever learned to love *unconditionally!* That means someone doesn't have to be like me for me to love them. And–that means I don't have to be like them in order for them to love me! A truth so simple we refuse to accept it!

On the surface, I find Ecclesiastes depressing but when I remember its just a mere human definition of life then I can understand why life as we know it can be so demoralizing. God can teach us a much better way. That is why this Holy Bible was written. It is our guide book to glory. The more times we read it, the better our chances will be that we will eventually learn how simple truth, honor and love can lead to greatness. God's definition of greatness is based on how full our hearts are–not how full our pocket books are! I'm not knocking wealth, but let us remember what true wealth is!

Jesus said, "I have come so that you might have life more abundantly!" He is the "key" And to turn to Him is to turn the key of opportunity to a life beyond our wildest dreams! Well! What are you waiting for?

The "I Love My Bible" Commentary
Song of Solomon

SONG OF SOLOMON 1

Sometimes symbolism seems to show a weird
  example
And the Song of Solomon contains many
  A sample!
Maybe when a girl searches for her mate
And her mate searches for her
Lovely, haunting memories may begin to stir.
I must admit these passages do not inspire me.
Perhaps I have a weakness I've failed to see.
Yet I realize Christ calls the church His bride
And promises He will always be by our side!
There is a difference here, subtle it may be.
I can't imagine my Savior hiding from me!
Maybe this was written so we would know
Our God is a One of a kind God
And don't we love that so!
Our '*husband*' is faithful, just, and true
And His love for us is always good as new!

SONG OF SOLOMON 2

I have no time to seek an evasive shadow.
Spring is here!
The *Promise of the Ages* comes
To make the shadows disappear!
The *Lily of the Valley* blooms in magnificent
  beauty
And the roses have no thorns to prick hands
That hurry to perform their duty.
Night gives way to the *Morning Star*
And the voice of that lonely dove
Haunts us from afar.
"Come," we say, "O King, like a gazelle"
And like Solomon's bride we declare
"Thou doest all things well!"
So–the symbols continue here
As we picture the KING we hold so dear
So great is His grace we have nothing to fear!

SONG OF SOLOMON 3

If I were the maid of Shunem I'd wonder
What other girl had gotten hold of him
And whose fancy did he tickle?
One who is gone so much
Will find himself a reason to be fickle!
But she loved this king
Who had such a mighty army
Perhaps to control this thing called love
That can be so unmanageable and stormy!
Yet, no amount of competition
Could lessen her desire
For she was so lonely
And her heart was a flaming fire!

SONG OF SOLOMON 4

Does Christ consider His 'bride"
As beautiful as did Solomon?
Have we been pure and holy
In all we have said and done?
Can we stand on the mountain top
With our King
And hear Him say, "Your beauty is like
That of a garden in the Spring?"
Will we welcome our Lord with open arms
And hearts aglow?
Will our lives have said for us
"Lord, we love you so?"
Good deeds are like a sweet perfume
And love for God keeps our *benevolent flowers*
Constantly in bloom!
What a wonder it would be to hear God say
He sees beauty in us
As we walk with Him each day!
Well, beauty is in the eyes of the beholder
If the beholder sees beauty in the soul.
And if we are loyal and obedient to our Lord
We will gradually see that beauty unfold!

Comment on Song of Solomon

SONG OF SOLOMON 5

The Bridegroom says, "Behold, I stand at
The door and knock.
My love for you is as solid as a solid rock!"
I must not open the door too late.
The One with such a tender heart
May not choose to wait!
He has a love beyond compare
A love that can never be found elsewhere!
There is none who can rival Him.
Is not my heart His private *Jerusalem?*
His invitation extends to all.
No one *ever* has to fall!
Oh, earth, earth, earth, hear His voice!
Make our Beloved King
Your high priority choice!

SONG OF SOLOMON 6

I bet every time Solomon confiscated
A new wife, his problems would double
Proving his amorous prowling
Only led him into serious trouble.
One plus one , in God's sight is *one*
Not one plus one hundred or more
Which is really not worth counting
Unless you are keeping score!
The important fact is-lust seeks many partners
Love seeks only one!
If there is a hidden truth here for us to see
It is, though Christ has many He loves
It is an undiminished love He gives to me!
Don't ask me how He can do that
I don't know!
But it is a wonderful feeling
To know He loves me so!
It seems, in our physical feelings
We seek only self satisfaction
But the love found through God's Holy Spirit
Causes an entirely different reaction!
God helps us to reach out and love others
For, after all, aren't we all sisters and brothers?

SONG OF SOLOMON 7

There is a feeling of love and mutual respect
We don't want to miss
For nothing earthly can be more beautiful
And fulfilling than wedded bliss!
We humans judge things by the physical realm
And it supercedes
All other reasons as to the rationale
Of our many deeds.
Whether it is friendship, love, or hatred
Which is intense
It seems we base more on feeling
Than we do on common sense!

SONG OF SOLOMON 8

A life of love is poetry in motion
With each line an expression of kindness
Joy and utter devotion!
It is not concerned with the attributes
Of a lovely frame.
This love of which I speak
Is to glorify our Father's Name!
And, like the bride who takes pride
In this man of her choice
We exult in our God and listen to our hearts
Longing to hear His voice.
The bride is saying
 "Come quickly my beloved, like a deer!"
If you will listen closely to His church
Those are the words you will hear!
When He comes life will be a poetic marvel
Moving as gracefully as a speedy carvel!
We will rejoice in life's most beautiful union
The day we share in that heavenly, holy
communion!

The "I Love My Bible" Commentary

NOTE: Now we have come to the end of part four. We've seen Israel's ups and downs, her glory days, and her gory ones too. Remember Ecclesiastes said there is nothing new under the sun? Haven't you noticed man still makes the same mistakes-the only difference is now it seems to be more universal. And now that the end of time is drawing near it seems infinitely more frightening! We've become more educated and less moral. We either dismiss God as a myth or have expected His spiritual integrity to have disappeared along with ours. Adultery is committed wholesale and glamorized. Greed has overcome honesty and life is not worth a plugged nickel. Look how many are slaughtered every day! God is saying again, His people sin as if they were commanded to! Christ said it would get worse before it gets better. Is that the poetry we seek?

Some times poetry is like a prairie dog,
hiding in a deep dark hole
picturing dirt and debris
holding down a wounded soul.
And some times poetry soars
like an eagle in flight
lifting anxious souls swiftly to the light!
In reading these poetic books
I some times felt truly lifted
and I considered David extremely gifted.
Ah, but there was many a sad part
that brought sorrow to my heart
sometimes a recipe of pain
through Job to Song of Solomon
and then a trace of joy and instances of fun!
Perhaps life is that way
meant to have mixed emotions on any given day.
But through and around it all
is God's everlasting arms
and no matter the chill in life
He gives us a love that warms!
So, what is the story these books tell?
Through it all our God does all things well!

Remember now thy Creator
in the days of thy youth,
while the evil days come not,
nor the years draw nigh,
when thou shalt say,
I have no pleasure in them.

....

For God shall bring every work
into judgement
with every secret thing,
whether it be good
or whether it be evil.

(Ecclesiastes 1:1 and 12)

PART FIVE

THE MAJOR

PROPHETS

ISAIAH TO DANIEL

Come now,

and let us reason together,

saith the Lord;

though your sins be as scarlet,

they shall be as white as snow;

though they be red like crimson,

they shall be as wool.

If you be willing and obedient,

ye shall eat the good of the land

But if you refuse and rebel,

ye shall be devoured with the sword

for the mouth of the Lord

hath spoken it.

(Isa: 1:18-20kjv)

The "I Love My Bible" Commentary
The Book of Isaiah

ISAIAH 1

If my precious, holy, heavenly Father
Would want to sit down and talk
Why would I , or anyone
Ever have a reason to balk?
But we must say what we mean
When we cry to Him to make us clean.
I can't walk with my eyes looking
To the heavens when they are glued
To the ground.
Every part of me must be given to Him
If I would be Heaven bound!
Though I think there are no idols
In my life today
I must stop and consider what it is
That makes me stray!
I want a love that is not here today
And gone tomorrow.
I'm tired of a life that brings only sorrow.
I must open my heart
And let the Father's love come in.
How much better it is to know His presence
Than to wonder what might have been!
But very few want to say they are "sorry"
And want to repent.
No one understands what the Father meant.
Can you imagine God wanting to draw near
To us as weak as we are?
Yet it still concerns Him
When we follow from afar.
His reasoning is based on love
And His love is founded on need.
And there is no greater need than for us
To walk with Him-no greater, no indeed!
Our Lord will always be willing to "reason"
For His love will *never go out of season!*
You see–He cries out for His children
The ones He cherishes.
*He wants back the backslider who perish*es!

Sadly He has to say,
"Where are those I've cared for day after day?"
"Come now and let us reason together"
Says the Lord of all the ages.
That great love has been misunderstood
Even by the world's greatest sages.
Do we realize God can truly make us
White as snow?
Well, He says He will and that's enough
For me to know!
Those who think the Christian life
Has not panned out to be what it seemed
Have never known how marvelous it is
To be God's redeemed!
One day God took away our shame
And, more than anything else
We need to glorify His name!

ISAIAH 2

Those who seek the 'wonders' of the world
Miss God's main attraction!
Only at His place of worship
Will His people find satisfaction!
And in the days of which Isaiah speaks
Man will find the glory of the ONE he seeks!
Isaiah says, "Puny man, frail as breath
Don't ever put your trust in him!"
He knew the truly wise would someday
Worship God in Jerusalem!
Man will find his own belligerence
Merely a travesty
For every knee on earth will bow
To God's majesty!
Man will worship the ONE he spurns
When the Holy One of the ages returns.
And when God's ship of judgement docks
Unrepentant man will hide among the rocks!
But it will be too late.
Many will have already sealed their fate!

Comment on Isaiah

ISAIAH 3

It is not God's will for His people to fail.
It displeases Him to see anarchy prevail.
Neighbors fighting neighbors
And friends no longer friends.
A loving peacemaker finds
He wastes the precious time he spends.
People brag about their sins and are unashamed.
They take pride in every horror ever named.
And God says He will judge the haughty women
Who walk with wanton eyes
Who think their beauty is the world's only prize.
Goodness! It looks as if God is talking
About today!
But notice what Isaiah says.
All the wicked will get their well-earned pay!

ISAIAH 4

Whenever God speaks of judgement
The subject of mercy is soon to follow
In spite of our sins being endless
And our faith weak and hollow.
Oh how can I describe
Our God who loves us so much?
How can I explain the joy in my soul
Just to feel His heavenly touch?
We've yet to see the beauty
Of God's glorious Holy Land.
Canopied night and day by God's
Protecting hand!

ISAIAH 5

Sad songs inflict our souls with melancholy.
Such gruesome tunes usually depict
Man's worst felon-folly.
God had given these people so much
But their outrageous defiance
Put them completely out of touch.

So bitter were their sins they could only grope
And drag their indiscretions on their idiot rope.
Their 'shrewdness' spurned their many woes
These who were only pseudo-heroes.
No matter the punishment.
"It could wait," they said, "until tomorrow."
Meanwhile their souls grieved
In self-inflicted sorrow!

ISAIAH 6

No Olympic medal
and no sweepstake prize
could equal the thrill
of getting to see the Lord
with my own eyes!
No amount of glitter
nor the world's greatest reward
could ever be as magnificent
as getting to see my Lord!
But I can tell you something
better still.
My God has discovered a way
to help me do His will!
The Lord whose glory fills the skies
wrapped himself in a molecule
and has come to fill my heart
with His atomic fuel!
Yes, He lives in your heart
and mine
and its our turn
to let His glory-light shine!
Now we can say
"Here we are Lord,
what can we do
to show the world your great love
and glorify you?
For no Olympic medal
and no sweepstake prize
can equal the glory of lifting
You up in other people's eyes!"

The "I Love My Bible" Commentary

ISAIAH 7

Immanuel! Immanuel!
What a contrast to my failure
And I will never feel successful until the day
I get to see my Savior!
Immanuel! Immanuel! Please come again
And straighten up this mess
Made by unrepentant man!
Mankind still does not believe
What you can do
And failure looms at his outcast rendevous!
Thou art the vine! We are the branches.
Help us live the life your love enhances.
Blessed Savior, thou doeth all thing well!
And we fervently cry
"Come, oh come, Immanuel!"

ISAIAH 8

God still demands that we remain true to Him.
We must not embrace the sins of Jerusalem.
Since the days of creation
God has been man's only way of salvation.
Only those who maintain loyalty to the Lord
Will walk in safety with their spirits unscarred.
What should God's people be thinking of ?
How dainty are His morsels
And how matchless is His love!
It is foolish to ask for help
From a decaying habeas corpus!
Isaiah asks, "Why not ask your God?"
If we don't, shame on us!
For why should we go to spiritual zombies
Who walk in the dark
And can not produce even the tiniest spark?
Our God will show the road called 'right'
If only we will walk in His light!
His light is prettier than a rainbow
That surrounds us with a gentle glow
And its that light which helps our faith to grow!

ISAIAH 9

"Nevertheless" can be a powerful word
When God promises joyful sounds
Would soon be heard!
Isaiah told them, "The promise is here!"
God's glory would illuminate this sphere!
Those who walked in darkness
Could bask in the *light*
For *The Love of All The Ages*
Would banish the shadows of the night!
He would be known as the *Prince of Peace!*
Cruelty, injustice, and all the horrors
Of war would cease!
Yet Israel gloried in her own might.
She refused to repent and maliciously sinned
In God's sight.
Such people were destined to be crushed.
Even the filthy mouthed and all liars
Would be hushed.
Pity these people who walked the paths
Of ruin and seduction
For they carelessly sought
Their own destruction!

ISAIAH 10

Judges who issue unfair laws
Will face many a woe.
Retribution will haunt them
Wherever they go.
To whom much is given, much is required!
God was their gracious employer.
Those who disgraced Him would be fired!
How tragic to hear the Lord say
"I will not help you.
Doomed and dammed are the wicked today!"
Though God warns judgement follows
Deliberate disobedience
His loving heart would save them
With eager expedience!

Comment on Isaiah

Those enemies of Israel could form
Their destructive packs.
    No problem!
God would cut them down as easily
As a woodsman using his trusty axe!

ISAIAH 11

Someday there will be peace
Among the wild animals and the tame.
Someday God will send David's descendant
Who is also His Lord to glorify HIS name!
When the *"TREE"* was cut down
God said it would seem
As if Israel was left without a single dream.
Yet someday soon we will get to see
How glorious God's blessings can be!
Israel has already returned
The *second time around!*
She stands now on God's holy ground.
God says someday it will be so safe
Babies can crawl among snakes.
    Count on it!
Sooner or later God *always* fulfills
The promises He makes!

ISAIAH 12

Do I trust Jehovah God? I must! I must!
Trust banishes the fear that once
Banished my trust.
Oh, the joy is indescribable when I drink
Deeply from the fountain of salvation!
Only the Lord can be the strength and song
Of a soul–no matter his nation!
Great and mighty is the Lord of hosts.
Deep, deep in our souls
We must love Him the most!
It surely pleases Him to hear us say
We WILL praise and glorify our Lord today
For He has placed us on the Kings highway!

ISAIAH 13

The Lord looks beyond Babylon
–looks beyond the cross!
He looks at the glitter we see
And says it is only dross.
Wealth and power do not control His hand.
Instead, it causes perversion across our land.
God not only said He's destroy Babylon
But the world also.
Our wicked culture will be shaken
For it has no place to go!
Man cannot run and hide
When God punishes us with strong finality.
Those who ignore the message of the cross
Will soon face a gruesome reality.
The unbeliever is a merely unwholesome
Disobedient jerk
Who will not be among the survivors
When God finishes His work.
This is not popular for those who turn away.
But none of us can run from
God's final judgement day.

ISAIAH 14

There is hope for God's people
Who seem to have lost the battle
And have now retreated.
Lucifer-once glorious, beautiful, and mighty
Has been thoroughly defeated!
He cannot ascend to the heavens anymore.
He and his servants have abused God's people
And God has evened the score!
But he still walks this earth
Defeating the doubtful and disobedient
And those who have not considered
Faith in God to be expedient.
The apostle Peter later would say
The devil stalks this earth
Seeking those he can destroy.

The "I Love My Bible" Commentary

But strength is given us.
We must not let him rob us of our joy.
No matter how dark the skies may be
Remember–Satan was defeated
    at Calvary!!!!!!!

ISAIAH 15

Moab–So close to Israel and so far
    away from God.
Yet she and Israel were sinful people
Like two peas in a pod!
Moab would weep and her streams
Would run blood red
For she refused to listen to what the Lord said.
These people whose lives were so unkempt
Would discover their sins were not exempt.
God would send lions to hunt them down.
They would all be destroyed
The lowly as well as the renown.
Moab's greatest warriors would cry in terror
For they had not sought the One
Whose love protects even the lowly sparrow!

ISAIAH 16

Proud Moab pleads for protection.
She came to Judah and sought direction.
Even they knew God rewards kindness
And were able to see His love
Even though in deep spiritual blindness.
Sometimes the heathen see
What God's people cannot.
They know where help can be found
When they find themselves in a 'spot!'
Yet Moab's glory would be ended.
God would give her no help because of
The false gods on whom she had depended.
There would be no harvest joys
And no future for her little girls and boys
-truths the winds of time lifts and stirs!

The rejector would become the rejectee
For she never claimed Israel's God as hers!

ISAIAH 17

How can man carry in his heart
That which cannot carry itself?
There is no power in that which man
Can place on a shelf.
But speaking of worshiping
What hands have made
People today have coveted articles
Produced in every trade.
Cars, boats, fancy homes, and many a treasure
Have lured many away to seek only pleasure.
Idols? We have them in places unexpected
And as we *pursue* them
Our God waits though utterly rejected.
Those idols of old had a different name
But self-effacing *"I want it"* people
Still cling to their 'idols' just the same.
And–there are more ways to plunder people
Than with an iron rod.
Unconcern, indifference, and apathy
Have also devastated the people of God!

ISAIAH 18

We can still stand by the river side
to watch similar winged sailboats glide!
And the message echoes in the waves
despite man's endeavors
only the Heavenly Father saves!
God watches quietly
from His glorious home
and His heart breaks as His prodigals
continue to roam.
Are we like ancient Egypt
in our souls
arrogant, empty people
with no lofty goals?

Comment on Isaiah

We cam almost hear
Egypt's groans
and see those wild animals
gnawing on decaying bones!
But God, who destroys
also lifts!
And He says someday Egypt, too
will bring Him gifts!
His warnings are merely
to put living substance
in these old dry bones!
We can be sure God sees
our sorrow
and hears our moans!
<u>So</u>
we stand by the riverside
waiting.
Christ is coming
for His "bride!"

ISAIAH 19

The "City of the sun" will see the *true light!*
A sign of loyalty to the Lord
Would soon erase their plight!
He promises to restore the people He smote.
It would be so-o-o impressive
All Egypt would take note!
But what of Egypt's counselors-of what
Could they boast?
They had lost the carnal knowledge
They valued the most.
But now, in wisdom, they worship God alone.
God had tenderized their hearts of stone!
No matter what Egypt had done
God still loved them all!
He is not willing that any soul slip and fall!
And God would unite Israel, Egypt, and
Assyria with His own 'interstate!'
They would be allies and it would be
A time that could be utterly great!

ISAIAH 20

The Philistines would cry for help
After Sargon captured Asdod.
And when they sought help from Egypt
They received this message from God
"Don't count on Ethiopia's power
Nor her glorious ally.
Egypt cannot help you win your battles
Nor help you when you cry/"
Egypt would be shamed like a man
Caught without his pants
And he would be as helpless as a child
Walking barefoot among fiery ants!
Isaiah's messages were written
On hearts of stone.
Even he could not teach these people
To worship God alone!
How inevitable reality can be
No matter how pitiful and fervent the plea.
All would be treated like Ashdod
For they had not believed in Jehovah God.

ISAIAH 21

Darkness falls and the watchman stares.
Trembling, he sees riders coming in pairs!
The prophecy is coming true.
The ruthless reign of Babylon is through!
Vengeance comes faster than an arrow.
Babylon had been ruthless
Now she faces incredible terror!
God had told those who trusted Him
To look for good news.
Those who doubted would change their views.
Seek him my friend
And trust Him until the end.
For the 'end' is the beginning of a new life
Where we will find victory over earthly strife!
Someone asks, "Watchman what of the night?"
And he says, "Ah, I see rays of morning light!

The "I Love My Bible" Commentary

ISAIAH 22

Isaiah moans, "Let me alone to weep.
My people are dying and I can't sleep!"
Death echoed across the mountainside.
Wherever he ran, he found no place to hide.
It was that way because Israel had become
So sinful and very unfair.
God could stand them no longer
So He removed His protecting care!
Mighty men's lives were shattered and broken
Because they refused to believe
What God had spoken.
They had said, "Let us eat and be merry.
Lets drink all the booze we can carry!"
They thought it useless to repent
And they missed that mercy train
That God had lovingly sent!
"So let me alone," Isaiah said.
"My people are as good as dead!"

ISAIAH 23

The ships of Tarshish return
To find their harbor gone.
Only silent ruins remain where once
Was many a beautiful lawn.
No one would welcome sailors from afar.
It was as if they had set their course
According to the wrong star!
Tarshish had shown too many people
Their ugly side.
Now the God of the universe destroyed
Their unbridled anger and their pride.
But He gave Tarshish the same promise
He had given Israel.
After *seventy years* her waves would swell!
Water splashing against her sea wall
Would wash away the ugliness of her fall!
Hope must have set her heart on fire
When the Lord promised to restore Tyre!

ISAIAH 24

Like Isaiah's Israel we are defiled by crime.
God's laws have been horribly twisted.
Even when our leaders sensed the trend
Very few of them resisted.
Now gladness is slipping away.
Psychiastrists with heavy case loads
Are getting richer by the day.
But their counsel turns no one to the Lord
And fearful people imprison themselves
In their own homes with all doors barred.
Times will continue to grow steadily worse
And it will seem as if the whole earth
Lies under God's curse.
It will be when fallen angels are punished
Along with arrogant, unbelieving mankind.
Darkness will prevail until
God comes to *'lighten'* those who do His will!

ISAIAH 25

My Lord is a refuge from the storm!
The driving rain of hellish indifference
can do me no harm.
My Lord is a shadow from the heat.
Cool winds directed by His spirit
guide my weary feet.
My Lord is a shelter from evil men
who would carelessly
lead us into sin.
My Lord is all these things-and more
And-because of Him
there will come a day
when we will stand on heaven's shore!
I'll know what Isaiah meant
when he said
"God's people must not fear!
Better days are just ahead!"
They are! For you! For me!
Just you wait and see!

Comment on Isaiah

ISAIAH 26

All may enter in who love the Lord.
Heaven's gates are open wide!
Love, Joy, and peace are given
To all those who dwell inside.
God, who has lived in our hearts
Will stand in our midst for all to see.
There will be no doubters
When we walk with Him for all eternity!
These promises in Isaiah are so profound
None can doubt we will walk on holy ground!
Those who hide behind crooked lawyers
To commit their crimes
Will be found and convicted
As time on earth slowly unwinds.
Only when God sends punishment
Will evil men see his need to repent.
May they learn to walk in righteousness
Before God's final judgement has been sent.
For nothing can ever be as hard
As knowing we can never live
In the presence of the Lord!

ISAIAH 27

It is true that Israel was purged
But it would not have happened
Had she done what Jehovah urged!
Crime, crookedness, and adultery
Haunted her streets
And are ugly weaknesses man still repeats.
But idols were the straw that
"Broke the camel's back."
And Israel's belligerence was the "hair"
That over-weighed the pack.
Isaiah seems ambivalent here
Yet he makes it plain.
God would restore His people
Like hand-picked grain!
But soon God showed them no pity.
It was *one too many times* they turned away.
But, like the prodigal's father
He longed for them day after day.
When they repented, would it matter?
Oh yes, His pardon came on a silver platter!
God's salvation is an endless fountain.
There will be inexpressible joy
When we worship Him on His holy mountain!

ISAIAH 28

It did no good to be the pride
Of drunkards and bums.
We see Israel's "crowing" glory
Swiftly fading as judgement comes.
Samaria would be demoted to the gutter.
Serious errors and mistaken messages
Were all she could mutter.
Even Jerusalem was led by drunks.
Those who had been priests
Were now following arrogant punks.
They could have had rest
If they had been good and kind
But they stumbled on the words of God
And grew spiritually blind.
Yet God knew when to crush
Or to beat gently with a feathered flail!
Those who trusted Him knew
He would never fail!

ISAIAH 29

Mere words cannot save a soul.
Man must *reach up* to obtain his goal.
If he is truly righteous he will do just that!
And we must *practice* goodness
If we're to get God's righteousness down pat!
Over and over God has said
Man's words are ineffectual
When his "works" are *dead*.
God says "To be alive, you must live in me!"

The "I Love My Bible" Commentary

Then He says here in Isaiah
That scoffers will cease
But when He rules here on earth
We will live in peace!

ISAIAH 30

Many people have cut themselves off
From the Lord and are like lonely trees
On the distant mountain tops.
No one sees their tears nor hears their cries.
Hope grows dimmer as their morale drops!
But the pattern for happiness is plain to see.
God says, "you can have quietness
And confidence if you will come to me!"
Read this chapter over and over
Until it *sinks in*
Despising God and disobeying His words
Is a horrible sin.
But–there is a voice that whispers in my ear.
It says, "This is the way! Walk here!"
I know God is concerned about
My and your behavior.
Long ago He sent the Holy Spirit
Through the auspices of our Savior!
His purpose was to instruct and guide
And give us the comfort
That makes us feel good inside!

ISAIAH 31

God says, "Woe to those who run
To "Egypt" for help
(or America, or anyplace in between)
And refuses to seek the help of the Lord!
Somehow they end up finding more trouble
Than they have ever seen.
There are not enough horses, not enough men
To overcome the battles the Lord can win.
The Israelis were not to trust
In Egypt's chariots
For the Lord would hobble them
With His mighty heavenly lariats!
God gave warning but they failed to hear it.
The Egyptians were mere men
And their horses were only flesh-not spirit.
The best men could do was terribly shoddy.
God's people were to trust in no earthly body!
Only the Lord could rescue them
And restore hope to Jerusalem.

ISAIAH 32

God is like a shadow of a great rock
In a weary land.
In the shadow of His presence
Israel's people were to take their stand.
In that day they would be willing to hear
For God's Words would be clearly plain!
God would end the cruelty of the sinners
And punish those who were vain.
The heart has to be cleaned, the spirit purified
Before people will live in peace, side by side!
The Lord can do the impossible
But peace seems that way.
Man talks much about it
Yet there is no peace today.
But when God gives a promise
It will be our hoped-for situation.
God's people will someday live quietly
In peaceful habitation!

ISAIAH 33

Who is it who will dwell on high?
Who will see the Lord in all his beauty?
It will be all those who deny
That righteousness is just a duty.
It goes far beyond that for it is love fulfilled!
It is joy in doing what our God has willed!
I'll see Him, it says in this chapter
And I will live happily forever after!

Comment on Isaiah

Wisdom and knowledge shall be
The pattern for my stability.
I know God has made His heavenly home
My accessible facility!
The strength of salvation cannot be measured
And is more valuable than all the gold
Man has ever treasured.
Isaiah says those who doubt God shall
Conceive chaff and bring forth stubble.
They will have nothing good to remember
Despite all their trouble.
He says, "Look on Zion!
There is beauty there!"
It will be a place of magnificence
A place way beyond compare
A place of great rivers and glorious streams.
And it will be a time when God will lead
To beautiful pastures where His light beams!
The Lord is our precious law giver
And He will lead us across His peaceful river!

ISAIAH 34

We hate bad news and refuse to look
At the inevitable prophecies in this book.
It should make God's people sad
To have lost the good news
Because they had earned the bad!
Some people think God has no right
To indignation
And refuse to admit we are His creation!
And–children of the King sometimes act
Like children of the devil
By making promises that are not on the level!
So–God will level his creation
From even beyond the stars
For there has been so much evil
We can never count all the scars!
But look on the bright side!
The God who destroys can also restore
And make the heavens and the earth
Much better than before!
He forgives the repentant too
And will make us all as good as new!

ISAIAH 35

There is nothing dryer than a desert
Nothing more succulent than a rose!
Soon we will rejoice in a blooming desert
And live to see how God's glory glows!
God strengthens the trembling hands
And supports the feeble knees.
He will direct us toward the King's highway
And away from troubled seas!
The ransomed of the Lord will find
No potholes there!
There will be no broken down vehicles
Needing repair.
Each person will be encouraged
By the things he sees
When "our desert" blooms like a rose
And our ruthless shadow flees!

ISAIAH 36

It doesn't make sense for a man of renown
To think he can usurp God's holy crown.
Israel was not ruled by Hezekiah-but the Lord
And every profanatory insult Sennacherib, the
King of Assyria spoke, God would record.
Sennacherib thought Israel depended
On the Egyptians she had befriended.
But Israel had a friend he didn't know
Though he claimed he did and told Israel so.
His problem was he thought he was bigger
Than the King of the universe
And expected even God to tremble
As he continued to threaten and curse.
He had a lot of guts but no gumption.
Otherwise he would never have made
Such an ignorant presumption!

The "I Love My Bible" Commentary

ISAIAH 37

Sennacherib came with a great army
But left with only a few.
God replied with incredible speed
To show what He could do.
Sennacherib could not harm one hair
On even one Israeli head
And he would have to "eat" all those
Nasty things he said.
Hezekiah mourned in sackcloth and ashes
And complained that "Sennacherib
Destroys everyone with whom he clashes!"
He was in agony because he couldn't bear
This heathen who was so unfair.
But Sennacherib came up a dead-end street.
He would turn and run the opposite direction
In total chaos and utter defeat.
He wasn't fighting mortal Israelis
But Israel's immortal King
And he was destined to learn
What such arrogance would bring.
Jerusalem, the city he could not deprave
Would be the cause of his early grave.
Sennacherib would be shown no pity.
When God stepped in to save His city!

ISAIAH 38

Many a child of God lives with what
He considers, a soul half-scarred
Because he fails to see he has been healed
Thoroughly and completely by the Lord!
It is such a tremendous thing to know
And it gives our souls an inward glow!
It is a life-time shot in the arm
When our Lord saves us from harm!
Hezekiah rejoiced in God's healing
And would not restrain the joy he was feeling!
He said his life was only half done
And it seems he thought The gates of Sheol
Would hide him from the sun!
But he cried, "Lord heal me please?"
And God took the sun back ten degrees!
That was the sign Hezekiah needed
To prove God had done what he pleaded!
It was the gift the Lord was willing to give
When Hezekiah cried, "Lord, let me live!!"

ISAIAH 39

Once again a man falls because of pride.
Hezekiah had been healed by the Lord
And he felt good inside.
Bragging about his possessions gave him pleasure
But he should have remembered
It was really the Lord who was his treasure!
He wanted to impress the Babylonian envoy
And showing them his treasures gave him joy.
The Babylonians enjoyed it too.
Now, nothing was hidden from their view.
But shame on Hezekiah's response
To bad news when he said
"Well at least when it happens I will be dead."
And once again it seems too late to suture
The fraying seams of Israel's future!

ISAIAH 40

God's mercy shines again!
He spoke tenderly to Jerusalem.
Whispered softly in her ear.
Now her sins were pardoned.
She had nothing more to fear!
What can make hope stronger
than comforting words from the Lord?
What makes burdens lighter
that were once so very hard?
Well, we know don't we?
It's the Lord, Himself
who makes life sweet as it can be!

Comment on Isaiah

*Over and over God had told them
to destroy idols made of gold
and His mercy embraced them
when they did what they were told!
He loved those homesick sinners
whose hearts yearned
and welcomed them when they returned!
How can we describe our God?
To whom can He be compared?
Certainly not to those wicked people
His great love had spared!
They were His lambs
so He would see
The people He loved
would be strong and free!
He would give power
to the tired and faint.
God would and will take care
of every repentant saint!
So! Why is God, God
to rule the universe? Oh no!
It is to comfort His people
where ever we go.
It is to look on us with love!
It is to turn our eyes from failure
to seek the ONE above.
He is God because
He wants to give us power!
He is God because
He wants to be our strong
and mighty tower!
We shall walk and not be weary
because He walks by our side.
He is the "Rock of Ages"
where we can run and hide!
He is God so he can heal
our scars.
He is God so we can reach up
and touch the stars!
Thank God, He has no equal!
HE IS GOD!!!!!*

ISAIAH 41

Only in silence can we hear what the Lord
Wants to say.
His silence whispers in our hearts
"I will give you joy today!"
"Today" is the day to realize
God is still in control!
He listens when the needy cries
And soothes his troubled soul!
"I am God," God says!
Why don't we trust as we did once before?
Why don't we hear Him say
"Don't fear people anymore?"
He is not an idol and He makes no idle threat.
What He says will happen, will happen
And that is life's one sure bet!
We must not rely on things that are as empty
As the wind.
We have a holy God who is our dearest friend!
How many times have we prayed
And still failed to hear Him say
"You must not be afraid?"
Listen to our Lord proclaim
"I still direct those who call on my name!"
We can be sure our facilitator is on the way!
God is still in the business of helping us today!

ISAIAH 42

See God's chosen One
who has His Holy Spirit
Who is His delight!
His holiness is as different
from ordinary man
as day is from night!
God had only this <u>one</u>
faithful servant until the end!
Man has only One
who has proved
to be a faithful friend!

The "I Love My Bible" Commentary

The glory of the skies
cannot portray this One!
His love is deeper than the ocean
and more brilliant than the sun!
He can fill our hearts with love
and He only!
He came to show us
we never need to be lonely!
God would and will not
give anyone else His glory.
This is the story of love!
This is the Messiah's story!

ISAIAH 43

God says He can do much better
Than anything we can do!
He said, " Take notice, with only one word
I have saved you!"
No one can oppose Him. *God is His Name!*
He has lived through all eternity!
Can we say the same?
He is our redeemer! He is our great King!
Is it any wonder that the angels sing?
Just think, this great God has chosen me
So he can make me all I want to be!
And who of us can ever understand
His loving willingness to forgive?
He, and only He alone can teach us
What it really means to live!
Oh Great God of the universe, I plead my case
For I am *nothing* without your amazing grace!
I want to be a witness, faithful and true
And I want to tell the whole world
There is nobody just like you!

ISAIAH 44

Israel was supposed to listen to God
But they did not.
Pages of records meant to post good deeds
Only were filled with a huge black blot!
Their hopes remained unanswered because
They looked in all the wrong places.
Deluded fools follow paths the atheist traces.
The Lord alone stretched out the heavens!
The Lord alone created the earth!
Those wicked, doubtful hard headed NATS
Would soon despise the days of their birth!
When God speaks, the rivers obey.
Only He causes the sun to rise day after day!
He forgives our sins no matter
How long the list.
When His sun rises in our hearts
Our sins disappear like morning mist!
Wealth and fame can be a lie
For they give little comfort when we cry.
But when we cry, God will hear it
And will soothe us with His Holy Spirit!

ISAIAH 45

God raises up Cyrus for Israel's benefit.
Cyrus, who was Israel's friend
Put on his boxer's mitt
And pummeled Israel's enemies
Where ever he went!
God was telling them this man of the future
Would be heaven sent!
Yet Israel, God's disobedient "clay"
Questioned Him day after day.
But, someday, God's people would declare
Our Great God is completely just and fair!
Israel was very lucky way back then
For God refused to give up on these men.
He also said, "Let all the world look to me!"
He opened the door of His kingdom
And He did it at Calvary.
God saw that old rugged cross
Long before Jesus came.
He pictured a time of incredible love
When Christ would come to erase our shame!

Comment on Isaiah

ISAIAH 46

"Who can equal me?" God asks.
"To whom can I be compared?
The only blessing you can claim
Are those I have shared!"
God tells them to let the heathen rage.
He had promised to walk with them
Even in their silver haired old age!
Talk about a commitment that never fails!!!!
Beside our Blessed God, all else pales!
And His promise to abide with us
Is deeper than a casual walk!
We are bonded, God and I
By His tenacious calk!
There is no other like my God
Whose word is just and true!
He saves us so we can pass His good news
To others too!

ISAIAH 47

Could this chapter be written
to America?
(Or any modern nation today)
"Your knowledge and wisdom
(so-called)
have caused you to stray!"
Let us hope the next verse
does not extend to our generation
because it describes
a horribly destructive situation.
But the human disaster
is not the worst.
There is no remedy
for those God has cursed.
Yet they cursed themselves
with their evil ways.
Oh my people
doesn't this chapter describe
what is happening in these days?
A pleasure mad nation
forfeits its future
and has no hope.
It will face gloomy days
and many heartaches
with which
it will be unable to cope.
God is saying to us
"There could be a day
I won't answer when you call!"
You see, pride does go
before destruction
and a haughty spirit
before a fall.
Before the good days disappear
Let us return to our Lord
while He is near!

ISAIAH 48

Peace flowing like a river, righteousness
Greater than the ocean waves
Is God's will and ultimate inheritance
For the people He saves!
But once again He finds many people
Spiritually worthless and no good.
People refuse to obey His commandments
Or do as they know they should.
Must our Lord label us as hardheaded as brass
Because of the many holy tests
We have failed to pass?
We have not been refined in the furnace
Of affliction!
Instead, His gentle rebuke has been
Our only restriction..
But it still concerns Him to hear us swear
Our allegiance day after day
And not mean a word we say!
Still, our Lord remembers the *honor*
Of His name
And reminds us of His heavenly fame!

The "I Love My Bible" Commentary

ISAIAH 49

God sneaks in a prophecy of the Messiah
Once again.
He has done it many times
Yet countless people
Have rejected His glorious plan
And chosen to walk in darkness
Committing many crimes.
Someday, though, prisoners of darkness
Will come to the light!
Sheep grazing peacefully will be
A marvelous sight
Even wild beasts will be tame
And will walk with man side by side!
God also tells us He has a special place
For us to run and hide!
And He adds those who wait for Him
Will never be ashamed!
Those who reject His protection
Will know He can't be blamed!
They can't say, "God made me do it!"
Nothing evil ever comes from His Holy Spirit!
Many have claimed there are discrepancies
In Isaiah–or called him an idle dreamer
But someday the world will know
He truly depicted Christ as our redeemer!
God adds He will save the Savior
From premature harm
For countless people would need the security
Of God's mighty , loving arm!

ISAIAH 50

The Lord does not "sell us out!"
No one is taken for our debt to Him.
He, himself, paid the debt
For our hopes were bleak and slim!
He has given us His words to help the weary.
With His glory to surround us
No day we face will be dreary!

But "face" is the operative word.
When people keep their eyes on heaven
Hope has always spurred-gigantically spurred!
The Lord will tell us what to say
If we will not rebel and turn away.
Oh, to trust in the Lord and not walk
In my own light
Means I will feel His holy spirit
And experience joy in His sight!

ISAIAH 51

Our ancestry has been defined!
We Christians know of this quarry
From which we are mined!
Christ is our solid rock!
We come from pure and noble stock!
It makes no difference should unbelievers
Not understand
That we love the Lord and have placed
Ourselves under His command!
We who have chosen the Christian walk
Must not fear or take part in slanderous talk.
Our God is the same God who dried up the sea
And His indescribable miracles
Continue to set His people free!
The "right" we do not have
Is to fear evil men.
God will not help those living in sin!
We are hidden safe within His hand.
It is as if we are already living
In the Promised Land!

ISAIAH 52

Wake up, wake up, Jerusalem.
You have slept way too long!
Your enemy has slipped through open doors
And discovered you are no longer strong!
Desolation and destruction haunt you now.
No one comforts you. *Not a soul knows how!*

Comment on Isaiah

Wake up, wake up, Jerusalem!
    Same song!
    Second verse!
The nation that sins lives under God's curse!
Wake up, wake up, Oh Christian!
Where have your morals gone?
Down TV tubes or picture screens
Neither of which cares what evil means.
Wake up! Wake up! Its time to see
What God's people are meant to be!
    Pure and true!
    Holy and free!
That is what God desires for you and me!
God's great "servant" will come to declare
That our God gloriously reigns
And the universe will echo
Those beautiful, melodious strains!
But--we see here in God's word
First the sad song will be heard!

ISAIAH 53

*One would expect
our Lord's anger to boil
even if it were slowly
for how could He stand to see
the treatment of One so holy?
God must have prepared Himself
for a million years
to face that one brief moment.
He must have vaccinated Himself
with a powerful grief potion
in order to ignore
earth's vicious, evil rodent.
It would be the devil's day
to hold all that is holy at bay.
God, Himself
would face great loss
when His holy Son
pure and magnificent
would hang on the cross!*

*It would be such trauma
God would say(in Isaiah's time)
"See Him bloodied and disfigured
paying for man's crime!"
I think God must have created
the mourning dove
to cry in sorrow
when mankind would reject
His great love!*

ISAIAH 54

The mountains will depart and the hills
Will disappear
But look for the Lord. He will still be here!
The shame of our youth will disintegrate
When God exiles His anger for our sake!
Isaiah says God's kindness will not leave
The blessed people who truly believe!
His people may be tempest tossed.
We may have felt we were utterly lost.
But hope springs eternal
From our eternal King
Who will route the terrorist
And ease the "hornets" sting!
Whatever the problems that are such a bother
They will be conquered by our "Father!"
This is the heritage of the people of the Lord!
Incredible blessings will be our reward!

ISAIAH 55

The *"Living Water"* is for anyone who thirsts!
Mankind need not hunger or fear the worst.
Bad news flees when God is in control.
God says there is still good news available
For every living soul!
God stands at our hearts' doors and knocks!
He is willing to forgive and cleanse
The dirtiest of spots.
Don't try to understand His ways

The "I Love My Bible" Commentary

Or why He will abundantly pardon.
God has been in the *"forgiving business'*
Every since man's fall at the *garden*!
His ways are higher than ours
And we cannot reach that high!
Even Science can achieve wonders
Yet when it thinks of God
It wonders "how" and "why!"
Only the Holy Spirit can explain
God's thoughts and ways.
God's knowledge will only be given
So we can lift Him up in praise!
Notice what God says about His word.
Its effect will certainly increase
And His ultimate purpose
Is that we live in joy and peace!
Man cannot supply our many needs
No matter how much he boasts.
So–is anyone hungry or thirsty?
Let him come to the Lord of hosts!

ISAIAH 56

Let our enlightened souls be still!
Gentiles, sit up and take notice!
Israelis are not the only ones
Permitted to bask in God's glory solstice!
When the Israelis got off track
God lovingly brought them back!
And He does the same for Gentiles too.
The *Father's* message to all of us is
    "I love you!"
There will be no second class citizens
In His heavenly reign.
No soul there will have reason to complain!
The only reason anyone will be left out
Is because he turns from God
And lives in sin and doubt.
God's temple is to be called a house of prayer
And when God's *"temples"* walk in his light
He will surely be there!

It is an everlasting name He gives
I know I shall live because my *"Father"* lives!

ISAIAH 57

The Godly die before their time
And no one wonders why
But God brings them home to rest....
These godly ones who die!
The end is so much different for adulterers
And murderers, robbers, and liars.
Their lives have seemingly ignited
Hell's unquenchable fires.
But in this day it is unpopular to think
We must be responsible for our deeds
So mankind justifies his actions by saying
He has unrequited needs.
And God grieves because such men
Give Him no thought
Yearning only for the pleasures or treasures
They have sought.
And man thinks his righteousness
And good works cinch his salvation
And hopes he will gain a glorious vacation!
But haughtiness spoils good works
And blinds the self-righteous
To his evil hidden quirks.
Contrite, humble spirits dwell with God
In His high and holy place
Because they eagerly accepted His forgiveness
And His wonderful grace!
Those who have repented will hear His
    "Peace be still!"
One glorious day, they made the decision
    to do His will!
Don't worry that the godly die young.
He(or she)is having "a time" in heaven!
Skies here were never so blue
And rivers never so still!
Saints are waiting there for me and you!
And God waits too-for all who do His will!

Comment on Isaiah

ISAIAH 58

The voice seems to say, "Don't act so pious
My people, I see your sins."
We cannot deceive God.
He has built-n long distance lens!
What is it God wants of us anyway?
Well, He's certainly made it clear!
He wants us to help the needy every day
And spread His good cheer!
That is how our light shines
If we let it shine from within.
Sharing God's love helps us be
What we wish we'd always been!
Every ill of mankind can be cured
By God's potent prescription
But only obedience brings healing
Which is beyond human description!
One more thing Isaiah had to say
God wants His people to honor "His" day!

ISAIAH 59

Some people think God has grown weak
In these modern times.
Mankind lies, grumbles, and opposes the good
Yet wonders about the growth in crimes.
We blame God for our evils
When we, ourselves, are wrong.
No, God can still hear us
And His saving power is still strong!
But He says He won't bless those
Who are a blessing to no one.
No wonder we seem to grope in the dark
And stumble as if there were no sun.
Though our sins keep piling up
Do we say we commit no sins?
Perhaps we overlook the fact
That God expects us to make amends!
And repentance is an unwelcome word
In our vocabulary

So, instead of a happy state of mind
We end up being mean and contrary.
But our *Redeemer* comes
To all who turn from sin
And He gives His Holy Spirit to strengthen us
When He comes to live within!
We surely do not want our God to turn away
For we need His help, His strength
And, most of all, we need His love today!

ISAIAH 60

Isaiah must have said
"Let the good times roll, Lord!
Come live with us!
Let your glory undergird our hearts
like a mighty truss!"
The Lord says
we will share His home.
The Lord never lies!
All Israel rejoiced
because she knew
the Lord heard her cries!
Someday many will come
to Jerusalem
to drink from God's fountain.
Jerusalem will be called
the city of the Lord
and His most glorious mountain!
Though Jews are hated now
they will be respected then.
They will forget all the
unhappy places they have been!
Someday all God's people
will rejoice in His light
Days of mourning will be gone
and there will never be
another night!
There will be glory for every soul
when God returns
to let the good times roll!

The "I Love My Bible" Commentary

ISAIAH 61

Planted like a mighty oak, the people would
Be rooted deeper when the Father spoke!
And someday their ashes would replaced
By incredible beauty.
Joy would motivate God's people
To eagerly perform their duty!
Praise will be so glorious it will permeate
The atmosphere.
Such rejoicing can not be contained
When our Lord comes near!
*Beauty, joy, and praise
Are God's three musketeers!*
Our Lord will not allow robbery and injustice
To fill our hearts with their nefarious fears!
What has He done for me?
He has blessed me with His sanctity!
The songs of the sanctified soul
Reaches to heaven and beyond!
And if we listen to our hearts
We will hear the angels respond!
No one has ever loved us as much as our Lord.
He is more than willing to bless!
His garments of salvation
And His righteous robe
Are the most beautiful garments we possess
For they are our ticket to that heavenly place
Where we will live in His amazing grace!

ISAIAH 62

Jerusalem, Jerusalem, how lucky you are
That God has considered you
His most blessed and brightest star!
Many times God has yearned for His holy city
And His heart also yearns to show us pity!
Joyful emotions lift me up
And I feel as if my heart will burst!
Such joy comes from my "Father"
When He knows I put Him first!
It is only by His love, mercy, and grace
That I can take part in His glorious prediction.
How can the name "God" describe my God?
He is beyond description!
No one cares?
Don't you believe it!
God's love is constant and true
And He will always do what He says
He will do for you!
One life-saving day God smiled at me
And I know He has set me free!

ISAIAH 63

Have you ever sung a song so beautiful?
Can you imagine anything so sweet?
Can anything lift up our hearts like God's
Invitation to walk salvation's holy street?
The thrill is gone?
No way!
The joy of our Lord grows greater day by day!
He comes in crimson glory to reaffirm
His power and might.
He comes to show the joy that results
From walking in His light!
He comes to hand out judgement
To His people's foes.
Yet His Spirit grieves as their rebellion grows.
We must question why people can disown
The greatest friend they have ever known.
He is our redeemer from distant ages past.
How can we harden our hearts so fast?
Blaming the other person isn't new.
Look at what the Israelis said!
"Why Lord, you made us turn against you."
Blame Society! Blame your folks!
Blame your Lord!
After all its been done so long it isn't hard!
Like us they refused to listen to-or believe
These judgements they had heard.
After all, reality is such a *very* dirty word!

Comment on Isaiah

ISAIAH 64

Like the Israelis we, too, must ask
"How can such as we be saved?"
At one time or another we have been sinners
Unworthy and depraved.
Yet our "Father" is the *potter* and we the *clay*.
  We lie broken, Father.
  Remold us now we pray!
Ever have a Sarge who said, "Move it
  and move it on the double?"
And you did, just to keep out of trouble!
Well, our Lord is a Commander-in-chief
And we'd better move despite our disbelief!
Sometimes we wonder why God stands
Silent and still.
Perhaps it is because we have failed
To do His will!
If we must remind Him we are His people
Something is wrong.
We have been heading the wrong direction
And have no reason to sing the victor's song.
How can we be saved and lifted up?
Try drinking from the Master's salvation cup!

ISAIAH 65

Thank the Lord for "good grapes"
That preserve God's style of goodness
For our sakes!
Godly people uphold the land
They are the ones who dare to take a stand!
A nation is preserved when God has
True servants there–those who love justice
And are kind and fair.
But God doesn't think much of the attitude
"I'm holier than you."
That is caused by pride and it contaminates
Every thing we try to do.
And many a nation has fallen
Because of fallen ideals
And now, again, the world seems to idolize
The adulterer, the violent, the one who steals.
Still----someday----God's will, will be done
And our future will be brighter than the sun!
Jerusalem will welcome the "Morning Star"
When Christ returns
Even the earth will welcome Him and
The desert will bloom with flowering ferns!
There will be no hearts that are broken
And, better still, God will answer prayers
Before they are spoken!
Listen for the celebration. Listen for the cheer!
It's a cinch! God will soon be here!!!!!!!

ISAIAH 66

God's business is top priority! No nonsense!!
He warns us taking Him lightly will bring
Just recompense!
Heaven is His throne–the earth His footstool!
The man who refuses to honor His word
Is considered to be a fool!
Yet He shows pity to the man whose heart
Is humble and contrite.
Such a man's future will be gloriously bright!
God promises His people He will intervene.
Earth has yet to behold such an ineffable scene!
Isaiah makes it clear!
The nation of Israel will never disappear!
In these days that Isaiah mentions
No one will be spiritually blind
For God *will be recognized*
And worshiped by all mankind!
It will be a day hard to describe.
In those days no politician will take a bribe!
No gangster will draw a gun.
No violence will be done.
People will cherish one another
And no child will be without a father or mother.
It will be a time of miraculous love
When we are joined by our Father from above!

The "I Love My Bible" Commentary

Note: Isaiah is one of my favorite Old Testament books. It shows God's mercy and love as well as His power. I've read it many times and I never cease to wonder at God's patience with His people. You would do well to study it over and over!

We live in a time when few
want to say they are sorry.
Few want to repent.
Few seem to care
what the "Father" meant!
Can you imagine
God wanting to draw near
to us as weak as we are?
Yet it still concerns Him
when we follow from afar.
His reasoning is based on love.
His love is founded on need!
Man's greatest need through the ages
is the *Ageless One*
Is there any one greater?
No indeed!
And our Lord will always be willing
to reason
for His love will never go out of season!
God is God!
He was God
when Adam sinned
when David sinned
and He is still God
even though we sin.
God is real!
God is alive!
He will always be God!
Because of *that* the world
is in awfully good shape
for the shape it is in!
God seems to be harsh sometimes
but we call that "tough love!"
I think perhaps we need it
if we want promotion
to His glorious home above!

Who hath believed our report?
And to whom is the arm of the Lord revealed?
For he shall grow up before him as a tender plant,
and as a root out of a dry ground:
he hath no form nor comeliness, and when we shall see him,
there is no beauty that we should desire him.
He is despised and rejected of men;
a man of sorrows ,and acquainted with grief;
and we hid as it were our faces from him;
he was despised, and we esteemed him not.
Surely he hath borne our griefs,
and carried our sorrows;
yet we did esteem him stricken,
smitten of God, and afflicted.
But he was wounded for our transgressions,
he was bruised for our iniquities:
the chastisement of our peace was upon him;
and with his stripes we are healed.
All we like sheep have gone astray;
<u>we have turned every one to his own way;</u>
and the Lord hath laid on him the iniquity of us all.
He was oppressed, and he was afflicted,
yet he opened not his mouth;
he is brought as a lamb to the slaughter,
and as a sheep before her shearers is dumb,
so he openeth not his mouth:
He was taken from prison and from judgement:
and who shall declare his generation?
For he was cut off out of the land of the living:
for the transgression of my people was he stricken.
And he made his grave with the wicked,
and with the rich in his death;
because he had done no violence,
neither was any deceit in his mouth.
Yet it pleased the Lord to bruise him; he hath put him to grief:
when thou shall make his soul an offering for sin,
he shall see his seed, he shall prolong his days,
and the pleasure of the Lord shall prosper in his hand.
(Isaiah 53:1-10kjv)

The "I Love My Bible" Commentary
The Book of Jeremiah

JEREMIAH 1

God considered the Israelis full of hot air.
He told Jeremiah not to flee from there!
Jeremiah was so young and tender
The Israelis must have considered
His assignment only a "weekender!"
But God knew Jeremiah was not too weak
For Him to give this innocent young man
His soul-searching words to speak.
To those who think Jeremiah's words
Were only to scorn
Listen to God say, "Jeremiah, I knew you
Before you were born!"
Those Israelis viewed this young "upstart"
With "you're wet behind the ears
And don't even know your own heart!"
But God's call was so vivid and real
Jeremiah knew non-performance
Would bring him no appeal!
And none of these people
Were mighty enough to fear.
God had demanded he tell them
Their judgement was drawing near.

JEREMIAH 2

The prayer I most desperately need to pray
    is---- "Lord,
Let me see you moving in my life today!
Let me feel your heart beat deep in my soul.
I won't fail when I know You are in control!"
It was a concern to God when His people
Young and old, turned him down flat!
And He asked them,
"How can you treat your God like that?"
His love for His people is deep and eternal
And, so we can understand it, He describes it
As paternal!
And because we do not obey Him
The world is not at peace
And we still seek elusive "idols"
As our sins increase.
It looks as if the whole world has gone mad.
We look for hope but the news is always bad!
We anesthesize ourselves with pleasure
And fail to cherish our greatest treasure.....
    the right to be free!
Jesus offered it when He said, "Come to me!"
God chose Jeremiah as a little boy
Because His message was simple.
"Be good, honest, and pure
And I will meet you at the temple!
Even in the Old Testament
A little child was chosen to lead the way.
But Jeremiah wept because
They would not listen
And insisted on going astray.

JEREMIAH 3

The adulterous, idolatrous Israelis
Were always in trouble because they couldn't
See their guilt
And they stumbled blindly over those
Self-willed walls they had built.
Sometimes we need bifocals if we would see
What we should cherish dearly
But more importantly, in matters of the spirit
Using God's "nigh-focals" will help us
Focus clearly!
With God's vision we can see the obscure
Sign posts that point us to a brighter day
And we can experience the elegantly simple
Pleasures that are ours when we pray!
Then we can see to hold on tight
No matter how utterly dark the night!
The sun beams down tracers of hope
To tumble down faith's mountain slope.
Whether we see clearly or not

Comment on Jeremiah

Is our decision.
But we'll never have God's "winsight"
Without the presence of His inner vision!
The Israelis were always turning
To someone else because
They trusted in wooden gods
With built-in hidden flaws.
"Come back to me" God said
And He says it now
For we cannot see to walk His paths
Until He shows us how!

JEREMIAH 4

Instead of worshiping God man seeks
Self-satisfaction and the latest sensation.
"Self" builds walls between God
And His favorite creation!
Self-satisfaction is sin in God's eyes
And that is why He often ignores our cries.
Sin is self inflicted neurosis
And it sets up an invisible necrosis.
Like cancer, its effect is not felt
Until the final stages
And becomes more evident as its victim ages.
The stronger it grows, the harder it is to evict.
It is often a welcome tenant
With hidden dangers we fail to predict.
But the word "sin" cannot aptly describe
Its own condition
Which can be worse than the chain reaction
Of a nuclear fission!
"Such a little word!" My Mother used to say.
But look at all the devastation it has caused
   today!
The best way to describe sin is
Its against everybody and is so unfair.
There is no harmony in the soul
And no peace anywhere.
Yet, we insist in doing our own thing
And ask why we have no happy songs to sing.

"Self" and "sin" go hand in hand
And bring many sorrows we fail to understand.
It seems that is the way we are!
We suffer because we follow
Our heavenly Father from afar.
The same thing happened to the Israelis
In Jeremiah's time so long ago.
There was much about this spiritual life
These belligerent people didn't know!
How much intelligence can we claim
We who foolishly dishonor His name?

JEREMIAH 5

God told Jeremiah to search every street.
To see if Jerusalem had at least one man
Devoid of dishonesty and deceit.
There is a simple equation in life
As easy as two plus two.
Have no place in your life for the Lord
And He may have no place for you.
Think of nothing but running after pleasure
   and fun
And there will come a day in your life
That you will have no place to run.
Essentially that is what God told this nation
Who loved foreign gods and sought
The latest recreation.
God said they committed adultery wholesale
And today we have something similar
People are equally guilty-whether *him or her!*
We have eyes that do not see
Ears that do not hear.
People sin viciously against the Lord
And do not even fear.
We need to read what God is stressing.
These sins rob us of God's blessing!
Jeremiah says the priests were ruled
By false prophets and the people liked it so.
So--they would find themselves
With no worthy place to go!

The "I Love My Bible" Commentary

JEREMIAH 6

God told Israel to refrain from idolatry
But they wouldn't stop.
He called them swindlers and liars
From the least on up to the top!
They refused to walk the paths
God wanted them to walk.
And they wearied Him with their willingness
<u>Only</u> to talk.
God said Israel spouted evil like a fountain
And had desecrated His holy mountain.
Jerusalem had been colorfully attired
And gloriously plumed.
She had been beautiful and delicate
But now she was doomed.
God found NO pureness in her to bring out.
When He sent His *not accepted* correction
All she did was pout.
"I have discarded them." God said.
And Jeremiah mourned for these people
He considered good as dead.

JEREMIAH 7

God looked into Israeli hearts
And discovered only wrong desires.
He told Jeremiah He abhorred their use
Of strange unholy fires.
Think of Nadab and Abihu, Aaron's sons
And what happened in Leviticus ten.
They offered *strange fire* before the Lord
And God destroyed these two men!
Same song–umpteenth verse!
Only Israel had grown even worse!
How tragic it is to be so flauntingly evil
      that God would say,
"Jeremiah, pray no more for these people!"
See the great truth hidden there?
When God's *faithful, <u>obedient</u>* people pray
(<u>His</u> definition of obedience-not ours)
God is honor bound to answer their prayer!
There are many sins listed in this chapter.
Because of them, Jerusalem would no longer
Resound with joy and laughter.
Her people would weep upon the mountain
And shave their heads in shame.
For they had continued to dishonor
The blessed Father's Holy Name!

JEREMIAH 8

There is no balm in Gilead!
No salve will ever do.
There is no anti-biotic
for hearts that continue
to be untrue.
What the false prophets
taught the people
was merely slush.
They were so wicked they didn't
even know how to blush!
When the people found themselves
on the wrong road
they wouldn't turn back.
Life was more exhilarating
on the downward track!
Though they chose to remain
depraved
they would cry
"Summer is over and
we are not saved!"
Heathen prophets and
Israel's false prophets, too
had become like two peas
in a pod
yet they had the audacity
to blame their troubles
on the Lord God!
Like I said in chapter seven
Same song, umpteenth verse!

Comment on Jeremiah

JEREMIAH 9

God did not approve of men harassing
One another
So it broke His heart to have to say
"Beware of your brother!"
They were all adulterous, treacherous, and
Deceitful men
Who piled lie upon lie and sin upon sin.
Instead of repenting, the Israelis constantly
Grumbled
Even as Jerusalem's power swiftly tumbled.
Through the ages God has said
"Let not the wise man bask in his wisdom.
His wisdom comes from me!"
And no one is wealthy without His help
Nor can the mighty set anyone utterly free!
If we boast it must be in God alone.
His power is like *holy marrow* to the bone!
God despises heathen rites.
Only love for Him can take us
To nobler, grander heights!
God told Jeremiah the kind of lives He prized
Came only from *hearts* that were circumcised.
My chances to be rich, mighty, or wise
May be awfully slim
But you can bet I can stake my bets
    betting on Him!
God's love is steadfast every day
    and wonder of wonders
He graciously loves to be that way!

JEREMIAH 10

Over and over God had to say
"You run after idols and turn me away."
They acted like a bunch of confused astro-nuts
Who based their fate on *ifs* and *ands* and *buts!*
They revered an idol made of *dead* wood
They could wad
And then stupidly asked it to be their god.
Idols were only wood whittled quacks
Who could lift no burdens from their backs.
And to think these people kneeled and tarried
Before a god that had to be carried!
In our hearts is the only way
To carry our *Living God* day after day!
Our Lord who had courted them so sweetly
Was ignored and blasphemed completely.
Jeremiah knew mankind's actions
Would only bring strife
Because they lacked the knowledge
To map their own life.
But Jeremiah knew the One who could!
And he refused to worship a piece of wood.

JEREMIAH 11

Again, God has to say, "Pray no more
For these people–they've gone too far.
They bow at the alters of shame
Coating their faces with unremovable tar.
God implied they were babes, all de-brained
Who didn't have enough sense to come in
Out of the cold when it rained!
Had they obeyed the words God had spoken
Contact with Him would not have been broken.
They lost their temple rights
For they followed the godless too many nights!
Jeremiah depended on God to keep him alive
But those who plotted his death
Faced a disaster they would not survive.

JEREMIAH 12

There is an eloquence in equality
That anarchy can never picture!
Man has never learned that his rebellion
Creates a devastating stricture.
They would harvest a crop of shame.
For their lawlessness had brought dishonor
To God's Holy Name.

The "I Love My Bible" Commentary

Jeremiah reminded the Lord
How faithful He had been
He was weary and in spiritual danger
From daily confrontation with these men.
God implied there is a "jungle"
Jeremiah must travel though.
He could not stumble or fall and still remain
God's messenger to the Jew!
But even in judgement
God mentioned compassion
God's mercy, love, and tenderness
Will always be in fashion!
All He asks is for us to obey
And He promises to strengthen us
To face another day!

JEREMIAH 13

If we'll read between the lines we'll see
We need daily cleansing to keep us rot-free!
We cannot bury our heads in the sand.
We must cling to God in order to stand!
It is so easy for us to get the wrong impression
And it leads us into a bewildering depression.
Look closely and you will see
When His people's sins were *stormy*
God sent his discipline through
An unmerciful army.
The reason the Israelis could do no good
Was because they put God out of their minds
And He exposed them to gross judgement
Of all kinds.
And it seems even God was unsure
How long it would be
Before these people would be pure.
They had records with awesome blots
Because they refused to repent
And ask God *to erase their evil spots!*
Here, I must add a negative plus.
We must be careful *how we act*
Or those judgements could apply to us!

JEREMIAH 14

Servants covered their heads in grief.
It was so dry they saw no relief.
The people's sins had left them confused
And hopelessly baffled.
They thought God's power had been raffled!
"We carry your name," they said
Admitting their hopes were good as dead.
They accused God of deserting them
When it was the other way around.
"You wander away from me," God said
"And walk on contaminated, unholy ground."
War and famine came as the people grieved.
They chose to listen to false prophets
Who themselves were deceived.
God demonstrated His grief
Through Jeremiah's tears
For He knew the people would not repent
Despite their many fears.
Though they didn't repent they complained
And wondered why it never rained.
Their actions would state their unholy state
For holiness would bring a responsibility
They seemed to avoid with barbarous hate!

JEREMIAH 15

Jeremiah moaned and cried helplessly.
"Where are the good times I expected to see?"
He knew he couldn't walk the path
Of service alone
For without the Lord, he was as useless
As an old dry bone!
He thought he'd walk trails that were higher
But found himself in the mud and mire.
And look at the chance he took
When he said God's help was as uncertain
As a seasonal mountain brook!
Well, the Lord told him a thing or two!
"I told you not to let them influence you!"

Comment on Jeremiah

And, we too, are not to moan and fuss
For the Lord says the same thing to us!
Meanwhile the Lord warned Jeremiah
Unless he trusted Him again
God would cast him aside
And choose another man!
I bet he acted like a cowed pup
And begged the Lord not to give him up!
And I bet he never again acted so sassy
For we see his service was totally classy!

JEREMIAH 16

Man can become so evil God will grant him
  no favors
Because he wallows in the depths of the sins
  he savors.
These people sinned to their hearts content
And then had the audacity to wonder
What *in the world* the Father meant!
But harsh as was God's judgement
His promise was greater still!
Those people of Jerusalem would return
To stand someday on the very same hill!
But first they would have to be cleansed
Of their evil deeds
Then they would understand why it is our God
That man desperately needs!
Other nations would come to God also.
Sooner or later they would learn
There is *no sweeter* place to go!
But now these people ridiculed Jeremiah
No matter what he said or what he would do.
They decided God's threats through Jeremiah
Would never come true.
God used the word "if" as He had done
Many times before.
"If" they would obey and follow Him
He'd restrain His judgements just once more!
They didn't believe one word
As if God was one of whom they never heard.

Yet there is something better God wants us
  To know
Though His words cut deeply like a sharp knife
He is saying, The pot of gold we are seeking
Is not at the end of the rainbow.
It is at the end of a godly life!

JEREMIAH 17

Imagine God having to say, "These men
Act as if I have commanded them to sin."
And to make matters even worse
They think they have not earned the "curse!"
So the heritage that was theirs
Has slowly slipped from their hands
As they follow heathen gods of other lands.
Foolish people fail to see
Where man's loyalty needs to be.
The Lord knows man's heart is grievously
Wicked and full of deceit
And longs for strange heathen delicacies
He considers to be tasty and sweet.
And from that comes the sad story.
God says they were registered for earth
And NOT for glory!

JEREMIAH 18

God says His people cannot be counted on.
They ran after every pervert and wanted Him
To leave them alone.
They hired their own prophets and wise men
But their advice spurred only wickedness
  within.
Israel needed help from a more reliable source
But she would have to seek it in humility
And genuine remorse.
Jeremiah knew how much they had dishonored
God's word
But he felt no thrill when he had to say
"Let screaming be heard."

The "I Love My Bible" Commentary

These were the words of a bitter man
Whom Israel had rejected again and again.
He had been faithful to give them
Godly advice day after day
And he told them their *"Great Potter"*
Was willing to remold His marred
And crippled clay!

JEREMIAH 19

I would think the Lord would become
   deathly ill
At just the thought of forgiving people
Who had no intention of doing His will.
God said these people had done an awful
thing
For they shed innocent blood
When they killed their own offspring.
Because of that they would be destroyed.
How would they feel then about
The terrible sins they had enjoyed?
 Their's had been unbelievable slaughters
When they aborted the lives of their own sons
   and daughters.
They were heartless, hopeless, incorrigible
   people
Who did their "own thing" and went their
"Own way!"
Now their *back pocket of hope* would empty.
They would have to pay.
They had sunk so low
God wouldn't reach down even to touch them.
Such were the depths of the sins of Jerusalem!
God does not-will not-change His rules.
His people must obey.
I shudder when I think of the consequences
Of what even *God's people* are doing today!
This Prophet God, this Priestly King
Must be terribly, terribly sad
When His people insist on
Doing their own thing.

JEREMIAH 20

What an unpriestly priest was Pashur
As useless to God as an ankle-burr.
To think, he had Jeremiah beaten
And put in chains!
It is the hypocrites of God's people
Who often give us the most grievous pains!
But Jeremiah's answer was Pashur's dry bones
Will soon be buried under Babylonian stones!
It concerned Jeremiah he couldn't speak
A word of kindness
To people who walked in spiritual blindness.
He was so discouraged he swore
He'd never again mention God's name
But the words God had planted in his heart
Burst into an unquenchable flame!
God wanted Jeremiah to get His people
Our of their unholy rut
And He simply would not allow Jeremiah
To keep his mouth shut!
But depressed Jeremiah didn't seem very brave
When he wished he'd died in infancy
To be buried in an untimely grave.
I'd hate to think what he would say
If he were trying to witness to people today!

JEREMIAH 21

It puzzles me that we can turn so quickly
Against the will of our Lord
When He has always told world leaders
"You must not treat my people hard!"
It is not His fault that judges take bribes
And there is dishonesty in our leaders
Similar to what Jeremiah describes.
It is NOT His fault when men rape and kill
In a sadistic perversion of His will.
God kindly gives man a chance to choose
His own "breaks"
And will judge him on the choices he makes!

Comment on Jeremiah

Those who choose to lie, rob, kill, and cheat
Increase their chances of facing defeat.

JEREMIAH 21

It puzzles me that we can turn so quickly
Against the will of our Lord
When He has always told world leaders
"You must not treat my people hard!"
It is not His fault that judges take bribes
And there is dishonesty in our leaders
Similar to what Jeremiah describes.
It is NOT His fault when men rape and kill
In a sadistic perversion of His will.
God kindly gives man a chance to choose
His own "breaks"
And will judge him on the choices he makes!
Those who choose to lie, rob, kill, and cheat
Increase their chances of facing defeat.

JEREMIAH 22

God's man can not *beat around the bush.*
He must be direct!
Some people need a definite push
To make them show our Lord respect!
Our Lord is always concerned about our needs
So, those He puts in priestly authority
Must be full of good deeds!
But evil king Jehoiakim built injustice
Into his palace walls.
As we read history can't we see injustice
Is why many a person or nation falls?
And mansions do not make a nation great.
It is mercy and kindness
That makes 'its soul' a beautiful estate!
Yet Jehoiakim was a disobedient whelp!
God would refuse to give him any help.
Even his son who took his place
Was considered a hopeless disgrace.

All Israel held God in such disregard
That Jeremiah had to say
"O earth, earth, hear the word of the Lord!"
My goodness what a shame
That the Lord had to *beg* the people
To glorify His Name!

JEREMIAH 23

The shepherds of God's sheep
Thought there was no commandment
They should have to keep.
Who would think God's leaders would mock
The lonely, the needy of His frightened flock?
Their adulterous lies made matters worse.
Priest, prophet, and the people
Were all under God's curse.
They closed their ears to God's reprimand
As wickedness devastated their land.
But there is a remedy for one who strays
When he turns to God and forsakes evil ways.
God's word is like a hammer covered
In sheep skin.
It may smack the stubborn head
But it soothes the broken heart within!

JEREMIAH 24

Isn't it strange that God chose to say
"I am with those people I sent away!"
Though they looked at Babylon as a land
That defiles
It was their sins that exported these exiles!
But those left at home were considered to be
Worthless alloy
God would not bless any of them
And they would feel no joy!
Zedekiah was considered a rotten fig
Too bad to be used.
He was repulsive to God
Because of the many people he abused..

The "I Love My Bible" Commentary

He, who had been a 'ravager'
Would have to watch his own sons' massacre!
And he would be mocked, taunted and cursed
For his penalty needed to be reimbursed.
This man who considered himself
Such a fancy Dan
Would never see his majestic home again.

JEREMIAH 25

All Israel was serving a life sentence
-seventy years which would surely
   lead them to repentance!
She had shown no pity or repentance before
And now had forced God to even the score.
The Lord also had a case against other nations
And if they didn't repent they'd face
That *'heated'* place of lower elevations!
God's whirlwind of wrath would arise
On those people whose favorite game
Was to demoralize!
All the wicked leaders would weep and moan.
In their time of slaughter they would be alone.
People laughed at the thought
Of God's retribution
And never believed He would ever make
   restitution.
But "Drink from my cup of wrath," God said
And those who laughed would cry instead!
These rebels would have to understand
God undergirds
Only those who honor His words.
We know our Lord has said
"If you will be true to me.
Your life will be full of joy and victory!"
But they weren't true to our Lord
And they didn't have enough brains or brawn
To keep them out of Babylon!
It was just around the corner, across the fence
Or it may as well have been
For these people who live in incessant sin.

JEREMIAH 26

If you are faithful to the Lord.
It could cost you your life! Jeremiah found out
These people thought he was a heretic
Who didn't know what he was talking about.
No matter how faithful or how obvious
God's judgements are
Most people consider God's servants
To be irrational and bizarre.
No one wants to face reality.
In this case, Jeremiah's warnings held such
A horribly gruesome finality.
"Go away little boy ," they must have said.
"You've got strange things in your head!"
They did not harm Jeremiah this time
But they still committed the awful crime
Of killing another servant of God.
Urijah had been warning them they faced
God's powerful disciplining rod!
He tried to run to Egypt and hide
To evade his inevitable homicide.
But the wicked man who wore the crown
Sent his servants to hunt Urijah down.
Urijah didn't have a prayer
They took him home and killed him there.
But God saved Jeremiah who was not through.
There was much more work he needed to do.
People have not changed.
God's word is still ridiculed
For people doubt it and continue to be fooled.

JEREMIAH 27

For years man had ignored God's message
And he still won't listen.
Murder, rape, adultery, and theft are the walls
Of his own prison.
He has wrapped himself in mystery and deceit.
Even in Zedekiah's day
God was warning them of their defeat!

Comment of Jeremiah

These people got too big for their britches
To repair these people's hopes
Would have taken a million stitches!
The Israelis would have nothing left
No seams to repair because of their own theft.
False prophets had stolen their hearts away
And, whether they liked it or not
They were going to Babylon to stay.

JEREMIAH 28

A false prophet has a big mouth
And questionable virtues.
It would be foolish to base any decisions
On the knowledge he construes.
Hananiah had the nerve to tell the people
A big fat lie!
But Jeremiah essentially told him
The proof of the pudding was in the pie!
God had not changed His decree
And would not intervene to set Israel free.
The people were all spiritually broke
And none of them understood the message
Of the 'yoke!'
Worst of all, Hananiah would have to pay.
He would die for telling all those lies
That fateful day.
He stumbled over a truth so very simple.
It was double deadly to tell a lie
    in God's name
Especially at HIS Holy Temple!

JEREMIAH 29

God's people can't be moved so far that
God's promises can not follow in pursuit!
God told them to pray for Babylon
-her peace would be theirs to boot!
The very young would grow to be
Grandparents there
And if they spread God's message
They would have hope to spare!
God's people *are to act like God's people*
    wherever they are
Though they had been taken in an act of war!
But those false prophets who had stooped
To adultery with their neighbor's wives
And who had been so utterly rotten
Would have to pay with their lives.
And Shemaiah would dream no more
He had paddled his leaky dream boat
With a tattered oar!
There was much better news for those
Who would look for God in earnest.
They would escape Babylon's burn list!
They would live to freely worship God again
But it would be *after* that seventy year span!

JEREMIAH 30

Could this be God's own to whom he speaks?
"Your sins are so many your stench reeks!"
Their sins became an incredible bruise
-skinless skin they could not bear to lose!
Even though they made them selves outcast
God considered their troubles in the past.
God looks so far ahead we can't possibly see
The promises He sends in great multiplicity!
He would also give His people
Their *own* ruler-their *own* man
And extend His people the invitation
To come to Him again!
But God's devastating whirlwind
   would burst on those
Whose spirits would not bend!

JEREMIAH 31

   Since time began
  God has had one concern
   a very precious truth
   man has yet to learn

The "I Love My Bible" Commentary

"Act like my people"
God said.
He has love, mercy and truth
for us to spread!
We are delinquent children
out on bail.
Yet He still loves us
though we continue to fail.
We should have learned
from Israel's mistakes.
One goes through trouble
from the trouble he makes.
God had to send them away
to make them want
to come back.
It took punishment
-then mercy
-then grace
to get them on
the right track!
Only love can find a way
to open doors
of opportunity.
Only love erases
sin's viral threat
with God's immunity!
God went way out on a limb
to help these people
come back to Him!
He talks about a new contract
which we know He gave.
It would inscribe His laws
in the *hearts* of the people
He wanted to save!
Think of the times
God has answered our prayers!
Think of the love and mercy
we've enjoyed!
It will be even better
when He sets up His kingdom
here on earth

which can never be destroyed!
I will truly be His
and He will truly be mine!
It will be a magnificent song
when we sing our heavenly
Auld Lang Zine!

JEREMIAH   32

Guess What!
Dungeons can't keep God's word
From bursting through!
God said, "Your cousin, Hanamel, has land
He wants to sell to you."
Did you ever feel really low
And in your dungeon of blues
Thought you had no place to go?
Israel did when God said she would be overrun
Yet He would set her free.
What you call that, is long range planning
All Israel failed to see.
They had seen freedom and not treasured it.
They had seen prison and not learned one bit.
They had seen love and turned away.
Now they thought God had sent them
To Babylon to stay.
And those who were left behind
Were still spiritually blind.
Seeing, they saw not
That their sins were a deadly blot!
Seeing, but not seeing, they ignored
Their only chance to be restored.
They had hardly done one thing
God had told them to.
Is it any wonder He told them He was through!
But God's mercy overruled His anger.
They would not stay in Babylon
Except for the seventy years they would linger.
They'd learn God was their harbor of hope
Their anchorage of strength and of stability
Just as He was in Jerusalem's Holy Facility!

Comment on Jeremiah

JEREMIAH 33

Jeremiah remains in jail
    but God's message
    osmosis through the bars!
Iron, steel, brick, or stone
    cannot keep out the
    One who made the stars!
It is another message of warning
    to hard headed men.
God had abandoned them
    because of their wickedness
    and sin.
Though His right hand
    held messages of woe
His left hand held the love
    that would soften the blow!
There would be happiness
    in Jerusalem someday.
They would praise the Lord
    for bringing them home to stay!
You see, God had a plan in mind
    He would send
His servant David's descendant
    and he would be unusually kind!
God continued to send the news.
    "I will *never* abandon the Jews!"
But the Jews abandoned Him
    and there would be
    more bad news for Jerusalem.
They turned Christ away
    in wary resentment
    for they didn't believe
    He was David's descendent.

JEREMIAH 34

Zedekiah must have thought reassurance
From the Lord was his license to sin
But his ego would be deflated with just
The prick of God's holy pen.
Zedekiah promised to be good but acted
    otherwise.
It was the straw that broke the camel's back
When added to his other lies!
He had let his Israeli slaves go free
But then reneged.
He should have known God would see
The awful things he did.
He would regret his insidious act
For it was deadly to break God's contract!

JEREMIAH 35

Obedience to God brings continuity and self
    respect.
When we lift God up, we'll do nothing we
    regret!
God admired the family of Rechab.
They didn't consider conformity to be drab.
Their father left rules for them
And our Lord saw
How faithfully these people obeyed
Their father's wish-their father's law!
God held them up as an example to the Jews.
Their lives would have been much better
Had they held similar views.
"But no, you go your own way
And refuse to obey." He said.
They could have chosen to follow Him
But turned away instead.
God blessed the Rechabites who continued
Jonadab's nomadic life style
And refused to drink wine.
You can feel the sadness when the Lord says
"I wish I could say the same
About those who claim to be mine!"
If it was such an honor to honor Jonadab
Then why was it so hard
For those Israelis to honor our Lord?
And why is it so hard for us to see
God also expects obedience from you and me?

The "I Love My Bible" Commentary

JEREMIAH 36

The Lord must have grown weary of sending
Warnings these Israelis ignored.
Yet He promised to forgive them again
If they turned from those sins He abhorred.
Seeing where the responsibility lies
Might have ended impervious, insolent replies
But 'reality' was unpopular even then!
And Israel's disparate monarch
Ardently refused to bend.
As Jehudi read the scroll
Jehoiakim cut each section away.
And then burning God's precious word
Was Jehoiakim's order of the day.
But flood, fire, fallacy, or ferocity
Cannot destroy God's judgement
Or, for that matter, prevent His generosity!
He patiently repeated the message
But sent a little more.
It seems Jehoiakim should have painted
A picture of that crown he wore.
It would soon be a memory
Because he failed to see
<u>God's</u> *order of the day*
Would be to put this evil man away!

JEREMIAH 37

The 'blind' led the blind toward destruction
As Israel's power faced immediate reduction.
One was taken prisoner and another reigned
But Zedekiah didn't listen with his heart
When Jeremiah complained.
Yet he knew Jeremiah had influence
With the Lord
And he wanted desperately to know about
His future reward.
Zedekiah occasionally tried to be good
But he was easily swayed.
He could have strengthened his 'back-bone'
If only he had prayed!
He did release Jeremiah from the dungeon
Where he had been thrown.
At least Jeremiah would not die there all alone.
It seems Zedekiah did have an open mind
And, in spite of himself, managed to be kind.

JEREMIAH 38

No man ever changed his mind so much.
One would think this king had no control
And was completely out of touch!
At least there were holy men in his cabinet
And once again Jeremiah would not die
 -at least not yet!
Ebed-melech came to Jeremiah's rescue.
He told the king, "It's an evil thing you do."
Zedekiah kept Jeremiah's rescuers busy.
He changed his mind so many times
He must have gotten dizzy!
Finally he sneaks away from everyone's sight
To ask Jeremiah about his plight.
Feature this, the king, who should fear no one
Seemed to fear everyone under the sun!
Well, he didn't like that 'subject' of doom
But he couldn't say, "drop it!"
He *knew* Jeremiah was God's holy prophet.
We've called Jeremiah the weeping prophet
   but would I cry if I were hungry
   would I stumble if I were blind?
  Would I accuse my Heavenly Father
   of being terribly unkind?
  And if I were king would I put
   thoughts of Him away
  and walk in darkness every day?
  Dare I judge this ambivalent king
  who had no joyful songs to sing?
   I, too, like so many others
   sometimes seem to stray
   and disappoint my 'Father'
   when I forget to pray.

Comment on Jeremiah

JEREMIAH 39

Finally! Zedekiah faced Jeremiah's prophecy.
Through prison and ridicule his message
Was one of constancy!
Over and over he warned King Zedekiah
Of sin's result.
But getting him to listen was very difficult.
When Nebuchadrezzar broke through
There was no place to run.
Zedekiah's sons were killed and he was taken
Blinded and in chains to Babylon.
Jerusalem was burned, the walls torn down..
He lost his home, his freedom, and his crown.
There is only one positive message found here
And it is the word God sent to Ebed-melech
To say he had nothing to fear
Complete safety was his reward
For all those years he trusted the Lord!

JEREMIAH 40

The line has been drawn tight, there is
No room for slack.
God had grown weary of listening to
Their faithless flack!
Jeremiah's pleading had been to no avail.
He had spent years delivering that *holy mail!*
'Payday someday' had come at last
And now their joy faded into the past!
A few people were left behind
To harvest the grapes and drink their wine.
Even the Babylonian Captain knew
Of God's judgement on the Jews
He told Jeremiah, "go where you choose!"
The Jews were defeated but their passion
For life kept growing.
Many returned from Moab, and Ammon
With their faces glowing!
Even though they would be under foreign rule
They hoped Babylon would be less cruel.

JEREMIAH 41

When one rejects bad news, bad news
Hounds him anyway.
Had Gedaliah been cautious he would have
Held Ishmael at bay.
Ishmael carried more guilt on his shoulders
When he killed <u>all</u> the Jewish officials
And Babylonian soldiers.
Then more men came to worship at the temple
But notice their idolatrous trait.
Cutting themselves was forbidden by the Lord
So it is likely that is why they fell
For Ishmael's bait!
Johanan rescued the people Ishmael had taken
And Ishmael's hopes were badly shaken.
Yet Johanan would take his people to Egypt
Because he lacked the articulation
To adequately describe the situation.
He and the people expected no sympathy
From the country that was their potent enemy!

JEREMIAH 42

Why do people seek good news from the Lord
And still hold on to their fear?
Johanan and the people sought God's advice
Yet were very insincere.
They didn't impress the Lord who had looked
Into their hearts
But can't you see the good advice our Lord
Willingly imparts?
Our Lord knew these people would not listen
Or obey
And when Jeremiah told them what He said
They would turn away!
But God warned them first
It may be bad news where they were
But Egypt would be worse!
The war they feared would follow
On their coat-tails

The "I Love My Bible" Commentary

And the paths they chose to walk
Would turn to treacherous trails!
They and Jeremiah held vastly different views.
And they simply would not listen
To this important, though gruesome, news!
These proud men told Jeremiah
"You lie to the people!"
Proud men now say, "God is dead.
Disband the church. Tear down the steeple!"
Dis-belief is a chronic contagious ailment
That always seeks truth's curtailment!
Men obey the Lord if it suits their plans.
Yet these men knew the fate of the other clans.
But did it do any good at all?
No, they still went to Egypt though they knew
They were destined to fall.
Who cares about history?
What do we learn from the lessons it teaches?
Man still considers himself beyond the arm
Of the Lord, no matter how far it reaches!
These people went to Egypt hoping to be free
Yet Nebuchadrezzar would rule them there
From his royal canopy!
He would plunder Egypt, picking it clean.
Johanan would finsd he could place no hope
In Egypt's king or queen.

JEREMIAH 44

'Back talk' put their lives in spiritual reverse
For God had warned them their sins
Would bring an awesome curse!
They didn't listen to a word Jeremiah said
Not even when God implied they were all
Just as good as dead.
These Israelis offered no apology
And belligerently continued their apostasy.
Sin is like putting cotton in your ears
And you fail to hear you are badly in arrears!
That was the problem these people faced.
They turned their backs on God

And were ultimately disgraced
God did promise to withdraw His wrath
If His people would follow His noble path.
But those who followed their idol queen
Hoping to please her
Would face burial by Nebuchadrezzar!

JEREMIAH 45

Baruch had faithfully recorded God's word
Yet the man's vision was painfully blurred.
He thought he had more troubles
Then he could handle
And he feared Israel's vicious reigning vandal.
He could not face a man so disdainful
And feared an encounter that would be painful.
He experienced no rest but only languor
As long as he felt Jehoiakim's anger.
But he received a great promise from the Lord.
He would be spared as a well earned reward!
God knows our fears and our heartaches
And can *dramatically* fulfill the promises
He makes!

JEREMIAH 46

Silent as a serpent gliding away
Egypt is too frightened even to pray!
What can a bull god do anyway?
Bellow?
It was so useless you could only color it *yellow!*
This bull-god of Egypt weeps
but his subjects still fall in heaps!
Amon, god of Thebes, would be punished too.
Those who worshiped him would find
all those idol gods are, and can only be untrue.
Only God can save His people!
Only God is strong!
And He would see to it
His people would return
to where they belonged!

Comment on Jeremiah

JEREMIAH 47

Every dog has his day—so they say.
A flood would destroy those Philistines
—they couldn't get away.
Time marches on and swallows its prey
And turns sunshine into a dismal gray.
The colonists from Caphtor would suffer
From the winds of war.
Retribution is such a thorn
But God says they, too, must mourn.
Men would flee for their lives
And leave their children all alone.
Clattering hoofs and rumbling wheels
Declared their judgement was full-blown.
Jeremiah felt pity for the Philistines
And wanted God to end such dismal scenes!
He was truly a man who cared.
And even wanted these heathen spared.

JEREMIAH 48

When Israel was destroyed
Moab had not thought it mattered.
She never thought she'd see
The day she would be broken and shattered.
They shaved their heads in anguish
Slashed their hands in shame.
She would soon forget the days
She gloried in her fame.
Moab had been fruitful
But now no one would tread the grapes.
No one had felt threatened by war.
Now only a few escapes.
Moab was filled with tears and a trembling
She could not hobble.
It was as if she knew she'd be smashed
Like a broken bottle.
God always said
"Don't rejoice in another's bad luck
Or your own fate may run amuck!"
Moab refused to listen.
Now she would see those swords glisten!
And almost before she sneezed
All her mighty strongholds would be seized!
She had watched while Israel cried in sorrow.
Now it was her turn to face the same horror!

JEREMIAH 49

Many nations hear predictions of their doom.
They would find themselves in Israel's same
'Bad news room!'
Ammon and Edom would find they, too
Would be called to account!
When God finished with them
There would be no steeds to mount.
The poor, the hungry, the innocent
Who had suffered at the hands of every creep
Who came along
Must have asked how long before
God would stop those who were doing wrong!
"Flee for your lives," God said.
He knew the deadly virus of war
Would continue to spread!
Nations that had lived in peace when Israel
Trembled in fear
Would almost be immobilized in shock
To see their judgement drawing near!
It would be no use to hide for they would
Be scattered to the four winds!
For them, the gory, the enemy, and the
Uncertainty of war would be a mixture
Of unpalatable blends.

JEREMIAH 50

Oh Babylon, your turn is coming.
Your fate will set your victims humming!
No one has been more wicked.

The "I Love My Bible" Commentary

No one has been more cruel.
In your fires of unjust judgement you added
Too much fuel!
You were a mighty hammer heavy as a sledge.
Now you hear of your coming destruction
And it sets your teeth on edge.
Assyria had faced annihilation.
Now God predicts the same for this nation!
Cruelty is a chain letter that circles ominously
And exposes an evil heart's incompetency!
God would spread terror to her rotten heart!
But first He would allow many to depart.
Babylon's turn for utter terror
Would be the worst of all!
The whole world would shudder
At this evil nations fall!

JEREMIAH 51

During the fourth year of Zedekiah's reign
God sent a message to Babylon's evil domain.
She would sink like a stone into the
Euphrates River
The scroll Seraiah carried contained
All the judgements God said to deliver!
Though he read it out loud he wasn't arrested.
Evidently no one believed the judgements
To which he attested.
It takes gumption to look ahead seventy years!
Its difficult enough to understand 'today!'
That may be the reason no one listened
To what Seraiah had to say.
Babylon didn't believe God made the earth
By *His* wisdom and *His* power.
Her wise men had little, or no, spiritual I.Q.
So, naturally, all their plans would turn sour!
Compared to God, all men are stupid beasts
Even though knowledge has greatly increased.
Yet I hesitantly confess
In matters of the spirit, we continue to regress!
The ghosts of unbelieving Babylon
Prowl all of our University(s) corridors
And haunt our PHD's
Hoping they can solve the riddle
Of why we still act like the aborigines!

JEREMIAH 52

Wickedness and pride caused Zedekiah to rebel
And Nebuchadrezzar ordered him expelled.
But before Zedekiah was taken to Babylon
He beheld a terrible scene.
All Israel's princes and his sons were killed
And he had no power to intervene.
Zedekiah had been told to help Israel
-to extend a righteous rule
But he mistreated the people and ultimately
'Played the fool!'
He believed nothing Jeremiah had spoken
And this man eventually died heart broken!
Because he refused to 'see'
He truly could see no more
That his opportunities were gone.
God had shut the door!

Note:

Jeremiah has come and gone but this weeping prophet will never be forgotten. His heart stayed as tender as when he was called as a youth. The tears he shed were more for his people than for himself. God's love is stronger than that!
L-o-v-e like HIS, we should always remember
For it will never fade into a dying ember!
But Jeremiah possessed a huge impatience and his impertinence almost cost him his place in God's employment. When he told God He was as unreliable as a seasonal meandering brook, God almost rejected him. Truly, I don't remember any prophet being so bold with God except for Moses. Still, God has always honored *hallowed searching of the heart!*

For thus saith the Lord;
sing with gladness for Jacob,
and shout among the chief of the nations:
publish ye, praise ye and say,
O Lord save thy people
the remnant of Israel.

Behold, I will bring them
from the north country,
and gather them for the coasts of the earth,
and with them the blind and the lame,
the woman with child
and her that travaileth with child together;
a great company shall return thither.
....

Hear the word of the Lord O ye nations,
and declare it in the isles a far off,
and say,
He that scattereth Israel will gather him,
and keep him,
as a shepherd doth his flock.
(Jeremiah 31:7-8; 10kjv)

The "I Love My Bible" Commentary
The Book of Lamentations

LAMENTATIONS 1

Nothing was sacred to these people anymore.
Many times Israel had defiled the temple.
Now her enemies have done the same.
And Israel was discarded like dirty rags
Because her sins disgraced God's name!
It seems Israel had no allies
Who would come to her rescue.
Though she groaned, begged, and pleaded
God ignored her too!
"Is it nothing to you?" She cries.
And no one seems to hear.
Israel's beauty and majesty are gone
And she has no heroes to cheer.
God saw her sins and she no longer brags.
Sin took away her beautiful garments
And replaced them with filthy rags!
"Oh Lord," Israel cries. "Make them let us be.
Punish those heathen as you punished me!"
The wheel of misfortune keeps turning
And now it seems
America is on the precipice of learning
About the rewards we seem to yearn
But are they the equivalent of what we earn?
Have we ever discovered when sin
Covers a heart with deadly plaster
It could die slowly from choosing
The cursed-aid of the wrong master?

LAMENTATIONS 2

A cloud of anger hovers over us
When we disobey our blessed Lord.
Even though it breaks His heart
He must show us discipline can be hard!
It has never been God's nature
To act without mercy.
Yet, Israel chose to shake her fist in His face
And said, "I dare you to curse me!"
God had forgiven them so many times, they
Refused to believe He would draw the line.
How could God punish them when He said
"I love you and you are mine!"
Repetition seemed to benefit a very few.
No matter the numerous warnings
That revealed what God would do.
Reality was a word for others to face
For surely, God would not remove His grace!
Sin grows slowly, insolently, finally in spurts
Yet we seem unaware of its growth
Until it hurts!
Its *our* sins that become so heavy we go under
And still we do nothing until they scatter
Our hopes asunder!
And then all we can do is *one thing*.
We must turn our lives over to our King!

LAMENTATIONS 3

Buried in deep waters, held by heavy chains
Israel cannot escape her punishment
And no hope remains.
Jeremiah sees their pain and cries for pity
But only bears and lions stalk their holy city.
But Jeremiah knows Israel is to blame
And he says his soul will live in utter shame.
He begged his people to repent
As he had for many, many years.
But it is too late; now they hear only
Their enemies jeers.
Ah–but there is one ray of hope.
The Book of Lamentations tells us
God's compassion never ends!
For He is lenient to the people He befriends.
So Jeremiah tells the people to wait.
He knows the Lord will return
Before its too late!

Comment on Lamentations

LAMENTATIONS 4

The finest gold loses it luster when sin
And treachery prevails.
It happens when people refuse to return
To the God of the ages though all else fails.
Ever learning, but truly not learning at all
That-when one sins he is destined for a fall.
The picture of Jerusalem painted here
Seems evident today in our putrid atmosphere.
Life is cheap and dreams fade away.
Rivers of despair wash them into the sea.
News grows more frightening by the day
And terrorists make it a mockery to be free.
Take a close look at Jerusalem's woes
And remember that is the way bad luck goes.
But it is the bad luck *we make*
For there are many of God's commandments
We continue to break!

LAMENTATIONS 5

The unrepentant Israelis cried in pain
But their sins had been so terribly ugly
All their tears were in vain.
And look at who they blamed!
You'd think they were innocent victims
Who had been unjustly framed.
God *didn't punish them for their father's sins.*
It was their own indiscretions that kept them
On needles and pins!
Those who were first were forced to be last
And their slaves willing service
Was now in the past.
Now servants bossed their 'bosses'
And took pleasure in those rich men's losses.
All Israel asked if God was angry still
Though they continued to disobey His will.
These people should have realized
As they spoke
The King of the Ages was their only hope!

Note:
*Lament
is such a depressing word
because we look
at its ugly side.
But it depicts an awesome love
Jeremiah couldn't hide!
It lays bare the depths
of his soul.
He cared so much
for his people
he sometimes lost control.
He lamented often
but his concern
was for others
and he would continually
weep for his brothers!
It is unpopular
to cry today.
Cry
and you cry alone!
But tears are
the soul's catharsis
and can melt
the heart of stone!
Though Jeremiah's tears
fell on unrepentant ears
lamenting
was the only way
he could demonstrate
his fears!
It seemed Jeremiah
would always lament
because his people
refused to repent!*

The "I Love My Bible" Commentary
The Book of Ezekiel

EZEKIEL 1

I don't believe God would have held
Ezekiel's attention
Had He not shown Ezekiel things that were
Almost too glorious to mention!
It was a resplendent vision God gave
To Ezekiel to view!
The Magnificent Creator sat on a throne
Of translucent blue!
He was surrounded by strange creatures
And Ezekiel must have cringed
At their unusual features!
Close your eyes and imagine the beauty
He beheld.
When he saw that glorious halo, how odd
He must have felt!
Man has developed no camera that could
Depict such beauty.
And who could ever describe how Ezekiel
Would react to his awesome duty?
Ezekiel had to be overwhelmed by this scene.
No wonder he fainted!
God had to strengthen him for him to draw
Those pictures of judgement
He must have reluctantly painted!

EZEKIEL 2

Fear knocked Ezekiel flat on his face
But God picked him up!
The news God wanted him to give would be
An overflowing, bitter cup.
He would need all the strength he could find
So the Lord was firm with him
Yet incredibly, lovingly kind!
Israel was a bunch of rebels, God said.
He warned Ezekiel not to be a rebel too.
And God used Ezekiel's *hard head*
To get His message through!

Ezekiel was to 'chew on' the messages
God gave him to share.
It would surely strengthen him to return
Any threatening stare!
Finally-*the piper must be paid!*
It would take courage to face them unafraid.
No one wants to give others news of doom
Because the bearer feels the heinous gloom!
Yet Ezekiel discovered he could jump on
Some people and stomp them in the ground
And his words would still be as useless
As if they never heard a sound!
That is why God made Ezekiel so strong.
He knew people hate to admit it whenever
They are wrong.

EZEKIEL 3

God gave Ezekiel words that were sweet
To the taste but bitter to hear!
He said, "Tell Israel what I'm going to do
And be sure you make it clear!"
Ezekiel would have to face stubborn rebels
And shatter 'rock' hard heads into pebbles!
But he had to internalize God's solemn news
For he needed *rock hard* courage to face
Those with vastly different views.
He would have to rise morning after morning
To give these evil people God's unwelcome
  warning.
And if Israel denied God's news and remained
  in unrepentance
They would have to face this fore-warned
Awfully bitter sentence.
It seems God gave Ezekiel little choice
And it he wanted to save his own life
He must adamantly lift his voice!
He *must* share his God given vision
And then he would not be held responsible
For any man's decision

Comment on Ezekiel

EZEKIEL 4

People who stray from God are spiritually
   paralyzed.
Yet, when Ezekiel remained immoveable
Israel must have been surprised.
Would Ezekiel have been one God could trust
Had God not reminded him he was only dust?
Ezekiel's ego must have been incredibly large
For God kept reminding him, God Himself
Was still in charge!
Israel's rebellion was so evil
God wanted them to think of the consequence
And certainly to fear it!
Yet, even Ezekiel failed to penetrate
Their unwilling spirit.
That is why God took such extreme measures
For His people had turned from Him
And were seeking strange unholy treasures!
Now there sustenance was gone
And they fed on terror.
Sin had made them as helpless
As a tiny unprotected sparrow!

EZEKIEL 5

The symbols Ezekiel uses grow stranger!
Hairs scattered to the wind were used
To warn Israel of impending danger.
Those that were not scattered were set on fire.
It was such an awful price for wallowing
In evil mud and mire.
There is not one word of comfort spoken.
Israel would be hounded, starved, and broken!
She had defied God's temple without restraint
And therefore Israel would weaken and faint.
        There was no hope!
           No hope!
           No hope!
But they refused to listen when Ezekiel spoke.
So God said to let their record stand.

Since they had sinned so grievously
Famine, disease and war would stalk
This evil, ungodly land!

EZEKIEL 6

Ezekiel was like a sandstorm with dust
Swirling everywhere.
God's name for him, "son of dust" was
Surely a picture of the news he had to bear!
Faces of the strongest men wince and pale
As they fall along a rugged mountain trail.
They had not believed in the God of peace.
Maybe war would open their eyes.
Yet they were unaware God wouldn't answer
Their feeble, desperate cries!
It is demoralizing to read these warnings here
As we watch these people cringe in fear.
Is it not strange that God must make life hard
Before people will recognize that He alone
        is Lord?

EZEKIEL 7

The bad news bear bears bad news!
He tells Israel she will see trouble coming
From four different views.
They surely heard by 'word of mouth'
Trouble would swirl from the North
And then around to the South!
Wicked men learned God would not budge.
No one could buy off this Holy irate Judge!
The worst kind of heathen would occupy
Their spacious homes
Homes taken by infidels while Israel roams.
False prophets would not, could not
Guide them away from their fiasco.
Since they would not go to God
They had no place to go!
Hands and hearts and bodies would be scarred
When they rejected God in one accord!

The "I Love My Bible" Commentary

EZEKIEL 8

I can see now why God gave
Such glorious visions to Ezekiel, His prophet
For the news was so thoroughly depressing
He must have cried, "Lord, please stop it!"
So God showed him what the people were
Doing secretly.
Ezekiel needed to see they had turned
From God completely.
These men who thought they had the 'smarts'
Were unaware that God could see into
The depths of their hearts!
Well, I know of no professional 'shrink'
Who can look into my eyes
And tell me what I think!
But *they* could not hide from God's power
And they denied themselves the protection
Of David's '*high and mighty tower!*'
God said they thumbed their noses at Him
And He would destroy these idol worshipers
Of Jerusalem.

EZEKIEL 9

Such solemn news he brings, the man carrying
The writer's case.
Following orders, he marked those who were
Full of God's grace!
These were the ones who had wept and sighed
Hating the sins in which others took pride.
Men of Israel had defiled the temple.
Now God defiled it too.
Seventy elders were the first to feel
The *final* judgement that was long overdue.
The land of Israel was full of injustice
God knew they said, "God has gone away.
He doesn't see us.!"
Now even as this plain spoken prophet pleads
And pleads fervently
God still repays them for their evil deeds.

EZEKIEL 10

Once again Ezekiel is privileged to see
God's incredible glory and awesome beauty!
The resplendent throne was no less spectacular
Than it was before!
Ezekiel stood in silence as awe
Filled his heart once more!
God did not speak to him, but to the stranger
Who carried the writer's case.
He was told to scatter coals all over the city.
I wonder
Had any of those coals contained any pity?
At least God's glory filled the temple
From end to end.
His magnificence is undoubtedly far beyond
These words Ezekiel penned!
Notice where the Lord is, He is surrounded
By incredulous beauty!
And notice also, how seriously those
Who love Him perform their duty!

EZEKIEL 11

Ezekiel says, "Then the Spirit lifted me!"
What a happy state to be!
But sometimes the Spirit directs His prophets
To declare doom
Instead of yellow roses, black dahlias bloom.
Dark thoughts of evil men could not be hid
Because, sooner or later, they were revealed
In what these people did.
They had considered their city an iron shield
But evil made it no safer than an open field!
Yet God spoke words of tenderness
Hearts of stone would soon turn into
Hearts *of loving bliss!*
Soon it would be joyously reported
God would return those exiles He deported!
God had cleansed those sins He exposed.
They had been punished enough. Case closed!

Comment on Ezekiel

EZEKIEL 12

All delay is ended! God says He will act.
Now, will they consider God's judgements
To be a viable fact?
No one cared to listen as Ezekiel
Shared his testimony
For they thought him to be a pathetic phony!
The prophecies he had staged
Were no less scoffed than the times he raged.
Nothing he did seemed to matter
For they chose to think he was madder
Than the 'mad hatter.'
All the scenes he staged for their benefit
Failed to profit them one bit!
They had not honored the Lord enough
To keep a single vow
So God says, "There punishment is overdue.
I *will* do it *now!*"
The time for mercy was gone
                  finished
                          past!
They had gone too far. Now the die was cast!

EZEKIEL 13

Lying prophets are a scourge on society.
They have no conscience and no propriety!
Even while Ezekiel was telling them this
They were listening to a self-styled prophetess.
She wore bracelets on her arms
And fooled the people with her 'charms.'
The male prophets, too, were a disgrace.
They could tell their lies with a straight face!
God said, "I *never* spoke to them at all.
Their trickery is causing my people to fall."
"I worry," He said, "about the news they give
When they say those who should live will die
And those who should die will live!"
These lying prophets gave God's people
Poison to drink-with a chaser

And God had to eradicate them
    with His great giant eraser!
Like them, we can't lift our heads without
Lifting our hearts also
For when we need proper guidance the Lord
Is the only one to whom we should go!

EZEKIEL 14

Though they would renounce their idols
And symbolically tore them apart
God knew they would not destroy an idol
Still imbedded in their heart!
We're so good at putting on false fronts
And hiding the fact we are spiritual runts.
But-like the Israelis we cannot hide
Our hypocrisy from God.
And we will inevitably feel the effect
Of God's fine-tuning rod!
God sees our spiritual defiance
And can correct our ambivalent alliance.
Paul said it would be hard to be a Christian
In the latter days
So we can't criticize the Israelis
As we, like them, fail to give God praise!
Well–it seems Paul was right
And no wonder we're all so uptight.
Experience tells us if Israel had obeyed
It is highly possible they would not have faced
War, famine, beasts, or plague!

EZEKIEL 15

The 'vines' of the Old Testament
And the VINE of the 'New'
Are worlds apart!
One was not fit to burn.
The Other was pure of heart!
One cannot trust a 'vine'
Of the Old Testament variety.
It contained a mix of strange potpourri!

The "I Love My Bible" Commentary

What about the 'mixture' of our world today?
Are we vessels of the spirit or just common clay?
We must be true if God would consider us "fit for hire!"
If not(true)it seems, we only jump out of
The frying pan into the fire!
Israel was not purified when her cities burned
For holiness was a lesson she never learned.
But those of this day who claim to be so wise
May be in for a terrible surprise!
Our 'vines' of knowledge may be spurned
God has told us many, many times
Spiritual truths must be spiritually discerned!
Despite the 'truths' on which we've relied
We fall so short of being purified!
*Ah–but the truths we find in the Bible
God assures us–are utterly reliable!*

EZEKIEL 16

I believe this 'son of dust' was so agitated
He must have thrown dust in the air
When he reminded Israel of God's great deeds
And still they didn't care!
"What a filthy heart you have."
God told him to say.
He added they were worse than a prostitute.
Their souls were so contaminated
Their spiritual illness had become acute!
"Oh prostitute, hear the word of the Lord"
He continues-but they closed their ears!
And no matter how vehemently Ezekiel grew
Their faith continued downward in arrears!
But are we as stubborn as a donkey that balks
And are we Christians thankless in addition
To all our other faults?
We are destined to swallow a bitter pill
As a result of *our* morales sliding down hill!
Look how far human nature fell
In one generation if you must.

Man-kind fell from Adam's biting the apple
To murdered Abel's 'biting the dust!'
How can we consider God unfair when
He had granted so much mercy to this nation?
In this day, for our nation, how many times
Has God's grace made its mercy rotation?
Look at Israel's sins(and look at ours too!).
They were pride, laziness and too much food
And response to the poor was very crude.
No wonder Israel was crushed, broken
And set aside.
All of the previous sins as well as the above
Gave them no place to run-no place hide!
Still God has His 'mercy plan'
For He said He would restore them once again!

EZEKIEL 17

Nebuchadnezzar had tried to treat him fair
But Zedekiah's trickery proved to be a snare!
Honesty would have been his best remedy
But Zedekiah stupidly 'two-timed' his enemy.
The 'eagle' he chose could not compete
To that *multi-colored feathered eagle*
Who downed him in defeat.
If birds of a feather are to flock together
They should come from the same nest.
Zedekiah thought he was hopping up
To a higher *limb*, instead he only regressed!
Egypt could do nothing God didn't allow.
Zedekiah must be punished
For breaking his solemn vow!

EZEKIEL 18

Oh, here comes the nitty-gritty
About a proverb people used trying to be witty!
Sour grapes, it says, sets teeth on edge
But the Lord says that is wrong
And He has given many a mis-judged person
Reason to sing a happy song!

Comment on Ezekiel

God gives victory to those who turn from sin.
The Lord said, "If you are good from now on
I will forget what you once have been!"
Who ever says the God of the Old Testament
Was a dirty bully
Has pulled the wool over his eyes so often
Even his eyes have grown densely wooly!
Our God does not like to see the wicked die
And He never fails to hear the souls deep cry.
But a man could not rely on *past* goodness.
It will be forgotten!
When God closes the books on 'our' today
Our deeds must not be rotten.
God continually says, "Turn and live"
For when people repent, He will still forgive!
This is one of those special golden nuggets
In God's Word
And still the best news we have ever heard!

EZEKIEL 19

It is very sad to see a nation destroyed
By its enemies
But utterly devastating to see it destroy itself
From within!
For its disunited citizens have contemptuously
Demolished themselves by sin!
They followed their own rules
And their own rules swallowed them!
So-in the river of life, they created a log jam!
You can't live without love if you love to live
And if you only give hatred, you receive back
That which you give!
Don't give me a set of rules.
Give me somebody to love
And I'll set my sights on those stars above.
Give me somebody to love-somebody
Like my Lord
And then being righteous won't be so hard!
Being righteous can be a 'piece of cake'
When I live holy for my Savior's sake!

That is what God wanted Israel to see.
Holiness makes life what it ought to be!
If only Israel had read *between the lines*
She would have lived where *His light shines!*

EZEKIEL 20

He was often ridiculed, poor old Ezekiel
who only wanted the best for his people!
He must have thought
"If only I can help someone else
make one less mistake
if I could prevent one more heartache
maybe I could turn the tide
and there would be one less person
who would hurt inside!"
But how can you help someone
who is insincere?
Even though Ezekiel warns
of the reality of sin
they showed no trace of fear.
Israel straddled a shaky fence
precipitating the kind of judgement
holiness prevents!
But they made their own plans
And God says, "Forget them!"
Their lives were so evil
it made their worship
an empty sham.
God swore to bring them
to His desert judgement hall
and teach them to loathe
those sins that had caused them to fall!
It seems God put Ezekiel
in the middle
of people who considered
his messages only a riddle.
I wonder did they dread the mornings
the predictions, the gruesome pictures?
Maybe not, because it seems
they ignored all those warnings!

The "I Love My Bible" Commentary

EZEKIEL 21

Had Oscars been given in Ezekiel's day
He would have won hands down!
He had the world's greatest dramatic coach
Who gave him poetic license to laugh, cry
  or frown!
But nothing he did seemed to affect
Israel's zombidic gouls
Who, having become calloused could only
Respond like soulless fools!
Many had celebrated how well their sins
Had thrived
But now their day of reckoning had arrived.
These sins at which the Lord had recoiled
In anger
Are the same sins that have placed
Our generation in danger.
So-what does God say about this prophecy
On which we border.
"I change not!" And *that* tells us
All His rules are still His *official order!*
Maybe our modern Zedekiah's, our modern
'False prophets' and these so-called humanists
Will learn someday the necessity of faithfully
Obeying our Lord's command!

EZEKIEL 22

Jerusalem receives a horrible indictment.
It was because idol lewdness filled her
With distasteful excitement.
She thought herself as clever as a wise old owl
But God considered her doomed, damned
Filthy and foul!
Adultery was common across the land.
Murderers, extortioners, and racketeers
Prospered by all the evil they planned.
But God snapped His fingers and
Demanded *instant recall.*
He would incinerate this worthless slag
That had caused His people to fall!
The priests did not teach His people
Right from wrong
Though righteousness could have made
His people strong!
God was immensely dissatisfied
Because the prophets claimed false visions
And the priests viciously lied.
None of them could stand 'in the gap'
Nor rescue Israel from her self-sprung trap!

EZEKIEL 23

People do not learn from other's mistakes.
Blind people followed other men's evil traits.
Foolish lovers play the game of 'prostitute'
Spiritually dying as they become blind
Deaf and mute.
Children were taken away as slaves
And their parents buried in common graves.
'Aholah' and 'Aholibah' so much in common
In their *common* behavior
Must bear the consequences of betraying
Their Savior!
God said His judgements would be a lesson
For all to see.
They would pay for their idolatry and harlotry.
These people, too hard headed to prod
Would live only long enough to learn
God alone is God!
They would not have come up short
Had they not been short on love.
Without it, we only learn to *push and shove!*
Had they lived for God's glory
Theirs would have been a different story.
Would you compare us with that ancient time
When the people considered Ezekiel
Imbedded in crime?
It was a crime to tell the truth, to be outspoken!
And black-sheep Israel rejected God.
Surely Ezekiel ended his days heartbroken.

Comment on Ezekiel

EZEKIEL 24

The 'best' sheep from the flock were still
Not good enough.
Sheep, soon with no Shepherd because
They mistakenly thought He could only bluff!
God wanted to cleanse His people
But His people refused
And their filthy lewdness rendered them
Unfit to be used.
God has a 'cleansing fire' but they would not
Come to be cleansed
And God considered them *wormy* chickens
Worthy only to be singed..
Later, God wouldn't allow Ezekiel to mourn
Even for his wife
In an attempt to show Israel the hopelessness
Of a decadent life.
Right is right and wrong is wrong!
God colors nothing grey.
But screens *big or little* beam into our lives
The immorality so many accept today.
Crime in our streets, our homes, our schools
And in corporate or legislative halls
Have weakened our well intentioned
Beautiful Spirit-built walls!
We can't blame a knowledge we've retired
When we face a future we foolishly hot-wired!
Ezekiel speaks to America-to the world-today
And says don't follow ancient Israel's
Evil pathway.
Israel came back to God. So can we!
God still says, "Please come back to me!"

EZEKIEL 25

Ezekiel was to look toward Ammon, Moab
And Edom, too
And was to tell those half-baked heathen
What God was going to do!
And he was not to leave the Philistines out.
They who had won many battles
Were now destined to lose the final bout!
And God keeps warning us and trying to show
How important it is for us to know
The wonders of His grace.
He keeps hoping we will do *'an about face!'*
What happens to those who refuse to turn?
I guess when you're tarred and feathered
Its like a slow burn!
Maybe that's going too far but its just a symbol
And maybe that's why God often told Ezekiel
To fear and tremble!
Ezekiel was willing to be a symbol even so far
As becoming lame
Hoping when Israel looked at God they would
Take off their dark glasses of shame!

EZEKIEL 26

Oh Lord, do it again!
Keep your messages coming!
Only 'your reality'
can keep back-sliding Christians
from slumming!
The high expectations
our Lord sets
are because He knows
what horrors sin begets!
This time God sent
His messages to a coastal city
who harassed others
because she didn't know
the first letter in the word 'pity!'
Tyre would feel God's judgement.
Tyre would feel His scorn!
Their penalty for inhuman acts
would be they also
would mourn.
It would be like God said.
She would disappear into
the nether world of the dead!

The "I Love My Bible" Commentary

EZEKIEL 27

This famous city made beautiful by architects
Will lose the fine homes she avidly protects!
Merchandise from many lands
Fill her warehouses to the brim
But a hurricane of horrors will turn
The bright light of her glory hauntingly dim.
Her fate was to perish beneath the seas
And those who watched wept bitterly
Wallowing in ashes down on their knees.
Surrounding cities would quake in fright
When her mighty vessels sunk in the night.
Ezekiel consistently brings bad news
Yet he shudders from the horror he views.
No one will have reason to rejoice
If his life shows he made the wrong choice.
I suppose it has always been safe to bet
What you 'do' is what you 'get!'

EZEKIEL 28

*In this chapter God addresses
the one who is behind
the heartaches and disappointments
of all mankind!
Satan's oratory has always been
to appeal to the selfishness of men.
He was egoistic and stupidly sought
his own acclaim
and foolishly refused
to glorify the Father's Name.
His great wealth filled him
with inner turmoil
and his rebellion
against the Lord began to boil.
He was said to be wiser than Daniel
and it seems to me
-cockier than a Cockier Spaniel!
And every since the day he fell
he has filled the men with pain
in whom he has instilled
the lust for earthly gain.
God already looked at Satan
as destroyed
because of the destruction
he would and had deployed.
But God also addressed
the king of Tyre
who would soon experience
his own hellish fire.*

EZEKIEL 29

Part of Israel's cleansing was to give her
No one else to lean on.
When she cried in grief and trouble
She was to cry to God alone!
Egypt had to be cut down to size.
She had to be unable to answer Israel's cries.
Israel had been told *never* to return
To Egypt's shore.
Because she had, Egypt would be left
Powerless and poor!
We wonder why God removes His blessing
When we take our eyes off of Him.
But it seems this old world has too much 'fat'
God finds it necessary to trim!
And God must wonder why His people
Keep turning away.
    Why?
Is it because we have been richly blessed
We think it is no longer necessary to pray?
*And do we forget how God's heart warms
Toward we who lean on His everlasting arms!*

EZEKIEL 30

It is sundown for Egypt and her allies.
The shadows lengthen and only bad news flies.
Anarchy leaves its footprints along the Nile
And no one is left to save man or child!

Comment on Ezekiel

The defeated king of Egypt would groan
As one who had a terrible wound.
And he would learn how Israel felt
When she was left hopelessly marooned.
Power slips through Egypt's hands
And she is to be dispersed to distant lands.
God's judgement was to be broadened
And lengthened
And for a little while, Babylon strengthened.
Egypt had not thought God's words mattered
But they would change their minds
When they, too, were scattered.

EZEKIEL 31

Strange that the whole world would be
Compared to the Garden of Eden!
And Egypt was considered to be
The *garden's* most glorious Tree!
It was God who fed and nurtured her
So she would be a welcome shade
For the tame, the wild and the free!
Her beauty was incomparable
For her 'roots' went deep
But pride denied her the privilege of a glory
She could no longer keep!
It was God who gave her the magnificence
He also took away.
Destruction was her fate
And it would do no good for her to pray.
This nation who held her head high
Above the clouds
Would be clothed in the vestige
Of hell's dark funeral shrouds

EZEKIEL 32

He considered himself a lion-this king
Who was merely a crocodile!
And he muddied the stream as he slithered
Along that beautiful Nile.
He would be caught in a net and left stranded
For God saw him as evil and under-handed.
The Nile would flow clean and clear
And there would be no idols left
For Egypt's people to revere.
Even the people would be doomed to burial
With an evil hoard
Because they faced annihilation from God's
Mighty avenging sword.
People who shared common sins would share
Common graves
Or to put it another way, man must walk
On the road he paves!
Egypt would destined to lose all she prized
And would lie in infamy
Beside those she despised!

EZEKIEL 33

The importance of a watchman can not be
Over emphasized.
People can be prepared for trouble if they
Are well advised!
But God's watchman has an awesome task.
There are deep spiritual dangers
He must be faithful to unmask!
How can God's people know to repent
Unless a man is faithful to the purpose
For which he has been sent?
God takes no pleasure in the death of a soul.
And He knows we all need guidance
To bring our lusts and iniquities under control.
God's ever lasting mercy and love
Is beautifully pictured here.
He who repents and lives righteously
Has absolutely nothing at all to fear!
But we also see a picture of spiritual *MIA'S*
Who would not repent nor change their ways.
Ezekiel searched high and low, far and wide
In obedience to the Lord
And he could not find one soul left unscarred!

The "I Love My Bible" Commentary

EZEKIEL 34

The shepherds of our country, like Israel
Care little for their 'sheep'
For laws favor the rich and there are very few
Promises our politicians remember to keep.
God was very displeased with these shepherds
Of old
Who were unconcerned that their people
Were hungry and cold.
God's message to those leaders who sowed
Wild oats
Was that He would distinguish the rams
From the billy goats.
And God could see the difference between
The *fat shepherds* and those *skinny sheep*
Who were pushed and butted so hard
They were afraid to lie down and sleep.
"I will be their Shepherd," God said
"And will give them their daily bread!"
His loving care continues around the clock!
And He still cares for His beloved flock!

EZEKIEL 35

Despising God's people was Edom's sin.
It really was foolish for her to hate
Her 'next of kin!'
Her judgement descended like a mighty flood
For she had enjoyed observing Israel's
Shed blood
And to think she said she didn't care
That Israel's magnificent holy God was there!
God's love for Israel was incredibly great
And Edom would be punished for her hate!
Though Israel wasn't good, Edom was worse
Because they didn't fear God-the lofty God
Of these people they chose to curse.
Too bad Edom was filled with so much hate
And chose to rejoice at Israel's fate.
Now her good fortune fled
For the turbulent tide had turned
And she must drink the 'sour milk'
She herself had churned!

EZEKIEL 36

Israel would again be adorned with flowers!
This land will receive God's merciful showers.
God forgave all who brought Him shame
By an astounding rescue that exalted His name.
He gave Israel new hearts and right desires
And they would no longer cherish idols
Nor bask in 'strange fires.'
God took away their hearts of stone
And gave them a gentle love
That honored Him alone!
We see God's people must loathe themselves
For their evil ways.
Prayer and repentance would(and will)
Bring much better days!

EZEKIEL 37

Movement begins from the ground up!
There is life for bleached and brittle bones!
Ezekiel must have shuddered when he heard
Those precarious grunts and groans.
The old graveyard is not a graveyard anymore!
Shouts and happy voices were heard as before!
Death is not the victor. Life reigns supreme!
God has proved over and over again
He is able to redeem!
No one knows the power of this One on high!
To those who say He's been defeated
We have one glorious reply!
He lives!
    He lives!
        He lives!
           And we will too!
There is no better news than God's promise
That He will make us all better than new!

Comment on Ezekiel

EZEKIEL 38

This awesome prophecy is yet to be.
Many will see this awful battle on satellite TV!
Men who rule with great aplomb
Will shudder at sight of this ultimate bomb.
In our wildest imagination we cannot picture
Even a fragment of such devastation!
"Its just an allegory," some people say
As they shrug off the reality of that bitter
Judgement day.
But no amount of liquor one can imbibe
Can erase a destruction too horrible to describe.
Yet we must remember-because of His love-
God's judgement is hesitantly sent
And inasmuch as it is, very few people believe
Our God is omnipotent!

EZEKIEL 39

Those who mock God's Word better enjoy
   it now
For they might step beyond the belligerence
God is willing to allow.
The man who will not even pray once
Severely tests our *FATHER'S* patience!
It can be a costly mistake
For people of any nation to make.
Atheistic Gog and Magog will pay
An eighty five percent penalty
When God intervenes to set His people free!
God will set their teeth on edge
When He fulfills His mighty pledge!
Though Israel had been a disobedient nation
God would protect her to justify His reputation.

EZEKIEL 40

The temple must be restructured when worship
Is once again restored.
And they must cleanse the area
Heathen people have explored.
God's pattern for worship had to be explained
And even the priests had to be diligently
retrained.
There was only one family of priests
God would allow to lead His flock.
It was those who carefully followed Him
As did their father, Zadok!
Every part of the temple must be examined
   in detail.
Ezekiel must pass these dimensions
On to others and he must not fail.
Choosing the sacrifice seemed the most
important of all.
Only a *proper sacrifice* could redeem man
From his fateful fall.
But still this fails to picture God's great grace
When He would send His Beloved Lamb
To die in our place!

EZEKIEL 41

Now Ezekiel is given a peek at the
'Most High Place'
where only the Cherubim can look
on God's face!
It was considered by the Israelis
to be very unique
a place were a chosen few
could hear God speak!
God has always been close
to His people
yet far enough away
that He not be contaminated
when they sinned each day.
Can't you see it.....?
Close enough to love!
Close enough to forgive!
And <u>close enough</u>
to give them
a glorious reason to live!

The "I Love My Bible" Commentary

EZEKIEL 42

That which is holy should not be contaminated
-even the garments they wore
Those holy vestments must be removed
Before they exited the temple door!
Those garments are described in Isaiah 61.
They are clothing in which the threads
Of salvation are delicately spun.
And the robe of righteousness is not given
To just anyone!
We can see the divine clothing of the priests
Is everlasting joy
For blessed is the one who works
In the Heavenly Father's employ!
        Notice!
There is a wall between the holy and profane!
Which has always been difficult
For the unspiritual to ascertain.
But God knows the difference and won't admit
A single soul whose garment is inappropriate!

EZEKIEL 43

The Lord's glory fills the temple!
It would be dark and dreary otherwise.
When one is filled with His Spirit
    it lights up in his eyes!
God's presence adds a beauty hard to describe
    but *only in His presence*
      is the temple purified!
God wants it that way-pure and simple!
Holiness, and only holiness, is the basic law
    for God's great temple!
We are the altars of His heavenly fires
And are the light of His presence that inspires!
A temple is not a temple if God is not there
For only He has an abundance of holiness
-a holiness only He can share!
Holiness-a gift one cannot carry in a purse.
It is a gift only the heart can disperse!

EZEKIEL 44

It is costly to desert the Lord
But to follow Him demands that we be
Of one accord!
For two cannot walk together except they agree
And I certainly need Him much, much more
Than He needs me!
But to think God says *He is our heritage!*
    (wonderful, wonderful!)
In the New Testament we are called His priests
And we will grow in grace only as we partake
Of His Word and salvation-His heavenly feast!
As we hunger for God's Word we can only
Whet our appetite
On His smorgasbord of living holy
And of living right!
God's people must see the difference between
    right and wrong.
Even God's food is digested better
When we pause to listen to salvations's song!

EZEKIEL 45

God comes first! Why shouldn't He?
He has done so much for you and me!
It has been that way since time began
And has always been His priority # one plan!
If our leaders-especially our leaders
Ever(which is not being done) put God first
No one will have to live in hunger
And no one will ever live in thirst!
Honesty does have a perpetual domino effect
But so does that which is evil and suspect.
    God says,
"Quit robbing and cheating my people
    and always be fair!"
And yet, from the top echelon to the bottom
    honesty is rare!
God also expects the people to pay their taxes.
Anarchy prevails when the honest host relaxes.

Comment on Ezekiel

Be vigilant! Be fair! Be clean!
And it will be easier to learn
what these sacrifices mean!

 EZEKIEL 46

The priest, the prince
the people
all lives intertwine
and there would be harmony
if they lived by God's design!
The priests were in charge
of proper sacrifice.
The prince had rules
to follow, too
that were clear and concise!
God's work must not be done
sloppily
if it was the prince's desire
to live properly.
And truly their land
would be a paradise
if and when
the people followed
the Lord's advice!
But there was a sacrifice *so holy*
it must be treated with care.
There is no such thing
as superficial sanctification.
The priest must beware!
If man maintains the balance
in that which is holy
He will do all things for God's glory!

EZEKIEL 47

The Major Prophets once covered
the market on *religious goods!*
They were God's
pre-grace Robin Hoods!
Certainly, no one was charged
with the information they shared
and the poor in spirit
knew how much they cared!
If we'd digest the good news
as well as we digest the bad
we'd not be influenced by the latest fad!
The good food and clothing of the spirit
are our basic needs.
And those garments of salvation
keep us warm when the cold winds blow!
Though the prophets words seem harsh
we need these truths to help us grow!
It seems Ezekiel was harsher
than all the rest!
But God wants we of the faith
to stand tall
on His holy mountain crest!
Now-as Ezekiel draws to a close
let us tarry where the living water flows!

EZEKIEL 48

The 'son of dust'
has just staged
his last sand storm!
He has obeyed the Lord
faithfully
and sounded every alarm.
He examined every path
his belligerent people trod
and he made 'no bones'
about their need to return to God.
Now he describes their land again
and divides God's inheritance
to every man.
Each tribe had its special place
and none could claim another's space.
God has a place where we, too
can stand.
Rest assured His people
will possess the Promised Land!

The "I Love My Bible" Commentary

NOTE:

We have come to the end of Ezekiel and what a character he was! He must have been very special for God to have used him the way He did. But, of course, when God uses someone, it makes them special! Ezekiel was known to be hard headed as brass. Israel had no leader he was afraid to sass! God had demanded he be that way in order to confront Israel's belligerence day after day. He challenged them-chin up and head on, because he was facing people whose hearts were hard as stone! Jeremiah wept, but Ezekiel roared at these people whose relationship with God was past being restored. God would have forgiven them, that's true, had they done what He wanted them to do. They were disobedient, hostile, and unfair. God wouldn't have spared them even if Job, Daniel, and Noah were there! These three men's righteousness combined would not have been enough to save these belligerent people whose 'hides' were impenetrably tough. They cared nothing for this God they had scorned and were as doomed in the cold winds of circumstance as sheep that had been shorn!

So-we can see the problems that Israel faced, but not only she alone, because all our lives-theirs and ours-we suffer because of that LOVE we disown. We certainly are like the Israelis as we stand on this precipice of time ready to throw ourselves who knows where......some to be dashed on retribution rocks below, some to glide on pockets of grace-filled pillows of air! What ever happens we will soon behold the ONE who is *more precious* than silver or gold! It is He who stands with arms outstretched who is always ready to keep our lives secure and our flight safe and steady! The choice is ours . We can take this plunge called life with Him-or alone. Israel didn't during this period of time and they saw only despair when they could have had a vision of His throne! We take that same plunge when we turn down grace and settle for grunge! We live in a 3-D world bordering on spiritual poverty though God is offering a life-time of fully guaranteed eternal prosperity! But we grovel before prime time slime and still wonder why our streets are full of crime. I fear we do stand today where the nation Israel stood, and fail to see the reason its so reasonable to be good!

Again, when I say unto the wicked,

Thou shall surely die

if he turn from his sin

and do that which is lawful and right;

If the wicked restore the pledge,

give again that he had robbed,

walk in the statutes of life,

without committing iniquity,

<u>he shall surely live</u>

he shall <u>not</u> die.

None of the sins that he hath committed

shall be mentioned unto him:

he hath done that which is lawful and right;

<u>he shall surely live.</u>
(Ezekiel 33: 14-16kjv)

The "I Love My Bible" Commentary
(The Book of Daniel)

DANIEL 1

These four young men who were away
From home must have been in pain
But their lives would touch the lives of others
And it must not be in vain!
Think about these young men who had never
Been out of 'their own back yard!'
Think about evil scenes and foreign kings
And queens who dishonored our Lord!
This is what they saw in Babylon
And they refused to be this idolatrous nation's
Helpless pawn!
Opportunity can knock in distant lands.
One must be prepared for what time demands.
Good times-bad times intermingle and merge
And sometimes one must put away
His independence urge!
These young men rose from obscurity
And then proved their God-given purity!
They did not sacrifice their ideals
And did not partake of kingly meals.
Israel fell victim to Babylon's invasion
But these young men resisted evil persuasion!
Daniel, <u>Hananiah, Mishael, and Azariah</u>
Known as Shadrach, Meshach, and Abednego
Stood faithful to this God
Our young people need to know!
To know Him is to love Him
And to love Him is to stand
Like a beacon light for others
      especially
When and where doubts of God are fanned!

DANIEL 2

A frightening dream led Nebuchadnezzar
   to realize
He needed the wisdom of Daniel's God
To open his eyes.
He could not see the future but God could
And Nebuchadnezzar had to learn wisdom
Does not come from gods made of wood.
He doubted his magicians had any power
(they didn't)and trusted them less by the hour.
Had it not been for Daniel, they would have
Been killed and that held them in derision!
But it was different with Daniel who had God
Who gave him a special vision!
This is one of the many symbols of Daniel
Men have criticized
But then we know it is because
God has not opened their eyes!
Because of his God-given knowledge
The King made Daniel great
When this faithful man of God became
Babylon's Chief Magistrate!

DANIEL 3

I believe Nebchadnezzar mocked God
In his own particular way
For he built a ninety foot golden statue
That actually must have had feet of clay.
In his mind, the kingdoms of this world
Were his own
And this worldly king pictured himself
On God's eternal throne.
Surely, should any rock come tumbling down
It could not harm the statue that wore
His golden crown.
He learned nothing from that ill- fated statue
Made of gold, silver, iron, and clay.
So he made a statue to himself
And made his biggest mistake that day!
He decreed all should worship it but he didn't
Get to first base with God's servants
And he recoiled in anger.
Yet the fire he ordered for Shadrach, Meshach
And Abednego put them in no mortal danger

Comment on Daniel

There was a fourth man in the fire
And they were not even singed!
They knew they might die
But not a one of them cringed!
Nebuchadnezzar finds himself once again
In God's great judgement hall
And once again he had to admit
God is the greatest ruler of all!

DANIEL 4

Nebuchadnezzar must have been pleasingly plump
Yet he was reduced to living with the animals
Around a worthless stump.
He had thought he could replace God or bust
And ended up with his face pushed in the dust.
It took seven years to change his frame of mind.
Enamored with his own power
He was spiritually blind!
God used his 'madness' to straighten him out
And we see no further proof that this king
Was ever full of unbelief and doubt!
His last words gave the Lord glory and praise
And he must have lived happily
The rest of his days!

DANIEL 5

Beltshazzar-an example of one who thought
God's laws were repealed
For the fortunate, rulers, and well-heeled!
There seems to be a level in all society
Where people feel they have risen above
The need for goodness and any propriety.
They think laws are for the 'other' fellow
Who must comply
Because there are *favors* in the law
Most people cannot afford to buy.
But God's favors are not for sale
And the message He sent to Beltshazzar
Caused his face to pale!
This heady, crafty king who was unrepentant
Was weighed in God's balances and found
To be seriously delinquent!
He discovered he would lose all he owned
Because God had marked him to be dethroned.

DANIEL 6

Ever have a boomerang hit you slap dab
In the head?
That is what happened to Daniel's enemies
Who fervently wanted him dead.
They deserved the punishment they got
After devising that insidious, inhuman plot.
Can't you picture Daniel looking those lions
Straight in the face
Knowing he was protected by God's grace!
Darius knew God was Daniel's great friend
And that God possessed a power that would
Never, ever end!
Our God performs great miracles which are
Definitely universal
And the help He gives His people
Is always available for His dispersal!
"Greetings!" Darius exclaimed. "God is great!"
He had learned God's people's safety
Does not depend on fate!

DANIEL 7

*There are various kinds of power
and man's beastliness
may take many forms
but he must account to
'The Ancient of Days'
for everyone he harms!
When God's court begins its session
and the books are opened wide
there will be no place then
for man to run and hide!*

The "I Love My Bible" Commentary

It is hard for us to depict
The 'Ancient of days'
when we forget to follow Him closely
and fail to give Him praise.
But there was a 'MAN'
who understood Him completely
who walked with Him
beside still waters
whose love was so strong
whose faith was so real
He considered his will
the same as the 'Father's!'
His body may have been human
but His soul and spirit
were divine!
And when God's holy Son
takes the throne to reign sublime
then-and only then-will
our streets be free of crime!
These four great kingdoms
Daniel described(future and past)
will soon discover
their power will not last.
'Reality' is a dirty word
we hate to face
but rest assured it will be easier
for those who have accepted
God's grace!
Each man will suffer great loss
who has refused to take the hand
of the One who conquered
the cross.
And all creatures great and small
will learn our God is over all!

DANIEL 8

Daniel is given another dream like the first
And though one beast defiled the temple
Years would pass before his deeds would be cursed.
This time a man approaches Daniel and
His presences seems so great
Daniel fainted from fear of an unknown fate.
But this holy being helped Daniel to his feet
And informed him many years must pass
Before the vision would be complete.
Men would grow more evil as their morals regress.
It is the time of the anti-christ that Gabriel
Seems to stress.
It must have been a spectacular vision
Because Daniel couldn't get it off his mind
And he eventually became ill wondering
How men could be so unkind.
But there would be a change of scene
For the Great God of Heaven will intervene!

DANIEL 9

Daniel prays a mighty prayer confessing
His people's sins
Noting there were very few who had even
Tried to make amends.
No man can pray with such fervor without
Being heard.
God's Word says we should always pray.
He will answer and He always keeps His word.
Again, God sends Daniel a message of hope
And the great love of our holy God
Must have helped Daniel to cope!
Do it again, Lord! Do it again!
And you do for truly repentant man!
And we know you show your mercy too.
When we repent, that's what you said you'd do!
God is the same as in Daniel's day
And He will bless all who walk His pathway.
Forgiveness is a lovely rose from God's garden
And *nothing* equals the thrill of His pardon!
He is slow to punish, quick to forgive
So man sins foolishly with no remorse
And never really learns how to live!

Comment on Daniel

DANIEL 10

The more Daniel prayed, the more fantastic
Were the visions he received!
Great was the love of God for this man
Who not only read God's Word but believed!
No greater word can be spoken to anyone,
For God said, "You are greatly beloved,"
Giving approval of what Daniel had done!
              Pleasing God!
There is a drought of that spiritual moisture!
Our tongues of praise have turned to dry lakes.
Even the food of the spirit is rejected and
              my heart aches!
      No wonder Daniel prayed
      As it is now, it was then
And he felt compelled to confess every sin..
God knows how desperate we can feel
And He continues to show us His love is real!
              Who knows?
Maybe in a dream in the shadow of the night
"Thou art greatly beloved of God" will be sent
To change our darkness into sunshine bright!

DANIEL 11

The kingdoms are mentioned again
And there seems to be nothing but trouble.
War and carnage will be so terrible
Many lands will lie desolate and in rubble.
No one seems to be honest as liars flourish.
'Flattery' and 'intrigue' spread contamination
Among the evil ones 'they' seem to nourish.
But the people that know God remain strong
Though they would be in danger from those
Dissidents who continue to do wrong.
They would be jailed, robbed, and abused
Despite their faithful teaching to those
Who remained doubtful and confused.
Even the most gifted of God would fall
For even the most spiritual are human after all!
But God will see to it that we are cleansed
And refined
For God's people or those Satan cannot bind.
Evil men will find their schemes are breakable
By the hand of the Omnipotent One
Whose own plans are unshakable!

DANIEL 12

    We can see why the book of Daniel
            is despised.
      It depicts God's awesome power!
       And those who disbelieve
        do not want to face
        that fateful hour!
  Many think they will be exempt
    and will not face judgement
   for their shame and contempt.
    But judgement will not be
         unsightly
      for God's people
whose reward for right living
will be their 'on switch'
     to shine brightly!
Here we see where volumes
of knowledge will be released
 as wells of wisdom overflow
and travel is greatly increased.
  Many will travel to and fro
   with freedom and dignity
     wherever they go.
But the greatest news of all
    is God's children
    will rise again
    in those days
and innumerable people
  will look on His face
     and finally
      finally
   be able to truly
   give Him praise!

The "I Love My Bible" Commentary

NOTE:

*Many biblical critics claim
there is nothing substantial
about the glorious visions
in the book of Daniel.
The criticism began in the days
of Porphyry
who claimed Daniel was merely
'hog-wash' history.
And many people have swallowed
a deception questionably
elementary
and it has continued
century after century.
Remember–God lets us
find what we seek.
Dare we seek for errors
of which others speak?
Nit-picking puts us
in the pits of despair.
And lack of faith in God
leaves us desperately bare.
History repeats itself
time and time again.
The lessons we need to learn the most
are never learned by unrepentant man.
But I'm not that concerned with history
All I need to know is God loves me!*

We have walked through Isaiah and heard him say "Here am I Lord, send me!" And we have watched Jeremiah weep for his people even in Lamentations and we've heard him proclaim that God's mercies never end. Every time you see a sunrise, remember God's mercies are new every day. Ah—we do get up in a *new world every day!* And Ezekiel--he must have possessed an ego astronomical in proportion ! Many times God reminded him he was a 'son of dust' to keep his estimate of himself in proper proportion! *It took quite a few times!* And then we come to Daniel who visions depicted more despair than glory–but yet they foretold a future glory which we have the privilege of seeing-almost in 3-D. Are we in the last times? It looks that way, but only God knows that for sure! We do see the fulfillment of prophecy accelerating! And Jesus said when that happens–"Look up!" Its certainly not promising to look around us is it? ***Look up!***

And at the end of the days
I, Nebuchadnezzar, lifted up mine eyes
unto heaven, and mine understanding
returned unto me,
*and I blessed the Most High
and I praised and honored
Him that liveth forever,
whose dominion is an everlasting dominion
and His kingdom is from generation
to generation.
And all the inhabitants of the earth
are reputed as nothing:
and He doeth according to His will
in the army of heaven,
and among the inhabitants of the earth;
and none can stay His hand
or say unto Him,
what doest thou.*
(Daniel 4: 34-35kjv)

Part Six

The Minor

Prophets

Hosea to Malachi

O Israel,
return unto the Lord thy God;
for thou hast fallen by thine iniquity.

I will heal their backsliding.
I will love them freely;
for mine anger is turned away from him.

Who is wise, and he shall understand
these things?
Prudent, and he shall know them?
for the ways of the Lord are right,
and the just shall walk in them;
but the transgressors
shall fall therein.
(Hosea 14: 1, 4, 9kjv)

The "I Love My Bible" Commentary
(The Book of Hosea)

HOSEA 1

It is a sad picture when God has to take pains
To teach a nation latched on to adulterous reigns.
Israel was pictured as a unfaithful harlot
A being she thought to be the lowest of all
But she continually refused to apply these words
To herself and she continued to fall.
Hosea must have wondered why
He should marry a flirt
Because every time she left him
Was another time to hurt.
But there was a message in the names
Of the children she had
A message of pain and of hope!
God would cherish Israel's wayward children
Freeing them from a slavery
In which none of them could cope!
Forgiveness brings a joy full and free
And joy teaches God's children to live in peace
And blissful harmony!

HOSEA 2

Name calling is ok when a name 'spells' hope!
God showed them He could reach down
And lasso them with His mercy rope!
Ammi—would walk in the sunshine
For God said his name meant, "Your are mine."
And Jezreel's sister could be pleased
With her momma
Because 'pitied' was another name for Ruhamah.
It seems God wanted Jezreel to 'intercede'
For maybe he could show his 'mother'
His great need.
God uses Gomer to picture Israel's indiscretion.
He had searched the land and all the people
Had failed His inspection..
"But I will pity you," God said.
And He promised to supply their daily bread!
Israel was to forget her idols
And turn to the Lord.
Then-love and mercy would be her reward!

HOSEA 3

Sin devalues a soul that turns to adultery
And loves to 'party.'
Look what Hosea paid for Gomer–only
Two dollars and eight bushels of barley!
But God paid more for us and He uplifts
His returning prodigals with mercy gifts!
But Israel would suffer for years before
God would draw her to Him once more.
Hosea told Gomer to live alone for many days
To be cleansed from her adulterous ways
-a picture of how long Israel would be
Living without God in squalor and misery!
God shows us over and over again
How much He wants to walk with man!
Why is it we have failed to see
Worship is walking with God in simplicity
-just simply loving Him that's all!

HOSEA 4

How awful this sounds and how could it be?
God says, "My people are destroyed because
they don't know me!"
They'd had the prophets and priests
And other godly men
But somewhere along the way
Even the most righteous had turned to sin.
There was no kindness
no faithfulness
no knowledge
of God in the land!
They stunk to high heaven
and sunk to low levels
and no one was able to stand.

Comment on Hosea

Weak knees and hard heads
  brought them up short.
It was hard to find even one
  faithful, trusting heart.
Sin kept them in suspense
  and it made true worship
  just a mere pretense.
They sang their songs
  in minor keys
  and unmelodic strains.
Wine, women, and song
  had robbed them
  of their brains.
It seems they would
  have reason to cry a lot
  knowing God would turn
  their flesh to dry rot!
Now take a look at what
  modern man has done.
*There is nothing new
under the sun!*

HOSEA 5

How many times has God had to say, "Listen!"
Hearts scrubbed clean and sterile souls
Would noticeably, willingly glisten
  but no one obeyed
And over and over again these Israelis strayed.
Fickle hearts intentionally closed their minds
To knowledge of the Lord
And they treated Him with unholy disregard.
Ephraim chased after dead, useless idols
And Judah loved to lie, murder and steal.
No one could be found whose faith was real.
No wonder our cast-off God turned away.
He didn't have the heart
To watch His precious people stray!
But still, we can see Him watching
Looking for His disloyal children to return.
Every day until they do--His heart will yearn!

HOSEA 6

They said, "Come, let us return to the Lord!"
They thought God would heal
The souls hideously self-scarred.
But their love vanished like morning dew
And our God bitterly cried,
 "Oh what am I going to do with you?"
They never learned how much God despises
Unconsecrated, insincere sacrifices.
It takes love to make an offering holy
And it takes love to honor His splendid glory!
He rejected their treachery and 'wolf packs'
That left a well worn trail of bloody tracks.
"Oh Judah," God said. "I hate your evil traits
And though I've wanted to bless you
Only your punishment awaits."
It would defile them like they defiled others
Because they had been utterly heartless
Toward their helpless brothers.

HOSEA 7

It does make a difference where we live.
It seems if we live among hate and treachery
Hate and treachery will be all we have to give.
Also drunkenness and adultery seemed to go
  hand in hand
And this fire that smoldered through the night
Raged throughout the land.
That sounds like what is happening today
And instead of *coloring ourselves happy*
We live in shades of gray!
We don't even realize how weak we are
For we have failed to keep our eyes
On the Morning Star!
And like a crooked arrow we fumble around
And completely miss the mark
So we must not blame the Lord
When it is we, ourselves, who have chosen
To stumble foolishly in the dark.

The "I Love My Bible" Commentary

HOSEA 8

A vulture only descends on the dying or dead.
Israel could have lived in obedience to God
But she chose death instead
So–those 'vultures' circled around
And foreign armies desecrated her ground.
She chose kings without God's consent.
She refused to believe He meant what He said
And said what He meant!
God called Israel a wandering wild ass
But we should not laugh. The way we act
God probably puts us in her same class!
We wander into areas where doubters fuss.
And like Israel, we think God's laws
Don't apply to us.
Israel put God out of their minds
But we have put Him out of our hearts
Hands once pure, merged in mire
Now are covered with pagan 'warts!'
So I wonder what my Savior thinks of me.
Is my worship-like Israel's-just a ritual
Or do I follow Him willingly?
Would the world have reason
To call *this Christian a faker*
And question my faithfulness to my Maker?
May those *vultures of doubt* fly on by
Because I am true to the one who lives on high!

HOSEA 9

Thorns and thistles would grow
Where grapes and figs had grown.
Israel would be unable to walk
Those beautiful paths she once had known.
Her hands were worse than warts, and filthy too.
She had continuously been unfaithful and untrue.
The people she called 'heathen'
Would walk her familiar trails.
Her future had been bright but now she watches
As her *light of hope* dims and fails!
Oh Israel, why are we so much like you?
Are you watching us do the same things
You used to do?
How tragic that day after day
Our people refuse to listen to God, or obey!
Move over Israel and make room.
It seems we, too, or headed for that rut
That we can only call *inevitable doom!*

HOSEA 10

When a farmer wants oats, he won't plant wheat
And when we want righteousness, and peace
We shouldn't plant deceit!
And if we should cultivate wickedness
And national disorder
We should expect our God to protect
Not one single border!
The Bible plainly states we should do our best.
Then we can know we are truly blessed.
God has always said the evil will be cursed
And their 'luck' will only go from bad to worse!
He had told Israel not to trust in lies.
And unless He was their Commander-in-chief
Her military was only in for a bitter surprise!
  "Not by power
     not by might
     but by My Spirit"
  says the Lord!
  That is how man survives!
Nations-like Israel, like America-living in ease
Never learn to guard against the worst disease.
It is to think they accomplish greatness alone
And dis-allow the Ruler of heaven's throne!

HOSEA 11

God asks
"How can I give you up, my Ephraim."
"How can I let you go?"
And He may ask you that question also!

Comment on Hosea

We can't blame God for deserting us
When its really the other way around.
Man seeks everything but God
Yet trouble is all he has found!
God is not helpless. He could force man to repent
But He knows true joy comes only
When we gladly accept the love He has sent!
The one authentic response He expects
From the ones He loves
Is to see us returning to Him
Like homesick, lonesome doves!

HOSEA 12

Chasing the 'wind' can be dangerous.
Israel discovered it can turn on you!
Have you noticed what God's winds
Of retribution can do?
Now once again God claims Israel strays
And tells them they will be punished
For their evil, treacherous ways.
Years before, Jacob had wrestled with God
And he prevailed.
Had Israel followed his example
They would have never failed.
Jacob was holding on with all his might.
He wept and pleaded for a blessing
And until God blessed him, he held on tight!
And oh how God continues to yearn
For His wandering unfaithful people to return!
We'll discover love and obedience
Has a powerful effect
When God receives our allegiance and respect!

HOSEA 13

.God took care of Israel in a dry and thirsty land
But she lost *living water* and failed His command.
Instead of getting better, they did their worst
And treachery placed them under God's curse.
He alone is God—has been forever and forever!
But evil negative Israel imagined herself clever!
Was she clever when she refused new birth
And turned from God who made this earth?
Israel faced the consequences of forgetting God
And she found lions of trouble blocking
The wayward paths she trod.

HOSEA 14

"Oh Israel, return to the Lord," was God's
Repeated invitation.
But she considered His pleas to be only
An insinuation.
Yet God would cure her of idolatry and deceit.
She would someday walk on God's easy street.
The paths of the Lord are true and right.
How do I know? His word says so!
And along those paths His light shines bright!
But sinners trying to walk them will fail
Because they prefer to walk their own trail.
And, of course, narrow is the way
That leads to life, and straight is the gate
And many think sin is fun so God can wait.
These people march to their own drum
And fail to seek this glorious life to come!
Meanwhile He remains loving and strong
And His principles of love and grace
Can fill us with a lovely song!

Note: It must have been quite a shock to Hosea when God told him to marry a prostitute to picture Israel's unfaithfulness to Him, but it was a shock to our Lord to see His people so unfaithful. Yet they never *got the picture* because they did not turn from sin. Do we see what they failed to see.? I'm afraid we do not. America courts sin and defies judgement and our courts turn the guilty loose every day. Seeing-we see not, and hearing-we hear not. We need a revival! *We need to empty our buckets and let the Holy Spirit fill them with living water! How about it? Lets do it!!!*

The "I Love My Bible" Commentary
(The Book of Joel)

JOEL 1

Sometimes man's gray matter resembles ashes
For he seems unaware with whom he clashes!
Now man would see the result of his tendency
To disobey God with arrogant consistency.
Destruction came wave upon wave
And not even the aged were worthy to save!
Contrary to popular opinion, God's Word
Does not always bring good news
And God's judgement is not swayed
Because of man's different views.
We live in a time when the ashes I mentioned
Have obscured black and white.
But-ashes or no-man's actions will be exposed
In God's revealing light!
They were disclosed in Israel's day.
They will be revealed once again.
God's wisdom, justice, and power
Cannot be superceded by any man!

JOEL 2

Sound the alarm!
Our souls are in peril!
Our deeds are rotten
and our thoughts unsterile!
We long for God's judgement
but we are not ready.
Our hearts are faint
and our faith unsteady.
There's was too
when God sent locusts
to destroy their crops.
*They were up a creek
without a paddle*
and I bet none of them could stand
that ear-splitting rattle!
Yet the pattern is given
in Joel again.
God will not punish
a truly repentant man!
God promised Israel
He would restore the crops
the locusts ate.
His forgiveness is one
of the many proofs
His love is great!
The tremendous promise here
is God will pour out His Spirit
on one and all.
He will truly save
those who seek Him
and will surely answer
when we call!

JOEL 3

The valley of decision stands out
Like a sore thumb.
There will be no excuse for the spiritually
Deaf and dumb!
The knowledge we need is on every page
And we should grow smarter as we age!
God put His Word on earth for us to use
There is so much there we can learn
And still-like Israel-we refuse.
Listen to Joel's 'voice'
And realize your need to make the right choice.
Armies from all over the world
Will tremble as God's flag is unfurled.
Those who have raped, robbed, and murdered
And those who are spiritually fickle
Will find themselves standing with the 'goats'
Awaiting God's mighty sickle.
Only then will the disobedient feel fear
When they discover the 'day of the Lord'
  is near.
It is a mighty case Our Great Judge has built
And He says He will by no means

Comment on Joel

Clear the oppressors of their guilt.
It will be different for the meek
Who will have all the many blessings
They have tried to seek!

In the valley of decision it will be
At the end of time and close of history!
Our waiting will be over and done.
Clocks will be gone when eternity has begun!

Note: They say dynamite comes in small packages and Joel and its truths are surely dynamite! Each of God's prophets essentially say the same thing but in a different way as God, over and over, strives to get the messages of purity over to His people. His grace says, "You are welcome to come." His law says, "This is the way!" It pointed to Christ who is the way, who showed the way, who paved the way! The world still stands in the valley of decision and the decision its people make will determine where they stand! We can be sure of holiness because God is holy. We can be sure of mistakes because we are human, but that valley lies at the foot of the cross and there we make our decision. To accept His invitation-or reject it-determines our destination. "Choose!"God says. "Choose!"

"I am the Way, the Truth, and the Life," our Lord says! Who will you choose?

The "I Love My Bible" Commentary
(*The Book of Amos*)

AMOS 1

God sends messages through Amos
One after another!
Even Edom would be punished
For abusing Israel, his brother.
Repetition of sin
Sooner or later gets under God's skin!
His justice over rules His love
When it comes to deliberately evil men.
Long before the kings of Persia established
Decrees no one could revoke
The living, unchanging God of heaven
Created an eternal justice when He spoke.
But even though man was to be
Punished for his crime
God gave him a chance to repent
Time after time!
Still those He forgave consistently
Severed His rope of grace
And lost their chance
To gaze on God's glorious face!
God has spoken!
The day will come when He will not mend
The rope unrepentant man has broken.

AMOS 2

God continues the judgements pictured
In chapter one.
But now its coming to Israel and she must
Face all that she has done.
God said they used stolen money
To pay for the sacrificial wine
When God had said, "You must not desecrate
That which is mine!"
The people told His prophets to hush
And didn't even have the modesty to blush!
God watched as they trampled the poor
And kicked the meek aside
And yet they held their heads up high
In unrealistic pride.
They had mocked the good and the righteous
And had ridiculed the simple
Going so far as to actually profane the temple.
Who can assess the depths to which they sunk?
No wonder God thought these people stunk!
Here is a thought for the spiritually deranged.
God's judgement will not/has not changed!

AMOS 3

How can two walk together
except they be agreed?
This is an age old question
which addresses our greatest need!
God is the One we need the most
to keep our hearts right.
Something, God said,
His people
had forgotten to do.
Of all the people on earth
God had chosen them alone.
Now their deeds had sprung
the traps of justice
and all Israel
would grieve and moan.
The unchangeable rule
of the universe
is we must face what we do
yet God will cleanse
and heal the pain
we put ourselves through!

AMOS 4

What awesome words!
"Prepare to meet your God
for your are dealing with the One
who formed the mountains

Comment on Amos

*created the winds
and gave light to the sun!"
God knows our every thought
sees our heart's intent
and when our sins disgrace Him
He demands that we repent!
Jehovah, the Lord
the God of hosts is His Name
and it seems unreal
that we would ever
want to bring Him shame!
All the hope He's given
all the hope He has restored
turns to shame
whenever He's ignored.
Despite all He's done
man holds him at bay
and seems to enjoy
turning our God away.
Israel would not listen.
She had strayed so far
her faith was in arrears.
She must have thought
"where is God?
We'll be ready
when He appears!"
But who of them was ready
when their faith was NOT
strong and steady?
I think we can see
there are strange days up ahead
and we must be prepared like He said.
Its still not easy
for our God to say
prepare to meet Him face to face
but He has saved us by His grace!
So, think of the joy
think of the love!
We're going to have to
hold each other down
when we reach our home above!*

AMOS 5

Amos said,
"Sadly I sing this song of grief.
Sadly I sing!"
Israel had become so evil
she was left with not one good thing.
Same song! Umpteenth verse!
The same old sins
bring the same old curse!
Men hate honest judges.
Many still lie and steal.
Politicians levy heavy taxes
not caring how we feel.
Fines and interest soar
out of sight!
Violence brings destruction
to those who cannot fight.
Courts claim justice
and its all a lie
for little is done
for the victims who cry.
God wants to see
a mighty flood of justice
and a torrent of doing good.
It can be done if we will stand
for right and holiness
like the saints of old have stood.
And then
"Sadly I sing"
will be a song no more.
For "happy" will be the song
we sing
when we reach that heavenly shore!

AMOS 6

Those living in luxury would not be exempt
For their indiscretions had been awfully unkempt.
God said their revelry was now at an end
And they would have no estates or land to defend.

The "I Love My Bible" Commentary

He had told them to change their ways
If they wanted to see much better days.
But they didn't, so even the richest of the rich
Would be captured and sold as slaves.
So many would die that few would be left
To carry others to their graves.
God seemed to ask,"Can horses run on rocks
Or can oxen plow the sea?"
He implied, "It is a stupid question to ask
But not as stupid as what you do to me!"
The richer and more powerful they grew
The more they placed themselves above
The limits of God's commandments
And they lost the joy of living in His love!
Didn't He once say their ears were fat
And I wonder, when He thinks of us
    does He say that?

AMOS 7

Amos thought Israel was way to small
To take such a tragic fall.
Don't think one person is not enough
To change God's mind
For its always His wish to be loving and kind!
But the plumb line was God's last resort.
He'd given in enough!
He was tired of His people coming up short.
But Amaziah ordered Amos to put on his
    walking shoes
He considered Amos just a fruit picker
Singing the blues!
Old Amaziah told Amos to take his visions
    elsewhere
And to quit laying those nasty rumors bare.
He should have left Amos alone
For now he created troubles of his own!
Amaziah did not change God's mind!
God said He would punish Israel with locusts
Or by a consuming fire.
But you know what Amos did?

He talked God out of it!
That is the wonder of prayer
A man of prayer has power to spare!!!
Dear Amos was terribly afraid
And didn't want Israel destroyed by any plague!
So God did what he asked–changed His mind!
We'll never be able to do an autopsy
On the heart of God and we would never
Understand what we would find!
For lying there would be unmeasurable love
-a love unending and unimaginably kind!
God never quit loving Israel, never will
Today, tomorrow, forever–He loves her still!

AMOS 8

Ripe fruit should depict beauty and fulfillment
But not this time!
It should have pictured Israel dominant and
Successful, thankful in her prime.
Instead, it brings deadly warnings.
There would be a famine of God's Word.
They wouldn't listen anyway.
This country could only be compared to fruit
In the last stages of decay.
They were spiritual shorties
With evil clogged arteries.
Merchants couldn't wait for the Sabbath to end
So their cheating could begin.
Those visions God sent did bring Amos pain
But his people who should have been
Giants of faith had grown spiritually insane.
They did not want Amos to interfere
But lets think about this, folks.
What do we do with the truths we hear?
Every day, in the pulpits, on Christian TV
We hear, "God says, My people, return to me!
We don't worry about locusts but today
Terrorists are the locusts who seek our decay.
But God has a way out.
Prayer will nourish our faith and erase doubt!

Comment on Amos

AMOS 9

Israel did not realize what her indiscretions
Would ultimately cost.
Yet God said not one "true" kernel would be lost!
God sifted this nation with a mighty sieve
Searching for those worthy to forgive.
Forgiveness was based on their repentance
For what they had done
And unless they repented there would be
No place to run.
Our God would search them out
And-in love-cleanse them of their doubt.
God, whose eye is on the sparrow
Spared this nation many times.
Yet those who boasted God would not touch them
Would have to pay for their crimes.
But the Lord loved Jerusalem.
It was King David's city!
And because of His promise to David
He would show them pity.
Now the Lord stands inside the altars
Of our hearts for we are His temple
And if only we'd *read between the lines*
Of His Holy Word we'd know
Why He wants our faith to be pure and simple!

Note: Amos was a simple man and we wonder why God would use him to pronounce such a complex warning. But, had he been a "big" man in the eyes of the people, they might have listened to the man but not the message! We often look at "big" men and *listen to their reputation*-not their words! (Maybe that is why we have "politicians" and not many true leaders!)

Nothing was to stand between these people and the message God was sending them. Amaziah tried it and I advise you to go back and read Amos 7: 10-17 and there you will see the futility of interfering with God's messenger. Amos was a fruit picker, an uncomplicated man close to the soil-but our God is BIG enough to use the smallest of people! God often picks the most unusual men to perform uncommon tasks or proclaim extraordinary events! And, definitely, Amos was a humble man such as were all the "true" prophets. Even Moses described himself as a humble man *and perhaps humility is more an attitude than a man's station in life.* God resists the proud but gives grace to the humble. Remember, Jesus made Himself of no reputation to draw peoples' attention to the works of God and not to Himself-though He was God for He said, "I and the Father are ONE!"

Amos–a small man with Big Words. That is the way we should remember him!

The "I Love My Bible" Commentary
(Comment on the Book of Obadiah)

OBADIAH 1

The Crossroads!
What a blessed place to stand
but Edom didn't use it well.
She misused her advantage
and the peace she had cherished
turned to a living hell.
She would no longer be safe
for she refused to save Israel
in her time of need.
And her betrayal of Israel
had soured like a musty seed.
Even her famous wise men
would have no counsel to give
for God had said
all the people of Edom
were unfit to live!
They had shown Israel
no pity at all
and Obadiah tells them
they are destined to fall.

Note: Obadiah did not have much to say to Edom. God didn't give him much! Finally, God seems to be as eager to be rid of them and their atrocities toward Israel as Esau was to rid himself of his birth right. And maybe Obadiah was just in a hurry to say, "Goodbye and good riddance." He had watched as Edom taunted Israel as she suffered. She had even abused them too.....sort of like kicking a man when he's down!

Though God had warned Israel many times to change her ways, it was not Edom's place to compound her punishment. God says, "Vengeance is mine!" And we'd better stay out of His way. He doesn't need our help–which, incidently would only be a hindrance. He knows what He is doing. We certainly don't. Usually we want to punish someone before we have all the facts. Proverbs says to hear both sides before you judge. We can be sure God knows the incidents from every angle. Sure, God had said Israel needed to be punished! But she was not to suffer from someone else's hand. Actually God's punishment is really discipline based on love. *And He is just!* Usually, man is not! Certainly Edom wasn't and she would no longer be a nation. Gone! Erased! Forgotten! Obadiah—one of God's *short* lessons!

(A very important question)

(God asks)

Can

two

walk together

Unless

they be agreed?

(Amos 3:3kjv)

The "I Love My Bible" Commentary
(The Book of Jonah)

JONAH 1

Jonah had to experience a whale of a death
In order to willingly preach about life!
Nineveh must hear God's message
And seek forgiveness for causing strife.
She must have a chance to repent
And that is why Jonah was sent.
He didn't want to preach to Nineveh
And his peevishness bordered on insurrection.
He needed to learn disobedience will not
Escape God's detection.
He did not care for Nineveh's lost
And he would dodge his duty at any cost.
He didn't realize it might cost him his life
So he ran!
One can become so self-righteous
He cares nothing for his fellow man.
Such was Jonah's case!
He thought no *alien* worthy of God's grace.
So Jonah ended up in the belly of a whale
In God's death row of an unusual jail!

JONAH 2

Jonah is a prime example of what prayer can do
For no matter how bad the circumstances
God can, and will, answer you.
But Jonah had to be willing to obey
The Lord's command
Before the whale would regurgitate him
Out to safety on dry land!
God did answer Jonah's fervent prayer.
And now Jonah had a real message to share.
God removed Jonah from the whale
So he could say
"Nineveh, I have a message of hope today!"
God did change Jonah's *sentence*
But it was only *after*
He prayed his prayer of repentance!

JONAH 3

God looks on our great cities and sees
Larceny everywhere.
And He still sends "Jonahs"
With a message to declare!
If people would listen as Nineveh did
Their future would be brighter.
Little children would be safe
And the burdens of the homeless lighter!
But there are so many strange voices
And many people offer confusing choices.
Flashing lights beckon the lonely
Who have no place to go
No one seems to hear that still small voice
That whispers soft and low!
Still, God's people have great news to give
And we can prove it by the way we live.
Not to witness is to be like Jonah
And just sitting under a *dying gourd*.
And that is an attitude we can not afford!

JONAH 4

Jonah is an excellent example of a Christian
Who doesn't get his way.
He pouted and complained when
God's forgiveness of others spoiled his day.
Sometimes we think we have the inside track
And our sanctimonious congregations
Fail to invite the strangers back.
We wonder why some churches are dying.
Look at the lesson of the vine!
God made it grow, but it quickly wilted
Under harshly *unfriendly* sunshine!
(God was saying, "Others, too, are Mine!")
Have we forgotten Gethsemane
And the lesson God wants us to see?
Like you–I must open this heart of mine
And help my Savior care for the vine!

Comment on Jonah

NOTE: I noticed two things about Jonah! God called him to witness to people he scorned so he purposely headed in the wrong direction. No way he was going to save those ugly sinners. No Way! But God spared them anyway. We know Jonah could not have saved them. A man who does not love will not witness. If we should take Jonah's name apart–again–we'd see two things. *Jo-rhymes with no* and in effect that is what he said. Actually 'nah' is slang for 'no' isn't it? *So--I took Jonah apart!* What would happen if someone did that to us? Would most of us have a big 'no' plastered on our hearts? We say not–but how many of us Christians actually witness to others? The second thing is–Jonah *pouted* when God saved them. Do we still have Christians who are only interested in their own salvation. Oh people, I've been there–done that! And I don't say it proudly.

Once I said "no" to God (actually, I bet you it was many more times than that). She was a redhead sitting in the pew in front of me. I argued with God about her. "How do I know she's not saved," I asked. *Stupid question!* I still remember that girl though I never met her or talked to her. *My opportunity faded into oblivion!* I've taught Sunday School on and off for about thirty five years but I've never forgotten her! Sometimes I think I was better at being Jonah than Jonah was!

It's a sad thing to say "no" to God! That "no" wraps itself around our hearts like a wet noodle and boy does it stick tight! Jonah probably knew that, but I see no evidence that he ever changed his attitude. Jonah sought to avoid the(heathen)lost. Jesus sought them! So—who's spirit should we have? *I'll let you answer that!*

The "I Love My Bible" Commentary
(The Book of Micah)

MICAH 1

Those in Judah and Israel who would prevent
Their hopes crashing
Had to give up their carved images
Which were only worthy of smashing.
It seemed that Micah lamented and wailed
As he walked barefoot in sorrow and shame
Grieving for those who failed.
He worried that his peoples' wounds
Were far too deep to heal
But they seemed not to listen
No matter how fervent his zeal!
So–many of them would lie sleepless
In the pale moon light
Listening to jackals and ostriches
Crying through out the night!
They would weep for their little ones
Who had been led away
But none of them would live long enough
To see a better day.
They would continue to weep in sorrow
Longing to escape the woes of 'tomorrow!'

MICAH 2

Harsh words can heal heartaches
If they cause us to pause and think.
Many a soul has listened to our Lord
And stopped short of falling in the brink!
Look at the awful sins Micah listed
And instead of obeying and repenting
God's belligerent people resisted.
Cheating, lying, robbery, and murder
Anyone of which is the wrong goal
Will be reflected in the mirror of the soul!
We cannot fool God.
Why do we think we should?
Even the punishment He sends us
Is for our own good.
This business of straying
And lying about it is getting old.
The Great Shepherd continually tells us
There is safety in the fold!
The Messiah would come.
The promise was (and is)sure!
Only then-*the second time around*
Can God's people really feel secure!

MICAH 3

"Because of you, dear leaders
Our country will be destroyed.
You listen to strange voices
And the spiritually unemployed."
Imagine Micah saying that God's leaders
And people were out of touch.
Their bribes and demands for reimbursement
Had become far too much.
The preachers hearts were empty
Unless their pockets had been filled
And sooner or later their voices
Around God's temple would be stilled.
God looks at the leaders first
For He begins at the top!
It is a poor country indeed,
When the leaders are a flop!
The trouble is, many leaders think
They are above scrutiny
And will stop at nothing short
Of spiritual mutiny.
But God says their days will come to an end.
They were the tethered refuse on whom
No one could depend!

MICAH 4

The last days are mentioned again.
Good and bad–God promised justice
-whatever-to every man.

Comment on Micah

We can't develop an Utopia.
Utopia will come to us in the form of a decree.
God will issue His laws and the keeping
Of them will utterly set us free!
If God has to arbitrate
It will not be because of international hate.
Instead, there will be universal peace?
Sound too good to be true?
Well–it is something *only the Lord can do!*
Even Israel did not understand His plan
For they were spiritually blind.
Someday Israel will rejoice when Mount Zion
Becomes the favorite of all man kind!
Our God-King of the ages-will rule from there!
He will be gentle with His people
And absolutely gracious and fair!

MICAH 5

Oh Bethlehem, Bethlehem, how small you are
And yet you will produce the One who is
The Bright and Morning Star!
Keep an eye on Bethlehem
Until Israel's spiritual rebirth.
And watch for *that light*
That will shine upon the earth!
Israel will be exceptionally blessed.
The day is coming when God will give
His chosen people rest!
There will be NO heathen shrines
Or devil worship then
When God has poured out His vengeance
On evil men.
Israel will never again be abused
Like helpless sheep.
Don't worry about it happening.
Its another promise God will keep!
Someday the sun will shine brighter
Than it ever has before
When God returns to earth
And lives with men once more!

MICAH 6

God asks, "Oh my people what have I done
Yesterday or today
To lose your love and make you turn away?"
Can you imagine these people having
No patience with the Lord?
He had rescued them from a slavery
That had been bitter and debasingly hard.
But through the years that memory faded
And their love for God slowly abated.
The Lord had asked so little in return
Yet, His was a love many would spurn.
All God wanted was fairness and justice
And a humble walk with Him.
They would have had free air to breathe
Beautiful homes, and fatted lambs to trim!
Bring these questions down through the years
Until today
And we can see-like Israel-many have
Turned away.
So the Lord must ask again
"Oh my people, what have I done
To make you turn away from me?"
And we will have no answer
For burned in our hearts
Is the vision of Calvary!

MICAH 7

Where is there another God like our God?
None can be found!
Only in the presence of Jehovah God
Can we stand on holy ground.
My God loves to be merciful.
My God is loving and kind!
He has thrown my sins into the depths
Of the ocean and views them
As one totally blind!
He set His love on us long ago
And sent His Son to tell us so!

The "I Love My Bible" Commentary

(Micah, continued)

We cannot judge Israel for doubting Him.	And the angels who have searched the
We have too.	Universe come to proclaim
We are survivors who have forgotten to ask	There is no one like Him and
"Where is there another God like you?"	In humble adoration they glorify His name!

Note: There is one verse that draws me back to Micah over and over again. It is a jewel of unmeasurable brilliance and indiscernible worth! You'll find it in the sixth chapter the eighth verse. "He(God)hath showed thee, O man, what is good; and what doth the Lord require of thee *but to do justly, and to love mercy, and to walk humbly with thy God?(!!!)*

I would venture to say it is one of the most important verses in the Old Testament.
Do justly so you won't hurt others!
Love mercy so you will be merciful to those who hurt you!
And
walk humbly with God so you will know how to do justly and how to extend mercy!

We carry all manner of cards in our pockets or wallets or purses. This is one we need in an obvious spot so that every time we open our wallets or purses the first thing we see is *do justly, love mercy, and walk humbly with thy God!* The world would not be in the troubles it is in-if inside our hearts and our pocket books we carried this holy healing scripture! Say it before you leave your home in order to take healing to the world. *AND say it before you return home in order to bring healing to your home!*

One more time!
What does the Lord thy God require of thee
but to do justly, to love mercy, and to walk humbly with thy God!

*But thou, Bethlehem Ephratah,
though thou be little
among the thousands of Judah,
yet out of thee
shall he come forth unto me
that is to be ruler in Israel;
whose goings forth
have been from of old,
from everlasting.*

----

*And he shall stand
and feed in the strength
of the Lord,
in the majesty of the name
of the Lord his God;
and they shall abide:
for now shall he be great
unto the ends of the earth.*
(Micah 5: 2 and 4kjv)

The "I Love My Bible" Commentary
(*The Book of Nahum*)

NAHUM 1

Nahum asks,
"Who can stand before an angry God
Whose fury is like fire?"
The Assyrians would perish
no matter how many
mercenaries they would hire.
An evil man must be careful
who he pushes and shoves
for God is very protective
of those He loves!
Sometimes evil is up
and sometimes evil is down
but the escalator of time
will eventually usurp its crown.
God gives the longsuffering
time enough to mend
and meantime brings the evil
to an untimely end.
If one has rejected God
a thousand years
is much too young to die
and even a king will find no solace
when God passes him by!

NAHUM 2

Destruction often comes at a moment of peace.
Security does has a delicate short-term lease!
(Think of the World Trade Center!)
And Nineveh never thought she would fall.
She had so many mercenaries on instant call.
All her silver and her gold were stripped bare.
And the Queen of Nineveh was led
Helpless down her exclusive thoroughfare!
The old and feeble had lived there unafraid.
Happy were the homes in which her children played.
But Nineveh's glory had been snatched
From the arms of others
Because of her, many nations had mourned
The loss of sons, daughters, sisters and brothers.
So, now the Lord of hosts turned against
That wicked city
And He would show her the horror
Of a lifetime without pity.

NAHUM 3

This city that claimed to be so full of beauty
Was crammed with her plunder.
And now all her ill gotten goods would be
Plowed under.
We have a popular saying today.
"What goes around, comes around."
So–if you plow someone's hopes under
You will find yours *buried deep underground!*
Such was Nineveh's case.
Her victims hopes were sunk, lost with no trace.
God called Nineveh a city of blood.
All the judgement it deserved
Would come in like a flood!
Nineveh would never rise to be the same.
All the world would see her '*nudity*' and shame.
Soon God's '*locusts*' would suddenly appear
And the bankruptcy of those evil rulers
Would be instantaneous and sure!
Power never makes greatness-then or now.
To be enshrined in the heavenly halls of fame
Takes the wisdom of God to show us how!

Note: All powerful, evil nations will fall. We can see that has happened throughout the Bible and all through secular history. And we can see when a nation turns to evil as did Israel, it, too, will fall. **God never blesses evil.** To successfully fight it, we must contend with our own evil first–adultery, murder, etc., and corporate as well as individual theft. *If we don't God will!*

(A GOOD VERSE TO MEMORIZE)

The Lord

is good,

A STRONG HOLD

in the day

of trouble;

and

He knoweth them

that trust

in Him
(Nahum 1:7kjv)

The "I Love My Bible" Commentary
(*The Book of Habakkuk*)

HABAKKUK 1

"Must I forever see this treachery?"
Habakkuk wails!
"Every where I look
crime and trickery prevails."
The law was not enforced
and there was no justice in the courts.
He admitted that Israel
had committed atrocious sins
and wondered how their punishment
could actually make amends.
"Oh Lord," he cries.
"Don't you understand our plight?"
There was oppression everywhere
and all men did was fuss and fight!
And though we know
our Savior promises that someday
we will have a life of bliss
we wonder why this generation
still faces a time of war
and of crime and hopelessness!
Yet, in these books of prophecy
sent by God to man
Habakkuk is a time capsule
that holds the heart of God
and preserves His golden rule!

HABAKKUK 2

*There is a silence so eloquent
it transfuses the soul!
It surrounds us in God's temple
and completely makes us whole!
Such silence feels the heartbeat
of a Holy God
who bids us walk in splendid paths
we have never trod!
"I will watch for God."
Habakkuk muses
"and not trust in that which confuses."
He hears the promise God always gives.
"The righteous man trusts in me and lives!"
So he says, " lets look to our Lord
for guidance
and while we are in the temple
let there be silence!"*

HABAKKUK 3

I have long contended Habakkuk contains
the greatest Old Testament compliment.
When he says, "I see God in brilliant splendor"
we can only imagine what he meant!
He declares God's loving dedication
and rejoices in His salvation.
Oh what faith it takes to say
"No matter how hard the times
I will walk with God each day!"
He knew God was his *living fountain*
and would bring him safely
over the 'mountain.'
Habakkuk is a precious jewel hidden
in the Old Testament gold mine
and proves God's *special polish
will always make this 'diamond' shine!*

Note: I believe the most beautiful statement of faith in the Old Testament is in Habakkuk. Its fervor addresses a residing faith. It says,(in essence)no matter how *bad* life is–with God it is *good! We cannot read Habakkuk without feeling we've had a spiritual hormone shot! Oh to have faith as great as Habakkuk's!*
If you want a shot in the arm(better still, in the heart)please read Habakkuk 3 verses seventeen through nineteen! He is saying if all resources fail our God never will–therefore he will rejoice and the description he uses shows *how much he will rejoice!* I hope you will find it contagious!

...the Lord is in his holy temple:

Let ALL the earth

keep silence before him.

(A great statement of faith)

Although the fig trees

shall not blossom,

neither shall fruit be in the vines;

the labor of the olive shall fall,

and the fields shall yield no meat;

the flock shall be cut off from the fold

and there shall be no herd in the stalls:

Yet I WILL rejoice in the Lord,

I will joy in the God of my salvation.
(Habakkuk 2:20 and 3: 17-18kjv)

The "I Love My Bible" Commentary
(The Book of Zephaniah)

ZEPHANIAH 1

Those who never loved God and
Never wanted to
Will never know the joy of the wonders
He can do!
They will never realize what it was
Their gold could not buy
For God's love will slip through their fingers
Without them ever knowing why.
God says strong men will weep
And all Judah will be purged
When He makes a clean sweep!
It seems Judah loved to walk a wayward path
And she was headed for a collision course
With God's wrath.
It is still risky business to sit contended in sin
For God still despises the trait of indifference
    in men.

ZEPHANIAH 2

God's shameless nation(now He has another)
Would forget how to laugh
When their opportunities to repent
Had blown away like chaff!
All of those who had tried to obey
-the humble ones, would surely pray!
Only those humbly doing God's will
Would escape the gloom
When God protected them
From His wrath in the *day of doom.*
God sent bad news first to His nation
But He included others in His proclamation!
The Philistines would also be rooted out
-Moab and Ammon too.
Ethiopia and Assyrians would experience
The same fate they had wished upon the Jew!
The cedar paneling of Nineveh would resound
With the hooting of the owls
And her great banquet halls would only shelter
The type of beast that freely prowls!
From glory to gory was her fate
Because she gave God's people only hate!
But which is worse–indifference or disdain?
In this time of weak Christianity, and atheists
Which gives Our gracious Lord the most pain?

ZEPHANIAH 3

The leaders of Israel were like those of today.
They will do anything to get their own way.
And did you ever hear someone complain
That preachers only preach for monetary gain?
Well then, let me be more personal
Though it may be hard.
We must ask ourselves how much
We trust and obey our Lord.
And if there is an antidote for dirty words
We must all take the 'cure'
For when God says He will change our speech
It means He wants it pure!
Some day He will gather us together
And give us a good name
But you can bet it will only be after
We turn our backs on shame.
Then the Lord will sing a happy song
And I want to be there so I can sing along!

Note: You would think, with all the prophets
giving the same message-it would soak in!
Same thing though today! Perhaps it is because
so many hearts have grown as hard as a metal
we have yet to discover!
God said He'd change our hearts of *stone* to
hearts of flesh-but that is only if we are willing.
*It seems history is only a vampire that sucks the
knowledge of God from our hearts.*
We certainly haven't learned from it, have we?
Thank God, the knowledge is still here. Seek it!

In that day it shall be said

to Jerusalem,

fear thou not,

and to Zion,

let not thine hands be slack.

The Lord thy God

in the midst of thee is mighty;

he will save,

he will rejoice over thee

with joy;

he will rest in his love,

he will joy over thee

with singing.
(Zephaniah 3:16-17kjv)

The "I Love My Bible" Commentary
(*The Book of Haggai*)

HAGGAI 1	HAGGAI 2
A drought of holy living devastated the land.	*Israel rejoice!*
And God's temple laid in ruins	*The desire of all nations*
Because they ignored God's command.	*is coming home!*
People wondered why their pockets	*He will rule from Jerusalem*
Were so full of holes.	*and no one will want to roam!*
They were unpaid actors enjoying evil roles.	*There will never be*
"Be careful how you *act*," God said.	*a greater story*
If they ignored His *directions*	*Then God filling Israel*
He would withhold their *daily bread!*	*with His glory!*
They were like children wanting candy	*But—in the meantime*
Giving nothing in return	*everything went wrong!*
But God had much for each of them to learn.	*The people with their selfish attitudes*
God said, "I will appear in my glory	*were writing a bitter song.*
If you want me there	*Yet when they turned their lives around*
But you will have show me that you really care!"	*what a marvelous future they found!*
Only when they put Him and His temple first	*God promised to bless them all*
Could they be happy	*and happy songs would resound*
In the roles they so carelessly rehearsed.	*in His great banquet hall!*

Note:

We're approaching the end of the fifth dispensation–the law! As a reminder, the first dispensation was the age of innocence-the second, the age of conscience and then the flood. The third was the dispensation of human government and the fourth was the dispensation of promise which lasted from Abraham to the Egyptian bondage. And then there was the dispensation of the law(the fifth) which lasted from the Exodus through the crucifixion of Christ.
        And then there was number six–the dispensation of grace!
This one is ours! There will be one more before the end of time–*the dispensation of the kingdom!*

In the meantime here we are(or here Israel is)still contending with God. Still believing it was all right to go their own way. Still acting like people are continuing to act today-even some Christians.
You would think with so many prophets giving the same message, it would eventually soak in!
It still doesn't. We can read these messages which have been repeated many times---and have we learned?   I wonder!   *But God had his faithful servants then, who never gave up!*
We have some faithful ministers today *who preach the word, or should I say the faith, <u>once delivered to the saints.</u>* Saints of God, we would do well to listen to them *and listen well!*

For thus saith the Lord of hosts;

yet once

it is a little while,

and I will shake the heavens,

and the earth,

and the sea,

and the dry land;

And I will shake all nations,

And the desire of all nations shall come:

and I will fill this house

with glory,

saith the Lord of hosts.
(Haggai 2: 6-7kjv)

The "I Love My Bible" Commentary
(The Book of Zechariah)

ZECHARIAH 1

If Zechariah contained
only three words
they would suffice!
"God's Word endures!"
Those who say obey it
give mighty good advice!
The Israelis paid no attention
to God at all
"and that," said Zechariah
led to their fall!"
God sent a vision to this prophet
deep in the night
to illustrate His plans
for Israel's homeward flight!
In a sense Israel was like a child
who had been spanked
and all its rights vigorously yanked!
Even so, God would comfort her
because He knew
how uncomfortable they were.

ZECHARIAH 2

Jerusalem is crowded now but we've seen
Nothing yet!
We've not begun to see how much bigger
She can get.
Jerusalem-bursting at the seams- will be bigger
Than the Jews wildest dreams!
Guess who will be the glory of the city
And the surrounding country side!
For once, Israel will have good reason
To be completely full of pride.
The Lord, Jehovah, will be there!
All people will stand in awe and silence
And no one will despair!
Oh, Jerusalem, Jerusalem, sing and rejoice!
Out of all the great cities
The Commander of the armies of Heaven
Has made you His choice!

ZECHARIAH 3

Satan has always stuck his nose in where
It doesn't belong
And he accused God's priest of doing wrong.
But, no matter how vile the accusation
God decreed mercy to Joshua and his nation!
In one day, God would cleanse the Jews
By any means He chose to use.
He said Joshua, the high priest
Would be his instrument to overcome the beast.
But first Joshua must be cleansed
For righteousness must prevail
Before all evil could end.
Zechariah asks for a clean turban
For Joshua's head.
It seems he thought Joshua should put away
Bad thoughts and think of good ones instead.
He was happy to hear the best news of all.
There is a way out for all those who fall!
In a single day God would remove all sin
And He would do it through
The One who gave himself for all men!
Joshua represented the *'Branch'*
Who was the temple's foundation stone
And the hope of all the world
Depends on faith in Him alone!

ZECHARIAH 4

Sometimes the foundations must be shaken
Before God's sleeping saints can be awakened.
Strength sometimes comes from being alert
To the knowledge of God's Word
And His was a message just waiting to be heard.
"Not by might, nor by power," says the Lord
"But only by my Spirit!"

Comment on Zechariah

Strength from His Word was sent to all
Who were willing to hear it!
God's people were not to cringe in fear.
Even mountains of trouble would disappear!
God gives opportunities people must not shirk
For His eyes are beaming on those
Who faithfully do His work!
And again, Zechariah hears the Lord's voice.
Even in small beginnings, God would rejoice.
Other symbols given are simply to advise
And they are sensed by those who are truly wise!

ZECHARIAH 5

Have you ever told a lie and then wanted
To crawl in a hole?
That might beat facing the message
Of the mighty flying scroll!
God wanted it to announce to all liars
They would be extracted by His mighty pliers!
Those who swore falsely by His name
Did not care if they brought Him shame.
It seems to me the flying articles represent haste.
God's in a hurry to rid the land of filth and waste.
It took a God size bushel basket to rid Israel
Of her prevailing sin.
God used a woman to picture adultery.
She was shoved into the basket and closed in.
Her destination was Babylon-so very sultry.
Babylon always pictured idolatry and adultery.
Both were filthy in God's sight
And they would plummet to Babylon
In their final flight!

ZECHARIAH 6

This is definitely not the "Swing low
Sweet Chariot" song.
These horses and chariots were sent everywhere
To punish those doing wrong.
Then another beautiful picture began to unfold.

Joshua receive a crown made of silver
And of gold.
And the announcement to follow
Will not be considered great
By the agnostics and unbelievers
Who would separate church and state.
Christ will reign as King *and* Priest
With perfect harmony between the two!
To separate morality from government
Guarantees a nation run askew!
But God said His righteous rule won't come
Until we learn to obey.
And unless we do we will face anarchy
Until God returns to stay!

ZECHARIAH 7

Our Lord must remind us over and over again
We must be kind and just to our fellow man.
Once again we see God punished the Jew
Because he blatantly ignored what God
Told him to do.
It does no good to seek God's blessing
If we are insincere.
God says "Be earnest when you come to my
Temple, otherwise I don't want you here!"
Do we go to church for fellowship and fun?"
God warns us it is an attitude
From which His people should run.
The building that houses the steeple
Must be full of reverent, worshipful people!
God honors worship that comes from the heart.
Ours is a glorious Covenant relationship
When we do our part!
Our part is to simply obey
And glorify Him in our lives each day!

ZECHARIAH 8

"Tell the truth," God says. "Be fair. Try to live
At peace with everyone."

The "I Love My Bible" Commentary

"Don't plot harm and don't tell lies.
How I hate what you have done!"
His advice to the Israelis was the basis
For a new relationship.
But their refusal to listen made this nation slip.
Different though, if they obeyed with dedication
For many could gather in a joyous celebration.
God promised obedience would bring peace
And prosperity that would last so long
Aged men and women would join hands
With boys and girls in a happy song!
We might think it sounds too simple
That mere obedience would restore the temple
But it did and if we who are 'called'
Are faithful and true
God will show us, there is no limit
To what He can do!

ZECHARIAH 9

The Great King would not enter suddenly
(not the first time anyway)
Like a lightening bolt
But he would come slowly riding on the back
Of a donkey's colt!
The time for glory and majesty would be
In the *Far Distant Future* at the end of history.
First He would bring peace
And great hope to prisoners seeking release.
But in their time, many cities would face doom
All mankind would share a staggering gloom.
Yet we see a heartwarming invitation
And their eyes would shine with the realization
That God was speaking to them
When He offered safety in Jerusalem!
Do you realize the way God's mercy goes?
He promises two mercies for each of our woes!
-twice the mercy and twice the grace
And He can do it!
What a blessed day that will be
When His holy realm stretches from sea to sea!

ZECHARIAH 10

Notice! God's people can go anywhere
And still be under His personal care!
It seems our strength will grow by the hour
For the Lord, Himself, will give us power!
And in those days no matter
How far away the Israelis were scattered
Seeking God and returning to Israel their home
Was all that really mattered!
Tho God's anger burned against Judean leaders
Who were rejected like waves of the sea
Held back by mighty receders
They would still cross their *sea of distress*
To live like people only God could bless!
It would be as if God never cast them away
And they would be under His personal care
  night and day!

ZECHARIAH 11

One admires a noble shepherd
Who tenderly cares for his sheep
But Israel's leaders betrayed their *flock*
Rejecting and selling them much too cheap.
Were they nothing but slaves to be set aside
These pitiful 'sheep' who had no place to hide?
Even the shepherds were of little value
For God considered them worthless too.
But it was the kind His people craved.
What other kind of shepherds should God give
To these people who so carelessly behaved?
That beautiful shepherd's staff called *'grace'*
Was broken and discarded
And losing their unity was one way
That they were justly rewarded.
Sometimes our will Lord send us
What we want (when we keep asking)
Instead of what we need
It must pain Him deeply to leave us alone
To wallow in our greed.

Comment on Zechariah

ZECHARIAH 12

Zechariah seems to have so much symbolism
Packed in his little book.
We can almost hear the waterfall
Changing to a meandering brook!
This chapter places beauty and chaos
Almost side by side.
One doesn't know whether to stand in awe
Or to run and hide!
Even as God promises horror
His mirror of love reflects
Courage, love, honor and power for His rejects!
He gave His people reason to rejoice again.
The people of Judah would return to God
And He would strengthen every clan!
But verses ten and eleven are full of a future
Ambivalent repentance.
People would mourn and yet at the same time
Had(will)given the Messiah an unfair sentence!
Here's another picture of the sacrificial lamb
Rejected and ignored
Until the end of time when His promise
(to return)would be restored!
Life seems a roller-coaster made with no brakes
Yet somehow God will end it safely
For He makes no mistakes!

ZECHARIAH 13

There is a glorious fountain for God's redeemed
That cleanses and purifies much purer
Than we have ever dreamed!
Yet Zechariah says the Shepherd who supplies
The fountain will be struck down
And His helpless sheep will be scattered
Never again to see their home town.
No one will be sure where he belongs.
Two-thirds will be destroyed by heathen throngs.
Its such a sad story this chapter tells.
Instead of the *'fountain'* God's people
Had drunk from contaminated wells.
But someday the surviving third would return unmarred
And will declare allegiance only to the Lord!

ZECHARIAH 14

Watch for the
'Day of the Lord!' It is coming soon!
There will be no sun to light the skies and no
Romantic moon.
It will be a time of war more devastating than
We have ever seen.
The Mount of Olives will split apart
And God's people will escape
Through the valley in between!
How can beauty and horror be mixed?
But it is here!
Many will be assaulted and many will
Simply disappear.
Those who fight Jerusalem will suffer
A horrible fate
But it will be the last time any man
Will be allowed to display so much hate.
From then on, Jerusalem will belong to the King
And even the bells on the horses
Will have a holy ring!
And what about the light?
The Lord will shine with such brilliance
There will never be another night!
Note: This speaks of the time we've been waiting for! Love and peace will reign because we will be with Him! Not all prophecy is bad. God sends hope to the righteous. We'll never see another horror movie or no dirty sexual shows. Those who insist on living in adultery, who lie and cheat, rob and murder will have no ticket to enter. It will be a place they never desired. Don't ask me why! Paul later said their understanding was darkened because they didn't believe. What an incredible sadness that will be!

The "I Love My Bible" Commentary
(The Book of Malachi)

MALACHI 1

Some people seem to think it incredibly hard
To believe we are greatly loved by the Lord!
And some might say
"When Lord, can you name the day?"
God's answer to us also
Will be, "Can't you see I'm with you
Everywhere you go?"
They couldn't see. Neither can we!
God walked beside them everyday
They didn't see
Because they were looking the other way.
How it must have hurt Him to feel their hate
And to see them bringing sacrifices
That were merely second rate.
"Sooner or later." God says, "You *must*
Put me first!
Those who never learned that lesson were
Inevitably cursed.
And don't we often say its too hard
To *take up our cross* and follow the Lord?
We have given Him *bottom drawer* hearts.
He gave us top drawer rules!
And in going our own way
We have been untrained, ungodly fools.
Our God is a great King who should be revered
Who could easily solve all the problems
We have ever feared!

MALACHI 2

Well! What do you know?
The Lord hates divorce!
And does He want us to guard our passions?
Of course!
We are united in God's plan
and are *ONE* in His sight.
Breaking faith with one another
is anything but right.
Our lives fail to give glory to His name.
We don't take holiness seriously
and I say that to our shame.
The greatest rift we face with God
is the rift we create
when we turn away from each other
and tumble into
the bottomless pit of hate.
Life was meant to be so sweet.
Where did we go wrong?
The *cream of the crop* has clabbered
and no one sings a happy song.
Some say its ok to do evil
that God doesn't care.
Wanna bet!
Just stop and think.
We haven't had to
pay the piper yet!
Many of us have failed to recognize
when God says to be holy
He will not compromise!

MALACHI 3

The soul's crippling contaminates must be
Destroyed by God's special fire.
Only purified Levites would be worthy to hire.
God would send His courier to prepare the way
For the Great One of the ages to come some day.
But there's no reason for us to fret
Most of what is mentioned has not happened yet.
Mankind does continue to commit the same sins
And though the Lord is merciful we seem to be
Barely hanging on by our chins!
We still rob God and say its not so!
Yet we still expect His blessing wherever we go.
But God sees us for what we are
And tries to turn us around.
Our Father wants us to walk
On heavenly higher ground!

Comment on Malachi

Remember how we've called our children
Our precious jewels?
Well, our Heavenly Father does the same!
God loves us deeply and we are precious to Him!
And if we don't feel that, He is not to blame!

MALACHI 4

No one can adequately describe our Lord
Though many have tried.
When He is near we can be *fully satisfied!*
He reaches down to dry our tears
And will help us conquer all our fears!
What a beautiful picture of hope He brings
When He say He will rise with healing
In His wings!
We've never known what freedom really means
But God pictures it as calves let loose
In pastoral scenes
Their actions seems to proclaim, "Oh boy!"
And I suppose we can call *that* jubilant joy!
He says the wicked will burn like straw
And warns us to carefully obey His law.
He always gives us ample time to repent
So we can't complain when His promised
Judgement has been sent!
That's it for the Old Testament.
And there will be a four hundred year silence.
It is as if the world stood still.
   (The lesson?)
Man goes nowhere at all when he refuses
To do our Heavenly Father's will!

Comment on Old Testament

In the beginning God's creation
Displayed a glorious splendor
Until sin raised its ugly head
And that questionable character
    whispered,
"God did not mean what He said!"
And man kind never learned the glory
Of the God of the 'Garden'
Was His eternal willingness
To abundantly pardon!
They seemed to fight their battles
With no holds barred
And because they ignored
The judge of the ages
Countless lives were scarred.
When they refused to listen
God refused to speak
And they were devoid of the counsel
God wanted them to seek.

So man cried, "God where are you?"
And only the echo answered back
    "God where are you.....
        are you...
           ....are you.....?"
And that echo would wrap its sound
Around the universe to haunt all men
Who would become untrue.
It seemed man sinned and became
    steadily worse
Like the same old song umpteenth
    verse!
Though God's thunder rumbled
Man could not hear
For when the gentle whisper came
He turned a deafened ear.
Finally man recoiled in bitter surprise.
    Even the echo ignored
    his feeble, desperate cries!

Official Silence

Oppressing Silence

Osmosing Silence

For, behold the day cometh,
that shall burn as an oven;
and all the proud, yea, and all that do wickedly,
shall be stubble:
and the day that cometh shall burn them up,
saith the Lord of hosts,
that it shall leave them neither root nor branch.

But unto you that fear my name
shall the sun of righteousness arise
with healing in his wings;
and ye shall go forth,
and grow up as calves of the stall.

And ye shall tread down the wicked;
for they shall be ashes
under the soles of your feet
in the day that I shall do this,
saith the Lord of hosts.

Remember ye the law of Moses
my servant,
which I commanded unto him in Horeb
for all Israel,
with the statutes and judgements.

Behold I will send you Elijah the prophet
before the coming of the great and dreadful
day of the Lord:

And he shall turn the heart of the fathers
to the children,
and the heart of the children
to their fathers,
lest I come
and smite the earth with a curse.
(Malachi chapter 4kjv)

The Blessed New Testament

*In the beginning was the Word,
and the Word was with God,
and the Word was God.
The same was in the beginning with God.
All things were made by Him;
and <u>without</u> Him
<u>was not anything made that was made.</u>
In Him was life;
and the life was the light of men.
And the light shineth in the darkness:
and the darkness comprehended it not.*

----

*He was in the world,
and the world was made by Him,
and the world knew Him not.
He came unto His own,
and His own received Him not.
But as many as received Him
to them gave He power
to become the sons of God,
<u>even to them that believe on His Name:</u>
which were born, not of blood,
nor of the will of the flesh,
nor of the will of man,
but of God.
And the Word was made flesh,
and dwelt among us,
(and we beheld His glory
the glory as of the only begotten
of the Father;)
full of grace and truth.*
(John 1:1-5; 10-14kjv)

Introduction to the New Testament

Through the ages man has trudged up
the lonely hill of hatred and bad breaks
which contains the insurmountable barriers
his undisciplined behavior creates.
But there came a time
when it seemed time stood still
and mankind could see
the One who came to do the Father's will!
Angels held their breath
when the decision was made
for this <u>Great One</u> of the universe
to come and make a trade.
He would trade His life for ours!
His intercession would free us
from death's unholy powers.
On top of Jerusalem's hill
stood a Ray of Light
so powerful He overcame
the weight of the darkest night!
No one needs to wonder why He chose to roam
for God's great love compelled Him
to show us the way back home!
The ones who follow Him
walk no lonely trails
and rejoice in the presence
of the One who never fails!
It was the darkest day on earth
that day Christ was crucified
but He arose to show us
no matter what side of life's hill
we walk on now
it will be on the sunny side!

*Then said Jesus unto them again,
verily, verily, I say unto you
I am the door of the sheep.*

*All that ever came before me
are thieves and robbers:
but the sheep did not hear them.*

*I am the door:
by me if any man enter in,
<u>he shall be saved,</u>
and shall go in and out,
and find pasture.*

*The thief cometh not but for to steal,
and to kill, and to destroy;
I AM COME THAT THEY MIGHT HAVE LIFE,
and that they might have it
more abundantly.*

*I AM THE GOOD SHEPHERD;
The Good Shepherd giveth His life
for the sheep.*

----

*My sheep hear my voice.
And I know them,
and they <u>follow</u> me:*

*And I give unto them eternal life;
and they shall never perish,
neither shall any man pluck them
out of my hand.*
(John 10:7-11; 27-28kjv)

Part Seven

The Morning Star

Matthew
Mark
Luke
John
Acts

Arises

Come unto me,

all ye that are labor

and are heavy laden,

and I will give you rest.

Take my yoke upon you,

and learn of me;

for I am meek

and lowly in heart:

and ye shall find

rest for your souls.

For my yoke is easy

and my burden is light.
(Matthew 11:28-30)

The "I Love My Bible" Commentary
(The Book of Matthew)

MATTHEW 1

What does genealogy have to do with us?
Everything!
In the line of events
in the passing of time
genealogy would bring us peasants
kinship to the King!
He planned it that way-way back when
He had to expel Adam from the Garden
And had to develop His 'salvation' plan!
Adam was the old covenant.
Jesus is the new!
Like a new link in our DNA
meant to make us
better in every way!
Three-fourteen generations mentioned
from Abraham to Christ..each
and there we view the 'crest'
of the mountain we need to reach!
God's genealogy
the genetic 'stock market'
rising from Abraham to David
falling from David to the exile
and the 'ticker tape' ran quietly
until fourteen generations later
at the birth of the Christ child!
And then
God's spiritual stock market
rose above the charts
when God gave heavenly wealth
to lonely human hearts!
God sent heaven to earth
and offered men the great investment
of a miraculous new birth!
And
that is what genealogy
has to do with man!

MATTHEW 2

A little Judean village
an out of the way spot
throngs pressing in to pay
for beds no better than a cot.
He deserved a feather bed.
They couldn't even find one feather!
And that manger didn't protect Him
from Israel's inclement weather.
But angels kept Him warm
and love kept Him safe from harm!
He was sent by
the God of all the ages
who ages not!
His love is pure and holy
without a single blot!
We don't have to worry.
Our God is in control!
I KNOW that because
He sent Jesus to save my soul!
And it all started in that little town
when He put on simple clothes
and laid aside His crown!
It must be
the longer my God lives
<u>the sweeter He grows</u>
and every time I think of
His love
the brighter it glows!

MATTHEW 3

John said he was just a messenger
preparing the way
but he was unprepared
to baptize the King that day!
But Jesus said it must be done
and God sent the snow-white dove
to glorify His Son!

Comment on Matthew

Feature a snow white dove
announcing the Son
of God's great love!
And when Jesus went
down into the water
He drug the old devil under
and when He came up
He turned life into a miracle of wonder!
Imagine a simple river side
and then picture our Lord
changing the 'tide!'
His grace is an overflowing stream.
Life without Him was a nightmare.
He turned it into a beautiful dream!
We are over our heads
in God's river of grace
but all we understand
of it is like
we're sitting on the river bank
wiggling our toes in the "Rio Grande!"
So---you've sinned
and you're on needles and pins!
Take heart!
God's grace is greater
than all our sins!

MATTHEW 4

Once I described Moses
as a giant of a man in a lonely place.
This "Man" was in a lonely place too
but His stature was not measured
in feet--but in grace!
And man has no instrument
to calibrate that!
Grace-almost greater than love
Grace-sweeter than honey
Grace-wonderfully free
yet unobtainable
with any amount of money!
So--here stands the One
bound now by time
but clothed in eternity.
He came to face trouble
so trouble could never
defeat you and me!
This "Man" left love along the trail
and if we embrace that love
we should never fail.
We may never be giants
but a "Giant" lives in our hearts
and this world will never
be a lonely place
when we take hold of that great love
and accept His incredible grace!

MATTHEW 5

The Sermon on the Mount
displays
a hill of responsibility
a mountain of grace
far more than we need
to help us reach that Holy Place!
To stand in His presence
to look on His face
is to feel the fresh air
of Heaven.
Heaven! Gloriously ours because
Jesus made it our home base!
He always had a message
for the multitudes who came
and everything He told them
glorified His Father's name!
Many ears were open to His message
but countless more shut Him out.
His was the voice of authority
but disbelief nudged their heart with doubt.
They wondered how could one
who lived so simple
have the power He claimed
but had they done what He said

The "I Love My Bible" Commentary

none would ever have been ashamed.
He talked of love because
He knew it first hand!
He was awesome, but in gentleness
He gave each command.
Could anyone doubt He loved people
as they listened to that beautiful voice?
He was simply telling of a better way
and offering a better choice!
"Love others," He commanded
"as God loves you!"
Love is the road to perfection
and love helps us
keep our heavenly home in view!
If we'd only *read between the lines*
we'd see how gloriously
His *love* shines!
The message still rings out
from every church steeple.
Godliness exalts a nation
and gives hope to its people!
He challenged us to be perfect
and to walk in our Father's ways
for the Heavenly Father leads us
toward bright and cloudless days!

MATTHEW 6

Do we understand there is to be no pride
in our giving?
Do we realize honest, wholesome prayer
brings joy to living?
Even when we deny ourselves
we are not to gloat.
There are many holes and dropped stitches
in a self-righteous coat.
And could there be any doubt
what our Lord thinks of greed
yet He never denied one
who came with a legitimate need!
He longed for people to understand
God's provision.
Christ came unto His own
but following Him must be *their* decision.
He never promised blessings
for unbelievers.
"Seek God first," he said.
We must all keep our hearts open
in order to be *heaven's* receivers!
Consider the examples He gave
of God's magnificent care.
So His people must not fret.
We'd always have beauty to wear!
But century after century
we humans live in sorrow
because we still choose
to worry about tomorrow!

MATTHEW 7

We cannot judge others because
our judgement is seldom just
and many evils are hidden
under its malevolent crust.
So very few have the spiritual
expertise
to know who to condemn
and to release.
Even our so called Superior Court Judges
release deadly criminals to walk the streets
and they thumb their noses
at the innocent victims
their viciousness defeats.
Our country's morals and legal system
are built upon the sands
and if we are destroyed
it will be at our own hands.
"Straight is the gate and narrow
is the way," our Savior cried
and we will utterly sink
in quick sands of despair
if His teachings are denied!

Comment on Matthew

MATTHEW 8

They followed Him, these folks of all classes
For no one before Him had been able
To heal the masses!
They came-the leper, the Roman, the meek
The scorner, and even the man from Gadara.
Had not Christ told them that God loved
All creatures, even the tiny sparrow?
Even His disciples did not understand
That He had come to set them completely free
And were amazed when He quieted the winds
And calmed the stormy sea!
God's love is a love no one can describe
Yet He had to overcome the foolish questions
The unconcern, the vicious jibe.
And He chastised the foolish one who said
"Sir I'll follow you after my father is dead."
But Jesus' message has always been
"Follow Me now,"
He was not to shun Jesus for his next of kin!
Faith follows Him unafraid, and undaunted
He had so much to give, but it wasn't
What many wanted.
The citizens of Gadara begged Him to leave.
Though a man was healed, they lost money
And they were grieved.
Money was their God and its hideous effect
Was a needy fellow human was shown
   no respect.
Their love and concern came up short
And Jesus left them without a single retort!

MATTHEW 9

There was power in every word He spoke
Love in every act.
They called it blasphemy when
He called Himself God
And refused to accept it as a fact.
"Talk is cheap," He said
And He knew their thoughts were sour.
So he went ahead an healed the paralyzed boy
In order to show them His great power!
Those who considered themselves
   authoritative
Followed Him like furtive pests
And those notorious word swindlers
Became unwelcome guests.
They ignored Him when He preached
That the self-righteous could not be reached.
Many with their old ways, questioned the new
But Jesus understood their point of view.
He knew their tradition was so entrenched
In their minds
It was as if someone had closed the blinds!
How can I describe One so great?
His love transcends the universe.
Yet those who doubted Him
Would have loved to place Him under a curse!
They could not stop His healing.
They could not shut His mouth!
He came to heal wounded spirits
And to end a spiritual drought!
He walked through this chapter healing
As He did in the one before.
He was the object of Pharisaical hate
Yet the people loved Him all the more!
Christ felt pity for the ones that came
And He healed them in His Father's Name!
"The harvest is great," He said, "and the
Laborers or few."
His time on earth was short and He must do
What He must do!
Our Lord knew His love would harvest
Abundant yields
From this earth's soul-starved carnal fields!
Now He tells us to pick the fruit
Of souls lost in sin
Tells us we must be faithful to witness
Of His love for all men
For we'll never know how many we can win!

The "I Love My Bible" Commentary

MATTHEW 10

Twelve special men were chosen
But not to do as they pleased.
They were to heal the many who were
Tormented, crippled and diseased!
They would be representing the Lord
And had a significant command to keep.
"Go," Jesus said. "Go not to the gentiles
But go to the Israelis, God's lost sheep!"
The people along the way could make two
  choices.
They could send these men away, or listen
To those gentle voices!
God's people are not to bless the ungodly
-not now, not then.
God will *not* bless those living in sin!
Cities that would not welcome them
Would fail to measure up.
And they would regret not drinking
That Living Water straight from His cup!
As always, these men were not to dread
The enemies' deadly arrows.
God would care for them as easily
As He cared for the insignificant sparrow!
And don't think a cup of water
To a man of God will go unrewarded
For it was and is meant
That God's people be highly regarded!
The Lord said it and its certainly true.
God will reward us though no man
May cherish what we do.
He said, "Endure to the end!"
      Why not?
In us-beside us walks our Dearest Friend!

MATTHEW 11

John was in deep despair for was no longer
  free
But Jesus sent these comforting words
"Blessed are those who don't lose faith in me!"
He called John a great man-the Elijah of that
  day
And because of John many were walking
Once again on the *King's* Highway!
But Jesus heard the doubters too
And said, "Sodom-will be better off than you."
"When funeral songs are sung," He said,
"You bellyache!"
"And when happy songs are sung," you say
'Be sad for goodness sake!'"
Even when *they* gorged on mutton
They accused Him of being a glutton.
He came to love, to heal; He was the very best!
   "Come unto me," He said,
      and I will give you rest!"
So I '*came*' one day to walk on holy ground
But I've learned I must always hold His hand
For it is in *close communion* that I learn
My Lord is absolutely grand!
And I cannot write about His Words
Without listening to His heart
For there I see His many miracles
Were truly precious works of art!
Everything He does is forever just and right!
   Truly, His yoke is easy
      and His burdens are light!

MATTHEW 12

Sun light must have bounced off temple walls
And enhanced its beauty!
But here was One greater than the temple
Who considered mercy far more glorious than
  duty.
The Pharisees cared more about legality
Than a poor suffering cripple
But Christ's love reached out and stirred
Healing water into an ever widening ripple!
No one ever met Him and left unaffected.
He was either totally hated or fondly respected!

Comment on Matthew

Many were filled with the animosity that blinds
—evil men who were the products of castrated minds.
They despised Him because
He knew the value of a soul.
Lost sheep were His primary concern.
The Pharisees had made money their goal.
Christ would allow these spiritual perverts
To blaspheme the Giver but not 'the gift!'
Speaking against The Holy Spirit
Would cause an unrepairable rift.
There were many truths He tried to teach
But His words went in one ear
And out the other
When simply to believe would have brought
Brother closer to brother!

MATTHEW 13

*Jesus said much about the Kingdom
and it is very important that we see
nothing can compare to its value
or its incredible integrity!
Those who were experts
in the Jewish laws may have earned
their bachelors degrees
But only Christ's disciples
who had double treasure
were qualified to be
Doctor's of Divinity!
Yet, His home town citizens
would not honor His teachings
or His commands.
They didn't believe in His miracles
because they could only see
a carpenter's hands.
He was many things
-a farmer who sowed good seeds
-a great King who saw His peoples needs
-a renowned merchant who sought
heavenly pearls among the weeds
but He wasn't just a bystander.
He was-and is-
our Universal Great Commander!
How blessed those people were
to hear and see
the messages and the healing
of the Man from Galilee!*

MATTHEW 14

When Jesus learned of John's death
He wanted to be alone.
But the crowds came anyway.
He was the greatest being
they had ever known!
Jesus taught the many people who came
but it was his healing power
that actually brought Him fame.
He never disappointed those
who came in hunger or thirst
but ministering to the needy
always came first!
His disciples would have sent
the people away
because they didn't realize
Jesus wanted them to stay!
Wherever or whatever the need
Jesus could provide.
That was the *biggest lesson*
He had to teach those
who walked by His side!
He walked on the water
and into hearts that were shamed.
"Why, you really are the Son of God,"
they exclaimed!
They had doubted the truths He revealed
despite the thousands He had healed!
"Why did you doubt me?" He asked
and they knew their ambivalence
had been unmasked!

The "I Love My Bible" Commentary

MATTHEW 15

Our Lord was so great
He had power left over to heal
the *untouchables*
–those the Jews called "swine."
It was as if He wanted to say
to His disciples
"the helpless, hopeless heathen
are also mine!"
Those self-righteous Jews would not
eat the crumbs
from the Master's table
but those who longed for
love, hope, and healing
were ready, willing, and able!
He just kept getting better
as He went along.
He healed all who came to Him
and they responded
in a happy praise filled song!
Once again He feeds the crowds
but more than just food and drink
and we'll discover later, even this
did not make His disciples
sit up and think!
He always seemed to be in a hurry
for He had such a limited time span
so our Lord sends the people home
and heads for Magadan!

MATTHEW 16

The Pharisees and the Sadducees
Came to test Jesus's claim
He just DIDN"T do things their way!
And His love for the people
Grew sweeter every passing day!
No wonder they hated him.
They held a terrorist hold on the people.
Jesus gave them love!
They shoved the law down the people's throats.
He set their sights on the stars above!
Their hypocrisy was darker than midnight.
His yoke was easy and His burden light!
Christ warned His disciples
about the yeast of the Pharisees
because their sermons
would put no soul at ease.
His gloriously wonderful presence
went mostly uncherished and unrecognized
but Peter and the apostles knew how highly
our Savior should be prized!
The first great confession came from Peter.
True!
No sweeter confession can ever be made
for no other went through such great horror
or paid the price Jesus paid!
Our Lord gave the keys of the Kingdom
to Peter but only to open doors!
The Samaritans and gentiles must also be free
To walk the heavens where the spirit soars!
Only Jesus knew the value of a soul
and only He could(and can) make us whole!
But He cautioned Peter not to think like a man
For such earthly thinking could sabotage
God's glorious plan.
"Thou art the Christ" still rings
out from souls tired of doubt and fear.
"Thou art the Christ"- a galactic truth
all mankind needs to hear!
"Thou art the Christ" ascends the heavens
And way beyond
And we hear, "Thou art the Christ"
as the angels joyfully respond!
It's a "thing," you know
the kind that gives our heart
a glow.
"Thou art the Christ" we say
as we feel those living waters flow!

Comment on Matthew

MATTHEW 17

*The first hint of our Lord's true glory
was given to only three!
And even they could not understand
this majestic vision
they were privileged to see!
Isaiah saw His glory
Ezekiel and Moses, too!
But our Lord had been so gentle
with His disciples
they couldn't comprehend
this heavenly view!
Peter seemed to have the same problem
we have today.
In the presence of such awesome power
he should have knelt to pray.
There is a time to be silent
and to bow in reverent awe
but dear old Peter spoke
inappropriately
in response to the phenomenon
they saw.
I believe we can identify with Peter
in more ways than one
and God has to say to us
"Be quiet in your hearts
and listen to My Son!"
Nothing should have detracted
from this moment
and the King of all the ages
had to put Peter in his place
so Peter could look beyond himself
to see the wonder of God's grace!
Then we see Jesus returning
from the mount
to reproach a faithless, inept group.
He still had much to do
to form His "army"
into a powerful and faithful troop!
And, He seemed to give them
the command
to also honor the laws of the land!*

MATTHEW 18

*There is nothing as great as faith
like that of a little child!
The adoration of simple faith
is the basis for greatness
in those who are meek and mild!
FAITH IS THE ROPE
THAT TIES US TO HEAVEN!
(And no one can cut that rope!)
Faith is the sunshine in our souls!
Jesus knew when we fail to have faith
we will never reach our goals.
He dearly loved to hold
a little child in His arms!
Those who cause His children to lose faith
will face the souls most deadly storms!
There are many who need to know
faith in God is within their reach.
Ah! This is a holy message
He has given us to teach!
Our Lord talked much about
our behavior toward one another
And how often we should be
willing to forgive an erring brother.
Our relationships can be as delicate
as a frightened, elusive wraith
if we forget to diligently apply
Our Lord's teaching on faith!*

MATTHEW 19

*God's unequal and profound
mathematical enquiry surfaces
once again!
And it is the most misunderstood
equation known to man!
How in the world, man wonders*

The "I Love My Bible" Commentary

can one plus one equal one!
Forget it!
Man won't even try!
Divorce has become synonymous
with the mournful words, "bye, bye!"
Faithfulness is what?
"It is a burden," he says
he doesn't want to carry.
And we have adapted
a popular saying to read
"Eat, drink, and re-marry!"
But if we truly love our spouses
we will be able to see
the quick-sand suction of adultery.
God considers it a vicious crime
and He demands moral purity
even in this day and time!!!
And they had another saying
that seems to have been perverted
to hypocritical leaven.
The people seemed to think
only the rich went to heaven.
Well, they were partly right!
The rich in faith do.
And that is a great lesson
for me and you!
Anyway, Jesus knew the rich
could be in spiritual ill health
if he foolishly depended
on his own wealth.
It must have blown their minds
for many of them thought
riches were a sign of godliness
and heaven could be bought!
That was common knowledge before
Jesus taught heaven was also for the poor!
And those who think
fairness to be a haunting thirst
need to hear Jesus say
"those who are last now
shall someday be the first!"

MATTHEW 20

The Kingdom of God is so precious
Christ repeated His stories.
Even the seven wonders of the world
failed to depict the simplest
of heaven's glories!
And once again Jesus says
the last shall be first
and the first last!
Our Lord wants to be sure we know
God's mercies can never be out classed!
The disciples had as much trouble
understanding that as we do.
As much as He taught humility
the question was still asked
"Can my sons rule next to you?"
And to the ten who were indigent
about her question concerning the throne
He warned
"I came to serve and your attitude
should be like my own!"
As He left Jericho many people
followed along behind
and all of them should have understood
His purpose for healing those two
who were blind!
Had he not been trying to open
His disciples eyes?
His illustration of this teaching
should have held no surprise.
Our prayer should be
"Open our eyes so we can see
the glory of true humility."
We need to learn the moral
of that lesson too
for we are so apt to want recognition
for everything we do.
Jesus never sought the limelight!
He just spread the message of love
to open up our unilluminated sight!

Comment on Matthew

MATTHEW 21

What is this?
A King riding on a donkey's colt!
They must have thought
"Who is he kidding?"
They knew the King of the Ages
would arrive triumphantly
enthroned on a lightning bolt!
The aristocrats would not worship
one so humble.
And if He was the hope
of the poor and helpless
the "old" teachings
would surely crumble!
But this world system
had to be turned upside down
before the people would understand
the mighty glory
of this One's modest crown!
And the purpose of the Temple
was actually revealed.
Those who cried to Him
were indisputably healed!
"My Father's House is to be called
a House of Prayer"
And then He healed many
to show how much He cared!
And Jesus declared faith could demand
"Move over Mount of Olives"
and it would!
But unless they had perfect faith
that demand would do no good.
Our Lord's authority was questioned
again and again.
No wonder the people considered Him
only a prophet to be admired by man.
And the leaders
who should have given God glory
were pictured as wicked tenants
in His story.

He was the Rock of Ages
they could not crush
a noble messenger of truth
they would never be able to hush!
"Who is this?" The leaders cried.
"He is Jesus of Nazareth,"
the crowds replied!
But He was not just a prophet
as they thought.
For no prophet ever taught
the truths
our precious Savior taught!

MATTHEW 22

The Kingdom of God was such
a mystery
only Christ could clear the air!
It is a banquet for the hungry
but only the worthy
can feast in assurance there!
One must wear the robe provided
in order to feast
-a covering purchased in blood
by our magnificent High Priest!
Many will come from back alleys
and the corners of lonely streets
but sadly, few will be chosen
to taste Heaven's incomparable sweets!
People still test our Lord
with questions they consider hard
but His questions in return
surely cause our hearts to burn!
Who is the Messiah to me
a stranger
a friend
my one and only blessed Lord?
And the answer buried in my heart
will surely determine my reward!
And–who the Messiah is to you
will certainly determine what you do!

The "I Love My Bible" Commentary

MATTHEW 23

It has always been difficult for God's leaders
To practice what they preach!
And it seems these Pharisee's non-exemplary behavior
Badly contaminated their speech.
It must grieve our Lord when
Our so called holiness is just for show
And we forget it is Him we must honor
Everywhere we go!
He said our service must be humble
If we long to be great
And Jesus knew we are the victims
Of the problems our haughtiness can create.
We are to put our hands in His hands
And follow where He leads.
It is in humility we can realize
It is He who supplies all our needs!
And, we must serve as He served
—love as He loved
—pray as He prayed!
If we overlook His brand of mercy and faith
We will stray as foolishly
As the Pharisees strayed.
We cannot hold on to a holy God
And pat ourselves on the back
At the same time.
Acting like sinners and trying
To look like saints
Is Christiandom's greatest crime.
If we do not learn the lesson of Jerusalem
It will be a pity.
For if our worship is merely a ritual
We will be as desolate
As that once ghostly city!

MATTHEW 24

Did the Lord not want to see the temple
Because He knew it would soon be gone?
It seems, for the wise as well as the simple
His spiritual truths were much too deep
For those who only saw
The results of brain and brawn.
Jesus talks of a time of *"forever after!"*
Readiness is the theme of this chapter!
—readiness for the expected and unexpected.
For Christ will come at a time
When His moral codes are often disrespected!
Even His *"living temples"* may not be prepared
Though He has warned us only the wise
And faithful will be spared.
There is a *separate* and *holy* route
Laid out by our Lord
And our decision whether or not to follow Him
Will ultimately determine our reward.

MATTHEW 25

Responsibility can be a shelter
of repose
an elegantly beautiful fragrant rose
or
it can be a dark and threatening tornado
showing no mercy or favor
and it all depends
on our response to our Savior.
Responsibility is the oil of readiness
for the one who serves
and his loyalty to the Kingdom
never falters and never swerves!
We may not be given much to do
but do it we must.
And whatever we do must be
merciful, kind, and just!
So where will we stand
-to the left or to the right?
Will we scurry into darkness
or walk in His blessed light?
The choice is ours.
We can walk among beautiful flowers!

Comment on Matthew

MATTHEW 26

Oceans cannot hold the tears of failure
God's people have shed through the years
for denial sneaks in
on the bitter side of life
and adds fuel to our fears.
Its so easy to say
"I'd never do that!"
And then our pride betrays
and crucifies our Lord
over and over again."
Yet He says
"Stay with me! Stay with me!"
But the strength He needed then
would not come from any man.
"Stay with me," He says today.
We must watch and work
and weep and pray!
The weak and fainthearted
must drink from His cup.
It will not go away!
Will we declare like Peter
"I never knew Him"
and then run and hide in despair
or will our faith be as fresh
as cool morning air(!)?
What message will the rooster convey
as he crows beneath our windows
at the dawning of the day?
The echo comes
"Stay with me! Stay with me!"
If we do we will not need
to sulk away in sorrow
crying bitterly!

MATTHEW 27

When the mobs drug Him
through the streets
He was strong enough
to be weak!
And His was an elegant silence
when they wanted Him to speak!
And though He cried
"My God, my God
why has thou forsaken me?"
He stayed to the bitter end
there on Calvary!
He heard all the mockery
-felt all the shame
-knew of their hatred
but loved them just the same!
Death could not kill His love!
Their hate could not change
His mind!
Even through the vilest death
known to man
our Savior was loving and kind.
Now man tries to crucify
the truths Christ left behind
and the curtains they draw
before their eyes
have left them spiritually blind.

MATTHEW 28

Good things happen
early in the day!
The air is clear.
The sun is new
And dawn is on its way!
But this particular day
was brighter than the rest!
And those who came were unaware
how much they would be blessed!
"Don't be frightened"
the angel said.
"The One who suffered at evil hands
is no longer dead!"
"He is risen" can not be silenced
by those who don't yet understand

The "I Love My Bible" Commentary

*life and death
and the effects of both
are under His command!
We must climb that mountain
of faith
if we would meet Him
face to face!*

*We must believe He is risen
in order to share in His grace.
And until the end of time
this truth will survive
He is alive, folks!
HE IS ALIVE!*

Note: God knew beginning the New Testament demanded action on a grander scale than He had ever done. *So He gave Himself!* What more could be done? Man had become so blind he had lost the purpose of fulfillment, the joy of love, the overwhelming result of faithfulness. We had a glimpse of it when Abraham fully trusted God with his son Isaac, when Moses defended a fellow Israelite and then went back, under God's direction, to rescue them all! We see it again when the prophets stood up against an evil nation(their own)though it often cost them their lives!

Man has no excuse for evil. The pattern for goodness has always been before us. And the Great Designer came down, sewed that pattern in love, grace, and healing in order that we all could see the beauty of holiness. Man tried to kill His holiness by hanging Him on a cross BUT He arose! Today man attempts to kill His truth through ridicule, through refusing to allow His Word in the grade schools of this country, through mis-guided judges and lawyers who accept no one with a higher authority. His Word says " *a nation that forgets God shall be turned into hell!*(Psa.9:17) There is hell in America's streets today(and other nations, too) No one can be sure he is safe. There was hell in New York when the devil's advocates destroyed the World Trade Center. There is hell in homes that have become divided because of adultery and thousands of children suffer. There is hell because untold numbers of unborn children are viciously murdered. Yes, America is paying for her sins.

But go back to the promise of Second Chronicles 7:14 for the remedy! It is as glorious now as it was then!

"If my people which are called by my name
shall humble themselves
and pray
and seek my face
and turn from their wicked ways
then
will I hear from heaven
*and will forgive their sin
and will HEAL their land!*

And *that* is the formula for peace and safety. So–what's holding us up?

And Jesus answering said unto them,
do you not therefore err.
because ye know not the scriptures,
neither the power of God?

For when they shall rise from the dead
they neither marry
nor are given in marriage,
but are as the angels which are in heaven.

And as touching the dead,
that they rise;
have you not read in the book of Moses,
how in the bush God spoke to him,
saying, I am the God of Abraham,
and the God of Isaac,
and the God of Jacob?

He is not the God of the dead
but the God of the living:
ye therefore do <u>greatly err.</u>
(Mark 12: 24-27kjv)

The "I Love My Bible" Commentary
(The Book of Mark)

MARK 1

Mark seems in a hurry to get the message out.
Maybe it was because he felt he had no clout!
He told of John coming from the wilderness
To announce the Kingdom
And it was to the wilderness Jesus withdrew.
It is alone in the wilderness of life
God sometimes makes us new!
Part of the gospel of the Kingdom tells us
We must turn aside
To find that eternal shelter
Where our weary souls can rest and hide!
We think the wilderness holds trauma
But it strengthened both Jesus and John
And there we discover how elegantly
Our hopes, too, can dawn!
Alone in the *wilderness garden* of the Spirit
Where gorgeous flowers of faith can grow
We find the strength that comes from Him
In paths where the heavens glow!
Mark *was* in a hurry to tell the good news!
Jesus guides us beyond man's wilderness
Where we can feast on heavenly views!
But we Christians do not have to hurry
As it sometimes appears.
There may be haste in the telling
But our joy will last through countless years!
How does God share His love?
Well, He just passes it through you and me
And unless we release it
We'll be as lonely as a trackless sea.
It is like an unpaid debt now in arrears
And the loss will be ours
If this matchless treasure of love disappears!

MARK 2

To say our Lord was busy is putting it mild!
And when Jesus forgave a young man's sins
It drove His enemies wild!
Those who cared dug through the roof.
Those who didn't *raised it!*
The Pharisees denied the people love.
And our Lord constantly displayed it!
They considered tax collectors
And notorious sinners merely scum.
    Jesus said
 "They are the reason I have come!"
And Jesus told them, in effect
That law and grace won't mix.
Old attitudes must go, in the news He depicts!
"I am the Master of the Sabbath," Jesus said
And when His people were hungry
Our Savior gave them bread!
Cataracts must have dimmed their sight
And they were never were able to realize
The significance of the panorama
Unfolding before their eyes!

MARK 3

Never did a man get in so much trouble
for doing good!
Great was their desire to kill him
and they would have done it then
if they could.
They made a mockery of holiness.
Jesus made a mockery of deceit!
They were indifferent to human needs.
He offered a healing sure and complete!
Well, the demons recognized
God's Holy Son
even though the Pharisees
scoffed at all He'd done.
Here we see, we can't give in to tyrants
because tyrants don't give in.
And that same policy applies
when I must deal
with my own sin!

Comment on Mark

When I give in-or give up
is when I give out
and my faith is pushed aside
-smothered by my own doubt.
But Jesus had no doubt
though He knew
His ministry would soon
come to a close
so He carefully trained those
twelve men He chose.
Peter, James, John, and Andrew
Philip, Thomas, James and Matthew
were joined by
Thaddaeus, Simon, Judas
and Bartholomew.
Even they often misunderstood
His holy zeal
and must have questioned
if their faith was real!
They learned the Christian life
would be a struggle
but the rewards were also great
Like us, they eventually learned
with God in their (our) hearts
His followers are not consigned
to the ambiguity of fate!

MARK 4

If you have ears
if you have hearts
listen!
Good seeds are planted
by the Master
and like gold, they glisten!
And when evening falls
as it must
we can place our lives in the hands
of the only One we can trust!
God expects our faith to grow
like the plant from the mustard seed
and no matter how strong the storm
He knows what we need!
When He says,
"Cross to the other side,"
He leads the way
and will remove the obstacles
that stand in our way!
Then as now our Savior 'sleeps'
with just one eye closed!
He knew the peril they were in
even though He dozed.
And had His disciples really listened
when He said, "Lets cross the lake,"
they would have known
it would be a cinch to reach
the other side
no matter how hard
the wind would have blown!

MARK 5

Had the demons been able
to fully control this man
he would never have gone to Jesus!
Don't you know they would like
to hinder you and I?
For they know how marvelously
His love can please us!
It was no big thing for Jesus
to calm the troubled man.
He saw Jesus coming
and *there* he ran!
I'm sure the demons would
loved to have held him back
for this poor soul
had been the home
of this unwelcome pack!
We see Jesus placing this man
far above money any object brings.
He always taught a *person*
is much more valuable than *things!*

The "I Love My Bible" Commentary

Imagine these people
asking Jesus to go away
after they had seen such a
tremendous miracle that day!
Jesus left this man behind
to tell others
how merciful God had been
–just one of the many examples
of His power to save from sin!
So Jesus travels on.
Others were seeking Him out!
It is touching here
how one would touch Him
in order to be healed
while others sneered in doubt.
Jesus told the woman
her faith had made her whole.
And–that means
He had also saved her soul!
And, the parents in this story
believed in His power
so their little girl was revived
that very same hour!

MARK 6

Who would think Jesus would find the people
In His home town hard to convince?
But those unbelievers remembered
His humble origins and so they took offence!
It seems the thicker the clouds of doubt
The dimmer the light
And the heavy torrents of envy
Played havoc with their sight!
They could only see flesh and blood.
His mighty Spirit hid!
Because they refused to believe in Him
They couldn't accept the miracles He did.
At this time He shares His power
With His dearest friends.
Those villages refusing their messages
Were left to the fate of evil winds.
Even Herod heard of Jesus
And he thought John had come back to life.
John had been killed
For criticizing Herod and his wife.
Jesus fed the crowds, walked on water
Calmed the angry sea!
Where ever He went the hurting, the hungry
The hopeful were there
And He answered every legitimate plea!
Our Lord had come to do the Father's will.
He looked into troubled souls and told them
"Peace be still!"

MARK 7

The Religious CIA
came to Jesus one day
and they took Jesus to task!
They had been watching His disciples.
"Why don't your disciples wash?"
They asked.
Jesus told them their rituals
were deadly
for they did not teach
discipline of the heart.
They broke the laws of God
through their tradition
and actually thought they were smart!
But the Lord could see
through their masquerade.
"Its not what you eat," He implied
"that makes you afraid.
Fear comes from sin
and sin comes from wicked thoughts
which leads to the vile pollution
your hypocrisy wroughts!"
Again, a woman begs for His help
and falls at His feet.
She wanted Him to touch her daughter
and make her healing complete!

Comment on Mark

MARK 8

The great crowds always came
seeking more!
"How can we feed them?"
The disciples asked.
"There is nothing left in store!"
But somebody had
a few loaves of bread
and several fish too.
They must have known our Lord
could take almost nothing
and make it do.
The Pharisees were there again
hoping they could *do Him in!*
"You must do more miracles!"
And Jesus sighed.
"How many more miracles
do you need?"
Our Lord replied.
His disciples even felt His disdain.
When Jesus mentioned yeast
He still had to make His message plain.
"Think of all I did!" He said.
"And you think its because
we have no bread?"
Of course they had bread!
Wasn't He there?
No matter how much He fed them
there was always more to share!
Our Lord had so much interference
even from His own.
No wonder He felt He had to face
that ugly cross all alone!
They never learned
how much He had to give
or understood that He must die
so they could live!
Jesus knew
there is nothing more precious
than a soul
and we, too, must believe
only our Savior can make us whole!
There is power in His name
and we (who believe in Him)
should *never* cringe in shame!

MARK 9

The closer we draw to our Savior
the more glory He lets us see!
And if we are to awe in His presence
the more silent we should be.
Quiet hearts are wrapped
in His holy essence
and feel the warmth
of His loving presence!
Peter, James, and John
saw His glory
and would later tell this story!
But they would return to a scene
of a defeat very grim.
For it seems as yet His disciples
considered healing power
belonged only to Him!
And so He said
"Bring the boy to me!"
Don't you know there is a lesson here?
When we fail and see only despair
we can take our problems to Jesus
and leave them there!
"Just have faith," Jesus said
"like a little child!"
He knew doubt leaves us
paralyzed and defiled!
And He gives our souls
their greatest release
when He shares His love
and gives us peace!
"We are the salt of the earth!"
That's what He said!
So—lets share this heavenly bread!

The "I Love My Bible" Commentary

MARK 10

The Pharisees questioned Jesus but
Their motives could not be hid.
Don't you suppose He can see through us
When we act as shallow as those Pharisees did?
Jesus said there is no other recourse.
Only adultery can be *an excuse* (not a reason?)
For the trauma of divorce!
But, it seems the courts have made it easy
For a marriage to break apart.
I wonder if they care, that whenever there is
A broken marriage, there is a broken heart?
And when a marriage dies, many vultures
Gather around
As if there is *any thread of hope,* it too
Must be thoroughly unwound!
But our Lord can give a marriage CPR
And restore it back to life!
For it is not God's will that a wife leave her
    husband
Or for a husband to desert his wife.
No divorce should be allowed
Until counseling has been tried
-until the two have prayed for guidance
   and until all hope has died!
But remember, faith keeps hope alive!
And if we turn to Him who created
   marriage number one
*All the harm we've done each other
   could surely be undone!*
Man and wife may have to face
Some terribly stormy weather
But man must not dissect
What God has joined together!
Of course Christ covered other issues
In this chapter, but we do need to see
The importance of marital integrity!
And when society says, "Be all you can be."
Remind them only Jesus can truly set us free!
And that's how you can be *all that you can be!*

MARK 11

The musical choir in heaven must be building
To a howling crescendo!
Tension mounts and our Lord must realize
Jerusalem is not the place for Him to go!
The doubters, the assassins, the evil are there
Using the temple to make money
Cheating God's children and being unfair!
The King of the Ages rode in on a donkey
Wanting His people to see
*True greatness rides in on the splendor
Of genuine humility.*
It seemed His teaching came to naught
In the presence of the Pharisees
But I suspect His words to them
Were not meant to please!
And our Lord taught His disciples
Another lesson on prayer.
Belief in Him, and forgiving others gave them
The awesome power only faith can declare!
This chapter closes in a heavenly stand-off
For Jesus did not choose to answer
Those evil men who chose to scoff!

MARK 12

The higher one is in the power echelon
   the greater the temptations
     to think of others as non
       persons.
And the greater one considers
   himself to be
   the more likely he is to have
   the mind of a *Pharisee.*
Though these Jewish leaders
and Pharisees never gave Jesus glory
   they were wise enough to know
they were the wicked men in His story!
But now a man who knew
Christ knew well of what He'd spoken

Comment on Mark

asked about
the One Glorious Commandment
that should never, ever be broken!
Christ answered
"Thou shall love the Lord thy God
with all the strength
in your heart, soul, and mind!"
And we know God also wants us
to be loving and kind!
The more we love God and others
the less we will roam
from the presence of the One
my heart calls home!
My Lord had much to say
about the piously insincere
but He marveled at a widow
who gave her *all*
in benevolent cheer!
Need we wonder who
He wants us to imitate?
Our Lord said
it is a giving heart
that truly makes us great!

MARK 13

Beauty turns to ashes
even in the temple
and keeping beauty in our hearts
is never easy or simple!
Jesus sat on the slopes
across from Jerusalem
and answered the questions
the disciples asked of Him.
But His words were full of bad news
and their hearts must have been
sadly bruised.
"Watch," He said
so as not to be deceived.
Many *woes* are mentioned.
Many hearts will be grieved.

"Now, learn a lesson from the fig tree,"
Jesus said.
There will be trouble
but those who are alert
will be *one step ahead!*
We *will* watch if we yearn
for our blessed Lord's return!
To *watch* is our duty
if we wish to walk
in incredible beauty!

MARK 14

The Passover draws near
and the Lamb is ready.
Though He knows what is to come
His will is strong and steady!
No lamb ever went to its slaughter
with so much confidence!
His love *is a love*
of which He *never* repents!
There is joy, gladness, and hope
in this chapter
also awful betrayal and doom.
But the future and the history
of the Church began
in the holy atmosphere
of that *Passover room!*
He sang a song with His disciples
and then went to meet His fate
but those deadly hours
germinated a love
that overcomes all hate!
Jesus knew, until His disciples
could see Him as their Risen Lord
their eyes would remain closed
and their spirits scarred.
It was as if the earth
revolved in reverse
the day He died in order
to lift sins awful curse!

The "I Love My Bible" Commentary

MARK 15

*Early in the morning
when the stars begin to yawn
sleepy people notice it is darkest
just before the dawn!
But this dawn was different
than the rest.
Though our Lord would die
the world would be blessed!
But-it was the darkest day
earth has ever known
because man placed
Jesus on the cross
instead of on the throne.
He knew
He could not rule
in the minds of men
until their hearts submit.
And until His disciples
could picture His great love
He could never quit!
So He kept His eyes on the Father
and His feet on
the cross-directed road.
He gave us His easy yoke
and took our heavy load!
This story is old but ever new!
On Mount Calvary
Jesus gave mankind
a holy different view!
Now we can see eternity
Because Jesus died
for me and you!*

MARK 16

*Rainbows everywhere.
Exceptional beauty to declare.
Dew freshens the morning air.
JESUS HAS RISEN!*

*Wordless people stand
and stare!
Where is the One
who was lying there?
The tomb is empty
the coffin bare!
JESUS HAS RISEN!*

*Evil men didn't care.
Doubtful men still unaware.
His was a power
extremely rare.
JESUS HAS RISEN!*

*Say there!
Have you some time to spare
for the One who has gone
to prepare
for that meeting in the air?
Then–others will say
we have risen!*

Note. They say dynamite comes in small packages and if Mark is an example than we have to say "Mark is a dynamite of a book!" Mark doesn't cover our Savior's birth, for he wants to get to the *business at hand*! His was the shortest of the gospels and he seems to have these great truths at his command! Don't short change Mark even though it is short! Beauty doesn't need an encyclopedia. It just needs to be told–and this time it was told, short and sweet!
Jesus sometimes preached long sermons and sometimes short. The length doesn't matter as long as the content is holy and true! He said 'I am the Way, the Truth, and the Life." That doesn't need to be long! All He is was summed up in that short sentence. It shouldn't take us long to decide to follow Him! Should it?

*Then said Jesus unto them again,
Verily, verily, I say unto you,*
I AM
*the door of the sheep.
All that ever came before me
are thieves and robbers;
but the sheep did not hear them.*
I AM *the door;
by me, if any man enter in,
he shall be saved,
and shall go in and out
and find pasture.
The thief cometh not, but to steal,
and to kill, and to destroy;*
I AM *come
that they might have life,
and they might have it more abundantly.*
I AM the Good Shepherd:
*the Good Shepherd giveth His life
for the sheep.*
(John 10: 7-11 kjv)

The "I Love My Bible" Commentary
(The Book of Luke)

LUKE 1

"Dear friend who loves God" is the world's
Greatest salutation
For there is no sweeter life or dearer love
That can give us cause for celebration!
To love our God completely sets our feet
On higher ground!
No song sung ever so sweetly can describe
A love so profound!
If only we could hear that sacred choir rehearse
Their song of love to the King of the universe!
They rehearsed for the time God sent an angel
To tell Zacharias a seemingly impossible story
Of One who was incredibly pure
Coming from His home in glory!
And his son John would prepare the way
For this One who brought an unequaled love
To this earth *to stay!*
We'd said, "you gotta be joking," if we were him
Which was almost what he said
For he was too old to have a son
And considered himself reproductively dead.
Its not safe to question an angel as he found out
And was struck dumb until time erased his doubt!
But Mary excepted Gabriel's news
Though she had more to lose
At least as far as this world is concerned.
She could have been stoned by the Jews
-or burned!
But then God is bigger than the Jews
Or the Romans, or all the world combined.
Sure–she would be ostracized, because they were
Spiritually blind!
But no man could erase the fact
God considered it time to act!
If this story was written in the skies
How many people would pause to lift their eyes
And would they view it(heaven forbid)
As lovely clouds drifting slowly away
Or, better still, would they let it
Change and bless their lives each day?

LUKE 2

In a sleepy little Judean village
obscured by most
sounds carried on the wind
to convey the glory
of the Lord of hosts!
But not even angels beautiful voices
could signify
the depth of the love or yearning
of this One who came to die!
He knew He would be rejected
and He was never truly respected.
But, earth couldn't wait
and time couldn't wait.
Man had become so evil
only evil was his fate.
Just a little love will do you
if you love Him in return.
He has too great a love
for any of us to spurn.
We can live without wealth.
We can live without fame.
But we just exist in empty space
if we refuse to praise His Name!
Now let the words we carry
be those He can commend!
When are we gong to realize
man has no greater friend?

LUKE 3

John was a great man of the hour
a hell-fire and brimstone preacher!
Jesus was the Son of God
yet they considered Him only a teacher!

Comment on Luke

But they both preached about the kingdom!
John could point the way.
Jesus told them *He was the way!*
John lost his head.
Jesus lost his heart!
For this was evil times
and men would not relinquish
their devilish crimes.
John was a voice crying
in the wilderness.
Jesus came to conquer it!
So different-yet so much alike.
But they killed John
and told Jesus to take a hike!
He wouldn't go away
He came to rescue His own!
He was different than anyone
they had ever known.
He came to set things straight.
Bigotry had turned love to hate!
God had said, "Love one another"
but hate had reigned
since Cain killed his brother.
It was a case of "show and tell"
a way to keep us out of hell.
Jesus said, "Come unto me!"
And that is about as simple
as simple can be!
He came
He saw
He conquered all
so that we would never
have to fall!

LUKE 4

Luke also tells of Jesus's temptation.
The devil resists the Holy Spirit
but it's a lost cause.
He couldn't keep Jesus from teaching
everyone of God's holy laws!
Over and over again he would try.
If not Jesus, he'd try another.
In the meantime Jesus's glory
was so great it was impossible
for this deceiver to smother.
Jesus returned from the wilderness
full of the Spirit
and spread God's truth to everyone
who longed to hear it!
He came to do so much
to free the captive
open blinded eyes
to answer all His people's
desperate cries.
He never failed a one who came
The weak, the weary, the hopeless
never were the same!
Only love can do so much!
Only love can heal our heartaches
with just a gentle touch.
And His touch was gentle
His love pure
His power impossible to describe!
Only love can feed a multitude
and leave them fully satisfied!
His doctrine was purer than the heavens
His teaching supreme!
No one left with their souls untouched
but many left unredeemed.
His stories brought wonder-and wrath.
-a wrath so strong they tried
to throw Him off a dead-end path.
He told the truth-nothing more
-nothing less
but he was rejected by hard hearted men
He had wanted to bless.
He had to keep moving on.
His mission officially began
when He faced temptation all alone!
He faced a long road ahead.
Many needed His living bread!

The "I Love My Bible" Commentary

LUKE 5

Jesus seemed to possess a knack for getting
Into trouble with the *"big shots!"*
It was because He loved the down and out
And the have-nots!
When He honored the prayers of the "little guys"
The "big" guys considered Him deranged.
And the more He loved *the little folks* the more
He and the Jewish leaders became estranged.
Consider the lepers who kneeled at His feet
Or the fishing boats that held a catch
Hard to beat!
Consider the paralytic who left his sleeping mat
And the Pharisees and other leaders complaining
  "Did you see that?"
They all griped when He didn't fast.
"The old ways are best," they said.
But Jesus knew they wouldn't last.
And to think these people had the chance
  to choose
The incredible joy of walking 'in His shoes!'

LUKE 6

Jesus healed a man who was crippled
And his enemies were wild with rage.
He came to bring them love but they lived
  in the hating age!
No one was ever watched as closely as He.
And no one understood the matchless glory
They were privileged to see!
They followed him like vultures waiting to tear
Every good deed into shreds of despair.
His love was 100% high octane fuel
Yet their hatred drove them to be unusually cruel.
But, somewhere scattered among that crowd
Were twelve men who longed to be
Citizens of that kingdom He called eternity!
He drew them to Him in a kind and gentle way.
They would need His strength to face
The spiritual perverts of His day
And always-always-His message was love
  loud and clear!
Every other emotion would dissipate and decay
But the holy, precious love of God would never
  ever fade away!

LUKE 7

The greatest joy in the world did not come
From pleasure- mad people at play
But from those who were able to declare
"We have seen the hand of God at work today!"
The greatest faith did not come from those
Who crowded near
But from a hated gentile who considered
His servant very dear!
Even John would question God's great power
Could prison have caused this man to cower?
Jesus's answer should encourage all
Whose courage falters and whose faith is small.
"Blessed is he," He said
"Who does not lose faith in me!"
And He added there was no one
Greater than John in all humanity!
Yet, in that kingdom no greater than Jesus
Could be found.
Still the wolf pack hung around!
But, everyone who felt His touch
Knew why He said of the woman
"She has loved me much!"
And, still those who come kneeling
Receive a gloriously magnificent healing!

LUKE 8

Wherever Jesus went
the needy came
to receive healing
and left
praising His name!

Comment on Luke

Whenever He spoke
the demons fled.
They knew there was power
in what He said!
Winds could not resist Him
nor waves overcome His will
and even the forces of nature yielded
when He told them
"Peace be still!"
But isn't it strange to hear these men ask
"Who is this man?"
They had walked and talked
and ate with Him
from the time His work began!
Ask the woman who touched His hem
and then fell at His feet!
Ask the little girl who had
tasted death
and then found life utterly sweet!
Would they ask, "Who is this man"
when His power had flowed
through their veins?
And what about the demoniac
who discovered God truly reigns!
Our Lord had an answer
for every question
hope for every need
and we can say today
"He is Lord indeed!"
Though He knew of the pain to come
-could see Himself hanging
between two thieves
and knew he would be labeled
only a bum
our marvelously glorious Savior
made Himself a non-person
so all people could have the chance
to feel like a king!
He hung on a cross
where He asks us to kneel
and accept the hope
only He can bring!
It was also important to Him
that every man
refuse to be distracted
from God's holy plan.
He bids us walk
the straight and narrow.
"Don't worry," He says.
"Remember the little sparrow!"

LUKE 9

When Jesus said to do something
He always had the means even though
The 'pickings' were small!
After these men having seen His power
I marvel at them doubting Him at all!
It seems to me they were unnecessarily rude
When Jesus told them to share their food.
If only they'd realized His food for the soul
Was to teach them *the cross was His goal!*
After Jesus told them of His impending death
Three of them witnessed His transfiguration!
It's as if He said, "Don't worry about the cross
Because I will overcome that situation!"
Our Lord showed displeasure very few times
For He had such a patient heart
But He knew His disciples had little faith
And His time was so short.
So, another man and his little boy
Left the Savior's presence full of joy.
Later He tell His disciples the importance
Of having faith as a little child
For the Father's heart *is wide open*
To those who are meek and mild!
Then He talks about spiritual offense
And assures them it makes absolutely no sense!
We are the *salt of the earth*!
We are to be kind to others.
And our goodness can be a flavor of life
To our unsaved brothers!

The "I Love My Bible" Commentary

LUKE 10

Our Lord has an universal love
that will overcome a world of hate
and He told these people it takes love
to get them through heaven's gate!
But He has chosen to use
people like you and me
to tell others how much
He longs to set them free!
He said the harvest is ripe
but the laborers are few
and many need to know
what our Father is willing to do!
Those seventy rejoiced
at their might
but Jesus told them
to rejoice only that their names
were written in heaven
and they had been chosen
to walk in the light!
He is willing to teach us
how to help each other
and that His *flame of love*
is one no one can smother!
It was to His words Mary heeded
because she *knew* what she needed.
And, like Martha we must learn
to walk in the light of His words each day
and then we will gain a great faith
that will never go away!

LUKE 11

God has no midnight.
We can go to Him at any hour!
His is a loving concern no demon
anywhere can devour.
Jesus said keep on asking
for God will reply
and He will give His Holy Spirit
in answer when we cry!
After all the miracles they saw
our Lord perform
How could these people ever
have wished Him harm?
No matter what He did
they considered it a spoof
and refused to believe though
He gave them ample proof!
Have you noticed those who doubted
were those who claimed
to know the most
and they hated Him because
He showed them they had nothing
in which to boast?
Yes, they hated Him because
He ridiculed their demands
and, despite the hardness
of their hearts, they knew
they deserved His reprimands!

LUKE 12

First of all, it was His disciples
who needed the Sermon on the Mount!
For what else could give them
courage on which they could count?
Jesus added a few parables
to confuse those who thought
they were wise
and used them to open
His disciples simple and trusting eyes!
His people didn't need
mighty sermons to help them grow.
Just down home love
and heavenly truths
was all He wanted them to know!
Wisdom's greatest truths
can be spun
with common threads!

Comment on Luke

*and the golden tongue
of our Messiah
would weave marvelous tapestry
in hearts instead of heads!*
He had so little time
and longed to teach them
so very much.
Our Lord wanted them to always
remember His Word
and to feel His gentle touch!
It was(and is)
our Heavenly Father's desire
to feed His flock
and through the ages
we are to remember
He is our solid Rock!
Now, if we want our lives to count
we must be careful to live
by the Sermon on the Mount!

LUKE 13

*Christ walked among many
but 'knew' only a few
for they sought not the Master
but only what He could do.
They did not say
"Lord, touch my soul
for it is there I need you most!"
Instead, they wanted signs
and wonders in which
they could boast.
And when they piously told of others
on whom they considered
God's judgement to be sent
our Lord searched their hearts
and then replied
"Yours will be a similar fate
unless you repent!"
He helped a woman stand
straight and tall
and they used the "Sabbath"
as an excuse to hide
they had no love for her at all!
I marvel that the Lord continued
to walk among these hypocrites
for the greater His mercy
the bigger their fits!
But I feel His heart break
when He has to say
"You've rejected me Jerusalem
and now I have to turn away!"*

LUKE 14

*Where the dove lights
there will be hawks.
Wherever there is simple
eloquent goodness
someone squawks!
They used a sick man
to bait their prey.
Still the Lord healed him
before He sent him away.
They set themselves up.
He put them down!
But it was only because
they refused to honor
this One worthy of a crown!
"Be open," He said.
"And be ready!
And let your love for Me
be strong and steady!"
His disciples would climb
to heights unknown.
They had accepted the King
who was worthy
of a heavenly throne!
The 'Mountain' had come
to these men
and in loving, eternal forgiveness
had saved them from their sin!*

The "I Love My Bible" Commentary

LUKE 15

Man says, "A bird in the hand
is worth two in the bush."
But it is the ones in the bush
that God seeks!
The misguided
the wayward, the lost, the fearful
are those of whom our Savior speaks!
And it seems the value of heaven
is not cherished until it is missed!
Explaining that was an opportunity
our Savior could not resist!
But even the story of the prodigal son
was at its best
a faded, elusive picture
of the loving heart
beating in the Father's breast!
And we would witness at any cost
if we could fully understand
how much our heavenly Father
loves the lost!

LUKE 16

The choices we make are the balancing act
That determines whether we rise or fall.
The tight rope of faith pulls us forward
To the greatest life of all!
But what if we leave the Lord out
And choose money instead?
And fail to reverence the One
Who gives us our daily bread?
Though the rope may stretch just a little bit
It may be enough to send our hopes
To the deepest pit!
Yet the ones who see us falter fail to perceive
How anxious our Lord waits
To grant us reprieve!
And those who choose money will never feel
The glorious salvation from a love that is real!

Those were our Lord's ultimate goals.
To show us true wealth and to save our souls!

LUKE 17

It's no light thing for one to lead another astray!
An awful punishment awaits that person
On God's final judgement day.
Even 'faith' has been misused by the masses
For there is a much reduced level of faith
Where pride and humility clashes.
"Be not proud of your faith," Jesus was saying.
But–to keep pride out of our hearts
Takes a *lot* of praying!
Of course, faith in God will be our defense
When the world comes to an end
Because-you see-grace is kind and gentle
But the *law won't bend!*

LUKE 18

The blind man could not see
  yet he could see better
   than those who could look
    into the Savior's eyes!
   He was a *nobody*
    an indigent debtor
   but the greatness of his faith
    took the others by surprise!
   Our Lord allowed no one to
    to turn him away
  because he had the kind of childish faith
  Jesus had mentioned earlier in the day!
   He was merciful to the one
  who beat on his chest and cried out loud
    but Jesus pictured unforgiveness
     for the self-righteously proud.
    Every city our Savior entered
     every path our Savior trod
      He displayed the forgiving
      tender, loving side of God!

Comment on Luke

LUKE 19

A man named Zacchaeus, short in stature
Needed to see Jesus, so he climbed a tree!
He was a man of great riches but he felt
His heart would never be free.
How could he know he would someday
See the Savior face to face
And receive an immeasurable portion
Of God's amazing grace?
The Publicans complained of course
But they could have until they were hoarse
And Jesus would have saved him anyway.
Again, our Lord showed His mercy
By forgiving Zacchaeus that day!
He considered Zacchaeus one of Israel's
   lost sheep!
And He forgives every sin no matter how deep!
He went to Jerusalem to visit the temple there
But the crooked merchants brought him despair.
For you see, it was supposed to be
A serene and beautiful house of prayer!
He won no honor from the 'big shots' that day
Because He turned all the crooks away!
When ever you see a church and its steeple
Remember, it is a house of prayer for all people!

LUKE 20

Wherever the Lord preached the *good news*
He was confronted by the *goody-two-shoes!*
They wanted to know who gave Him authority
To drive the merchants away
Even though they knew God's glorious temple
Was primarily a place for His people to pray.
He answered them with a question.
"Was John a prophet?"
And they said they didn't know.
His question was so *hot*, they had to drop it
And of course they changed the subject!
They showed a coin that bounced in their faces
When His remark put them in their places.
What He said is still relevant today!
The Government demands their piece of pie
Even before we can give God His share.
But then the governments of this world
Think they come first
And mistakenly think God doesn't care.
God only asks for a tenth.
Look at what they take!
And its hard for most to get by
On the measly amount of money they make!
But always remember the temple is a place
Where God solves your needs with His grace!

LUKE 21

Its an equation we don't understand
When one so poor gave all in her hand.
The widow-though what she gave was small
Was credited with giving more than them all!
So—giving is measured by the heart
When we joyfully give our *little part!*
But there is more He wanted us to remember.
Giving of yourself is not a weekender!
Its all of us every day, when at work or at play.
Once Jesus implied we would not thirst
If we'd only learn to put God first!
He knew His followers would be hated
As was He.
But He has a love that will guide us
Safely into eternity.
Though it seems today's wickedness
That creates a blinding mist
Will cause people to think God's promises
Have ceased to exist
God will prove they certainly do.
Watch for the day He will rescue me and you!
He has a love many will spurn
And there will always be doubters who jeer
But I'm still looking for Him to return
And He will find me waiting here!

The "I Love My Bible" Commentary

LUKE 22

And now, the Passover!
The reason for His coming
-the coming of a new age!
It was time for Him
to exit this world's stage.
He had confronted His enemies
and listened to them rage.
He had gathered His lambs
to His heart
and now it was time
for Him to depart.
But first the Passover!
He had come to the Jew
the Gentile
displayed His power
to every believer
but many refused to wear
the garments of salvation
woven by the Master Weaver!
Now He gives His disciples wine
to picture His blood
and to picture His body
as the <u>bread</u> of life
he gives His disciples each
a slice!
Yet, when He needed His disciples
they slept
while He suffered in agony
all alone.
The drops of blood
He sweated in the garden
were for unbelieving hearts
made of stone.
Yet, His disciples slept
and He suffered all alone!
He was seized and ridiculed
by the Pharisees
and Peter denied
ever knowing Him.
It seems He would die friendless
rejected-as He said-by
the leaders of Jerusalem!
And we imagine Him saying again
"Oh, Jerusalem, Jerusalem
I would have gathered you
as a mother hen
but you have chosen instead
to live in sin."

LUKE 23

Herod and Pilate
two peas in a pod.
Neither had any moral
aptitude for God.
Yet Pilate did believe
Jesus had committed no crime
and he tried to release Jesus
one more time.
But the rabble rousers began to fuss.
"Kill Him," they said
"and release Barabbas to us."
They chose a filthy assassin
and turned the King of truth away
So Pilate delivered Jesus
to His enemies that awful day.
Even in death He promised
life to a thief
who hung on an adjoining cross.
They entered Paradise together
while those who killed Him
faced a terrible loss.
He gave Himself back to God!
THAT was their plan
when they discussed His coming
to bring new life to man!
So give your 'self' to Jesus
He gave Himself for you!
To gain a love so great
-that's the least we can do!

Comment on Luke

LUKE 24

They had gone home, weeping.
Darkness had come to everyone.
They had watched Him die
and saw the darkness
of the midnight sun!
Bound by matchless grace
the circle of love is now closed
and we see that grace is greater
than man ever supposed!
Now!!!
The hope of the ages reappears
to erase all fears
to dry all tears!
And very early in the morning
when hope rises to 'high C'
He who is the melody of the ages
performs the living notes
for you and me!

His circle of love
has closed in
and His matchless grace
has included all men!
No matter how far we may go
we cannot leave
His circle of love.
No matter how lonely
we may feel
we can have the joy
Of that presence from above!
The circle of love
may it grow!
And may I never forget
His is the sweetest love
I will ever know.
It's a love tried and true!
It's a love available to you!
And all the angels will rejoice
when you make Him your choice!

Note: Now–as He said, "It is finished!" He did His part. He gave His all for us. Now, new life is available for us. It sounds so simple some do not believe it. Why would God send His son to suffer? Why? It was so we could know we can triumph over sin! It was so He could arise to show us incredible victory! *It was so we could have a personal relationship with God!* It was so we would never have to suffer all alone, never *feel all alone*, never think we have to earn our way to heaven, which we can't! *AND THAT IS WHY JESUS CAME, DIED AND ROSE AGAIN!*

Paul said we earn rewards, but he knew we could never earn heaven.

"For by grace are you saved
through faith
and that not of yourselves:
it is the gift of God *not of works*
lest any man should boast.
For we are *His Workmanship*
CREATED IN CHRIST JESUS
unto good works....
(Ephesians 2:8-9)

The "I Love My Bible" Commentary
(The Book of John)

JOHN 1

In the beginning was the Word!
In the beginning!
It was God's Word that set
the world to spinning!
In the beginning was God's love!
In the beginning!
Because of God
from day one Adam was
accustomed to winning!
But Adam turned his back
on God
and suddenly God was gone
and Adam was left
with no great friend
to help him carry on.
It grew darker through the years.
The more men walked away
from God
the greater his fears!
Now we see Christ
coming to claim His own.
Here he was!
He made the world
and the world knew Him not.
Many still don't know Him today.
Many still don't care
that He came to show the way.
It's a straight and narrow path
and so is the gate.
There are so few who love
really love
and so many who hate.
But why hate when love is near?
Why be confused
when the facts are clear?
He came to claim His own
yet many still struggle all alone.
So, I ask again
Why do we struggle?
He is still God!
He brought us love and joy
and peace and rest.
All that He gives or gave
is the very best!
Fortunately there were a few
who would accept His love
and cling to His grace!
Those who did
discovered the joy
of looking on His face!
And-according to the Word
they were looking at the One
who lovingly, carefully
<u>*began the beginning!*</u>

JOHN 2

The first miracle Jesus performed
was to honor wedded bliss
-a blessing on a marriage
from the very first kiss!
The show and tell of God's delight
was to bring purity to
the wedding night!
Old traditions never die.
Humanity just sweeps them
under the rug
and wants no commitment involved
in any kiss or hug.
God says. " make marriage
last a life time!"
Mankind ties the knot
and then *turns on a dime.*
Worse yet
he doesn't seem to know
what *knots* are for
nor worries about the innocent lives
he might carelessly mar.

Comment on John

Honesty in relationships
should be a *must*
yet mankind is more changeable
than were those
our Lord didn't trust!

JOHN 3

(The truth starts with this and ends with this!)
"For God so loved the world that He gave
His only Begotten Son, that *whosoever*
believeth in Him should not perish, but have
everlasting life!"
EVERLASTING LIFE!

Jesus said that to one
who came *'to the Light'*
(and He was the Light)
in the obscurity of the night.
Jesus looked into his heart
and knew what he really needed.
And in that soft plowed ground
of readiness
eternal life was seeded!
Our Lord compared himself
to the serpent lifted on the *pole!*
He said
*"When I am lifted up
I will make you whole!"*
He came to show God's love for man
and brought along salvation's plan.
This plan so great has bogged in the mire
of the doubt and disbelief of man
who have never felt God's holy fire!
"Those who don't believe," He said
will feel God's wrath
and their disobedience will take them
down an ignominious path.
Yes!
*God so loved the world
that He gave the One
He loved the most.
And that, my friends should compel us
to witness from sea to sea
and from coast to coast!*

JOHN 4

Jesus sat down at the well on a shaded bench.
The woman came with a thirst
No one else could ever quench!
Jesus gazed into her heart and discovered
Her life was sinful and broken.
She was surprised that it was to her
Whom a Jew had spoken!
The water He gave her was in life-giving
Perpetual motion!
Our Lord not only saved her, but won
The whole town's devotion!
He knew the woman had sinned. So did they!
In curiosity, they all followed her that day.
The woman at the well has many counter-parts
Who need the Savior to heal their broken hearts!
Jesus considered it nourishing to do God's will
And He lovingly says to us, "Peace be still!"
Though we may never know how lonely
Another person may feel
We can guarantee they will receive God's help
When their worship is spiritual and real!

JOHN 5

Some people never give up hope!
Consider the man at the pool.
Don't you suppose after all
those years of waiting
some called him a fool?
And when Jesus told him
to take up his mat
(and walk)
many must have thought
"Why couldn't I do that?"

The "I Love My Bible" Commentary

Our Lord healed souls
even more dramatically
than He healed the lame.
His power to heal spiritually
or mentally or physically
is still the same!
But many people doubt the many miracles
of which we've heard
but it is because so many of them
do not know His word.
I'm speaking of heart knowledge
that watches for God to act
for indeed, everything He says
is an irrefutable, eternal fact!
In His day
many claimed they believed Moses
but He said that wasn't true
for, He said
"Had you believed Moses
you would have believed me too!"

JOHN 6

The Bread of Life
soothes life's hunger pains
And His blood, though red as crimson
removes sin's ugly stains!
Why was what He said
so insulting to the crowd?
They had eaten the food He offered
and in His presence humbly bowed!
The truths He revealed in this chapter
caused many to turn away.
Those who were seeking
only physical food
disgustedly left Him that day.
But dear old Peter said
"To whom shall we go?
Thou has the Words of Life!"
But he didn't see too well
for when He rebuked Jesus
for saying He was going to the cross
Jesus knew that fact came
from the one who inhabited hell.
Even Peter was not 100% right
and had to be corrected.
Remember, Jesus searches our hearts
and only in Him, are we perfected!

JOHN 7

The world didn't love Him, for He was such
A sharp contrast
To the fickle traditions He said wouldn't last.
He was "forever"
But they didn't see, or accept, Him that way
And they knew they were going to kill Him
And it would make their day.
And they did. But He came back anyway!
Ignorance of the scriptures will pervert
A stubborn , unbelieving heart.
Remember how those Pharisees viewed Him
–as a devious upstart!
Their blinded hearts did not know Jesus
Nor from where He came
And their lust for life *became a dying flame.*
"How can He know so much?" they asked.
"He's never been to *our* schools."
(They didn't know He was the true Professor)
And all those who loved the our great Messiah
Were considered ignorant fools.
But this one they called a Galilean
Was so much more!
He was the *bridge* over the Jordan river
That joined them to Heaven's shore!

JOHN 8

"You don't know me!" Jesus said.
They were spiritually deaf and dumb.
They doubted our Lord so much
Their hearts had grown numb.

Comment on John

The good news He brought
though it shouldn't be, was alien to them
and not the answer these people sought.
If and when they followed Him
it was to ridicule
especially when He said
He had come to rule!
They brought Him a woman caught in adultery
to test His 'expertise'
but He sent them packing when He granted
her precious soul release!
She met the Living One
whose *light* would flood her path!
He was older than Abraham He said
and those Pharisees questioned
His heavenly knowledge of math!
"Sure," they said mockingly.
"You're not fifty years old.
Sure, you've seen Abraham!"
They didn't know, could not see
they were talking to *The Great I Am!*
He tried to convince them
that everything He said was on the level
and they responded with
"You are possessed by a devil."
Most importantly, He advised them
to live as He told them to.
Then they would have the power of truth
to give them a freedom fresh and new!
Truth is God's middle name!
Love is His first!
And He promises Living Water
to everyone who thirsts!
Yes, all His claims were true and right
and when we follow Him
we'll always have His light!

JOHN 9

The age old question was asked
about the man born blind.
Jesus's disciples wondered if his parents
had been sinful, or at least unkind.
And Jesus must have thought
it was the living end
for them to imply an innocent baby
had already sinned
even before he had the chance
thereby saying that God punishes
even in advance!
What a foolish question
and what a cruel thought
when Jesus felt love for this man
who was one of the needy He sought!
The Pharisees played the *bad guys* again
for they ostracized this lucky man.
But–he was wiser than they.
He believed in the One who said
I am the Life, the Truth, and the Way!
Those who were spiritually blind stood by
never grasping the glorious truth
their unwilling hearts chose to deny!
For didn't Jesus say
"I have come that you might have life?"
You bet He did!
His work is to see that salvation
will not, cannot be hid.
Jesus is the Soul Specialist
-just one of a kind!
He brings food to the hungry soul
sight to the spiritually blind.
He says emphatically
"I love you so very, very much"
and He heals the broken hearted
with the miracle of His touch!
But in this day He has chosen
our hearts, our hands, our feet.
Its His way of involving us
to make His work on earth complete.
We will not stumble in *heavy mist*
if we will only rely on the expertise
of the Soul specialist!

The "I Love My Bible" Commentary

JOHN 10

There is a gate for the sheep
formidable, impressive, never closed!
This Living Gate easily overcomes
any problem ever posed!
The "Gate" becomes the "Shepherd"
when the sheep leave the fold.
Wherever they wander, He wanders
for there could be frightened sheep
He may need to hold!
Jesus proved His Messiahship
by His love for the sheep!
The Father had given Him many souls
—and these, He had sworn to keep!
No one else ever gave so much
for so many
and was cherished by so few.
But He gave life to His followers
—fresh, wholesome, brand new!
Only He could love
unconditionally
until the end!
Only He could give protection
on which His lambs
could depend!
This keeper of the sheepfold
is enfolded in our hearts
and when my time on earth is over
and my soul departs
the Shepherd will go
where I go
stay where I stay
for He has promised me
He will never go away!

JOHN 11

Jesus viewed death as sleep
-a time when one's soul
journeys from earth to awake
on heaven's shore!
And He illustrated His power to raise the dead.
Therefore many believed on Him
who had not believed before!
But, still there were questions asked
that angered our Lord
and I suppose even Mary thought
raising Lazarus would be too hard.
Did this miracle please the Pharisees?
Heavens no!
This was when they really decided
Jesus had to go!
They offered great resistance
and were thoroughly organized.
But they found out our Lord
was not easily mesmerized!
And though he would be arrested
brutalized, and killed
the great mission of the ages
would soon be fulfilled!
Many Jews would come to the temple
to partake of pesach
(pronounced pa sock)
and to meet the One David had called
"Israel's solid rock!"
Now the time was drawing near
for the event
that brought our Blessed Savior here!
But the 'hurricane' was off the coast
waiting to blow in
waiting for the day
that human nature would seem to win.
What is the saying?
You can't keep a good man down!
We'll soon see Jesus coming back
and this time
He will be wearing a crown!
Its not over until its over
and we will get to see
the King of all the Ages
returning for you and me!

Comment on John

JOHN 12

"We've lost" is not for sons of the King!
Ask Lazarus who escaped
 death's unholy sting.
Ask Mary who brought expensive perfume
 to anoint our Lord.
And, even ask those who waved
 their palm branches in one accord!
But, first think deeply about our Savior.
 Think of how His goodness
 contrasted with man's evil behavior.
Think of how the Pharisees stood aloof
because their blinded eyes could not see
 nor did their tainted souls
 long to be free.
"We've lost" was the confession
 of tainted souls
 *laced with the strychnine
 of unholy goals.*
And the battle of disbelief
 still rages
 supported by those who oppose
 the King of the Ages!

JOHN 13

Our Lord gave a sign of humility
For His disciples to embrace and pass on!
And all God's people, to be successful
Must walk within that humility zone!
But Peter would not stick out his feet!
"My gosh," he said. "You can't wash me!"
He flunked his first lesson in humility!
But he quickly changed his mind
When Jesus insisted
For he knew how much he needed cleansing
And should never have resisted.
But humility tears at our egos-rips pride apart
And plays havoc with a haughty heart!
Yet we must learn-like Peter-how pride ends
In a dark and lonely street
And-like Peter-realize how badly we need
Our Savior's cleansing to make our lives
 complete!
But we still wonder why would Jesus kneel
At the feet of those unworthy to untie his shoes
And I suspect we'd be like Peter who was
Thoroughly shocked and chose to refuse!
But, we need our Lord's cleansing daily
Just like He said
Because, as He says, there's *glory* up ahead!
 And then the meal!!!
This meal pictured His eternal propitiation
 *Only He could do so much
 with unswerving dedication!
 His body given for me!
 Wonder of wonders
 He sets me free!
 Someday I will be able to meet
 This One who made my cleansing
 pure and complete!
 And we will share His bread and wine
 in that heavenly Palestine!*

JOHN 14

*"Let not your heart be troubled!"
 Those who heard Him
 had double treasure.
With God in heaven and Jesus on earth
 their faith could grow
 to double measure!
There would be one more surprise.
 The Holy Spirit would come
to be a constant, comforting friend!
"Let not your heart be troubled!"
Our Savior whispers soft and low
 for I have sent a friend
 a special Holy Friend
 to go with you
 wherever you may go!*

The "I Love My Bible" Commentary

Our Lord's only demand is that
we love and obey Him
but think of our great reward!
In return we are promised
the triune presence of our Lord!
Our Savior's love for us was so great
He willingly faced a horror
we cannot describe
and a dilemma we can never recreate.
Jesus knew God hated sin so much
He would have to turn away.
But He had to open the door
for the Holy Spirit
to walk into our hearts
and He did it on what is known
as the earth's darkest day!
Our Lord tells us
"Let not your hearts be troubled"
because He knows
someday
sometime
somewhere
somehow
we will accept His offer
of the glorious life
the Holy Spirit bestows!

JOHN 15

Only the true vine can wind
His tendrils around our hearts
and our hearts around His
little finger!
Apart from Him
we are pathetically inadequate.
So...close to Him is where
our hearts must linger!
We must live within His love
walk within His light.
If our cup of joy would be full
we must keep our blessed Master
close within our sight!
We didn't choose Him.
He chose us to walk by His side!
And wonder of wonders!
Because of Jesus
I am fully satisfied!

JOHN 16

Our Lord wanted to teach His disciples
   much, much more
But His time on earth was running out.
He knew they would scatter at His arrest
For their hearts were still full of doubt.
But He would send the Holy Spirit to be their
   guide
And soon they would not hide
Behind locked doors, trembling inside!
The Holy Spirit would give them strength
And boldness to testify
Of Jesus and all the events that just passed by!
You might say they were given a blank check
   to spend
Knowing all the soul's expenses would be paid
By Jesus who proclaimed He was their friend!
He overcame the world and gave them peace
   of mind
And left us the knowledge that our Lord
Is indisputably kind!
"Cheer up," Jesus whispers in our ears!
"I have come to conquer all your fears!"
He told them all His heart in His discussion
During the Passover meal.
It would be their last before His death
And He knew the devastation they would feel!
But had they really be listening they would
Have known it was only for a little while
He would rise again and light their faces
With a triumphant, happy smile!
It would be over. Yes?   No!!!
There would be one more thing left to show!

Comment on John

JOHN 17

Take note, dear Christian
when you feel all alone
and it seems no one cares for you.
You are strictly on your own.
You feel as if no one prays in your behalf.
Troubles have overwhelmed you
and you've forgotten how to laugh.
Read John chapter seventeen.
Read it again!
Read how Jesus prayed for you
and, never again, should you feel
no one cares what you do!
Jesus reached out and touched you
two thousand years ago.
He made a point of mentioning us
so *all* of us would know
there will never be a time
we are not loved and cherished!
And of all those who accepted Him
(for whom He prayed)
none have ever perished!
We may be living in a deadly hour
but remember unbelief
has no lasting power.
He WILL come again for His own
and we'll rejoice
around that great white throne!
I'd like to inject a thought
from chapter ten
of how easily He protects us from sin.
"My sheep hear my voice
and they follow me!"
The thought is not that Jesus
will lead us through green pastures
but that all pastures will be blessed
by the touch of His feet!
Not that He draws us to the mountain tops
but He gives us a dream
of a mountain top meeting
that will be incredibly sweet!
That was the crux of His prayer.
He wants us all to meet Him there!

JOHN 18

Earth must have trembled
at the stomping of their feet.
They were approaching the One
they were not worthy to meet.
The betrayer who walked among them
should have trembled too.
The world, heaven, nor hell
would forget what he chose to do.
He saw Jesus heal
but his heart clutched the money
in his hands.
It would never save a soul
nor fulfill one heart's demands.
Our hearts demand peace.
Jesus freely gave it!
Life is precious.
Jesus came to save it!
But
they marched on to confront the One
who knew His work was almost done!
Did they see how calmly
He faced them?
Did they see the love in His face?
Did they ever stop to think
He had come to save them
by His marvelous grace?
The night had begun
with the songs
Jesus and His disciples had sung.
And now the music fades
into unmelodic deep dark shades!
And we see the idiots choose Barabbas
and turn Jesus away.
And this was the beginning
of a long, dark day!

The "I Love My Bible" Commentary

JOHN 19

Our Lord's greatest pain
was not on that cross
silhouetted against the sky.
It was when Pilate said
"Behold the man"
and the crowd yelled, "crucify!"
Those nails only pierced
His hands and His feet.
It was their words that hurt
deep in His heart
when their rejection was complete.
And though the clamor would increase
it was *their* shame He died to release!
They looked on Him
whom they had pierced
but could not see the "Light"
and those who were so cruel
could not imagine their plight.
Pilate's words have drifted down
To this time span
and we, too, must
"Behold the Man!"

JOHN 20

Mary Magdalene was still in shock
when the sun peeked over the hill
and the morning she walked
to the Lord's tomb.
His death had broken her will.
He, who had over come Lazarus's death
had not prevented His own!
His enemies had made thorns His crown
and the cross His throne.
But little did she know
nor could even guess
at the incredible power
this Holy One possessed!
Raise others? Maybe!
Himself? No!
Now that HE was dead
to whom could He go?
But He turned death into a flower
that bloomed in the night
and Mary found Him
in the garden
much to her delight!

JOHN 21

They met one more time
by the lake of Galilee.
They didn't realize
when the Savior left
how lonely they would be.
But the Lord put in an appearance
-maybe His last!
And once again Peter and John
seemed to head the cast.
There must have been jealousy
between the two
for when Peter asked about John
Jesus answered
"What is that to you?"
He wanted Peter to feed His lambs.
John might tarry!
Could that be?
But, most importantly
our Lord still asks the question
"Do you *really* love me?"

Comment on John

Note: John wrote with his heart because he had leaned on Jesus's breast and heard His heartbeat, felt His love, cherished His grace, and believed on His miracles. It was at the Passover meal that Jesus let His *hair down* and opened His heart to His disciples who hung on to ever word He said!

They had walked with Him, gazed on His face, slept on the same hard ground He did, and felt the pillow of His love! Especially John! It was inevitable that the book of John would be more spiritual than the others. Maybe he gained that spirituality by osmosis, but I suspect it was through love! He seemed to have that trusting-child kind of love Jesus sought.

No where did Jesus open up His heart as completely as He did(as told)in John chapters 14-16, and no where else do we hear Him praying for us as He did in John 17. Read John 17 and then re-read John 14-16 and, incidently it would be ideal to memorize and carry daily in your heart. It's the way Jesus wants us to draw near to Him and it's the way He wants to draw near to us. Otherwise we become full of doubt and fear. Doubt is a tight corset that squeezes our faith and fear is a heavy fur coat that smothers it! Jesus offers us the fresh air of His love. Read about it in the book of John.

The "I Love My Bible" Commentary
(The Book of Acts)

ACTS 1

Can one look up and look forward
    at the same time?
    Ask our Lord's friends.
    Our Lord had taught them
    about love, about life
and about a hope that never ends!
Though He disappears into a cloud
    the cloud could not obscure
    the gift of life He had given
which was holy and wonderfully pure!
    "Forward" is His battle cry
    upward His only direction
    and He has given us the "Church"
    to help us find perfection!

ACTS 2

The leaders of Israel considered the apostles
To be men of lowly estate
But as they listened to Peter and the others
They realized these men were offering them
Something wonderful, something great!
Think of their response, their thoughts!
O my soul, don't consider a moments hesitation
For these men offer the guarantee of salvation!
Take it! For the greatest joy you'll ever know
The sweetest words you'll ever hear
Is that gentle voice of Jesus saying
"Child, I am with you! I am here!"
It was a golden opportunity for each soul.
God was offering them salvation!
Did He really want to make them whole?
Hadn't He said that always?
Coming to Him would bring better days!
Life is not life without His presence!
He speaks of a sweet smelling savor
–a holy essence.
Yet our Lord has been denied
By countless, thoughtless, evil men
Who never admitted He came to save us
From even our deepest, darkest sin.
    But I say
    as for me–O my soul,
    I will never forget
    the day my Jesus
    made me whole!
In these times, just like the days of Pentecost
There are many people confused, many lost!
And evil events like those of nine-eleven
Remind us how much we need more of heaven!

ACTS 3

Peter and John take part in a meeting
  none of them would ever forget.
And to the one who had been crippled
    the beautiful gate was more
    beautiful yet!
    I bet when he left that temple
  he must have jumped over that gate
    for he felt a happiness
    no one could possibly abate!
  But, Peter and John took no credit.
    They gave the credit to our Lord
    and those hypocritical Pharisees
    who watched and listened
must have had their consciences jarred!
    The wonderful message
    the Apostles preached
encouraged many to turn from sin
    for our Savior came because
  it was His desire to save all men!
    Thousands were saved that day
    and joyfully walked
    along the King's Highway!
And for those who continue to roam
    we say
Jesus is the way back home!

Comment on Acts

ACTS 4

The power of faith was revealed
when a forty year old man was healed!
Then the apostles were told
not to preach in Jesus's holy name.
But they told the Pharisees
salvation is much too important
not to proclaim!
Opposition seems to fire
their faith to new heights
and the Lord's people react
in a way in which He delights!
Oh, how they loved Him
and could not rest.
Even if they would lose their lives
they had to do their best!
There were countless new professions
and those who believed
showed their faith
by sharing their possessions.
No wonder those Pharisees fumed.
The saving and healing power of Jesus
had now been resumed!

ACTS 5

People trying to fool the Holy Spirit. Oh, my!
It is certainly foolish to try to tell God a lie.
They thought they were fooling dear old Peter
But their deception
Brought them an unwanted final rejection.
This story of Ananias and Sapphira
Was included as if to say
"Fool not the Holy Spirit who lives in you today!"
The Lord knows when we are untrue
And He knows everything we do.
So why try to fool the one who lives in me
When He saved me from lies and hypocrisy?
Let us be like those apostles who were proud
And honest men
Who humbly told about Jesus who came
To save all men from their sin!
They met plenty of opposition
From the establishment
But still preached that forgiveness is available
For ALL who repent!

ACTS 6

As the believers increased
so did the discontent.
Equality was being introduced
to people who didn't know
what equality meant!
Now that the church was growing
so large
it almost became a business
needing men of integrity
to take charge!
The apostles would do the preaching!
The deacons would take care of
the people's needs.
But whether it's the soul
needing substance
or sustenance for the body
it's the Lord who feeds!
Obviously, there are many ways
we need to be reached
but our growth is more dramatic
when God's Word is preached!

ACTS 7

First the apostles face harassment
and now the deacons felt their wrath!
Stephen told how their ancestors
had persecuted holy men
and now the Jewish leaders
had chosen the same hideous path.
Stephen began with Abraham

The "I Love My Bible" Commentary

and took them through David's time.
He told them they were stiff-necked
heathen
with hearts full of crime!
They couldn't take it anymore
and, whipped to mob-madness
decided to even the score.
But Stephen had seen the Glory
of God!
He could not be scathed
and he worried that God
would punish these men
for the way they behaved.
He looked beyond their hatred
to that throne above
and in glorious anticipation
walked toward the God of love!

ACTS 8

I believe Stephen's death haunted Saul
Though he persecuted other Christians
Trying to kill them all.
But the believers fled in all directions
Taking along the story
Of the love that Jesus brought to earth
And everywhere they went
They told of our Savior's glory!
Peter, John, and Phillip had great influence
On people in far away places.
Even Simon, the magician, coveted their power
And the love he could see on their faces!
Phillip met an eunuch returning to Ethiopia
And taught him that our Lord died to give
His people passage to an eternal Utopia!
Then the Spirit of the Lord caught him away
But not until the eunuch's life was changed
On that eventful day!
Our Lord works in marvelous ways
His wonders to perform
And here He spirits Philip far away from harm!

ACTS 9

Paul is a startling example
Of how God can turn a man around!
As Saul, he had hated Christians
And punished everyone he found.
But there is always a 'Damascus Road'
Waiting somewhere in our path
To turn us away from hate and a harmful wrath.
There, our Lord comes to say
"I want you to turn around
And follow me today!"
To be a chosen vessel like Paul
Is truly the greatest, sweetest life of all!
Well, those other Christians feared the worst!
Many of them refused to accept Paul at first.
But it didn't take them long
To see that Paul was singing a different song!
This chapter briefly switches to Peter
Who was gong from place to place
Teaching new believers about God's grace!
Grace that is greater than all our sin
Is still God's greatest gift to men!

ACTS 10

God proved His arm was not short
When He reached out and pulled Cornelius in!
It wasn't just the Jew
Our Savior longed to save from sin!
This concept was not new.
Salvation was *never* just for the Jew.
But somehow their inclusiveness made it hard
To draw but few gentiles to our Lord.
Peter couldn't doubt our Lord's intent
When Cornelius received the Holy Spirit
That our Father sent!
Our God is FULL of glory and grace!
He has provided a way so all who come to Him
Will have the joy of looking on His face!
Thank God for the story of Cornelius!

Comment on Acts

ACTS 11

Now, sadly we see even Christian Jews
not wanting to embrace the gentiles.
They should have welcomed
those new converts with loving hugs
and friendly smiles!
But, old habits are hard to break
and old ways hold on
for old times sake.
They forgot Jesus taught love
for everybody
not just for the Jew
and-good Christian friends-that's
a reminder for me and you!
Do we accept people who are *different*
whether *class* or *race*?
Do we sometimes think only we
are worthy of God's grace?
Christians and Jews have sometimes been
like two peas in a pod
thinking only we are worthy
to receive the grace of God!
But the message is plain
if only we will hear it.
"Witness, witness, witness"
Says the Holy Spirit!

ACTS 12

It was no big deal for God to deliver Peter
When He had once delivered a whole nation!
Peter was just *one man* but he was so highly regarded
His friends were filled with elation!
Peter had to pinch himself to be sure he was awake
But he realized God was delivering him
For the church's sake!
He was a *walking answer* to all their prayers.

*Just when we think we are defeated
God reaches down to show us
how very much He cares!*
From the beginning of time God's people
Have faced obstacles that are utterly distressing
But God merely takes us by the hand and
Turns our problems into an eternal blessing!

ACTS 13

*The Church can go nowhere
without fasting and prayer!
Neither can I, Lord
so teach me to pray.
Lead me to seek you
even before the sun rises
everyday!
I don't ask to be like Paul.
I just want Your Spirit.
That is all!
Help me discern
what is best for my soul
for I cannot help others
unless
I am spiritually whole.
People need the same message
given by Barnabas, Paul, and Peter.
Though we love each other
the love of God is much, much sweeter!
And, when we tell of God's
salvation
the spiritually hungry
will willingly hear it
provided we are filled
with God's Holy Spirit!
The need for wholeness
never changes, never will.
It is in His Presence
we hear the gentle voice
bidding us, "Peace be still!"
It is the gift we can be certain He gives
because we KNOW He lives!*

The "I Love My Bible" Commentary

ACTS 14

Paul and Barnabas preached from Iconium
  to Antioch
And in spite of the area's growing hostility
They nurtured and fed God's flock!
"You are my sheep," Jesus had said.
Their orders were to move on and move out
Though they faced many full of doubt.
Even though Paul and Barnabas proved
They healed a cripple who jumped to his feet
Those people's grasp of the *Good News*
Was certainly incomplete.
How quickly they changed their mind
And became dangerously unkind.
Almost overnight these apostles lives
Here in Iconium were at stake
Because of fellow Jews whose faith was fake.
But not once has it ever been said
That they retreated.
In fact they returned before they left for Antioch
Where they rejoiced because their task
Had been joyously and fully completed!

ACTS 15

Trouble again from *the old flask*
Trying to contain
A Christianity *fresh as new wine!*
Adhering to old customs proved to be
An impossible task.
We have a *newness in life* we still fail to define!
It would be like defining the universe
That lies beyond the black hole
Which would be more difficult than walking
From the North to the South Pole!
But still they argued back and forth
—these gallant men
All concerned with man's obvious need
To be saved from his iniquities and sin!
Their interpretation of the law
Was just a technicality.
For these men knew being saved was actually
A vibrant, glorious reality!
Jesus released men from the curse of the law
But to those who still held to Judaism
The wound was still fresh and raw.
The tragedy in this chapter is when Paul
And Barnabas sharply disagreed
And maybe this was the first tremor
In the world's most noble creed.

ACTS 16

Often God describes us as His temple
and the way He lives in us
is so beautifully simple!
How wonderful is God's salvation!
It is a way of life that gives us
tremendous inspiration!
Paul was wholly committed to God
and that is why that whole prison
was shaken!
Those Philippians didn't realize
who they had taken.
God was on Paul's side
and those infidels had no place to hide!
But this time God
gave beauty for ashes
-so much-all those prisoners
forgot the pain from those 40 lashes!
It is very simple to follow
the road Jesus paved.
Paul said
"Believe on the Lord Jesus Christ
and thou shall be saved!"
And that is the message of this chapter
-saved now, always, and forever after!
Our God does not leave us
to our fate.
Say it over and over again.
"Our God is truly great!

Comment on Acts

ACTS 17

*God's man confronts man's wisdom
at Mars Hill.
Had their minds really been opened
they could have learned God's will!
But the wisdom of God
is foolishness to men
who mistakenly think their strength
comes from the knowledge
they carry within.
Paul tells them that God gives life
and breath to everything
and His purpose in all of His creation
was to bring
people of all races
people of all places
back to His throne of grace
-back to that noble
and inspiring holy place
where man was meant to be!
Only in being true sons of God
could any man stand tall and free!*

ACTS 18

Now Paul more or less acquires a second home
As he befriends a couple exiled from Rome.
Leaving their home must have been depressing
But meeting this vibrant and noble apostle Paul
Turned their deportation into a great blessing!
Priscilla, Aquila, and Paul shared God's love
And their tent making expertise.
It was their mutual love for Christ, though
That brought these thoughtful people peace!
Paul stayed in Corinth for a year and a half
Teaching the Word
And during that time, many hearts were stirred.
Later when Paul leaves, heading for Jerusalem
Apollos, fluent in the scripture, takes his place.
And he, too, proclaims *God's Amazing Grace!*

ACTS 19

Even in the early church there were some
Who neglected the Holy Spirit
Though He shared a great message to those
Willing to hear it!
*He is our teacher, our guide, our comforter
Our great friend.
His wisdom, His knowledge, His love
Are without end.
Jesus said we could do nothing apart from Him.
He is the sacrificial lamb! He is the vine!
And He sent the Holy Spirit to remind us
He is our life, the new and living wine!*
But, so much has happened to the Church
So much love stripped away like bark
And as the Holy Spirit is neglected
We walk a loveless trail in the dark.
We must not concentrate on empty programs
That try to replace the dynamic, vibrant story
Of God's incomparable grace!
His Holy Spirit is a beautiful, love-blessed gift
Which is definitely heaven sent.
Its just a part of Himself, God willingly lent!
Let's be like the people in Paul's day
Who threw their charms away
Because they knew, such was not needed
   on the *King's Highway!*
And, whether we are *early* Church or *late*
We all have passage through that
   wonderful golden gate!

ACTS 20

*Fifteen minute sermons!
What a joke.
One took his breakfast
dinner and supper
when Paul spoke!
But, finally, Paul's sermon
lulled Eutychus to sleep.*

The "I Love My Bible" Commentary

It must have been like still waters
pure and deep!
But, God's spirit given to Paul
would raise this man
to testify of God's power
again and again!
Now Paul heads for Jerusalem
not knowing what he faced
but knowing the good times
he'd shared with his people
would never be replaced.
But his life meant nothing
unless he used it
for God's work!
It was a precious, sacred duty
he refused to shirk.
He entrusted his friends to God
and to His Holy Word
convinced their faith would grow
with every scripture verse
and sermon they heard!
Yes, we are set apart
and that should bring joy
to every trusting heart!

ACTS 21

Dear old beloved Paul, heading for Jerusalem
Stops to see an old friend.
Philip, the deacon/evangelist was one of
The last stops before his journey's end.
Remember he told the people he must report
All that God had accomplished through him!
But "tradition" would raise its ugly head
Once he returned to Jerusalem.
He was warned over and over
To stay away from there.
"You're breaking my heart," he said.
But it was his heart they wanted to spare!
His heart would be broken by truths
Falsely altered
But Paul's faith in God would stand the test
And he never faltered!

ACTS 22

Paul could have been a 'giant' as an Orthodox
  Jew
He had studied at the feet of Gamaliel
And knew what good Jewish men should do.
But, one day, on the road to Damascus
Paul saw the "Light!"
And only then did he learn the tremendous
Privilege
Of loving God with all his might!
He would testify of that meeting with our Savior
Numerous times
And, oh how he grieved over his previous
Hideous crimes.
But, though being as strict a Jew as was Paul
He still needed the same salvation as do we all!
We are all destined for that meeting
With Jesus face to face
And if we turn away from Him
We'll never walk in the *light* of His grace.
Paul was triple blessed; he was born a Jew
—was a citizen of Rome by *birth*
And by *birth* he was a citizen of Heaven, too!
But he needed salvation to cleanse his heart
  of hate
And maybe, more than one unnecessary trait!
This message of salvation is *old as the hills*
  yet it is forever new!
  Remember that gate I mentioned?
  We need the ticket of salvation
  before the Lord will let us through!
Paul made a long and clear defense because
Many of these Jewish leaders who should have
Known the Lord didn't really know His laws.
And, Paul used the Roman law to evade
The Jews evil intent
For he was aware of what their treachery meant!

Comment on Acts

ACTS 23

How wonderful is Paul's steadfast confession!
Would we be able to conquer such repression?
"Brothers," Paul said. "I have always lived
In good conscience before God!"
Nothing less than that can keep our lives clean
On these earthly paths we trod.
HOLINESS IS ONLY A MIRACLE AWAY!
And comes as we walk with God each day.
Holiness gave Paul a courage that came
From the Messiah they had denied.
Therefore they could not understand why
Paul was so satisfied!
"*I KNOW in whom I have believed,*"
He would say one day.
Knowing our God is the only way to walk
His life-giving, gloriously golden pathway!

ACTS 24

Paul heartily testified
"By the way they call heresy
worship I my father's God!"
He could say that triumphantly.
His feet were gospel-shod!
He was a man who spoke from the heart
<u>not</u> with a 'forked' tongue.
His enemies clung to *the law*
-he to a spirit forever young!
He constantly strived
to keep his conscience clear.
Being an embarrassment to our Father
was Paul's only fear.
He was *not the ring leader*
of a fanatic religious group
but he had found a loop in the law
in which only *LOVE*
could be its loop!
That is why it wasn't hard
for Paul to proclaim
"Jesus is my Savior
and I will always try
to bring honor to His Name!"

ACTS 25

Agony and alienation walked hand in hand
    with Paul.
But it could have been worse
Had he returned to Jerusalem's judgement hall.
Paul had not tried to overthrow the Jewish laws
But he was persecuted because he held tightly
To the Christian cause.
Paul would go through anything for Jesus
Because Jesus had done so much for him.
Paul's faith would grow even beyond Rome
Because Jesus gave his all at Jerusalem!
Paul–the early Christian tormenter
Had *completely turned around*
For his feet had been firmly planted
On heaven's higher ground!
Paul had gained a love beyond compare
And he never found any alienation there!

ACTS 26

Paul always shared his Damascus story
More than willingly
And it broke his heart to recall the question
"Saul, why are you persecuting me?"
He'd gone after people—he thought
But our Lord was really the one he sought.
Ah! But, our Lord was really seeking Paul
On that Damascus Road
And He turned Paul around with the grace
He bestowed!
Paul was *set apart* for the Lord that day
And, indeed, his sins were all washed away!
Paul never forgot to whom he belonged
And no one can deny Paul's faith was strong!
But King Agrippa could not be convinced

The "I Love My Bible" Commentary

Nor could this king see how very desperately
He needed the power of Jesus to set him free.
And we do not know if King Agrippa's life
Came to an untimely end
But we do know that Paul, though facing death
Continued to walk with his *great eternal friend!*
      Yet----he appealed to Caesar
        and to Caesar he would go
          his head held high
          and his faith in tow!

ACTS 27

Seas were turbulent and the journey rough.
The heaviest of ships were not strong enough!
One would think the ship's captain would know
How quickly and fiercely the winds could blow!
He refused to respect or even listen to Paul
Feeling certain he could make Rome
Before the end of Fall!
The seas grew higher and those scared sailor's
Fears increased and no one would eat.
All but Paul believed they were on a journey
They would never complete!
Though the ship wrecked, it was only a delay.
Soon Paul would walk the Appian way.
It is not the journey we must pursue.
But only the faith that brings us through!

ACTS 28

There are far more possibilities for Paul
in a prison cell
-more time to pray
-more time to sing
-more time to write
all that 'good news' he wanted to tell!
Blessed news we would never
have heard
Had not it been put into
the written word!
You see, our Lord has a reason
for every test.
Because Paul was imprisoned
millions have been blessed.
I'm sure Paul's faith was tested
over and over again
but I venture to say few people
loved God more than this man!
Paul would consider this prison
his home away from home
and he refused to lose faith
even in Rome!
He wrote many 'loving letters'
to his converts everywhere
and they must have read them eagerly
knowing he was under God's loving care!

Note: So the church is established and is here to stay until the Lord, himself, takes us away! Its seen many a revival, many a cold dark night. It has been hated cruelly but claimed God's love and held on tight! It has pointed the way to heaven, glorified the Lord and has rescued many from sin. Now it is suffering the indifference of people incredibly blessed but spiritually poor. The world has never needed our Savior more, though it thinks it does not need him at all. *Thank Hollywood for that. Thank TV also—that is, if it makes no difference to you where you go.* But beware, my friend. God's truths are without end and His Word says "what you reap IS what you sow. He advises us to sow a crop of righteousness. "I HAVE NOT CHANGED," He says. Yes, society has changed. Morales have changed. But, if you want to reach heaven its imperative to remember *God has not changed!*

Then Peter said unto them,
repent, and be baptized everyone of you
in the name of Jesus Christ
for the remissions of sins,
and you shall receive the gift of the Holy Ghost.
For the promise is to you, and to your children,
and to all that are afar off,
even as many as the Lord our God shall call.
(Acts 2:38-39kjv)

Neither is there salvation in any other:
for there is none other name under heaven
given among men
whereby we must be saved
(Acts 4:12kjv)

And they said believe on the Lord Jesus Christ
and thou shalt be saved and thy house.
(Acts 16:31kjv)

But this I confess unto thee,
that after the way that they call heresy,
so worship I the God of my fathers,
believing all things
which are written in the law and the prophets.
(Acts 24:14kjv)

And Paul dwelt two whole years
in his own hired house,
and received all that came unto him,
preaching the kingdom of God,
and teaching those things which concern
the Lord Jesus Christ,
with all confidence, no man forbidding him.
(Acts 28: 30-31kjv)

Part Eight

The Loving Letters

Romans

to

Revelation

And Final Farewell!

*Therefore being justified by faith,
we have peace with God
through our Lord Jesus Christ:*

*By whom also we have access by faith
into this grace wherein we stand.
and rejoice in the hope
of the glory of God.*

-----

*But God commendeth his love toward us,
in that, while we were yet sinners,
Christ died for us.*

*Much more then,
being justified by his blood,
we shall be saved from wrath
through him.*
(Romans 5:1-2; 8-9kjv)

The "I Love My Bible" Commentary
(The Book of Romans)

ROMANS 1

The Roman Road!
The Road to Salvation
paved by the blood of Christ
lined by martyrs and saints!
And smoothed by the Hope
of the Ages
which our Father
so lovingly paints!
Its God's way to point us home
-to call the prodigal
who has chosen to roam.
There's no place like home
for God's own.
We'll not know complete peace
until we gather around
His throne!
Even though Paul was in prison
he found a way to feed his flock!
God's truth was a truth
his enemies could not block!
For faith finds a way
to enlighten God's people
on their way!
Faith is the spot-light of this chapter
but what happens
when the light is turned off?
People lie, cheat, and steal
and if they mention God
it is only to scoff.
Strange that Paul would start Romans
with such a strong contrast
but we must learn to follow God closely
if we want our faith to last!
Faith needs love!
Faith needs light!
Man knows not where to turn
when he walks
in the darkness of spiritual night.
Those awful traits Paul mentioned
are raging today
and if we are to overcome them
there is only one way.
The one powerful method
that leads men to glory
is lovingly explained
in God's salvation story!
Like Paul, I am not ashamed
of the gospel of Christ.
It was for me
my Lord was sacrificed!
He willingly came to earth
because He knew
*just how **much***
even ONE soul was worth!

ROMANS 2

"Wait a minute!" Paul exclaimed.
"You, yourselves, should be ashamed!"
All those negative traits
Paul listed in the first chapter
were exactly the same ones
these Christians(?)
were running after!
All such people are under
God's judgement
who walk in evil ways.
There will be sorrow and suffering
for everyone who strays.
If we would desire that our conversion
be dynamic and real
we must be careful
what our thoughts, our actions
and our words reveal!
Paul said to be a "real Jew"
was to have a changed heart
and we are to live as those
who are set apart!

Comment on Romans

ROMANS 3

All that man has ever needed—Jew or Gentile
Is to completely trust our Lord
And only in trusting do we learn that obedience
Brings its own reward!
If we are to be saved by faith, faith must do its work
Where man walks earthly trails in which
Trials and temptations lurk!
We may be tempted to think our good deeds
Are the only keys to heaven anyone needs
But we fall short of God's ideal
No matter how religious we may feel.
Why do we complicate God's perfect plan?
Only God's Messiah was destined
To save earth's delinquent man!
Good deeds won't work without faith
Nor faith without God's laws.
Our Father knows that our good deeds
Are full of hidden flaws!
Dear friends, it is very hard
For me to understand
Why so many fail to trust our Lord!
Paul said God's Words would always prove true and right
And indeed they show us how
To walk paths of endless delight!

ROMANS 4

*To have faith like Abraham
draws us to the Great I Am!
There is no other God
only One for us to choose.
And faith in Him discloses
His many marvelous virtues!
If only we'd observe that His 'staff'
is gentler than His rod
We'd know how easily
we can find mercy in our God!*

*Faith is holiness bared to the bone!
But Paul did not mean
that faith is really alone.
You see faith ties us
to God's apron strings
and obedience just rides along
on the happiness faith brings!
It is not 'works' we must desire.
Only faith sets our souls on fire!
When we rely on works
we won't give our Heavenly Father credit
and everything we do winds up heavily
in the minus column of debit.
Nothing—no one—less than God
can cleanse and make us whole.
It is not works, my friend
but faith in God
that will save your soul!*

ROMANS 5

*Trust God
-to save you
-to hold you
-to lift you!
Thank Him
-for great privilege
-for wonderful joy
-for hope whatever you do!
To trust God
is to hold our heads high
never helpless because
our Lord stands nearby!
God's kindness is His Royal Diadem
and now we are kings of life
because of Him!
Can we say we've earned the good life?
Heaven forbid!
It is only given
based on what our Savior did!*

The "I Love My Bible" Commentary

Adam plowed us under
Jesus pulled us up
and we drink the nectar of life
from God's golden cup!
Grace has given us
an eternal reward
and we owe it all
to our Blessed Lord!

ROMANS 6

My bond was set so high it couldn't be paid
And I shuddered because I was so afraid.
I had received my 'pay check' and it said, death
-a sentence so horrible I couldn't get my breath.
Thank God, my God gave me a chance
When He handed me His eternal gift!
The wages of sin held me down
But God's love gave me a lift!
Paul reminds me I stand
Safely, serenely and completely in God's hand!
Now I live forever in glorious hope
For God has given me a different view of life
With His celestial telescope!
Very, very slowly I have learned
I have a love I have not earned!
For God reached down and took me in
And saved me from a life of sin!

ROMANS 7

One who is dead to the law will not face
A death sentence
Provided he has turned to the Savior
In true repentance!
Some say the law is evil
For it arouses forbidden desires
And ignites raging, lustful, destructive fires.
Some say if we had no laws to break
There would be no evil and not one heart ache.
How foolish !

No guide lines would mean no life lines to hold.
Who would know to be good to his neighbor
Unless we were told?
Man needs to know the right path
Much more than he needs science or math!
Paul says we have a deadly nature that will
Naturally decline.
I for one need the Savior
And I thank God He is mine!

ROMANS 8

There is only a sunny side
to God's boulevard
where my souls basks
in resplendent wonder
and angels stand on guard!
No condemnation lurks to frighten me
I've been safe every since
I passed through Calvary!
Though I face daily problems
God diffuses them when I pray
and the Holy Spirit intercedes
when I don't know what to say.
God offers a golden nectar
of which I can imbibe
and I drink deeply of that love
no one can describe!
Greater than the heavens
-deeper than the sea
-that's how big God's love is for me!
Once I was a pauper
in the 'loving' field
but, oh what mighty love
my Father has revealed!
Can anyone steal it away from me?
No way!
For He has promised
to walk with me each day.
God's love is always
in the present tense.

Comment on Romans

He is my loving Savior
and my ultimate defense!
Yes, He is a rock
where I can hide
and I proudly proclaim
all who rest in Him
are thoroughly satisfied!
Nothing can separate me
from His love.
NOT A SINGLE THING!
No wonder my spirit soars.
He has given me
a glorious new song to sing!

ROMANS 9

You can almost feel the pain in Paul's heart
As he reasons with the Jews.
He knew the life God offered them
Was much too precious to refuse.
Still they turned God away and Paul asked why.
And down through the ages we read
Of his heart rending cry.
"Why won't you come, my people?"
    "Why won't you come?"
Even the woman of Samaria(remember her?)
Had coveted just one lonely crumb!
Our *Bread of Life* offered His people so much
Yet, they considered His gift unworthy to touch.
And, then they called God unfair
Often going so far as to say
"Our God doesn't care."
Lack of faith in God became their personal
    stumbling stone
And they, like all who reject our God, will face
This earth's uncertain future all alone.
But, those who have made God their choice
Will live forever to rejoice!
Paul left no reason for doubt.
He could safely promise
No trusting saint would *ever* be left out.

ROMANS 10

Having a zeal of God
but not according to knowledge
is like walking on a treadmill.
We feel we are going places
but we're only standing still!
We struggle through thoughts of doubt
and times of strife
though it is so simple
to trust in Christ
who freely gives us life!
To believe in one's own heart
that God's salvation is real
will draw us close to Him
and no one can doubt
the great love we feel!
But, I know its up to me
to share what I see
—that God is in the business
of saving you and me!
And despite all the current
conflicting views
it's a privilege to share
God's precious and everlastingly true
good news!

ROMANS 11

Sometimes we can develop an Elijah complex
When we look at others as spiritual rejects.
Need God remind us we are not alone?
There are many who worship Him
And to Him they are known!
Some worship in private, some in lonesome awe
Some seek His grace and others hold to the law.
Whoever they are, and whatever they do
Remember our God can easily save them too!
We, who are grafted into grace, should reach out
And show those lacking in faith
They have no reason to doubt!

The "I Love My Bible" Commentary

God must wonder why so many folks complain
And why so many spiritual dissidents remain.
It is not only a trait of God's own nation
For people all over the world
Are turning their backs on His salvation.
Surely false religionists must sit on tacks
Knowing they are destined to feel God's axe.
But-in mercy-God endures man's spite
Allowing the foolish to walk in the *night!*
And, many people are *sitting on the fence*
Instead of walking the *narrow road*
While others who are treasure seekers
Swear they have found the 'mother' lode.
But, if we desire to have faith without measure
We must remember God has said
He is our *greatest treasure!*
Someday He will reveal His glory
And withdraw His grace.
Those who have rejected Him
Will HAVE to meet Him face to face.
Paul is not just telling us an idle story.
Our God IS a God of incredible glory!

ROMANS 12

Essentially Paul is saying
"Be an engine, not a caboose!"
"Walk the narrow road
instead of play*ing* fast and loose!"
If you just *have* to measure your worth
use the golden rule
for those who use God's measure
will never play the fool.
And Paul knew perfecting our talents
would never be hard
if we faithfully use them
to honor our Lord.
Paul wanted us to have lives
of quality
-the kind that brings hope to others
and joyful harmony!

*The good life can put us
on God's one way easy street
where we can be shining examples
to every one we meet!*

ROMANS 13

Paul advises us to obey our government
For God is the one who put them there.
But-anarchy says, "I want to do what
I want to do therefore the Law is very unfair."
It isn't easy to discipline the maddening crowd
Those who flaunt their disbelief
As if they have reason to be proud.
Disobedience is based on hatred of the things
God calls holy and pure
And because hate flaunts justice, that person
Can never feel secure.
Paul said, "love does no wrong to anyone!"
I bet you, it is Love that upholds the sun!
Love completely fulfills God's laws.
To be loving and kind to others
Is life's greatest cause!
Living up to Paul's standards may be hard
But he says we can do it
If we ask for help from our Blessed Lord!

ROMANS 14

*We Christians need to read this chapter
until we know it by heart.
It could ease all the tensions
that have torn this world apart.
Paul considered it very important
to spread love, joy, and peace
to one and all!
Harmony should be the church's goal
And we must not forget
criticizing others
Does not make us whole.*

Comment on Romans

We can lead no one to Christ
when we are mean and spiteful
but the love the Lord gives us to share
is utterly delightful!
Now, the hardest part of all
is to walk worthy of our calling
always realizing
we must live in such a way
as to help keep others from falling!
"Living or dying," Paul said.
"we follow the Lord"
That is so those who follow us
will not stumble
nor think the Christian life is hard.

ROMANS 15

Love is "*state of the art*"
direct from heaven's shore
and no matter how much
we love each other
we know our Lord loves us more!
Paul knew love honors others
more than self
as proved by our Savior
for nothing less than love promotes
likewise noble behavior!
And, goodness and mercy
are somewhere between grace and love
that has been sent to us
from that home up above!
Knowing this caused Paul to roam
down many treacherous trails.
He wanted others to learn
of this love of God that never fails!
Paul's messages, his demeanor
his miracles
were packaged in godly signs
of the kind of changed lives only God refines!
At last Paul's work was finished.
At last he could go to Rome!

And he seeks prayer-partners
to pray for him
as first he travels to his home.
He knew danger lurked
on those trails he would trod
but, in happy harmony, he would
always walk with God.
We know Paul loved God
with all his heart.
Truly, his love was
"*state of the art!*"

ROMANS 16

In summing up Romans
I must agree
only the *grace of God*
could ever set me free!
And only that *balm of Gilead*
can open my eyes of faith to see!
I can see Heaven.
I can see home.
I can see a love
from which I will never roam.
I can see God's love is richer
than any earthly treasure
and I can see His greatness
is beyond all measure!
He is wiser than all of history's
noble sages
Truly, He IS my Rock of Ages!
In summing up Romans I must agree
Great is the grace God has given me!

Note: Paul paints many road signs that point to heaven–*many signs but only one way!*
He never doubted the power of Christ to save us and he knew beyond doubt that it was God's love that sent Him here to die for us, but he couldn't understand why they rejected God's great love! *Neither can we!*

The "I Love My Bible" Commentary
(The Book of 1st Corinthians)

1ST CORINTHIANS 1

Modern 'Corinthians' prance
across the stage of grace
arguing(like those ancient ones)
who deserves the most important place.
Modern 'Corinthians'
think they have God alone
and those not in their group
they willingly disown.
Paul warns us of such
a negative attitude.
Christians are not to be
narrow minded, selfish, and rude.
And Paul said no ONE preacher
was more important than the others.
God has commissioned all of them
to teach us how to treat
our Christian sisters and brothers.
We modern 'Corinthians'
should hold our heads in shame
because, when we back-bite
and complain
we bring dishonor
to our Savior's holy name!

1ST CORINTHIANS 2

"I came," Paul said, "with simplicity.
I kneel before One
who is full of glory."
But Paul appeared as one
weak and fearful because
nothing and no one should cast a shadow
on life's most beautiful story!
He said, "No eye has seen
no ear has heard
no mind has conceived
the glory, the wonder, the grace
and the love of God
which are greater
than many have ever believed."
It takes the mind of Christ
To see the love of God.
It takes a wisdom greater than ours
to see the treacherous paths we trod.
And it took the sacrifice of One
holy and pure
to actually make us feel
safe and secure!
Because the mind of Christ
reveals His light
we will never grope in darkness
fearful of the night!

1ST CORINTHIANS 3

Was Paul saying baby talk pleases only babies
Because it shows growth retardation
And milk-fed anemic Christians cannot learn
The art of holy separation?
Paul speaks of bread and strong meat
And the grace spread by love that we need
To make our souls complete.
He wondered why they would say
"I belong to Apollos or Paul"
When it was God who was over them all.
"Who am I or who is Apollos?" He asked.
If these Corinthians depended on them
To save them, their souls had already crashed!
"It is God." he said, "God who saves your soul."
Sure, Apollos was eloquent, and Paul was bold!
But God–only God–could save them from sin.
Paul never played the 'big shot.'
Souls were too precious and hell was too hot!
That is why he so emphatically said,
 "Other foundation can no man lay
Than that is laid which is Christ Jesus."
Remember what Jesus said about foundations?
He said those who obeyed him had a solid one!

Comment on 1ˢᵀ Corinthians

All our faith should be on what He has done!
Paul's preaching may have been bold
Apollos's speech more beautiful and eloquent
But Paul assured these contending Corinthians
He and Apollos were *both heaven sent!*
And he closed with the sweetest news of all
Sweetest for anyone who belongs to Christ!
And its because Jesus paid a high price for us
Because–you see–our souls **are** high-priced!
We are full of grace and holy(plural) powers
Because God had Paul say all thing are ours!

1ˢᵀ CORINTHIANS 4

We have a *jump rope called 'conclusion.'*
The faster we jump, the greater our confusion!
We judge harshly one day, and lax the next
Therefore we should carefully read this text.
Paul would never judge himself.
He said, "The Lord must decide
The various and sundry reasons
I walk by His side!"
We walk by faith(as did he) and not by sight
And the Lord will reveal who truly
Walks in His light.
We think we are full, spiritual, and contented
And sometimes we carelessly accuse others
Of being slightly demented.
Though Paul seems to be harsh
He loved those he had brought to the Lord.
So, as we read these words he sent to them
We might say he was *gently* hard!
But his message to them and to us
Applicable for then or any hour
Was if we would be loving Christians
We must live by God's power.

1ˢᵀ CORINTHIANS 5

Now we read of one who had tasted 'new wine'
And because of his adulterous, sinful heart
Thought it unnecessary to confine.
He had much to learn
For he didn't treasure this life he didn't earn.
And he could never earn salvation anyway
He had a gift so great, yet chose to stray.
Evidently those in his church, spiritual so called
Seemed to portray a faith that stalled.
Were these church leaders 'out to lunch'
Not caring that one spoiled *apple*
Can ruin the whole bunch?
Though this man's sin was hideous
Paul cared for his soul hoping perhaps discipline
Might make this sinner whole.
Of course we know he'd have to repent.
Adultery is definitely NOT heaven sent.
It is a waterfall destroying everyone in its path
Because it brings to all who are guilty
The certainty of God's eternal wrath.
Yet judging others in the church may keep us
On needles and pins unless we do it graciously
But we MUST deal with the one who sins
For they should know it is God's kind of love
That will heal from sin and set them free!

1ˢᵀ CORINTHIANS 6

Paul said don't go to outsiders when judgement
  is desired.
Maybe he thought judges outside the church
Were unscrupulous and should be fired!
We should resolve our claims righteously
And we all need to be as patient as we can be.
Paul talks about immorality once again
And how we should act before our fellow man.
              Imagine!
Our precious Lord wants to fill us with Himself
In order to make us *a part of Him!*
If God's people would remember that
Surely our *light* would *never grow dim!*
Me-a part of God-and Him a part of me!
There can be no greater glory for all eternity!

The "I Love My Bible" Commentary

1ST CORINTHIANS 7

*If God says it is good to be married
you can bet it is so!
And His Holy Word just happens
to give marriage a special glow!
Paul was concerned about
those difficult times.
Its good he didn't live today!
Surely our God
who says He abhors sin
must have to look the other way.
It breaks His heart to see so many
involved in so-called free sex
yet paying a high price
with that deadly viral hex.
Paul emphatically states
that marriage is NOT sin.
If we had all pleased God
in marital sexual honor
this nation would not be
in the shape it is in.
The Bible says the nation
that forgets God
shall be turned in to hell.
Well!
God has given men and women
a lot of love to give
but only to the one
with which we are willing
in honor to live!
Paul emphasized what he considered
the most important thing.
And that is
we must live holy lives
that show the world
we honor our King!*

1ST CORINTHIANS 8

People argued about their diets in Paul's day.
Though it pertained to religion, Paul told them
What they ate didn't help in any way.
Some seemed to think they had all the answers
And used their *so called cutting truths*
As contaminated lancers.
Did you ever notice how *cutting* people can be
Never realizing the only *cutting* should come
From God's two-edged sword(His Word)
Which is the only tool that can set us free!
Were Paul's problems different from ours?
   Were they really?
Can we say we have no false gods
When many watch the TV for hours?
As to the matter of eating, Paul's words
Don't seem so grim
Unless we continue to stuff ourselves
While still wishing we were slim!
I wonder! Could an idol be that extra piece
Of pie or that big helping of potatoes
You thought you just **had** to fry?
   (and eat of course
   'cause you were hungry
     as a horse!)
And when you are tempted by a special treat
Ask yourself, *"Do I eat to live
   or do I live to eat?*
Though we don't offer food to idols-not at all
We do eat as if we're in a great banquet hall.
We could desire God's gourmet food
Which is what David called *honey from the Rock*
And its sustaining power lasts twenty four hours
Completely around the clock.
Now that is real vitamins, minerals, and such
And that is something of which we can never
   get too much!

1ST CORINTHIANS 9

Long ago God offered man His holy nature
So we could walk without fear
But many ungodly men

Comment on 1st Corinthians

Consider that holy, righteous name
In the context of a sneer.
*To be called of God overcomes any name
we may be called!*
But in this chapter Paul suffers when
His good name is mauled.
It seems some supported Peter and not Paul.
They seemed to think Paul had no rights at all.
Paul did hurt deeply inside
For here he is, *on another roller coaster ride!*
Sometimes he's up; sometimes he's down
No in between for him, for his flock
Wears either a smile or an unwelcome frown!
What kind of friends are they? Fair weather?
I guess they could never get their act together!
But–don't we often favor one man over the rest
Not considering preachers are God's servants
And all are doing(we hope) their best?
Even though we may disagree
The blessings come when we *let them be!*
Now, what might that be you may ask
And I ask you, who was the One
Who gave him his task?
It seems to me Paul is saying preaching is a race
And the ones who finish
Only finish by God's grace!
And more often than not
We'd be wise to keep our hands *out of the pot!*

1ST CORINTHIANS 10

Warning signs are everywhere
but we don't listen
and we don't care.
We have a 'it can't happen to me'
philosophy
and go on our way
oblivious to any spiritual injury.
Paul said, "Remember the wilderness
where God extended His provision.
Remember the Jewish rebellion
which brought so much derision!"
If we want to enjoy the future
we must learn from the past
and not obscure God's light
with the sinful deeds we might cast.
Paul reminds us others
have faced our same problems
experienced the same temptations
made the same mistakes
but God helps us overcome our wilderness
and brings us out of the *cedar breaks!*
It seems Paul feared their attitudes
for even at the Lord's table
the contentious ones continued
their feuds.
There is a beautiful picture here
of a spiritual toddy
when we share the blessings
of Christ's blood
and the benefits of His body!
And though the body of Christ
has many parts(us)it is still one!
We are members only
of a growth
Christ, Himself, has begun!
*One apart
One together
Strengthened for this world's
so called fair or stormy weather!*
We must never be a stumbling block
to anyone whom God has said
is a part of His flock.
Certainly we can express ambivalence
others won't understand
unless we fully commit ourselves
to live the way our Father planned!

1ST CORINTHIANS 11

Two controversial doctrines emerge-especially
The one about women!

The "I Love My Bible" Commentary

Paul outrageously precipitates a female anger
That leaves our heads *swimming.*
But we must remember Paul wanted order
In the church.
Ladies of that age had too little knowledge
To knock the preacher from his perch.
Still–Paul's greatest concern
Was improper communion and bad attitudes!
Some were living in evil and some
Were acting like judgmental prudes.
Possibly, it is an unwritten law
When we obey Him, love comes
In the hush of reverent awe!
Remember, attitudes will affect our behavior
And often bring no glory to our Savior.
"Oh, people," Paul said. "Its time we behaved
As those who are longing to see others saved."
How many souls turn away badly scarred
Because we fail to glorify our Lord?
Perhaps we leave a soul injured and reeling
When we fail to show true Christian feeling!

1ST CORINTHIANS 12

We have special abilities given us by the Lord
And His Spirit tell us which message to accept
And which one to discard!
So many people say they are right
And we must ask them how they know.
Do they really have God's knowledge
Or is it their own horns they blow?
We shouldn't be suspicious
But we should be able to discern
The purity of the truth others say we must learn.
God's Spirit lifts up Jesus and to pass the test
We must rid ourselves of garbage
And save that which is best!
Jesus, only Jesus, can turn our lives around.
It is through His Spirit we can walk
On holy, solid ground!
Now we know, He gives different assignments
So that His *body* can grow!
Prophets, preachers, apostles and teachers
Are gifted to help us walk this earth below.
*Discern while you learn God's Word
And then search the Scriptures
To prove what you've heard
For God's truths truly stand the test
And only through His Spirit can we say*
We are truly blessed!

1ST Corinthians 13

*God has a love that splits
the black hole of doubt
into a million splinters
and love thaws the icy ponds
of life's fear-filled chilling winters.
Love is beyond description
even for Paul who was so eloquent
but somehow he manages to present it
as far-r-r more than benevolent!
Love hold us in its arms!
Love erases fear!
Love looks into the heart of God
and knows that He is near!
How can anyone describe* that
*in the confines of human understanding
but is it adequate to say
love is not fierce and never demanding?
I think not!
Maybe we ARE unable
to describe how love sits us
triumphantly at God's banquet* table!
*For now it is enough to know
God will lead us out
through that black hole of doubt
where we are told
faith will truly make us bold!
Faith, hope, love, these three
but love and only love
will make us what we want to be!*

Comment on 1st Corinthians

1ST CORINTHIANS 14

I believe this world has gone
from bad to worse
simply because it ignores
the instructions in the first verse!
Love is the name of the game!
Love is to be our greatest aim!
When love gets hold of you
you are never the same!
And
love brings glory to our Father's name!
So–we'd do well
to follow Paul's advice.
It was love that compelled our Savior
to pay such an awesome price!
Love speaks in a language
all people understand.
Even the most illiterate need that love
to gently hold his hand.
Love will erase every border
and will prove someday
how terribly the world has needed
God's style of law and order.
God spells law, l-o-v-e
and that is what makes us
what we ought to be!

1ST CORINTHIANS 15

The world is full of reminders that God doesn't change.
Yet, those who don't believe in God
Still consider His salvation strange.
"Its not realistic," they say, not knowing what 'realistic' really means!"
I believe Paul spent 99% of his time explaining
The simplicity and reality of grace
Because the world would not believe
That One so great would die for the human race.
Why did Christ come to be wrapped in flesh?
It was so we can be wrapped in eternity!
Why did He have to die?
It was so we could live triumphantly!
Paul says knowing of victory-present or future
Makes us strong and steady
And with God's help-when He returns-we *will be ready!*

1ST CORINTHIANS 16

Paul encourages interaction between churches
  because
No matter where he was working he'd pause
To remind the churches of his concern.
He never refused to teach those willing to learn!
We speak of *tall* men to today but who could be
Taller than Paul?
His love gave him a stature envied by all!
His advice is needed today.
He said, "stand true to the Lord"
And when he said, "act like men,"
He must have known it would be very hard!
Love people! That is what so many lack!
Its hard to love one who *stabs you in the back!*
But Paul chose to remember all those who had
Helped him and he was passing it on
For he knew no church could reach faith's
Glorious heights
If it faced its problems all alone.
He prays that the Lord would extend to all
His love and favor.
Of course He will! Why else is He our Savior?

Note: Paul seemed to have more problems with the Corinthians than he did any other church therefore he seemed to love them more-like the father of the prodigal, he longed to pull them close to the Lord. Look for that kind of love between Christians today. It is here–all around us. Why do I know that? Because the great love of the Lord still lives in our hearts!

The "I Love MY Bible" Commentary
(The Book of 2nd Corinthians)

2ND CORINTHIANS 1

After all Paul had been through with these men
He still called them friends!
So we find it is true!
A true consecrated Christian's love never ends!
Paul had been criticized, crushed, overwhelmed
And felt the chilly breath of doom.
Yet Paul had been straightforward and sincere
Speaking from his heart where doubt could find
  no room!
He knew God's Holy Spirit was
The first payment on God's installment plan
And, he knew nothing could be better
Than God's presence in the heart of man!
Therefore Paul constantly patterned himself
After our blessed Lord
And when people rejected him
No wonder he was broken hearted and scarred.
He worried when people didn't believe what
  he said
Even though he assured them he spoke
In Christ's stead.
He swore he didn't want to make anyone sad
And it was because of the great love he had!
The more I have read through Paul's letters
The more I admire this man.
For he expressed more love than most can do
In an entire life span!
OK! It WAS tough-love
Which is definitely the **best** kind!
For this kind of love removes the cataracts
  from blinded eyes
  and cobwebs from the mind!

2ND CORINTHIANS 2

Sometimes love makes you cry
as in Paul's case
but even though a man
sinned horribly
Paul would say
"Lets shower him with God's grace!"
United discipline laced with love
would show
a comfort and forgiveness
only a child of God
is privileged to know!
Sometimes Paul wrote with a
punctured heart
wounded and bleeding
because-though he worked so hard
response to God's Word
seemed to be receding.
Yet he speaks of God's perfume
giving a soothing fragrance
that overcomes a foul doom.
Paul knew his purpose for living
was to share the grace
God was giving!
And, in this day, this hour
we must continue to tell
of God's marvelous saving power!

2ND CORINTHIANS 3

Paul begins to wonder about himself.
What about his image?
It seemed faith had become
an endless scrimmage!
Paul was struggling to avoid
the Christian cancer
better known as "paranoid!"
False teachers had to bring
an unearned recommendation
but Paul reminded the Corinthians
they knew of his dedication.
Their changed hearts could testify
the messages they received
came from the One on high!

Comment on 2nd Corinthians

The one great truth
Paul would consistently confess
was *only in the pure gospel*
of Christ
could they find success!
Grace could never be veiled
because He who gave it
never failed!
And only in Christ
could they understand
God's way up
was to hold His hand!

2ND CORINTHIANS 4

It all begins with God
our life, our hope
our joy, our beliefs
for there is NO one else to trust.
No one else can erase our griefs!
God in His mercy
God in His love
God in His grace
far surpasses
man's puny ambivalent pace!
If the Good News is hidden
it is hidden to the unbelievers
who inadvertently listen
to the atheistic deceivers.
God has said
"Let there be light."
And the joy He puts on our faces
is incredibly bright!
There is nothing like
God's precious treasure
(His Word)
that can give His people
indescribable pleasure!
We don't know why things
happen as they do
when troubles seem many
and pleasures seem few
but we do know, like Paul, we can say
we will never give up or give in
for God's richest blessings are for us
who have turned from our sin!

2ND CORINTHIANS 5

Christianity isn't guesswork.
Our future is secure!
When these 'tents' are taken down
we will have bodies strong and pure!
Yet, every moment we're away from home
every strange and winding trail we roam
it seems our disappointments grow.
So we wonder if there are rewards
for we who love the Savior so.
Now we question if we are doing right
for when troubles come
we take flight!
How many of us are honestly sincere
though sometimes considered
spiritually insane
and do we look on others
with suspicion and disdain?
Yet, this new life
this great love
is God's marvelous gift.
Who else but God can give our hearts
such a glorious lift?
His love enables us to love
but it is a love completely pure
and His is a love in which
we can feel perfectly secure!

2ND CORINTHIANS 6

There are no yesterdays or tomorrow's in the word *salvation!*
It is in the <u>current</u> beat of the heart obsessed with heavenly dedication!

The "I Love My Bible" Commentary

Salvation runs on *direct current* from our
Electrifying Savior
And depends on Him to jump start His style
Of high voltage behavior!
It's a challenge to be like Him
But He took the plunge first and now
We who are saved are all *in the swim!*
Paul wanted his Corinthian friends to see
It was only Christ who could set them free!
God's people should have no admiration
For people living in sin.
Their *darkness* must never overcome our light
That God has gloriously planted within.
There will be *nothing negative* permitted
In God's heavenly territory
And we must separate ourselves from sin
If we want to partake of His purity and glory!

2ND CORINTHIANS 7

Great promises!
Greater motivation!
After all, doesn't God say
He is our relation?
That was all Paul needed
to keep him going.
His confidence, his pride
were in knowing
God stood by his side!
And the arrival of Titus
gave him a joy he couldn't hide!
And, even though it changed
those Corinthians lives for the better
he still grieved
having scolded them in a letter.
A good man like Paul
should have an influence on his peers
and he could see as they followed
his advice, it alleviated their fears.
Once again he had established a rapport
with people who now loved him as before!

2ND CORINTHIANS 8

No church can survive without God's grace
Nor without first seeking to *look on His face!*
And those who dedicate themselves to Him
Will help enlighten others whose hearts
Have grown weak and whose hopes are slim!
Paul told these Corinthians they'd not know
The true joy of Christian living
Until they had shared their love through their
Sacrificial giving.
We give to others when we love dearly
And all who love God can see that clearly!
A man of integrity like Paul
Could be trusted to forward *it all*
-always for the purpose it was shared!
Somewhere out there, he knew, an indigent soul
Would know *somebody cared!*
Its God's way of giving others a lift
When they see we care enough to send a gift!

2ND CORINTHIANS 9

Speaking of gifts, we have one incredibly great!
It is God's grace brought by the One who will
Eventually overcome all hate.
Such generosity! Such colossal caring
-the prime example of true magnificent sharing!
Paul puts it at the end of this chapter
But giving has always begun with our Lord
And when we give, God multiplies our 'seed'
As the fruit of our reward!
And as long as we have this godly love
We keep revealing
Others will thank the Lord for our gifts
With deep fervor and a hearty joyous feeling!
God's love provides a bond no one can sever
And our good deeds will honor Him forever!
Honoring Him should be our greatest aim.
Loving Him—we'll never be the same.
And in serving Him, we will glorify His name!

Comment on 2nd Corinthians

2ND CORINTHIANS 10

If these people were filled with the Holy Spirit
Why should Paul have to plead?
He had told them they were *kings of life*
And Christ could fulfill their every need.
It seems they had turned into a wild bunch
Sinning freely because they obviously thought
God had gone *out to lunch!*
Where was the love they once had
And why this rebellion that made Paul so sad?
It seems as if they wanted earthly fame
And were choosing preachers who felt no desire
To glorify the Heavenly Father's name.
Paul's goal was to live up to God's measure
And, because of his love for these people
He considered them his personal treasure.
Love does that, you know.
What was it Ruth said? "I'll go where you go!"
Its still that way and as our love grows
Folks won't doubt us when they see it shows!
Love can't be hid
if we love others like Jesus did!

2ND CORINTHIANS 11

It is quite a feat for one who is darkness
To portray himself as 'light'
But Satan has duped many a person causing
Them to lose their sight.
Our 'sights' should be on Jesus
Our hopes on Him only!
To turn away from Him is to face life
Bleak and lonely.
Many have posed doctrines contrary to the cross
And have crossed the line of faith
Much to their loss.
Paul tells the people how true he has been.
His simply said, "God can take away your sin!"
The wisest preacher must not stray.
There is one gospel to be presented God's way.
Jesus is our propitiation
And only He can give us salvation!
No greater news can we share.
Heaven is our home and He will meet us there!

2ND CORINTHIANS 12

Paul considered boasting to be very vain
And even though he bragged he would also complain.
It seems he has to put these men back in touch
For they began to doubt his message too much.
I believe Paul had most of his trouble
From preachers who were turning the gospel
Into *wood, hay, and stubble!*
So he told them of God having given him
An amazing revelation
Even though he did it with a hint of hesitation.
How could Paul explain something so great
It could not be explained?
"You have made me act like a fool." he said
In a style painfully strained!
And his last words in this chapter
Could've been, "what are you adulterers after?"

2ND CORINTHIANS 13

Paul spoke of love in 1st Corinthians thirteen
But they must have said, "what does he mean?"
And, *they say*, the third time is the charm
And perhaps Paul thought, trying one more time
May not help but should do no harm.
It seems these people's skulls were made
Of iron and clay
Truths hard to get in and easy to slip away!
His advice to them is obviously his last
And comes down to us from a Christian past.
"Check up on yourselves," he said
And if they discovered they were truly Christian
They would not live in fear and dread.

The "I Love My Bible" Commentary

"Are you really Christians?" He asked.
For, you see, hypocrisy can make holiness
An impossible task.
Essentially he said, "If you do what I say
You'll be happy as you grow in Christ?"

"You will have a glorious love and friendship
Though free to us, was highly priced!"
So we can say that none of us, too, need to fall
For the grace of the Lord Jesus and God also
Will be with us all!

Note: I suppose if one would say love shines brighter through discipline, one would have to say it at least with a grin! For nobody likes discipline as Paul was well aware. And he knew when he chastised his people, they thought he didn't care. But Paul had a heart as big as Texas, tenderly fine tuned with strong reflexes! Many times he admitted crying over the harsh words he had to write, and he must have wondered why his people often recoiled in spite.

True, godly love is so strong and deep it can not be displayed in movies, or tv, or in any photograph! Therefore people can not understand how it is often portrayed through God's rod(strong though it may be)and in the form of His tender loving staff! Remember what David said? "Thy rod and thy staff, they **comfort** me!" If God disciplines those He loves, as He says He does, then its His way of **pruning us** to receive AND give a greater love. *Love never fails!* If Paul had a theme for 1st and 2nd Corinthians–that is it! *Love never fails!*

*Grace be to you
and peace from God our Father,
and from the Lord Jesus Christ.*

*Blessed be God,
even the Father of our Lord Jesus Christ,
the Father of mercies,
and the God of all comfort;*

*who comforteth us in all our tribulation,
that we may be able to comfort them
who are in any trouble,
by the comfort wherewith
we ourselves are comforted of God.*
(2 Corinthians 1:2-4kjv)

The "I Love My Bible" Commentary
(The Book of Galatians)

GALATIANS 1

We say with Paul
"All glory to God through the ages
Amen!"
There is no end to the reasons
and we surely know not
where to begin!
No wonder Paul was incredulous when people
Turned away from God to seek a path to heaven
No angel would dare to trod!
Though Paul's words were at times unpleasant
That dear man stands at the top of faith's
  crescent.
Paul knew to whom he belonged
And his soul ached for the One he had wronged.
No one could change Paul's message
Nor could any one weaken his stand.
Christ had been lovingly revealed in him
And he refused to retreat despite any reprimand.
Chosen to be born anew
Paul would stand tall and true!
"Glory to God," he would say
and it echoes down to us today!
And we who have this old, old story
join Paul in giving our Savior glory!

GALATIANS 2

Like Paul I say
"I am crucified with Christ.
I was there(in spirit)when He died.
He took my hand in His
and I felt Him shudder when he cried
'My God, my God
why has thou forsaken me?'
But He knew all along!
It was through His death
I could sing salvation's song.
I was there when my Savior peered
through the darkness of man's soul
and I felt the fear that grew
with the vengeful thunder's roll!
I was there when He arose
to give me life anew
and I basked in the warmth
of His glory
that sheds a golden hue!
Kept in protective custody
guarded by the law
I now have His promises
on which I can draw.
Only He died
but I am crucified
to live as He lives
to show all people
the magnificent love He gives!"
And Paul says I am
born again to be the spiritual child
of Abraham!

GALATIANS 3

Could Paul have said to us, "Oh foolish people
Have you been hypnotized?"
Would he say we doubt the chasteness
Of this gospel he so highly prized?
If we are easily led away through traditions
Handled carelessly
We may forget the beauty of our salvation's
Great simplicity.
We do not depend on works though we work
With diligent zeal.
Its our ultimate trust in Him that creates in us
A resilient faith that is real!
If we are to be foolish, lets be foolish for Him
For *none* of God's promises will ever grow dim!
We are told that faith holds on, holds up,
  holds out
And will never, never cause us to doubt!

Comment on Galatians

GALATIANS 4

Have you ever been down a road with fog
So thick you couldn't see
With only a broad yellow stripe to show you
Where you ought to be?
Have you ever tried to walk at night with just
Enough light to give you the edge
And to keep you from straying close to a ledge?
The law was like that, one not knowing for sure
If he had tried hard enough to be regarded pure
      -always walking in fear
      -never knowing if harm was near!
One can call that introspection and it causes
One to focus in the wrong place
For looking at one's self keeps our eyes off
Of God's loving face!
And that is the difference between
  law and grace!
Law and grace are two brothers longing
For the same spiritual gift
But the one who depends on the law discovers
A deep and ever widening rift!
It is simply hard to understand
Why God merely asks us to hold His hand.
Grace walks beside the Lord
While those who claim they keep the law
Walk far behind!
And their vision of spiritual oneness grows
Progressively blind!
Law never brought the warmth of walking
By His side
Nor the assurance that the penalty for sin
Had been fully satisfied.
Somehow that emptiness and loss
Had to be satisfied at the cross!
And where the law says maybe
Grace guarantees us we are free!
Our Savior took away the law's futility
When He said, "Come and follow me!"

GALATIANS 5

I am free!
I am loved!
I am saved!
I count on nothing at all
  except God's grace!
Nobody is going to tell me otherwise
  for Jesus is my blessed hope
  and my greatest prize!
This is the "Spirit" chapter
  and under His control
I have no doubt I can reach my goal!
We are clothed in garments of salvation
  and robes of righteousness
    (see Isaiah 61:10)
  God's holy suits!
And in every pocket we can find
  the Holy Spirit's fruits!
There is love, joy and peace
  to give our troubled hearts release.
  And longsuffering, gentleness
  goodness, faith, meekness
  and temperance
  requires no need for recompense!
We have nailed our evil natures
  to our Savior's cross
  and we who love God's salvation
  know its wise to let Him boss!
God's hands cover mine
  like a mighty glove
  and I am kept completely safe
  in the circle of His love!

GALATIANS 6

Will there be grief instead of laughter
Because we have disobeyed the good advice
We find in this chapter?
Do we gently and humbly help others
Who have fallen into sin

The "I Love My Bible" Commentary

Or do we, like that self-righteous Pharisee,
Wag our tongues at the trouble he's in?
To share each others troubles is to obey
Our Lord's command.
Someday we may be the ones too weak
To make a stand.
We won't make comparisons if we do our best
To help one who is weaker to *pass his test.*
And Paul says we should never tire
Of doing right
Some day we'll earn a great reward
If we are faithful *in the fight!*
It is wonderful to know the cross of Christ
Can truly save
Whether I'm famous or infamous, rich or poor
Cowardly or brave!
It is His cross only that turned me around
And sent my soul seeking His higher ground!
And I say to you as did Paul.
May the grace of the Lord Jesus be with you all!

No note here.
Just Paul's words!

The fruit of the Spirit is

Love
Joy
Peace
Longsuffering
Gentleness
Goodness
Faith
Meekness
Temperance

Against such there is no law!

'Nuff said!

*Be not deceived;
God is not mocked:
for whatsoever a man soweth,
that shall he also reap.*

*For he that soweth to his flesh
shall of the flesh reap corruption;
but he that soweth to the Spirit
shall of the Spirit reap life everlasting.*

*And us not be weary in well doing:
for in due season we shall reap,
if we faint not.*

*As we have therefore opportunity,
let us do good unto all men,
especially unto them that are of
the household of faith.*
(Galatians 6:7-10kjv)

The "I Love My Bible" Commentary
(The Book of Ephesians)

EPHESIANS 1

Who says I'm not loved?
Who says I'm not wanted?
Those mean and ugly innuendoes
only leaved me undaunted.
God's Word tells me
He loved me even before
the world began
and back in the days He designed salvation
I was included in His plan!
In the richness of His grace
God covered me with His salvation!
He understands me fully
and how I feel in any situation.
When I think of how God delights in me
I give Him praise
and because of what my Lord has done
I will walk in beauty all my days!
But, can you imagine God being richer
because of me when I'm so spiritually poor?
Still, the less I think of me
I'm sure He loves me all the more!
We cannot begin to imagine
how God fills us with Himself
when we're so tiny and finite
but neither can we understand
how He gives us His love
His life and His glorious light!
God's salvation is not based
on *anything* I can do
He reached down and saved me
just because He wanted to!

EPHESIANS 2

God's curse is stronger than an atomic bomb
But man keeps marching to a different drum
Flaunting his own aplomb.
Why does anyone ignore the greatest love
In this seemingly endless universe?
Can't he see his denial leads him through doubt
To a future much, much worse?
He still counts on his own righteousness
(see Isaiah 64:6)
Which leads him down a dead-end street
Where he will learn he designed his own defeat.
Christ has done it all
and no one has to fall.
It is only God's mercy
that saves us from sin
only God's love
that extends grace to all men!
Oh, the matchless grace
of our Lord and King
who puts hope in our hearts
and gives us a joyous song to sing!
His kindness cannot be described.
We, who were strangers, are now
completely His and fully satisfied!
He gave us pure love!
He gave us new life!
We sit in heavenly realms
far away from earthly strife.
Oh, we walk this earth all right
but we are bathed
in the glory of His light
-not a reward
for what we've done
-only because we believe
in God's Son!
We are growing pillars
in the temple of grace
and someday, we'll know the joy
of seeing our Savior face to face!
(For by grace are you saved through faith
and that *not* of yourselves
it is the gift of God, not of works
lest any man should boast.)
Ephesians 2:8 & 9 KJV

Comment on Ephesians

EPHESIANS 3

(If Paul could say this
so can I and I'll put
my name in his place!)
I, Jean, the servant of Christ
have imprisoned myself
in fear and doubt
though Jesus gave His all to break
the shackles of fear and brought me out!
I have full share in the riches of His grace
so why in the world do I persist
in falling flat on my face?
Just think!
If Paul didn't deserve God's grace
I deserve it much, much less
but I still have the endless treasures
of Christ
and I know I am blessed!
Oh, how perfectly wise
God has proved Himself to be
and to think the wisest King of the Ages
has extended His love to me!
I'll never be able to comprehend
the great love of this One
who calls Himself <u>my friend</u>!
Will I stop loving Him?
No, never!
I will love my God
forever and forever!

EPHESIANS 4

It is strange that we have to beg people to be
Humble and gentle and kind.
Paul says we are parts of ONE body
So, in effect, we should be of one mind!
We have the same Spirit!
We have the same love!
We have been called to share a future of glory!
We have the same God who has shared with us
His incredible love story!
He is over us all, and in us all and is living
Through us all and He imparts
Special abilities out of His rich house of gifts
To strengthen and encourage all our hearts!
Why did He do all this for us?
It is so we can be full of His love
-full of His strength and most of all
So we will not bring the Holy Spirit sorrow
For He has chosen us to share in His great
And *golden one time tomorrow!*
We are not to live as the unsaved do
-not driven by evil things and reckless lust
But by hearts pure and true.
For His salvation is a mighty elegant eagle
That soars graciously high.
Imagine riding its wings to the *sweet by and by!*

EPHESIANS 5

Guide lines for Christians are grossly ignored.
Try to talk about them and others act bored.
But they are so beautiful and bring a happiness
We can't describe.
God's laws are an uplifting toddy in which
We all can imbibe!
"No sex sin," God says, "and no foul talk
Or coarse jokes.
We, who love the Lord, must be pure, gentle
And humble folks!
And we honor Christ when we show our love
And honor to one another
And it pleases God when we respect each other!
Paul speaks of marriage and says we are one
We should be as bonded as Siamese twins
And when one cheats nobody wins.
How can we excuse adultery and deceit
When God's style of love is so utterly sweet?
Life is good relationships and all else is wood,
Hay and useless stubble.
When we fail to love, all we gain is trouble!

The "I Love My Bible" Commentary

EPHESIANS 6

I may not be a soldier but I have armor anyway
And faith is my shield to help me win everyday!
And, every time the old devil has roared
I only have to banish God's mighty sword!
God's *belt of truth* keeps me strong
And I know as I yearn for His approval
I will do no wrong!
And I know my enemies are mighty
But our mighty God is stronger still
And he hears when I pray in the light of His will.
Isn't it marvelous to know we can claim
All God's blessings and His grace?
        Just think!
Someday we'll see Him face to face!

Note: Paul had such love for his people that he wanted to be sure they were equipped to live the *good life. What people call the good life today has nothing to do with life.* It has to do with things. God's word assures us that loving others is truly the good life. All the things we have now will rust or rot but the love we have for one another will live forever. Paul's test for love seemed to be–if you loved someone you would not cause him or her to sin against the Lord. We need to stop thinking of 'things' as having quality and re-qualify love! Paul stressed that over and over. I used to think Paul was harsh. and yet I began to see there is a difference between harshness and *tough love. God's tough love gets us through the hard times. Try it!*

*But God, who is rich in mercy,
for his great love wherewith he loved us,
even when we were dead in sins,
hath quickened us together with Christ,
(by grace ye are saved;)*

*And hath raised us up together,
and made us sit together in heavenly places
in Christ Jesus:*

*That in the ages to come
he might shew the exceeding riches
of his grace
in his kindness toward us
through Christ Jesus.*

*<u>For by grace are ye saved through faith</u>
and that not of yourselves;
it is the gift of God:*

Not of works lest any man should boast.

*<u>For we are His workmanship,
created in Christ Jesus unto good works,</u>
Which God hath before ordained
that we should walk in them.*
(Ephesians 2: 4-10kjv)

The "I Love My Bible" Commentary
(The Book of Philippians)

PHILIPPIANS 1

There is no better wish
for a man like Paul to make
than that Christians love each other
for the Savior's sake!
Paul's longing was deep and sincere
and he also prayed
that we hold our Savior dear!
He is just talking through
the Philippians to us.
"Be inwardly clean," he says
"and don't ever fuss!"
We must do *all* that we do
in order to honor our Lord
and that means we must
always be on guard.
We may even wish we could
leave this world behind
to live in an atmosphere
where everyone is loving and kind.
But, whatever happens
Paul wants us to know
only in trusting God
can our faith find a chance to grow!
We can live in eager expectation
for-bad or good- the Lord holds our hands
in any situation.
And-dear friends don't ever forget
why Paul said dying is better yet!

PHILIPPIANS 2

Paul wanted these people to know
The reason our Lord came in the form of a slave
Was so even the lowest of the low could see
Even they were eligible for the gifts He gave.
He considered everyone a lost and lonely child
None were beyond God's reach and none were
  too defiled.
Christ obeyed our Heavenly Father to the end
When he told that repentant thief on the cross
He was there to be his friend.
In the darkness of fear Christ shared His light
So none of us would ever have to cower
In despairing fright.
Paul implies that we, too, are to be like
Beacons of light speaking no words of blame
-shrinking back from ever disgracing Christ's
Holy name!
As Paul needed many helpers, so do we
For many people do not know the love of God
Can set them free.
So-dear friends of mine
freely share the light
God has given us to shine!

PHILIPPIANS 3

"Whatever happens, be glad!"
This from the man who had
many reasons to be sad.
But whether in prison or out
Paul's love for God
left no room for doubt.
Paul knew the heavenly life
had been highly priced
and it came straight to us
through the love of Christ.
That is why Paul laid aside
those many traditions and laws
and committed himself
to God's higher cause!
He strained to reach
the end of his "race"
and challenged us
to keep up the pace.
He knew we'll get to see
that glorious future
God has waiting for you and me!

Comment on Philippians

PHILIPPIANS 4

"I love you," are the sweetest
words ever spoken
and were it true of all of us
no hearts would ever be broken.
Paul was always concerned
about the spiritual state
of his Christian brothers
and, in love, he taught them
to look for the fine, good things
in others!
Only if *true love* is given
free reign and full release
can we children of God
ever experience ultimate joy
and eternal peace!
But, we must remember
*God's definition of love is
that it is holy and pure
and it is like a blanket
that keeps us safe and secure!*

God says His ways are higher than ours
and it is far more exquisite than
the world's most beautiful flowers!
Life would never be so grim
if only we'd give the love
He has given us back to Him!
Maybe then, we could understand
why Paul closes with the mention
of generosity's well-earned reward
because we need to be aware
when we have a loving, giving spirit
we truly love and honor our Lord!

Note: Paul seems to be growing mellower
and I suspect its because these people are
growing in grace. And in *grace, there is always
room to grow!* And-I haven't counted the times
he used this word *love* but I believe he used it
more than any other word and *it* is definitely the
greatest word in God's heavenly dictionary!
*I venture to say no one would ever go wrong
following Paul's advice!*

The "I Love My Bible" Commentary
(The Book of Colossians)

COLOSSIANS 1

It feels like love, this joy that fills our days!
It seems like light-*pure holy light*-that guides
Our path ways!
And, its surely like faith that keeps us going
When the Spirit sets gentle winds to blowing!
God did so much to eliminate any walls
We may have built
When Christ carried away all of our guilt!
*Paul says we stand before God covered with
His great love
And it's the only thing that comes with an
Eternal guarantee from our Father up above!
Christ is our only hope of glory
And its His energy in us that compels us
To tell this blessed story!*

COLOSSIANS 2

*In Christ lie hidden mighty treasures
that far surpass
all of earth's fleeting pleasures!
Christ is our 'knitting' machine
and he also weaves us a life
that is holy, pure, and clean!
We can never imagine the scope
Paul covers when he says
Christ is our only hope!
This vital union Paul mentions
will keep God's people
from unholy dissension.
No earthly philosophy
has ever contaminated
a soul (trusting in Christ)
who is fully consecrated.
Our Savior has taken us
out of the shadow of the law
into the sunshine of His grace
and given us a love
no one any where can replace!
We know we cannot trust ourselves
to keep the law
so we fully depend on Christ
to cleanse our souls
from every flaw!*

COLOSSIANS 3

Love should be as natural
as breathing out and breathing in
but, because we have neglected it
horror haunts the hearts of men.
No Christian should be remiss
in that of which Paul speaks of
which such clarity
as he reminds us to keep our hearts
full of charity.
Paul advises us to have love
for our children
wives for their husbands
husbands for their wives
plus all other relationships
that bless us all our lives!
"Love is a privilege," Paul said
"and a responsibility!"
Love draws all people together
in holy humility!
Paul found this to be factual.
Truly, love is a natural!

COLOSSIANS 4

Paul speaks of the mystery
of Christ
but the biggest mystery
is why so many Christians(?)
do not truly love or honor Him!
So many walk on the edge
of the obedience circle

Comment on Colossians

dangerously off balance
on the edge of the rim!
The part I like the best
is when Paul says
"Let your speech be always
with grace
seasoned with salt
that you may know how
to answer every man"
(face to face!).
And Paul should have quoted
the Savior-the one he loves
for Jesus said
"Be wise as serpents
and harmless as doves!"
He mentions many helpers
who stood by his side
-men whose love for Paul
was always deep and wide!
Paul always closed with
"Grace be with you!"
He'd experienced the grace of God
and knew what it could do!
And it would be sin
if they didn't do good to all men!

Note:
In summation, Paul seems to be saying
don't be weary!
Prayer will subdue a heart
that is dark and dreary.
The sun shines when God sends answers
that are strong and sweet.
No other can possibly create a life
so absolutely complete!
So our witness should be
sensible and loyal.
The Good news is
our Lord is utterly
and omnipotently royal!
But even slaves could approach
the Lord as well as their owners.
You see, when we walk
with our Lord
none will ever be *loaners*!
Even though in prison
Paul was concerned
about his Christian friends
and he greeted one and all
with the assurance
that God's love never ends!

The "I Love My Bible" Commentary
(*1ˢᵗ and 2ⁿᵈ Thessalonians*)

1ˢᵗ THESSALONIANS 1

The power of the Holy Spirit spread
To all churches large and small!
Paul's intent was to remind the Thessalonians
The Holy Spirit would not let them fall.
But it was, and even now must be,
A two-way street for those who follow.
Unless we open our hearts
To God's blessed Holy Spirit
Our faith will be hollow!
Oh, to know the God who is living and true
—to know how much He is concerned
     with everything we do
  is a miracle spawned by His grace!
God did bring Jesus back to life
And one day we will see Him face to face!
The names may change(Romans, Greeks, etc.)
But the message is the same!
To know we belong to God compels us
To glorify His name!

1ˢᵗ THESSALONIANS 2

To speak as messengers from God is *job one*
And none preached more sincerely
Than the precious preacher Paul had done!
Trusted to tell the truth, anchored in faith alone
Paul never changed the message
He had received straight from God's throne!
He never stooped to pretending.
His faith in God was sure and unbending.
We should live for the same One he did
For Paul always longed to do all our Father bid!
The Good News is still the same Good News!
It was God's saving message Paul proclaimed
And we should live in such a way as to
Never embarrass God or never be ashamed!
And we will all practice what we've heard
If we remember *God's Word IS God's Word!!!*

1ˢᵗ THESSALONIANS 3

We're so close to being bad
  too far from being good
  but Paul has given us
  an example to follow
  if only we would!
Pray and work and love each other
  for God would not have us
  take advantage of one another.
  He helped Paul put into practice
  the things
  that inevitably pull at our
  heart strings!
For, you see, a deeper understanding
  of God's love
  draws us into the circle
  of His grace
  where we stand blessed of God
  in His high and holy place!
We may be close to being bad
  yet the bad will go away
  when we place our hands in His
  and *never, never forget to pray!*

1ˢᵗ THESSALONIANS 4

The cry of the archangel
and the great trumpet call
of God
awaits us yet
so living holy and pleasing God
are two necessities
we must not forget!
We often say we are
going to heaven or bust
and then engage ourselves
in questionable lust.
Only careless fools
refuse to live by God's rules.

455

Comment on Thessalonians

We must let brotherly love
guide us always
for we know the Lord is coming
in the latter days!
Who knows?
It might be tomorrow
when we welcome Him in joy
or hang our heads in sorrow.
Indeed, we must watch
for the clouds to part
for there will stand the One
who will bring joy
to every watchful heart!

1ST THESSALONIANS 5

Like a thief sneaking in the night
like the wings of an eagle
suddenly taking flight
like a million volt
lightening bolt
that appears from nowhere
our Lord will appear
suddenly out of thin air!
We are to be on constant alert .
We know the man who guards his house
will never lose his shirt!
Over and over our Lord has warned
"Be ready!"
And He demands that our faith
always be strong and steady.
In the meantime we can honor Him
by respecting the leaders
of our church
and His words will guide us
if we indulge in heavenly research!
We do know His desire
is that we do no wrong
and develop a love pure and strong.
We will, if we follow
the Holy Spirit's direction.

When He comes He must find
his people
Striving for perfection.
Out of the blue
our Lord will appear
and we who love Him dearly
hope that day is drawing near!

2ND THESSALONIANS 1

Our greatest glory will be that we belong
to our precious Lord
and because of His tender mercy
He will give
each of us His own special reward.
How tenderly God loves His own!
He is sweeter and more dear
than anyone we have ever known!
How can we ever thank Him enough
for His wonderful gifts?
Paul says thank the Lord
for every downcast soul He lifts.
Think about the One to whom you belong
and you will lift your voices in joyful song.
Someday our greatest joy will be
to see the One who set us free!

2ND THESSALONIANS 2

Rumors pierce the world's translucent skin
Threatening, frightening, numbing from within.
We spend too much time listening to rumors
And being deceived
Getting upset and excited and easily grieved.
But the rumor to which Paul refers
Is the worst of all
And has caused many a Christian to fall.
We can see the trick of those who lie
Is to trip us up.
They are dogs who act like an innocent pup.

The "I Love My Bible" Commentary

The one who lied to Adam and Eve
Still looks for victims to deceive.
He causes rebellion to anarchy itself
On the world stage
Bringing hatred, fear, crime, deceit
And consuming rage.
People do not know what is real anymore
And we get up every morning wondering
What the day holds in store.
Paul did say Satan was full of rebellion and hell
And would bury countless people under his spell.
But–if we hold on to the truth with a steady grip
We'll know when our enemy slips in
An unsavory tip!
He has planted many a doubt
But we know our Lord will straighten him out!
Gossip—we shouldn't ever pause to hear it.
    Our hearts should be tuned
        to the blessed Holy Spirit!

2ND THESSALONIANS 3

*Paul ends his letters
with such love and grace
sharing a godly love with his converts
that no one anywhere can replace!
His wish is my wish, too.
May God send a deeper understanding
Of His love from Himself to you!
And in this day of sin
we need to pray like Paul.
May God keep us safe from sin
and give courage to us all!
Paul's philosophy would not be popular
to the man on the street.
He said, "them that will not work
shall not eat!"
He may be harsh but we feel
he is encouraging a healthy ideal!*

Note: I really don't need to add much to this since the comment on chapter three seems to summerize these books well. I do think I should add, we should be like Paul- always faithful to our call!
We know our God of whom Paul speaks so lovingly will someday come for you and me!
I'd like to close this with the words John wrote in Revelations 22:20B. *Even so, come, Lord Jesus!*

*See that none render evil for evil
unto any man;
but ever follow that which is good,
both among yourselves, and to all men.*

Rejoice evermore.

Pray without ceasing.

*In everything give thanks
for this is the will of God in Christ Jesus concerning you.*

Quench not the Spirit.

Despise not prophesyings.

Prove all things, hold fast that which is good.

Abstain from all appearance of evil.

*And the very God of peace
sanctify you wholly;
and I pray God your whole spirit and soul and body
be preserved blameless
unto the coming of our Lord Jesus Christ.*

*Faithful is he that calleth you
who also will do it.*

Brethren, pray for us.
(1 Thessalonians 5: 15-25kjv)

The "I Love My Bible" Commentary
(1st and 2nd Timothy)

1ST TIMOTHY 1

Think we're not a family?
Look how Paul addresses Timothy!
He starts with three ideals
to keep *his children* from all wrong.
We are (Timothy especially) to be
filled with love
that comes from pure hearts
and clean minds
to keep our faith strong!
But, if you want to see a Christian
on a spiritual see-saw
then watch one who is consumed
with just keeping the law!
We are under grace
and it is grace that undergirds
*and sets us free to fly
higher than the birds!*
So, we are to cling tightly
to our faith in Christ
and keep our consciences clear.
Indeed!
Bringing shame to the name
of Christ
should be our biggest fear!

1ST TIMOTHY 2

Can you get the picture?
God is on one side
and we are on the other
and the *only one, Christ
who can bring us together
is willing to call himself
our brother!*
Read the prayer our Lord prayed
in John seventeen
and again you'll see
the power of prayer
(especially His)
and how much it can mean!
Paul said, "pray much
plead, and give thanks
for it pleases our Lord!"
It is the best way to fight
the fight of faith
with no holds barred!
So Paul advises us to pray
free of anger, resentment and sin.
It makes us one with Christ
who gave himself for all men.
But it looks as if
there might be a thorn in Paul's crown!
Was it a loving, forgiving heart
that so obviously put women down?
Maybe that is why Paul had to say
we must never forget to pray!

1ST TIMOTHY 3

If we are earnest, wholehearted followers
Of Christ–of course
We will know for sure He is our soul's
Great hidden source!
And Paul says a man who wants to be
A preacher or deacon has a good ambition
But he, of all people, needs a huge supply
Of our Lord's spiritual nutrition!
For he must know we need the guidance
Of godly ministers who walk close to our Lord
And they must be the first to know earthly greed
Brings no heavenly reward!
All the good deeds we need to follow after
Are mentioned by Paul in this chapter.
We can't go wrong following Paul's advice
For he encourages us to be utterly
and consistently nice!
Paul's heart was certainly in the right place
-next door to love and next door to grace!

Comment on Timothy

1ST TIMOTHY 4

Our hope is in the living God who died for all
In order that those who were spiritually dead
But now alive, will never have to fall!
He has given us the Holy Spirit to direct
Our deepest thoughts and tell us what to do.
We can not go wrong as we listen
To God's guidance flowing through!
He sends us love, faith and His clean thoughts
As our ideal.
*We **cannot** base our decisions on how we feel!*
And-obviously we are unable to surmise
The benefits of God's spiritual exercise.
But-we must practice in God's holy
And perfect incomparable "gym"
For our strength does come from Him!
We need His strength to overcome devils
Who practice hypocrisy and lies.
We can't let them *pull the wool over our eyes!*
Paul ends with "take heed"
For God's Word and Holy Spirit is all we need!

1ST TIMOTHY 5

This chapter states what we need today
when preachers seem to be
falling like flies!
God says here that many pastors
may be sinful and many of them
may seem to get away with their lies
but judgement day is coming
as surely as the sun rises and sets
and *unless they repent*
they must face the fact
God never forgets.
Paul also speaks of helpless widows
and their needs
and the church must remember
taking care of them
is one of its most noble deeds!
He also says our response
to all people must be holy and pure
for living holy in God's love
is the only way we can feel secure!

1ST TIMOTHY 6

We need sound, wholesome doctrine
as much as they did then!
Here, I think, Paul is saying
the harder men work for God
the more they encourage other men.
Remember, God's Word
is a powerful cleaner
for the *windows of the soul!*
It keeps His light coming through
cleaning our thoughts
to give us a perfect view!
The thought here is
though work is good for our souls
a monetary reward should be
the least of our goals!
For goodness and happiness
are like having money in the bank
for then we are truly rich
no matter our station or rank!
If we'd only remember the words
of our Lord
we won't get uptight
and we won't listen to accusations
that detour us from doing right!
God's love, His mercy and His grace
is evidenced in all Christ did for us
and is the reason God's people
join in
as all heaven sings
The most important thing
in heaven or on earth is to know
our God is Lord of lords
and King of kings!

The "I Love My Bible" Commentary

Paul must have thought some preachers
were hopelessly insane
for he closes, telling Timothy
to avoid vain babblings (doctrines?)
that were false and profane!

2ND TIMOTHY 1

Remember, dear Christian, God has not
given us the spirit of fear
but of power, of love
and of a sound mind.
He has blessed us richly
with faithful followers of the cross
who are loving and kind.
Paul reminded Timothy of his faith
which he had inherited
from his mother and grandmother.
And Paul convincingly assured Timothy
he could find salvation in no other!
(Than our Lord)
Paul fought hard
for his faith in the Lord.
And the reason he fought
was to encourage us to hold tightly
to the pattern of truth we've been taught.
Remember the everlasting life
God has given you.
Pass this great hope on to others
just as Paul would want you to do!

2ND TIMOTHY 2

*God's truth stands firm
like a great rock!
Our Lord affirmed it when He said
"Fear not little flock!"
But Paul had to tell Timothy
to "be strong in the strength
Christ Jesus gives you
even though you may suffer as I do!"
We should be faithful to this life
of grace
this life Paul calls "an endless race!"
He says work hard like a farmer
who raises a large crop.
Of ALL people, we have no reason
to stop!
But, we will never carry out
these great acts
unless we faithfully stick to the facts!
The facts!
Jesus came to save sinners!
Our Lord gave His all
and **that** is the basic formula
of our call!*

2ND TIMOTHY 3

What a stinging rebuke and what an awesome
Statement that comes from Paul.
He says many will love only themselves
And the love of money will cause many to fall!
Children will be disobedient ingrates
And many will have no redeeming traits.
People will be unloving, unfaithful, unkind
Refusing to worship, unsettled in the mind.
This is how Paul describes saint-less sinners
Who care nothing for the Heavenly Olympics
Or its gold medal winners.
Though they may go to church they will sneer
At the pure holy commandments they will hear.
*Frightening as it may seem
we live in that age of doubt
and we must face the fact this is the age
Paul was talking about.
People say wrong is right
and right is wrong.
More than ever now
the people of God must be strong!*

Comment On Timothy

*We know the scriptures make us wise
and we who love the Lord realize
His way will prevail.
People of God
we will NOT fail!*

2ND TIMOTHY 4

We must proclaim the Word of God
urgently
every time we get a chance
day in and day out, constantly!

No matter if people won't listen
to the truths He gives
we must tell the world
our Savior lives!
God is not dead!
He's not even asleep!
The Great Shepherd still cares
for His little sheep!
He steadies us with His mighty arm
and though we may suffer
He will deliver us from all harm.
People who are truly clever
will praise the Lord forever and forever!

Note: 1st and 2nd Timothy (also Titus)are the pastoral letters and its plain to see Paul expected no more out of Timothy than he did of himself. Paul certainly would not have made headlines in the papers or on TV. The media seems to enjoy only pointing out the failures and I could name several. But—none of us Christians are perfect! Our Lord knows that! **But**–He has made it possible for us to be. He's given us directions(or His map as I said in Genesis 1).And those directions are in His Holy Word– ***The Bible!*** Most comforting of all, He forgives us when we fall.(Read 2Chronicles 7:14 again).And be sure to read 1st John 1:9-10.
What our preachers need to realize is-their responsibilities are greater because their call is greater. Because of that we need to pray earnestly for them every day! Thank God for true and faithful preachers. Try to stay away from those who are not!

The "I Love My Bible" Commentary
(Titus and Philemon)

TITUS 1

Like Paul told Titus, we are sent
To give the Word its true meaning-interpreting
It as God meant.
Paul was controversial, but his heart was true
And he wanted Titus to be faithful, too.
He never tried to confuse anyone.
No one can doubt how much Paul loved
    God's Son!
He speaks of truths alien to many in these days!
To be a fair, sensible man, clean minded
And level-headed, was his rule always.
Paul says a person who is pure of heart
Sees goodness in every thing
And, unless we act accordingly, how can we
Come to know our Great King?

TITUS 2

Whatever we say for the Lord
    is more precious than gold!
Then why are so many of us so timid
    instead of courageous and bold?
God offers the free gift of life
    to everyone
    made available to us
    through believing in His Son!
His requirements are still the same.
Only in living God-honoring lives
    do we glorify His name!
How we treat each other
    shows how much(or how little)
    we have grown in grace
    and showing each other love and respect
    makes this old world a better place!
ALL of these things are what we teach.
    We may walk this earth
    but loving and obeying God
    definitely puts Heaven in our reach!

TITUS 3

All the words of Paul has written
    are forever true
    given to help us Christians
    to examine what we do.
He says we cannot earn salvation
    when Christ has already
    washed our sins away!
It is in following Jesus
    we experience joy every day!
Paul tells Titus not to become involved
    in arguments about God's laws
    for we have been saved by love
    that binds us to a higher cause!
    And I want you to know
    to Jesus is still the only way to go!

PHILEMON

In prison himself, Paul's empathy prevailed.
He would beg Philemon to forgive Onesimus
Who, himself, could have been easily jailed.
Onesimus was seeking freedom from slavery
In those days, that took considerable bravery!
Paul considered himself free though in chains
And his style of freedom still remains!
    Love is the great emancipator
    And comes only from our Creator

Note: Paul successfully pleaded for Onesimus
because he knew the true meaning of freedom
and the trauma of slavery. But the real slavery
was slavery of the soul. That is the reason for
his directions in the Timothy and Titus letters.
No one is free if his soul is enslaved! Paul's
desire was to free the spiritual slaves even more
so than the physical ones–like Onesimus!

I charge thee before God,
and the Lord Jesus Christ,
who shall Judge the quick and the dead
at his appearing and his kingdom;

Preach the Word;
be instant in season, out of season;
reprove, rebuke, extort
with all longsuffering and doctrine.

For the time will come
when they will not endure sound doctrine;
but after their own lusts
shall they heap to themselves teachers
having itching ears;

And they shall turn away from the truth,
and shall be turned unto fables.

But watch thou in all things, endure afflictions,
do the work of an evangelist,
make full proof of thy ministry.

For I am now ready to be offered,
and the time of my departure is at hand.

I have fought a good fight.
I have finished my course,
I have kept the faith.

Henceforth there is laid up for me
a crown of righteousness,
which the Lord, the righteous judge
shall give me at that day:
and not to me only,
but all them that love his appearing.
(2 Timothy 4: 1-8 kjv)

The "I Love My Bible" Commentary
(The Book of Hebrews)

HEBREWS 1

God's glory shines out through God's Son!
Regulating the universe is just one
*of the **minor** things our Lord has done!*
(See Job 26:7-14LB)
But-His crowning achievement
was sacrificing His life for all men
for only He could rescue us
from all our sin!
God opened His one way street
and gained a victory
in which no devil can compete!
Through Christ, God met us face to face!
Through Christ, He sent us His grace!
No other bears such great esteem
no matter how great they may seem.
Even all the kings through out the ages
have been unworthy to tie His shoe laces!
Those who have dishonored our Lord
face a devastating retreat
down to the bottomless pit
charged with atomic heat.
But those who worship God
and claim Him as their friend
know the honor of loving Him
will never come to an end!
And Paul says, concerning angels
that they are ordained
with the dedication
to cherish and care for
those who have been given
the glorious gift of salvation!
It is an unlimited credit card
that gives eternal access to our Lord!

HEBREWS 2

A tumble weed drifts with the wind
here and there
and unless we listen to God's Word
we, too, will tumble in despair.
And when we pause to wonder
why we are weak
we must admit we fail to listen
when God's preachers(prophets)speak!
But there is no one who can
adequately describe
the strength Christ has given me
and *no way* I can ever repay Him
for giving me eternity!
How could One so perfect
suffer for one with so much guilt
and cleanse me to the uttermost
completely to the hilt?
He devised a way to make my soul divine
and He is not ashamed to say
all He has and all He is-is mine!
He is more-much more
than any mere angel
this One who became a Jew
to be God's High Priest
in order to give abundant life
and do it lovingly for me and you!
No book has ever held a message so sweet.
God sent His Son to make our lives complete!

HEBREWS 3

After reading chapters one and two
knowing all of the above
we have every reason to serve our Lord
with thankful hearts
and boundless love!
Paul uses the word "therefore"
as icing on the cake.
All that Christ did for us compels us
to do all things for His sake!
But there is a limit to God's patience
when we try to limit Him.

Comment on Hebrews

Those who did, saw the promised land
but heard a message sadly grim.
God would never let them in
and He proved to them
(and to us)
unbelief is a terrible sin.
Consider those who failed the test
and were never able to enter
God's perfect place of rest!
We must beware for we could see also
that Heaven is a place we might never go.
Ah! But knowing all of the above
should give us the incentive
to honor and obey
the One who gives us such great love!

HEBREWS 4

"Believe me," God says. "I know what I say!"
"You must walk with me in faith each day.
You think I don't know when you don't trust me
And that you have secret thoughts I cannot see."
Great is the heart of my God and it will beat
Far beyond the time our rest in Him is complete!
He is full of living power
With ever-seeking eyes that watch tenderly
Over His children, hour after hour after hour!
And His promise stands like a great rock
Jutting from the sea.
God says, "those who love me will come to me!"
Clouds floating gracefully in the sky
Only show how swiftly time is passing by.
He knows us to the depths of our hearts
  -inside and out!
And our Lord's precious heart is broken
When we are full of doubt.
Still He watches, eagerly waiting
Wishing we would go beyond just contemplating.
Meantime God holds out powerful, loving hands
And as He has done from the beginning of time
-waiting and watching, there He stands!

HEBREWS 5

I am powerless but I worship One
whose power knows no limit
and, as always, He has promised
to be where I need Him
minute by minute!
He lingered at the cross
so I would not have to linger in fear.
When ever I need Him
this one much more powerful
than Melchisedec is here!
They nailed His hands to the cross
but no one could nail His heart.
Strange that I should be saved
because He hung on a 'T' shaped weapon
unsafe for Him.
Stranger still, that I walk in a light
that on that day grew so dim!
And now I have a love
that will never go away
because He delivered himself
to suffer on that day.
Endless should be our love and respect
for this One who is greater
than Melchisedec!
Paul knew how necessary it would be
for us to "preach"
its there, this heavenly land
we want to reach!
And the One who lives on
that eternal throne
knows we can't make it on our own!
Where Jesus is
love comes out of the woodwork
faith comes from the depths of despair
joy springs up like a fountain.
Where Jesus is
those who walk in darkness
see a great light.
Where Jesus is!

The "I Love My Bible" Commentary

HEBREWS 6

We 'stomp' over the same old ground
Until it hardens
And we spoil the hallowed soil of the soul
Where God abundantly pardons.
Instead of becoming mature from holy 'food'
We should eat
We want *fast foods that ferment to rotten meat.*
God's great food grows stale in the darkness
Of the unrepentant heart
Where the bacteria of sin thrives
Until we pull God's curtains of light apart!
We have tested the wonderful food of heaven
-shared it in the light of His love.
We walk this earth below but keep our eyes
On our home above!
And the truths we hear will abound
To help us walk on hallowed ground
Where the 'Bread of Life' is our only leaven
And partaking of Him is our way to heaven!

HEBREWS 7

Just as Melchisedec came to Abraham
that faith filled man
so does our High Priest
but Paul says
He brings us a better plan!
Melchisedec could not live
in the heart of Abraham
as does the Lord in ours.
Abraham walked a barren land.
We live among
faith's most fragrant flowers!
High priests come and go
but **not** the True High Priest.
He lives forever to save unto the uttermost
even the ones the world considers
to be the very least!
Never once was Jesus weak and sinful.
Never once did He fail!
Those Priests who served before Him
stand in His shadow-forever pale!
Will He disappoint us? Never!
Jesus is our High Priest
forever and forever!

HEBREWS 8

God looked at the lambs but they wouldn't do.
He rejected the bulls, and the billy goats, too.
They just covered men's sins
Like God had covered Adam and Eve.
Lambs or goats could not change a heart
Bent on following doctrines meant to deceive.
Man who deliberately follows those
Who are utterly sinister
Need the guidance of God's heavenly minister.
Only Christ could take His pen
And write God's new agreement deep within.
One can turn from the altar and forget all
In which he took part.
But we can't forget what God has written
In the depths of the heart.
And how exciting it is that our greatest reward
Is in the wonderfully marvelous privilege.
Of knowing Christ Jesus our Lord!
Paul would not have us forget
Christ is much greater and kinder
Then was Melchisedec!

HEBREWS 9

Until I accepted Christ's death in my behalf
The sins God held against me
Were likely stored in the world's largest vault.
Because Christ died for me I can gladly say
God sees me now without a single fault!
Once for all, He took his blood to that holy place
And now, in Heaven, my name is written
Once for all time because of His grace!

Comment on Hebrews

Moses sprinkled the blood of animals.
Our Lord sprinkled His own!
Moses walked wilderness trails.
Jesus reigns now on His throne !
There is no comparison between the two
For Moses only told us what to do
But our Savior showed us how!
Through His death and resurrection
And because we know He lives
We have eternal salvation
And we *know* we have it *now!*

HEBREWS 10

Paul says the "old" has gone down the drain!
The law can't save a soul or ease our pain.
He says the law is too hard to keep.
The one who depends on only keeping the law
Will cause himself to weep.
For the law only proves we are sinful fools
Who never did, never could, and never will
Completely fulfil God's holy rules.
But we have an advocate who did not falter
    when He came to say
"Oh, God, I will lay myself on the alter!"
He is the *only sacrifice* that can make us perfect
In God's sight.
Christ is our *Morning Star*, our brightest light!
Now we can go to our *Father* without fear
For He bids us all to come and draw near.
In Christ, God sees us as being clean and pure!
And, because of His love we are infinitely safe
And eternally secure!

HEBREWS 11

Faith does not know the meaning of defeat.
Faith conquers every problem that we meet.
Though we know we know not what we face
We move forward, convinced of God's grace!
Faith bids us look beyond pain
To see our love for God will never be in vain.
Like others who have walked unknown trails
In the past
We will learn by our own experience
How long God's love will last!
He will never let us walk these trails alone
And His is a love we should never disown.
We join others in this heavenly caravan
Where millions of the faithful have walked
Who could not be swayed no matter how much
Or how long the doubtful and skeptics talked!
We are wrapped in God's love
And life has no unbearable load
Because our Savior walks beside us on this
Long and dusty earthly road!

HEBREWS 12

Since we have such a huge crowd
watching us
we must keep our eyes on Jesus
as Paul advises
for sin wraps itself around our feet
denying us life's most golden prizes!
Jesus was willing to die
a shameful death
so we can live a glorious life!
His love, power, and advocacy
prepares us to overcome
life's most traumatic strife.
There are so many sins
we must guard against
especially those unintended personal sins
we once romanced.
Now God expects us to live
purer and cleaner
avoiding any behavior that might suggest
unsavory demeanor
for God has invited us to Zion's holy hill
where we can bask in His glory
and exult in His will!

The "I Love My Bible" Commentary

HEBREWS 13

Continue to love each other!
What better advice can we hear?
Oh how closely it brings us
to being completely pure!
If you've ever felt uncertain
if you've ever felt great fear
you need this loving advice
to help keep your soul secure.
Our Lord's love is forever.
There is no one as great!

There at the cross
where He gave himself He proved
no one should immerse himself
in hate.
He left Heaven's walls of safety
to walk with us in love
He walked on this earth
next door to hell
so we could walk
those heavenly trails above!
We can have great joy now
and His love shows us how!

Note: Hebrews, the great epistle of faith, was certainly written by one whose faith seemed as great as ALL those he mentioned combined! His faith carried Paul through all circumstances which he described in other letters. He was beaten, robbed, left for dead, almost drowned and seemingly experienced every trauma known to man, yet in faith he said, he was very much alive! We do not see him questioning the trials he went through as we often do today. Each trial seemed to make him a little stronger. Why was this book written? To show us no circumstance, no matter how devastating has the power to undermine our faith–only to test it. I wonder what my score will be when God judges my faith? Certainly nowhere near the quality of Paul's! But when my faith seems to crack and fall to pieces, God's Word picks it up and puts it back together again. That's why I love it! That's why I read it, and that's why I've written this commentary to encourage others to seek the comfort-from the God of all comfort-that only these precious Holy Scriptures can bring.

Give up?
Never!
(well, almost never!)
Hold on?
Ah! Yes!
Forever!
Why?
Because I know my Heavenly Father has never given up on me
and THAT is the miracle that has given me the faith
to hold on, to hold out and to hold up!
I challenge you to have faith in God!
Only faith finds out how great He is!

But this MAN , because he continueth ever,
hath an unchangeable priesthood.

Wherefore He is able also to save them
to the uttermost
that come unto God by Him,
seeing He ever liveth
to make intercession for them.

For such an high priest became us,
who is holy, harmless, undefiled,
separate from sinners
and made higher than the heavens;

Who needeth <u>not</u> daily
as those high priests, to offer up sacrifice,
first for his own sins,
and then for the people's:
for this He did once,
when He offered up himself.

For the law maketh men high priests
which have infirmity;
but the word of the oath,
which was since the law,
maketh the Son,
who is consecrated forevermore.
(Hebrews 7: 24-28kjv)

The "I Love My Bible" Commentary
(The Book of James)

JAMES 1

James-a servant of God
a man with a great spiritual gift
looked beyond troublesome times
difficulties and temptations
to give his people a much needed lift!
He knew God was the answer
for every problem men faced
and one who sought wisdom from Him
would never be disgraced.
And if we want a noble character
grown to full bloom
we should put aside our doubts
and give faith its rightful room!
Wisdom compels us to seek faith
and faith draws that wisdom
from our hearts!
To follow God wisely
gives us a wisdom
full of joy filled sparks!
*God sends us all that is perfect and good
and He teaches us how to act
as He would!
James says we should look constantly
into God's law for all men
for it sets us free
not to be soiled or dirtied ever again!*
Always look into the mirror of your soul.
There-God's wisdom make can you whole!
No other can give us so much hope.
No other is so sweet.
God gives the ultimate wisdom
that will fill our souls
and truly make us complete!

JAMES 2

If our faith is dead our deeds will be rotten.
Without faith, all we've ever learned
is quickly forgotten.
Like the man who sees himself in the mirror
and quickly turns away
we can forget the vision of holiness
God planted in our hearts to stay!
But-faith keeps us on track.
Faith bids us never look back.
It motivated Abraham and even Rahab
but a little dab of faith won't help you
if you don't use that little dab!
Faith is the substance of things
hoped for
the evidence of things not seen.
It holds our hearts along the trail of life
from beginning to end
and all the places in between!
Let it not be said of us
that our faith is useless and dead
because we don't try to honor
all those precious things he said.
Believing is not enough.
James says we must act
otherwise others will look on our faith
as 'fiction' instead of fact.

JAMES 3

Watch dogs of the faith
don't look at shadows or grovel in gloom.
And they don't look for fault in others
in order to *lower the boom!*
James seems to think some people
need muzzles for their tongues.
They are only pin-heads
who shrivel even smaller
when over expanding their lungs.
He says only a tiny rudder can turn
a big ship
but a big mouth causes
many a Christian to slip.

Comment on James

and if we should think we are wise
we should realize it shines through
in loving, courteous replies!
Now, if we can control our tongues
we have control in every way
but who does in this changeable
ambiguous day?
God wants us to be wholehearted
straight forward and sincere
and maybe we will give all people
the kind of news they need to hear!

JAMES 4

What causes dissention among the masses?
Is it because the upper forty
Disdains the lower classes?
Or could it be wanting that
Which belongs to a neighbor
Because one is to lazy to lift
Even a little finger in honest labor?
If we want *what we want*
To consume it on our lust
It could cost us a loving relationship
Purely built on trust!
James says to make friends with lustful people
Only brings us sorrow and the wrath of God.
He(James)seems to be harsh and unkind
But he wants us to have joy and a satisfied mind!
He knew that Christ had calmed the sea
Which was tossed by angry winds
And James tried to show his people
How God's love comes with amazing dividends!
Some say James knew our Savior
Heart to heart and face to face
And that is why he was so eager to write
Of God's incredible love and amazing grace!
James asked why we fuss and fight.
Maybe we are all frustrated from inaction
And from not walking in the *light!*
He said knowing to do good was not enough
Where are the good deeds if we only bluff?
To say we'll do something and not to do it
James said is s-i-n, sin!
And that leads to the ruin of insincere men.
Life won't be as uncertain as the morning mist
If doing the Father's will is at the top of our list.

JAMES 5

James was a man of honest and noble character
And strong will.
The One who had calmed the storm within him
Had merely spoken, "peace be still!"
He spoke of rich men, and poor men
Men of happiness and men in deep grief
But he wanted them to know, through patience
They could know God would send them relief.
Now-can you count the many times you've
   heard
   "Be ye doers of the Word?"
And James also wrote of Elijah who he said
   was likewise made of common clay
And if we pray as earnestly as did Elijah
   God will surely answer us today!

Note: James's letter may have been short but
it was long on advice–very good advice! He
stressed purity and godly action which never
harmed a soul. Lets hope his love for the sinner
is as important to us as it was to him! So–it
seems we should prove our faith by loving
deeds. There are many people who have no way
of caring for even their simplest needs.
If its happiness we want then we may find it by
helping others who need us today!
He knew faith to be an energizer when he said
faith without works is merely dead. For real
faith puts God's energy in our hearts and it
becomes impossible for us to do nothing!
And that seems to be the theme of this letter!

The "I Love My Bible" Commentary
(1st and 2nd Peter)

1ST PETER 1

Peter is saying reverent love holds on
to the Father's arms
holds on to His love and has no fear
of life's deadly storms!
Ransomed souls try harder
to please the Lord
because they know the lifeblood of Christ
guarantees them a heavenly reward!
Radiant hearts know the joy
of being *born again*
not of corruptible seed
but with seed that is purified
and given to us when our Savior died.
Our Savior's love is our greatest prize
and His guarantee is written in the skies.
His Word will lead us beyond
the depth, the width, the height
and length of eternity.
That is what God's love
has done for you and me!
And through the centuries
this story has been told.
Our faith is more precious to God
than all the world's purest gold!

1ST PETER 2

Because God's Word is so great
because His love cannot be explained
because every since we've known Him
our lives have been changed
because of that and much, much more
we need to cling to Him
more than ever before!
Christ is our 'Rock of Ages'
the great cornerstone
chosen carefully by God to be
the greatest friend we've ever known!
If only we could really imagine
the greatness of His salvation
surely we'd live our lives
in strong dedication.
Still, we wonder why
this great 'Cornerstone'
this builder of men's lives
loves us so much
that He consecrates Himself
to free us from our enemy's clutch.
That is why Peter said to hate no one.
We must pass on this life
God gave us through His Son!

1ST PETER 3

If we would love each other
as much as the Lord loves us
if we would remember we dishonor Him
when we fight and fuss
if our lives were so godly
no one could fail to see
the reasons we live in harmony
maybe there would be
no crime in the streets
no broken homes
no crippling defeats.
If we would love each other
with tender hearts and humble minds
not repaying evil for evil
and really cherishing the tie that binds
we certainly would have a happy life.
Every woman would honor her husband
and every man
would cherish his wife!
We can do it if we quietly
put our trust in Christ
and always be ready to say
why we choose to behave
in a God honoring, respectful way!

Comment on 1st and 2nd Peter

We know Christ died for us so we can be
loving, forgiving, tactful people who know
we are completely and eternally free!

1ST PETER 4

We should be people of prayer
more than ever now
and use our special talents
to fulfill every vow.
God's deep love will keep us
on the *straight and narrow!*
*Remember, we worship God
who even cares* for the little sparrow!
Peter tells wives to be beautiful inside.
Our lives must be so pure
we'll have nothing to hide!
And husbands, he says, must be
full of good deeds
always being thoughtful
of their wife's needs.
For the Lord is watching
and listening to our prayers.
Not until the end of time
will we understand how much He cares!
We read here that judgement starts
at the house of God.
If we keep on doing right
God will spare us from His rod!
And, if we are *barely* saved
will there be any pity
for the wicked and depraved?
That is why we must tell of our faith
in gentle and respectful ways
and then we will be honoring
our Heavenly Father
who is worthy our praise!

1ST PETER 5

Dear Peter, that old elder of the church
passes on his gift to his peers.
His gift was love and faith in God
which would certainly allay all their fears.
He had fed the flock as our Lord commanded
and he could not bear to see
people who loved the Lord
helplessly stranded.
There is no generation gap here.
The Lord molds all ages together!
Such a love as His makes us all
strive to be better.
God will lift us up if we are humble
and we don't have to fear
when we hear old Satan grumble!
Consider this!
God will set us firmly in place
not because we deserve it
but because of His incredible grace!

2ND PETER 1

Peter always remembered
he was a servant of the Lord
and his faith in our precious Savior
could never be shaken or jarred!
He had come through the trial of failure
at the cross
and he had seen the loving forgiveness
in his Savior's eyes
and would never again
feel such loss.
Neither would he cower or run in fear.
That faith the Lord had given him
would never disappear!
He had learned the recipe
for endless joy and peace.
It is to serve our Lord
until He freely gives us
loving and heavenly release!.

The "I Love My Bible" Commentary

God rescues us from rottenness and lust
but if we want to live holy
letting God have His way is a must!
Peter never tired of telling the story
of how, with his own eyes
he had seen the Lord in *all His glory!*
This Great Light, our Morning Star
will shine in our hearts
wherever we are!

2ND PETER 2

Peter said false teachers would sneak into the
Church, and they have haunted it every since.
Some of these deceitfully evil pedagogues
Declare sex sin is not wrong(by their example)
And they leave God's people with no defense.
Purity and holiness demanded by God
Has been mocked and ridiculed
And no one knows the number of people
These evil instructors have fooled.
Like Lot, we must be rescued
From these lustful and sodomistic liars
For they will continue to spread their venom
Until God destroys their stubble with His fires!
God did destroy Sodom in order to commit
The wicked to oblivion's curse
Yet men still ignore His laws
And the world is growing steadily worse.
We must remember Paul says we are slaves
To whatever we give control
And lust-baited wickedness can prevent us
From reaching even one righteous goal.
How can we forget so easily
That God has given us life fresh and new
And our love for Him should encourage us to be
Responsible in all that we say and do?
Peter compares those who return to sin
To a pig or a dog
Who do not care where they wallow
Nor can avoid sin's endless fog.

2ND PETER 3

Can you imagine a thousand years
seeming like just a day?
When we think of our Lord's return
we wish it was that way.
but in our pain
a day seems like a thousand years
and the higher we pile our sins
the greater grows our fears.
Sin leads to depression
and depression to despair
and we begin to wonder
does anybody care?
And it seems many believe
the Lord will never return.
They never repent
and almost thumb their noses
at this Great One they spurn.
Peter said these scoffers
would do as they please
not knowing this One who rules
the heavens
will bring them to their knees!
So, if they insist on resisting God
let them!
But don't let them lead you astray.
There is incredible joy coming
for all who look forward to that day!

Note: I love Peter. He certainly grew in faith! From a man who couldn't keep his mouth shut and who even failed to listen to his own words when he swore he'd never forsake the Savior to a giant of a man whose faith never wavered, he proved to be one of the greatest saints of his time. He eloquently encouraged those saints he had won to the Lord to grow in grace and faith. And through these epistles, he encourages us to do the same. Dear old Peter, we would do well to observe these things he tells us to do!

Blessed be the God and Father
of our Lord Jesus Christ,
which according to his abundant mercy
hath begotten us again unto a lively hope
by the resurrection of Jesus Christ from the dead.

To an inheritance incorruptible, and undefiled,
and that fadeth not away, reserved in heaven for you,

Who are kept by the power of God through faith
unto salvation ready to be revealed in the last time.

For as much as ye know you were not redeemed
with corruptible things, as silver and gold,
from your vain conversation
received by tradition from your fathers;

<u>*But with the precious blood of Christ*</u>
as of a lamb without blemish and without spot.

Who verily was foreordained
before the foundation of the world,
but was manifest in these last times for you,

Who by him do believe in God,
that raised him up from the dead, and gave him glory;
that your faith and hope might be in God.

Seeing ye have purified your souls in obeying the truth
through the Spirit unto unfeigned love of the brethren,
see that ye love one another with a pure heart fervently:

Being born again, not of corruptible seed,
but of incorruptible, by the Word of God,
which liveth and abideth forever.
(1 Peter 1: 3-5; 18-23kjv)-

The "I Love My Bible" Commentary
(1ˢᵗ, 2ⁿᵈ, and 3ʳᵈ John)

1ˢᵗ JOHN 1

"Christ was alive!" John said.
He should have known!
He touched our Lord
and never again felt alone.
That touch would last him forever!
John, born again in Christ, knew a bond
no one could sever.
"Christ was alive!" He said.
John had seem Him!
His eyes feasted on a vision
that would never grow dim.
And-John had loved Him
who is the "Light."
No darkness could ever threaten John.
Christ had illuminated his sight!
John, how I envy you!
You walked with my Lord
got to hold His hand
and gazed on His face.
Who could hope for more?
Who could ever imagine so much grace?
But His love also walks with me
and leads me to that glorious place!
Then I can touch my Lord
feel the scars my fingers trace.
He did it all for me
when He washed my sins away.
Yes, I will touch Him
and I can hardly wait
until that holy, glorious day!

1ˢᵗ JOHN 2

Christ Jesus took the law away
and replaced it with His love!
Yet, His love is the Greater Law
He brought to earth
from His home up above!

When love-light floods our hearts
the darkness disappears
and we no longer stumble
with fear-darkened tears.
His way is always up.
His way is always new!
Knowing we are forgiven
changes everything we do!
Because of that we must display
no greedy ambition, no foolish pride
nor any immoral behavior
that makes us want to run and hide.
We live in the circle of His arms
the One who said
"Peace be still!"
This forever love compels us to live
within God's loving will.
Led by the Holy Spirit
in happy fellowship with God
we'll never have to be ashamed
of the godly paths we've trod.
John says we must live "in Christ"
never to depart
for He has given us love
without measure
from the depth of His heart!

1ˢᵗ JOHN 3

There is a little of "John" in each of us
longing for peace
longing for love
longing to lean on the Savior's breast.
There is a little of "John" in each of us
wanting a closer walk
longing to hear His voice
longing for God's perfect rest!
We want to be number one
but like John who grew in grace
we must learn its far more important

Comment on 1st, 2nd, and 3rd John

to be able to look on our Savior's face!
John was so vulnerable
John was so 'real'
and he continued to seek that love
that is surely strong enough
for all God's people to feel!
Its all right to be like John
for he loved our Savior
and always sought to live
in God's loving favor.
Until we can experience
earth's final dawn
lets hang on and be
just a little more like John!

1ST JOHN 4

Love has no rhyme or reason.
Love will never go out of season!
Love is God's own border patrol
and it is used by Him
to build a fence around our soul.
Love is like a hoe
and it weeds out hate
for hate cannot not thrive
where love is great!
And John reminds us
our love is incomplete
when we love God but hate
the brotherly stranger we chance to meet.
John says perfect love eliminates
all fear and dread
if we'd only love each other
the way John said.
Can you get the picture?
I could go on and on
and never tire of saying
great is the One who sends us love
from His heavenly throne!
John said, "God is light"
so we should love Him with all our might!

1ST JOHN 5

If God has His rightful place
in your heart
let no one take Him away.
Hold on to that marvelous gift
urgently, every day.
For God is love
and God is grace
and God is definitely real.
God gives eternal life
and how great that should
make you feel.
We know in our hearts
what God says is true.
His promise to give us eternal life
does make us good as new!
Therefore, we will not practice sin
when we realize God surrounds us
and we are safe within!
Where sin reigns God's grace departs.
Dear people
keep God's love deep in your hearts!

2ND JOHN 1

Anyone known to be God's own
will never have to feel alone!
Anyone full of God's mercy and grace
will show it by the light
on his(or her)face!
Dear Cyria must have been
such a one as this
truly full of love and blessed
with an angel's kiss!
"She followed the truth," John said
and had no fear to dread!
Yet, John felt it was necessary
to reiterate

The "I Love My Bible" Commentary

she must never walk
in the shadow of hate.
And, she was to stay within
the guidelines
where only God's light shines!
We, too, must seek our full reward
which can only be
given from the Lord for only He can see
if we walk with Him faithfully!

3RD JOHN 1

Dear Gaius must truly have loved John
and John certainly loved him!
But there is trouble in paradise.
One who passed himself off as a leader
possessed the church's most deadly vice!
It seems he hated John
hated the missionaries
must have hated the Lord
for he ostracized his church
and made their lives unbearably hard.
How could he criticize one
who praised love so highly
or ridiculed John who had walked
with the One who is so mighty?
John displayed a good example.

This man's was bad, *bad!*
He probably never repented
of the negative influence he had.
But John writes of another
whom he considered his brother!
And John would wish the best
on Gaius and Demetrius whose love
had put their souls at rest!

Note: This great man who, tradition says, always lifted his hands and admonished his people to love one another, was truly the apostle of love! Maybe the love of Jesus osmosed into John as John leaned on His breast! I've always loved John because in the act of leaning on our Savior's breast, he showed us how close we can be to God-close enough to hear His heart beat, close enough to feel His love.

I think this proves that the closer we live to our Lord, the easier it is to share our love. How many of us draw as close to the Lord as did John? And, how many of us can almost hear that precious heart beat? But, because love does make us vulnerable we hesitate to reach out and love our glorious God or our neighbor or the stranger we chance to meet. It is easier when we realize the more we love, the greater our faith! Blessed people, like John said, love each other!

*This then is the message
which we have heard of him,
and declare unto you, that God is light,
and in him is no darkness at all.*

*If we say that we have fellowship with him,
and walk in darkness, we lie,
and do not the truth:*

*But if we walk in the light,
as he is in the light,
we have fellowship one with another,
and the blood of Jesus Christ his Son
cleanseth us from ALL sin.*

*If we say that we have no sin, we deceive ourselves,
and the truth is not in us.*

*If we confess our sins,
he is faithful and just to forgive us our sins,
and to cleanse us from all unrighteousness.*

*If we say that we have not sinned,
we make him a liar,
and his word is not in us.*

----

*My little children, these things I write unto you,
that ye sin not, and if any man sin,
we have an advocate with the Father,
Jesus Christ the righteous:*

*And he is the propitiation for our sins:
and not for ours only,
but also for the sins of the whole world.*
(1John !:5-10; 2: 1-2kjv)

The "I Love My Bible" Commentary
(Jude, the last Epistle)

JUDE 1

How very kind Jude begins his letter
wishing kindness, love, and peace!
Yet he had to remind his people
God's truth is never on a leash!
Truth must be free
to keep without change or error!
But, at this time, there were some
teachers who would not keep
God's people on the straight and narrow!
A teacher who worms the church
underground
precipitates its spiral
downward bound.
Jude reminded his precious people
what could happen
when we doubt and disobey.
We will *not* find the Lord walking there
because there are no tunnels
on the King's highway!
But, there is a place
a special place
where we can bask in the glory
of God's grace
if only we would develop
the sense
to realize love is a protecting fence!
Jude said to stay within the boundaries
where God's love can reach you!
Its like coloring your life
rainbow colors when you do!
I must live within His love
and never drift away
for I need God in my life
every single day!

Note: We don't hear much of Jude in the Bible, but he left God's people the pattern for a glorious heritage. "Stay," he said, "within the boundaries where God's love can reach you!" Its not that he meant God could not reach us anywhere for He can. But He will not reach out and encircle one in His arms who chooses not to be there. The choice is ours. Do we want to be that close to the most glorious being in the universe? I certainly cannot imagine anyone not wanting to be there. But, it is obvious many do not! Many thumb their noses at His commandments. Many deny there is a God or say God is dead. Those who do not say it verbally, say it by their actions. We stay within those boundaries when we worship and obey Him. Jesus said not every one that called Him Lord would enter the Kingdom of Heaven, but only those who did the *will* of the Father. And, that is why Jude said we should stay within the boundaries where God's love could reach us. There is a glorious future awaiting God's people. Why in the world would anyone want to risk losing it?

*But, beloved, remember ye the words
which were spoken before of the apostles
of our Lord Jesus Christ;*

*How that they told you there should be mockers
in the last time,
who should walk after their own
ungodly lusts.*

*These be they who separate themselves
sensual, having not the Spirit.*

*But ye, beloved, building up yourselves
on your most holy faith,
praying in the Holy Ghost,*

*Keep yourselves in the love of God,
looking for the mercy of our Lord Jesus Christ
unto eternal life.*

----

*Now unto him that is able
to keep you from falling
and to present you faultless
before the presence of His glory
with exceeding joy,*

*To the only wise God our Saviour,
be glory and majesty, dominion and power,
both now and ever. Amen.*
(Jude vv 17-21; 24-25kjv)

The "I Love My Bible" Commentary

*(The final book in the Bible
the Book of The Revelation
the book of endings
and beginnings!
The beginning of eternity)*

THE REVELATION 1

God's Word has always stood the test!
Now John says, "read God's Word
and be blessed!"
First, we must see Jesus
as John saw Him
alive forever more!
He is the Alpha and Omega
richer than the rich
and a refuge for the poor!
John saw Christ
in His magnificent glory
and thus he has the right
to share with us
God's last incredible story!
Christ Jesus has the keys
of death and hell
and now He gives John
a story to tell!
Though most of us shy away
from this blessed book
its great and awesome warnings
deserve another look!
Warnings were always given
in order to turn God's people
to the light!
Those who love the Lord
and obey Him
will not tremble as he reads
nor will he close this book in fright!
Christ is our Alpha and Omega
and His love for us will never end!
Take heart, all of you, who cherish
this One as your greatest
and dearest friend!

REVELATION 2

The GREAT ONE walks among
the candlesticks to see
if they are shedding their light!
Are they?
Down through the ages He has searched
to find light bearers
overcoming the darkness of the night!
Do we?
He seeks churches looking for love.
Where is the Spirit He sent
by His Holy Dove?
Will His hand remove our candlesticks
because they hold no light?
Do our churches seek a lesser love
thus sinning in His sight?
How much good will He find in us
who seek to share His name?
When He left,   the church
dearly loved Him.
Will He find it still the same!
We see Him telling the First Church
of Ephesus
they have left their first love
and they surely must return.
To Pergamos He said
they had remained loyal yet
but they seemed to forget
that sex sin was a sin He hated
and He hinted
They were followerers of Baalim
Who led Israel into that sin.
It was, then and now, the blight
Of all men
and He promised those who repented

Comment on Revelation

*would be given a new name
one that was glorious
and would bring them heavenly fame.
He told Thyatira He was aware
of their good deeds
and noticed their improvement
but they, too, fell short
in morals which surely mattered.
Did they forget that was the reason
Israel's bones were scattered.
He promised them death
if they continued to follow
'that woman Jezebel'
who was leading them into
the depths of hell.
Punishment for adultery
is heaven sent
and those who commit it
must repent!*

REVELATION 3

*Oh, its sad what He says to Sardis.
They thought they were active
but He said they were dead.
Their deeds were far from right
and He threatens to banish them
from His sight.
He said they must go back
and believe as they did before.
It seems they didn't love Him
anymore!
Evidently they had sunk
to self-righteousness
and had lost their spiritual spunk!
"Self" can never get us to heaven.
"Self" can never get us home
for God considers "self" only putrid foam.
Our trust must be in Him
not in programs, not in fame
but only in His holy and glorious name!*

*But, goodness knows
there were many who had not
soiled their clothes
with sin or self.
He promised them garments of white
fresh and pure.
They would walk with Him
and always feel secure!
This next church is different!
I think I must belong
to the Church of Philadelphia
because He said it wasn't strong!
Oh, how that describes me!
But
He says He knows I'm trying to obey
and He has opened a door for me
no one can shut today!
This church I belong to
has not denied His name
has not forsaken Him whose holiness
always remains the same!
He promises this church will stand
on holy ground
and no one can take away its crown!
Now He mentions one more church
the church of Laodicea
the church thought to be bold
thought to be rich
but neglected the truths
it was meant to hold
the church that was neither
hot nor cold.
Christ said they were poor
and naked and blind.
Self righteousness had caused them
to be lukewarm and unkind.
"Behold," He said, "I stand
at the door and knock!"
It was His church but they
had put Him outside
and denied this "Rock of Ages"*

The "I Love My Bible" Commentary

where they were meant to hide!
He still says, "I stand at the door
and knock!"
He longs to feed His earthly flock!
Open the door, church
open the door!
Let our Lord be our <u>first</u>
and greater love once more!
We need Him now more than
we have ever needed Him before.
So He says, "let us hear!
Indeed we must!
For how else cane we lift up
this Noble One
in whom we all should trust?

REVELATION 4

John must have opened his heart
to Jesus
because now Jesus opens a door
for him.
But this open door revealed a future
that would be very grim.
First, John saw the glory of the throne
a likely occurrence for first
we must see Him
in order to understand
how much He considers us His own!
Then John saw the elders
on lesser thrones
all clothed in white
dazzling because they walk
in the presence of this One
who sheds His glorious light!
That place was glowing
with life magnificent
because the One they worship
is truly omnipotent!
"Holy, holy, holy," they said.
We do, too!

Lord, how worthy you are
for you created all things
from the tiny atom
to the most dazzling star!
One very evident truth in this chapter
for you and me
is the closer we draw to God
the more we can see!
It is in His presence we can behold
a glory and honor
more precious than gold!
And, truly it will be a time
we will know the meaning of the words
"peace be still"
for then we will understand
the glory of
God's creative will!

REVELATION 5

There are symbols in chemistry
and there are symbols in math
and the Bible tells us
God has set us signs
along earth's treacherous path.
But God's symbols for the future
sometimes blows our minds
and though we need His light
we hurriedly draw the blinds!
People shy away from Revelation
though its promises are great.
Even when we understand
doubt comes to cloud
that holy symbolic slate.
We know lambs are gentle creatures
but our Symbolic Lamb
reveals the scroll's secret features.
And only He is worthy to reveal
the awesome contents
of each and every seal!

Comment on Revelation

Heaven's creatures sang a new song
that will never go out of date
for worthy is the Lamb
whose love will overcome
the treacherous depths of hate.
Seven things He is worthy of
all because of His great love!
Count them one by one
    1. Power
    2. Wealth
    3. Wisdom
    4. Strength
    5. Honor
    6. Glory
    7. Praise
and those creatures sang
"worthy is the Lamb
for ALL He has done!"

REVELATION 6

The first seal reveals a conqueror
bent on conquest
but who was he to conquer
and what was his test?
Must power be demonstrated
by the shedding of blood?
It seems it has
every since the flood!
And, inflation always seems
to be a result of blood shed.
The more man fights
the less he has of daily bread!
Of course, fighting and famine
always lead to death.
In these times of havoc
surely the Lord holds His breath!
But it does take patience to wait.
God will rescue His people
and He's never a minute late!
Now we see destruction
and more to come
when the Lamb becomes a Lion
who takes command.
In that great day of His wrath
who can possibly stand?
They asked that–those who pleaded
for the rocks to fall on them
because now they knew
they had been defeated.
They had tried to "put God out"
but instead, He ended up
hitting a Grand Slam!

REVELATION 7

Before the havoc
there is a witness
has always been!
Even in judgement God pauses
to offer His mercy to men.
It is here we read
"God will wash away their tears!"
So great will be the washing
we'll no longer have
any doubts or fears.
144,000 strong
serving the Master
with a heartfelt song.
144,000 dressed in robes
dazzling white
now come to serve the Lord
constantly day and night!
They will never hunger
or thirst again.
The sun will not send its
blistering heat
on any single man.
They live where God's living water
springs.
The Lamb is their Shepherd
and they will live as kings!

The "I Love My Bible" Commentary

REVELATION 8

Now we come to the seventh seal
and shudder at what it might reveal.
Before Jesus came the first time
There was silence on the earth.
(no revelations.)
It was as if He'd spent 400 years
dreading the day
of His 'human' birth.
Before He comes to earth
the second time
there will be silence in heaven
as angels stand in utmost grief
because after all these years
many men continue to wallow
in unbelief.
This time the angels grieve because
there is no longer an advocate
for sinners
who continue to break God's laws.
Once there was silence
before the calm of His presence.
Now the silence is before the storm!
Judgement is on the horizon
and God has sounded the alarm.
At this time, those who refused
to face reality
must face defeat.
There will be no place to hide
and no place to retreat.

REVELATION 9

The first four trumpet blasts
in chapter 8 still resound
and now the abyss is opened
and awesome agony is unbound.
Pain will be worse
than the sting of a scorpion
where only death brings relief
but death could not be found
to alleviate their grief.
Now a third of mankind will be killed.
If hope EVER had a voice
now it seems its voice is stilled.
Plagues seemed to be pictured
as being one hundred million troops
but yet mankind would not repent
of his murders, thefts, and witchcraft's
or abandon his sexual hoola hoops!
He still had his idols
of gold, silver, stone, and wood
(things, things, things)
and despite God's judgement
turned their backs on God
and refused to do good.

REVELATION 10

What was the message of the scroll
that the angel handed John?
All we know is John's prophecies
will last until the final dawn.
The message is sweet
but it turns sour
possibly because mankind becomes
more wicked by the hour.
In the day when
the seventh angel sounds
the Great Physician will have finished
making His final rounds.
There will be no balm in Gilead
(a medicinal gum)
no medicine for the
ugly behavior of the bad.
(see Jeremiah 8:22)
Those who refuse to honor the One
who wears that holy crown
will not know the future will be uncertain
for the angel told John
not to write it down!

Comment on Revelation

REVELATION 11

Remember the rule of two witnesses?
That was God's requirement
before any judgement could be passed.
*Now, **God's two witnesses***
have appeared
and judgement comes at last.
Zechariah writes of them
and now they come to Jerusalem!
It will be awful how they
will be treated so cruel
but its just a continuance
of good and bad's constant duel.
But–the two witnesses come to life
and victory is sweet
and that is because
our Great King will never face defeat!
When God intervene's
for His people's sake
it will be with a mighty earthquake.
And when the seventh trumpet sounds
God takes control!
He keeps His promise
*to save every **trusting** soul!*

REVELATION 12

Feature a woman clothed
with the sun
with the moon as her platform.
She was priceless to God
yet the devil would try
to cause her harm.
Heaven interceded because she carried
righteousness within
From her womb came
the Savior of all repentant men.
How many times has an innocent child
caused such a war as this?
But Heaven must be cleansed
and the devil couldn't resist.
He and his demons were cast to earth.
He could not stop the salvation
begun at that holy birth!
Now he takes vengeance
on all of us.
That old devil is going to have his way
or bust.
But let him stand beside the sea.
(of souls)
God will see to it that we will
defeat him eventually!

REVELATION 13

Out of the sea of faces rises a beast.
It is tragic that he considers
the souls of men his greatest feast.
Can you believe that people
would worship so foolishly
one who slanders God
and acts so mulishly?
Though his head was wounded
he was healed
but his heart was D. O. A.
When he fought with God
he would rue the day!
Now comes an imitation 'lamb'
whose heart was dark
for he would let no one eat
unless they had his mark.
It doesn't take wise calculation to see
this one was as wicked as could be.
But, his jig was up!
He would drink the dregs
of his wickedness
to the bottom of his cup!
This is where the numbers 666
are mentioned
and was a symbolic way of saying
*this one was **not** well intentioned!*

The "I Love My Bible" Commentary

REVELATION 14

Always the Lamb!
Always the Lion!
Always the King!
And John thrilled to hear
those 144,000 sing!
Can you imagine men who are blameless?
Can you imagine men who never lie
who will follow the righteous 'Lamb'
and will never die?
Even the angels now get involved
in telling the great story
that all men must give
our great Jehovah glory!
Yet, they warn the saints
*they will succeed **only***
if they hold to holy restraints!
Then we hear(like John)
that happy voice
saying, "now the saints can rejoice!"
You see, it is the time for the harvest
when God's wrath
*will allow **only the saints***
to walk His glorious path!

REVELATION 15

These awesome symbols
cause us to tremble
as we wonder
"what in the world do they resemble?"
But, through the horror
drifts a song!
Victory would come out of the pits
to right all wrong.
But God is not limited
to signs or symbols.
He is the artist of them all!
We who fear and reverence Him
will not be injured in the 'fall.'

Only He is holy!
Only He is great!
Revelation is really saying
"Worship Him before its too late!"
It seems that purity and plagues
picture quite a contrast
but what we see here
is God having His way at last!

REVELATION 16

Oh, that voice!
Bear in mind
no one in Heaven wants to be
this unkind.
Men have been warned
for thousands of years
men who have shed blood
men who have caused tears.
Because they had no mercy
because they didn't care
they had dared to be different
and caused many despair.
Now, what goes around
comes around
and the awesome news these vials bore
brought a judgement
weighed out by the pound.
Not one of those seven angels
whom you might ask
would say he enjoyed
fulfilling his task.
But not one of those men
would repent
and where ever you look
not a single knee was bent!
Proof that what fell on these men
was justice for their great sin!
And surely we've found
what goes around
does come around!

Comment on Revelation

REVELATION 17

*No matter how great exterior beauty
may be
unless it soaks all the way through
to cleanse notorious hearts
what good will it do?
I suppose it is a mystery why adultery
haunts so many souls
and why humanity prostitutes itself
and forgets its heavenly goals.
Heavy sin descends with
traumatic power
and will cause the Babylonian spirit
to split to pieces in that final hour.
No more will immorality be seen
or heard or felt
along with the unexpected terrorists
and the horrors they dealt.
Man will feel that awesome hail
(mentioned in chapter 16)
and learn too late
how tragic it is to fail.
Its true we can't 'weigh' sin
but it has weighted down
far too many men.*

REVELATION 18

*Now an angel comes to say
the Babylon system has
fallen to pieces.
Mankind cannot dodge
the hideous weapons
God now releases.
So, whether or not we see the symbols
or feel the fiendish fear
whether or not we believe the prophecies
time passes swiftly while
we linger here.
It is time to eradicate evil
and send the devils away.
God is coming to earth and no evil
can be concocted on that holy day.
Those who have deceived the masses
will see the panorama of holiness
only briefly when it passes.
They have refused to take hold
of this life more precious than gold.
No wedding bells for them!
They will be permanent aliens
outside God's holy Jerusalem.*

REVELATION 19

*The symbols teach us
God **will not** be ignored.
He will reign supreme
when His earthly kingdom
is restored.
And if Revelation is closed to our minds
our hearts hold the key.
Jesus said, "I will reveal my truths
to those who love, obey
and honor me!"
We cannot peak through the keyhole
of truth
and see in God's dimension
for just a peak denies us
more than a grain of comprehension!
Jesus told us in Chapter three
He wants us to "open the door!"
And unless we swing wide
the doors of our hearts
He will not tell us more.
His great truths are like the waves
that pound against the shore.
They keep coming
bringing us more power
than we've ever known before.
Now we are living in the latter days.
Truly, we must lift our voices in praise.*

The "I Love My Bible" Commentary

*for just around the corner
just around the bend
God's great beginning appears
as this world's system
comes to its bitter end.
It will not matter how hard
the old devil and his system fights.
They will be destined to face
God's punishment of fervent heat
and torturous nights.*

REVELATION   20

*The second greatest news
of the millennium
is the old devil will be fastened down.
Bound in chains for a thousand years
he won't be able to muster
even a tiny frown
-at least not one we can see!
That will be a heavenly preview
of a peaceful eternity!
For a thousand years, there will be
joy on earth
a continuous celebration
full of heavenly mirth!
But when the thousand years are over
the devil tries again
and somehow manages once more
to pervert the heart of man.
His rebellion restores anarchy
and starts the final war
but he is soundly defeated
by our Bright and Morning Star!
He cannot defeat God
though it be his greatest desire.
He-and his followers-will be
destined to the second death's lake
of sizzling eternal fire.
Our God has his book of life
and He is **never** unfair.*

*Take care, my friends, to be sure
your names are written there!*

REVELATION   21

*We think it is an impossible duty
to create such incredible beauty!
God will remake a new heaven
and a new earth with no troubled seas.
Cloudless skies enhance that city
where joy, faith, and peace
are its only keys!
Our Alpha and Omega
puts on that final touch
to welcome the home coming
of those He loves so much.
That city, that precious holy city
will be full of the glory of God
with no empty trails to follow
no helpless paths to trod.
There is way too much beauty to describe.
It is enough to know we'll be home
and fully satisfied!*

REVELATION   22

*The river of life flows to God's sea
crystal clear in purity
offering the water of life completely free!
Trees that stand nearby
provide food for you and me.
Life as we've never known it
will be so complete
it will have no room for evil
no visage of deceit.
The Lamb is there and God the King!
We'll join in heaven's choir
as the angels sing.
"Come," He says. "Let the thirsty drink!"
And while the ages roll
I'll praise **Him** for saving my soul!*

*And, behold I come quickly;
and my reward is with me,
to give every man according
as his work shall be.*

*I AM ALPHA and OMEGA,
the beginning and the end,
the first and the last.*
(Revelation 22: 12-13kjv)
------

*I Jesus have sent mine angel
to testify unto you
these things in the churches.
I am the root and the offspring of David,
and the bright and morning star*

*And the Spirit and the bride say,
Come.
And let him that heareth say, Come
And let him that is athirst come.
And whosoever will,
let him take of the water of life freely.*
(Revelation 22:16-17kjv)
----

*He which testifieth these things sayeth
Surely I come quickly.
Amen.
Even so, come. Lord Jesus.*

*The grace of our Lord Jesus Christ
be with you all.
Amen.*
(Revelation 22: 20-21kjv)

The "I Love My Bible" Commentary

(Now you know why I love this book
why I know God loves me
why I know what promises
He has not fulfilled — He will!
Why —because He is always the same!)

What is it like to reach
the top of the mountain?
You never want to descend!
God has led us into a land
of great promises that will
never end!
From Genesis to Revelation
God is devoted to our consecration.
And none of these blessed stories
will ever grow old.
Even the valleys they describe
contain great beauty
for us to behold.
Though the glory of the Old Testament
stands in the shadow of the New
still, together, they unfold
all the wonders God set out to do!
Flowers of faith grow tall as Redwoods
that shade deep rivers
and God's light shines down
on still waters
where barely a ripple quivers!
Yet, the greatest miracle of all
will be when we see
that final curtain fall.
And God's greatest glory
will be
when He writes
"The end is the beginning"
on the world's greatest love story!
You'll see!

Something

extra

The Christian Life Is A Love Song ©

1997

Jean Heizer

1. The Christian life is a love song my mother used to say
We will share this melody as we walk thru life each day, for
Those we need to do a good deed to help them on their way
Use the Christian life as a love song to cheer the world each day

Chorus
With a song in your heart and a smile on your face don't forget each
Share God's love and wherever you go the world will sing, your Christian
life is a

Ending
Love-ly thing. The Christian life is a love song - A love song - A love

Jean Heizer — Mansfield, TX 76063

arrangement by Louise Taylor & Carol Robinson

The Christian Life Is A Love Song©
(By Jean Heizer)

(1.) The Christian life is a love song
    My Mother used to say.
    We must share this melody
    As we walk through life each day.
    There are those in need
    Would be a good deed
    To help them on their way.
    Make the Christian life your love song
    As you walk through life each day!

        And with a song in your heart
        And a smile on your face
        Don't forget each day
        To share God's grace
        And wherever you go
        The world will sing
        Your Christian life
        Is a lovely thing!

(2.) Now she sings the songs of Jesus
    In perfect harmony
    With the saints of all the ages
    What a glorious rhapsody!
    Her life is sweet
    She's at His feet.
    She's with Him constantly.
    Her Christian life was a love song
    And now she's been set free.

        And with a song in her heart
        And a smile on her face
        She never forgot
        To share God's grace
        And wherever she went
        Her friends would sing
        Her Christian life
        Was a lovely thing!

(3.) Father help me show I love you
    As I live here joyfully
    May my witness in your name
    Be done consistently.
    My life's complete.
    It can't be beat
    My Savior is the best!
    I made my Christian life a love song
    And my God has done the rest!

        And with a song in my heart
        And a smile on my face
        I never forget
        To share God's grace
        And wherever I go
        I'll always sing
        This Christian life
        Is a lovely thing!

(4.) Make the Christian life your love song
    As you walk this earth today.
    Take time to help each stranger
    You may find along the way.
    It's plain to see
    Love'll set you free
    When you help those who stray
    Make the Christian life your love song
    To cheer the world each day.

        And with a song in your heart
        And a smile on your face
        Don't forget each day
        To share God's grace.
        And wherever you go
        The world will sing
        Your Christian life
        Is a lovely thing!

Excerpts of various comments

....from comment on Genesis 3..
**the God of the Garden would become
The "God of the Cross!"**
God gave our Savior as a
Bridge across the Gap
And because we needed directions
Back to Him, God provided
The Bible as our map!

......from comment on Genesis 4
**...oh to be separated from my God
forever
I have no doubt
Though the fires of hell should die
The fire in my soul will never
go out!**

.............from comment on Deut. 7
*No thought
no feeling
no expression
of this body of sod
no word
no sound
no melody
can ever express
the magnificent holiness
of Jehovah our God!*

.......from comment on Deut. 10
*God IS our praise
Wonderful
Forgiving
Loving always!
God is like this
more than a soft breeze's
gentle kiss
more consistent
than the seasons
guiding us
like seaside beacons!*

..............comment on Psalms 23
*This gentle shepherd knew a Shepherd
more gracious than he.
This gentle shepherd knew our God
was much greater
than he could ever be!*

..............comment on Isaiah 40
*......why is God, God?
To rule the universe? Oh no!
It is to comfort His people
wherever we go!
It is to look on us with love
It is to turn our eyes from failure
to seek the ONE above.
He is God because
He wants to be our strong
and mighty tower!....
..... because He wants to give us power
We shall walk and not be weary
because He walks by our side.
He is the 'Rock of ages'
where we can run and hide!*

..............comment on Matthew 2
*A little Judean village
an out of the way spot
throngs pressing in to pay
for beds no better than a cot.
HE deserved a feather bed.
They couldn't even find one feather!
And that manger didn't protect Him
from Israel's inclement weather....*

*Closing comment at end of book.
.......From Genesis to Revelation
God has dedicated Himself
to our consecration!......
...flowers of faith grow tall as Redwoods
that shade deep rivers
and God's light shines down
on still waters
where barely a ripple quivers
....yet the greatest miracle of all
will be when we see that final curtain fall
and God's greatest glory   will be
when He writes
"The end is the beginning"
on the world's greatest love story
You'll see!*

Wake Tech. Libraries
9101 Fayetteville Road
Raleigh, North Carolina 27603-5696

WAKE TECHNICAL COMMUNITY COLLEGE
3 3063 00141541 2

WN DATE DUE

APR 2 5 2013			

GAYLORD — PRINTED IN U.S.A.

Printed in the United States
95729LV00003B/411/A

9 781432 712839

DEC — 02